BILLS, QUILLS, AND STILLS

BILLS, QUILLS, AND STILLS

AN ANNOTATED,

ILLUSTRATED,

AND ILLUMINATED

HISTORY OF

THE BILL OF RIGHTS

ROBERT J. MCWHIRTER

Cover design by Andrew Alcala/ABA Publishing.

Design and layout by Quadrum Solutions.

The materials contained herein represent the opinions of the authors and editors and should not be construed to be the views or opinions of the law firms or companies with whom such persons are in partnership with, associated with, or employed by, nor of the American Bar Association or ABA Publishing unless adopted pursuant to the bylaws of the Association.

Nothing contained in this book is to be considered as the rendering of legal advice for specific cases, and readers are responsible for obtaining such advice from their own legal counsel. This book and any forms and agreements herein are intended for educational and informational purposes only.

Printed in the United States of America.

19 18 17 16 15   5 4 3 2 1

Library of Congress Cataloging-in-Publication Data

McWhirter, Robert James, 1961- author.

  Bills, quills, and stills : an annotated, illustrated, and illuminated history of the Bill of Rights / by Robert J. McWhirter.

    pages cm

  Includes index.

  ISBN (hardcover): 978-1-60442-097-5

  ISBN (paperback): 978-1-61438-380-2

  ISBN (ePub): 978-1-61438-381-9

1. United States. Constitution. 1st-10th Amendments. 2. Civil rights—United States. 3. Constitutional history—United States. I. Title.

  KF4750.M39 2014

  342.7303—dc23

2014028403

Discounts are available for books ordered in bulk. Special consideration is given to state bars, CLE programs, and other bar related organizations. Inquire at Book Publishing, ABA Publishing, American Bar Association, 321 N. Clark Street, Chicago, Illinois 60654-7598.

www.ShopABA.org

DEDICATION

To the living memory of Fr. Robert Leo Plasker, CSC,
my uncle for whom I am named, who spent his life
walking with the poor of Latin America.

To his brother, Fr. Alexander Plasker, OSB, who teaches us
loyalty and faith.

To my parents, J. Jeffries McWhirter, Ph.D, a teacher and
library, who gave us the world of ideas, and Mary Clare
McWhirter, who gave us the drive to make the world better.

To Gina, my wife, whose grace makes a family. To our boys,
Robert, also named for his great Uncle Bob, a bright and
winsome boy; his twin brother, the quick witted and sensitive
Ryan; and their younger brother, Gabriel, another bright boy
who brings happiness to a room.

TABLE OF CONTENTS

Prequel and Preamble:
Did They Forget to Pay the Bill?

*"The Conventions of a number of the States, having at the time
of their adopting the Constitution, expressed a desire, in order
to prevent misconstruction or abuse of its powers, that further
declaratory and restrictive clauses should be added . . . ."*

— From the *Preamble* to the Bill of Rights

Chapter 1: Of Dogma and Desire:
Saying What You Believe About the
First Amendment

*"Congress shall make no law respecting an establishment of
religion, or prohibiting the free exercise thereof; or abridging
the freedom of speech, or of the press; or the right of the people
peaceably to assemble, and to petition the Government for a
redress of grievances."*

— The First Amendment

Chapter 2: Shooting Your Mouth
Off About the Second Amendment

*"A well regulated Militia, being necessary to the security of a free
State, the right of the People to keep and bear Arms, shall not be
infringed."*

— The Second Amendment

"In all criminal prosecutions, the accused shall enjoy the right to a speedy and public trial, by an impartial jury of the State and district wherein the crime shall have been committed, which district shall have been previously ascertained by law, and to be informed of the nature and cause of the accusation; to be confronted with the witnesses against him; to have compulsory process for obtaining witnesses in his favor, and to have the Assistance of Counsel for his defense."

—Amendment VI

"In Suits at common law, where the value in controversy shall exceed twenty dollars, the right of trial by jury shall be preserved, and no fact tried by a jury, shall be otherwise re-examined in any Court of the United States, than according to the rules of the common law."

—Amendment VII

"In all criminal prosecutions, the accused shall enjoy the right to a speedy and public trial, by an impartial jury of the State and district wherein the crime shall have been committed, which district shall have been previously ascertained by law . . . "

—Amendment VI

"No person shall be held to answer for a capital, or otherwise infamous crime, unless on a presentment or indictment of a Grand Jury, except in cases arising in the land or naval forces, or in the Militia, when in actual service in time of War or public danger . . ."

—Amendment V

"The Trial of all Crimes, except in Cases of Impeachment, shall be by Jury, and such Trial shall be held in the State where the said Crimes shall have been committed; but when not committed within any State, the Trial shall be at such Place or Places as the Congress may by Law have directed."

—Article III, Section 2

Epilogue: How We Ponied – Up to Pay the Bill

"Section 1. Neither slavery nor involuntary servitude, except as a punishment for crime whereof the party shall have been duly convicted, shall exist within the United States, or any place subject to their jurisdiction.

Section 2. Congress shall have power to enforce this article by appropriate legislation."

—The Thirteenth Amendment

"Section 1. All persons born or naturalized in the United States . . . are citizens of the United States and of the State wherein they reside. No State shall make or enforce any law which shall abridge the privileges or immunities of citizens of the United States; nor shall any State deprive any person of life, liberty, or property, without due process of law; nor deny to any person within its jurisdiction the equal protection of the laws.

Section 2. Representatives shall be apportioned among the several States according to their respective numbers, counting the whole number of persons in each State, excluding Indians not taxed . . . .

Section 5. The Congress shall have power to enforce, by appropriate legislation, the provisions of this article."

—The Fourteenth Amendment

"Section 1. The right of citizens of the United States to vote shall not be denied or abridged by the United States or by any State on account of race, color, or previous condition of servitude.

Section 2. The Congress shall have power to enforce this article by appropriate legislation."

—The Fifteenth Amendment

ACKNOWLEDGMENTS

"No way am I going to write this book!"

I would have said that if you told me how long it would take. And my "long suffering wife" would have said, "no way are you writing this book, buddy!" But thousands of hours, reams of paper, and three laptops later, here we are.

But it would have not been possible without very important people.

Tim Brandhorst, my editor, is a gem—a calm guiding hand who allowed me to vent my insecurities during the project. His well placed encouragement was all it took. As I scrivend, I knew that Tim believed in the book and gave it a home at ABA Publishing. Whatever they pay you is not enough!

Tim Blake, Margaret Ackroyed, and Mary Baily are the Federal Courts Library in Phoenix, Arizona. It is a treasure trove and these people are the key. They helped me in their spare time out of support and love of learning. Margaret has a knack for getting material from repositories that for anyone else would have been "lost to history." Mary has her fingertips on every inch of the library. My friendship with Tim has been a great reward. I could not have done it without you all.

Tim Eigo (I seem to know a lot of very literate guys named "Tim"), editor of *Arizona Attorney* and a fine writer himself, approved the publication of four of this book's chapters in article form, starting with *Molasses and the Sticky Origins of the Fourth Amendment*, June 2007 and ending with *Baby, Don't Be Cruel: The Illustrated Eighth Amendment*, January 2010. He and art director Karen Holub did a wonderful layout that assured the articles´ success. Thank you both for the encouragement.

Gary Stuart, the don of Arizona legal writes, sought me out to write a feature about my writings for the *Arizona Attorney Magazine*. It came just when my courage for the project was flagging. Gary's book, MIRANDA—THE STORY OF AMERICA'S RIGHT TO REMAIN SILENT (2004) is a must read. Gary also gave me the honor of letting me read the manuscript of his upcoming book, INNOCENT UNTIL INTERROGATED: THE STORY OF THE BUDDHIST TEMPLE MASSACRE AND THE TUCSON FOUR, which reads like a novel but stings like a bee. It is an important contribution to a crucial issue of false confessions in the criminal justice system. Thank you, Gary.

I owe a great debt to Helen Koop who donated many sketches to this book. When you see how she brought the topics to life, you will feel indebted to her also.

"There are no great writers, only great editors!"

I thought this was one of my original statements but the one attributed to many great writers is "there are no great writers, only great rewriters." My following friends prove the point.

Chief Justice Stanley G. Feldman of the Arizona Supreme Court selected me as one of his law clerks for the 1988-89 term. I could not have planned a better first job to learn legal writing or a better mentor and later friend. Thank you, Judge (o.k., after your insistence for some 20 years, "Stanley") for your patience with a somewhat immature law clerk just finding his way in the legal world! My writing is so much better and all the ways you prepared me for the profession are incalculable.

When you entered the courtroom of the Honorable Pendleton Gains of the Superior Court of Maricopa County, you saw heritage: James Madison's painting, a map of old Virginia, replicas of the Constitution and Bill of Rights. For this reason, I asked him to review my manuscript. He took it on as a labor of love brining to bear his knowledge of history and religion, not to mention the finer points of grammar. (As my eight year old boys would say, I got "schooled" in comma placement). Scarcely a page of this book is not better because of him. With great sadness I write that Penny succumbed to cancer before he saw this book in print. I mourn the loss of a friend and the many fine conversations that will not now happen.

I had the honor of serving on the American Bar Association Criminal Justice Council and Book Board with Mike Wims, a man steeped in history and good writing. The book is better for his helpful review, citations to further sources, and knowledge of English culture. I have reviewed his book How To Try A Murder Case: Pretrial and Trial Guidelines for Prosecution and Defense (ABA, 2011) and heartily recommend it.

I often had cases against my friend Emery Hurly of the United States Attorney's Office in Phoenix Arizona and we have argued in the Ninth Circuit. He would argue well; I would argue well—then we would go out for breakfast. He is a fine lawyer prosecutor; far more concerned about justice than "winning." His knowledge of firearms made the Second Amendment chapter worth reading. I look forward to sharing our next pitcher of cheap beer and conversation.

Randy Howe and I have been friends since the first day of law school (or thereabouts), over 25 years! He not only reviewed the First Amendment chapter but was a patient ear over the years as I vented my thoughts and frustrations about this book. Randy is dignified and thoughtful; somebody needs to make him an appellate court judge!

Kathleen Sweeney's fine eye for citation form and correct presentation was a great help. This was especially true for First Amendment chapter. Thank you for the time you put in to make the book better.

Four law clerks worked on this project: I meet Laura Curry when she was a baby. She is the daughter of two distinguished lawyers and will be one herself. Part of Melissa Fanoe's charm is that she does not know how good she is at this "law stuff." Michael Clancy, Judd Nemiro, and Gabriel Mueller were all my students in Trial Advocacy at Phoenix School of Law. They are talented young lawyers with great futures–hire them!

Three people, out of many teachers, most taught me how to write. My father, J. Jeffries McWhirter, Ph.D., poured over our high school papers and taught us not only the mechanics, but that writing can touch souls.

Rebecca Berch, Chief Justice of the Arizona Supreme Court, was once the director of the writing program at Arizona State College of Law. She taught scores of us from her tiny office (I think it once was the first floor broom closet) not only legal writing, but better writing. I am grateful for the personal attention she gave me, among others, all while running a writing program for hundreds of law students.

Regretfully, I don't remember the name of my third significant writing teacher. She was a grad student teaching English 102 in my second semester at Arizona State University. She tormented me, or so I believed, by making me rewrite a perfectly good paper—again and again! She told me to think of writing like a microscope with each edit subjecting the subject to a stronger and clearer lens. (At least I remember her metaphor!). I suffered though it for the "A" (hell, at that point I would have washed her car for the "A"). In retrospect, she may have seen potential–she certainly saw laziness. I can only now acknowledge her and all the other teachers struggling to get their students to find more in themselves.

I thank my wife Gina, accomplished lawyer and conscientious judge, for the grace she showed during this project. All the times Gina held down the fort made this book possible. Our three boys, Robert Anthony, Ryan Alexander, and Gabriel Adam, were also a great help and more than made up for their lack of substantive contribution with enthusiasm!

These paltry acknowledgments hardly do justice to everyone's contribution. But it is all I have to give. Thank you all.

Robert James McWhirter
August 2014

INTRODUCTION

(If you like history)

"To not know the events that happened before one's birth is to remain always a child."

Cicero wrote that - people who like history read it and say "ah" (If you didn't say "ah", you may want to go to the next column).

"Originalism" is the rage! It says you must read the Constitution and Bill of Rights as the Framers would have read them (o.k., that's a little simplified but this is an Introduction). With this in mind, this book takes the history of the Bill of Rights from as far back as I could find up to around 1791-the history the Framers knew.

As Justice Oliver Wendell Holmes wrote,

"A page of history is worth a volume of logic."

New York Trust Co. v. Eisner, 256 U.S. 345, 349 (1921). Writing clever stuff like that is why he got his own postage stamp.

Some of this history is well known, some used to be well known, and the rest is not well known but should be. As Justice Luis Brandeis observed,

"[t]he greatest dangers to liberty lurk in insidious encroachment by men of zeal, well-meaning but without understanding."

Olmstead v. United States, 277 U.S. 438, 479 (1928) (Brandeis, J., dissenting). Brandeis is as pertinent as ever.

Or as Samuel Beckett wrote in WAITING FOR GODOT, Act I (1954),

Estragon: *We've lost our rights?"*

Vladimir: *"We got rid of them."*

Getting "rid" of rights is all too easy when we don't know where they came from or what they are. Avoiding such a loss is the point of this book.

(If you don't like history)

"History is just gossip about dead people!"

People who say they don't like history often like gossip. (Hell, who doesn't?). Gossip is just history, so this book is for you, too! In fact, if you want to look smarty, you can throw out my quote at a party or bar. I did a *Google* search to make sure I hadn't accidently ripped it off from somewhere and came up with this nice one from Oscar Wilde:

"History is merely gossip. But scandal is gossip made tedious by morality."

This was from his play *Lady Windermere's Fan: A Play About a Good Woman* (1892), which is about people not having sex with their spouses.

Oscar Wilde

With this in mind, I make you a pitch:

History is not boring. Boring history teachers are boring!

This is an original quote, too (I think). But it calls to mind that I don't want this book to be like the history teacher (Ben Stein) in FERRIS BUELLER' DAY OFF (Paramount Pictures 1986). I promise, I will not call out to a comatose class,

"Anyone?, Anyone?"

"Save Ferris!" Image by Helen Koop

What I present in this book is a lot of what "they" don't bother to teach you in school– the juicy stuff! So, how about taking a chance and buying this book (which could help me send my kids to trade school).

Then take an even bigger chance and read it to see why the Bill of Rights is worth the effort.

Prequel and Preamble:
Did they Forget to Pay the Bill?

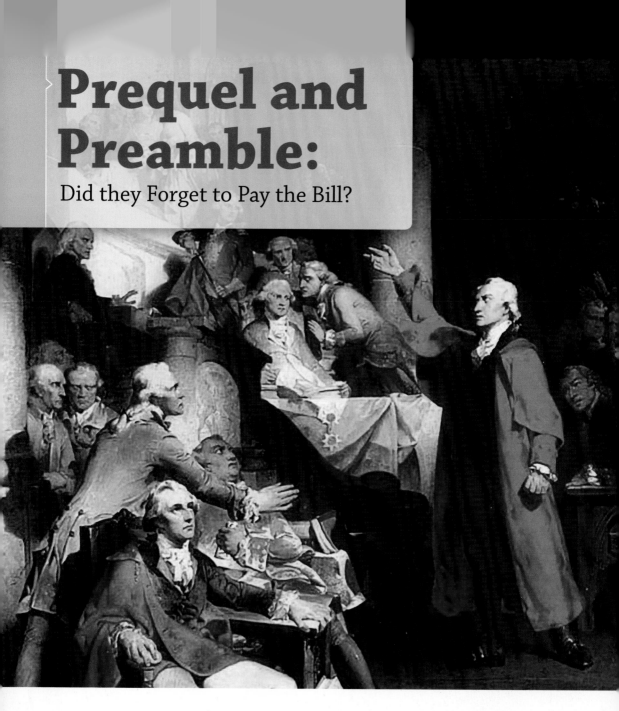

"THE Conventions of a number of the States, having at the time of their adopting the Constitution, expressed a desire, in order to prevent misconstruction or abuse of its powers, that further declaratory and restrictive clauses should be added . . . ."

From the *Preamble* to the Bill of Rights

The Constitution doesn't give you many rights,

. . . at least not the Constitution that made it out of Philadelphia on September 17, 1787. Sure you have the right to a civil jury, a habeas corpus petition,[1] and a prohibition on ex post facto laws.[2] But beyond those, the main right that the 1787 Constitution gave you was to keep your slaves[3]—hardly a promising start!

1. Article III, § 2 states that *"The Trial of all Crimes, except in Cases of Impeachment, shall be by Jury, and such Trial shall be held in the State where the said Crimes shall have been committed, but when not committed within any State, the Trial shall be at such Place or Places as the Congress may by Law have directed."* Article I, § 9 states that *"The privilege of the writ of habeas corpus shall not be suspended, unless when in cases of rebellion or invasion, the public safety may require it."*

3. The Constitution's slavery provisions. Unlike other constitutions, ours has no eraser—i.e., a way of deleting the superseded, obsolete, or rescinded parts. Thus, we cannot sweep our sins under the rug and the original four clauses allowing slavery are still there. Article I, § 9 allowed the continued "importation" of persons, Article IV, § 2 prohibited helping escaping persons and required their return if they successfully escaped, Article I, § 2 defined other persons as "three-fifths" to calculate each state's population, and Article V prohibited any amendments or legislation changing these provisions until 1808. The original Constitution, though, does not use the word "slavery."

The Constitution

2. Article I, § 9 prohibits ex post facto laws. The English jurist and commentator William Blackstone noted that the Roman Emperor Caligula *"wrote his laws in a very small character, and hung them up upon high pillars, the more effective to ensnare the people."* 1 WILLIAM BLACKSTONE, COMMENTARIES ON THE LAWS OF ENGLAND 46 (1765). But for a law to have effect, authorities must promulgate it. *See e.g.,* St. Thomas Aquinas, *"Promulgation is necessary for the law to have force. Promulgation that takes place now, extends to future time because of the durability of writing, by which means it is continually promulgated."* SAINT THOMAS AQUINAS, TREATISE ON LAW 6 (Richard J. Regan 2000). As for Caligula, John Hurt played him in the good TV series *I Claudius* (1976) and Malcolm McDowell played him in the bad movie CALIGULA (1979).

Blackstone

Caligula

Aquinas

Signing the Constitution

One of the few who objected was George Mason—they voted him down ten to zip.[1] In terms of what we think of today as the individual rights the Constitution protects, the Framers don't even get an "A" for effort![2]

To be fair, the Framers were busy forming a functioning republic.[3] Their brilliance was putting into practice Enlightenment political theory and proving that people could govern themselves.[4]

And through wars (including the Civil War), depressions, population explosions, and territorial expansion—to name but a few challenges—it worked.

The original Constitution is an owner's manual, not a manifesto.

The Framers, for the most part, honestly believed a Bill of Rights unnecessary. Their thinking was that the states kept every right the

---

1. "It would give great quiet to the people," said Mason, to include a Bill of Rights. *Quoted in* Shlomo Slonim, *The Federalist Papers and the Bill of Rights,* 20 CONST. COMMENT. 151 (2003), *citing* 2 Max Farrand, THE RECORDS OF THE FEDERAL CONVENTION OF 1787, at 587–88 (Sept. 12, 1787) (1937). *See also* Leonard W. Levy, *Bill of Rights, in* ESSAYS ON THE MAKING OF THE CONSTITUTION 258, 259 (Leonard W. Levy ed., 1987) (hereafter Levy, *Bill of Rights*). Elbridge Gerry of Massachusetts proposed adding a bill of rights and Mason seconded the motion, but the Convention, voting by states, voted it down 10 to 0. Later, Mason expressed greater objection, declaring that he *"would sooner chop off my right hand than put it to the Constitution as it now stands."* Levy, *Bill of Rights* at 260.

Gerry died in office as Vice-President under James Madison. "Gerrymandering" is named for him, which occurs when a party draws electoral districts to stay in

Gerry

power. Gerry was defeated as Massachusetts Governor in 1812 over his support for the "gerrymandered" redistricting bill. Issues of gerrymandering are still relevant today. *See, e.g.,* Robert Farley, Comments, *Preventing Unconstitutional Gerrymandering: Escaping the Intent/Effects Quagmire,* 38 SETON HALL L. REV. 397, 426 (2008). On Gerry's attempts to insert a right to a civil jury into the Constitution, *see* Matthew P. Harrington, *The Economic Origins of the Seventh Amendment,* 87 IOWA L. REV. 145, 181 (2001).

This political cartoon led to the term *gerrymandering.*

---

2. Benjamin Franklin may have agreed: *"I consent, Sir, to this Constitution because I expect no better and because I am not sure that it is not the best." Quoted in* CATHERINE DRINKER BOWEN, MIRACLE AT PHILADELPHIA: THE STORY OF THE CONSTITUTIONAL CONVENTION MAY TO SEPTEMBER 1787, at 256 (1966). For a full quote of Franklin's speech and an account of his personal charm in the Constitution's support *see generally* ROBERT A. DAHL, HOW DEMOCRATIC IS THE AMERICAN CONSTITUTION? 24–25 (2001) (noting that "[a] substantial number of

the Framers believed [in the necessity to] erect constitutional barriers to popular rule because the people would prove to be an unruly mob, a standing danger to law, to orderly government and to property rights.").

---

3. *See, e.g.,* Douglas O. Linder, *The Two Hundredth Reunion of Delegates to the Constitutional Convention (or, "All Things Considered, We'd Really Rather Be in Philadelphia"),* 1985 ARIZ. ST. L. J. 823 (regarding the Framers' motivations and purposes during the Constitutional Convention presented through an imagined conversation today with the key Founders themselves!–a good read).

Locke

4. The Constitution incorporated the ideas John Locke presented in his TWO TREATISES OF GOVERNMENT (1689) that civil society was created for the protection of "life, liberty, and estate." Each individual is free and equal in the state of nature, and rights are inherent to all individuals. He therefore believed people can govern themselves. The reason for the Constitution was that the Articles of Confederation did not work. *See generally* Douglas G. Smith, *An Analysis of Two Federal Structures: The Articles of Confederation and the Constitution,* 34 SAN DIEGO L. REV. 249 (1997).

Franklin on the $100 Bill

Constitution did not mention.[5] Moreover, the federal government had only the power the Constitution specifically gave it. Thus, there would be no need to say that Congress could not prohibit freedom of speech, for instance, because the Federal government had no power to do anything about speech.[6]

As it turned out, the Framers' failure to include a Bill of Rights almost blew the whole thing.[7] They failed to appreciate the states' fear of an oppressive national government that the Anti-Federalists were able to stir up.[8]

History would prove the Anti-Federalists correct;

the national government eclipsed the states in realms no one in 1789 ever imagined. But much of this expansion came through applying the Bill of Rights to the states; ironic because the Anti-Federalists wanted a Bill of Rights to protect them *from* the national government.[9]

McKean

5. As the Federalist Thomas McKean explained, the people did not need to reserve all the rights not in the Constitution because they stayed with the person. He gave the example of when a person sells 250 acres of 1,000 acres, it is not "necessary to reserve the 750?" Slonim at 153, *citing* 2 THE DOCUMENTARY HISTORY OF THE RATIFICATION OF THE CONSTITUTION 546–47 (John P. Kaminski & Gaspare J. Saladino eds., 1976). McKean continued, "*the [Constitution's] whole plan of government is nothing more than a bill of rights—a declaration of the people in what manner they choose to be governed.*" Slonim at 153, *citing* THE DOCUMENTARY HISTORY at 387.

6. William Blackstone, whose works were highly influential to all colonial lawyers, supported the view of a Bill of Rights being superfluous: "*Now the bill of rights was only declaratory, throughout, of the old constitutional law of the land . . .*" 4 WILLIAM BLACKSTONE, COMMENTARIES ON THE LAWS OF ENGLAND 372–73 (1769). Blackstone was referring, however, to the ENGLISH BILL OF RIGHTS of 1689.

7. "[T]he failure to attach a bill of rights to the Constitution . . . represented an Achilles' heel" to ratification. Slonim at 151, (*quoting* Robert Rutland). That "the Antifederalists stumbled upon one oversight in the Constitution that bore the appearance of an Achilles' heel," and they "assiduously promoted the idea that the failure to include a bill of rights was not an oversight, but a studied bit of Federalist deception." Slonim at 151 n.2, *citing* ROBERT ALLEN RUTLAND, THE ORDEAL OF THE CONSTITUTION: THE ANTIFEDERALISTS AND THE RATIFICATION STRUGGLE OF 1787–1788, 32–33 (1966). Regarding the passing of the Constitution and the ratifying documents in various states, *see* Documentary History of the Bill of Rights, http://www.constitution.org/dhbr.htm (last visited Mar. 12, 2008).

Henry- "Give me liberty or give me death!"

8. This included Patrick Henry, who fought vehemently against the Constitution's ratification with rhetoric reminiscent of his "*Give me liberty or give me death*" speech inciting the American Revolution. Henry spoke against the Constitution in the Virginia convention because it lacked a Bill of Rights: *I trust that gentlemen, on this occasion, will see the great objects of religion, liberty of the press, trial by jury, interdiction of cruel punishments, and every other sacred right, secured, before they agree to that paper. . . . My mind will not be quieted till I see something substantial come forth in the shape of a bill of rights.* 3 J. ELLIOT, THE DEBATES IN THE SEVERAL STATE CONVENTIONS ON THE ADOPTION OF THE FEDERAL CONSTITUTION 462 (1891).

9. On the relationship of the Bill of Rights to the states as they were incorporated as a limit on state power through the 14th Amendment, *see* Randall T. Shepard, *The Bill of Rights for the Whole Nation*, 26 VAL. U. L. REV. 27 (1991). For the Bill of Rights in American law, *see* William J. Brennan, Jr., *Why We Have a Bill of Rights?*, 26 VAL. U. L. REV. 1 (1991), and Thurgood Marshall, *Reflections on the Bicentennial of the United States Constitution*, 101 HARV. L. REV. 1 (1987).

To save the Constitution sallied forth James Madison, Alexander Hamilton, and John Jay with THE FEDERALIST PAPERS to argue for the Constitution's ratification.[1]

In FEDERALIST NO. 84, Alexander Hamilton argued that a Bill of Rights would be dangerous to liberty! Naming rights would enable the federal government to infringe on any unnamed ones. Thus listing them was

"not only unnecessary in the proposed Constitution but would even be dangerous. They would contain various exceptions to powers which are not granted; and, in this very account, would afford a colorable pretext to claim more than were granted . . . .*[2]

For why declare that things shall not be done which there is no power to do? Why for instance, should it be said, that the liberty of the press shall not be restrained, when no power is given by which restrictions may be imposed?"

Moreover, continued Hamilton, a Bill of Rights would be redundant. The states had their own bills of rights and

"the Constitution is itself, in every rational sense, and to every useful purpose, a bill of rights."[3]

Besides, it already protected the republican government, provided habeas corpus to prevent wrongful detention, and prohibited ex post facto laws and titles of nobility, and these were the most meaningful "securities to liberty and republicanism."[4]

Also, argued Hamilton, a Bill of Rights is appropriate to limit kings but has

1. THE FEDERALIST PAPERS are eighty-five articles advocating for the Constitution's ratification written by Alexander Hamilton (nos. 1, 6–9, 11–13, 15–17, 21–36, 59–61, and 65–85), James Madison (nos. 10, 14, 18–20, 37–58, and 62–63), and John Jay (nos. 2–5 and 64), under the pseudonym "Publius." These articles are a primary source for interpreting the Constitution. *See McCulloch v. Maryland*, 17 U.S. (4 Wheat.) 316, 433 (1819) ("*the opinions expressed by the authors of that work have been justly supposed to be entitled to great respect in expounding the Constitution*"); *see also* Gregory E. Maggs, *A Concise Guide to the Federalist Papers as a Source of the Original Meaning of the United States Constitution*, 87 B.U. L. REV. 801 (2007). For views questioning

THE FEDERALIST PAPERS' actual affect both historically and today *see* Melvyn R. Durchslag, *The Supreme Court and the Federalist Papers: Is There Less Here Than Meets the Eye?*, 14 WM. & MARY BILL RTS. J. 243 (2005), and Dan T. Coenen, *A Rhetoric for Ratifications: The Argument of the Federalist and Its Impact on Constitutional Interpretation*, 56 DUKE L.J. 469 (2006).

Madison became the fourth President, Hamilton the first Secretary of the Treasury, and John Jay the first Chief Justice of the United States.

Madison   Jay

2. THE FEDERALIST No. 84, at 513–14 (Alexander Hamilton) (Clinton Rossiter ed., 1961). This argument lead directly to the 9th Amendment. *See* **Chapter 9: The Ninth Amendment: Still a Mystery After All These Years.** Justice Joseph Story wrote that the 9th Amendment, "*was manifestly introduced to prevent any perverse or ingenious misapplication of the well-known maxim, that an affirmation in particular cases implies a negation in all others.*" 2 JOSEPH STORY, COMMENTARIES ON THE CONSTITUTION OF THE UNITED STATES 651 (5th ed. 1891); *see also* Randy E. Barnett, *The Ninth Amendment: It Means What It Says*, 85 TEX. L. REV. 1, 25 (2006).

Hamilton

"no application to constitutions, professedly founded upon the power of the people, and executed by their immediate representatives and servants."[5]

After all, Hamilton continued, the first words of the Constitution are better than any listing of rights:

WE, THE PEOPLE of the United States, to secure the blessings of liberty to ourselves and our posterity do ordain and establish this Constitution . . .

The Federalists succeeded in getting the Constitution ratified. No one can know whether this was because of (or despite) THE FEDERALIST PAPERS.

But one thing is for certain, Hamilton's arguments against having a Bill of Rights were utterly unpersuasive.[6] James Madison, at least, knew that to stop the movement to scrap the Constitution, he had to get a Bill of Rights through Congress and to the states.[7]

In this, Madison had a change of heart. Like Hamilton, he had argued in FEDERALIST

No. 38 there was no need for a Bill of Rights and that the old Articles of Confederation had none. Madison had not supported a Bill of Rights at the Constitutional Convention.

Two things changed his mind.

First, Madison's mentor, Thomas Jefferson, wrote Madison in December 1787, noting that unlike the Articles of Confederation, the new Constitution had no guarantee that the states kept *"every power . . . not . . . expressly delegated to the United States in Congress."* Thus,

---

3. *See* Slonim for an effective and concise analysis of Hamilton's FEDERALIST No. 84, as well as the relationship of Madison's FEDERALIST No. 10 and No. 51 on the lack of need for a Bill of Rights; *see also* Levy, *Bill of Rights* at 263 (discussing Hamilton's FEDERALIST No. 84 argument that the Constitution is itself a bill of rights). *See* Levy, *Bill of Rights,* at 262 (discussing the belief that states' bills of rights eliminated the need for a federal bill of rights. Regarding the remarkable number of state constitutions and their contribution to freedom and rights, *see, e.g.,* PATRICK T. CONLEY & JOHN P. KAMINSKI, THE BILL OF RIGHTS AND THE STATES: THE COLONIAL AND REVOLUTIONARY ORIGINS OF AMERICAN LIBERTIES (1992); Horst Dippel, *Human Rights in America, 1776–1849: Rediscovering the States' Contribution*, 67 ALB. L. REV. 713 (2004); Charles A. Rees, *Remarkable Evolution: The Early Constitutional History of Maryland*, 36 U. BALT. L. REV. 217 (2007).

4. Although the statement sounds quaint today, Hamilton wrote that the ban on titles of nobility *"may truly be denominated the corner-stone of republican government."*

....

5. *Magna Carta* of 1215, the PETITION OF RIGHT of 1628, and THE BILL OF RIGHTS of 1689 were wrested from kings. Levy, *Bill of Rights,* at 269. Americans believed that Parliament had irrevocably limited itself by reaffirming Magna Carta, the PETITION OF RIGHT of 1628, the HABEAS CORPUS ACT of 1679, the BILL OF RIGHTS of 1689, and the TOLERATION ACT of 1689. Levy, *Bill of Rights,* at 293. *See generally* BERNARD SCHWARTZ, THE BILL OF RIGHTS: A DOCUMENTARY HISTORY 4–41 (1971) (containing a copy of all the above documents and brief commentary). *See also* BERNARD SCHWARTZ, THE GREAT RIGHTS OF MANKIND 1–25 (1977) (for commentary on the American Bill of Rights and English antecedents).

The Constitution's Preamble.

....

6. As Supreme Court Justice Hugo Black wrote in 1960, "[i]t seems clear that this widespread demand for a Bill of Rights was due to a common fear of political and religious persecution should the national legislative power be left unrestrained as it was in England." Hugo L. Black, *The Bill of Rights*, 35 N.Y.U. L. REV. 865, 869 (1960).

....

7. *Quoted in* Levy, *Bill of Rights,* at 279.

"[a] bill of rights is what the people are entitled to against every government on earth, general or particular [i.e., national or state], and what no just government should refuse, or rest on inference."

On not listing all rights, Jefferson argued that half a loaf is better than none and *"let us secure what we can."*[1]

Second, Patrick Henry was a looming threat to Madison.[2]

Henry was intent on sending two Anti-Federalists to the United States Senate from Virginia and thus blocked Madison's election to the Senate. Henry then sought to gerrymander the congressional districts to keep Madison out of the House of Representatives as well. Madison's political future now depended on championing the Bill of Rights. He promised that if elected, he would append a Bill of Rights to the Constitution.[3]

Patrick Henry's threat, it appears, did more to create the Bill of Rights than Thomas Jefferson's reasoning.

On June 8, 1789, Madison proposed to the First Congress several amendments to the new Constitution that became our Bill of Rights.[4] He had to fight to even get the amendments heard.[5] Several members continued to think a bill of rights unnecessary and they shuttled the amendments, as well as Madison, off to a committee for review. Eventually, though, Madison got them out of Congress with revisions on September 25, 1789. By December 15, 1791, enough state

Jefferson   Madison

1. The fuller quote follows:
I will now add what I do not like. First the omission of a bill of rights providing clearly, for freedom of religion, freedom of the press, protection against standing armies, restriction of monopolies . . . . Let me add that a bill of rights is what the people are entitled to against every government on earth, general or particular; and what no just government should refuse, or rest on inferences. . . .
Letter from Thomas Jefferson to James Madison (Dec. 20, 1787).

Henry

2. Henry Counties in Alabama, Illinois, and Tennessee are named for him, and Virginia has both a Henry and a Patrick County for him. There is also a USS *Patrick Henry* submarine, and the first of the WWII liberty ships was named the SS *Patrick Henry*, all a tribute to Henry's pugnacity.

USS Patrick Henry

Madison

3. See Carl T. Bogus, *The Hidden History of the Second Amendment*, 31 U.C. DAVIS L. REV. 309, 360–62 (1998).

James Madison (1751–1836) was the fourth (1809–1817) president of the United States and was called the "father of the Constitution" and the "father of the Bill of Rights." But Madison never intended the provisions to be a Bill of Rights. Rather, he would have inserted the provisions throughout the Constitution. Levy, *Bill of Rights*, at 283–84 (noting that Roger Sherman argued that they be added at the end as "amendments"); *see generally* RICHARD LABUNSKI, JAMES MADISON AND THE STRUGGLE FOR THE BILL OF RIGHTS (2006). Moreover, the Bill of Rights was not, originally, *ten* amendments. Madison took over two

hundred proposals from the states and political leaders and submitted seventeen to Congress, which he largely based on George Mason's Virginia Declaration of Rights of 1776. The House approved all seventeen amendments, but the Senate rejected some (including Madison's favorite on protecting conscience and the press) and combined others.

A copy of the original U.S. Bill of Rights.

4. Why we call it the "Bill of Rights" when it wasn't a Bill? The Bill of Rights was never a "bill" in Congress. Indeed, the Founders were debating a "Bill of Rights" even before there was a Congress. The reason is that exactly 100 years earlier in 1689, the English Parliament passed an actual "Bill of Rights" aka "An Act Declaring the Rights and Liberties of the Subject and Settling the Succession of the Crown." As later Chapters in this book show, the English Bill

English Bill of Rights (1689)

legislatures ratified the Bill of Rights to make it law.[6]

Given that the original proponents were more interested in *states'* rights than in *individual* rights, this is unsurprising. As Madison predicted in a letter to federalists, the Bill of Rights *"will kill opposition everywhere . . . ."*[7]

Thus, the Anti-Federalist tactic of arguing against the Constitution because it lacked a bill of rights backfired when Madison succeeded in getting the Bill of Rights through the Congress and to the states.

But despite Madison's hard work, for most of our history, we have not paid much attention to the Bill of Rights.[8] One thing, at least, remains remarkable about the Bill of Rights; though it took the first Congress many weeks to take up the Bill of Rights, in passing it one of the first acts of the new national government was to limit its own power.[9]

So even though the Framers didn't even get an "A" for effort with the Constitution, their quick make-up with the Bill of Rights got them, and us, a pass—but barely. Slavery remained the American cancer.[10]

The history of the rights outlined in this book is one of struggle. Brave people struggled for the recognition of individual rights. They then struggled to make those rights universal.

We struggle to do the same.

---

of Rights (1689) influenced the U.S. Bill of Rights. For example, the 8th Amendment's prohibition against "cruel and unusual punishments" and excessive bail comes nearly verbatim from the English Bill of Rights. **See Chapter 8: *"Baby Don't Be Cruel":* Just What's So Cruel and Unusual About the Eighth Amendment?**

....

5. See Levy, *Bill of Rights,* at 283–84.

....

6. Several states, however, did *not* approve the Bill of Rights; Connecticut, Georgia, and Massachusetts never got around to ratifying it until the sesquicentennial of the Constitution in 1939!

....

7. Levy, *Bill of Rights,* at 285. Thus, Madison became not only "the Father of the Constitution" but "the Father of the Bill of Rights." LEONARD W. LEVY, ORIGINS OF THE FIFTH AMENDMENT: THE RIGHT AGAINST SELF-INCRIMINATION 421 (1968).

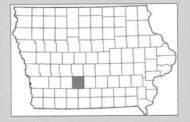

You would be hard-pressed to find any state or city that does not have something named for Madison, for example, Madison Country, Iowa, and its covered bridges where ROBERT JAMES WALLER, THE BRIDGES OF MADISON COUNTY takes place. The novel became the movie THE BRIDGES OF MADISON COUNTY (Warner Brothers 1995) with Meryl Streep (nominated for the Best Actress Oscar) and Clint Eastwood, who also directed it. (This one is definitely a "chick flick").

Madison County, Iowa is also the birthplace of Actor John Wayne, who said among other things, *"Courage is being scared to death—but saddling up anyway."*

Wayne

....

8. As Justice Hugo Black wrote, "Today most Americans seem to have forgotten the ancient evils which forced their ancestors to flee to this new country and to form a government stripped of old powers used to oppress them." Black at 867.

Black

9. "It was one of the great achievements of our Constitution that it ended legislative omnipotence here and placed all departments and agencies of government under one supreme law." Black at 870.

....

10. On slavery, Gouverneur Morris of Pennsylvania stated at the convention, *"the inhabitant of Georgia [or] South Carolina who goes to the coast of Africa, and in defiance of the most sacred laws of humanity tears away his fellow creatures from their dearest connections and damns them to the most cruel bondages, shall have more votes in a Government instituted for protection of the rights of mankind, than the Citizen of Pennsylvania or New Jersey who views with a laudable horror, so nefarious a practice."*
Quoted in Gene R. Nichol, *Toward a People's Constitution,* 91 Cal. L. Rev. 621, 623 n.6 (2003).

Morris

BILLS, QUILLS, AND STILLS

CHAPTER 1

Of Dogma and Desire:

Saying What You Believe About the First Amendment

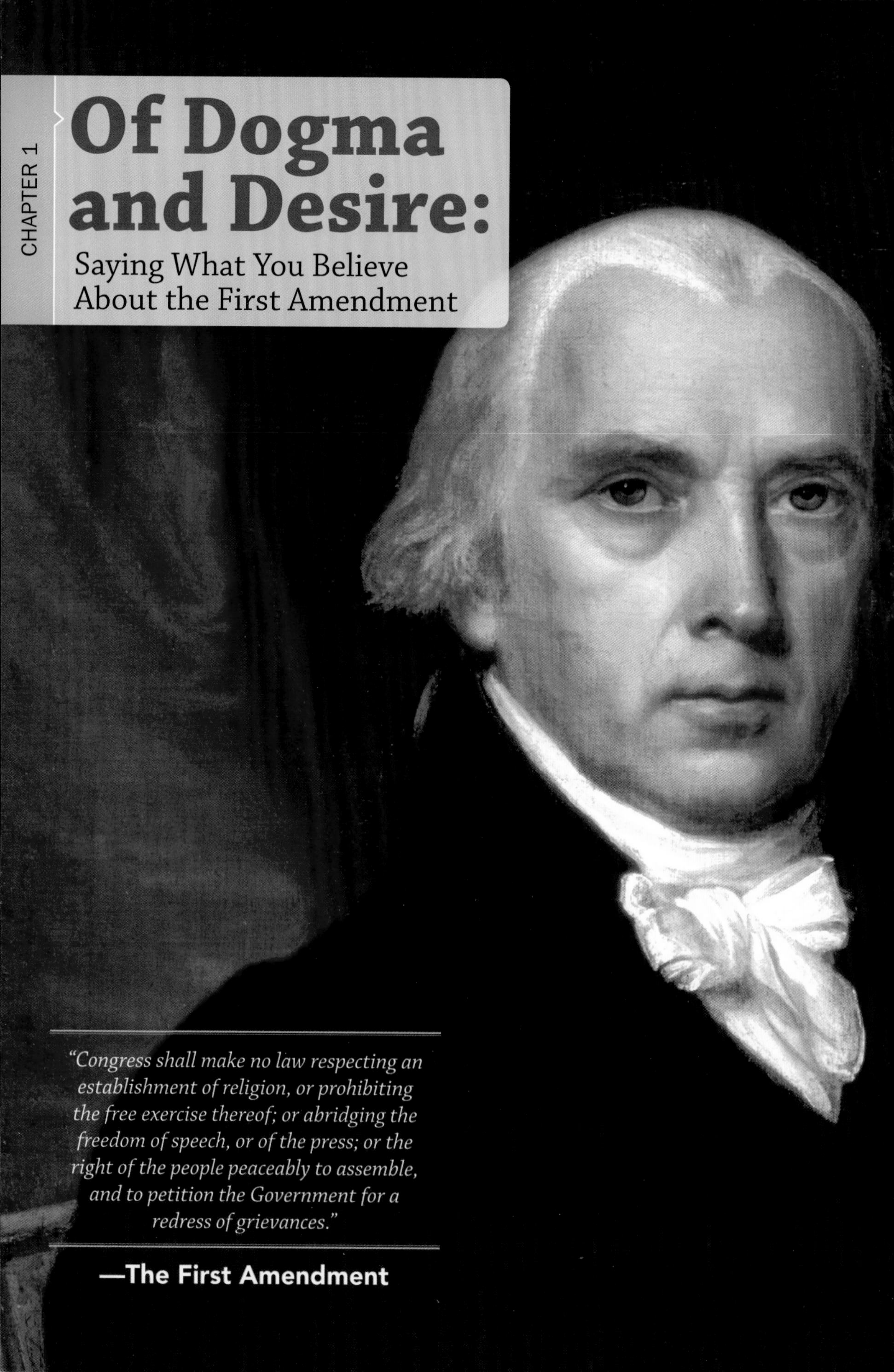

"Congress shall make no law respecting an
establishment of religion, or prohibiting
the free exercise thereof; or abridging the
freedom of speech, or of the press; or the
right of the people peaceably to assemble,
and to petition the Government for a
redress of grievances."

—The First Amendment

A high school kid unfurled a banner at an off-campus school activity reading,

"Bong Hits 4 Jesus." [1]

He got suspended for ten days and eventually lost his case in the U.S. Supreme Court. [2]

But was it speech or religion? Actually, it doesn't matter—it was the First Amendment.

Speech *and* religion! People fight wars about either, and especially about both, including the American Revolution. In fact, the kid got his suspension increased from five to ten days after he quoted Thomas Jefferson. [3]

1. Image by Helen Koop

Original Banner at the Newseum in Washington D.C.

2. *Morse v. Frederick*, 551 U.S. 393 (2007), held that the suspension did not violate the student's right to free speech, nor did confiscating the banner. The kid, Joseph Frederick, later settled his case just before the Alaskan Supreme Court was to decide it under the Alaskan Constitution. So, in Alaska at least, it appears that even a high school student can speak about or believe in *"Bong Hits 4 Jesus"*!

3. *Frederick v. Morse*, 439 F.3d 1114, 1116 (9th Cir. 2006). Jefferson had very clear ideas about Jesus, but he probably never used a bong.

Thomas Jefferson

A bong or water pipe is a smoking device for cannabis, tobacco, or other substances. The water cools the smoke.

As "*Bong Hits 4 Jesus*" shows, the First Amendment is front and center in the "culture debates." On any given topic—school prayer, "faith-based initiatives," abortion, the death penalty, health care, the Ten Commandments on public property—we debate the First Amendment's scope, both as to what we believe and what we can say about it.

But guess what? The First Amendment

wasn't originally first. It started out as the third amendment. (So much for the hortatory speeches that "*the First Amendment is so important because the Framers put it first!*"). In fact, the Framers originally put it after an amendment regarding the size of the Congress and another related to Congress's pay.[1]

Our current First Amendment, though, was the first that articulated individual rights, and thus was

always the start of the "Bill of Rights."[2] Even so, our modern understanding of freedom of speech and of the press is less than one hundred years old.[3] And as we will see, the Framers, for the most part, would not have considered the First Amendment the main definer of religious freedom and free speech.

This is not the case today.

Under the First Amendment's Free Press, Speech,

---

1. See ANTHONY LEWIS, FREEDOM FOR THE THOUGHT THAT WE HATE: A BIOGRAPHY OF THE FIRST AMENDMENT 9 (2007). The original "first amendment" concerning the size of the House of Representatives and congressional apportionment never passed, but the states did ratify the original "second amendment" concerning congressional salaries on May 7, 1992, making it the Twenty-Seventh Amendment: "*No law, varying the compensation for the services of the Senators and Representatives, shall take effect until an election of Representatives shall have intervened.*" U.S. CONST. amend. XXVII).

James Madison

2. The First Amendment was James Madison's personal project. Brent Tarter, *Virginians and the Bill of Rights, in* THE BILL OF RIGHTS: A LIVELY HERITAGE 12 (Jon Kukla ed., 1987). He gets credit for being the "father of the Bill of Rights" because he made a campaign promise to get it passed and sifted through piles of proposals and wording to do so. See **Prequel and Preamble: Did They Just Forget to Pay the Bill?**

3. Before World War I, the courts generally did not protect speech. Not until *Gitlow v. New York*, 268 U.S. 652 (1925), did the Supreme Court hold that the First Amendment applied to the states. *Near v. Minnesota*, 283 U.S. 697 (1931), was the first time the Supreme Court ruled for the press against a prior restraint by holding unconstitutional a state statute enjoining publication of an allegedly defamatory newspaper. That same year, the Supreme Court upheld the validity of symbolic speech in *Stromberg v. California*, 283 U.S. 359 (1931), by invalidating a California

law that forbade the display of a red flag "*as a sign, symbol or emblem of opposition to organized government.*" It took until 1965 for the Court to hold unconstitutional a federal law as violating the First Amendment in *Lamont v. Postmaster General,* 381 U.S. 301 (1965). See, e.g., David M. Rabban, *The Emergence of Modern First Amendment Doctrine*, 50 U. CHI. L. REV. 1205, 1213–15 (1983). See LEWIS 112–23 (discussing the lack of court protection to violations of speech and religious rights for most of American history); see also David M. O'Brien, *Freedom of Speech and*

Free Government: The First Amendment, the Supreme Court and the Polity, in THE BILL OF RIGHTS: A LIVELY HERITAGE 43, 48, 52 (Jon Kukla ed., 1987) (noting that the First Amendment shows two hundred years of expansion). For the growth of the First Amendment in the courts, see FLOYD ABRAMS, SPEAKING FREELY: TRIALS OF THE FIRST AMENDMENT (2005); Erwin Chemerinsky, *History, Tradition, the Supreme Court, and the First Amendment,* 44 HASTINGS L.J. 901, 916 (1993) (noting that the tradition of protecting speech and religion has changed profoundly over time).

Petition, and Assembly Clauses, people print, blog, speak out, protest, petition, argue, and march.[4] People are motivated to do all that printing, blogging, speaking, protesting, petitioning, arguing, and marching by their respective creeds. They demand to freely exercise their creed *and* to be free from someone else establishing a different creed over them.

In this sense, the First Amendment's two components of speech and religion define us. No other part of the Constitution has this scope.[5]

Both the political Left and political Right hold free speech as an article of faith, and whole political movements, such as the Moral Majority and the civil rights movement, have organized around religion.[6]

Although the First Amendment's current scope is a modern innovation, the aspiration it embodies and the rights it incorporates are products of history—and a rich history at that.

In fact, the kid with the *"Bong Hits 4 Jesus"* banner—a little turning point in history—now has something in common with Sir Thomas More, who in 1535 defied King Henry VIII—a big fat turning point in history.

"I die the King's good servant and God's first."

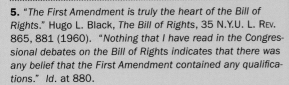

4. *"Stop the Presses!"* The press itself often becomes "the story" in movies that range from the suspense drama ALL THE PRESIDENT'S MEN, (Warner Brothers, 1976) about Watergate, to the comedy-drama THE PAPER, (Universal Pictures, 1994) in which the main character gets to yell, *"Stop the Presses!"* And of course, there is Orson Welles' masterpiece (and perhaps the best American movie of all time), CITIZEN KANE (RKO Pictures 1941), a fictional account of William Randolph Hearst and his newspaper empire. For a discussion of Hearst and "yellow" journalism, see Trevor D. Dryer, *"All the News That's Fit to Print": The New York Times, "Yellow" Journalism, and the Criminal Trial 1898–1902*, 8 NEV. L. J. 541 (2008).

5. *"The First Amendment is truly the heart of the Bill of Rights."* Hugo L. Black, *The Bill of Rights*, 35 N.Y.U. L. REV. 865, 881 (1960). *"Nothing that I have read in the Congressional debates on the Bill of Rights indicates that there was any belief that the First Amendment contained any qualifications."* *Id.* at 880.

6. King stating the dream.

So said More—knight, lawyer, judge, and once lord chancellor of England—just before King Henry VIII had his head chopped off.

Sure, More's statement is literally graver than the kid's *"Bong Hits 4 Jesus,"* but it is still about stating a creed.

A lot of people died for religion then, as they continue to do now. So what makes More special?

Aside from the fact that A MAN FOR ALL SEASONS is a great movie,[1] More represents the confluence of the First Amendment's two parts: speech and religion, the same as *"Bong Hits 4 Jesus."*

Ironically, it was not what More said that got him killed; it was what he refused to say. Specifically, he refused to swear an oath, the Act of Supremacy, regarding Henry's hostile takeover of the Catholic Church in England.[2] Speech, like religion, can be symbolic as well as spoken.

Henry killed a lot of people for speaking about such things.

That More lost his head for something he did not say is ironic because he was the greatest speaker of his day.[3] Henry knew this and sent a message to More that

"[t]he King's pleasure is further that at your

Henry VIII

1. A MAN FOR ALL SEASONS (Columbia Pictures 1966) won an Academy Award for Best Picture. Robert Bolt adapted his stage play for the movie. Courts have quoted both the film and play numerous times, including the U.S. Supreme Court in *National Ass'n of Home Builders v. Defenders of Wildlife*, 551 U.S. 644 (2007). Robert Bolt's final film project was his screenplay for THE MISSION (Warner Brothers 1986), which picked up on the themes of moral conscience and religion presented in A MAN FOR ALL SEASONS twenty years earlier.

2. *See* **Chapter 5: From Testicles to** *Dragnet*: **How the Fifth Amendment Protects** *All* **of Us,** discussing More's role in the history of the right to remain silent.

Sir Thomas More

execution you shall not use many words."[4]

It was not enough that Henry arranged to "legally" kill More; Henry also did not want an embarrassing execution.[5]

But though Henry could count on More's obedience to be brief, More knew the value of a good sound-bite. Aside from a few customary quips and exchanges, such as forgiving his executioner, More said only the words quoted above.

"I die the King's good servant and God's first."

They were more than enough.

The best speeches are often the shortest, and in just nine words More summed up the whole conflict about the right to say what you believe without government reprisal.[6] Although the confluence of speech and religion undid him, his words live on to indict Henry.

Today we effectively view the First Amendment as *two* amendments: one regarding religion and another regarding speech. But the First Amendment actually emerged from the interplay between the two.

Henry's break with the Roman Catholic Church, part of the Protestant Reformation, illustrates this interplay; what you believed and what you said about it became a government problem.[7]

---

3. In happier times, More had been speaker of the House of Commons and stood his ground against Cardinal Wolsey, who as lord chancellor and papal legate exercised both the power of the young King Henry and that of the faraway pope.

Thomas More Defending the Liberty of the House of Commons by Vivian Forbes

As we shall see, in 1523, Sir More wrote a PETITION FOR FREE SPEECH to Henry, arguing that the king was better served by a Parliament that did not fear reprisal from open and frank discussion of differing points of view.

4. More's son-in-law, William Roper, wrote of More's death about twenty years later. WILLIAM ROPER, THE LIFE OF SIR THOMAS MORE c. 1556–57 (Gerard B. Wegemer & Stephen W. Smith eds., 2003), *available at* http://www.thomasmorestudies.org/docs/Roper.pdf.

5. As Justice Hugo Black wrote, "[m]isuse of government power, particularly in times of stress, has brought suffering to humanity in all ages about which we have authentic history. Some of the world's noblest and finest men have suffered ignominy and death for no crime—unless unorthodoxy is a crime." Black at 879.

6. More did not become Saint Thomas More until Pope Pius XI canonized him in 1935. What he had to "say" about Henry, conscience, and political power applies just as well to totalitarianism under Hitler, Stalin, and Mussolini.

Contrary to popular belief, More is not the patron saint of lawyers—that is Saint Ives—but of statesmen.

Saint Ives (Ivo of Kermartin, canonized in June 1347 by Pope Clement VI), whose prayer reads:

"Saint Yvo was a lawyer, and not a thief, A thing almost beyond belief."

7. A contemporary engraving showing **Henry VIII** (already getting fat) enthroned on top of Pope Clement, with Bishop Fisher trying to help the pope and Henry's new archbishop of Canterbury, Thomas Cranmer, and new lord chancellor, Thomas Cromwell, supporting the king. The scene also shows Henry binding over monks for execution and confiscating the wealth of the church. All of this happens while Cramner hands Henry the printed Word, connecting religion and press.

Henry *established* himself as the pope in England and the Anglican Church as the official religion, which is why we have an *anti*-establishment clause that

"Congress shall make no law respecting an establishment of religion . . . ." [1]

But Henry and his successors had no idea what they had gotten themselves into, because in breaking with Rome, they not only had to suppress Catholics[2] but all manner of dissenters from established Anglicanism, most notably Puritans.[3] This is why we have a "free exercise" clause that

"Congress shall make no law . . . prohibiting the free exercise thereof [religion] .."

The dissenters, however, would not keep their mouths shut despite the crown's and the established church's best efforts to suppress them. They spoke out, and the Anglicans tried them, which

1. Religion and Dogma. Even today, Americans are a religious people, but they are much less *dogmatic. See* Richard Albert, *Religion in the New Republic*, 67 LA. L. REV. 1, 22 (2006). America has seen, for instance, the growth of Protestant "megachurches" having little or no connection with any Protestant denomination or predefined doctrine.

"Dogma" is a given religion or other organization's undisputable belief or doctrine. In the religious context, divergence from it is "heresy." The word comes from Greek, and the plural is either "dogmas" or "dogmata." Denominations, sects, and organizations spend a lot of time defining dogma. The Catholic Church, for example, has different

levels for defining dogma, which as history shows leaves a lot of room for interpretation. *See, e.g.,* Dogma, THE CATHOLIC ENCYCLOPEDIA, http://www.newadvent.org/cathen/05089a.htm (last visited Nov. 12, 2009). DOGMA (Miramax Films 1999) is an American adventure-comedy-fantasy satirizing the Catholic Church and belief.

Religion, though largely unknowable and impenetrable, is still central to most people. Albert at 8–9. Defining "religion" is difficult and attempts range from *"belief in the existence of a larger force; and adherence to a code of human conduct"* and *"[a] system of faith and worship usually involving belief in a supreme being and usually containing a moral or*

ethical code," to *"recognition on the part of man of some higher unseen power as control of his destiny, and as being entitled to obedience, reverence, and worship; the general mental and moral attitude resulting from this belief, with reference to its effect upon the individual or the Community"* to *"the voluntary subjection of oneself to God"* to *"any belief system which serves the psychological function of alleviating death anxiety."* Albert at 10–11, *citing* BLACK'S LAW DICTIONARY 1293–94 (7th ed. 1999); XIII OXFORD ENGLISH DICTIONARY 568–69 (2d ed. 1989); XII CATHOLIC ENCYCLOPEDIA 739 (1909); James M. Donovan, *God Is as God Does: Law, Anthropology, and the Definition of "Religion,"* 6 SETON HALL CONST. L.J. 23, 95 (1995).

The Lakewood Megachurch interior in Houston, Texas

The Crystal Cathedral in Garden Grove, California

is why we have a freedom of speech clause that

"Congress shall make no law . . . abridging the freedom of speech . . . ." [4]

They continued to write pamphlets and books, and the kings continued to burn them—both the books and

sometimes the Puritans—which is why we have a freedom of the press clause that

"Congress shall make no law . . . abridging the freedom . . . of the press . . . ." [5]

They petitioned for rights, which the church and crown

ignored, which is why we have the right to assemble and petition:

"Congress shall make no law . . . abridging the right of the people peaceably to assemble, and to petition the Government for a redress of grievances." [6]

---

2. Despite the admiration for More, anti-Catholicism became the norm in England. Catholicism went underground, which the story of Abbot Richard Whiting and his steward Thomas Horner shows.

Whiting was abbot of the great Glastonbury Abbey, built on the site of King Arthur's Avalon. In the early days of Henry VIII's stealing of church property, Whiting sent the king a pile of deeds to various manors in the abbey's possession. Because this did not occur in not an age of bank transfers, he sent the deeds hidden in a pie with his steward, Thomas Horner. The story is that Horner pulled out a deed for himself. What the record shows is that Horner testified against Whiting at his treason trial. Horner, for services to the crown, got the deed to the Manor of Mells, in Somerset, and a nursery rhyme:

"*Little Jack Horner sat in the corner, Eating a*

Christmas pie: He put in his thumb, and pulled out a plum, and said, 'What a good boy am I!'"

Abbot Richard Whiting

3. The Pilgrims seeking a new world away from the established Church of England.

---

4. This includes a Puritan named **John Lilburne**, known as Freeborn John, who would not shut up! Lucky for us, he didn't. We will hear more about him in **Chapter 5: From Testicles to** *Dragnet*: **How the Fifth Amendment Protects** *All* **of Us** and **Chapter 6: How the Sixth Amendment Guarantees You a Court, a Lawyer, and a Chamber Pot.**

5. The Puritan **John Milton**, who wrote the great epic poem Paradise Lost (1667), first wrote one of the greatest defenses of free speech, Areopagitica: A Speech of Mr. John Milton for the Liberty of Unlicensed Printing to the Parliament of England (1644). We will hear more about Milton later in this chapter.

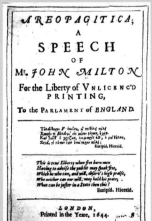

First page of Areopagitica (1644)

The Petition of Right (1628)

Protesters assembling to demand jobs during the civil rights movement

6. The Framers knew of Parliament's Petition of Right (1628), setting out specific liberties that the king could not infringe: only Parliament could levy taxes, martial law could be imposed only during war, prisoners could challenge their detention through the writ of habeas corpus, and bans on the king's billeting troops in homes (the precursor of the Third Amendment). *See* **Chapter 3: The Third Amendment: Don't Count It Out Yet!**

We will return to Henry later because he is central to understanding why the Framers knew we needed the First Amendment.

The Framers also knew that fighting a revolution for rights, like those the First Amendment articulates, requires something to push the cause. Certainly the Enlightenment's promise of a free and open society motivated Jefferson, Adams, and Madison.

But for most of our history, especially the history the Founders knew, it was not a philosophy that pushed the struggle for rights, including the right to speak. It was religion.[1]

RELIGION AND SPEECH IN HISTORY

The Hebrews:

The ancients had a utilitarian approach to their gods. Treat them well, and the gods (supposedly) treated you well. They would not have understood the later Judeo-Christian idea that God is inherently good to *everyone*.[2]

---

1. The English and American experience refutes Karl Marx's pronouncement that *"[r]eligion is the sign of the oppressed creature, the heart of a heartless world, and the soul of soulless conditions. It is the opium of the people."*

Far from being the thing that oppressed people, religion and speech motivated them to gain rights and democracy. *"They [the Framers] knew that free speech might be the friend of change and revolution. But they also knew that it is always the deadliest enemy of tyranny."* Black at 881; Susan Wiltshire writes that free speech *"does not ensure good government . . . [but] its absence does ensure totalitarianism."* SUSAN FORD WILTSHIRE, GREECE, ROME, AND THE BILL OF RIGHTS 111 (1992); *see also* Walter B. Hamlin, *The Bill of Rights or the First Ten Amendments to the United States Constitution*, 68 COM. L.J. 233 (1963) (*"I submit that these Ten Amendments are the best answer to those violent, turbulent men of Communistic leanings, both at home and abroad, who would place Might upon the pedestal which others have raised to Right."*).

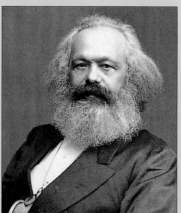

Karl Marx

2. The word "god" probably comes from the Indo-European "*ghut*" and the old German "*guth*" giving also the German "*gott*," the Dutch "*god*," and Swedish/Danish "*gud*." JOHN AYTO, DICTIONARY OF WORD ORIGINS 258 (1990). The salutation "good-bye" was originally "God-be-with-you," which Shakespeare rendered "God-be-wy-you" and "God buy' ye." *Id.* at 259. Interestingly, the word "god" is not related to "good," which instead comes from the prehistoric Germanic "*gath*" for "bring together," also the source of English's "gather" and "together." *Id.* at 259.

3. *Exodus* 20:2–3; *see also Deuteronomy* 5:6–21.

Exodus (Greek for "departure" and the source of the modern English word "exit"), the second book of the Jewish Torah and Christian Old Testament, tells how Moses led the Israelites out of Egypt. According to Exodus, Moses gave the Israelites the Ten Commandments. Tradition says Moses wrote the five books of the Torah: *Genesis*, *Exodus*, *Leviticus*, *Numbers*, and *Deuteronomy*.

4. *Exodus* 34:15; *see also Deuteronomy* 5:9; *Exodus* 20:5.

THE TEN COMMANDMENTS (Paramount Pictures 1956), staring Charlton Heston and Yul Brynner, was Cecil B. DeMille's remake of his 1923 silent film classic THE TEN COMMANDMENTS (Paramount Pictures 1923). Adjusted for inflation, the 1956 version is still the fifth highest grossing movie of all time and is the second highest grossing religious film after Mel Gibson's PASSION OF THE CHRIST (Independent Film 2004). *See* http://en.wikipedia.org/wiki/The_Ten_Commandments (last visited Sept. 13, 2005).

Cecil B. DeMille

Rather, as the Old Testament's First and Second Commandments show, God helps the Hebrews because they have an exclusive relationship with him:

I am the Lord your God, who brought you out of the land of Egypt, out of the house of slavery; Do not have any other gods before me.[3]

Moses brought forth these commandments from Mount Sinai into a world of competing peoples with their competing gods:

You shall worship no other god, because the Lord, whose name is Jealous, is a jealous God.[4]

So the Bible recognized many deities, but God and the Hebrews were going steady!

Take care not to make a covenant with the inhabitants of the land to which you are going, or it will become a snare among you. You shall tear down their altars, break their pillars, and cut down their sacred poles.[5]

4. *(continued)* The competition of peoples and gods shows in the Golden Calf story, where Moses, upon descending Mount Sinai, destroys the false idol. Also, the special effects centerpiece of THE TEN COMMANDMENTS was the parting of the Red Sea, which was about God beating the Egyptian's gods.

5. *Exodus* 34:13–14. Moses set the example and caused quite a stir by descending from Mount Sinai and destroying the original Ten Commandments by hurling them at the golden calf.

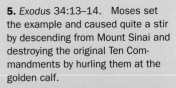

Moses with Ten Commandments by Rembrandt (1659)

Moses and the Golden Calf by Beccafumi (1537)

The Adoration of the Golden Calf by Poussin (1633–34)

Heston backed up by some serious special effects; the "walls" of the Red Sea were made of jello

The Ten Commandments did not allow the Hebrews to "play the field."[1]

As for religion and government, the Hebrews had an early separation of church and state.[2]

God made the judges (and later the kings) separate from the priests.[3] The kings of Israel were not to meddle in the priestly functions.

Once King Saul offered sacrifice to God before a battle because the high priest Samuel was late. When Samuel got there, he rebuked Saul:

"Thou hast done foolishly: thou hast not kept the commandment of the Lord thy God, which he commanded thee: for now would the Lord have established thy kingdom upon Israel forever. But now thy kingdom shall not continue . . . .[4]"

---

1. The Ten Commandments: Still the Center of Controversy!

In *Van Orden v. Perry*, 545 U.S. 677 (2005), the Supreme Court held by a 5–4 vote that the Ten Commandment display at the Texas State Capitol *did not violate* the First Amendment's Establishment Clause. At the same time, however, *McCreary County v. ACLU of Kentucky*, 545 U.S. 844 (2005), held by another 5–4 vote that the Ten Commandment display in a Kentucky courthouse *violated* the Establishment Clause. *See generally* Lael Daniel Weinberger, *The Monument and the Message: Pragmatism and Principle in Establishment Clause Ten Commandments Litigation*, 14 Tex. Wesleyan L. Rev. 393 (2008) ("Public displays of the Ten Commandments have been touchstones of Establishment Clause litigation ever since the Supreme Court ordered a public school to remove a plaque in 1980."); Susanna Dokupil, *"Thou Shalt Not Bear False Witness": "Sham" Secular Purposes in Ten Commandments Displays*, 28 Harv. J.L. & Pub. Pol'y 609, 635 (2005); Thomas B. Colby, *A Constitutional Hierarchy of Religions? Justice Scalia, the Ten Commandments, and the Future of the Establishment Clause*, 100 Nw. U. L. Rev. 1097, 1099–1101 (2006).

According to Justice Stephen Breyer, the "swing vote," the Texas monument had a civic/secular purpose whereas the Kentucky courthouse display was to establish religion. *But see* Douglas Laycock,

Cecil B. DeMille

Heston lays down the law

Towards a General Theory of the Religion Clauses: The Case of Church Labor Relations and the Right to Church Autonomy, 81 Colum. L. Rev. 1373, 1384 (1981) ("*Those who take religion seriously have reason to be alarmed when public officials proclaim that crosses and Christmas carols have no religious significance, or that the Ten Commandments are a secular code.*").

But just where did the Texas monument come from? The answer is Cecil B. DeMille. Working through the philanthropic organization, the Fraternal Order of Eagles, he sent hundreds of stone tablet "replicas" to state capitals and court houses just before the release of The Ten Commandments in 1956. ("Replicas" of what?— DeMille did not use one in the movie, and as far as we know, neither God nor Moses spoke the King James Bible's version of English.) But according to Breyer, one of the reasons the Texas monument was acceptable was because it served the very secular (and capitalist) purpose of being a Cecil B. DeMille publicity stunt!

In a dissenting opinion in *Perry*, Justice John Paul Stevens made an important point. How could the DeMille version of the Ten Commandments not establish religion when it presented the specific Protestant King James version?

Ten Commandments monument at the Texas state capitol

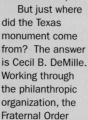

McCreary County Ten Commandment display

"The Eagles may donate as many monuments as they choose to be displayed in front of Protestant churches, benevolent organizations' meeting places, or on the front lawns of private citizens. The expurgated text of the King James version of the Ten Commandments that they have crafted is unlikely to be accepted by Catholic parishes, Jewish synagogues, or even some Protestant denominations, but the message they seek to convey is surely more compatible with church property than with property that is located on the government side of the metaphorical wall."

The books of *Exodus* and *Deuteronomy* give different wordings for the Ten Commandments, thus Jewish, Catholic, various Protestant, and Islamic versions exist.

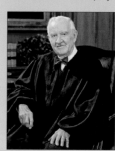
Justice Breyer

Justice Stevens

So much for Saul trying to gain a little God-power on his own—one word from Samuel, and Saul was out![5]

This was not the only example. When the priests got wind of Judean King Uzziah burning incense to God in the Temple, it was bad news for him:

"And they withstood Uzziah the king, and said unto him, It appertaineth not unto thee, Uzziah, to burn incense unto the Lord, but to the priests the sons of Aaron . . . go out of the sanctuary; for thou hast trespassed . . . .[6]"

For overstepping his proper jurisdiction, Uzziah got leprosy.

The Hebrew religious establishment protected its jurisdiction and was clear on what power was separate from the civil government.

---

2. *See generally* Robert Joseph Renaud & Lael Daniel Weinberger, *Spheres of Sovereignty: Church Autonomy Doctrine and the Theological Heritage of the Separation of Church and State,* 35 N. Ky. L. Rev. 67 (2008).

3. *See Exodus* 18:13–26 (regarding the office of judge); *Exodus* 28:1 (regarding the office of priest). Renaud & Weinberger at n.14.

Samuel lays down the law for Saul

4. *1 Samuel* 13:9–14.

6. *2 Chronicles* 26:18; see also Renaud & Weinberger at 70–71 (discussing King Jehoshaphat's respect for the separate jurisdictions of the priests and kings, *citing 2 Chronicles* 18:3–6, 19:11).

5. Getting God-power for the army is still in play. Geoffrey R. Stone, *The World of the Framers: A Christian Nation?* 56 UCLA L. Rev. 1, 2–3 (2008), begins his article with but one example from the religious "culture wars." An Air Force Academy graduate objected to the color guard at the Academy lowering the flag to the cross at a ceremony because the oath he took was *"to protect and defend the Constitution, not the New Testament."*

As for the irony of asking God for the power to kill God's other creations, no one summed it up with bitter irony better than **Abraham Lincoln** in his Second Inaugural Address on March 4, 1865:

"Both [sides] *read the same Bible and pray to the same God, and each invokes His aid against the other. It may seem strange that any men should dare to ask a just God's assistance in wringing their bread from the sweat of other men's faces, but let us judge not, that we be not judged. The prayers of both could not be answered. That of neither has been answered fully. The Almighty has His own purposes."*

The Persians:

The first significant instance of what we would recognize as religious tolerance was in the Persian Empire under Cyrus the Great.

In contrast to the Hebrews tearing down their neighbor's altars, Cyrus proclaimed that he

"repaired the ruined temples in the cities he conquered, restored their cults, and returned their sacred images . . . ."[1]

Even the Hebrews praised Cyrus's tolerance in allowing them to return to Jerusalem and rebuild the Temple:

"In the first year of King Cyrus, Cyrus the king issued a decree: Concerning the house of God at Jerusalem let the temple . . . be rebuilt . . . . And let the cost be paid from the royal treasury. Also let the gold and silver utensils . . . be returned and brought to their places in the temple in Jerusalem; and you shall put them in the house of God."[2]

Cyrus' proclamation went beyond toleration in that he publicly worshiped the

1. Cyrus's proclamation is on the **Cyrus Cylinder**, found in 1879 in modern-day Iran. Cyrus issued it in cuneiform script circa 539 BC, after he conquered Babylon.

See generally Hirad Abtahi, *Reflections on the Ambiguous Universality of Human Rights: Cyrus the Great's Proclamation as a Challenge to the Athenian Democracy's Perceived Monopoly on Human Rights*, 36 DENV. J. INT'L L. & POL'Y 55, 58–59 (2007) (arguing that Cyrus's proclamation recognized that nature gives individuals human rights that thus limits the ruler's power).

2. *Ezra* 6:3–5. The full quote shows the specificity of Cyrus's decree:
"In the first year of King Cyrus, Cyrus the king issued a decree: Concerning the house of God at Jerusalem, let the temple, the place where sacrifices are offered, be rebuilt and let its foundations be retained, its height being 60 cubits and its width 60 cubits; with three layers of huge stones and one layer of timbers. And let the cost be paid from the royal treasury. Also let the gold and silver utensils of the house of God, which Nebuchadnezzar took from the temple in Jerusalem and brought to Babylon, be returned and brought to their places in the temple in Jerusalem; and you shall put them in the house of God."

See also *Ezra* 1:1–11; *Isaiah* 45:1–6 (praising Cyrus's humanity and justice).

Medieval painting showing Cyrus the Great allowing the Hebrews to return to Jerusalem and the Temple's rebuilding (1470)

gods of the peoples whom he vanquished, such as the Babylonian god Marduk:

> *"[Cyrus] sought to worship him each day . . . . Cyrus, the king, his worshipper . . . May all the gods . . . say to Marduk, my lord that Cyrus, the king who worships you . . . ."*[3]

Certainly Cyrus made a good public relations move with this one! But it went beyond a mere PR stunt to show something else about rights and religion.

It was not the king and his god that subjected and ruled over people, or even the king/god of the Egyptians.[4] Instead, Cyrus' dynasty worshipped Ahura-Mazda.[5]

Unlike most ancient gods, Ahura-Mazda is a moral and spiritual essence rather than a material or natural force. Ahura-Mazda was preoccupied with the reign of justice and a struggle where the forces of light (justice) confront the forces of darkness (injustice) through law.[6]

3. *Quoted in* Abtahi at 66.

4. For much of Egyptian history, the pharaohs claimed to be incarnations of the god Horus.

5. Abtahi at 62.

Horus
Horus and Seth crowning Ramses III

Ahura-Mazda

Marduk

6. Abtahi at 62 (discussing how the Persians incorporated the beliefs of the ancient Iranian prophet and religious poet Zoroaster (Zarathustra) regarding the struggle of light and dark; good and evil). Zoroaster influenced the Greeks and Europe to the extent that Raphael included him in his painting *The School of Athens* (1509).

Scene from the Persian capital, Persepolis, showing the dark god Angra Mainyu killing the primeval bull and temporarily taking the universe out of balance

Detail of Zoroaster and a star-studded globe

In this cosmology, the king has the moral imperative to effect justice. Though maybe ethereal, it is objective; that is, outside the king. The king no longer rules just in his own interest but bows before a broader concept.

Cyrus, then, may have given the world its first separation between the secular (the king and positive law) and the spiritual (Ahura-Mazda and justice) spheres.[1] Or, as Thomas Jefferson would later say, a "*Separation of Church and State.*"

Taken to its fullest extent,

Cyrus and his notion of justice beyond the human realm would be the basis of natural law and even the premise of the DECLARATION OF INDEPENDENCE that

> "*We hold these truths to be self-evident that all men are created equal . . . .*"[2]

The Hebrews were not the only ones who admired Cyrus. The Greeks were also fans; remarkable because they often warred against the Persian Empire.[3]

Plato recognized the balance the Persians created

between slavery and freedom. When the Persians shared freedom with their subjects, government worked better because

> "*soldiers were friendly to their officers [and] wise men free to give counsel.*"[4]

The Persians, following Cyrus's lead, also allowed free speech because

> "*the king was not jealous but allowed free speech and respected those who could help at all by their counsel, such a man had the opportunity of contributing to*

---

1. Abtahi at 66, arguing that "[b]y referring to a reality beyond human reality, which constitutes humans' last resort to defend their rights against authoritarianism, Cyrus refers to what would be called natural law . . . ."

2. THE DECLARATION OF INDEPENDENCE, para. 2 (U.S. 1976). See Abtahi at 66–67, arguing that Cyrus and his proclamation may have prefigured Article 18 of the UNIVERSAL DECLARATION OF HUMAN RIGHTS that

"[e]veryone has the right to freedom of thought, conscience and religion; this right includes freedom to change his religion or belief, and freedom, either alone or in community with others and in public or private, to manifest his religion or belief in teaching, practice, worship and observance."

UNIVERSAL DECLARATION OF HUMAN RIGHTS, G.A. Res. 217A, at 71, U.N. GAOR, 3d Sess., 1st plen. mtg., U.N. Doc A/810 (Dec. 10, 1948), *quoted* in Abtahi at 66–67.

3. Probable relief of Persian King Xerxes, who launched the invasion of Greece in 480 BC.

Eleanor Roosevelt holds a Spanish version of the Universal Declaration of Human Rights

4. Abtahi at 83 (discussing Plato's *Laws*). This, of course, is not the Hollywood image of Persians from the "sandal epic" THE 300 SPARTANS (20th Century Fox 1962) to the fanciful but visually stunning 300 (WARNER BROTHERS 2007).

5. Abtahi at 83. Abtahi goes on to note that Plato develops the idea of a society based on the mutual exchange of reason as the bases of a *res publica* (citing PLATO, THE REPUBLIC (trans. Benjamin Jowett 2009), *available at* http://classics.mit.edu/Plato/republic.html).

Later in this chapter, compare Sir Thomas More's PETITION FOR FREE SPEECH in Parliament.

the common stock the fruit of his wisdom."

Because of free speech, men of ability rose in the empire and

"all their affairs made progress, owing to their freedom, friendliness and mutual exchange of reason."[5]

Speaking of The Greeks:

The Greeks prized this free mutual exchange of reason, at least in the abstract. The first historian, Herodotus, who wrote about the Persian War, noted that freedom and free speech were good for government:

"And it is plain enough, not from this instance only, but from many everywhere, that freedom is an excellent thing."

Indeed, because of the freedom to speak the Athenians had become fierce fighters:

"Even the Athenians, who, while they continued under the rule of tyrants, were not a whit more valiant than any of their neighbors, no sooner shook off

the yoke than they became decidedly the first of all."[6]

Herodotus explains the psychology of freedom:

"These things show that, while undergoing oppression, they let themselves be beaten, since then they worked for a master; but so soon as they got their freedom, each man was eager to do the best he could for himself."[7]

Herodotus's contemporary and successor in the western historical tradition, Thucydides, picked up on the same theme of connecting freedom and government:

---

6. See online text and translation at http://www.sacred-texts.com/cla/hh/hh5070.htm (last visited July 14, 2009).

7. Writing about a war 2,500 years after the Persian Wars, historian Stephen Ambrose quotes General Maxwell Taylor about the 101st Airborne Division during World War II: *"The men were hardened, the officers tested, their equipment upgraded and they had that wonderful flexibility and self-confidence imparted by a democratic society. No other system could produce soldiers like that."* STEPHEN E. AMBROSE, D-DAY JUNE 6, 1944: THE CLIMACTIC BATTLE OF WORLD WAR II 53 (1994). As Ambrose later analyzed in STEPHEN E. AMBROSE, THE VICTORS: EISENHOWER AND HIS BOYS: THE MEN OF WORLD WAR II 183–84 (1998), *"[t]he men fighting for democracy were able to make quick, on-site decisions and act on them; the men fighting for the totalitarian regime were not. Except for a captain here, a lieutenant there, not one German officer reacted appropriately to the challenge of D-Day."*

Herodotus

Fourth century BC Athenian warrior leaving for war

Gen. Taylor

General Dwight D. Eisenhower visits the 101st Airborne before D-Day and Athenians before battle

"Here [in Athens] each individual is interested not only in his own affairs but in the affairs of the state as well . . . . Of all people we alone do not say that a man who takes no interest in politics is a man who minds his own business, but we say that he is useless."

With respect to speech,

Thucydides specifically noted that

"the worst thing is to rush into action before the consequences have been properly debated."[1]

The Athenians, then, invented our notion of freedom of speech. Any citizen could address the assembly, the courts, or the

government and also could move legislation.[2]

Thucydides contrasts Athens with its rival, Sparta, showing that the Greek world was not unanimous regarding ideas of civil freedom and speech, and this underlay the conflict between the two Greek states.

Indeed, in terminology

Pericles

Brandeis

1. THUCYDIDES, THE PELOPONNESIAN WAR, *quoted in* WILTSHIRE at 113.

Thucydides is quoting the funeral speech of Pericles. Over two millennia later, Justice Louis Brandeis echoed that *"the greatest menace to freedom is an inert people."* *Whitney v. California*, 274 U.S. 357, 375 (1927) (Brandeis, J., concurring). Following Herodotus, Pericles notes the relationship between freedom and courage:

"[H]appiness . . . [is] the fruit of freedom and freedom of valor . . . ."

Quoted in Keith Werhan, *The Classical Athenian Ancestry of American Freedom of Speech*, 2008 SUP. CT. REV. 293, 310. Brandeis again picked up the theme: *"liberty . . . [is] the secret of happiness and courage [is] the secret of liberty."* *Whitney* at 375.

2. WILTSHIRE at 114–15. The Athenians called this *"isēgoria"* ("the equal right to speak") for everyone who wished to address the boule, ecclesia, or jury courts. WILTSHIRE at 112; Werhan at 300. *"[I]sēgoria"* is synonymous with democracy. *See* WILTSHIRE at 119 and 123 (*"[I]sēgoria"* was part of the freedom of assembly).

The ideal assembly speaker (*"rhētōr"*) was an "honest, ordinary citizen" who spoke simply and truthfully when he occasionally ascended the speaker's platform. Werhan at 303. This is the American ideal as well. In Norman Rockwell's *Save Freedom of Speech*, a man in a workshirt, with calloused hands, stands to voice an opinion at a town

meeting, while others, including men in suits and ties, look on. The *Saturday Evening Post* published this color lithograph in 1942 as part of the "Four Freedoms" series to encourage Americans to buy war bonds during World War II. Again, the image evokes Herodotus's and Thucydides's description of a democracy at war: *"so soon as they got their freedom, each man was eager to do the best he could for himself."*

The Greek world at the time of the conflict between Athens and Sparta

that reflects a modern free speech debate, the Athenian Demosthenes noted the role of speech in a free society rather than in a closed one:

"The fundamental difference between the Athenian and the Spartan constitutions is that in Athens you are free to praise the Spartan constitution, whereas in Sparta you are not allowed to praise any constitution other than the Spartan."[3]

So a very modern free speech debate played out in the ancient Greek world, with Athenian Greeks extolling the value of free speech and Spartan Greeks extolling the virtues of security. This language parallels the Cold War between the United States and the old Soviet Union about the nature of freedom and society.[4]

But just as America did not always stay true to its free speech foundation during the Cold War,[5] Athens did not always stay true to its own innovations of democracy and free speech.

3. *Quoted in* WILTSHIRE at 113.

4. Kruschev meeting with Kennedy during the Cold War. *See* Werhan at 313.

In *Debs v. United States*, 249 U.S. 211 (1919), the Supreme Court upheld his conviction. Debs eventually got a presidential pardon.

Election poster for Debs, Socialist Party of America candidate for president in 1904

In *Schenck v. United States*, 249 U.S. 47 (1919), the Supreme Court upheld the conviction of a person for circulating leaflets that argued that conscription is involuntary servitude. *Whitney v. California*, 274 U.S. 357 (1927), *overruled by Brandenburg v. Ohio*, 395 U.S. 444 (1969), upheld the conviction of an individual under the California Criminal Syndicalism Act for attending a Communist Labor Party convention. In *Dennis v. United States,* 341 U.S. 494 (1951), the Supreme Court upheld the convictions of the Communist Party leaders for advocating Marxist-Leninist ideology. Again, America has not always lived up to its free speech ideal.

5. **Communism Cases.** America has a history of trying to restrict communist speech.

Congress passed the Espionage Act of 1917 to target communists. O'Brien at 47. Presidential candidate and labor leader Eugene V. Debs was convicted and imprisoned under it for speaking against American involvement in World War I.

Eugene V. Debs

Debs in a federal penitentiary

World War I poster

In 399 BC, the Athenians put the philosopher Socrates on trial, not for anything he did but for what he said.

What we know of Socrates's trial comes from his student, Plato. In the *Euthyphro, Apology, Crito,* and *Phaedo,* Plato made Socrates's trial the central theme.[1] Socrates faced trumped up charges of *"corrupting the youth"* and *"disbelieving in the ancestral gods,"* showing once again the thematic connection between speech and religion. Plato's point is that speaking truth often offends the dogmatic.[2]

And for speaking the truth, the Athenians tried, convicted, and had Socrates kill himself with hemlock.[3] Even in Athens, the cradle of free speech, the right to speak and believe without government restriction was fragile.

---

1. *See* **Chapter 7: Trial by Jury or . . . by God!** for a brief discussion of the Socrates trial in the context of the history of juries.

"COME UNTO ME, YE OPPREST!"
—Alley in the Memphis *Commercial Appeal.*

Political cartoon of the era depicting an anarchist attempting to destroy the Statue of Liberty

Senator Joseph McCarthy chats with Roy Cohn at the McCarthy Hearings

2. *"Humans,"* said Socrates, *"do not know anything worthwhile."* He believed the human condition does not allow certainty of moral truth and therefore we never know for sure whether our belief regarding "truth" is correct. Werhan at 326, *quoting* Plato's *Apology.* For Socrates, only a god could possess true wisdom.

Socrates

3. For the effect of hemlock on the body, *see* **Chapter 8: "Baby, Don't Be Cruel": What's So Cruel** *and* **Unusual about the Eighth Amendment?**

The Death of Socrates by David (1787)

The Romans:

Romans of the republic and the early empire lived in one of history's most class-conscious societies. Not every citizen was free to speak, and Romans did not share the notion of freedom of assembly.[4]

They instead divided government along ideas of separating power among the classes: the monarchy (consuls), aristocracy (senators), and the democracy (people).[5] Only members of the senatorial class, the patricians, were supposed to speak their mind on politics, leaving normal citizens, the plebians, with only a representative voice in the office of the Tribune of the Plebs (*tribuni plebis*).

The Romans feared popular power and created an entire constitutional structure to hinder it. Ironically, all the constraints led to a government that lacked the ability to prevent that most popular of Romans, Julius Caesar, from usurping the whole thing.[6]

4. WILTSHIRE at 116.

5. WILTSHIRE at 127. This formed the precursor of the U.S. Constitution's separation of powers among the executive, legislative, and judicial branches of government.

The Supreme Court building of the judicial branch

The Capitol dome of the legislative branch

6. WILTSHIRE at 129. In 49 BC, Julius Caesar crossed the Rubicon River to march on Rome. This was the boundary that a Roman general could not cross while still commanding troops. By so doing, Caesar was in rebellion against the Roman Republic. Thus the term "crossing the Rubicon" has come to mean passing a point of no return.

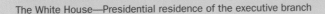

The White House—Presidential residence of the executive branch

But even the senators were not wholly free to speak their minds. The Romans had two elected "censors" (*censura*) to supervise counting the Roman population and to guard the "public morality" (*regimen morum*).[1] This is where we get our modern words "census," "censor," and "censorship."[2]

Defending public morality was a full-time job in the late Roman republic.[3] Censors did not just have to prevent crime and "immorality," they also had to maintain the traditional Roman character, ethics, and habits (*mos majorum*).[4]

But the job came with a lot of power. Because the censors controlled the census, they could expel a person from the list of Roman citizens and, thus, expel a senator from the Senate.

1. The census determined the senate list (*lectio senatus*) and the equatorial rank (*recognitio equitum*). Censors administered public buildings and the building of new public works.

2. This dour fellow is **Cato the Elder**, censor of Rome in 184 B.C., who was just the man to ferret out immorality! The word "*censor*" comes from the Latin "*senex*" ("old") and is also the root for "senator," "senior," and "senile." Aᴙᴛᴏ at 467.

3. *Romans in the Decadence of the Empire* by Couture (1847).

U.S. Cᴏɴꜱᴛ. Art. I, § 2, provides that the government must conduct a census every ten years. In modern America, census counters use handheld computers, and the count influences the distribution of public money and building projects, an interesting tie to the old Roman job of censor.

4. Activities that could get you in trouble with the censors included the following:

- living in celibacy when you ought to be providing new citizens;
- improperly dissolving a marriage or engagement;
- improperly treating your wife, children, or parents;
- spending money extravagantly;
- neglecting your fields;
- being cruel toward slaves or clients;
- having a disreputable occupation like acting;
- defrauding orphans.

Additionally, the censors policed public officials for malfeasance in office and perjury. But because it took two censors to act, a politician needed only to bribe one to get virtual immunity.

5. The censors are the origin of the modern "censure." The U.S. Senate and House still "censure" people, but it is only a public reprimand without legal consequence. In fact, it has no basis in the Constitution or Senate and House rules. On December 2, 1954, the Senate censured Republican Senator McCarthy for failing to cooperate with and insulting the subcommittee investigating him. Lᴇᴡɪꜱ at 123. "McCarthyism" ebbed with McCarthy's disgrace and death.

Joseph McCarthy

Because of this, censors were also known as *castigatores* ("chastisers").[5]

The censor could be useful to Roman politicians. The trick was to show your political enemy's immorality in a way that would trigger the censors' power of negating his citizenship, and thus his political voice. Indeed, public morality could easily expand to include what a person said rather than what he did.

The Roman censorship lasted from 443 to 22 BC, a total of 421 years. The office, in fact, did not really end. Emperors saw the value of having the power of censorship and thus took on the office under the title *praefectura morum* ("prefect of the morals").[6] Popes picked it up from there.[7]

6. Caesar Augustus, the first Roman emperor, took the censor job in 28 B.C.

The emperor also took over the job of *pontifex maximus*, heading the Ancient Roman College of Pontiffs and thus all religious institutions.

"*Pontifex*" means "bridge builder" ("*pons*" + "*facere*") and "*maximus*" means "greatest," as in the English "maximum." Originally, a "pontiff" probably built Roman bridges over the Tiber, a sacred river and deity. Thus, symbolically "pontiff" meant one who could bridge the divide between gods and men. In this sense, beginning perhaps as early as the late fourth century, the popes took on the title. *See* ENCYCLOPEDIA OF CATHOLICISM 1010 (Richard P. McBrien ed.,1995).

Ancient Roman bridge over the Tiber

7. The early Roman emperors took on the title *primus inter pares* ("first among equals") to reduce the appearance of a dictatorship.

In Christianity, the Eastern Orthodox Churches recognized the pope as *primus inter pares*, but Rome stayed with the idea of papal supremacy.

"First among equals" also describes the Chief Justice of the United States, who, despite having considerable administrative powers, has no direct control over the other justices' decisions.

The Roberts Court in 2009

Emperor Augustus in the robes of *pontifex maximus*

Pope Benedict XIV as *pontifex maximus*

Chief Justice John Roberts

Despite the Roman obsession with public morality, they were both tolerant and practical regarding religion, especially with respect to maintaining the power of the state.

As the Roman statesman Cicero noted,

"Jupiter is called Best and Greatest not because he makes us just or sober or wise but safe and secure, rich and prosperous." [1]

Roman religion, like the Old Testament Hebrew religion, centered on success.

For the Romans, more gods meant more success.[2] Incorporation was the policy; they simply added a newly conquered people's local gods to the Roman pantheon and often gave them Roman names. And as long as a religion was willing to give the emperor his due,[3] its adherents were free to practice as they pleased.

And so things went with the Romans, at least until somewhere around the year 30 AD, when they executed an obscure teacher (rabbi), challenging an obscure faith, from one of the empire's many backwater provinces. This rabbi's followers would create a religion that ended up taking over the Empire.

The rabbi was Jesus.

---

1. WILTSHIRE at 105, *quoting* CICERO, DE NATURA DEORUM 3.36).

"By Jove!"— Jupiter was the Roman version of the Greek Zeus. The names Jupiter, Jove, and Zeus all have a common Indo-European root that includes the Latin "*dues*," which translates into English as "God" and is the source of the English word "deity." *See* WEBSTER'S NEW INTERNATIONAL DICTIONARY OF THE ENGLISH LANGUAGE 691 (2d ed. 1942). The planet Jupiter is named for the Roman god.

Jupiter and Thétis by Ingres (1811)

5. "Christ!," "Jesus!," or "Jesus Christ!" are interjections or exclamations often used in surprise or anger, and they are not usually direct religious references. Some Christians believe they violate the Third Commandment against taking the Lord's name in vain and are thus blasphemous. To avoid the rebuke of "using the Lord's name in vain," circumlocutions and euphemisms exist, such as starting with "Jesus" and quickly adding "Mary and Joseph!" to make it sound like a religious invocation rather than like a curse.

2. WILTSHIRE at 104–05.

3. The empire brought a new fusion of state and religion with the "divine" emperor. WILTSHIRE at 106. For the Romans, it was not so much that the emperor himself was a god (unlike the Egyptian pharaohs) but that the emperor personified Rome's divine authority.

4. Jesus (c. 4 BC–c. 30 AD), also known as Jesus Christ or Jesus the Christ, is Christianity's central figure, and most Christian denominations venerate him as the son of God and God incarnate. Christians also believe he is the messiah (savior) that the Old Testament foretold. Judaism rejects these claims, and Islam considers Jesus a prophet.

"Christ" is English for the Greek "*Khristós*" ("the anointed") a translation of the Hebrew ("*Masía*" or "*mashiach*," which also means "messiah"), as in someone God has anointed for a special mission. The English spelling "Christ" comes

Christ the Savior, a sixth century icon from Saint Catherine's Monastery, Mount Sinai

from the seventeenth century, with Old and Middle English usually spelling it "Crist," with a short *i*, preserved in the modern pronunciation of "Christmas."

WWJD—WHAT WOULD JESUS DO—UNDER THE FIRST AMENDMENT?

Jesus did nothing; at least not anything that should have gotten the Romans to execute him.[4]

He committed no crime of which we know.[5] He did not lead armed revolutionaries. He conspired to commit no illegal deed.

Perhaps he blasphemed against the Hebrews' idea of God, but what would the Romans have cared about that?[5] Besides, the punishment for a blasphemer or a heretic was stoning, not crucifixion.[6] So what stake did the Romans have in the Hebrews' theological argument with the son of a carpenter?[7]

The answer is the power of speech and religion.

They killed Jesus for what he said.[8]

Jesus, through religious speech, challenged the powerful. For that they killed him:

"Then the whole assembly rose and led him off to Pilate. And they began to accuse him, saying, 'We have found this man subverting our nation. He opposes payment of taxes to Caesar and claims to be Christ/Messiah, a king.'"[9]

6. Indeed, the Romans specifically killed Jesus with crucifixion—the best audio-visual aid in the ancient world for making a political point. *See* **Chapter 8: "Baby, Don't Be Cruel": What's So Cruel *and* Unusual about the Eighth Amendment?**

A Byzantine crucifixion icon, Athens, Greece. An icon is a depiction of Christian religious art. It is not painted but "written," again showing the connection between speech and religion.

8. *Sermon on the Mount* by Bloch.

7. Historians generally accept that a man named Jesus lived, giving at least some credibility to the Bible as an historical source. Additionally, the Jewish historian Flavius Josephus wrote in 93 or 94 AD in his *Antiquities of the Jews* that

"[n]ow there was about this time Jesus, a wise man, if it be lawful to call him a man; for he was a doer of wonderful works, a teacher of such men as receive the truth with pleasure. He drew over to him both many of the Jews and many of the Gentiles. He was Christ. And when Pilate, at the suggestion of the principal men amongst us, had condemned him to the cross, those that loved him at the first did not forsake him; for he appeared to them alive again the third day, as the divine prophets had foretold these and ten thousand other wonderful things concerning him. And the tribes of Christians, so named from him, are not extinct at this day."

THE WORKS OF FLAVIUS JOSPEHUS 612 (William Whiston trans., 1847).

9. *Luke* 23:1–4.

The Tribute Money by Masaccio

Accusing Jesus of opposing taxes was a ploy to get the Romans to kill him. Jesus's opponents had asked him whether they should pay Roman taxes. He famously asked for a Roman coin and responded that they should

"[g]ive to Caesar what is Caesar's, and to God what is God's."[1]

In this statement, Jesus himself laid the groundwork for the separation of church and state. During his trial, Jesus expanded the theme when responding to Pontius Pilate, the provincial governor and his prosecutor:

"My kingdom is not of this world. If my kingdom were of this world, my servants would have been fighting, that I might not be delivered over to the Jews."[2]

But many Christians, both then and now, did not see this as a prescription to separate church and state.[3] Rather they saw it as delineating a Christian's role in the church-state struggle:

---

1. *Matthew* 22:21.

2. *John* 18:36. Jesus' trial before the Roman Pontius Pilate is a key part of the drama or "passion." Pilate usually comes across as sympathetic to Jesus; after all, Rome later became one of Christianity's centers. For Jesus' trial in film *see e.g.,*

THE LAST TEMPTATION OF CHRIST (Universal Studios 1988)

THE PASSION OF THE CHRIST (Newmarket Films 2004)

MONTY PYTHON'S LIFE OF BRIAN (Warner Brothers 1979)

JESUS CHRIST SUPERSTAR (Universal Studios 1973)

3. Christians recognize the duty from the Old Testament to acknowledge God:

"*Be wise now therefore, O ye kings: be instructed, ye judges of the earth. Serve the Lord with fear, and rejoice with trembling. Kiss the Son . . . .*"

Psalms 2:10–11, *discussed in* Weinberger at 410, *citing* 1 JOHN CALVIN, COMMENTARY ON THE BOOK OF PSALMS 22–27 (James Anderson trans., 1845; photo. reprint 2005) (commenting on the Protestant view of the individual's duty of acknowledgement); Pope Leo XIII, *The Christian Constitution of States*, Encyclical Letter Immortale Dei, Nov. 1, 1885, *in* JOHN A. RYAN & MOORHOUSE F.X. MILLAR, THE STATE AND THE CHURCH 1, 2–4 (1924), *available at* http:// www.ewtn. com/library/encyc/ l13sta.htm (stating the Catholic view of the individual's duty of acknowledgement).

Christ before Pilate (1881)

"We ought to obey God rather than men." **4**

This creed led many to the arena.

CHRISTIANS AND LIONS

Christians got into trouble because they would not give the emperor his due.

For the Romans, *pieta* ("piety") in religion was supposed to promote unity and loyalty to Rome; not the point of Christianity. Because the Roman view of religion was utilitarian, they believed bad things would happen if people did not properly respect the gods. After all, these traditional "pagan" gods had treated Rome pretty well, so why mess with success! **5**

This is where "throwing Christians to the lions in the arena" came about.**6** Generally, persecution of Christians was sporadic and not necessarily government policy. But some emperors did implement a broader persecution policy. The first and most famous was Nero.**7**

---

4. *Acts of the Apostles* 5.

5. The Roman Empire in 117 AD, at its greatest extent.

The Roman Empire in 117 AD

Senatorial provinces
Imperial provinces
Client states

6. *The Christian Martyrs' Last Prayer* by Gerome (1883).

A Christian Dirce by Siemiradzki. Nero (center) looks on at a martyred Christian woman.

7. Nero (37–68 AD) needed political cover in 64 AD, when Rome caught fire and he got blamed. In response, Nero blamed the Christians; after all, they did not honor the gods.

Following a long artistic tradition of presenting Nero in a bad light, Hollywood took a shot in Quo Vadis (MGM 1951), where Peter Ustinov gave the definitive Nero. *"Quo vadis"* is Latin for *"Where are you going?"* It refers to the story that Christ met Saint Peter on the Appian Way, fleeing Nero's persecution. Peter asked Christ, *"Domine, quo vadis?"* (*"Lord, where are you going?"*) and Christ answered *"Eo Romam iterum crucifigi."* (*"I am going to Rome to be crucified again."*). Peter took this to mean that he had to return to Rome to be crucified, so that Christ would not have to be crucified again. They crucified Saint Peter at the foot of Vatican Hill on the current site of Saint Peter's Basilica.

Peter Ustinov as Nero

Church of Domine Quo Vadis, where Peter met Christ

Crucifixion of Saint Peter by Caravaggio. Saint Peter asked to be crucified upside down so as not to be compared to Jesus.

Saint Peter's Basilica from the Tiber River

CONSTANTINE TO THE RESCUE

At least so Constantine said!

The traditional view is that Constantine embraced Christianity after God gave him a vision before the Battle of Milvian Bridge in 312 AD. Looking up, Constantine saw a cross of light and the words,

"Ev Toutw Nika" (or, in Latin, "in hoc signo vinces"; in English, "by this sign, conquer.")[1]

He had his troops, so the story goes, paint their shields with the Christian Chi Ro symbol.[2] Constantine won the battle and ended up emperor; otherwise we would not talk about him today.

From this point on, Rome tolerated Christianity throughout the empire.[3] For this, Constantine is known as the first Christian Roman emperor and was made a saint.[4]

But leaving aside Constantine's personal religiosity, his flirtation with the Christians paid off politically. If he had stayed with the old pagan faiths, the most he would

1. *Constantine's Conversion* by Rubens, showing him before the Battle of Milvian Bridge.

A coin of Constantine (c. 337 AD) showing the Chi Rho on the Roman standard (*labarum*) spearing a serpent

2. *Constantine the Great,* The Catholic Encyclopedia, http://www. newadvent. org/cathen/04295c. htm (last visited Aug. 2, 2009).

The Chi Rho is a very early Christian symbol made by superimposing the first two Greek letters of "Christ" ("Χριστός"); *chi* equals *ch* and *rho* equals *r*, to produce the monogram ☧.

Though not technically a cross, the Chi Rho invokes Jesus's crucifixion.

3. As the story goes, his mother, Saint Helena, prayed and prayed for him to accept Christianity. She then went to the Holy Land and found the True Cross. *St. Helena*, The Catholic Encyclopedia, http://www. newadvent.org/cathen/07202b.htm (last visited Aug. 2, 2009). The fact that she found it over 300 years after the crucifixion adds to the miraculous nature of the discovery. Of course, there were so many pieces of the "true cross" in Europe's churches that they would make a forest of crosses.

4. Not bad, given that he did not convert until his deathbed. The last-minute absolution must have been a good precaution. After all, during his reign he killed a number of rivals and courtiers. He also killed his wife Fausta by locking her in an overheated bath and his oldest son Cripus by poisoning him.

Helena and the true cross in Saint Peter's Bascilica

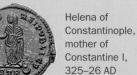

Helena of Constantinople, mother of Constantine I, 325–26 AD

The Baptism of Constantine by students of Raphael

have gotten would have been to be a "divine" emperor and the *pontifex maximus* ("chief of the pagan priests"). Roman history showed that neither title protected an emperor from assassination.

With Christianity, though, he got to be God's hand-picked savior, chosen under the sign of the cross at Milvian Bridge to kill everyone else.[5] And at the time, Christianity was a mess! In fact, it really was not Christianity but *Christianities* floating around the Roman world.[6] The "church" could not even agree on a basic creed or statement of belief.

Thus Constantine got to be God's broker— politically *way* better than being a dusty old "divine" emperor![7]

It was Constantine, not the bishops, who called the "church" to Nicaea (in modern Turkey) in 325 AD to have the bishops come up with the first truly universal statement of Christian belief.[8] This became known as the Nicene Creed, which most major Christian denominations use in some form even today.[9]

5. Constantine's colossal head. He is not portrayed as divine but chosen, with his gaze looking up to God. Overall, it gives the message that this is a guy you do not want to mess with!

6. Arianism was one of the Christianities. Bishop Arius from Alexandria, Egypt, in the early 300s denied that Jesus was fully God. Rather, the Father, in the beginning, created (or begot) the Son, and the Son, with the Father, created the world. This made the Son (Jesus) just a created being and not God. Regarding Arian Christianity, *see Arianism*, THE CATHOLIC ENCYCLOPEDIA, http://www.newadvent.org/cathen/01707c.htm (last visited June 12, 2009).

7. In fact, he got to be "Constantine the Great" and even Saint Constantine, as this mosaic centuries later shows. Hagia Sophia, Constantinople (Istanbul), c. 1000.

8. Constantine (center) and the Fathers of the First Council of Nicaea (325) holding the Nicene Creed in its 381 form.

9. The Modern Nicene Creed.

"We believe in one God, the Father, the Almighty, maker of heaven and earth, of all that is, seen and unseen.

We believe in one Lord, Jesus Christ, the only son of God, eternally begotten of the Father, God from God, Light from Light, true God from true God, begotten, not made, of one being with the Father.

Through him all things were made.

For us and for our salvation he came down from heaven: by the power of the Holy Spirit he became incarnate from the Virgin Mary, and was made man.

For our sake he was crucified under Pontius Pilate; he suffered death and was buried.

On the third day he rose again in accordance with the Scriptures; he ascended into heaven and is seated at the right hand of the Father.

He will come again in glory to judge the living and the dead, and his kingdom will have no end.

We believe in the Holy Spirit, the Lord, the giver of life, who proceeds from the Father [and the Son].

With the Father and the Son he is worshipped and glorified.

He has spoken through the Prophets.

We believe in one holy catholic and apostolic Church.

We acknowledge one baptism for the forgiveness of sins.

We look for the resurrection of the dead, and the life of the world to come. Amen."

Despite becoming a saint, Constantine could be perfectly pagan when it suited his political need. His arch of triumph in Rome makes no mention of Christ and uses no Christian symbols.[1] In his mix of Christianity, paganism, and state power, Constantine had the best of it all. Forget any separation of church and state; for Constantine it was his two "churches," Christian and pagan, that served the state, that is, him.[2]

Constantine would not have understood our modern concept of "the state." Rather, during this age it was the city, the Greek concept of the *polis*, that mattered. After all, it was the Roman Empire he ruled, named after the city of Rome. Even the later Byzantine Empire was named after Byzantium, Constantinople's old name before Constantine moved in.[3]

Constantine and his successors ruled for centuries over this "city" of Byzantium.[4] But it would take a Christian bishop and former pagan to define the place of something that was more than just the emperor's "city of men." There was something separate, which in many ways was a foundation for the later concept of separation of church and state.

This separate "place" is Saint Augustine of Hippo's CITY OF GOD.

1. The Arch of Constantine (315) in Rome commemorates Constantine's victory at Milvian bridge in 312. The fact that the Arch has no Christian symbols could be because the builders stole the art from older Roman buildings and monuments in a technique called "*spolia.*"

2. Constantine the Great crowned by Constantinople. It is the city, personified as a goddess, which crowns him, not a pagan priest or Christian bishop. Even in his symbols, Constantine would cede no power to the church.

As we will see, this is the type of power and status that Henry VIII of England lusted after.

3. In 1453 the Ottoman Turks took the city, renamed it Istanbul, and ended the Byzantine Empire for good. But you can still see the old Byzantine parts and ruins today, as featured in the James Bond movie FROM RUSSIA WITH LOVE (United Artists 1963).

4. At the risk of getting ahead of the story, **John Milton**, the author of PARADISE LOST, also wrote that Constantine was Christianity's worst corrupter. *See* John Witte, Jr., *Prophets, Priests, and Kings: John Milton and the Reformation of Rights and Liberties in England*, 57 EMORY L.J. 1527, 1562 (2008). For Milton, the early church had faithfully lived by "*rendering unto Caesar what was Caesar's*" and leaving God the rest. Despite persecutions, the church thrived for three centuries. Then Constantine came along and took "*things that were God's.*" Constantine sponsored the church, called the church councils, controlled church property, and appointed the bishops. For Milton, Protestants and Catholics alike had been "*enthralled*" and "*seduced*" by Constantine's (i.e., the state's) "*lavish superstition*" that church and state needed each other. According to Milton, Christians "*should not suffer the two powers, the ecclesiastical and the civil, which are so totally distinct, to commit whoredom together.*" *Id.* at 1562.

5. Botticelli's *Augustine* is a nice-looking Italian man at his desk. But given that Augustine was a Berber from North Africa, the older portrait is closer to the mark; Augustine was probably black. On Augustine generally, *see* PETER BROWN, AUGUSTINE OF HIPPO (1967); GARRY WILLS, SAINT AUGUSTINE (1999); *Saint Augustine*, THE CATHOLIC ENCYCLOPEDIA, http://www.newadvent.org/fathers/1201.htm (last visited Aug. 6, 2009).

Augustine by Sandro Botticelli (c. 1480)

Early sixth century portrait of Augustine

SEPARATING CHURCH AND STATE IN *THE CITY OF GOD*

Saint Augustine wrote THE CITY OF GOD (*De Civitate Dei*, also known as *De Civitate Dei contra Paganos* or *The City of God against the Pagans*) in the early fifth century.[5] The book is about God, martyrdom, Jews, and Christianity's relationship with competing religions and philosophies.

Augustine wrote it just after the Visigoths sacked Rome in 410 AD.[6] The Roman Empire, the "city of man," was failing. Augustine offered the "city of God" as consolation.

Even though Christianity was the empire's official religion, Augustine clarified that its message was essentially spiritual, not political. Human history was a conflict between the cities of God and man.[7]

In the city of God, people forgo earthly pleasure for Christian values. Conversely, the city of Man is always divided against itself, and the strong oppress the weak for their own interests and lusts. All of this was not supposed to happen in the church, the city of God on earth.

Despite Augustine, the centuries would show that it was hard to maintain the separation, especially when the church became the only real government in Europe.

6. *Sack of Rome* by Sylvestre (1890)

7. Augustine picks up on the Bible's BOOK OF REVELATION, which speaks of the *"Heavenly Jerusalem"* or the New Jerusalem, a better place than this earth.

This New Jerusalem becomes an important theme for the seventeenth century New England Puritans inspired to create it in America. John Winthrop, first governor of the Massachusetts Bay Colony, gave his famous "City on a Hill" sermon in 1630, extolling the ideal.

John of Patmos watches the descent of the New Jerusalem from God in a fourteenth century tapestry

Founding New Jerusalem

John Winthrop

MIXING THE CITY OF GOD AND THE CITY OF MAN: WHEN THE CHURCH *WAS* THE STATE

After Rome's fall, there was little struggle between church and state because there was no state. For the most part, kings— such as they were—ruled with personal oaths of allegiance.[1]

As for anything resembling government, the church was *it*. For one thing, clerics were the only ones who could read and write, and bureaucracy cannot run without writing.[2]

This is not to say that power struggles did not exist between kings and the church, only that this was not the institutionalized struggle that we mean today when we speak of the separation of church and state.

A famous event in medieval history illustrates the complicated relationship between the church and rulers: Pope Leo III's crowning Charlemagne as emperor.[3]

On Christmas day 800, Pope Leo III "surprised"

---

1. With feudal kings, government was personal and based on the oath of fealty (from Latin *"fidelitas,"* or "faithfulness")—a pledge of allegiance of one person to another. The oath was typically made upon a religious object such as a Bible or a saint's relic, thus binding the oath-taker before God. *See* **Chapter 5: From Testicles to *Dragnet*: How the Fifth Amendment Protects *All* of Us.** In medieval Europe, fealty was sworn between two people: the obliged person ("vassal") and a person of rank ("lord").

2. Judges and university professors, all of whom used to be clerics, still wear clerical "priest" robes, as do graduating university students. We get our modern word "clerk" from "cleric." *Cleric*, The Catholic Encyclopedia, http://www.newadvent.org/cathen/04049b.htm (last visited May 13, 2007).

Justice Oliver Wendell Holmes, Jr. in his robes.

3. Overlapping Politics. Ostensibly, this is a painting of Leo III crowning Charlemagne Holy Roman emperor in 800. But the painting has more to do with sixteenth century politics, because the pope is really Leo X, with Francis I depicted as Charlemagne.

Roland pledges to Charlemagne

The Coronation of Charlemagne by Raphael (c. 1517)

Charlemagne with the imperial crown, making him not just king of the Franks but *imperator augustus*, the first Holy Roman emperor.[4] This was an event loaded with symbolism and politics. Pope Leo was asserting that the pope could assume the power to recognize—i.e., select—the emperor, a very different deal from the one Emperor Constantine worked out four centuries earlier.[5]

But despite Leo's claims, the church still lived in a violent world.[6] In exchange for the church's recognition and legitimacy, kings and lords protected the church.

Only later did the Church gain more overt political power. In 1057, Pope Gregory VII declared that the pope was supreme not only over other bishops but also over secular authorities:

> *"Emperors must kiss the feet of the bishop of Rome."*[7]

Most emperors, kings, and other potentates did not comply. But what gave the church its real power was what it had to offer.[8]

---

4. **Voltaire** once quipped, *"[t]he Holy Roman Empire was neither Holy, nor Roman, nor an Empire."*

6. Charlemagne in 772 aids Pope Hadrian I (Leo's predecessor) with military assistance.

7. *Quoted in* Harold J. Berman, *Religious Foundations of Law in the West: An Historical Perspective,* 1 J.L. & Religion 3, 6 (1983). Before Gregory VII, the emperor was the head of the church and "vicar of Christ," with the pope being just the "vicar of Saint Peter." For most of history before this, the emperor actually chose the pope, not the other way around.

Pope Gregory VII

5. Compare Charlemagne getting the crown from Pope Leo with Constantine being crowned by the city of Constantinople.

Who got to put the crown on was still an issue a thousand years later when Napoleon crowned himself and then Josefina with the Pope and the church passively looking on.

Napoleon Crowning Josefina by David (1805–08)

8. Secular power began to support church decrees as when the Emperor Honorius provided in 412 that no clergyman should be accused criminally except before a bishop. Charlemagne later affirmed that a litigant could transfer his cause from a secular court to an ecclesiastical tribunal. Charles P. Sherman, *A Brief History of Imperial Roman Canon Law,* 7 Cal. L. Rev. 93, 102–04 (1918).

The church was the center of learning, culture, and law.[1] It invented universities, first to study theology but then other disciplines.[2] The church nurtured great scholars, jurists, philosophers, and theologians, who took old legal texts and systems and synthesized them.[3]

The church offered *law* to the people of western Europe.[4] Kings rose or fell, and empires grew or shrank, but the church unified the whole and endured. What this meant in practical terms is that nearly everyone in Europe lived under at least two legal systems:

the emperor's (or king's, or baron's, or lord's, etc.) and the church's. As this system of law evolved, each checked the other so that no power was absolute.

As we will see, Henry VIII of England eliminated the whole system. The later

---

1. Berman, *Religious Foundations*, at 3 ("*For over eight hundred years, from the late eleventh to the early twentieth century, law in the West was supported by, and in many respects based on, religious beliefs, both Roman Catholic and Protestant.*").

4. The first German law book, THE SACH-SENSPIEGEL (1220), says that "*God is himself law; and therefore law is dear to him.*" Quoted in Berman, *Religious Foundations*, at 12.

5. Berman, *Religious Foundations*, at 10. This church-state legal system with concurrent, concordant, and competing jurisdiction is a precursor to American federalism and the separation of powers. *See* **Chapter 9: The Ninth Amendment: Still a Mystery after All These Years; Chapter 10: "Are You Talkin' to Me?": Just Who Are Those "People" in the Tenth Amendment?**

2. Around 1087, the church created the first university at Bologna. Berman, *Religious Foundations*, at 7.

Medieval meeting of doctors at the University of Paris

3. The greatest was Peter Abelard (1079–1142), who first used the term "theology" in the modern sense of a systematic study of God and coined the term "positive law" to refer to enacted law rather than custom or natural law. Berman, *Religious Foundations*, at 8, n.7; *see also* WILL DURANT, THE AGE OF FAITH: A HISTORY OF MEDIEVAL CIVILIZATION—CHRISTIAN, ISLAMIC, AND JUDAIC—FROM CONSTANTINE TO DANTE: A.D. 325–1300, at 931–48 (1950). He was also famous for his love of Heloise. Artists have painted them for centuries, and their affair was made into the film STEALING HEAVEN (1988). Lovers still visit their tomb in the Paris cemetery.

Abelard and Heloise's tomb

Abelard and Heloise depicted in a fourteenth century manuscript

Abaelardus and Heloïse Surprised by Fulbert by Vanguard (1819)

Abelard and His Pupil, Héloïse by Blair (1882)

constitutional "revolutionaries," like our Founding Fathers, put it back.[5]

SPEAKING OF THE CHURCH IN ENGLAND

One day in sixth century Rome, Pope Gregory the Great saw tall, blond, and fair-skinned slaves for sale. With pity and curiosity he asked after them.

"They are Angles," replied someone.

"Not Angles but angels," reflected Gregory.

In 595, Gregory commissioned a Benedictine monk, later known as Saint Augustine of Canterbury, to convert the pagan King Æthelberht of Kent.[6] Thus was born the English Catholic Church.

6. Christianity actually came to Britain well before 300 AD. In Roman times, this Celtic Christianity had its own distinctive culture and Greek scholarship. See Thomas Cahill, How the Irish Saved Civilization: The Untold Story of Ireland's Heroic Role from the Fall of Rome to the Rise of Medieval Europe (1995), for an account of Celtic/Irish Christianity and its relationship with the newer Roman/Augustine Christianity. In the fifth century, non-Christian Germanic tribes invaded Britain. The Angles, Saxons, and Jutes conquered the native Celtic Christians and drove them into Cornwall, Wales, Scotland, Ireland, and Brittany, a peninsula in France. The King Arthur stories have their origin in a Celtic leader who resisted the invaders and ended up being a Hollywood favorite. See e.g., Excalibur (Orion Pictures 1981) King Arthur (Touchstone Pictures 1994) Knights of the Round Table (MGM 1953).

Richard Burton and Roddy McDowall in the Arthurian Play Camelot.

Saint Gregory and Saint Augustine

British stamps commemorating Saint Augustine baptizing King Ethelbert and establishing Canterbury Cathedral, Saint Augustine's Abbey, and Saint Martin's Church

A fifteenth century depiction of Arthur, the Round Table, and the Holy Grail

Centuries later, Rome cut a deal with William the Bastard for his invasion of England. William promised that if he won the English crown, the church could have greater power.[1]

In 1066, William won and became William *the Conqueror*—far better then being William *the Bastard* for all of history.[2]

Before the Norman Conquest, England had no separate ecclesiastical courts or independent ecclesiastical law.[3] The Norman king's introduction of church courts planted the seeds of the power struggle that was to play out over centuries, namely:

- Does king or pope or archbishop name a prelate or priest?

- Where are people tried, in the king's courts or the ecclesiastical courts?

- What about clergy who violate civil law? [4]

Over history, jurisdiction between the king's courts and the church courts was very fluid. For example, stealing and brawling were common-law crimes, but if they were done in a church, they became ecclesiastical crimes. On these and other questions, sometimes the king won and sometimes the church won.

But despite the church's jurisdictional power over court cases, the crown still usually controlled the church leadership. The archbishop of Canterbury,

William the Bastard

1. DAVID HOWARTH, 1066: THE YEAR OF THE CONQUEST 100–03 (1977) (discussing William's deal with the church and the trumped-up legal argument in Rome against his rival, Harold). As Howarth summed up, *"of all the novel weapons the Conqueror brought, the most effective was not the archery or the horsemen but the papal banner."* HOWARTH at 197.

2. William's half brother was Bishop Odo of Bayeux (c. 1036–97). He was either fourteen or nineteen years old when William made him bishop of Bayeux. Hardly a man of peace, he participated at Hastings and probably commissioned the Bayeux tapestry, showing himself fully engaged in the battle. But because he was a churchman he could not *"shed blood"* and thus used a mace or club rather than a sword. *See* DANNY DANZIGER & JOHN GILLINGHAM, 1215: THE YEAR OF MAGNA CARTA 102–03 (2003); COLIN RHYS LOVELL, ENGLISH CONSTITUTIONAL AND LEGAL HISTORY 55 (1962). Odo led the church in England after the Normans took over.

3. LEVY, ORIGINS OF THE FIFTH AMENDMENT 43 (1968). Under the Anglo-Saxons, bishops sat as judges. Regarding the Normans establishing separate church courts, *see* LOVELL at 69.

Odo rallies the troops with his club

An arrow in the eye kills Harold

4. Benefit of Clergy. This allowed churchmen to claim they were outside the king's jurisdiction and receive trial under canon law by compurgation, with the likely punishment being penance rather than hanging. It eventually passed into the common law and became a factor in the Boston Massacre trials. *See* **Chapter 8: "Baby, Don't Be Cruel": Just What Is So Cruel *and* Unusual about the Eighth Amendment?**

Tonsured monk

Boston Massacre

for example, was primate of England but was also a vassal of the king and thus remained the king's tenant.[5]

This was the backdrop to the struggle between King Henry II and his former friend, the archbishop of Canterbury, Thomas Becket.

"WON'T SOMEBODY RID ME OF THIS DAMNED PRIEST!"

Thus cried King Henry II about Thomas Becket. Henry's knights took him at his word and splattered the archbishop's brains at vespers on December 20, 1170.[6]

Becket had been Henry's great friend and chancellor. Henry made him archbishop of Canterbury on June 3, 1162. (To avoid the fact that Becket was not yet a priest, he was ordained the day before!) But their relationship soured as Becket began to take his job seriously, asserting the church's independence, jurisdiction, and tax exemptions.[7]

Henry was always trying to expand his power, organization, and control. Before 1166, for instance, both a bishop and the king's magistrate presided over most English courts. In that year (one hundred years after the Battle of Hastings), Henry passed new legislation at the Assize of Clarendon placing the king's courts exclusively under royal authority.

Becket's defiance of Henry led to his murder in 1170. Henry got the blame, probably deservedly so. He did public penance, including a scourging at the archbishop's tomb.[8] Although

---

5. LOVELL at 67. High churchmen swore to the king for their "temporalities" before they had their spiritual investiture. *Id.* at 75.

During this period, income from church lands in England was conservatively around £80,000 per year. DANZIGER & GILLINGHAM at 131. What this really means in today's dollars is anyone's guess—but we know it was a lot!

6. Earliest known portrayal of Becket's murder. The murderers were William de Tracy, Reginald FitzUrse, Hugh de Morville, and Richard le Bret. See DANZIGER & GILLINGHAM at 127–29 for a brief account of the Becket story and church/state power struggle. Becket sealed his fate when he called FitzUrse a "pimp." *Id.* at128; *see also* LOVELL at 94–99.

7. Henry and Becket disputing.

8. The story is still high drama. *See* T. S. Eliot's play MURDER IN THE CATHEDRAL (1935) as well as the movie BECKET (Paramount Pictures 1964), with Richard Burton as Becket and Peter O'Toole as Henry II. As for Henry's life and loves in film, *see* THE LION IN WINTER (Universal Pictures 1968), in which O'Toole again plays Henry, sparring with Katherine Hepburn's Eleanor of Aquitaine. Although these works have several historical inaccuracies, they make for good drama.

Page from The Canterbury Tales

Becket's shrine at Canterbury became the main pilgrimage site in England, with Geoffrey Chaucer's THE CANTERBURY TALES, set in the fourteenth century, two hundred years after Becket's murder, centering on the stories of pilgrims:

"When the sweet showers of April have pierced to the root the dryness of March and bathed every vein in moisture by which strength are the flowers brought forth then people long to go on pilgrimages to renowned shrines in various distant lands, and palmers to seek foreign shores. And especially from every shire's end in England they make their way to Canterbury, to seek the holy blessed martyr who helped them when they were sick."

In A KNIGHT'S TALE (Columbia Pictures 2001), Paul Bettany plays "Geoffrey Chaucer," who will later write "The Knight's Tale" as one of THE CANTERBURY TALES.

the church purged Henry of guilt for Becket's murder, he had to allow the church's privileges to continue. Becket was later canonized.[1]

After Henry II, the church continued as an *imperium in imperio* (a kingdom within a kingdom), with independent courts appealing to Rome.[2] Church courts also had different procedures, such as oral, sworn testimony, proof by paper (i.e., sworn depositions), and specialized pleading.

Henry II did not like the new deal. For example, in 1173, he ostensibly honored the ideal of free election for prelates when he wrote the following to the monks of Saint Swithin's Priory at Winchester:

"I order you to hold a free election . . . nevertheless I forbid you to elect anyone save Richard my clerk."[3]

This power struggle between church and state would continue through the centuries.[4]

MAGNA CARTA AND FREEDOM OF RELIGION

Under Henry's son, King John,[5] the church-state power struggle played out in grand fashion.

In 1205, archbishop of Canterbury Hubert died, and everyone claimed the right to fill his job.[6]

King John's insistence that he could fill the job led Pope Innocent III in Rome to put England under "interdiction," which meant that the clergy went on strike.[7]

For six years, from 1208 to 1214, no masses were said and no church bells rang. John did not care, because he kept all the revenue from

---

1. Three centuries later, a similar drama played out between Saint Thomas More, named after Saint Thomas Becket, and also the chancellor to a king Henry, this time Henry VIII. On More's echo of Becket, *see* LOVELL at 263.

Three years after More's death, Henry VIII summoned the bones of Thomas Becket to appear before him. SADAKAT KADRI, THE TRIAL: A HISTORY, FROM SOCRATES TO O.J. SIMPSON 168 (2005). When Becket's bones failed to appear, Henry had them hanged on a gibbet, burned to ashes, and shot from a cannon. Henry also stole all the contributed valuables from Becket's shrine, including just under 5,000 ounces of gold, 5,286 ounces of silver, 4,452 ounces of gilt plate, 840 ounces of parcel gilt, and a precious stone with gold angels that Henry made into a thumb ring. KURT VON S. KYNELL, SAXON AND MEDIEVAL ANTECEDENTS OF THE ENGLISH COMMON LAW 179–80, 185 n.35 (2000).

Pope Paul III later excommunicated Henry, partly because he *"surpass[ed] the ferocity of any heathen people, who, even when they have conquered their enemies in war, are not accustomed to outrage their bodies."* KADRI at 168.

2. LOVELL at 95–96.

3. DANZIGER & GILLINGHAM at 131.

4. A "prelate" is a high-ranking member of the clergy, usually a bishop or abbot. The word comes from Latin "*prælatus*," the past participle of "*præferre*," literally, "carry before," or "to be set above, or over," or "to prefer."

Prelates in the Catholic and other churches often wear mitres during ceremonies, which the chess piece, the bishop, symbolizes.

5. King John is the great wimp of English history. *See* **Chapter 6: How the Sixth Amendment Guarntees You a Court, a Lawyer, and a Chamber Pot.**

King John

vacant bishoprics (most of which he never returned). He also stopped paying the clergy their salaries under the theory that because they were not doing their job, they should not get paid.[8]

All this showed the king's power to control the church. Under feudalism, a priest was roughly equivalent to a knight and had a little fief called a parish. Ultimately, his holding of his parish depended not on his flock but on the next higher person in the feudal chain. The king was at the top, which meant that there was no real separation of church and state.

The pope was unable to get John to change until he was about to authorize King Phillip of France to invade England with the church's blessing. John submitted and accepted the pope's guy, Stephen Langton, as archbishop of Canterbury. The pope told Phillip to hold off, which he did, for a while.

Eventually, John's barons, the church, and the king of France all aligned against John. In 1215, the barons got him to sign and swear to *Magna Carta*, the first document in our constitutional history.[9] Stephen Langton wrote and negotiated most of it, which may account for the first clause:

> *"The English church shall be free, and shall have its rights undiminished and its liberties unimpaired."*[10]

From then on, English kings swore to *Magna Carta* as part of the coronation oath, as Henry VIII did three hundred years later in 1509. Henry later ignored his oath by making himself the pope of England.

But first an obscure monk named Martin Luther changed the world forever.

---

6. In a nutshell here is what happened:

- Archbishop Hubert died;

- The Canterbury monks and bishops wanted to vote for his replacement;

- King John got them all to wait (and incidentally got to keep all the revenues from Canterbury's lands in the meantime);

- Some of the monks went ahead and secretly elected a guy named Reginald, who went to Rome;

- The rest of the monks thought that was not a good idea, especially after the king showed up, and they elected another guy named John;

- Back in Rome, Pope Innocent III rejected the monks' claim to have had a vote and invalidated both elections;

- Pope Innocent put in his own guy named Stephen Langton;

- John rejected this and would not let Stephen take the job;

- Innocent put all of England under interdiction, closing all the churches for six years, from 1208 to 1214.

DANZIGER & GILLINGHAM at 132.

Archbishop Hubert Walter's tomb at Canterbury

7. Pope Innocent III.

8. DANZIGER & GILLINGHAM at 136–37. John also kidnapped all the "wives" and mistresses of the priests and would not release them until the priests paid him so that they could continue sinning.

9. DANZIGER & GILLINGHAM at 139. We will hear a lot more about *Magna Carta* in other chapters.

10. *Quoted in* DANZIGER & GILLINGHAM at 125. Langton probably was the one who preserved *Magna Carta* in the church archives.

Magna Carta

LUTHER AND CALVIN SAYING WHAT THEY BELIEVED

On October 31, 1517, Martin Luther nailed on the church door at Wittenberg, Germany, the Ninety-Five Theses, or questions on Catholic theology and practice.[1]

For centuries, the Roman Church had taught that with reason and free will, a man could live a good life, and by combining faith and good deeds achieve salvation.[2] The good deeds could be making a pilgrimage or giving alms to the poor or other charity.[3] By Luther's day, though, this teaching had become corrupted into the great moneymaker of selling indulgences.[4]

Luther strongly disputed Rome's claim that one could buy freedom from God's punishment. He taught instead that salvation did not come from good works but only from God's grace.

Regarding the relationship of church and state, Luther picked up on Saint Augustine's "city of God" and "city of man" theme. After all, Luther started as an Augustinian monk.[5]

In Luther's thinking, there were two kingdoms. A person could *not* work his way from the "earthly kingdom" into the "heavenly kingdom" because only God's grace could allow it. Still, though, a Christian in the earthly kingdom must

1. Martin Luther and a printed copy of the Ninety-Five Theses.

2. Berman, *Religious Foundations*, at 15.

3. Pilgrimage as a journey to redress sin played out in KINGDOM OF HEAVEN (20th Century Fox 2005).

Saint Peter's Basilica, the architectural and artistic marvel that prompted the Protestant Reformation

4. Indulgences were a great product for the church to sell because it could always make more! What you could buy was time out of purgatory for a relative or even yourself. Because only God knew how much time you had in purgatory, you could never know if you bought enough time out! So, the church could keep selling you ten years or one thousand years, depending on how badly you thought you had behaved.

A Dominican preacher, Johann Tetzel (1465–1519), had a great sales pitch: "*As soon as a coin in the coffer rings/ the soul from purgatory springs.*" His sales in Germany to raise money to build Saint Peter's Basilica in Rome prompted Luther to protest. Luther's Thesis 86 asked, "*Why does the pope, whose wealth today is greater than the wealth of the richest Crassus, build the basilica of Saint Peter with the money of poor believers rather than with his own money?*" Regarding Martin Luther see LUTHER (MGM 2003) a biopic starring Joseph Fiennes as Luther and Alfred Molina as Tetzel

5. The Augustinians still exist as religious orders of men and women in the Catholic Church following the Rule of Saint Augustine. Erasmus, Luther's contemporary, was also an Augustinian. As we will see, Erasmus was a great friend of Thomas More and a powerful voice for humanistic reform *within* the Catholic Church.

Leaving aside who was right about God, you cannot help but wonder how much bloodshed the world would have avoided had people both in and out of the Catholic Church chosen Erasmus's path of reform rather than Luther's.

Other Augustinians included a couple of popes and mystics as well as Gregor Mendel, whose 1850 to 1860 studies of pea pod plants in the monastery garden made him the "father of genetics."

Mendel

work to follow God. Thus, politics and law were not paths to grace and faith (as Rome taught), but grace and faith were paths to right politics and law.[6]

John Calvin (1509–64) jumped into the Protestant Reformation around 1530 and, like Luther, taught the doctrine of two kingdoms. But his concept of church and state expanded from Luther's community of the faithful to actual control of the state.

Calvin's "fellowship of active believers" was the seat of truth, qualified to control not only worship but also society's morals.[7] The Calvinist view of law was that it was to "*teach*" the faithful, as well as everyone else, the right path.[8]

The Calvinists expanded on these ideas of government and created theocracies in places like Geneva, Switzerland. As we will see, the English Calvinists, also known as the Puritans, sparked the English Civil Wars in the 1640s.[9] These same Pilgrim Puritans came to America to set up their New Jerusalem.

Luther respected civil authority and accepted a world where the prince was a *de facto* head of the church.[10] The Calvinists, however, sought to *establish* both church and state as a check on each other.

Luther as a young Augustinian monk

Erasmus of Rotterdam

6. Berman, *Religious Foundations*, at 15–17.

7. Berman, *Religious Foundations*, at 26, noting that the Calvinistic concept of law differed from the Catholic notion of law as something *given*. For the Calvinist, law was something *useful*.

John Calvin

9. Berman, *Religious Foundations*, at 27.

10. Berman, *Religious Foundations*, at 18.

8. Berman, *Religious Foundations*, at 30 ("*It was, of course, in Puritan New England more than anywhere else that the concept of reformation of the world was combined with the doctrine of the 'didactic' or 'pedagogical' use of the law to impose heavy criminal sanctions—indeed the death penalty—for moral offenses, especially those of a sexual or religious nature.*"). THE SCARLET LETTER was about pedagogy. NATHANIEL HAWTHORNE, THE SCARLET LETTER (1850). Set in seventeenth century Puritanical Boston, the novel tells of Hester Prynne, who gives birth after adultery, refuses to name the father, and struggles to create a new life of repentance and dignity. Several movie adaptations exist, including THE SCARLET LETTER (Hollywood Pictures 1995).

Classic Comics version of THE SCARLET LETTER

PRESSING RELIGION: LUTHER PUBLISHED, AND PUBLISHED, AND THUS DID NOT PERISH

To know God and grace, a man should read his Bible, said Luther, who obviously could no longer rely on the Pope or the Roman Church. So Luther translated the Bible into German, the language of his people. It exploded on the scene.

There are many causes of the Protestant Reformation, but in ages past, the Catholic Church had confronted pagans, heretics, schisms, religious movements, and constant challenges to its authority.[1]

1. For example, there were the Paulicans from the fifth through seventh centuries, the Bogomils in the eighth century, and the Cathars of eleventh through thirteenth centuries, who form the backdrop to Dan Brown's THE DAVINCI CODE (2003) and the subsequent film, THE DAVINCI CODE (Columbia Pictures 2006). Later came the Joachimites of the thirteenth century, and the Apostolic Brethern and Dulcinian heresies that form the backdrop of Umberto Eco's THE NAME OF THE ROSE (1980) and the film, THE NAME OF THE ROSE (20th Century Fox 1986). Eco's book is a good primer on medieval philosophy and theology.

2. And with printing, the books themselves became ever more dangerous.

Book burning did not start with the printing press. In fact, before printing book burning was more effective because books had to be hand copied, so replacing books was a long, laborious task.

Disputation between Saint Dominic and Cathers by Berruguete (fifteenth century), shows the story of Cathar and Saint Dominic's books thrown on a fire but Dominic's did not burn, showing the truth of his teachings. This story shows the early Dominican desire to convert heretics by persuasion.

Disputation between Saint Dominic and Cathers by Berruguete

In 1644, John Milton wrote against the destruction of books and their ideas: "*He who kills a man kills a reasonable creature, God's image; but he who destroys a good book, kills reason itself, kills the image of God, as it were, in the eye.*" Books, moreover, "*are not absolutely dead things, but do contain a potency of life in them to be as active as that soul was whose progeny they are.*" Thus for Milton, destroying a book is a "*kind of homicide,*" "*sometimes a martyrdom,*" even "*a kind of massacre.*" Witte,

John Milton

Milton, at 1592–93, *quoting* AREOPAGITICA: A SPEECH OF MR. JOHN MILTON FOR THE LIBERTY OF UNLICENSED PRINTING TO THE PARLIAMENT OF ENGLAND (1644). But though Milton defends books and their ideas perhaps better than anyone else, his defense also shows why book burning did not end. People who are willing to kill for their ideology will just as easily kill a book: "*On the evening of May 10, 1933, some four and a half months after Hitler became Chancellor, there occurred in Berlin a scene which had not been witnessed in the Western world since the late Middle Ages. At about midnight a torchlight parade of thousands of students ended at a square . . . opposite the University of Berlin. Torches were put to a huge pile of books that had been gathered there, and as the flames enveloped them more books were thrown on the fire until some twenty thousand had been consumed. Similar scenes took place in several other cities. The book burning had begun.*"

. . . Dr. Joseph Goebbels, the new propaganda minister, who from now on was to put German culture into a Nazi strait jacket, addressed the students as the burning books turned to ashes. The soul of the German people can again express itself. These flames not only illuminate the final end of an old era; they also light up the new. Id.

WILLIAM L. SHIRER, THE RISE AND FALL OF THE THIRD REICH: A HISTORY OF NAZI GERMANY

333 (1950, 1960). One of the books the Nazi's burned was the play ALMANSOR: A TRAGEDY (1823) by Heinrich Heine, who referred to the Spanish Inquisition's burning of the Muslim Qur'an and wrote "*[w]here they burn books, so too will they in the end burn human beings.*" The Nazis proved him right with the Holocaust. For reference to Heine's quote, see United States Holocaust Memorial Museum, http://www.ushmm.org/research/library/faq/details.php?topic=06#quote_heine (last visited Aug. 21, 2010).

Heinrich Heine

Ray Bradbury's FAHRENHEIT 451 (1951) is a cautionary tale of a world where books are burned to control ideas and people. According to Bradbury, "451" is the temperature at which book paper burns. (This is actually not accurate, with the actual temperature being closer to 450 degrees Celsius, which would be 842 degrees Fahrenheit, but Bradbury thought "Fahrenheit" made a better title.) Bradbury wrote it during the Cold War to critique American society. *See also* FAHRENHEIT 451 (Universal Pictures 1966).

There is a book burning in the movie PLEASANTVILLE (New Line Cinema 1998), which makes the point that new and different ideas are not always "pleasant," but they are necessary for any world with color and beauty that is worth living in. As for book burning in America, the New York Society for the Suppression of Vice, founded in 1873 by the antipornography crusader Anthony Comstock, advocated book burning and even inscribed it on its seal. Comstock burned tons of books that he considered "*lewed*" and successfully lobbied the U.S. Congress to pass the Comstock Act, 17 Stat. 598, on March 3, 1873, making it illegal to send any "*obscene, lewd, and/*

So what made Luther, and later Calvin, different?

It was the printing press.[2]

A mere generation before Luther, Johann Gutenberg started printing.[3] And Gutenberg's first book in 1455 was the Bible.[4]

In a very real sense, the Protestant Reformation was about printing: bibles, tracts, teachings, charters, covenants, institutes, and books. They were best sellers and gave men like Luther a living after they left the monastery.[5]

The press made religion, and religion made the press, underscoring why the First Amendment is about both.

---

or lascivious" materials through the mail, including contraceptive devices and information.

We can hope that the Internet may have made book burnings a thing of the past; you cannot burn the whole World Wide Web. But countries like China that limit access to the web are trying to do the same thing. According to Amnesty International, China blocks all information regarding subjects such as the Tiananmen Square protests and has the largest recorded number of imprisoned journalists and cyberdissidents in the world. *China: No Investigation, No Redress and Still No Freedom of Speech! Human Rights Activists Targeted for Discussing the Tiananmen Crackdown*, AMNESTY INTERNATIONAL, http://www.amnesty.org/en/library/info/ASA17/025/2010/en (last visited Aug. 15, 2010).

3. Gutenberg did not invent printing or the printing press, which existed long before using carved wooden blocks. What he invented was a practical way of making movable type with a metal alloy and a hand mould. Movable type allows the printer to place precast letters on a block that he can then "press" on paper. This is done for as many copies as needed, and then the printer reorders the type to press the next page. (This, of course, is the origin of "the Press" as the First Amendment uses the term.) In a day a printer can print thousands of identical copies of a page that would have taken medieval monks weeks to inscribe.

Johann Gutenberg

A case of cast metal type pieces and typeset matter in a composing stick

The 1959 Xerox 914, the first plain paper photocopier using xerography (from Greek *"xeros"* ("dry") and *"graphos"* ("writing").

A woodblock from 1568 showing one printer removing a page while another inks the text blocks

Cast metal type

4 Gutenberg's Bible was a prop in the apocalyptic THE DAY AFTER TOMORROW (20th Century Fox 2004), clutched by the librarian, Jeremy: who wants to save one little piece of "Western Civilization".

Gutenberg first page

5. The Typewriter. Think of the typewriter as a little printing press invented in the 1870s. A typewriter is a machine with movable type. Instead of putting lead type on a big block it has little levers called keys that you press in the order you want. Also, instead of having to ink all the type on the block beforehand, the typewriter's keys hit an ink tape just before hitting the paper, transferring the ink from the tape onto the page. Thus, the type never touches the paper, only the ink tape, which advances each time you push a key.

The standard layout of the typewriter keyboard—QWERTY—has a near alphabetical sequence on the "home row." But, by design, QWERTY is not the most efficient layout possible because it requires the typist to move his or her fingers between rows for the most common letters. This slows the typist to prevent the key bars from jamming. Now that word processors and computers have replaced the typewriter, there is no need for the QWERTY layout other than that we all learned it.

HENRY VIII: WHEN DESIRE BECAME DOGMA

Finally back to Henry![1]

One thing to remember about Henry VIII is that at heart he was a conservative Catholic all his life. He just decided to be Pope of England. In matters of heresy, both before and after he broke with Rome, Henry differed from other leaders of his time only by the greater severity of his intolerance.[2]

Before Henry's "great matter"—that is, his divorce from Catharine of Aragon—Pope Leo X had recognized him for writing, with Sir Thomas More's help, ASSERTIO SEPTEM SACRAMENTORUM MARTINUM LUTHERUM (DECLARATION OF THE

1. *Henry VIII* by Hans Holbein (1540) This Holbein painting shows a man bursting with charm and good nature. Trusting in that could cost you your head. Thomas More's biographer and son-in-law, William Roper, recounted a telling conversation with More:
"Roper: *How happy he was whom the King had so familiarly entertained . . .* More: *I thank our Lord, son, I find his Grace my very good Lord indeed . . . Howbeit, son Roper, I may tell thee I have no cause to be proud thereof **for if my head could win him a castle in France . . . it should not fail to fall.**"* ROPER at 13 (emphasis added). Roper wrote twenty years after More's execution in 1535. But adding credence to this conversation is what happened

William Roper

Holbein's sketch of More

two days after Henry's coronation in 1510. Henry VIII had arrested his father, Henry VII's two most unpopular but loyal ministers, Sir Richard Empson and Edmund Dudley. Henry VIII had them groundlessly charged with high treason and executed. They, like More, were lawyers.

2. Henry reserved for himself in the Act of Supremacy the power to "*repress and extirp all errors, heresies, and other enormities.*" LEVY, FIFTH AMENDMENT, at 68–69.

Sir Richard Empson (left) Henry VII, and Sir Edmund Dudley

Dickens at his desk in 1858

Charles Dickens wrote A CHILD'S HISTORY OF ENGLAND for his own children and it became part of the English school curriculum. Summing up Henry VIII, Dickens wrote, "*The plain truth is, that he was a most intolerable ruffian, a disgrace to human nature, and a blot of blood and grease upon the History of England.*" III CHARLES DICKENS, A CHILD'S HISTORY OF ENGLAND 59 (1853), *available at* http://www.archive.org/stream/childshistoryofe03dickrich#page/58/mode/2up (last visited Nov. 7, 2009).

3. And Henry VIII is still a star. Shakespeare started it with his play, THE FAMOUS HISTORY OF THE LIFE OF KING HENRY VIII (1613). In 1613 a cannon shot fired for special effect during a performance of HENRY VIII burned the original Globe Theatre to the ground. There is also an opera HENRY VIII (1883), by Camille Saint-Saëns. Henry is a character in Mark Twain's THE PRINCE AND THE PAUPER (1881). Charles Laughton won an Oscar for THE PRIVATE LIFE OF HENRY VIII (United Artists 1933), and Robert Shaw was bombastic in A MAN FOR ALL SEASONS (Columbia Pictures 1966), which won Best Picture in 1966. Television works have included *Henry VIII*, a two-part serial (Granada Television 2003) and the dumbed-down, sexed-up *The Tudors* (Showtime 2007–present).

Charles Laughton and Binnie Barnes in THE PRIVATE LIFE OF HENRY VIII (United Artists 1983)

4. You can still see the "FD" for *fidei defensor* on British coins today. Why Henry and his successors kept the title is odd. If they did not recognize the Pope as anything more than the "Bishop of Rome," why keep the title that he bequeathed? Never underestimate Henry's capacity for self-justification.

As for Leo X and his cousin Clement VII, see E.R. CHAMBERLIN, THE BAD POPES (1969), a slim history that nevertheless devotes a chapter to each.

Leo X

Seven Sacraments against Martin Luther). This book was a best seller and made Henry the first king to ever publish a book—again, the mix of press and religion![3]

Because of this book, Pope Leo dubbed him "defender of the faith" (*fidei defensor*), which to this day is still one of a British monarch's titles.[4]

But two popes later, Clement VII (who was Leo X's cousin) did not grant Henry the divorce he sought to rid himself of Queen Catherine of Aragon in favor of Anne Boleyn.[5]

Henry tired of appealing to Rome,[6] of Rome controlling a huge chunk of England, and of the church being a separate government. And, of course, he tired of having to wait to marry Anne Boleyn.[7]

---

5. Little of this had to do with the sanctity of marriage. At the time, Clement was a virtual prisoner of Emperor Charles V, who just happened to be Catherine of Aragon's nephew. Not wanting to see Aunt Catherine dethroned as Queen of England, Charles blocked Henry's annulment. This fiasco cost Henry's lord chancellor, Cardinal Wolsey, his job. (What good is a cardinal in your employ if you cannot get an annulment when you need one?) Anne Boleyn took a personal interest in Wolsey's demise and got his palace. En route to face the treason indictment, he died declaring "*[i]f I had served God as diligently as I have done the King, he would not have given me over in my gray hairs.*" *Thomas Wolsey,* The Catholic Encyclopedia, http://www.newadvent.org/cathen/15685a.htm218 (last visited Feb. 10, 2006).

Clement VII

Charles V

Wolsey

Cranmer

6. Wolsey Couldn't Cut It! Wolsey was Lord Chancellor of England, the highest official under the king *and* papal legate (i.e., delegate), exercising the Pope's powers in England. It should have been easy for him to get Henry's annulment. Regarding Wolsey's powers of both church and state, see Lovell at 254. He ended up sending Rome eighty petitions, all bound in the customary red tape. In the end, he could not cut through the red tape, which is the first recorded use of the expression "red tape" for bureaucratic obstacles.

Elizabeth of York holding a white (York) rose

Wolsey trying to cut the "red tape"

York

Lancaster

Tudor

7. To be fair, more than just lust drove Henry. He believed he needed a male heir (although the successful forty-five-year reign of his daughter Elizabeth proved him wrong). His father, Henry Tudor, came to the throne as Henry VII after defeating Richard III at Bosworth Field. Henry Tudor had a weak claim to the throne but married Edward IV's daughter, Elizabeth of York (who is the model for the Queen of Hearts in a card deck). Thus, Henry VII was able to unite the two great factions of the Lancasters, represented by the red rose, and the Yorks, represented by the white rose, thus ending the Wars of the Roses (1455–85) and giving us the red and white Tudor rose. *See generally* John Gillingham, The Wars of the Roses (1981). The fear of repeating the destructiveness of the Wars of the Roses drove Henry VIII and assured the complacency of a great part of England's political and religious power structure when Henry made himself Pope of England. *See* Lovell at 255.

Henry VII holding a red (Lancaster) rose

Richard III

It always gnawed at European kings that the church was outside their jurisdiction and taxing power. Henry put an end to it by taking the church's entire legal jurisdiction into his own hands. Henry, who had received a superior theological education, must have thought, why not control the church?[1]

So Henry decided to be the Pope in England.[2]

To become Pope, Henry had Parliament pass the Statute in Restraint of Appeals, which ended all appeals to the Pope and made Henry the final legal authority on all religious and jurisdictional questions.[3] As justification, Henry claimed that the

English crown was imperial, and thus, like Constantine, he wanted to establish (i.e., control) the church.

Henry later had Parliament pass the Act of Supremacy of 1534, which made him

"the only supreme head in earth of the Church of England called Anglica

---

1. Henry was Henry VII and Elizabeth of York's second son after Arthur. They trained him for the church, probably to be Archbishop of Canterbury. Arthur died in 1502, leaving Henry to take the throne and, because Henry VII did not want to see his political alliance with Spain harmed, he made his son, Henry (later Henry VIII), take Arthur's "wife" Catherine of Aragon. Even though Arthur and Catherine never consummated the marriage, Henry VII had to arrange a dispensation from Rome to allow the marriage to Prince Henry. When Catherine later did not give Henry VIII a male heir, he made himself believe, and got his paid churchmen and scholars to argue, that it was God's punishment for marrying his brother's wife against *Leviticus* 18:16: *"Thou shalt not uncover the nakedness of thy brother's wife: it is thy brother's nakedness."* And *Leviticus* 20:21: *"If a man shall take his brother's wife, it is an unclean thing . . . they shall be childless."* Thus, God clearly wanted Henry to marry his new inamorata, Anne Boleyn.

Holbein's original sketch of More

4. Act of Supremacy, 1534, 26 Hen. 8, c. 1, *available at* http://tudorhistory.org/primary/supremacy.html (last visited Feb. 10, 2006).

5. See John Witte, Jr., *Tax Exemption of Church Property: Historical Anomaly or Valid Constitutional Practice?* 64 S. Cal. L. Rev. 363, 364–69 (1991) (noting that *"the Tudor monarchs had consolidated their authority over religion and the church and subjected them to comprehensive ecclesiastical laws enforceable by both common law and commissary courts"*).

2. Regarding Henry's establishment of the Church of England, *see* Lovell at 253–70.

Arthur Tudor

Catherine

Henry

3. Otherwsie known as the Ecclesiastical Appeals Act, 1532, 24 Hen. 8, c. 12.

Henry had Parliament doing a lot, making his reign one of the milestones in the growth of parliamentary supremacy and even democracy. But Henry was no democrat! He controlled parliament.

Other Parliaments had appointed kings in the past, such as the election of King Henry IV on October 13, 1399, dispossessing King Richard. At the start of Henry VIII's reign, however, Henry insisted he was the *anointed* king: from God to pope to me! He later found it far more useful and flexible being the *appointed* king: from God to Parliament to me! *See generally* Lovell at 256.

6. Portraits of **Catherine** when Henry married her and how she looked when he divorced her.

Catherine was eight years older than the forty-two-year-old Henry, while Anne Boleyn was in her early twenties and looked pretty good to Henry. Although she was only queen for three years, from 1533 to 1536, she gets all the press! *See, e.g.,* Anne of the

Henry VIII and Parliament

The shadowy Richard Rich

This all figured in Thomas More's trial in 1535, when Richard Rich testified that More said that *"Parliament could not make the king the head of the church,"* which was malicious treason.

Ecclesia, and shall have and enjoy annexed and united to the imperial crown of this realm."[4]

Before Henry, the church's bishops, abbots, and clergy had an independent income, being supported by their own lands. Although the kings would appoint many of the bishops and abbots, or somehow work out a bribe or deal with Rome to do so, after the churchmen gave the king his due, they were relatively independent. But after Henry, clergymen became the crown's employees in his "established" church.[5]

By establishing his own church, Henry was able to do a number of things:

- put away old wife Catherine of Aragon and marry his new hottie, Anne Boleyn;[6]

- gain jurisdiction and taxing power over all of England, Wales, and Ireland; and

- steal church property.[7]

Anne Boleyn

THOUSAND DAYS (Universal Pictures 1969), followed by THE OTHER BOLEYN GIRL (Columbia Pictures 2008). She also figures in seasons one and two of *The Tudors* (Showtime 2007–present).

Cromwell

of which were top heavy and unseaworthy—a good metaphor for Henry himself.

Ironically, Henry's profligate spending led to parliamentary democracy. By selling off the land for short-term cash, he deprived the crown of a long-term source of revenue. Henry's descendants—Edward VI, Mary, and Elizabeth—were always cash challenged, as were his Stuart successors—James I, Charles I, Charles II, and James II. The Stuarts especially had to continually call Parliaments for money just to run a government that was becoming more expensively modern. As we will see, Parliament could then "petition" for freedoms and rights.

7. Dissolution of the Monasteries: Henry's main minister, Thomas Cromwell, promised to make him *"the richest man in England."* KYNELL at 177. Henry and Cromwell did it by breaking the back of English Catholic spirituality. From 1536 to 1541, Henry made a huge amount of money by stealing monastery property.

Not only were monasteries independent of the king, they were independent of local Catholic bishops. (Accepting independence was not Henry's strong suit.) Henry disbanded 825 monasteries, nunneries, and friaries throughout England, Wales, and Ireland and took their income. He did provide a modest pension to the former members. The Act of Supremacy (1534), the First Suppression Act (1536), and the Second Suppression Act (1539) gave Henry the legal power to act.

The monasteries were indeed rich, powerful, and independent; many were not very holy.

But they were also the main providers of education and social services in England. Henry took it all for his own ends and did not replace the hospitals or alms houses. He sold their lands (on the cheap) not only to rich lords but to a whole new class of up-and-coming "Tudor gentry," who entered Parliament with a personal interest in supporting the king. Henry's annual income before he stole the church's lands was £140,000 but afterward was conservatively about £50 million in relatively modern currency (i.e., the British pound for 1910). KYNELL at 179.

Henry spent lavishly, including on the two greatest battleships of the age, the *Mary Rose* and the *Great Harry*, both

The *Mary Rose*

The *Great Harry* had gold cloth sails for diplomatic missions

Glastonbury Abby before Henry and now

England under Henry became a deadly place for free thought and belief.[1]

Any deviation from Henry's new religious order, most especially refusal to swear to the Act of Supremacy, threatened him.[2] No matter whether it was loyalty to the "Bishop of Rome" or belief in new Protestant doctrines, expression of dissent was too much for Henry; he sent you to the chopping block for one and to the fires of Smythfield for the other.[3] The crimes of heresy and treason became indistinguishable.[4]

Henry's friend Sir Thomas More, among many others, paid the price for Henry's acquisitiveness, passions, and quest for a male heir.

SIR THOMAS MORE: SPEAKING TRUTH TO POWER THROUGH SILENCE

Sir Thomas More was Lord Chancellor, having succeeded Cardinal Wosley, who in 1535 became one of Henry VII's earliest and most distinguished victims.[5]

1. Being one of Henry's wives could also be dangerous. And of Henry's wives? Just remember their fates in two trilogies: **Divorced–Executed–Died; Divorced–Executed–Survived!**

Divorced — Catherine of Aragon; mother of the future Queen Mary.

Executed — Anne Boleyn for adultery (though the only adultery she ever committed was likely with Henry); mother of the future Queen Elizabeth.

Died — Jane Seymour; mother of the future King Edward VI.

Divorced — Anne of Cleves; the marriage was annulled after Henry saw her in person.

Executed — Catherine Howard for adultery; unlike Anne Boleyn, she did it.

Survived — Catherine Parr was probably more of a nurse for old, fat Henry. She has the distinction of being the only Queen of England to marry four times; twice a widow before marrying Henry, and then married after him.

2. One of Henry's favorite ways to eliminate people, including wives, was a bill of attainder. Stanford E. Lehmberg, *Parliamentary Attainder in the Reign of Henry VIII*, 18 Hist. J. 675, 688 (1975). Attainders were bills in Parliament for the specific purpose of finding persons guilty outside the normal criminal process under the common law. Henry did not invent them; during the War of the Roses, whatever side got power would commonly attaint the other side. Lehmberg at 676.

Henry did not use attainder for the first fifteen years of his reign, until he broke with Rome. *Id.* at 677, 681. Later, he attainted 130 persons: 96 for treason, 26 for misprision, 5 for felony, and 3 for heresy. *Id.* at 701; *see also* Kynell at 176 (on Henry using attainder to do away with habeas corpus).

Attainder extinguished a person's civil rights, making him dead civilly. For this reason, it was totally contrary to the foundation of America, that everyone has "*inalienable*" rights. *See* The Federalist No. 44 (James Madison). For this reason, the Constitution prohibits bills of attainder in three different places: "*No Bill of Attainder . . . shall be passed*," U.S. Const. art. I, § 9, cl. 3; "*No State shall . . . pass any Bill of Attainder . . . ,*" U.S. Const. art. I, § 10, cl. 1; "*The Congress shall have Power to declare the Punishment of Treason, but no Attainder of Treason shall work Corruption of Blood, or Forfeiture except during the Life of the Person attainted*," U.S. Const. art. III, § 3, cl. 2. Regarding attainders and the Constitution, see Jacob Reynolds, *The Rule of Law and the Origins of the Bill of Attainder Clause*, 18 St. Thomas L. Rev. 177, 194–97 (2005).

3. Among other methods, Henry controlled the press to advance his "*lust and thrust by greed.*" Kynell at 181.

4. As historian Colin Lovell puts it, "*the mass of men . . . accepted the Tudor idea that all things were now Caesar's.*" Lovell at 270.

5. Levy, Fifth Amendment, at 94. For a history of More, see the brief biography by his son-in-law, William Roper. Roper; *see also Saint Thomas More*, The Catholic Encyclopedia, http://www.newadvent.org/cathen/14689c.htm (last visited Aug. 22, 2005). *See generally* (among several biographies) Richard Marius, Thomas More: A Biography (1985); Peter Ackroyd, The Life of Thomas More (1999). For a less flattering view of More, from the Protestant perspective, *see* Michael Farris, From Tyndale to Madison: How the Death of an English Martyr Led to the American Bill of Rights ch. 3 (2007).

Sir Thomas More

Making his persecution particularly ironic was that More was "*silent*" on the whole matter. He had retreated from public life citing "*ill health*" after only three years as chancellor.[6] More was, however, writing a great deal at this time in support of the Church of Rome. Although he did not directly attack his old friend King Henry, the message was clear.

More was "*a man for all seasons*" as his friend Erasmus called him, a great light of humanist thinking not only in England but throughout Europe. More's book UTOPIA was an international best seller and a great book of western literature.[7]

To More's house sojourned some of the greatest literary men of the age, including Erasmus.[8] It was while visiting More in 1509 that Erasmus wrote IN PRAISE OF FOLLY, a satirical essay that is one of the most notable works of the Renaissance and, though neither Erasmus nor More intended it, a catalyst of the Protestant Reformation.[9]

---

6. The Lord Chancellor—now the Lord High Chancellor of Great Britain—is still one of the most important officers in British government. Today the sovereign appoints him on the prime minister's advice. He is Speaker of the House of Lords, participates in the cabinet, acts as the custodian of the great seal, and heads the judiciary. Thus, he has executive, legislative, and judicial powers. The British have limited the office in modern times. *See* Diana Woodhouse, *United Kingdom: The Constitutional Reform*

The lord chancellor

Act 2005—Defending Judicial Independence the English Way, 5 INT'L J. CONST. L. 153 (2007); Susanna Frederick Fischer, *Playing Poohsticks with the British Constitution: The Blair Government's Proposal to Abolish the Lord Chancellor*, 24 PENN. ST. INT'L L. REV. 257 (2005).

Originally chancellors were clergy and the king's chaplain/confessor and thus "*keeper of the king's conscience.*" They began to provide direct justice, dispensing with legal technicalities, later called the "law of equity." Because the chancellor used to be the king's confessor or chaplain, he thus worked behind the screen or *cancelli*, which is where the word "chancellor" originates. LOVELL at 90. In England, the office goes at least as far back as

the Norman Conquest of 1066.

Because usually only clerics could read during most of the Middle Ages, the lord chancellor was almost always a cleric. At this point, only the king's justiciar—essentially the viceroy for the absent Norman kings—outranked him, but when the justiciar office ended, only the king outranked the Chancellor.

The Lord Chancellor attended the *curia regis* (royal court), which evolved into Parliament. The Chancellor's judicial duties also evolved through the *curia regis*, and the High Court of Chancery developed to decide cases according to fairness or "equity" instead of the strict common law. Clergy dominated the chancellorship until 1529, after Cardinal Wolsey's dismissal.

---

7. Thomas More's UTOPIA (1516) (the full title of which is OF THE BEST STATE OF A REPUBLIC, AND OF THE NEW ISLAND UTOPIA or, in Latin, LIBELLUS VERE AUREUS, NEC MINUS SALUTARIS QUAM FESTIVUS, DE OPTIMO REI PUBLICAE *Statu deque* NOVA INSULA *Utopia*) describes More's fictional Atlantic island that is the site of a seemingly perfect society. The work presents More's social ideas, which stand up even today:
"For if you suffer your people to be ill-educated, and their manners to be corrupted from their infancy, and then punish them for those crimes to which their first education disposed them, what else is to be concluded from this, but that you first make thieves and then punish them." MORE, UTOPIA, Book 1.

Drew Barrymore's character, Cinderella, quotes this passage in Ever AFTER: A CINDERELLA STORY (20th Century Fox 1998).

UTOPIA is also social satire. More got the name "utopia" from the Greek: "oὐ," ("not") and "τόπος," ("place"), literally "no place." Thus, Utopia is either a place of perfection or nonexistence.

An imagining of More's island, Utopia

8. Both of these Erasmus portraits show books; he embraced the press just as we embrace a new laptop computer. Erasmus translated the Greek Bible, which Martin Luther used to translate the Bible into German. Thus, Erasmus, a Catholic and Luther detractor, contributed to the Protestant Reformation.

---

9. Both Erasmus and More had translated the Greek satirist Lucian into Latin, and both Erasmus's IN PRAISE OF FOLLY and More's UTOPIA show this influence. Both works share a dry humor with double or triple meanings throughout. For example, the title of Erasmus's work in Greek, *Moriae Enkomiom,* can also mean "In Praise of More." The essay starts as virtuoso foolery but then takes a darker tone in a series of orations, as Folly praises self-deception and madness and moves to a satirical examination of pious but superstitious abuses of Catholic doctrine and corrupt practices in parts of the Roman Catholic Church. Erasmus meant it to help the Catholic Church reform, but it also encouraged the Protestant Reformation.

The More household praised books and learning.[1] In today's parlance, we would describe More as "tied in" to the "new information highway" and the "world-wide web" of learning and culture. As noted, printing changed everything, just as the computer has changed everything for us.

In the case of heretical speech, More was constrictive.[2] But when it came to freely speaking political ideas and thoughts, he was expansive. As speaker of the House of Commons, he supported the relatively new idea that all members should speak freely and even criticize the king's policies.

In his PETITION FOR PARLIAMENTARY FREE SPEECH, More argued to Henry that if Parliament was to be of counsel to the king, the members needed to speak freely. Only this, pleaded More, would ensure the king the best advice possible.[3]

This was the first petition ever made in Parliament for free speech[4] and thus a precursor to the First Amendment.[5]

Unfortunately for More, it was his prominence as a man of speech and letters that made his silence so loud. For one thing, in the 1500s a king's servant did not simply resign. A minister such as Thomas More served at the King's pleasure. Thus, More's public resignation for "ill health" was a statement of his disagreement with Henry.

1. We have Hans Holbein's sketch of the More family portrait of 1527 but unfortunately fire destroyed the original painting. Reproduced here is one of two copies of Holbein's original. It shows a family that reads. Nearly everyone, including the women, hold books.

2. More was always concerned that "*the stretys were lykely to swarme full of heretykes.*" THOMAS MORE, APOLOGY OF SYR THOMAS MORE KNIGHT, 219a-227b (1533), *quoted in* LEVY, FIFTH AMENDMENT, at 65.

3. We have More's PETITION FOR FREE SPEECH from William Roper and confirmed in Parliament's records. Excerpts from a modernized version show an interesting insight into human behavior: "*There can be no doubt that the assembly is a very substantial one, of very wise and politic persons. And yet, most victorious Prince, among so many wise men, not all will be equally wise, and of those who are equally wise, not all will be equally well-spoken. And often it happens that just as a lot of foolishness is uttered with ornate and polished speech, so, too, many coarse and rough-spoken men see deep indeed and give very substantial counsel.*"

With this in mind More, always a lawyer, pleads that "*many of your discreet commoners will be hindered from giving their advice and counsel, to the great hindrance of the common affairs, unless every one of your commoners is utterly discharged of all doubt and fear as to how anything that he* happens to say may happen to be taken by your Highness." Accordingly, Henry should "*remove the misgivings of their timorous minds and animate and encourage and reassure them.*" Also, Henry should "*give to all your commoners here assembled your most gracious permission and allowance for every man freely, without fear of your dreaded displeasure, to speak his conscience and boldly declare his advice concerning everything that comes up among us . . . .*"

For a complete text of this petition, see Center for Thomas More Studies, http://www.thomasmorestudies. org/segn/control/context?docId=2&searchDocId=2&selectedDoc=2&offset=0&version=modern& xpath=/wp:Document/wp:Content/page[1]&allDoc=true (last visited Aug. 12, 2010). Regarding More and Parliamentary free speech, see LOVELL at 240.

More's signature

Henry sent Thomas Cromwell to actively induce More to publicly endorse the king as head of the church— or to kill More.[6]

Specifically, Cromwell made More publicly refuse to swear to the Act of Supremacy of 1534. This act had an added clause repudiating *"any foreign authority, prince or potentate,"* an obvious reference to the Pope. By its terms, anyone who was called upon had to take an oath supporting the act.

More asserted himself *"a faithful subject of the King."* This, however, was far less than the age demanded, and Cromwell sent him to the Tower of London, the monarch's special prison for political opponents.[7]

More stayed there until a "special commission" indicted him for high treason. He was tried in July 1535.[8]

Much of the trial involved Cromwell trying to get More to confess that the Act

of Supremacy was illegal. By so doing, More would have committed treason.

During his persecution More never compromised on his understanding of the difference between the law of God and the law of the realm, which *"was the difference between heaven and hell."* In this he follows Saint Augustine regarding the "city of man" versus the "city of God" and is also a precursor of ideas of separation of church and state.

---

4. G.R. Elton, The Tudor Constitution: Documents and Commentary 255 (1960).

5. The U.S. Constitution specifically enshrines the concept of parliamentary free speech, providing *"for any Speech or Debate in either House, [a senator or representative] shall not be questioned in any other Place."* U.S. Const. art I, § 6.

Cromwell

6. Cromwell and More had a collegial relationship, but Cromwell knew his job was to please a fickle Henry. Also, Cromwell, unlike the essentially Catholic Henry, was what we would call a Lutheran.

7. Cromwell's specific authority came from the fact that Henry made Cromwell his vice regent and authorized him in 1535 to exercise all ecclesiastical jurisdictions with a "special commission." Cromwell's commission expired with his execution in 1540. Henry's daughter, Queen Mary Tudor, however, liked the idea of "commissions" to root out heresy. This eventually led to the infamous Court of High Commission. See Levy, Fifth Amendment, at 76.

8. More's judicial murder was typically Tudor. Henry VIII's father, Henry VII, started the Tudor dynasty with an indirect claim to the throne supported by various legal arguments. Thus, the Tudors were always keen to use "legal" procedures to achieve their ends, which included a lot of judicial murder.

In A Man for All Seasons Paul Scofield won an Oscar for his portrayal of More. Screenwriter Robert Bolt presented well the issues that led More to the block. It is still common even today to see More's life invoked, especially in legal circles. *See, e.g.,* Blake D. Morant, *Lessons from Thomas More's Dilemma of Conscience: Reconciling the Clash Between a Lawyer's Beliefs and Professional Expectations*, 78 St. John's L. Rev. 965 (2004).

The Tower of London

More did not confess. Instead, Cromwell found a perjurer in the person of Richard Rich, the solicitor general.[1] Rich testified that in a conversation in the Tower, More had denied Parliament's power to confer ecclesiastical supremacy on Henry and that More had said something to the effect that Parliament could not pass a law that "*God was not God.*"[2]

Though More denounced Rich as a perjurer, Cromwell's picked jury sealed More's fate. He was condemned and beheaded within the week.[3] But what he lived and died for eventually became part of the First Amendment's foundation.

HENRY'S PROGENY: EDWARD, MARY, AND ELIZABETH TUDOR

Henry VIII died in 1547, and the young and sickly Edward VI took over. He, or his regents, abolished all of Henry's treason and heresy laws—a promising start.[4]

But six years later, in 1553, Edward died, and his half-

Richard Rich

2. For More's trial as it relates to the history of the right to remain silent, *see* **Chapter 5: From Testicles to** *Dragnet*: **How the Fifth Amendment Protects** *All* **of Us.**

3. More was to be hanged, drawn, and quartered, but Henry "commuted" his sentence to beheading and, as was customary, his head was parboiled and put on the pole on London Bridge. More's daughter, Margaret, bribed the Bridge watchman and got the head for burial so that it would not be thrown into the Thames river. Henry's commutation was actually something of a kindness, in that hanging involved being cut down while still alive, and then having your genitalia cut off and your "entrails" dissected and burnt in front of you (they seemed to be good at keeping you alive for this), finally having your head cut off and your body quartered and dispersed to the four corners of the realm after the executioner cut out your heart and held it up for public view. BLACK'S LAW DICTIONARY 645 (5th ed. 1979). Also see BRAVEHEART (20th Century Fox 1995) for a simulation—not too gory—of the procedure. See **Chapter 8: "***Baby, Don't Be Cruel***":** **Just What's So Cruel** *and* **Unusual about the Eighth Amendment?**

1. Rich had to resign as solicitor general to testify, but Cromwell made it worthwhile for him. Today's lawyers have MODEL RULE OF PROFESSIONAL CONDUCT 3.7, which directs that "*[a] lawyer shall not act as advocate at a trial in which the lawyer is likely to be a necessary witness . . .*" Rich was an ambitious and shrewd man, as shadowy as the Holbein sketch of him. Five years later he had a hand in Cromwell's execution. Rich died in his bed a wealthy old man.

Margaret More

Site of More's execution on the Tower of London grounds

4. During the six years of his reign only two heretics burned. In contrast, during four years of Mary's reign 273 burned.

Edward VI was also "the Prince" in Mark Twain's THE PRINCE AND THE PAUPER (1882), about a young prince being mistaken for a common boy who looks just like him. Twain's story has been adapted numerous times including *The Prince and the Pauper* (Classic Comics, Issue 29 1946) as well as film and television versions, including THE PRINCE AND THE PAUPER (1937), starring Errol Flynn, and a Disney short film THE PRINCE AND THE PAUPER (Buena Vista Pictures 1990), starring Mickey Mouse in a critically acclaimed dramatic performance.

Edward VI

sister, Mary, took over.[5] This daughter of Catherine of Aragon believed it her mission to take England back to the Catholic Church. What you believed and said about it again became a crime.[6]

Mary took a page from Henry's book and established a commission *"for a severer way of proceeding against heretics."*[7] Mary's commission eventually became the Court of High Commission, which was the ecclesiastical arm of the Privy Council, just as the Star Chamber was the judicial arm.

Under Henry, all ecclesiastical power came under the sovereign, not from a pesky archbishop or pope. Despite her Catholicity, Mary saw no need to change this particular power structure.

But despite Mary's best efforts, English Protestantism lived on. After her death in 1558, Mary's half-sister (the daughter of Anne Boleyn) Elizabeth I took over. Elizabeth repealed all Mary's legislation against heresy.[8] Elizabeth was personally a moderate in an intolerant age.[9]

Mary Tudor

5. Levy, Fifth Amendment at 75 (quoting the Catholic historian Philip Hughes that *"[t]he facts are that in the last four years of Mary's reign, between February 4, 1555, and November 10, 1558, something like 273 of her subjects were executed by burning, under laws that her government had revived for the capital crime of obstinately adhering to beliefs that contradicted the teaching of the Catholic Church .... In this respect alone, namely of so many executions for this particular offence in so short a time, the event is a thing apart, in English history: never before, nor ever since, was there anything at all quite like it."*).

The work of Mary's Commission and its 273 victims earned her the title Bloody Mary. *Id.* at 76–77.

Turning to a less grave historical point, Mary's historical nickname raises the question of whether the Bloody Mary cocktail was named after her. It is a mixture in varying proportions of tomato juice, vodka, and other flavorings such as Worcestershire and/or Tabasco sauce. If the drink was named for her, she certainly never had one. Mary died in 1558, and tomatoes and potatoes (the latter for the vodka) did not make it to England until the 1590s. Other variations of the Bloody Mary with alternate ingredients include the Bloody Maria, with tequila; Bloody Geisha, with sake; Red Snapper, with gin; Michelada, with beer; Bullshot, with beef bouillon instead of tomato juice; Caesar or Bloody Caesar, with Clamato; and the Virgin Mary, Bloody Virgin, or A Bloody Shame, all with no alcohol.

6. Given that publishing at this point was mostly about religion, Mary renewed the old punishment for libelous printers: amputating a hand. Her first victim was a publisher aptly named John Stubbes. Sadakat Kadri, The Trial: A History, from Socrates to O.J. Simpson 76 (2005).

7. One of these heretics who met his fate under Mary was Archbishop of Canterbury **Thomas Cranmer**. Granting the divorce of Mary's dad from her mom turned out to be a bad career move.

Cranmer burned as a heretic from Foxe's Book of Martyrs

8. She was called Good Queen Bess, Gloriana, and, because she never married, the Virgin Queen. Nobody believes she was a virgin, but the state of Virginia is named after her. Of course, if she really was a virgin, it would cut against the slogan *"Virginia is for Lovers."*

VIRGINIA IS FOR LOVERS

9. During her reign only four Anabaptists burned. At the time, all the major factions of Christendom agreed that Anabaptists were heretics. Anabaptists denied the validity of infant baptism and, therefore, practiced rebaptism for adults. The movement was prominent during the sixteenth century and lives on in the Mennonite religion. The Baptists later adopted Anabaptist teaching regarding infant baptism. *See Anabaptists*, The Catholic Encyclopedia, http://www.newadvent.org/cathen/01445b.htm (last visited Aug. 29, 2005).

But relying on this view of Elizabeth misses a subtlety about her reign. More than even under Henry, religious nonconformity became treason; her government was zealous in ferreting it out, sending scores to prison, torture, and the gallows.[1]

Much of this resulted from Elizabeth's weak position when she took the throne. Besides the problem of being Anne Boleyn's daughter, Elizabeth was still illegitimate under both canon law and statute when she became queen. She even had trouble finding a bishop to perform the coronation.[2]

Plus, Elizabeth had the unique problem of being a female sovereign. With the Acts of Supremacy and Uniformity, she reestablished Henry's break with Rome, but, unlike dad, she could not be the church's "supreme head." No Protestant reform of that age went so far as to accept a woman priest, thus precluding Elizabeth from becoming the Pope of England.[3] Instead, she became the church's "supreme governor"— certainly good enough for her ends.

Pope Pius V convicted her of heresy in 1570 (*in absentia*, of course) and excommunicated her. The papal bull[4] that followed deposed her as queen, absolved her subjects

1. Sir Francis Walsingham (c. 1530–90) was Elizabeth's "spymaster." He admired Machiavelli, as can be seen in his quote *"[t]here is less danger in fearing too much than too little,"* and was one of the most proficient espionage-weavers in history. His intelligence on the Spanish Armada contributed to its defeat, and he discovered the plots around Mary, Queen of Scots, and actively participated in the trial leading to her execution. Even the playwright Christopher Marlowe was one of his spies. The modern British spy services, MI5 and MI6, have their origins in Walsingham's networks. Without Walsingham there would be no James Bond or George Smiley. *See generally* ALAN HAYNES, INVISIBLE POWER: THE ELIZABETHAN SECRET SERVICES 1570–1603 (1992).

James Bond, or 007 (pronounced "double oh seven"), is a fictional British spy created by writer Ian Fleming in 1953. So far, six actors have played Bond in the official series: Sean Connery, George Lazenby , Roger Moore, Timothy Dalton, Pierce Brosnan, and, since 2006, Daniel Craig.

George Smiley is John Le Carré's fictional MI6 agent and the central character in the novels CALL FOR THE DEAD (1961); A MURDER OF QUALITY (1962), TINKER, TAILOR, SOLDIER, SPY (1974); THE HONOURABLE SCHOOLBOY (1977); and SMILEY'S PEOPLE (1979). Alec Guinness played him in two successful television adaptations. Smiley is stodgy and ponderous and thus the antithesis of Bond.

2. Elizabeth I's coronation painting (1559).

Sean Connery as Bond

3. LEVY, FIFTH AMENDMENT, at 85. The movie ELIZABETH (Gramercy 1998) depicts many of the issues facing the queen, including the religious tensions between Catholic and Anglican prelates. Though a historian could quibble with details and event timing, the movie presents the issues with great performances by Cate Blanchard as Elizabeth and Geoffrey Rush as Walsingham.

Daniel Craig also plays an assassin Jesuit "hit man," based on John Ballard, a Jesuit priest executed in 1586 for plotting to kill Elizabeth. Craig later brought that assassin quality to his James Bond role in CASINO ROYALE (Columbia Pictures 2006).

4. A papal bull is a special pronuncment by a pope and named for the lead seal (bulla) authenticating it.

Pope Pius V and Elizabeth

Papal bull (Pope Urban VIII, 1637) sealed with a leaden *bulla*

5. LEVY, FIFTH AMENDMENT, at 88. The Bull of Deposition, *Regnans in Excelsis* ("Ruling from on High") marked a turn in Elizabeth's policy of religious toleration, and she began to persecute her religious enemies after it.

The bull's relevant section reads as follows:

"And moreover We do declare her to be deprived of her pretended title to the kingdom aforesaid, and of all dominion, dignity, and privilege whatsoever; and also the nobility, subjects, and people of the said kingdom, and all others who have in any sort sworn unto her, to be for ever absolved from any such oath, and all manner of duty dominion, allegiance, and obedience; and . . . We do command and charge all and every the noblemen, subjects, people, and others aforesaid that they presume not to obey her or her orders, mandates, and laws; and those which shall do the contrary. We do include them in the like sentence of anathema . . . ." Quoted in LEVY, FIFTH AMENDMENT, at 454 n.5.

from obeying her, and, for good measure, excommunicated any who did.[5]

This made it dicey to be Catholic in England. It became high treason in 1559 just to say that Elizabeth was not queen and in 1571 to allege she was a heretic or schismatic. Her government imposed crushing fines on Catholics, closed Catholic seminaries, and executed priests, especially Jesuits.[6]

And yet the priests still came, often hidden by Catholics.[7] When they were found, though, the charge was not heresy but treason.[8]

All of this underscores the problem with an "established" religion: heresy, a belief outside the official religious norm or orthodoxy, becomes treason. This is exactly why the Framers of the Constitution wrote the First Amendment's Establishment Clause.

But Catholics were not Elizabeth's only problem; there were also the Puritans. Initially, Elizabeth's government gave them a pass because they counterbalanced the Catholics. But as the Catholic threat diminished, especially with the defeat of the Spanish Armada in 1588, things changed.[9] The queen, like her father, was personally conservative in religion, with no affinity for Puritan radicalism.[10]

---

6. In 1585 Parliament banished all Catholic priests as traitors with An Act Against Jesuits, Seminary Priests and Such Other Like Disobedient Persons. Elizabeth executed 200 Catholics for "treason," all the while maintaining that it was not because they were Catholic. LOVELL at 267.

....

7. Many were hidden in "priest holes," hiding places for priests built into many Roman Catholic houses of England, especially during Elizabeth's reign. Most are attributed to the Jesuit Nicholas Owen, who constructed them to protect persecuted Roman Catholic priests.

Concealed priest hole in Partingdale House, Middlesex

R. P. Edmundus Campianus Soc: IESv.

8. See generally LEVY, FIFTH AMENDMENT, ch. 3. English Catholic priests came back to England after training in special seminaries abroad and presented a threat to Elizabeth's government. For this, she had them killed. One was Jesuit Father Edmund Campion, executed in 1581 after a sham trial. For Campion's trial in the context of the right to remain silent, see **Chapter 5: From Testicles to** *Dragnet:* **How the Fifth Amendment Protects** *All* **of Us.**

....

9. Elizabeth in 1588, showing the defeat of the Spanish Armada in the background.

10. Starting in 1563, John Foxe published his BOOK OF MARTYRS, giving accounts of the religious persecutions and Protestant martyrs. For over a century only the Bible was more popular in England than FOXE'S BOOK OF MARTYRS. It became a primer on the values of freedom of religion and speech, at least from the Protestant perspective. See LEVY. FIFTH AMENDMENT, at 79–82. The book's full title begins with ACTES AND MONUMENTS OF THESE LATTER AND PERILLOUS DAYS, TOUCHING MATTERS OF THE CHURCH. Through many editions, it became the affirmation of the Protestant Reformation in England. Foxe wanted to show the Church of England's historical foundation as the true and faithful church over Roman Catholicism. Foxe's record is extremely partisan and became the primary propaganda piece for English anti-Catholicism. Among other objections, Foxe's claims regarding martyrdoms under Mary ignore the mingled political and religious aspects of the time.

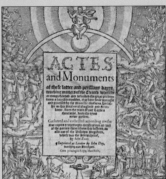

Leaving aside Elizabeth's religiosity, the issue was power. Elizabeth believed the state should control the church to effect her secular ends. The Puritans believed the church should control the state to affect heaven on earth. Here converges the Puritan and Catholic notion of the relationship between church and state. Both agreed that the church should control; they just had different notions of "the church."[1]

In Elizabeth's day, there were no grand political parties or movements. People instead articulated their politics through religion.

Among Elizabeth's tools of power were licensing and censorship, which her government employed more broadly than ever. In the early days of Henry VIII, printing and debate were much more open.[2] With the Elizabethan

settlement in 1559 began a system that required government licenses to speak or print.

Elizabeth's successor, James I, expanded the licensing to support his established church.[3] Religion and speech are locked in history, which explains why the Framers put them together in the First Amendment.

Elizabeth in 1575

1. Elizabeth saw the matter very clearly when stating that Catholics and Puritans "*join together in one opinion against me, for neither of them would have me to be Queen of England.*" Quoted in Levy, Fifth Amendment, at 147.

2. Elizabeth was no fan of parliamentary free speech, as Thomas More had advocated in the early days of Henry VIII.

For one thing, Parliament did not know the reason she called it until her opening speech, and it was to follow her agenda. Lovell at 233. In 1592, she advised the Speaker of the House of Commons that free speech was "*not as some suppose to speak . . . of all causes as him listeth, and to frame a form of religion, or a state of Government as to their idle brains shall seem meetest. She sayeth no king for his state will suffer such absurdities.*" Quoted in id. at 233.

The speaker of the House was a royal nominee to forward her agenda, and she severely treated speakers who failed her. Id. at 237. Ultimately, she could veto anything Parliament did. Id. at 238.

3. See Witte, Milton, at 1588, citing Cynthia Susan Clegg, Press Censorship in Elizabethan England (1997); Cynthia Susan Clegg, Censorship in Jacobean England (2001); David Loades, Politics, Censorship and the English Reformation (1991); S. Mutchow Towers, Control of Religious Printing in Early Stuart England (2003).

THE STUARTS

The Stuarts seem out of place.

Coming from Scotland may have had something to do with it. But they were not just out of place, they were out of sync; eventually, they were out of time.[4]

James I followed the popular Elizabeth in 1603. His son Charles I became king in 1625 but got his head chopped off in 1649. After Cromwell's "protectorate," Charles II took over in 1660 and tried to implement a French-style absolute monarchy but without the resources to make it work. When his less capable brother James II took over in 1685, he tried to do the same and lost the throne in 1688.

Although this book is not a history of the Stuarts, their story plays out over several chapters as it relates to the Bill of Rights. Religion and free speech especially bedeviled them.

James I: James I was a big advocate of the divine right of kings—being one, it came easily to him. In 1598, he wrote THE TRUE LAW OF FREE MONARCHIES, asserting among other things, "*rex est loquens*," ("the king is the law speaking").[5] James was an educated man and technically he was not saying he was above the law but that he embodied the law!

---

4. James I, king of England, was also James VI of Scotland and the son of Mary, Queen of Scots. Elizabeth had had Mary beheaded for treason. But in an historical irony, Mary's son James followed Elizabeth as king of England. Then followed Charles I, but Parliament deposed him, which led to Oliver Cromwell becoming "lord protector" (i.e., dictator) of England. Shortly after Cromwell's death, Charles II was "restored" to the throne, followed by James II. Finally, Mary (James II's Protestant daughter) ruled with her co-monarch husband, William of Orange.

William of Orange

Mary Stuart

5. *See* LEVY, FIFTH AMENDMENT, at 243.

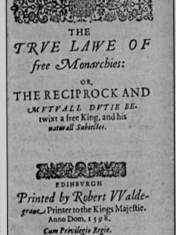

THE
TRVE LAWE OF
free Monarchies:
OR,
THE RECIPROCK AND
MVTVALL DVTIE BE-
twixt a free King, and his
naturall Subiectes.

EDINBVRGH
Printed by Robert VValde-
graue Printer to the Kings Majestie.
Anno Dom, 1 5 9 8.
Cum Privilegio Regio.

THE TRUE LAW OF FREE MONARCHIES sets out the doctrine of the divine right of kings. James saw it as an extension of the apostolic succession, the practice whereby bishops consecrate new bishops and priests by laying hands on them. The practice traces back in an unbroken chain to the original twelve apostles. During the reign of James's son Charles I, in 1644 Samuel Rutherford wrote LEX, REX (*The Law Is King*), expounding the theological arguments for the rule of law over the rule of men and kings.

See SAMUEL RUTHERFORD, LEX, REX, *available at* Liberty Library of Constitutional Classics, http://www.constitution.org/sr/lexrex.htm (last visited Dec. 5, 2005).

Samuel Rutherford

Either way, according to James, only God could judge him.

In a speech to Parliament, for example, James asserted that kings are not just God's

"lieutenants upon earth, and sit upon God's throne, but even by God himselfe they are called Gods."[1]

This makes you wonder whether James was all that clear that even God would judge him!

As did the Tudors, James believed in an established religion declaring, *"No Bish-* *ops, no King,"* meaning that crown and church were intertwined. James supported the established church and it supported him.

And because bishops got their jobs from James, they really tried to ingratitate themselves to him. During one theological debate, the archbishop of Canterbury, John Whitgift, pronounced:

"Undoubtedly your majesty speaks by the special assistance of God's spirit."[2]

The bishop of London, Richard Bancroft, one-upped Whitgift, proclaiming,

"I protest my heart melteth with joy, that Almighty God, of his singular mercy, hath given us such a king, as, since Christ's time, the like hath not been."[3]

These guys were obviously practiced and talented suck-ups. No wonder that upon Whitgift's death in 1604, Bancroft got his job as archbishop of Canterbury. This put Bancroft in position to oversee the KING JAMES BIBLE, which he tailored to suit James, reworking passages to make it monarch-friendly.[4]

---

1. *Quoted in* LEVY, FIFTH AMENDMENT, at 207.

Even today the head of the Anglican Church—that is, the Church of England— is not the archbishop of Canterbury but the monarch, who as of this writing is Queen Elizabeth II.

2. LEVY, FIFTH AMENDMENT, at 212–13.

3. LEVY, FIFTH AMENDMENT, at 212–13.

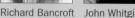

Richard Bancroft   John Whitgift

The Puritan **John Milton** would later accuse the Anglican clergy of following their medieval Catholic brethren having become

- *"a tyrannical crew"*
- a *"corporation of imposters"*
- *"halting and time-serving"* prelates

- *"Egyptian taskmasters of ceremonies"*
- *"a heap of hard and loathsome uncleanness"*
- a *"whip of scorpions"*
- *"illiterate and blind guides"*
- *"a wasteful band of robbers"*
- *"a perpetual havoc and rapine"*
- *"a continual hydra of mischief and molestation"*
- *"importunate wolves"*
- *"wild boars"*
- *"locusts and scorpions"*
- *"downtrodden vassals of perdition"*

Witte, *Milton*, at 1559.

Frontispiece to the KING JAMES BIBLE, 1611

4. The KING JAMES BIBLE is an English translation of the CHRISTIAN BIBLE begun in 1604 and completed in 1611. King James gave the translators instructions to guarantee that the new version would support both the Church of England and the monarchy. This was the third such official translation of the Bible into English, after THE GREAT BIBLE under Henry VIII and THE BISHOP'S BIBLE of 1568. All of these texts relied on William Tyndale's 1525 translation. Tyndale was the first to translate the Bible into English from Greek sources. He created new English words and expressions that we use even today, both in common speech and for their poetic value:

- *"Jehovah"* (from a transliterated Hebrew construction in the Old Testament, from "YHWH")
- *"Passover"* (as the name for the Jewish holiday "Pesach" or "Pesah")
- *"Atonement"* (at + onement), which goes beyond mere "reconciliation" to mean "to unite" or "to cover"
- *"scapegoat"* (the goat that bears the people's sins),
- *"let there be light"*
- *"the powers that be"*
- *"my brother's keeper"*
- *"the salt of the earth"*
- *"a law unto themselves"*
- *"filthy lucre"*
- *"it came to pass"*
- *"gave up the ghost"*
- *"the signs of the times"*
- *"the spirit is willing"*

Despite his arbitrary quirks, James would probably have had a relatively quiet reign but for the Puritans. To the Puritans, the religious power structures of the Tudors and Stuarts, like James's High Commission for Ecclesiastical Causes, represented the pope's law, and if there was one thing that a Puritan could not abide, it was "popery."[5]

What made matters worse for James was that these Puritans would not shut up.[6] James responded by trying to hinder speech itself. Indeed, James's restrictions on speech focused on both the religious and the political.

In 1621, James warned Parliament that it had no role in foreign affairs, saying it should not

"meddle with anything concerning our government or deep matters of state."[7]

Parliament, which by this point had become far more than the king's advisors with whom he could "parley," sent a protestation. James formally ripped the protestation out of the *Journals of the House.*

Edward Coke (pronounced "Cook"), later Lord Chief Justice of England, challenged James in a speech in the House of Commons. Members of Parliament, Coke declared, have an

"ancient right" and *"undoubted inheritance"* to a *"freedom to speak what we think good for government, either in church or commonwealth and what are the grievances . . . [T]he freedom of the House is the freedom of the whole land . . . . We serve here for thousands and ten thousands."*[8]

- *"live and move and have our being"*
- *"fight the good fight"*

Douai-Rheims New Testament

See Michael Farris, From Tyndale to Madison: How the Death of an English Martyr Led to the American Bill of Rights 23 (2007); Tyndale's New Testament (David Daniell ed., 1996). Many of these terms ended up in The King James Bible. The Catholic answer was The Douai-Rheims Bible of 1582 (New Testament) and 1609–10 (Old Testament), which also borrowed from Tyndale.

William Tyndale burned in 1536 for translating the Bible into English

5. The Puritan John Milton, living in the aftermath of King James, wrote of the need to protect the individual's liberty of conscience and freedom of worship from what he called *"the greedy idols"* of established Anglicanism, the *"spiritual tyranny of idle ceremonies,"* *"corrosive customs,"* and *"erroneous beliefs."* Witte, *Milton,* at 1529.

6. For more on the Puritan legal battles with James's courts, see **Chapter 5: From Testicles to *Dragnet*: How the Fifth Amendment Protects *All* of Us.**

7. *Quoted in* Steve Bachmann, *Starting Again with the Mayflower . . . England's Civil War and America's Bill of Rights,* 20 Quinnipiac L. Rev. 193, 216 (2000).

8. Witte, *Milton,* at 1588–89. Regarding James I's struggles with Parliament on free speech, including his jailing of Coke, *see* Lovell at 303.

Sir Edward Coke

James did not want the *"thousands and ten thousands"* involved in politics either. James encouraged them to engage in traditional village sports on Sundays (the original "weekend warriors") to prevent them from wasting time in the alehouses talking sedition. Bachmann at 222. You have to wonder whether the same things goes on today where men obsess about golf and the Super Bowl and repair to the modern sports bar only for buffalo wings, rather than dare talk politics.

Coke, like Sir Thomas More before him, was invoking a speech, petition, and debate tradition going back to the thirteenth century. Thus, when James I, and later Charles I, suspended Parliament and tried to curtail speech, Parliament indignantly rose up.[1]

These risings eventually killed James's son Charles I.

Charles I: As a modern commentator notes,

"[t]he most interesting thing about King Charles the First is that he was five feet six inches tall at the start of his reign, but only four foot eight inches tall at the end of it."[2]

In 1625, James's second son, Charles, took over and ruled until his head was chopped off in 1649. Like dad, he was a big fan of the divine right of kings, which led to a fruitless power struggle with Parliament.[3]

Charles was hapless,[4] but much of his problem was a changed world.

During the Middle Ages, the human condition limited the king's power. Even if the king was "divinely appointed," what did it really matter to his subjects? They probably never saw him or much of his government. If they had a legal dispute, for instance, they would seek justice from the local lord or church court, and only then voluntarily seek appeal to the king's common-law courts.[5]

But with the gradual development of modern taxing and bureaucracy, the monarch could directly or indirectly control everything. By Charles's time "divine right" was going out the door; people were starting to agree to government only if they had a stake in it and a voice about it.

John Lilburne

1. Coke's use of history became an important part of the English Revolution's ideology. John Lilburne, who we will hear more about in **Chapters 5, 6, and 7,** used to go into the House of Commons during the 1640s with a Bible in one hand and Coke's law books, THE INSTITUTES, in the other. Harold J. Berman, *Law and Belief in Three Revolutions,* 18 VAL. U. L. REV. 569, 600 (1984).

2. "Oliver Cromwell," on *Monty Python Sings* (Virgin Records 1991), sung to the tune of Frederic Chopin's Polonaise Op. 53 in A Flat Major. Actually, Charles was 5'4."

3. Charles was compensating. He was Britain's shortest king. ANTONIA FRASER, THE LIVES OF THE KINGS AND QUEENS OF ENGLAND 181 (1975). His elder brother Henry was the heir apparent, but Henry died of typhoid in 1612.

Anthony van Dyck in this famous *Charles I, King of England, from Three Angles* (1636), masked Charles's small stature and also solved Charles's problem of deciding between his three favorite suits for the portrait.

4. As Levy comments, *"[i]f supreme political stupidity in a king merits his execution, Charles richly deserved his fate."* LEVY, FIFTH AMENDMENT, at 266. Lovell describes him as a *"kindly, obstinate, and rather stupid man . . . ."* LOVELL at 309.

5. See several of the following chapters, especially **Chapter 6: How the Sixth Amendment Guarantees You a Court, a Lawyer, and a Chamber Pot.**

6. *See* Bachmann at 216–17; *see also* Witte, *Milton,* at 1532–36 (detailing the history of the English Civil War with Charles I).

7. *See* Harold W. Wolfram, *John Lilburne: Democracy's Pillar of Fire,* 3 SYRACUSE L. REV. 213, 220–21 and n.29 (1952).

The king summoned the **Long Parliament** in November 1640, so called to distinguish it from the **Short Parliament** he had summoned in April–May 1640. The Long Parliament also caused the king's advisers to resign and forbade its own dissolution without its members' consent. Tension between the king and Parliament increased until the English Civil War in 1642. After the king's defeat in 1646, the army exercised political power and in 1648 expelled all but sixty members of the Long Parliament. The remaining group, the **Rump Parliament,** brought Charles to trial and execution in 1649. It then stayed around until Cromwell forcibly ejected it in 1653.

Cromwell ejecting the Rump Parliament

Among the mistakes that led Charles to the chopping block were his struggles with Parliament in the 1620s. He fined and imprisoned members for speaking.[6] The Parliamentarians, especially the Puritans, pressed on, and Charles responded by dissolving Parliament.

Charles also tried to introduce a modified Anglican prayer book in Presbyterian Scotland, which led to a costly and unsuccessful war. His ineptitudes and financial need forced him to finally call a Parliament in 1640, after eleven years.[7]

This Long Parliament immediately sided with the Puritans, and in 1641, it abolished the courts in which Charles persecuted religious dissent and speech: the Court of High Commission for Ecclesiastical Causes and the Star Chamber.[8]

The Star Chamber in particular had been the court for prosecuting crimes such as counterfeiting and printing without a license.[9] Under the licensing laws, the bishop of London or archbishop of Canterbury reviewed all books, censored the illicit ones, and sent the unlicensed printers and authors to the Star Chamber for prosecution and punishment.[10]

When Parliament abolished the Star Chamber, the Tudor-Stuart licensing system became unenforceable, and the size of the press exploded.[11] For the first time, normal people could get their hands on cheap newspapers and political pamphlets.

A person's own voice limits the power of speech to those who can hear it or to those who "heard it said." The printed page, though, can literally go across all England and even across the ocean to colonial America.

---

8. The Star Chamber was particularly infamous among Puritans, many of whom came to America. *See Watts v. Indiana*, 338 U.S. 49, 54 (1949) (*"Ours is the accusatorial as opposed to the inquisitorial system. Such has been the characteristic of Anglo-American criminal justice since it freed itself from practices borrowed by the Star Chamber from the Continent whereby an accused was interrogated in secret for hours on end."*). THE STAR CHAMBER (20th Century Fox 1983) uses the Star Chamber's historical infamy as a plot basis. Michael Douglas stars as a frustrated judge who joins a shadow court that hunts down "criminals" who "get off" because of legal technicalities. The movie works as a thriller, more or less, but relies on the tired (and false) premise that the criminal justice system is not convicting enough "bad guys."

9. To the English of the time, printing a book was like minting a coin. Indeed, the manufacturing process of producing the movable type for printing is similar to minting a coin. Without a license, the publication was presumed "counterfeit," and printing, selling, or possessing it was an actionable crime. Witte, *Milton*, at 1589–90.

10. The Stationers' Company, the monopoly that enforced the licensing law, could "*search what houses and shops (and at what time they shall think fit)*" for illegal publications. Witte, *Milton*, at 1589–90. Regarding the history of search and seizure, see **Chapter 4: Molasses and the Sticky Origins of the Fourth Amendment.**

11. By one count, the number of pamphlets published during the year 1640 was 22, but by 1642 it was 1,966. Witte, *Milton*, at 1589; *see also* Bachmann at 220.

For centuries, kings had licensed and censured printing with varying degrees of success.[1] Now, who could turn back the tide of free speech?[2]

An alarmed Parliament tried to do so in June 14, 1643, by issuing a new licensing law to stamp out the "*many false, forged, scandalous, seditious, libelous, and unlicensed Papers, Pamphlets, and Books to the great defamation of Religion and government.*"[3] A dozen Protestant ministers replaced the bishop of London as censor and Parliament replaced the Star Chamber as enforcer.

But "free expression" had become its own political end, not just a way to get religious freedom or other rights. Thus, it deserved its own defense. The Puritan poet John Milton rose to the challenge with the masterful AREOPAGITICA (1644).[4]

By 1642, the English Civil War had begun. Parliament eventually defeated the royalist forces for good in 1648. Kings had been deposed before, but Parliament specifically tried Charles

1. Official censorship in England started before the Tudors, in 1275, with *De Scandalis Magnatum* for "seditious words" about the king or his officials. O'Brien at 43. But the printing press of the mid-1400s and Henry VIII's break with Rome made the practice a royal imperative. Henry VIII had a licensing law in 1530. The later Tudors and Stuarts broadened it with a dozen later acts, culminating in Charles I's Star Chamber Decree of 1637. Witte, *Milton*, at 1589–90.

2. Even today dictatorial regimes bring to bear all the resources of modern police technology against the expression of free speech and democracy. So far, they have all eventually failed as the fall of the Berlin Wall showed. But they often only fail after much human misery, and many have yet to do so, as the Tiananmen Square protests of 1989 showed.

Berlin Wall at the Brandenburg Gate, November 9, 1989

3. *Quoted in* Witte, *Milton*, at 1589–90.

"Tank man" was an anonymous man who blocked Chinese tanks on June 5, 1989, after the Chinese removed protestors from Tiananmen Square
Image by Helen Koop

William Blake's version of John Milton

4. John Milton (1604–74) wrote during the throes of the English Revolution, 1640–60. His PARADISE LOST (1667–68) is a masterpiece of English literature. In AREOPAGITICA: A SPEECH OF MR. JOHN MILTON FOR THE LIBERTY OF UNLICENSED PRINTING TO THE PARLIAMENT OF ENGLAND (1644), he defended freedom of expression:

• a nation's unity is created through blending individual differences rather than imposing homogeneity;
• the ability to explore the fullest range of ideas on a given issue is essential to find truth;
• censorship acts to the detriment of material progress;
• if the facts are laid bare, truth will defeat falsehood in open competition, but this cannot be left for a single individual to determine: "*Let her and Falsehood grapple; who ever knew Truth put to the worse in a free and open encounter?*";
• each individual must uncover his own truth because no one is wise enough to act as a censor for all individuals: "*Each person has the law of God written on his and her heart, mind, and conscience, and rewritten in Scripture, most notably in the Decalogue.*"
Quoted in Witte, *Milton*, at 1529, 1586.

Regarding Milton's influence on America and the First Amendment, John Adams wrote in 1776 that Milton was "*as honest a man as his nation ever bred, and as great a friend of liberty.*"

for high treason.[5] Charles refused to enter a plea, claiming that no court had jurisdiction over a monarch and that the court's power was nothing more than what grew out of a barrel of gunpowder. This sealed his fate.

As Milton noted, England was ready to embrace democracy. Give people education and

"all the Lord's people . . . become prophets . . . [T]he right of choosing, yea of changing their own government is by the grant of God himself in the people."[6]

Poor Charles never "got it." He, too, wanted the people's liberty,

"but I must tell you," declared Charles, *"that their Liberty and Freedom consist in*

having government . . . . It is not their having a share in the government—that is nothing appertaining to them."[7]

From his scaffold, Charles I looked over a changed world; how much insight he had into the change is impossible to know because they chopped his head off before he could say.[8]

First page of the 1644 edition of AREOPAGITICA. The title "Areopagitica" alludes to an analogous written oration of Isocrates presented in 355 BC to the Athenian Ecclesia, advocating a return of certain powers to the aristocratic Council of the Areopagus.

Title page of the first edition of *Paradise Lost*, 1668

PARADISE Lost has been just too good for Hollywood to pass up. SEVEN (New Line Cinema 1995) includes quotations from the poem; THE DEVIL'S ADVOCATE (Warner Brothers 1997) alludes to it and includes the line "better to reign in Hell, than serve in Heaven," and Al Pacino's Satan is named "John Milton." (The "devil's advocate" was originally a canon lawyer in the Roman Catholic Church appointed to argue against a person's canonization or beatification. Pope Sixtus V institutionalized the office in 1587. KADRI at 146.) THE CROW (Miramax Films 1989) quotes from the poem, as does THE PROPHECY (Dimension Films 1995) and THE SENTINEL (Universal Pictures 1977).

The Temptation and Fall of Eve by William Blake (1808), from PARADISE LOST

5. Trial of Charles I.

6. *Quoted in* Witte, *Milton*, at 1596, 1598.

7. *Quoted in* Wolfram at 227. Bachmann at 195–96 gives Charles's fuller quote from the scaffold: *"For the people . . . truly I desire their liberty and freedom as much as anybody whatsoever; but I must tell you, their liberty and freedom consists in having government, those laws by which their lives and their goods may be most their own. It is not their having a share in the government; that is nothing appertaining to them. A subject and a sovereign are clear different things."*

8. Execution of Charles I (contemporary German print).

Petitioning Cromwell for Everything: Charles was gone. A nice story would be that his demise ushered in an era of toleration, rights, and freedom that transplanted to America. Unfortunately, this was not the case.

Oliver Cromwell eventually emerged as the military dictator of England from 1649 until his death in 1658.[1] This was an unprecedented time of petitions, including THE HUMBLE PETITION OF THE LEVELERS (1647), AN AGREEMENT OF THE PEOPLE (1647),

and THE HUMBLE PETITION AND ADVICE (1657).

The power in these petitions lay not so much that they were printed but in the process by which they came about. Large groups produced them, which showed political power. They were symbols as much as proposals.[2]

Cromwell generally ignored the petitions and famously put the greatest petitioner of all, John Lilburne, on trial.[3] But

the power of petitions and the way in which they could marshal people and politics is exactly what the First Amendment guarantees. It is no accident that the Framers put the right to "*assemble*" and "*petition*" in the same clause.[4]

Restoration of Charles II: The Puritan Revolution, which had devolved into Cromwell's Protectorate, ended with the Stuart Restoration.[5]

In an historical inversion, Charles II was

---

1. Cromwell in his famous "warts and all" painting. Cromwell wanted this painting to distinguish himself from the way monarchs had themselves painted, most notably Charles I's flattering portraits to increase his stature.

Cromwell turned out to be as despotic as a king—perhaps more so because he was capable. It so happens he was Thomas Cromwell's (from Henry VIII and Thomas More's time) great-great-great-nephew.

2. Bachmann at 225. Parliament later illustrated the power of petitions as political rallying points and symbols when it passed a law during the Restoration of Charles II that neither king nor Parliament would accept a petition from more than ten people.

3. For the history of Lilburne and Cromwell, see **Chapter 5: From Testicles to** *Dragnet*: **How the Fifth Amendment Protects** *All* **of Us** and **Chapter 6: How the Sixth Amendment Guarantees You a Court, a Lawyer, and a Chamber Pot.**

Van Dyck's 1634 portrait with Charles on a raise making him look taller than his horse

But Cromwell still took the title "His Highness" and signed documents not as "Oliver Cromwell" but "Oliver, P" (for Protector) to emulate King Charles's "R" (for Rex). LOVELL at 350.

Contemporary Satirical print of Cromwell usurping Royal power

See CROMWELL (Columbia Pictures 1970) had Richard Harris in the title role and Alec Guinness as Charles I

AN AGREEMENT OF THE PEOPLE (1647)

John Lilburne

4. "*Congress shall make no law . . . abridging . . . the right of the people peaceably to assemble, and to petition the Government for a redress of grievances.*" U.S. CONST. amend. I.

5. Bachmann at 222.

6. *Quoted in* Bachmann at 208.

7. Again, this history underscores why the First Amendment's Framers coupled the Establishment and Free Exercise Clauses—they learned from history and wanted something better for America.
"*Congress shall make no law respecting an establishment of religion, or prohibiting the free exercise thereof . . .*" U.S. CONST. amend. I.

the one who wanted toleration; Parliament wanted restrictions on both speech and religion. As Charles declared,

"no man shall be disquieted or called in question for differences of opinion in matter of religion which do not disturb the peace of the kingdom."[6]

This was a far cry from his grandfather James I's exclusive support of the established Church of England. But Parliament and society were divided between Anglicans and Puritans, who each wanted to freely *and* intolerantly exercise their faith.[7] With the mix of speech, politics, and religion in mind, the Anglicans got the upper hand in Parliament and codified intolerance with the Clarendon Code.[8] The point was to restrict Puritanism.[9]

Charles tried to soften the law in 1672 by allowing meetings if they secured the crown's preapproval.[10] He also issued two Declarations of Indulgence suspending all penal laws against dissenting Protestants (usually Puritans) and Catholics.

But the Stuarts did not get credit for Charles II's toleration. Part of the reason for this is because he tried to establish a government around an absolute monarch along the French model, which never worked in England.[11] The political reality was that Charles II, just like his father, needed money, and only Parliament could grant it.

---

8. Bachmann at 208–09. The Clarendon Code included:

The Corporation Act (1661) providing that only those who received the Anglican communion could be members of the municipal government that controlled elections to Parliament.

The Act of Uniformity (1662) expelling two thousand Puritan clergy from their paid positions in the established Anglican Church for not consenting to everything in the PRAYER BOOK.

The Conventicle Act (1664) forbidding "*meetings held 'under color or pretence of any exercise of religion' of five or more persons not members of the same household.*" This law punished meetings for religious rites other than for the Anglican Church with imprisonment and, for the third offense, transportation to America (and later Australia) upon pain of death for returning to England. Parliament renewed the act in 1670 "*to prevent and suppress seditions conventicles.*"

The Five Mile Act (1665) forbidding any clergy or school master from coming within five miles of a city or town unless he declared he would not "*at any time endeavor any alteration of Government either in Church or State.*" Quoted in Bachmann at 209.

Although the Conventicle Act allowed freedom of worship in the home, the point of the Clarendon Code was to target Independent Puritans, the "dissenters," from the Church of England. These were the folks who loaded up on the *Mayflower* for America.

9. LOVELL at 370–71.

10. Bachmann at 221, *citing* His Majesty's Declaration to All His Loving Subjects (March 15, 1672). Later, Charles's brother James II tried to do the same thing with his 1687 Declaration of Indulgence.

Concurrently, in 1670, a juror named Edward Bushel refused to convict two Quakers who were speaking out in public. One of them was William Penn (later of Pennsylvania). This case ended up being a key to the history of juries and the origin of the Sixth Amendment. See **Chapter 7: Trial by Jury or . . . by God!**

William Penn (1644–1718)

11. LOVELL at 375–77. Charles tried to run the country without Parliament with a "cabal." The political connotation we have for this word comes from the first letters of Charles's five ministers:

Clifford—lord treasurer
Arlington—secretary of state
Buckingham—master of horse
Ashley (Earl of Shaftesbury)—lord chancellor
Lauderdale—secretary for Scottish affairs.

LOVELL at 374. Charles's CABAL was a precursor to a modern cabinet, but its members were not really united to form a government per se. They had their offices because they controlled votes in Parliament.

Flexing its political power, Parliament passed the first Test Act in 1673, requiring all office holders to deny under oath the Catholic doctrine of transubstantiation.[1] This law effectively prevented the king from appointing Catholics to high civil or military posts and disqualified them from serving in Parliament.

Charles II died unexpectedly on February 16, 1685 with no legitimate heir.[2] His brother James II took the throne. James II started out popular but Parliament and the people quickly came to despise him. In addition to the fact that he lacked his brother's tact and ability, he was something even worse: unforgivably Catholic.[3]

In late seventeenth century England, rumors of Catholic plots, conspiracies, and outrages abounded.[4] Beyond rampant prejudice, James II's Catholicism created a constitutional crisis. Since Henry VIII, the king was the head of the Church of England, which James promised Parliament he would defend and support. But how could a Catholic do this?

When James created a new Court of Ecclesiastical Commission to enforce conformity, it was not to Anglicanism, but to Catholicism. This was, to say the least, a bad political move, especially because this court's name was so close to the old Court of High Commission that Parliament had abolished in 1641.[5]

James opened a Catholic chapel in London; surrounded himself with Catholic advisers; and began appointing Catholics to the Privy Council, the faculties of Oxford and Cambridge, and, most disturbing of all, as officers in his rapidly expanding army.[6]

In 1687 and 1688, James issued two Declarations of Indulgence granting free-

---

1. Shown is a **Catholic monstrance** for holding the transubstantiated host. Part of what caused Parliament to pass the Test Acts was the Great Fire of London in 1666, which Londoners blamed on Catholics.

   Despite Charles's and later James's attempts to repeal it, the English Test Act remained in effect until The Catholic Relief Act of 1829 (10 Geo. 4, c. 7 (Eng.)). As we will see, the Framers of the U.S. Constitution prohibited "test acts" of any kind at Article VI, section 3: *"no religious Test shall ever be required as a Qualification to any Office or public Trust under the United States."*

2. On his deathbed in 1685, Charles proclaimed himself a Catholic. Bachmann at 205. The back story is that King Louis of France had been giving Charles a large subsidy under a secret treaty. The deal was that Charles was to declare himself a Catholic and in return he would get French troops to help him. LOVELL at 375.

   Charles's unexpected death never gave him the chance to carry out the whole plan. But the fact that he went ahead and declared himself a Catholic shows that he at that point must have had some religious feeling—or maybe he was just hedging his bets.

James as lord high admiral

3. LOVELL at 389–90 (James II *"was stupid and egocentric"*). James's conversion to Catholicism had come to light with the Test Act. James resigned the office of Lord High Admiral, a post in which he had served honorably and bravely, rather than conform to the Church of England rites.

4. See more on this history in later chapters, especially **Chapter 8:** *Baby, Don't Be Cruel":* Just What's So Cruel *and* Unusual about the Eighth Amendment? (discussing the Titus Oates Popish Plot and the Bloody Assizes).

5. LOVELL at 390; Bachmann at 214.

6. See Bachmann at 205–06, 209; LOVELL at 376.

dom of worship to Catholics and Protestant dissidents, abolishing the Test Acts. He also ordered bishops throughout the realm to have the declaration read during church services on two consecutive Sundays.

But instead of earning James credit for toleration, the declarations resulted in seven bishops, including the archbishop of Canterbury, refusing to read the declarations, arguing that the king lacked authority to issue them.[7] James had the bishops arrested for seditious libel.[8]

In our modern way of thinking, what James did was fair and makes him look like a man of principle. After all, why not give Catholics with ability a chance?

The problem was the way he went about it.

James arranged to have a court case to uphold his appointment of Catholic military officers despite the Test Act. He then stacked the deck by making sure the case went before the Court of King's Bench, which he had packed with judges who would give him the ruling he wanted. They held that *"the laws of England are the king's laws,"* and that the king could therefore dispense with the law *"in particular cases and upon particular necessary reasons."*

Thus, what Protestant England now saw was a Catholic king, creating a Catholic army, with a court that he controlled, saying he was above the law.

Adding to Protestant paranoia was that James's second wife, the very Catholic Mary of Modena, had a baby boy.[9] Thus, unlike his brother Charles II, who kept his Catholicism secret and had the bad fortune (or good sense) not to have a son, James II was starting a Catholic dynasty.

---

7. Bachmann at 206; *see also* Eric Schnapper, *"Libelou" Petitions for Redress of Grievances: Bad Historiography Makes Worse Law*, 74 Iowa L. Rev. 303 (1989) (noting that the First Amendment's Petition Clause owes its origin to the Seven Bishops Case in 1688, which led to the English Bill of Rights of 1689, providing an absolute privilege for the content of petitions to the government); Chemerinsky at 913–15 (noting that in light of the history, the Supreme Court wrongly decided *McDonald v. Smith*, 472 U.S. 479 (1985), which upheld a civil verdict for defamation for the content of letters to President Ronald Reagan and others).

8. Group portrait of the seven bishops imprisoned in the Tower of London in 1688. They were acquitted of charges of seditious libel.

Mary of Modena

Mary's son, James Francis Edward Stuart

Bonnie Prince Charlie

9. Many English regarded Mary of Modena as the Pope's agent. Mary's son was James Francis Edward Stuart, known as The Old Pretender or The Old Chevalier. He was the leader of the first major Jacobite rebellion attempting to regain the throne. "Jacobite" comes from *"Jacobus"* (Latin for "James"). The First Jacobite Rebellion and the Second Jacobite Rebellion were known, respectively, as "The Fifteen" and "The Forty-Five," after the years in which they occurred (i.e., 1715 and 1745). The second significant Jacobite rebellion centered around James II's grandson, Charles Edward Stuart, or Bonnie Prince Charlie. David Niven played him in Bonnie Prince Charlie (London Film Productions 1948).

An example of how speech is often symbolic is that those supporting a Stuart restoration would pass a wine glass over a water jug while drinking a toast to "the king" as a clandestine way of toasting the "king over the water," which is to say the Stuart "pretender" in exile in France. *See, e.g.,* Walter Scott, Redgauntlet 42 (1824) (describing such a toast but with the words *"[o]ver the water"* expressly added).

Prominent Englishmen arranged for James's daughter from his first marriage, the comfortably Protestant Mary Stuart, to take over with her comfortably Protestant husband, William of Orange.[1]

Under the banner "the Protestant Religion and the Liberties of England," William landed in England to knock his father-in-law off the throne. In the end, neither James nor his army was up to the fight. Perhaps remembering the execution of his father, Charles I, James fled with his family to France and never returned to England.

Meanwhile, London crowds stormed Catholic churches, and the mayor ordered the disarming of all Catholics. William arrived in London on December 28 and called a "convention."[2] This convention negotiated William and Mary's taking the throne as co-rulers and provided the basis for the English Bill of Rights.

The English Bill of Rights, of course, was the model for our own Bill of Rights. But the English version barred Catholics from the throne of England:

"[I]t hath been found by experience that it is inconsistent with the safety and welfare of this Protestant kingdom to be governed by a papist prince . . . ."[3]

The monarch also had to swear at his coronation he would maintain the Protestant religion.

Thus, we leave the story in Europe and switch to the history the Founders knew in America.

RELIGION AND SPEECH IN PURITAN AMERICA

Puritans and God had a special deal.

God contracted with them,

1. William of Orange

Mary Stuart

2. William technically could not call a Parliament because James II, on his way out of England, burned the writs convening Parliament in December. Parliament could not lawfully be convened unless it was summoned by writs impressed with the Great Seal, but James threw the Great Seal into the Thames River! The convention to work out the outlines of constitutional government set the precedent for America, culminating in the Constitutional Convention of 1789.

3. Through a complicated formula passing though Mary's sister, Princess Anne of Denmark, this would eventually lead to the Hanoverian dynasty in England, which included King George III.

George III

5. Governor John Winthrop of Massachusetts, in his "City on a Hill" sermon, *A Model of Christian Charity,* laid out the deal: *"Thus stands the cause between God and us, we are entered into covenant with him for his work; we have taken out a commission . . . . We must be a city on the hill . . . a light to the nations of the world. We must entertain each other in brotherly affection . . . for the supply of other's necessities . . . . We must delight in each other, make other's conditions our own, rejoice together, mourn together, labor and suffer together, always having before our eyes our commission and community in the work, our community as members of the same body . . . . [S]o shall we keep the unity of the spirit in the bond of peace; the Lord will be our God, and delight to dwell among us, as his own people, and will command a blessing upon us in all our ways . . . ."* Quoted in Witte, *Blest,* at 591–92.; also quoted in John Witte, Jr., *How to Govern a City on a Hill: The Early Puritan Contribution to American Constitutionalism,* 39 EMORY L.J. 41, 47 (1990).

4. John Witte, Jr., *Blest Be the Ties That Bind: Covenant and Community in Puritan Thought,* 36 EMORY L.J. 579, 590–91 (1987). According to John Milton, they were *"to be agents of His Kingdom, . . . to set a standard [of] truth, . . . to blow the evangelical trumpet to the nations, . . . to give out reformation to the world."*

Winthrop

and they contracted with each other, to be the New Jerusalem and chosen people.[4] If they acted *"godly,"* God would give them peace and prosperity. It was like the Hebrews' Old Testament deal—take care of God and he will take care of you.[5]

The Puritans, though, expanded the deal, making it not just between God and the chosen people, but between God, the ruler, and the people. This meant that if the people failed, the civil ruler would reprimand them, including the ultimate punishments of banishment or execution.

Conversely, though, the people could compel the ruler to discharge his divine office, and if he failed in his duty toward God or them, they could protest and disobey. And taking a page from the English Civil Wars, they could unseat him *"by force and arms."*[6]

This idea of a special deal with God explains why Puritans both in England and America were so passionate about law and politics.[7] To their way of thinking, a civil ruler had to be godly and the civil law was to reflect divine law and godly order.

Such a covenant implies a theocracy where the state must root out nonconformity and get after the devil.[8] For the Puritans, church and state were technically separate but both under contract with God to achieve the godly end.[9]

At least part of the Puritans' attitude toward government is still with us, notably the idea that the United States is a chosen land and specially blessed people.[10] As a chosen people, we believe in rooting out evil. This has sometimes led to worse evil. But it has also been part this country's drive toward forming a true democratic republic.

The "city on a hill" metaphor comes from *Matthew 5:14*: *"You are the salt of the earth. But if the salt loses its saltiness, how can it be made salty again? It is no longer good for anything, except to be thrown out and trampled by men. You are the light of the world. A city on a hill cannot be hidden. Neither do people light a lamp and put it under a bowl. Instead they put it on its stand, and it gives light to everyone in the house. In the same way, let your light shine before men, that they may see your good deeds and praise your Father in heaven."*

6. Witte, *Blest*, at 592–93; Witte, *City on a Hill*, at 59–61. The Puritans insisted that all officials have as *"godly a character"* as possible, notwithstanding their sin. See also Renaud & Weinberger at 80–84 (discussing the nature of church and state government in Puritan America).

9. Witte, *City on a Hill*, at 55.

7. Witte, *Blest*, at 593–94.

8. A sampling includes Anne Hutchinson's heresy trial of 1638, which led to her banishment; Mary Dyer, one of four Quakers known as the Boston martyrs, hanged for repeatedly defying a law banning Quakers; and the notorious Salem witch trials.

10. This approach to religion and society is the jumping off point for many Christian groups such as the Moral Majority, which Jerry Falwell cofounded in 1979 with a "pro-family, pro-life, pro-defense, pro-Israel" agenda. During the 1980s it was one of the largest political lobbies.

After the September 11, 2001, attacks, Falwell said on *The 700 Club*, a daily Christian Conservative TV show: *"I really believe that the pagans, and the abortionists, and the feminists, and the gays and the lesbians who are actively trying to make that an alternative lifestyle, the ACLU, People for the American Way, all of them who have tried to secularize America, I point the finger in their face and say 'you helped this happen.'"* Falwell further stated that the attacks were *"probably deserved."* After heavy criticism, Falwell apologized, though he later stood by his statement, declaring *"if we decide to change all the rules on which this Judeo-Christian nation was built, we cannot expect the Lord to put his shield of protection around us as he has in the past."*

By the late 1980s the Moral Majority dissolved, and Falwell died in 2007. The Christian Coalition of America continues much the same political agenda. Regarding early nineteenth century religious fundamentalism of the Second Great Awakening, John Adams warned that *"instead of the most enlightened people, I fear we Americans shall soon have the character of the silliest people under Heaven."* Stone at 14, *quoting* Letter from John Adams to Benjamin Rush (Dec. 28, 1807).

John Adams

The Puritans did wish to create a Christian community.[1] But the Founding Fathers were generations removed from Puritan zeal. As we will see, the Framers of the Constitution and Bill of Rights were reacting to their own forefathers to create a secular state.

PRESSING RELIGION IN ENGLAND AND AMERICA

The Puritans were keen on getting their message out; the printing press was how they did it. By 1638, the Massachusetts Bay Colony had its own printing press.[2]

With the Puritans' "city on a hill" mentality, the division between church and state was only technical.

If you disagreed with one, you disagreed with the other. A statement about religion was political, and a political statement was religious.

Thus licensing continued in the American colonies long after it ended in England in 1695.[3] With government and religion mixed, controlling the press became very important. All the colonies outlawed or censored "*blasphemous*"

---

1. Islands of Tolerance in an Intolerant World: Rhode Island and Pennsylvania. Albert at 39–40. Pennsylvania and Rhode Island had no established church: "*Pennsylvania, because its founding Quakers believed in it, and Rhode Island, because Roger Williams thought everyone but him so reprobate that they might as well worship as they pleased.*" RICHARD BROOKHISER, WHAT WOULD THE FOUNDERS DO? 26–27 (2006); see also J. WILLIAM FROST, A PERFECT FREEDOM: RELIGIOUS LIBERTY IN PENNSYLVANIA 18 (1990) ("*In Pennsylvania, there would be no legal church establishment, no tithes or forced maintenance of any minister.*"). Pennsylvania was not quite as open as Rhode Island because its religious freedom only applied to those "*who acknowledge[d] the being of a God*" and, like other states, had a religious requirement for holding public office. Nevertheless, it was a place where a man with freethinking ideas like Benjamin Franklin could live, prosper, and thrive.

Benjamin Franklin

Roger Williams

Colonial Pennsylvania

Colonial Rhode Island

2. Robert A. Rutland, *Freedom of the Press, in* THE BILL OF RIGHTS: A LIVELY HERITAGE 32 (John Kukla ed., 1987). Indeed, the press came before the colony's first legal code, The Massachusetts Body of Liberties of 1641.

3. Regarding licensing in England and the relative freedom of the press, see LOVELL at 399.

4. Milton's liberal thoughts on free speech did not extend to blasphemy, treason, or defamation, and they must be subject to "*the sharpest justice*" against the "*malefactors.*" But not even this bad speech justified a prior restraint for Milton. To censor a book is to deny human nature. Witte, *Milton*, at 1594–95.

Of course, many would consider "*Bong Hits 4 Jesus*" blasphemy. Blasphemy is clearly subject to interpretation.

Is Morgan Freeman or George Burns playing God blasphemy in BRUCE ALMIGHTY (Universal Studios 2003), EVAN ALMIGHTY (Universal Studios 2007) and OH, GOD (Warner Bros. 1977)? What about other depictions of religious symbols for humor or dramatic impact? And what about artistic expression in a free society?

Image by Helen Koop

speech, such as denying the soul's immortality or the Holy Trinity.[4] Generally, the laws that outlawed blasphemy also prohibited speaking badly of ministers and royalty.[5]

If blasphemy is putting a religious truth in a negative light, then *libel*, the putting of a person or entity in a negative light, is closely related.

LIBEL LAW IN ENGLAND AND COLONIAL AMERICA

Libel is a kind of *defamation*, which is when someone publishes (i.e., makes public) a statement that makes someone else look bad.[6] If you couple the libel with a statement against the government it becomes *seditious libel*, i.e., encouraging sedition.

The concept of seditious libel was always accordion-like, dependent on the whim of kings and their judges.[7] William Blackstone in 1769 clarified that English law allowed no prior restraint or censorship:

"Every freeman has an undoubted right to lay what sentiments he pleases before the public, but if he publishes what is improper, mischievous, or illegal, he must take the consequences of his own temerity."[8]

Piss Christ was Andres Serrano's 1987 artistic photo of a small plastic crucifix submerged in a glass of his urine. The piece won the Southeastern Center for Contemporary Art's "Awards in the Visual Arts" competition, which the National Endowment for the Arts (NEA), a United States government agency, sponsored. Religious groups such as the American Family Association and legislators objected, and the NEA nearly lost government funding.

NATIONAL ENDOWMENT FOR THE ARTS

A great nation deserves great art.

5. Regarding speaking in a religious assembly against the government and its prohibition, *see* Levy, Origins of the Bill of Rights 113–14 (1999).

6. If the offending material is "published" as spoken words or sounds, sign language, gestures, etc., it is *slander*. But if it is published in writing, film, CD, or DVD, it is *libel*. *Calumny* and *vilification* are synonyms for defamation. In the Bible, *Proverbs* 10:18 states: "*He that uttereth a slander, is a fool.*"
  See J.W. Ehrlich, The Holy Bible and the Law 155 (1962).

7. Seditious libel was malicious, scandalous political falsehoods that tended to breach the peace, instill revulsion or contempt in the people against their government, or lower their esteem for their rulers. Levy, Bill of Rights, at 122.
   One of the key sources on this history, if not the key source, is Leonard W. Levy, Emergence of a Free Press (1985). Several commentators, however, take exception to Levy's earlier work, Leonard W. Levy, Legacy of Suppression (1960), including David A. Anderson, *Levy vs. Levy*, 84 Mich. L. Rev. 777 (1986) (reviewing *Emergence of a Free Press*). Levy has responded in various articles, including Leonard W. Levy, *On the Origins of the Free Press Clause*, 32 Ucla L. Rev. 177 (1984) and Leonard W. Levy, *The Legacy Reexamined*, 37 Stan. L. Rev. 767 (1985). *See* David M. Rabban, *The Ahistorical Historian: Leonard Levy on Freedom of Expression in Early American History*, 37 Stan. L. Rev. 795 (1985) (book review).
   Also taking on Levy is Larry D. Eldridge, A Distant Heritage: The Growth of Free Speech in Early America 3 (1994) (arguing "*that colonists experienced a dramatic expansion of their freedom to criticize government and its officials across the seventeenth century*").

8. *Quoted in* O'Brien at 44. Blackstone's *Commentaries* was *the* book every colonial lawyer used for both his training and practice.

William Blackstone

Thus, the law allowed for later prosecution of "bad" speech:

> "[W]here blasphemous, immoral, treasonable, schismatical, seditious, or scandalous libels are punished by the English law . . . the liberty of the press, properly understood, is by no means infringed or violated."[1]

And, for such "bad" speech, the defendant "shall on a fair and impartial trial be adjudged of a pernicious tendency . . . ."

This, for Blackstone,

> "is necessary for the preservation of peace and good order, of government and religion, the only solid foundations of civil liberty."[2]

Eighteenth century England, however, saw few prosecutions for seditious libel because the press was part of one political faction or another and "even the most scummy had powerful political backers."[3]

Thus, even though no written constitution protected it, the eighteenth century English press in practice was relatively free. In fact, it was ahead of the American press in its freedom to criticize as it pleased.

Perhaps owing to its longer tradition of control over the press for religious reasons,

---

1. William Blackstone, Commentaries *151–52 (1769), *reprinted in* L. Levy, Freedom of the Press from Zenger to Jefferson 104–05 (1966). Many of the founding generation agreed with Blackstone. *See* Levy, *Free Press Clause,* at 205, noting that in 1788 Jefferson urged Madison to add a bill of rights to the Constitution, stating that "[a] declaration that the federal government will never restrain the presses from printing anything they please, will not take away the liability of the printers for false facts printed." Letter from Thomas Jefferson to James Madison (July 31, 1788). One of Jefferson's political rivals, Alexander Hamilton, in 1804 defended a Federalist editor prosecuted by the New York attorney general for libeling President Jefferson, saying that "the liberty of the press . . . [is] publishing the truth, for good motives and for justifiable ends . . . ." But an editor could not "use the weapon of truth wantonly . . . for relating that which does not appertain to official conduct [or for] disturbing the peace of families." According to Hamilton, this was not "fair and honest exposure" and was thus libelous. *Quoted in* Brookhiser at 161.

2. Blackstone's fuller quote follows: [W]here blasphemous, immoral, treasonable, schismatical, seditious, or scandalous libels are punished by the English law . . . the liberty of the press, properly understood, is by no means infringed or violated . . . The liberty of the press is indeed essential to the nature of a free state; but this consists in laying no previous restraints upon publications, and not in freedom from censure for criminal matter when published. Every freeman has an undoubted right to lay what sentiments he pleases before the public; to forbid this is to destroy the freedom of the press; but if he publishes what is improper, mischievous, or illegal, he must take the consequences of his own temerity. . . . But to punish (as the law does at present) any dangerous or offensive writings, which, when published, shall on a fair and impartial trial be adjudged of a pernicious tendency, is necessary for the preservation of peace and good order, of government and religion, the only solid foundations of civil liberty. Thus the will of individuals is still left free; the abuse only of that free will is the object of legal punishment. Neither is any restraint hereby laid upon freedom of thought or inquiry: liberty of private sentiment is still left; the disseminating or making public of bad sentiments, destructive of the ends of society, is the crime which society corrects. *Quoted in* Levy, Freedom of the Press, at 104–05.

3. Levy, *Free Press Clause,* at 183–84.

4. In 1722, for example, a young Benjamin Franklin and his brother James, publisher of Boston's *New England Courant,* were brought before the Massachusetts Assembly to reveal the authors of several "libelous" articles. They refused, and the Assembly censured and jailed James for one month but let Benjamin off with a warning. Scott J. Street, *Poor Richard's Forgotten Press Clause: How Journalists Can Use Original Intent to Protect Their Confidential Sources,* 27 Loy. L.A. Ent. L. Rev. 463, 465 (2007).

Benjamin later attacked censorship in Poor Richard's Almanack (1757): "This Nurse of Arts, and Freedom's Fence, To chain, is Treason against Sense: And Liberty, thy thousand Tongues None silence who design no Wrongs; For those that use the Gag's Restraint, First rob, before they stop Complaint." *Quoted in* Street at 463.

Franklin also supported the written word by helping start the first public library in America—and inventing bifocals! Brookhiser at 19.

 1739 edition of Poor Richard's Almanac

5. Levy, Bill of Rights, at 108.

or because America consisted of colonies under England's control, the colonial press did not enjoy the same freedom.[4] Through the 1760s colonial governments held publishers criminally liable if they abused the right to speech.[5]

The test of whether an accused in a libel case could have a *"fair and impartial"* trial happened in America.[6] In analyzing libel law, Blackstone left open two fundamental questions:

- Is truth a defense, and

- Does the jury or judge decide if there was a malicious libel?

A court case called *Zenger* would decide both questions for America.

THE ZENGER TRIAL

John Peter Zenger's 1735 trial revolutionized the law of seditious libel.

Zenger's *New York Weekly Journal* printed essays as well as advertisements and letters about local issues (generally printed under pseudonyms).[7] Its specialty, though, was attacking New York's royal governor, William Cosby. Sometimes Zenger would print a letter and leave a few dashes followed by,

"Something is here omitted, for which I beg my correspondent to excuse, as not safe for me to print."[8]

---

6. The Small Penis Rule: Modern American libel cases often involve an author making a fictional portrait of a real person, and that person suing. The "small penis rule" is an informal strategy that allows an author to evade a libel suit. A 1998 *New York Times* article describes the rule as follows:

"'For a fictional portrait to be actionable, it must be so accurate that a reader of the book would have no problem linking the two," said Mr. Friedman. Thus, he continued, libel lawyers have what is known as 'the small penis rule.' One way authors can protect themselves from libel suits is to say that a character has a small penis. "Now no male is going to come forward and say, 'That character with a very small penis, that's me!'"

Dinitia Smith, "Writers as Plunderers; Why Do They Keep Giving Away Other People's Secrets? *N.Y. Times*, Oct. 24, 1998, *available at* http://www.nytimes.com/1998/10/24/books/writers-as-plunderers-why-do-they-keep-giving-away-other-people-s-secrets.html?sec=&spon=&pagewanted=2.

7. Street at 462–66, noting the Founders' familiarity with Zenger's case.

Sir William Cosby

8. James Alexander, A Brief Narrative of the Case and Trial of John Peter Zenger, Printer of the New York Weekly Journal 9 (1963).

The slogan of the *New York Times* is "all the news that's fit to print" not "all the news that's safe to print." The Pentagon Papers put the slogan to the test. The Pentagon Papers (officially titled United States–Vietnam Relations, 1945–1967: A Study Prepared by the Department of Defense) was a top secret U.S. Defense Department history of U.S. involvement in Vietnam from 1945 to 1967. Defense Secretary Robert S. McNamara commissioned the study in 1967–68. They revealed that the United States had deliberately expanded the war by carpet bombing Cambodia and Laos, raiding North Vietnam's coast, and expanding Marine Corps attacks, all previously unreported.

heard the case and rejected the government's argument. *New York Times Co. v. United States,* 403 U.S. 713 (1971). In a concurring opinion, Justice Hugo L. Black wrote: *In the First Amendment the Founding Fathers gave the free press the protection it must have to fulfill its essential role in our democracy .... The press was protected so that it could bare the secrets of government and inform the people. Only a free and unrestrained press can effectively expose deception in government. And paramount among the responsibilities of a free press is the duty to prevent any part of the government from deceiving the people and sending them off to distant lands to die of foreign fevers and foreign shot and shell.*

Robert McNamara   Daniel Ellsberg

After Daniel Ellsberg leaked *The Pentagon Papers* to the *New York Times*, President Richard Nixon got a federal court to stop publication. The Supreme Court quickly

For Ellsberg and the events leading to the Pentagon Paper's publication, see the very good documentary, The Most Dangerous Man in America: Daniel Ellsberg and The Pentagon Papers (First Run Features 2009)

The speculation from this statement probably caused more impact than if Zenger had actually printed it. Zenger also would often use made-up ads,[1] one of which described Cosby as a monkey.

Zenger celebrated the September 1734 city elections of antiroyalist magistrates with an anonymous article calling Cosby and his supporters "*pettyfogging knaves*" and asserting that the new magistrates would

"*make the scoundrel rascals fly.*"[2] Zenger refused to divulge the author.

Zenger was obviously looking for trouble, and governor Cosby gave it to him.

Cosby tried to have a grand jury indict Zenger, but three different colonial grand juries refused. Cosby eventually had to convince the New York Council to arrest Zenger, and it also issued a warrant to burn four issues of the *Weekly Journal*.

For his 1735 seditious libel trial, Zenger could not find a New York lawyer to help him. The governor had disqualified some, and the rest thought his case a loser. Finally, a Philadelphia lawyer named Andrew Hamilton (no relation to Alexander Hamiton) took his case.[3]

Hamilton vigorously defended Zenger and an individual's freedom to criticize the government:

1. Over 250 years after *Zenger*, *Hustler Magazine* publisher Larry Flynt was still using made-up ads ridiculing opponents. In *Hustler Magazine, Inc. v. Falwell*, 485 U.S. 46 (1988), the Supreme Court dealt with Flynt's made-up ad featuring a "Jerry Falwell" interview about having sex with his mother.

In small print the "ad" disclaimed "*ad parody—not to be taken seriously.*"

Falwell was not amused. He sued Flynt for libel, invasion of privacy, and intentional infliction of emotional distress. The trial court dismissed the invasion of privacy claim and the jury found in favor of Flynt on the libel claim but for Falwell on intentional infliction of emotional distress, awarding Falwell $150,000 in damages.

The Supreme Court eventually heard the case and unanimously ruled that the First Amendment prohibits awarding damages to public figures for emotional distress. Any other ruling would "*chill*" valid political speech. "*The appeal of the political cartoon or caricature is often based on exploitation of unfortunate physical traits or politically embarrassing events—an exploitation often calculated to injure the feelings of the subject of the portrayal.*" Thus, even though Falwell argued that the *Hustler* ad was too "*outrageous*" for First Amendment protection, "outrageous" is a subjective term, and such a standard "*runs afoul of our longstanding refusal to allow damages to be awarded because the speech in question may have an adverse emotional impact on the audience.*"

THE PEOPLE V. LARRY FLYNT (Columbia Pictures 1996) depicts Flynt's story and his legal clashes, including the *Falwell* case. Flynt had a cameo as the trial judge.

Flynt and Falwell after the Supreme Court arguments, and Flynt and Falwell appearing together on *Larry King Live* on January 10, 1997. Both apparently got a lot out of the controversy.

Image by Helen Koop

"I beg leave to insist that the right of complaining or remonstrating is natural; and the restraint upon this natural right is the law only, and those restraints can only extend to what is false."[4]

Hamilton was advancing a new idea in libel cases that government regulation could only restrain what was false. Rather than focusing only on whether the publisher *"maliciously"* put the government in a negative light, whether true or not, truth was a defense. And the jury decided the truth.[5] What this meant is that a jury could nullify any government prosecution of a publisher or writer.

With this approach, Hamilton challenged the law itself, not just the facts. The jury bought it; the one-day trial ended with the jury deliberating for a few minutes and acquitting Zenger.[6]

Zenger's trial expanded the idea of press freedom, and this idea shaped colonial journalism leading to the Revolution.[7] And incorporating this concept is the First Amendment:

"Congress shall make no law . . . abridging the freedom of speech, or of the press . . . ."

Zenger's trial created an environment that allowed a freer press than ever before.[8]

---

2. ALEXANDER at 13–14, 111.

3. Hamilton, ironically, had participated in Pennsylvania's prosecution of publisher Andrew Bradford for seditious libel in 1729. ALEXANDER at 22. *See also* R. BLAIN ANDRUS, LAWYER: A BRIEF 5,000 YEAR HISTORY 109–10 (2009).

Andrew Hamilton

5. LEVY, BILL OF RIGHTS, at 104–05, 114.

6. Hamilton was already one of the greatest lawyers of his day. After Zenger's trial the term "Philadelphia lawyer" became synonymous with smart lawyer.

Andrew's son, James Hamilton, also became a prominent lawyer and Pennsylvanian politician. He died in 1793, but had owned a large track of land in Lancaster, Pennsylvania, where investors later established the Hamilton Watch Company—named after him—in 1892.

Hamilton 1904 watch

7. For a brief discussion of the Zenger case in the context of the growth of the American jury system, see Albert W. Alschuler & Andrew G. Deiss, *A Brief History of the Criminal Jury in the United States*, 61 U. CHI. L. REV. 867, 871–74 (1994). Clarence Darrow cited the William Penn and John Peter Zenger trials and juries in the closing argument of his own trial. *See* GEOFFREY COWAN, THE PEOPLE V. CLARENCE DARROW: THE BRIBERY TRIAL OF AMERICA'S GREATEST LAWYER (1993). *See also* **Chapter 7: Trial by Jury or . . . by God!**

8. *See McIntyre v. Ohio Elections Comm'n*, 514 U.S. 334, 361 (1995) (Thomas, J., concurring) (noting the Zenger trial's significance).

Only later in England did the Fox Libel Act of 1792 allow the jury to return a simple verdict of not guilty in libel cases. LOVELL at 457.

Hamilton's closing argument

4. ALEXANDER at 84.

REPUBLICAN JOURNALISM

People who bemoan the state of modern American journalism and politics should compare it to that of colonial America through the early republic.[1]

Today most media outlets maintain at least the semblance of objectivity, trying to present both sides of an issue.

Back then, most of the reporting looked like op-eds.[2] Many newspapers, in fact, were not independent but aligned with one party or the other.[3]

Journalists, in fact, were often proxies for the politicians or parties.[4]

But because journalists were not "gentlemen," they did not bother dueling each other or their targets, unlike the politicians for whom they worked.[5]

During the colonial period after the *Zenger* case, the crown could not use the criminal law to control libel.[6] Thus the greatest American journalist of the

1. Critics point to the *Howard Stern Show* as but one example of modern journalism gone amok. But, though more sexual, Stern would have fit right into early America. *See* Levy, *Reexamined*, at 768 ("*For the most part, people understood that scummy journalism unavoidably accompanied the benefits to be gained from a free press.*"); *see also* Levy, *Free Press Clause*, at 218 ("*Anyone who has read American newspapers from 1776 to 1791, when the first press clauses in the state constitutions and the first amendment were framed, would realize that the American press, like the British, was astonishingly scurrilous.*").

2. Partisan politics increased the number of newspapers in the United States from 92 in 1790 to 329 at the end of Thomas Jefferson's presidency, with all but 56 identified with a political party. *See Thomas Jefferson: Establishing a Federal Republic,* LIBRARY OF CONGRESS, http://www.loc.gov/exhibits/jefferson/jefffed.html (last visited Nov. 20, 2009).

3. *See*, for example, the *National Gazette,* the Jeffersonian Republicans' first newspaper (Nov. 14, 1791). Jefferson and Madison financially supported it and gave its editor, Philip Freneau, a position in Jefferson's State Department.

4. "Infant Liberty Nursed by Mother Mob."
The Federalists hoped to regain the presidency with this anti-Jefferson political cartoon. It failed with James Madison's election in 1809.
Jefferson got it turned back on him with "The Providential Detection" (1797–1800), showing Jefferson

kneeling before the altar of Gallic despotism as God and an American eagle save the Constitution. Jefferson's alleged attack on George Washington and John Adams in a letter to Philip Mazzei falls from his other hand. Satan, the writings of Thomas Paine, and French philosophers support Jefferson.

5. BROOKHISER at 142–45. Partly to maintain their stature as gentlemen, the Founders all used pseudonyms for their writing and reporting. Even James Madison, Alexander Hamilton, and John Jay wrote THE FEDERALIST PAPERS under the pseudonym "Publius".
In one famous case it did not work. Hamilton and Burr sparred in the papers for years, each doing the best he could to destroy the other's reputation. Finally, their cold war went hot, and Burr mortally wounded Hamilton in a duel on July 11, 1804, ending both their careers.

Brur-Hamilton duel

age, Benjamin Franklin, had all the freedom he needed to both become a rich man and a leader of the Revolution.[7] This, combined with his job as deputy postmaster for the colonies, put Franklin in position to influence events.[8]

Like good journalists today, Franklin the journalist protected his sources—and it cost him.

In 1773, a Franklin paper, *The Boston Gazette,* published private letters of Massachusetts royal Governor Thomas Hutchinson and Lieutenant Governor Andrew Oliver. In the letters, Hutchinson encouraged London to crack down on his fellow Bostonians, writing *"[t]here must be an*

abridgement of what are called English liberties."[9]

Back in London, where Franklin had been living for nine years, recriminations flew as to who leaked the letters. Two "gentlemen" fools even fought a duel while protesting their innocence. Because of this, Franklin admitted he leaked the letters.[10]

A colonial press

John Wilkes

7. Regarding Franklin, the press and mail, and the advanced state of journalism in the colonies, see BROOKHISER at 19–20 (reporting that there were twenty-five newspapers in the thirteen colonies, many set up by Franklin or his apprentices).

6. Levy, *Free Press Clause,* at 218. Just before the Revolution, America was abuzz about Englishman John Wilkes and his case, *Wilkes v. Wood.* Rutland at 33. In 1763 Wilkes, a prominent Parliament member, published anonymous pamphlets called *The North Briton,* including No. 45, which sharply criticized King George III. Government officials searched Wilkes's home, seized his papers, and arrested him. Such general warrants were common at the time to muzzle the press and squelch political dissent. Wilkes sued and won! See **Chapter 4: Molasses and the Sticky Origins of the Fourth Amendment,** which extensively discusses Wilkes as a precursor of the Fourth Amendment. *See* Daniel J. Solove, *The First Amendment as Criminal Procedure,* 82 N.Y.U. L. REV. 112 (2007) (noting that the First, Fourth, and Fifth Amendments share a common background concerning seditious libel). *See also* Levy, *Free Press Clause,* at 216 (noting that Wilkes held orthodox opinions regarding the common law of seditious libel).

One of Franklin's newspapers was the *Pennsylvania Gazette*

The word "gazette" for newspaper came from sixteenth century Venice, where Venetians would use a "*gazeta,*" a small coin, to buy their newspapers, a "*gazeta de la novita,*" literally "a pennyworth of news." AYTO at 251; ROBERT HENDRICKSON, QPB ENCYCLOPEDIA OF WORD AND PHRASE ORIGINS 289 (2004).

8. Franklin's political cartoon "Join, or Die" urged the colonies to join together during the French and Indian War. This is the first political cartoon in an American newspaper. STEPHEN HESS & SANDY NORTHROP, DRAWN & QUARTERED: THE HISTORY OF AMERICAN POLITICAL CARTOONS 24 (1996).

JOIN, or DIE.

9. BROOKHISER at 139; *see also* Street at 463.

Thomas Hutchinson

Andrew Oliver

10. Franklin's protestations that he only released the letters to a few local leaders to show that their problems were just with an overzealous Hutchinson ring disingenuous. BROOKHISER at 140. Franklin was sixty-eight years old, having made his first fame and fortune as a journalist. He knew better than anyone the way of the press.

But he would not reveal his "Deep Throat."[1]

In January 1774, a committee of the Privy Council called him in for interrogation; Franklin wouldn't budge.[2] Just like Zenger in 1735, Franklin stood on the principle that a journalist should not reveal his sources.[3] He took it to his grave.[4]

Confidentiality of sources became a principle of American journalism.[5] But because Franklin would not reveal the source of the Hutchinson letters, he lost his lucrative job as deputy postmaster general for all North America and could no longer serve as lobbyist for four American colonies.[6]

Franklin left London in March 1775, never to return as a British subject.

---

1. "Deep Throat" refers to the main whistleblower in the Watergate scandal. The name came from the 1972 pornographic movie DEEP THROAT (Plymouth Distribution and Bryanston Distritbution 1972) and is now synonymous for confidential whistleblower.

Washington Post reporters Bob Woodward and Carl Bernstein broke and followed the story of the burglary of the Democratic headquarters at the Watergate complex. The trail led to the downfall of President Richard Nixon in 1972. Dustin Hoffman and Robert Redford played Woodward and Bernstein in ALL THE PRESIDENT'S MEN (Warner Brothers 1976).

Nixon leaving office

The Watergate complex

Nixon announces Resignation

Resignation Letter

2. Even after an hour of abuse from Solicitor General Alexander Wedderburn who harangued, *"I hope, my lords, you will mark and brand this man [Franklin], for the honour of this country, of Europe, and of mankind . . . . . . Men will watch him with a jealous eye; they will hide their papers from him and lock up their escritoires. He will henceforth esteem it a libel to be called a man of letters."* Quoted in BROOKHISER at 140–41. This interrogation finally turned Franklin into a revolutionary.

Wedderburn

Franklin in 1777

3. Regarding the importance of *Zenger* as precedent of keeping a reporter's sources confidential, *see McIntyre v. Ohio Elections Comm'n*, 514 U.S. 334, 361 (1995) (Thomas, J., concurring) (Zenger's trial *"signified at an early moment the extent to which anonymity and the freedom of the press were intertwined in the early American mind"*).

4. Woodward and Bernstein never revealed their source either. No one was sure for thirty years until FBI deputy director W. Mark Felt revealed he was Deep Throat on May 31, 2005.

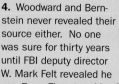
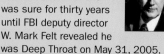

5. The Big Fat Freedom of the Press. In 1958 journalist Marie Torre quoted a CBS network executive that *"something is bothering [Judy Garland] . . . I don't know, but I wouldn't be surprised if it's because she thinks she's terribly fat."* Garland sued CBS and her lawyers eventually deposed Torre, who refused to identify her source because if she did *"nobody in the business [would] talk to [her] again."* *Garland v. Torre*, 259 F.2d 545, 547–48 (2d Cir. 1958). The court put Torre in jail for ten days for contempt of court for refusing to divulge her source. The courts of various states remain split on whether reporters can refuse to name their sources. *See, e.g., State v. Knops*, 183 N.W.2d 93, 95 (Wis. 1971) (constitutional privilege exists but subject to public's overriding need to know in the interests of justice); *State v. Buchanan*, 436 P.2d 729, 732 (Or. 1968) (reporters have no constitutional right to protect sources though it could be created by statute). *See generally* Street at 469.

Garland in the Wizard of Oz (1939)

Garland putting on makeup in 1957

Marie Torre

When the British eventually implemented Governor Hutchinson's advice and "abridged" "what are called English liberties," the colonies predictably reacted. The Stamp Act of 1764, for instance, would have put a modest tax on colonial newspapers, but in defiance not a single newspaper appeared on stamped paper.[7]

As for the press and journalism during the Revolution, there was a double standard. Patriot newspapers were free but not the pro-British loyalist ones.[8] This set a precedent that has carried through American history: freedom of speech and press suffer during war.[9] If we accept, as the Framers did, the vital role free speech plays in a healthy democracy, then hindering speech even during war is a contradiction and betrayal.

6. But Franklin ended up on the first U.S. postage stamp in 1847. And, he later made it onto the $100 bill, perhaps  for his quote from POOR RICHARD'S ALMANAC: *"A penny saved is twopence dear"* (misquoted as *"A penny saved is a penny earned"*).

7. Rutland at 33.

8. Rutland at 34. *See also* Levy, *Reexamined*, at 767 (noting *"that tarring and feathering a Tory editor because of his opinions shows a rather restricted meaning and scope of the freedom of the press. Indeed, one may ask whether there was free speech during the Revolutionary era if only the speech of freedom was free."*).

9. *See generally* GEOFFREY R. STONE'S PERILOUS TIMES: FREE SPEECH IN WARTIME, *From* THE SEDITION ACT OF 1798 *to the* WAR ON TERRORISM (2004) for a historical survey of freedom of speech during America's wars and an eloquent defense of free speech. *"[T]he national government has never attempted to punish opposition to government policies, except in time of war."*

• Shortly after the Revolution, President John Adams and the Federalists enacted the Sedition Act of 1798 prohibiting any person from writing, publishing or uttering anything of a *"false, scandalous and malicious"* nature against the government. Though supposedly because of an impending war with France, the act served primarily as a political weapon to strengthen the Federalists.

• During the Civil War, President Abraham Lincoln suspended the writ of habeas corpus eight times for persons who had been arrested for speaking or writing against his administration. A president can suspend habeas corpus during war, but Lincoln would refer to the Civil War as a "war"—rather than an insurrection— only when it suited him.

Lincoln as a Phoenix raising himself by burning free speech and habeas corpus

See Rutland at 38, noting that during the Civil War the Confederacy allowed more free press than in the Union, where federal marshals and mobs intimidated the war's Northern critics.

• During World War I, the government prosecuted around two thousand people for opposing the war and the draft under the Espionage Act of 1917 and Sedition Act of 1918. These people generally received ten-to twenty-year sentences. President Woodrow Wilson, while arguing to *"make the world safe for democracy,"* unsuccessfully pushed for a censorship law, arguing that *"authority to exercise censorship over the press"* was *"absolutely necessary to the public safety."* See O'Brien at 47, noting that by the end of World War I, thirty-two states had laws against criminal syndication or sedition.

• Just before World War II, a congressional committee began investigating *"the extent, character and objects of un-American propaganda activities in the United States"*; the FBI established an aggressive informer program and Congress passed the Alien Registration Act of 1940 (the Smith Act), which forbade individuals to advocate the propriety of overthrowing the government by force. Ironically, much of these provisions had to do with a perceived fight against communism, but the Soviet Union ended up our ally in World War II. Much of World War II propaganda was to try to get people to talk less with *"loose lips sink ships"* as the slogan.

• During the Cold War, President Harry Truman established a loyalty program for all civilian government employees; the House Un-American Activities Committee, or HUAC, cited 135 people for contempt (more than the entire Congress had cited for contempt in the history of the country to that point); and Senator Joseph R. McCarthy launched his virulent rampage.

• During the Vietnam War, the FBI carried out a wide-ranging program to *"expose, disrupt and otherwise neutralize"* dissident political activities, and protesters were prosecuted for burning their draft cards and expressing contempt for the American flag.

One of the Alien and Sedition Acts

But so far, America has always bounced back from these wartime restrictions with expanded liberty.[1] This expansion conforms to James Madison's original vision of an expansive freedom of speech and press,[2] often despite the wishes of our government.[3]

If the press of Madison's day is any indication, blatantly partisan, rasping, corrosive, and offensive discussions on all topics of public interest were the norm.[4] In fact, it makes much of what passes for

J. Edgar Hoover was the director of the FBI, from March 22, 1935 to May 2, 1972

1. Again, *see generally* STONE noting that "*the major restrictions of civil liberties of the past would be less thinkable today than they were in 1798, 1861, 1917, 1942, 1950 or 1969,*" and that "*in terms of both the evolution of constitutional doctrine and the development of a national culture more attuned to civil liberties, the United States has made substantial progress.*" Stone notes, among other examples of progress, *New York Times Co. v. United States (Pentagon Papers)*, 403 U.S. 713 (1971), where "*the Supreme Court,* for the first time in American history, stood tall—in wartime—for the First Amendment.*"

As Stone argues, "*we may learn slowly, and only in fits and starts, but we do learn.*" For example, a congressional report declared that the Sedition Act of 1798 had been passed under a "*mistaken exercise*" of power and was "*null and void.*" The Sedition Act of 1918, which was repealed two years later, helped give birth to the modern civil liberties movement. In 1976, President Gerald Ford formally prohibited the CIA from using electronic or physical surveillance to collect information on domestic activities of Americans and FBI Director Clarence Kelly publicly apologized for abuses under J. Edgar Hoover.

Jefferson in 1791

3. Levy, *Reexamined*, at 769. Jefferson's draft of the 1783 constitution for Virginia proposed that the press "*shall be subject to no other restraint than liableness to legal prosecution for false facts printed and published.*" LEVY, BILL OF RIGHTS, at 109.

But when Jefferson became president, he happily persecuted Federalist newspapermen. In 1806, his administration prosecuted six Connecticut citizens for seditious libel against him. Two of the defendants committed the crime while preaching sermons and the others in newspaper. Levy, *Free Press Clause*, at 177. Jefferson also had Harry Croswell, an obscure Federalist editor, prosecuted for seditious libel. LEVY, BILL OF RIGHTS, at 131. Thus Jefferson, once in power, asserted that the rival press could criminally assault the government, giving the government legal recourse. *Id.* at 109.

Jefferson in 1800

2. Alien and Sedition Acts. In 1789 the Federalist Congress passed and President John Adams signed An Act for the Punishment of Certain Crimes against the United States, four laws making it a crime to publish "*false, scandalous, and malicious writing*" against the government or its officials. The point was to punish criticism of Adams. Of course, gagging the Republican press and criticism of Adam's onetime friend and then political rival Vice President Thomas Jefferson was fair game! LEVY, BILL OF RIGHTS, at 125–26; Rutland at 38.

A court fined Vermont Congressman Matthew Lyon $1,000 and sentenced him to four months in an unheated cell in winter for suggesting that Adams be sent to a madhouse. BROOKHISER at 44. When Jefferson took over as president in 1801, he pardoned all the journalists convicted under the act, which expired on March 3, 1801. Rutland at 38. Lyon has the distinction of being the only man elected to Congress from jail—and the first to have an ethics charge against him for spitting on Roger Griswold.

But, something not generally understood is that the Sedition Act embodied Zengerian reforms in that it allowed the defendant to plead truth as a defense and confirmed that a jury would decide guilt, exactly what eighteenth century libertarians had fought for. Levy, *Free Press Clause*, at 199–200. Supreme Court Justice William J. Brennan, Jr. cited the Sedition Act in *New York Times v. Sullivan*, 376 U.S. 254, 273, 276 (1964), because it "*first crystallized a national awareness of the central meaning of the First Amendment*" and although "*never tested in this Court, the attack upon its validity has carried the day in the court of history.*"

Contemporary cartoon of fight in Congress over the Alien and Sedition Acts between Matthew Lyon (with tongs) and Roger Griswold of Connecticut

4. The ancient Athenian Demosthenes explained that "*of all states,*" democracies are "*the most antagonistic*" to political leaders "*of infamous habits*" because "*every man is at liberty to publish their shame.*" Indeed, "*even the lone individual, uttering the deserved reproach, makes the guilty wince.*" *Quoted in* Werhan at 318.

Demosthenes

Such was the Monica Lewinsky sex scandal with President Bill Clinton in 1995. The tabloid press devoted months to the issue, and the mainstream media eventually followed.

journalism today appear tame.[5]

But what type of nation was reading all those newspapers? Was it a Christian nation?

A CHRISTIAN NATION?

Whether this country was founded as a "Christian nation" depends on what you mean by that term.[6]

In fact, it has less to do with history than today's "culture wars."[7]

---

5. Clinton's was hardly the first sex scandal in America politics. Thomas Jefferson hired a freelance journalist, James T. Callender, to attack Federalists like Alexander Hamilton and John Adams.

In 1797, Jefferson secretly paid Callender to expose Hamilton's affair in 1791 with a banker's wife, Maria Reynolds. The banker, James Reynolds, was arrested for counterfeiting. Hamilton insisted he committed no public misconduct— he only had an affair with Maria Reynolds. After Hamilton left public life he felt compelled to stop rumors of misconduct in office by publishing a detailed confession of his affair. *See* RON CHERNOW, ALEXANDER HAMILTON 529–30 (2004).

Jefferson then turned Callender on Adams. Callender wrote a pamphlet attacking the Federalists called *The Prospect Before Us*. In June 1800, the Adams administration prosecuted Callender under the Sedition Act, and his trial was before Supreme Court Justice Samuel Chase. (The Jeffersonian Republicans later impeached Chase in part for his handling of the Callender trial; *see* WILLIAM H. REHNQUIST, GRAND INQUESTS: THE HISTORIC IMPEACHMENTS OF JUSTICE

SAMUEL CHASE AND PRESIDENT ANDREW JOHNSON (1992)). In addition to a $200 fine, Callender received a jail term under the Sedition Act and was not released until the Adams administration's last day in March 1801. Jefferson pardoned all journalists,

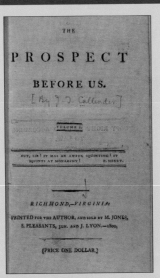

including Callender. Callender then asked Jefferson to appoint him postmaster of Richmond, Virginia. When he did not get the job, he switched sides and began editing the Federalist *Richmond Recorder*. Callender eventually targeted Jefferson, revealing that Jefferson had funded his pamphleteering and published Jefferson's letters to him to prove it. Callender later wrote in a series of articles that Jefferson fathered children by his slave, Sally Hemings. This prompted Adams's wife, Abigail, to comment to Jefferson that the serpent he "*cherished and warmed*" had "*bit the hand that nourished him.*" *Quoted in* DAVID MCCULLOUGH, JOHN ADAMS 577 (2001), and the discussion of the whole incident at 577–85; *see also* REBECCA L. MCMURRY & JAMES F. MCMURRY, JR., THE SCANDALMONGER AND THE NEWSPAPER WAR OF 1802 (2000), with reprints of the newspaper articles of the time detailing the Jefferson/Hemings controversy. Callender drowned on July 17, 1803, in two feet of water in the James River, too drunk to save himself.

A Philosophic Cock by James Akin (c. 1804), showing Jefferson's rooster courting the hen Hemings. The cock was also a symbol of revolutionary France, which Jefferson was known to admire.

6. Scholars argue from two camps: (1) the Founders intended to strictly separate religion from the government; and (2) the Founders were deeply religious people who believed that religion and government should work together. *Compare* Patrick M. Garry, *The Myth of Separation: America's Historical Experience with Church and State*, 33 HOFSTRA L. REV. 475, 476–78 (2004) (the Framers viewed religion as indispensable to government), *with* LAURENCE H. TRIBE, AMERICAN CONSTITUTIONAL LAW §§ 14-3, 14-4 (1978) (the Framers separated church from state for effective government).

7. *See generally* Stone regarding the culture wars. For example, see *Lee v. Weisman*, 505 U.S. 577 (1992), where the Supreme Court outlawed prayers at public school graduations. There are also the nativity scene cases, *Lynch v. Donnelly*, 465 U.S. 668 (1984), and

County of Allegheny v. ACLU, 492 U.S. 573 (1989), where the Supreme Court held against public expression of religious belief.

The Puritans: Certainly, the Puritans were founding a New Jerusalem.[1] Indeed, not just the Puritan colonies were motivated by their relationship with God. The first charter of Virginia, granted by King James I in 1606, was to propagate Christianity, and the other colonies had the same charge.[2]

The Puritans, however, were separatists by definition; they had fled the established government and Church of England. Thus, though the Puritans may have intended both the church and state to be "Godly," they did not necessarily intend to create the type of theocracy in America where the church

and the state were the same entity. Though the idea was a "Godly" place on earth, church and state were a check on each other to reach that end.

The Revolutionary Generation: Long before the American Revolution, the Puritan vision proved unattainable. By

---

1. The *Mayflower* Pilgrims came *"for the propagating and advancing the Gospel of the kingdom of Christ in those remote parts of the world."* Tupi at 215, *quoting* WILLIAM BRADFORD, HISTORY OF PLYMOUTH PLANTATION 24 (Little, Brown & Co. 1856).

2. Virginia's 1606 Charter declared: *"[T]o make habitation and to deduce a colony of sundry of our people into that part of America commonly called Virginia in propagating of Christian religion to such people as yet live in darkness."* Tupi at 215, citing 1 HISTORICAL COLLECTIONS: CONSISTING OF STATE PAPERS AND OTHER AUTHENTIC DOCUMENTS: INTENDED AS MATERIALS FOR A HISTORY OF THE UNITED STATES OF AMERICA 50–51 (Ebenezer Hazard ed., T. Dobson 1792).

In *Holy Trinity Church v. United States*, 143 U.S. 457, 465–71 (1892), the Supreme Court traced America's Christian heritage to Christopher Columbus's commission. *Discussed in* Tupi at 211–12. Even John Locke's 1669 Carolina Constitution provided that no man could be a citizen unless he acknowledged God, belonged to a church, and refrained from abusive language against religion. *Id.* at 211–12.

Columbus commissioned to bring God to the New World and get all the gold for Spain that he could lay his paws on

---

3. Stone at 3–5 ("By the time the Framers began drafting the United States Constitution, church membership had dropped to the point that "not more than one person in . . . ten" was affiliated with a Christian church.").

The Great Awakenings had a good part to do with the decline of the established churches. These were periods of rapid and dramatic religious revival in Anglo-American religious history beginning in the 1730s. Traveling preachers encouraged many to abandon the established churches for dissenting Protestant sects, causing the established churches to

increase their persecution of religious dissent. Matthew C. Berger, Comment, *One Nation Indivisible: How Congress's Addition of "Under God" to the Pledge of Allegiance Offends the Original Intent of the Establishment Clause*, 3 U. ST. THOMAS L.J. 629, 642 (2006); *see also*

BROOKHISER at 27. There were actually several Great Awakenings. Jonathan Edwards (1703–58) and George Whitefield (the cofounder of Methodism, along with John Wesley) were early leaders, and modern evangelical Protestantism traces its roots from them.

the 1770s, American Christianity was in decline, at least the *established* version.³

The DECLARATION OF INDEPENDENCE referenced some type of God when it famously declared:

*"We hold these truths to be self-evident, that all men are created equal, that they are endowed by their Creator with certain unalienable Rights, that among these are Life, Liberty, and the pursuit of Happiness."*⁴

But this God is not a traditional Judeo-Christian God.⁵ The "creator" it cites is "Nature's God," who gives "divine providence." This is not the God of Isaac and Jacob, but of Isaac Newton, who demonstrated the universe was knowable because it was rational. It is the Deist God, also called the "Creator," the "First Cause," and the "Grand Architect."

Thus, THE DECLARATION side-stepped Christianity.⁶

---

4. THE DECLARATION OF INDEPENDENCE para. 2 (U.S. 1776). *See* Brookhiser at 60 (discussing the Declaration and Jefferson's *"oblique"* references to God).

5. Stone at 22.

Newton by Blake (1805); man with the instruments of his own construct pierces the darkness

To use an old analogy, it is the "watchmaker God," who set the great clock of the universe in motion for us to discern. Brookhiser at 62. This creator embedded morality and inalienable human rights within nature's laws, and a person could discern them through reason, just like Newton's physics. Stone at 7. Many of our Founding Fathers, including Thomas Paine, Thomas Jefferson, Benjamin Franklin, Ethan Allen, and Gouverneur Morris, were Deists, and many others, including John Adams, James Madison, Alexander Hamilton, James Monroe, and George Washington, were at least partial Deists. Many, such as Patrick Henry, Sam Adams, and John Jay, were traditional Christians. *Id.* at 7–8.

6. Thomas Paine and a "Christian nation." Any modern "Christian nation" proponent must contend with Thomas Paine. Paine's works, COMMON SENSE, THE RIGHTS OF MAN, and THE AGE OF REASON, *"became the three most widely read political tracts of the eighteenth century."* Stone at 21. To the orthodox Christians of his day, and ours, he was *"a villain and an infidel."* Paine declared in THE AGE OF REASON:

> *"I believe in one God, and no more . . . . I believe in the equality of man; and I believe that religious duties consist in doing justice, loving mercy, and endeavoring to make our fellow-creatures happy. . . . I do not believe in the creed professed by the Jewish Church, by the Roman Church, by the Greek Church, by the Turkish Church, by the Protestant Church, nor by any church that I know of. My own mind is my own church."*

Stone at 19–20, *quoting* THOMAS PAINE, THE AGE OF REASON: PART ONE (1794).

In fact, the full title is THE AGE OF REASON; BEING AN INVESTIGATION OF TRUE AND FABULOUS THEOLOGY, which he published in three parts in 1794, 1795, and 1807. Paine certainly had no use for organized religion and wrote that the Christian doctrine of turning the

Thomas Paine

other cheek meant *"sinking man into a spaniel."* Discussed in BROOKHISER at 68–69. Paine was a Deist who advocated reason in the place of revelation, rejected miracles, and viewed the Bible as ordinary literature. Paine's engaging and irreverent style, as well as his book's inexpensive price, made Deistic ideas available to a mass audience. The fact that he was a best seller in America cuts against the current "Christian nation" argument. Regarding his view on freedom of the press, Paine generally agreed with Blackstone, and in an essay on "Liberty of the Press," he wrote that *"a man does not ask liberty beforehand to say something he has a mind to say, but he becomes answerable afterwards for the atrocities he may utter."* Levy, *Free Press Clause*, at 179.

Compare William Blake's illustration of God as the "Grand Architect" with Michelangelo's traditional image ruling the earth and sky like an old pagan Zeus. Blake's God created the grand watch of the universe symbolized by his compass, the same compass Blake's Newton uses to pierce the darkness.

Franklin, for example, edited Jefferson's original draft that said these truths were *"sacred and undeniable"* to *"self-evident,"* making the clause the document's most moving.[1]

This is not to say the Framers intended to establish an irreligious or anti-Christian nation. Most of them called themselves Christian, even if of a Deist type.[2] And as John Jay noted in

THE FEDERALIST PAPERS, Americans were

"one united people . . . professing the same [Protestant] religion."[3]

Also, the Framers lived in the legal world of the common

---

1. Brookhiser at 60. *See also* Tupi at 203–04 (discussing God in the DECLARATION OF INDEPENDENCE).

2. THE VIRGINIA DECLARATION OF RIGHTS OF 1776 mixed Deism with traditional Christianity:

> That religion, or the duty which we owe to our CREATOR, and the manner of discharging it, can be directed only by reason and conviction, not by force or violence; and therefore all men are entitled to free exercise of religion, according to the dictates of conscience; and that it is the mutual duty of all to practice Christian forbearance, love and charity towards each other.

Quoted in Herbert W. Titus, *God's Revelation: Foundation for the Common Law,* 4 REGENT U. L. REV. 1, 31 (1994). *But see* Tupi at 198 (steadfastly arguing that the Founders were "men of [Christian] faith")

3. THE FEDERALIST No. 2 (John Jay), *quoted in* Brookhiser at 26.

Jay

4. See **Chapter 6: How the Sixth Amendment Guarantees You a Court, a Lawyer, and a Chamber Pot** for more on the history of the common law.

5. CATHERINE DRINKER BOWEN, MIRACLE AT PHILADELPHIA: THE STORY OF THE CONSTITUTIONAL CONVENTION, MAY TO SEPTEMBER 1789 63 (1966).

6. *See, e.g., Vidal v. Girard's Executors,* 43 U.S. 127, 198 (1844) ("*It is also said, and truly, that the Christian religion is a part of the common law.*"). *Vidal* followed a long common law history.

For Edward Coke the common law was "*written with the finger of God in the heart of man . . .*" and Moses "*was the first reporter or writer of law in the world.*" *Quoted in* Titus at 2. William Blackstone began his influential COMMENTARIES ON THE LAW OF ENGLAND with the chapter "*The Nature of Laws in General,*" stating the Christian basis of the common law:

> *Man, considered as a creature, must necessarily be subject to the law of his creator, for he is entirely a dependent being . . . [A] state of dependence will inevitably oblige the inferior to take the will of him, on whom he depends, as the rule of his conduct . . . And consequently, as man depends absolutely upon his maker for everything, it is necessary that he should in all points conform to his maker's will . . . This will of his maker is called the law of nature . . . . Further, law . . . signifies a . . . rule of action, which is prescribed by some superior,*

and which the inferior is bound to obey. *Quoted in id.* at 3. For Blackstone the ultimate "superior" is the traditional Christian God.

Justice Joseph Story later found ample evidence to support the opinion that "*[t]here never has been a period, in which the Common Law did not recognise Christianity as lying at its foundations.*" *Quoted in id.* at 3. All of this contrasts with THE DECLARATION OF INDEPENDENCE's articulation of "nature's God." But, even Justice William O. Douglas, considered an activist liberal, wrote "*[w]e are a religious people whose institutions presuppose a Supreme Being.*" *Zorach v. Clauson,* 343 U.S. 306, 313 (1951).

But even before Christianity, humans agreed that law comes from the gods. Shamash, the sun god, handed down edicts to King Hammurabi; Jehovah did the same to Moses, and every nine years Crete's King Minos climbed Mount Olympus to get legal advice from Zeus. KADRI at 3.

Coke

Blackstone

Story

Shamash, the god of the Sun, seated on his throne

Moses bringing down the law

Zeus schooling Minos

law.[4] After all, thirty-five of the fifty-five delegates to the Constitutional Convention were lawyers or judges.[5]

And the common law's basis is Christianity.[6]

In fact, several common-law crimes such as blasphemy and heresy directly reflect Christianity.[7] States were still prosecuting these crimes in the early years of the republic.[8] But, such prosecutions are directly contrary to both freedom of religion and speech. The very existence of a heresy or blasphemy law means that someone is not free to believe or express his or her belief.

Again, the mix of religion and speech is still what it is about.[9]

---

7. Blackstone devoted another chapter to "*offenses against God and religion*," where he affirmed the common-law crimes of apostasy, heresy, reviling the ordinances of the church, blasphemy, witchcraft, and Sabbath breaking. Titus at 30.

8. Albert at 37 (noting that blasphemy laws reflected Christianity's infusion into the common law).

Potter Stewart

---

9. What Is Obscene? Justice Potter Stewart could neither describe obscenity nor hard-core pornography, but famously quipped, "*I know it when I see it . . .*" Jacobellis v. Ohio, 378 U.S. 184, 197 (1964) (Stewart, J., concurring) ("*I shall not today attempt further to define the kinds of material I understand to be embraced within that shorthand description [i.e., "hard-core pornography"]; and perhaps I could never succeed in intelligibly doing so. But I know it when I see it, and the motion picture involved in this case is not that.*"). Jacobellis was about the French film THE LOVERS (Les Amants) (Zenith International Films 1958) dealing with adultery and rediscovering love, pretty tame stuff by today's standards, with the Supreme Court holding that the film was not obscene.

Common-law courts were not always the final arbiter of public morality; the Star Chamber and church courts used to do this. But in 1641, the English Parliament did away with the Star Chamber and most of the old church court jurisdiction and gave it to the common-law courts, from which our Supreme Court descends. In a famous case in 1664

Sir Charles Sedley (also spelled "Sidley") got into trouble for "*having shown his nude body in a balcony in Covent Garden to a great multitude of people, and had said and done certain things to the great scandal of Christianity.*" The Court of King's Bench ruled that it was "*the custos morum ["guardian of morals"] of all the subjects of the King, and it is now high time to punish such profane actions done against all modesty . . .*" Quoted in Berman, *Law and Belief*, at 602. Sedley got a 2,000 mark

Sedley

fine, a week in jail, and three years' probation. Still, Sedley eventually became Speaker of the House of Commons.

As for showing the nude body "*to the great scandal of Christianity*" in America, no laws criminalized pornography at the time of the Bill of Rights. *Roth v. United States*, 354 U.S. 476, 482 (1957). By 1792, though, thirteen of fourteen states prohibited libel and criminalized either blasphemy, profanity, or both. *Id.*; see also Chemerinsky at 903. This is the origin of modern obscenity prosecutions.

Prophets versus Profits. Today, the proponents of obscenity prosecutions are usually conservative religious groups who object to pornography on religious and moral grounds. Thus, they assert their rights under the First Amendment's Free Exercise Clause to fight for their faith. On the other side is the pornography industry and consumer market that relies on the First Amendment's Free Speech Clause to fight for their expression (and profit).

The Framers and Religion: In addition to being part of a Christian culture, the Framers specifically extolled the value and even the necessity of religion.[1]

Our form of government "*required*" a religious people, said John Adams, because

"*our constitution was made only for a moral and religious people. It is wholly inadequate to the government of any other.*"[2]

Indeed,

"*[r]eligion and virtue are the only foundations of republicanism and of all free governments.*"[3]

For Franklin,

"*only a virtuous people are capable of freedom. As nations become corrupt and vicious, they have more need of masters.*"[4]

Franklin also recognized religion's role in sustaining morals:

---

1. Tupi at 202 (distinguishing between the French "atheistic" revolution and the American one).

Regarding the Founding Fathers' religious beliefs, *see generally* STEVEN WALDMAN, FOUNDING FAITHS: HOW OUR FOUNDING FATHERS FORGED A RADICAL NEW APPROACH TO RELIGIOUS LIBERTY (2009), debunking the myths of both the Christian Right and the secular Left. *See also* GARY KOWALSKI, REVOLUTIONARY SPIRITS: THE ENLIGHTENED FAITH OF AMERICA'S FOUNDING FATHERS (2008); BROOKE ALLEN, MORAL MINORITY: OUR SKEPTICAL FOUNDING FATHERS (2006) (arguing that the Founding Fathers did not establish a "Christian nation"); DAVID L. HOLMES, THE FAITHS OF THE FOUNDING FATHERS (2006); JON MEACHAM, AMERICAN GOSPEL: GOD, THE FOUNDING FATHERS, AND THE MAKING OF A NATION (2007). For the view arguing the Founding Fathers were a species of modern evangelical Christian, *see* TIM F. LAHAYE, FAITH OF OUR FOUNDING FATHERS (1996).

2. Tupi at 255, *quoting* John Adams; *see also* David K. DeWolf, *Ten Tortured Words*, 85 DENV. U. L. REV. 443, 451–52 (2007) (reviewing STEPHEN MANSFIELD, TEN TORTURED WORDS: HOW THE FOUNDING FATHERS TRIED TO PROTECT RELIGION IN AMERICA AND WHAT'S HAPPENED SINCE (2007)).

A young Abigail and John Adams

3. *Quoted in* Tupi at 227.

Adams as a young man, in his 1765 DISSERTATION ON CANON AND FEUDAL LAW, defended the "*sensible*" New England Puritans against those "*many modern Gentlemen.*" The Puritans were, for Adams, "*illustrious patriots,*" and the first "*to establish a government of the church more consistent with the scriptures, and a government of the state more agreable to the dignity of humane nature than any other seen in Europe: and to transmit such a government down to their posterity.*" Quoted in Witte, City on a Hill, at 41.

But a middle-aged John Adams became increasingly suspicious of religious dogma. As he wrote to Benjamin Rush, "*there is a germ of religion in human nature so strong that whenever an order of men can persuade the people by flattery or terror that they have salvation at their disposal, there can be no end to fraud, violence, or usurpation.*" Quoted in Stone at 13–14. Though a Congregationalist, Adams more closely identified with Unitarianism, a seventeenth century religious movement from England related to Deism. By Adams's time, the English scientist Joseph Priestly was its chief proponent. Adams, Franklin, and Jefferson avidly read Priestly. *Id.* at 14.

An old John Adams wrote to Jefferson, "*[t]wenty times, in the course of my late Reading, have I been upon the point of breaking out, 'This would be the best of all possible Worlds, if there were no Religion in it'*" but then added "*[w]ithout Religion this World would be Something not fit to be mentioned in polite Company, I mean Hell.*" *Id.*, *quoting* Letter from John Adams to Thomas Jefferson (Apr. 19, 1817).

A middle-aged Adams   Adams at 89 (1823)

4. *Quoted* in Tupi at 255.

5. Franklin wrote this to a young friend who had stridently attacked religion, preceding it with the following:

"*You yourself may find it easy to live a virtuous Life without . . . Religion; you . . . possessing a Strength of Resolution sufficient to enable you to resist common Temptations. But think how great a Proportion of Mankind consists of weak and ignorant Men and Women . . . who have need of the Motives of Religion to restrain them from Vice, to support their Virtue, and to retain them in the Practice of it till it becomes habitual. . . . If Men are so wicked as we now see them with Religion what would they be if without it?*"

Quoted in Stone at 23–24.

"If Men are so wicked as we now see them with Religion what would they be if without it?"[5]

George Washington believed that religion was useful both to public morality and republican government because

"reason and experience both forbid us to expect that national morality can prevail in the exclusion of religious principle."[6]

Also,

"true religion affords to government its surest support."[7]

Thomas Jefferson did not care if his neighbor believed in twenty gods or no God because

"it neither picks my pocket nor breaks my leg."[8]

Franklin would not pass as a Christian today. He admitted at the end of his life that *"I have . . . some Doubts as to his [Jesus's] Divinity, tho' it is a Question I do not dogmatize upon, [having] never studied it, & think it needless to busy myself with it now, when I expect soon an [opportunity] of [knowing] the Truth with less Trouble."* Stone at 9, *citing* Letter from Benjamin Franklin to Ezra Stiles (Mar. 9, 1790); *see also* Brookhiser at 64–65.

"*Here is my Creed.*" Franklin wrote, "*I believe in one God, the Creator of the Universe: That he governs the World by his Providence. That he ought to be worshiped. That the most acceptable Service we can render to him, is doing good to his other Children.*" Stone at 8–9.

With an ecumenical nod, Franklin commented that these are *"the fundamental Principles of all sound Religion."* Like Jefferson, Franklin thought Jesus was okay, but that people had corrupted his teachings: "*I think the System of morals & his Religion, as he left them to us, the best the World ever saw or is likely to see; but I apprehend it has received various corrupting changes.*"

Invoking his civic-minded God, Franklin called for a prayer each day at the Constitutional Convention and used the invocation of God to smooth the debates. *See, e.g.,* Brookhiser at 62; David L. Wardle, *Reason to Ratify: The Influence of John Locke's Religious Beliefs on the Creation and Adoption of the United States Constitution,* 26 SEATTLE U. L. REV. 291, 301 (2002). John Adams noted that Franklin was a mirror in which people saw their own religion: "*The Catholics thought him almost a*

Catholic. The Church of England claimed him as one of them. The Presbyterians thought him half a Presbyterian, and the Friends believed him a wet Quaker."

If anything, ethics was his religion. When he was twenty years old, in 1726, he listed the thirteen virtues to follow:

1. "*TEMPERANCE. Eat not to dullness; drink not to elevation.*
2. *SILENCE. Speak not but what may benefit others or yourself; avoid trifling conversation.*
3. *ORDER. Let all your things have their places; let each part of your business have its time.*
4. *RESOLUTION. Resolve to perform what you ought; perform without fail what you resolve.*
5. *FRUGALITY. Make no expense but to do good to others or yourself; i.e., waste nothing.*
6. *INDUSTRY. Lose no time; be always employ'd in something useful; cut off all unnecessary actions.*
7. *SINCERITY. Use no hurtful deceit; think innocently and justly, and, if you speak, speak accordingly.*
8. *JUSTICE. Wrong none by doing injuries, or omitting the benefits that are your duty.*
9. *MODERATION. Avoid extremes; forbear resenting injuries so much as you think they deserve.*
10. *CLEANLINESS. Tolerate no uncleanliness in body, cloaths, or habitation.*
11. *TRANQUILLITY. Be not disturbed at trifles, or at accidents common or unavoidable.*
12. *CHASTITY. Rarely use venery but for health or offspring, never to dullness, weakness, or the injury of your own or another's peace or reputation.*
13. *HUMILITY. Imitate Jesus and Socrates.*"

Franklin as the homespun American original

6. *Quoted in* Stone at 19.

7. *Quoted in* Tupi at 227.

8. *Quoted in* LEVY, BILL OF RIGHTS, at 108.

Washington

But though Jefferson was at least an agnostic, if not an atheist,[1] he was friendly to most "sectarian" religion for ordering republican life.[2]

More generally, a Frenchman, Alexis de Tocqueville, traveling in America in the early 1800s, noted American religion's role in tempering liberty:

> "[W]hile the law allows the American people to do everything, there are *things which religion prevents them from imagining and forbids them to dare.*"[3]

A Religious People versus a Christian Nation:

When the Framers wrote of the civic value of religion, they generally did so in the context of Protestant Christianity. But that does not necessarily mean they were speaking just of Protestantism or even Christianity.

Most certainly spoke in the context of the religion they knew, Protestant Christianity. But men such as Franklin, and even Washington, showed a broader tolerance. (Or in the case of Jefferson, a broader intolerance of any organized religion, be it Protestant Christianity or anything else!)[4]

Thus, just because the Framers may have recognized religion in society as a stabilizing influence, it does not mean that they intend-

---

1. Jefferson is the secularist's patron saint.

Jefferson cautioned his nephew in 1787 to "*shake off all the fears, & servile prejudices under which weak minds are servilely crouched*" and to "*question with boldness even the existence of a God; because, if there be one, he must more approve of the homage of reason, than that of blindfolded fear.*" *Quoted in* Stone at 10. Jefferson, like Washington, did not believe Jesus was divine but that he was the greatest teacher of all time. *Id.* at 10–11. In fact, Jefferson made his own Bible by cutting and pasting. He removed all sections of the New Testament containing supernatural aspects as well as what he perceived to be misinterpretations that the Four Evangelists had added. Several editions are in print. *See, e.g.,* THOMAS JEFFERSON, THE JEFFERSON BIBLE: THE LIFE AND MORALS OF JESUS OF NAZARETH (2010).

A self-confident and even whimsical Jefferson

2. Tupi at 255. But nothing changed Jefferson's anticlericism and his beliefs regarding the "*irritable tribe of priests.*" BROOKHISER at 72–73. Christian doctrines such as predestination, the inefficacy of good works, and original sin were for Jefferson "*nonsense,*" "*dross,*" "*distortions,*" "*abracadabra,*" "*insanity,*" "*demoralizing dogmas,*" "*deliria of crazy imaginations*" and "*hocus-pocus phantasm.*" Stone at 11, *quoting from* various Jefferson letters.

3. *Quoted in* Tupi at 217.

Alexis deTocqueville

4. As Jefferson once wrote, "*I have sworn upon the altar of God eternal hostility against every form of tyranny over the mind of man.*" *Quoted in* BROOKHISER at 73.

5. Berger at 648. Martin E. Marty, *On a Medial Moraine: Religious Dimensions of American Constitutionalism,* 39 EMORY L.J. 9, 13 (1990) ("*The Constitution and like documents were not written to save souls, to make sad hearts glad, to build denominational communities or encourage them, to promote public or civic virtue, to invoke God or the gods, or to encourage morality.*").

6. Berger at 638.

"Hocus pocus"—Magical conjurors still use this phrase. It most likely comes from "*hax pax max Deus adimax,*" a pseudo-Latin phrase that parodies the Roman Catholic Mass, which contains the phrase "*Hoc est enim corpus meum*" ("this is the body"). Others believe that it is an appeal to the Norse folklore magician Ochus Bochus or the Welsh "*hovea pwca*" (a "goblin's trick"). It is also the origin of the word "hoax." HENDRICKSON at 351; AYTO at 284

A 15th century mass

ed to establish a "Christian nation."

The Framers, moreover, specifically created a secular government.[5] They wanted to prevent a Church of the United States similar to the Church of England.[6]

The Constitution, for instance, refers to "*We the People*" as its source of legitimacy, not God:

"We the People of the United States . . . do

ordain and establish this Constitution for the United States of America."[7]

The Constitution does twice refer to religion.

The Constitution's first religious reference states it was

"Done . . . in the Year of our Lord one thousand seven hundred and Eighty seven and of the Independence of the United States of America the Twelfth."[8]

This was a common manner of dating documents, which we generally still use today.[9] This way of dating does not change the fact that the Constitution lays out a secular government, which its second religious reference explicitly shows:

"No religious Test shall ever be required as a Qualification to any Office or public Trust under the United States."[10]

---

7. Preamble to the Constitution. This contrasts with the constitutions of most of the states, which explicitly recognized religious obligation. Albert at 45.

Regarding the Framers purposefully leaving God out of the Constitution, as compared to the DECLARATION OF INDEPENDENCE, see Martin E. Marty, *Freedom of Religion and the First Amendment, in* THE BILL OF RIGHTS: A LIVELY HERITAGE 19 (Jon Kukla ed., 1987).

The Constitutional Convention

The Constitution spells out John Locke's philosophy on government with authority flowing from a social contract between each member of society. Berger at 640–41. Locke, whose writings most directly shaped the intellectual and political worldview of eighteenth century Americans, warned against "*claims to sacred truths.*" Stone at 6–7.

John Locke

8. U.S. CONST. art. VII. The Constitution also excludes Sunday from the day count before a president can veto a bill. Marty, *Freedom of Religion*, at 24.

9. See Marty, *Freedom of Religion*, at 24, arguing "Our Lord" sneaked in only as part of the date. *See also* Berger at 658 n.162 ("in the Year of our Lord" was colonial America's customary way of counting years).

BC and AD: Dionysius Exiguus ("Dennis the Short"), a Scythian monk, introduced "*anno Domini*" ("in the year of the Lord") in about 527. The years following his calculation of Jesus's birth he designated "*anno Domini*" (or "AD"). Thus, all years before we abbreviate as "BC" for "before Christ."

English texts used this system as early as the seventh century. Although modern references include using "CE" ("the common era") and "BCE" ("before the common era"), they are still based on Christ's birth date as the cutoff point. Thus, the old BC and AD system remains current.

Catholic Europe adopted the Gregorian calendar on October 4, 1582, to correct the errors of the then 1,628-year-old Julian calendar (from Julius Caesar). To fix the problem, the Gregorian calendar took out ten days. Because of England's break with Rome, England did not adopt the Gregorian calendar until 170 years later, in 1753. This is why it is hard to fix the birth date of people like George Washington. But the Gregorian calendar is still what we use today, and is inaccurate only one day every three thousand years. *See* RICH BEYER, THE GREATEST STORIES NEVER TOLD: 100 TALES FROM HISTORY TO ASTONISH, BEWILDER & STUPEFY 26–27 (2003).

Dennis the Short—or just a monk in a scriptorium?

Pope Gregory XIII

Detail of Pope Gregory's tomb celebrating the Gregorian calendar

10. U.S. CONST. art. VI, cl. 3. Marty, *Freedom of Religion*, at 24, and Tupi at 204–06 note that Article II, Section 1, provides that before taking office, the president "*shall take the following oath or affirmation: — 'I do solemnly swear (or affirm) that I will faithfully execute the office of the President of the United States and will, to the best of my ability, preserve, protect, and defend the Constitution of the United States,*'" and that Article VI, Clause 3, similarly provides that senators and representatives, state legislators, and all executive and judicial officers of the federal and state governments "*shall be bound by oath or affirmation to support this Constitution.*" Although Tupi argues that God is in the "*oath or affirmation,*" this neglects that oaths existed long before we humans had any concept of the Judeo-Christian God. For a brief history of oaths, see **Chapter 5: From Testicles to *Dragnet*: How the Fifth Amendment Protects *All* of Us.**

As we have seen, religious tests went back to Charles II and James II, when Parliament wanted to exclude Catholics from military and public office.[1] The Framers did not want that for America.[2]

The fact that the Constitution does not endorse or even evoke Christianity did not go unnoticed.[3]

In 1789, religious leaders from New England wrote President George Washington "*that the Constitution lacked any reference to the only true God and Jesus Christ, who he hath sent.*"[4] Washington replied that

"*the path of true piety is so plain as to require but little political direction . . . [only ministers of the gospel could further the] advancement of true religion.*"

A unanimous first Senate was even more explicit than Washington about

---

1. American Baptists were vocal proponents of the no religious test clause. Berger at 642.

The distinguished Baptist Reverend Isaac Backus, during the Massachusetts ratifying convention, stated that "*[n]othing is more evident, both in reason and The Holy Scriptures, than that religion is ever a matter between God and individuals; and, therefore, no man or men can impose any religious test without invading the essential prerogatives of our Lord Jesus Christ.*" He also stated that "*the imposing of religious tests had been the greatest engine of tyranny in the world.*" Id. at 642–43.

Later, Supreme Court Justice Joseph Story explained that Article VI made it possible, on the federal level, for Catholics, Protestants, Calvinists, Jews, and even

Backus

"*the Infidel, [to] sit down at the common table of the national councils without any inquisition into their faith or mode of worship.*" 3 JOSEPH STORY, COMMENTARIES ON THE CONSTITUTION OF THE UNITED STATES 731 (1833).

Story

2. Berger at 649. According to Maryland delegate Luther Martin, the "*no religious test clause*" was "*adopted by a very great majority of the convention, and without much debate.*" James Madison's notes indicate that only one state voted no and one state delegation was divided on the question.

3. The Post Office. Even the Founders had their "culture wars." In the early years of the republic, the nation debated the federal government's secular nature. Congress in 1810 and 1828, despite great pressure from religious groups, required the postal service to work on Sunday. Petitions inundated Congress declaring that the statute made "*it necessary to violate the command of God.*" Postal officials countered that frequent mail was essential to the nation's economy and national defense. Congress followed the reasoning that "*[t]he Framers of the Constitution recognized the eternal principle that man's relation with God is above human legislation and his rights of conscience unalienable*" and the federal government lacks the authority to "*define God or point out to the citizen one's religious duty.*" New technology eventually eroded the need for Sunday mail service and in 1912 Congress officially closed all Sunday postal service. *See* Berger at 651. *See also* Anuj C. Desai, *The Transformation of Statutes into Constitutional Law: How Early Post*

Persian Empire

Office Policy Shaped Modern First Amendment Doctrine, 58 HASTINGS L.J. 671, 673 (2007).

The unofficial Postal Service motto, "*Neither snow nor rain nor heat nor gloom of night stays these couriers from the swift completion of their appointed rounds,*"chiseled in gray granite on the New York City Post Office on 8th Avenue, actually comes from Herodotus's THE PERSIAN WARS (Book 8, ¶ 98). The Persians operated a system of mounted postal couriers who served with great fidelity under that motto. Postal Service Mission and Motto, http://www.usps. com/postalhistory/_pdf/ MissionandMotto. pdf#search= 'motto' (last visited June 12, 2009).

N.Y. City Post Office

the secular American government when it stated in the Tripoli Treaty of 1797 that the United States is

"not, in any sense, founded on the Christian religion" and thus had *"no character of enmity against the laws, religion, or tranquility of Musselmens . . ."*[5]

The First Amendment followed this secular path:

"Congress shall make no law respecting an establishment of religion . . . ."

At the state level, however, the First Amendment had it detractors. Critics believed it rejected Christianity and delegates to the state ratifying conventions complained that it would open control of the national government to atheists, Catholics, Jews, and Muslims.

---

4. Berger at 648.

Washington. Which Washington do you want to see? There is the pious one, beseeching God's help during the dark days of Valley Forge.

1866 engraving

Washington praying at Valley Forge is a persistent American image despite no documentation that it happened. Some people have this Washington as an article of faith in their Christian America. *See, e.g.,* JANICE CONNELL, FAITH OF OUR FOUNDING FATHER: THE SPIRITUAL JOURNEY OF GEORGE WASHINGTON (2003). But the real Washington spoke as a Deist, referring to *"Providence,"* the *"Almighty Ruler of the Universe,"* the *"Great Architect of the Universe,"* and the *"Great Disposer of Events."* *Quoted in* Stone at 17–18. According to historian Joseph Ellis, at his death, *"Washington did not think much about heaven or angels; the only place he knew his body was going was into the ground, and as for his soul, its ultimate location was unknowable. He died as a Roman Stoic rather than as a Christian saint."* JOSEPH J. ELLIS, HIS EXCELLENCY: GEORGE WASHINGTON 269 (2004). But one thing is clear; he was a man of tolerance. He said he was *"no bigot myself to any mode of worship."* Stone at 17, *quoting* George Washington's Letter to Lafayette (Aug. 15, 1787). Indeed, he went beyond mere toleration. To the Jews of the Touro Synagogue he wrote in 1790 that America did not practice *"toleration"* as it was not *"by the indulgence of one class*

of people, that another enjoyed the exercise of their inherent natural rights . . . . All possess alike liberty of conscience and immunities of citizenship." Quoted in BROOKHISER at 63. For Washington, toleration was a winning strategy, both for society and the battlefield. In November 1775 Washington barred the *"ridiculous and childish custom of burning the effigy of the Pope"* on Guy Fawkes' Day because it would interfere with attempts to get *"the friendship and alliance of the people of Canada."* Quoted in ALF J. MAPP, THE FAITHS OF OUR FATHERS: WHAT AMERICA'S FOUNDERS REALLY BELIEVED 75 (2005). Washington's order had the effect of ending the practice in America.

English Guy Fawkes Day

Ryan, in first grade, doing a stellar Washington

The English practice was to burn an effigy of Guy Fawkes every November 5. Fawkes conspired to bring back a Catholic monarchy by blowing up King James I and Parliament in the Gunpowder Plot of 1605. England still celebrates it, but now it is generally called "Fireworks Night." In the graphic novel V FOR VENDETTA (1982–89) and the movie V FOR VENDETTA (Warner Brothers. 2005), the main character, V, wears a Guy Fawkes mask.

5. BROOKHISER at 62–63.
"As the government of the United States of America is not in any sense founded on the Christian religion—as it has in itself no character of enmity against the laws, religion, or tranquility of Musselmen [Muslims],— and as the said States never entered into any war or act of hostility against any Mahometan [Islamic] nation, it is declared by the parties that no pretext arising from religious opinions shall ever produce an interruption of the harmony existing between the two countries."
Treaty of Peace and Friendship between the United States of America and the Bey and Subjects of Tripoli of Barbary, art. XI (Nov. 4, 1796), *available at* http://www.yale.edu/lawweb/ avalon/diplomacy/barbary/bar1796t. htm (last visited Oct. 14, 2006).

Would any senator today have the courage to vote for such a measure even though our America is far less religious, and more religiously diverse, than the Founders'?

In response, the First Amendment supporters pointed out that it says

"Congress shall make no law . . . ,"

leaving the states free to be as bigoted as ever,[1]

and especially anti-Catholic.[2]

Most of the new states, in fact, had established—meaning state-supported—churches. Although the American colonies

themselves were formally under the Church of England, colonial charters, religious dissent, and the Atlantic Ocean allowed diversity.

The northern states generally favored Puritanism

---

1. *See* Tupi at 209, noting that the First Amendment's main purpose was to only restrain the federal government from establishing a national religion. Justice Story confirmed that the First Amendment left the whole subject of religion exclusively to the states. STORY at 731.

2. Anti-Catholicism: As American as Apple Pie! Americans did not like Catholics. Given the fact that not many were around in colonial America, this tells a lot about cultural prejudice. *See, e.g.,* BROOKHISER at 17, 26 (in 1785 Catholics were less than 1 percent of the population, numbering only approximately 24,500). The fact is that all the states but Virginia had religious tests to disqualify those of nonestablished faiths, especially Catholics.

- THE DECLARATION OF INDEPENDENCE indicted King George III for upholding the rights of Catholic Canadians: *"He has . . . abolish[ed] the free [Protestant] system of English laws in a neighboring province."* This is ironic because both George III and George IV opposed Catholic emancipation in England. LOVELL at 417.
- **John Adams,** an enlightened and educated man, wrote his wife Abigail regarding Catholicism: *"Here is everything which can lay hold of the*

eye, ear and imagination. Everything which can charm and bewitch the simple and ignorant. I wonder how Luther ever broke the spell." Quoted in BROOKHISER at 26.

- **Benedict Arnold** justified his treason because of America's alliance with Catholic France, *"the enemy of the Protestant faith."* *Id.* at 17. (How much this had to do with Washington favoring French General Lafayette over him is an open question.)
- **Milton** traced all the evils of licensing and censorship to Roman Catholicism. It was the Vatican's 1418 campaign to suppress Wycliffe and Huss, precursors of the Reformation, that started systematic censorship, with this culminating after the Reformation in the Council of Trent and Spanish Inquisition. For Milton, Catholics did not get the toleration he preached for others because they had nothing to contribute to spiritual truth ; he said that one thing *"we know"* is the utter falsity of the *"teachings of the Roman Catholic faith."* In his earlier writings, Milton hinted vaguely that the class of heretics included Jews, Muslims, *"atheists"* and those given to *"popery, and open superstition."* By 1659 he had narrowed the list to just one: *"the papist only; he is the only heretic,"* for he *"counts all*

heretics but himself." Catholicism is not so much *"a religion, but a Roman principality."* Quoted in Witte, Milton, at 1569–70.

- **Locke** advocated in his Letter Concerning Toleration (1689) that every person *"has the supreme and absolute authority of judging for himself"* in matters of faith. Everyone that is but Catholics, Muslims, and other believers *"who deliver themselves up to the service and protection of another prince."* Locke was also intolerant of *"those . . . who deny the being of a God"* for *"promises, covenants, and oaths which are the bonds of human society, can have no hold upon an atheist."* Witte, Milton, at 1603–04.
- **Blackstone** justified treating Catholics as second-class citizens under the law because of their allegiance to the Pope: *"As to papists, what has been said of the Protestant dissenters would hold equally strong for a general toleration of them; provided their separation was founded only upon difference of opinion in religion, and their principles did not also extend to a subversion of the civil government. If once they could be brought to renounce the supremacy of the pope, they might quietly enjoy their seven sacraments, their purgatory, and auricular confession; their worship of reliques and images; nay even their transub-*

Adams

Arnold

Milton

Locke

Blackstone

(later Congregationalism) and the southern states Anglicanism (later Episcopalianism).[3]

State governments supported the established clergy from taxes that everyone had to pay, regardless of faith.[4] Taxes also supported church buildings.[5]

One thing to keep in mind, however, is that churches were the main social service agencies of their day. Today we expect government to provide and support our hospitals, orphanages, poor houses, and social welfare.[6] We also view public education as a constitutional and secular right.[7] In the Framers' world, churches did these things.[8]

---

stantiation. But while they acknowledge a foreign power, superior to the sovereignty of the kingdom, they cannot complain if the laws of that kingdom will not treat them upon the footing of good subjects." 4 WILLIAM BLACKSTONE, COMMENTARIES *54. DeWolf at 452. But one example in English law is that the Toleration Act of 1689 applied to Protestant nonconformists (mostly Puritans) but not Catholics, ironic because Catholics are theologically closer to Anglicans than Puritans. LOVELL at 400. The English colonials brought their anti-Catholicism to America, which flourished to the point of costing Al Smith the presidency in 1928 against Herbert Hoover and was still an issue in John F. Kennedy's election.

Smith   Hoover   Kennedy

3. Berger at 633–34 (noting that nine of the thirteen colonies had some form of established religion by the Revolution); *see also* Tupi at 209–10; Marty, *Freedom of Religion*, at 20.

4. *See* Witte, *Tax Exemption*, at 371 (these taxes included "tithe rates" to meet general ecclesiastical expenses and "church rates" to maintain church property. Nonconformists, usually Baptists, Quakers, Catholics, and Jews still had to pay the taxes.

A modern argument is that public education is religion and that *"No one in America would require an atheist or agnostic to pay taxes to support the church or the church school. Yet millions of American Christians are required to pay for an educational program that assumes that there is no God, or that, if He exists, He is irrelevant to history, science, and language. American school children study subjects as if the Author of these subjects does not even exist."* Titus at 35. *See also* ANN COULTER, GODLESS: THE CHURCH OF LIBERALISM (2006) (arguing that liberalism is a religion that seeks to supplant "traditional" Christianity).

5. Boston's Old North Church.

6. In 1935, the Social Security Administration was the first major federal welfare agency.

7. Regarding the role of churches in education see LEVY, BILL OF RIGHTS, at 97–98, discussing Article III of the Massachusetts Declaration of Rights.

On the national level, Congress appropriated money to pay for missionaries among the Native Americans, mostly for educational reasons. Berger at 650. The Northwest Ordinance in 1789 explicitly encouraged schools in the territory to teach "*religion, morality, and knowledge.*" Tupi at 225.

8. The founders of two of the oldest America universities, Harvard (1636) and Yale (1701), intended them to be Christian. The 1636 Harvard University rules declared: "*Let every student be plainly instructed and earnestly pressed to consider well the main end of his life and studies is to know God and Jesus Christ which is eternal life (John 17:3) and therefore to lay Christ in the bottom as the only foundation of all sound knowledge and learning.*"

Yale's rules of 1787 declared: "*All the scholars are required to live a religious and blameless life according to the rules of God's Word, diligently reading the holy Scriptures, that fountain of Divine light and truth, and constantly attending all the duties of religion. All the scholars are obliged to attend Divine worship in the College Chapel on the Lord's Day and on Days of Fasting and Thanksgiving appointed by public Authority.*"

Quoted in Tupi at 216–17; *see also* BROOKHISER at 18.

Dissenters from the established churches suffered civil disabilities, such as exclusion from universities and/or disqualification from office.[1]

Often though, especially in New England, states supported multiple established churches,[2] breaking from the European tradition.[3] At the time, one could speak of Lutheran Sweden, Anglican England, Catholic Spain, and Presbyterian Scotland, but no one church for America.[4]

America was, after all, a land of dissenters. We still cherish the image of the lonely Pilgrims who fled the Old World for freedom and opportunity.[5]

True, most of the dissenters were intolerant when they got here. But especially by the Revolution, enough conflicting dissenters led to toleration.[6]

In Virginia, for instance, men like Jefferson, Madison, and Washington did not believe the state should force people to support a church.[7] Both Jefferson's Statute for Religious Freedom and the Virginia Declaration of Rights allowed for real toleration and ended the state's established religion.[8]

This was Madison's background when he prepared the drafts of the Bill of Rights, most especially the First Amendment.[9]

---

1. Levy, Bill of Rights, at 90. Virginia passed laws in the late 1600s, for example, that prohibited Quakers from assembling. Also, non-Anglican preachers had to get a special license to preach. Between 1765–78, Virginia jailed forty-five Baptist ministers for not getting the license. Tupi at 209–10.

2. For variations of the establishment formula in the colonies, see Levy, Bill of Rights, at 97. Generally, the New England colonies adopted a system of multiple local establishments. New York, for example, had a dual establishment of the Anglican and Dutch churches. Berger at 633–34. Massachusetts maintained an established church but endorsed the principle of no preference, allowing for other churches to freely exercise their faith. Levy, Bill of Rights, at 83. See also John Witte, Jr., "A Most Mild and Equitable Establishment of Religion": John Adams and The Massachusetts Experiment, 41 J. Church & St. 213 (1999).

3. Levy, Bill of Rights, at 101. See also Levy, Bill of Rights, at 91, noting that American establishment was never as bad (i.e., discriminatory) as in Europe.

Colonial Maryland

5. Pilgrims landing on Plymouth Rock.

4. But, even in more tolerant America, no colony ever established (i.e., supported) all religions without exception. They always supported Protestantism or at most Christianity—no Judaism, Buddhism, Hinduism, Islam ("Mohammadism"), or any other "ism"!
    Maryland used the term "Christian" religion to be established rather than "Protestant," to allow for its Catholic population. Levy, Bill of Rights, at 99. Maryland was actually founded as a Catholic colony.

6. The Declaration of Independence triggered gradual disestablishment, and the Bill of Rights accelerated the trend. See Albert at 23–24 regarding the disestablishment of religion in the various colonies/states, noting that four colonies in 1776, and one each in 1777 and 1786, had disestablished religion. Establishment did not end until 1818 in Connecticut and 1833 in Massachusetts. Marty, Freedom of Religion, at 21; Levy, Bill of Rights, at 98. Massachusetts being the last may have been due to the relatively tolerant nature of its establishment to begin with.

7. Marty, Freedom of Religion, at 20. See also Berger at 647, noting that Virginia adopted the Lockean perspective on religious freedom, as demonstrated in Madison's Memorial and Remonstrance against Religious Assessments.

8. To get it through the Virginia House of Burgesses, Madison had to help Patrick Henry become governor. This got Henry out of the legislature, which opened the way for the Declaration of Rights, allowing for religious toleration. Marty, Freedom of Religion at 21. See also Levy, Bill of Rights at 85–86, noting most of the Founders, especially Madison, thought established religion not good and that he believed in the high wall of separation of church and state. Regarding Madison's Memorial and Remonstrance against Religious Assessments and the Virginia General Assessment Bill of 1784, see Levy, Bill of Rights at 85.

MADISON AND HIS FIRST AMENDMENT

The First Amendment was Madison's special project.[10] It was, in fact, his progeny, and though not initially all he wanted, it grew into itself.

Madison believed in individual conscience and the right to express it. Thus, the First Amendment embodies not only the free exercise and anti-establishment of religion, but also freedom of speech and press.[11]

In 1789, most of the Constitutional Convention delegates thought explicitly protecting speech and religion unnecessary.[12] As Alexander Hamilton argued in THE FEDERALIST No. 84,

"[w]hy should it be said that the liberty of the press shall not be restrained, when no power is given by which restrictions may be imposed."[13]

History showed Hamilton's argument unpersuasive.

As noted in this book's Prequel and Preamble, original Constitution's lack of a Bill of Rights left Madison having to contend with a very powerful Patrick Henry during the Virginia ratifying convention.[14] To win his seat in Congress, Madison agreed to champion a Bill of Rights, including what is now the First Amendment.

9. All of this disestablishment gave us English's reputed longest word and a spelling bee favorite: "antidisestablishmentarianism." (Two good movies revolving around spelling bees are BEE SEASON (Fox Searchlight PICTURES 2005) and AKEELAH AND THE BEE (Lionsgate 2006).)

The word actually means going against religion's disestablishment back to establishment. Thus you could say antidisestablishmentarianism is contrary to the First Amendment's anti-establishment clause.

Antidisestablishmentarianism originated in nineteenth century Britain against disestablishing the Church of England. The word has 28 letters and 12 syllables.

10. Marty, *Freedom of Religion*, at 19.

11. *See* O'Brien at 44–46, and LEVY, BILL OF RIGHTS, at 118, noting Madison's original 1789 proposal went well beyond Blackstone to protect the free press.

12. Charles Pinckney of South Carolina proposed "*that the liberty of the Press should be inviolably observed*." Roger Sherman replied, "*It is unnecessary. The Power of Congress does not extend to the Press*." Quoted in Leonard W. Levy, *Bill of Rights in* ESSAYS ON THE MAKING OF THE CONSTITUTION 258, 259 (Leonard W. Levy ed., 1987). Also, all agreed that the federal government had no power over religion. LEVY, BILL OF RIGHTS, at 81, 83–84 (listing several of the Founders on this point).

13. In fact, Hamilton argued, writing it down just invites encroachment because "*[w]ho can give it any definition which would not leave the utmost latitude for evasion?*" Ultimately, Hamilton contended, "*its security . . . must altogether depend on public opinion.*"

THE FEDERALIST No. 84 (Alexander Hamilton), *discussed in* O'Brien at 45; *see also* THE FEDERALIST No. 51 (James Madison) (discussion of religion). Hamilton's excuses regarding the lack of a Bill of Rights did not satisfy the Anti-Federalists. *See, e.g.*, Thomas B. McAffee, *The Bill of Rights, Social Contract Theory, and the Rights "Retained" by the People*, 16 S. ILL. U. L.J. 267, 278 (1992) (noting that among the natural rights the Anti-Federalists were most anxious to protect was freedom of the press).

Alexander Hamilton

14. Regarding Madison's debates with Henry during the Virginia ratifying convention and how Madison's arguments disarmed Henry and allowed for Virginia to ratify the Constitution, *see* Gregory C. Downs, *Religious Liberty That Almost Wasn't: On the Origin of the Establishment Clause of the First Amendment*, 30 U. ARK. LITTLE ROCK L. REV. 19 (2007).

Roger Sherman   Charles Pinckney

James Madison   Patrick Henry

Regarding religion, Madison's first draft of June 8, 1789, read:

> *"The civil rights of none shall be abridged on account of religious belief or worship, nor shall any national religion be established, nor shall the full and equal rights of conscience be in any manner, or on any pretext, infringed."*[1]

Through the legislative process, this eventually became the First Amendment.[2]

Madison also wanted the First Amendment to apply to the states. But what Congress wanted was a guarantee that the federal government would not impose a national religion.[3] Congress was more interested in protecting each state's right to establish its own religion than in protecting freedom of religion itself.[4]

Given the thinking at the time regarding the First Amendment, we can only now look at what most of the Framers wanted as nascent. They gave us a First Amendment that had the potential to be

---

1. Berger at 635–36, *citing* 1 ANNALS OF CONG. at 451. *See* LEVY, BILL OF RIGHTS, at 86–87 (regarding Congress and especially the Senate defeating Madison's original motion).

2. Responding to criticism that his draft would harm religion, Madison responded with the thinking of Milton and Locke that he *"apprehended the meaning of the words to be, that Congress should not establish a religion, and enforce the legal observation of it by law, nor compel men to worship God in any manner contrary to their conscience."* Berger at 636, *citing* 1 ANNALS OF CONG. at 758.

3. Berger at 645–46, noting that while debating proposed constitutional amendments, Congress considered and rejected an amendment applying many of the First Amendment protections to the states:

> *"No State shall infringe the equal rights of conscience, nor the freedom of speech or of the press, nor of the right of trial by jury in criminal cases."*

1 ANNALS OF CONG. at 783. The intent was to leave these matters to the states. LEVY, BILL OF RIGHTS, at 119; Marty, *Freedom of Religion*, at 24–25; *see also* Albert at 6.

4. The same was true for the press, where the First Amendment originally reserved to the states the authority to legislate speech and press. Levy, *Free Press Clause*, at 207. *See also* Rutland at 35–38 (outlining early state bill of rights guarantees of free press, especially Virginia's). *Gitlow v. New York*, 268 U.S. 652, 666 (1925), finally held that freedom of the press is protected from state interference under the Fourteenth Amendment's Due Process Clause. *See* Rutland at 39.

5. The Establishment Clause Today. The original intent of the 1789 Convention does not today control our reading of the First Amendment. Instead, the original intent of the Congress and people that passed the Fourteenth Amendment controls. *See* **Epilogue: How We Ponied Up to Pay the Bill.** In *Everson v. Board of Education*, 330 U.S. 1, 15–16 (1947), Justice Hugo Black for the Supreme Court defined the modern Establishment Clause:

> *"The 'establishment of religion' clause of the First Amendment means at least this: Neither a state nor the Federal Government can set up a church. Neither can pass laws which aid one religion, aid all religions, or prefer one religion over another. Neither can force nor influence a person to go to or to remain away from church against his will or force him to profess a belief or disbelief in any religion. No person can be punished for entertaining or professing religious beliefs or disbeliefs, for church attendance or non-attendance. No tax in any amount, large or small, can be levied to support any religious activities or institutions, whatever they may be called, or whatever they may adopt to teach or practice religion. Neither a state nor the Federal Government can, openly or secretly, participate in the affairs of any religious organizations or groups and vice versa. In the words of Jefferson, the clause against establishment of religion by law was intended to erect 'a wall of separation between Church and State.'"*

Hugo Black

See Berger at 654; Albert at 14. Justice William Rehnquist, dissenting in *Wallace v. Jaffree*, 472 U.S. 38 (1985), a case striking down a state law requiring *"silent meditation or voluntary prayer,"* argued *Everson* was flawed because *"[t]he Establishment Clause did not require governmental neutrality between religion and irreligion nor did it prohibit the federal government from providing nondiscriminatory aid to religion."* *Discussed in* LEVY, BILL OF RIGHTS, at 80.

6. The Establishment Clause's Evolution. A philosopher of religion would probably say whether God exists has nothing to do with *how* God chose to create man and nature. This is basically the Catholic Church's position. *See Dogma*, THE CATHOLIC ENCYCLOPEDIA, http://www.newadvent.org/cathen/05089a.htm (last visited Nov. 12, 2009). Despite this, Creationism seems to make God's existence contingent on disproving Darwinism.

The 1926 Scopes Monkey Trial, *State v. Scopes*, 152 Tenn. 424 (Tenn. 1925), *Scopes v. State*, 278 S.W. 57 (Tenn. 1925), tested the Butler Act, which made it

unlawful in any Tennessee state-funded school and university *"to teach any theory that denies the story of the Divine Creation of man as taught in the Bible, and to teach instead that man has descended from a lower order of animals."* In reality it was a staged presentation for

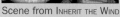
Scene from INHERIT THE WIND

what Madison wanted all along.[5]

And what he wanted was for America to separate church and state.[6]

THE "WALL" SEPARATING CHURCH AND STATE

Nowhere does the Constitution or Bill of Rights say "separation of church and state." But the principle is the way the Supreme Court has worked out how the First Amendment's Establishment and Free Exercise Clauses function together.[7] The concept makes the United States the first society to separate church and state.[8]

Jefferson gets credit for the phrase "the wall of separation of church and state" and thus our modern law on the subject.[9] Jefferson responded to the Danbury Baptist Association of Connecticut in 1802, which suggested that he declare a day of fasting for national reconciliation following his bitter political campaign against Adams:

---

the controversy culminating in Clarence Darrow's cross-examination of William Jennings Bryant and tripping him up on the Bible's inconsistencies. The film INHERIT THE WIND (United Artists 1960) culminates in this exchange and was really about McCarthyism. The play's title comes from *Proverbs* 11:29: "*He that troubleth his own house shall inherit the wind.*"

Creation science attempts to support the Bible's account of creation and disprove accepted scientific theories about the Earth's history. Fundamentalist Christians are its most vocal proponents, advocating that it be taught in public schools.

In *Epperson v. Arkansas*, 393 U.S. 97 (1968), the Supreme Court invalidated an Arkansas law that prohibited teaching evolution in public schools because "*teaching and learning must [not] be tailored to the principles or prohibitions of any religious sect or dogma.*"

Later the federal judge in *McLean v. Arkansas Board of Education*, 529 F. Supp. 1255, 1258–64 (E.D. Ark. 1982), held that the Arkansas Balanced Treatment for Creation-Science and Evolution-Science Act violated the Establishment Clause. In *Edwards v. Aguillard*, 482 U.S. 578 (1987), the Supreme Court ruled that a Louisiana law requiring the teaching of creation science along with evolution unconstitutionally sought to advance a particular religion. Supporting *Aguillard* were seventy-two Nobel prize-winning scientists, seventeen state academies of science, and seven other scientific organizations, describing creation science as religious.

Darwin as "A Venerable Orangoutang" (1871)

Darrow and Bryant

---

7. *In Everson v. Board of Education*, 330 U.S. 1, 18 (1947), the question was whether a local school board could reimburse parents, including some with children in Catholic schools, for costs of transportation. Justice Hugo Black wrote, "*the First Amendment has erected a wall between church and state. That wall must be kept high and impregnable. We could not approve the slightest breach.*"

Separating Church and State in Concord, New Hampshire

---

8. Marty, *Freedom of Religion*, at 20.

In the United States we use the word "minister" to refer to a religious person, usually clergy, who performs functions or services such as teaching, weddings, baptisms, or funerals. In other countries a "minister" can be a government official, such as the British prime minister. Americans use the term "secretary" for these functions, as in secretary of state. "Minister" comes from a Middle English phrase, from the Old French "*ministre*," originally "*minister*" in Latin, meaning "servant."

Prime Minister Winston Churchill

---

9. Barbara A. Perry, *Jefferson's Legacy to the Supreme Court: Freedom of Religion*, 31 SUP. CT. HIST. 181 (2006). Starting with the first significant Establishment Clause case in the nineteenth century, *Reynolds v. United States*, 98 U.S. 145 (1878), the Supreme Court pointed to Jefferson as "*an acknowledged leader of the advocates of [the Establishment Clause]*," and then went on to say that his views "*may be accepted as authoritative declaration of the scope and effect of the [Establishment Clause].*" *But see* Mark J. Chadsey, *Thomas Jefferson and the Establishment Clause*, 40 AKRON L. REV. 623 (2007) (documenting and arguing that Jefferson's thinking had little or no effect on the Establishment Clause's adoption). *See also* John Witte, Jr., Book Review, 16 J.L. & RELIGION 565 (2001) (reviewing DANIEL L. DREISBACH, RELIGION AND POLITICS IN THE EARLY REPUBLIC: JASPER ADAMS AND THE CHURCH-STATE DEBATE (1996)) (discussing Jasper Adams (1793–1841) of South Carolina as an exponent of a typical early nineteenth century American view of religious liberty that was not Jeffersonian).

"Believing with you that religion is a matter which lies solely between man and his God . . . I contemplate with sovereign reverence that act of the whole American people which declared that their legislature should 'make no law respecting an establishment of religion, or prohibiting the free exercise thereof,' thus building a wall of separation between Church and State."[1]

Jefferson was a good writer; thus, he did what most good writers do and stole metaphors from others, in this case the *"wall of separation."*[2]

Jefferson probably stole it from Roger Williams. In 1643, Williams called for *"a wall of separation between the garden of the Church and the wilderness of the world."*[3] In his case the wall of separation was to protect religion, not necessarily government.[4]

But Jefferson may have also stolen the *"wall of separation"* metaphor from Milton and Locke.

For Milton, the mixing of government and religious power was *"a whoredom"*:

"[S]uffer[ing] the two powers, the ecclesiastical and the civil, which are so totally distinct, to commit whoredom together, and, by their intermingled and false riches, to strengthen indeed in appearance, but in reality to undermine, and at last to subvert one another."[5]

Locke closely tracked Milton regarding religious liberty:

"The care therefore of every man's soul belongs unto himself, and is to be left unto himself."[6]

Because of this, the state has no more business trying to care for a man's soul than it has in trying to prevent him from neglecting his finances. For a man to care for his own soul, it was crucial that the church be *"absolutely separate and distinct from the commonwealth . . ."*

---

1. *Quoted in* Berger at 649 n.125 (added emphasis); *discussed in* Berger at 634–35 and 649–50. Ironically, Adams believed the same as Jefferson about the separation of church and state. *"Nothing,"* he wrote Benjamin Rush, *"is more dreaded than the national government meddling with religion . . . . I mix religion with politics as little as possible."* When a clergyman entered Congress, Adams wrote his wife Abigail that *"as he is the first gentleman of the cloth who has*

John Adams

appeared in Congress, I cannot but wish he may be the last. Mixing the sacred character with that of the statesman . . . is not attended with any good effects." *Quoted in* Stone at 15.

2. Regarding metaphors, Jefferson would have known that Aristotle wrote *"the greatest thing by far is to be a master of metaphor . . . since a good metaphor implies an intuitive perception of the similarity in dissimilars."* ARISTOTLE, POETICS 1459a (McGill–Queen's University Press 1997).

3. *Quoted in* Witte, *Milton*, at 1573; *see also* Berger at 639–40.

4. The Wall Protecting Religion. Roger Williams cofounded the Baptist faith in America, though he left that church only a few months later. Today, Baptists and Evangelicals often push for more government support of religion. Secularists conversely look with distrust on programs like President George W. Bush's White House Office of Faith-Based Initiatives.

But for most of the Framers, the wall between church and state was not to protect government but to protect religion *from* the government. *See* Marty, *Freedom of Religion*, at 24; LEVY, BILL OF RIGHTS, at 86–88; Downs *generally* (noting the role of the Virginia Baptist leader John Leland in establishing religious freedom); Berger at 643; Robert A. Sedler, *Essay: The Protection of Religious Freedom under the American Constitution*, 53 WAYNE L. REV. 817 (2007) (noting the overriding purpose of the religion clauses is to protect religious freedom). The Founders' concerns are as relevant today. *See, e.g.,* Douglas Laycock, *"Noncoercive" Support for Religion: Another False Claim about the Establishment Clause*, 26 VAL. U. L. REV. 37, 69 (1992) (*"Government by its sheer size, visibility, authority, and pervasiveness could profoundly affect the future of religion in America. For government to affect religion in this way is for government to change religion, to distort religion, to interfere with religion. Government's preferred form of religion is theologically and liturgically thin. It is politically compliant, and supportive of incumbent administrations."*).

FAITH-BASED
COMMUNITY
INITIATIVES

5. *Quoted in* Witte, *Milton*, at 1562–63. Milton often returned to this theme, calling it *"absurd"* that Christians have *"not learned to distinguish rightly between civil power and ecclesiastical."* The Bible makes clear that *"Christ's kingdom is not of this world,"* and his church *"does not stand by force or constraint, the constituents of worldly authority."* *Id.* at 1563. Also, *"the combining of ecclesiastical and political government . . . is equally destructive to both . . . ."* *Id.* at n.147.

Milton

Locke was important for the founding generation, especially Jefferson.[7] So when Jefferson was looking for a source for the metaphor regarding the "wall of separation," among Williams, Milton, and Locke he had plenty from which to choose.

SYMBOLS OF RELIGION AND SPEECH

People have always used symbols to make a statement,[8] especially in the context of religious and political expression.[9] America at the time of the Framers was no different. For example,

- Colonists burned the pope in effigy during "Pope Day" (still called Guy Fawkes Day in England).

- Protesting the Stamp Act, colonists placed various effigies on a "Liberty Tree" (a large elm), including a devil looking out of a boot, which was a pun on the name of British Prime Minister Lord Bute (pronounced "Boot") who the colonists (erroneously) thought was responsible for the Stamp Act.

- After the Declaration of Independence, Americans burned King George III's effigy, emblems, portrait, and coat of arms. Later, they burned effigies of unpopular governors and people like John Jay, coauthor of THE FEDERALIST PAPERS and Supreme Court Chief Justice, for negotiating the much opposed treaty with England.

- Englishmen and Americans honored John Wilkes for his printing *The North Britain* No. 45, with forty-five toasts at political dinners where forty-five diners ate forty-five pounds of beef. At other dinners, the meal was "*eaten from plates marked 'No. 45.'*" Colonists also thinned out Boston's Liberty Tree to forty-five branches.[10]

---

6. Locke went on:

"*But what if he neglect the care of his soul? I answer, what if he neglect the care of his health, or of his estate; which things are nearlier [sic] related to the government of the magistrate than the other? Will the magistrate provide by an express law, that such an [sic] one shall not become poor or sick? Laws provide, as much as is possible, that the goods and health of subjects be not injured by the fraud or violence of others; they do not guard them from the negligence or ill husbandry of the possessors themselves. No man can be forced to be rich or healthful, whether he will or no.*"
JOHN LOCKE, *A Letter Concerning Toleration, in* TWO TREATISES OF GOVERNMENT AND A LETTER CONCERNING TOLERATION 227–28 (Ian Shapiro ed., 2003); *quoted in* Toll at 421.

John Locke

7. *See* Berger at 640 (discussing Locke's influence on the American Constitution). *See generally* Wardle (discussing both Locke's deep personal Christian faith, belief in religious tolerance, and influence on America's Founders).

. . . .

8. Death by crucifixion was a Roman symbol of political power. Christians made it a symbol of faith, depicted millions of times from the ornate Calvary scenes to the simple cross.

Calvary by Paolo Veronese (16th century)

. . . .

10. *See* Eugene Volokh, *Symbolic Expression and the Original Meaning of the First Amendment*, 97 GEO. L.J. 1057, 1061 (2009) (discussing the various examples of symbolic speech during the Framer's era).

9. The symbols abound, from variations between sects, such as the Eastern Orthodox cross to the symbols of different religions and political movements: the Jewish star of David, the Taoist yin and yang, the Islamic star and crescent, the Hindi swastika to the Nazi swastika and the Communist sickle and hammer. Symbols used together can be symbols of a political statement, such as variations of the popular "COEXIST" bumper sticker.

If this history shows anything, it is that symbols have been powerful speech in America.[1]

People pray and pledge not only to what the symbols represent but to the symbols themselves.[2]

Almost by definition, their purposeful desecration or destruction is a statement and speech[3]— perhaps ugly and bigoted, but *speech* nonetheless.[4]

THE FIRST AMENDMENT AS YOUR PERSONAL SAVIOR

Religion and speech are a powerful combination:

"But when men have realized that time has upset many fighting faiths, they may come to believe . . . that the best test of truth is the power of the thought to get itself accepted in the competition of the market . . . . That at any rate is the theory of our constitution."[5]

So wrote Justice Oliver Wendell Holmes, and his marketplace of ideas metaphor guides the

---

1. "It's a Grand Old Flag/ A High Flying Flag!" Federal law, 36 U.S.C. § 301, attempts to preserve the symbolic power of the American flag by specifying conduct during the national anthem—hand held over heart, etc. Thus, the American flag itself is *speech*; coupled with the "Star Spangled Banner," it makes a powerful statement.

The flag during the War of 1812

Surviving 1814 broadside of the "Defense of Fort McHenry," Francis Scott Key's poem that later became the "Star Spangled Banner"

A fifteen-star, fifteen-stripe "Star Spangled Banner"

---

2. "*I pledge allegiance to the flag*" is how millions of America school children begin their day. When Francis Bellamy wrote it as a children's recitation for the 400th anniversary of Columbus's discovery of America, it originally had no reference to either God or the United States: "*I pledge allegiance to my Flag, and to the Republic for which it stands: one Nation indivisible, With Liberty and Justice for all.*"

In 1923 and 1924, the National Flag Conference claimed that immigrants would confuse the words "*my Flag*" for the flag of their native land and consequently added "*of the United States of America.*" It was not until 1942 that Congress even recognized the Pledge of Allegiance. Berger at 631.

As for "*under God,*" on April 22, 1951, the Catholic Knights of Columbus added it for its organization's meetings, and a year later called for Congress to insert it into the pledge. Congress did so in 1954, citing other examples of religion in American history, including the 1620 Mayflower Compact, the 1776 DECLARATION OF INDEPENDENCE, President Abraham Lincoln's

Original Pledge Salute (Bellamy Salute) of the Pledge of Allegiance.

1863 *Gettysburg Address*, and the 1864 inscription of "In God We Trust" on American coins. Such a reference, Congress asserted, distinguished America from "*the atheistic and materialistic concepts of communism with its attendant subservience of the individual.*" Berger at 632, citing H.R. Rpt. 83-1693; Sen. Rpt. 83-1313. This amendment brought the pledge to the form we know today: "*I pledge allegiance to the Flag of the United States of America, and to the Republic for which it stands, one Nation under God, indivisible, with liberty and justice for all.*" 4 U.S.C. § 4 (2000). When President Eisenhower signed the change into law on June 14, 1954, he declared: "*From this day forward, the millions of our school children will daily proclaim in every city and town, every village and rural school house, the dedication of our nation and our people to the Almighty . . . . In this way we are reaffirming the transcendence of religious faith in America's heritage and future; in this way we shall constantly strengthen those spiritual weapons which forever will be our country's most powerful resource in peace or in war.*" Berger at 633.

It shocked many when in June 2002 the U.S. Court of Appeals for the Ninth Circuit, in *Newdow v. U.S. Congress* (*Newdow I*), 292 F.3d 597 (9th Cir 2002), held the 1954 statute unconstitutional. The Senate unanimously denounced the decision, President George W. Bush dubbed it "*ridiculous,*" House Minority Whip Tom DeLay called it "*sad*" and "*absurd,*" Senate Majority Leader Tom Daschle referred to it as "*nuts,*" and Senator Robert Byrd of West Virginia called the judges "*stupid.*" *See* William Trunk, *The Scourge of Contextualism: Ceremonial Deism and the Establishment Clause*, 49 B.C. L. REV. 571 (2008). Congress reaffirmed the pledge with "*under God.*" Pub. L. No. 107-293, 116 Stat. 2057 (2002). Though the Ninth Circuit later narrowed its decision, the Supreme Court granted a review to great fanfare. Then, as a great letdown to Court watchers, it dismissed the case on a procedural ground.

Thus, the questions remain about what the Constitution allows our government to state about God. Can government state there is a God—a fundamental, religious belief? Can government state that there is a singular God? Finally, can government define one aspect of the nature of God, namely, that our nation is under God, implying that God specially endorses the United States? Berger at 656.

reading of the First Amendment.[6] Though Holmes gets the credit,[7] he was following Milton:

"Let her [Truth] and Falsehood grapple; who ever knew Truth put to the worse in a free and open encounter?"[8]

Holmes would have also known that Jefferson preached that the people *"may safely be trusted to hear everything true and false, and to form a correct judgment between them . . . ."*[9]

If one reads Holmes's statement closely, however, he does not say that the free and open marketplace of ideas will always produce truth but only that it is *"the best test of truth."*[10]

After all, regarding both expression and belief, the ancient Athenian Demosthenes warned that

"it would be dangerous if there ever happened to coexist a considerable number of men who were bold and clever speakers, but full of . . . disgraceful wickedness. For the people would be led astray by them to make many mistakes."[11]

---

3. The American flag and invoking the national anthem are powerful symbols.

"O'er the ramparts we watch" (from the "Star Spangled Banner") in a 1945 recruiting poster

Saint images destroyed during the Reformation at the Cathedral of Saint Martin, Utrecht

Thus, it begs the question: When a person burns the flag is he *doing something* or *saying something*? If he is just *doing* something, the First Amendment does not protect him. But if he is *saying* something, it does. So far, despite calls from senators and lower court judges, the Supreme Court has affirmed that burning a flag in a political context is *"speech,"* both *"inherently"* and *"conventionally"* expressive. *Rumsfeld v. Forum for Academic & Institutional Rights, Inc.,* 547 U.S. 47, 66 (2006); *Barnes v. Glen Theatre, Inc.,* 501 U.S. 560, 577 n.4 (1991) (Scalia, J., concurring in the judgment).

Burning flags as speech?

5. *Abrams v. United States,* 250 U.S. 616, 624–31 (1919) (Holmes, J., dissenting, joined by Brandeis, J.).

4. *Cohen v. California,* 403 U.S. 15 (1971) highlights both symbolic and written "speech." Mr. Cohen walked into a Los Angeles courthouse wearing a jacket inscribed with "Fuck the Draft." Writing for a 5-4 majority, the conservative justice John Marshall Harlan II wrote that "one man's vulgarity is another's lyric" and that in the context of opposing the Vietnam War, the "unseemly expletive" was used as a political protest. If Mr. Cohen can wear such a jacket in political protest, he most certainly can burn the same jacket as political speech. Thus, if he wears a jacket with the American flag, he could do the same.

6. Through various opinions, Holmes and Justice Louis Brandeis formed the foundation of modern free speech law. *See Whitney v. California,* 274 U.S. 357, 372–80 (1927) (Brandeis, J., concurring, joined by Holmes, J.); *United States v. Schwimmer,* 279 U.S. 644, 653–55 (1929) (Holmes, J., dissenting, joined by Brandeis, J.). These cases led to *Brandenburg v. Ohio,* 395 U.S. 444, 447 n.2, 449 (1969), punishing "mere advocacy" without *"incitement to imminent lawless action"* violates the First and Fourteenth Amendments. *Compare* Stanley Ingber, *The Marketplace of Ideas: A Legitimizing Myth,* 1984 Duke L.J. 1 (1984) (arguing that Holmes's marketplace is a flawed forum). Holmes may not always have been such a prophet of free speech. During World War I, he joined a more restrictive Court deciding the extent of the Espionage Act of 1917 and its 1918 amendments, where he wrote that even the *"most stringent protection of free speech would not protect a man in falsely shouting fire in a theatre and causing a panic."* *Schenck v. United States,* 249 U.S. 47, 52 (1919).

Holmes

Brandeis

7. Holmes remains the most celebrated justice of all time, with his own stamp and even a movie (highly fictionalized), The Magnificent Yankee (MGM 1950).

8. Areopagitica, *quoted in* Witte, *Milton,* at 1529, 1586; *see also* Werhan at 322.

10. John Stuart Mill regarded the premise that truth would trump falsehood in a free society as nothing more than *"a piece of idle sentimentality."* John Stuart Mill, On Liberty (1859).

John Stuart Mill

9. *Quoted in* Jeremy D. Bailey, Thomas Jefferson and Executive Power 218 (2007).

11. *Quoted in* Werhan at 332.

Thus, the notion that what is true or best will win is not a given.[1]

A person's "truth" encompasses conscience and privacy, the very essence of what it means to live free. For the individual and society, what conscience and privacy mean evolves.

As the Framers designed it, the First Amendment allows for evolution.[2] The Framers addressed the future, not the past.[3] By any measure we have more freedom of speech and religion today. The World Wide Web, for instance, has given us greater scope than ever, and no state has an established religion.

But who is listening?

Do the media inform or lead with "*bold and clever speakers*"?[4] "The media" seeks to manipulate us every day, to influence who we vote for to the toothpaste we buy.[5] And the lines between advertising, entertainment, and news are often so blurred as to be indistinguishable.[6]

This is where religion comes in, not just in the sense of a specific religion like Catholic, Baptist, or Muslim, but more broadly to refer to a world view that provides fundamental values and understanding.

We need something to help see the lines between the messages we get. That something can be traditional religion, a code of ethics, a philosophy, or principles by which to live. In this sense, even an atheist can have "religion."

Protecting that religion from the government is the First Amendment.

As Justice Robert Jackson eloquently wrote,

"[i]f there is any fixed star in our constitutional

---

1. Validating Demosthenes's warning is the documentary film, SHOUTING FIRE: STORIES FROM THE EDGE OF FREE SPEECH (Moxie Firecracker Films 2009), showing how both government and private interest groups can still violate the First Amendment's sprit, if not its letter.

Demosthenes

2. A train ride that changed how we speak: Holmes was riding a train with another famous Judge, Learned Hand, on June 19, 1918, between New York and Boston, and their conversation helped "shape" Holmes' views. *See* Gerald Gunther, *Learned Hand and the Origins of Modern First Amendment Doctrine: Some Fragments of History*, 27 STAN. L. REV. 719 (1975), (discussing Hand's 1917 decision in *Masses Publishing Co. v. Patten*, 244 F. 535 (S.D.N.Y. 1917), *rev'd*, 246 F. 24 (2d Cir. 1917), as a precursor of Holmes's opinions). *See also* Stephen M. Feldman, *Free Speech, World War I, and Republican Democracy: The Internal and External Holmes*, 6 FIRST AMEND. L. REV. 192 (2008) (discussing the scholarly debate on whether Holmes really changed his views on speech when comparing *Abrams* with his prior cases). Holmes also had read Zechariah Chafee, Jr., *Freedom of Speech in War Time*, 32 HARV. L. REV. 932 (1919). Chafee concluded that Framers like Madison intended "*to wipe out the common law of sedition and make further prosecutions for criticisms of the government, without any incitement to law-breaking, forever impossible in the United States.*" *Id.* at 947. Chafee (1885–1957) was an early free speech scholar and Harvard law professor who Senator Joseph McCarthy once pronounced "*dangerous*" at a 1952 U.S. Senate subcommittee hearing. *See* John Wertheimer, *Review: Freedom of Speech: Zechariah Chafee and Free-Speech History*, 22 REVS. IN AM. HIST. 365 (1994).

3. *See* Levy, *Free Press Clause*, at 180.

4. The 2004 presidential campaign showed how an organized media campaign could derail the candidacy of a decorated Vietnam War veteran. The Swift Boat Veterans for Truth had the sole purpose of questioning John Kerry's war record and helping derail his bid for president. A person can now be "swift-boated" as part of a political smear campaign.

The "Birthers" mounted a similar claim against President Barack Obama, claiming he was not born in the United States and therefore could not be president. The tabloids picked up on the myth as well

Swift Vets for Truth

Holmes

Chafee

Judge Billings Learned Hand (1872–1961) was a federal judge who served on the District Court for the Southern District of New York and later on the Second Circuit. Legal scholars and the Supreme Court have quoted Hand more often than any other lower court judge.

constellation, it is that no official, high or petty, can prescribe what shall be orthodox in politics, nationalism, religion, or other matters of opinion or force citizens to confess by word or act their faith therein." [7]

So you can believe what you want and say what you want, and the government can't do anything to you— at least in theory.

Just two years after Jackson wrote the words quoted above, he dissented from the Supreme Court's decision that upheld interning all persons of Japanese ancestry, including almost 100,000 citizens, in concentration camps:

"A military order, however unconstitutional, is not apt to last longer than the military emergency . . . . But once a judicial opinion rationalizes such an order to show that it conforms to the Constitution . . . the Court for all time has validated the principle of racial discrimination in criminal procedure and of transplanting American citizens. The principle then lies about like a loaded weapon ready for the hand of any authority that can bring forward a plausible claim of an urgent need." [8]

Jackson articulated the great worry regarding expanding government power during an ill-defined "war on terror;" all it takes is *"a plausible claim of an urgent need* "to justify curtailing liberty." The collapse of the Twin Towers on September 11, 2001, created a plausible claim. [9]

Rights and the rule of law are fragile things in a violent world. In the face of *"plausible claims,"* freedom of speech, press, and religion are always at risk. So far, after a crisis has passed, they have tended to come out stronger.

But the future does not guarantee it.

---

as CNN's Lou Dobbs, despite the fact that the state of Hawaii has released his birth certificate. The White House released the long version on April 27, 2011 to remove all doubt.

bama's birth certificate

5. We all grew up with *"Sticks and stones may break my bones, but words will never hurt me."*

A good enough lesson for children that most adults learn is not true. As the philosopher Jean-Paul Sartre wrote, *"Words are loaded pistols."*

Or as the Australian rock band INXS (pronounced as "In Excess") sings, *"Words are weapons shaper than knives, makes you wonder how the other half dies."*

Sartre

6. The film NETWORK (MGM 1976) showed how news can become entertainment and vice-versa. Peter Finch won a posthumous Oscar for playing Howard Beale, yelling *"I'm mad as hell, and I'm not going to take this anymore!"*

7. W. *Va. Bd. of Educ. v. Barnette*, 319 U.S. 624, 641–42 (1943).

8. *Korematsu v. United States*, 323 U.S. 214, 246 (1944), *reh'g denied*, 324 U.S. 885 (1945) (Jackson, J., dissenting).

Korematsu (finally) receiving the Presidential Medal of Freedom in 1998

Fred Korematsu was the original plaintiff challenging internment

9. The Twin Towers burning on 9/11.

Robert H. Jackson

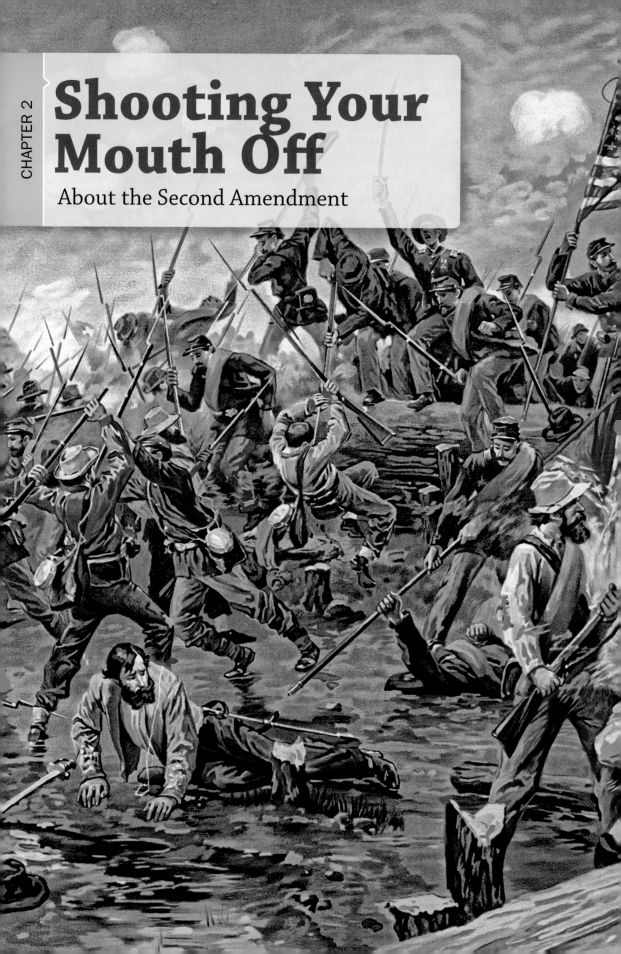

CHAPTER 2

Shooting Your Mouth Off

About the Second Amendment

"A well regulated Militia, being necessary to the security of a free State, the right of the People to keep and bear Arms, shall not be infringed."

—The Second Amendment

Nobody really wants the Second Amendment.

On the one hand are the gun contro*lists*, armed with violence statistics, who say it is all about *"a well regulated Militia."* We must regulate guns, they argue, because some guns are so simple even a child can use them.[1] They ignore, or at the least find inconvenient, the part that says *"the right of the people to keep and bear Arms shall not be infringed."*[2]

1. The **AK-47** was an icon of the Cold War. AK-47, for "Kalashnikov's automatic rifle model of year 1947," is named for its inventor, Mikhail Kalashnikov. He began design work in 1944 and the Soviet Armed Forces officially accepted the rifle in 1949. All Warsaw Pact nations used it, as does the People's Republic of China. The weapon also became a symbol of not only the Cold War but revolutions throughout the world. It even ended up on the Mozambique flag. Its durability and ease of use made it the most popular assault rifle of all time, with more AK-type rifles produced than all others combined. Literally, a child can use it.

An original AK-47

A modern AK-47

2. See John Levin, *The Right to Bear Arms: The Development of the American Experience*, 48 Chi.-Kent L. Rev. 148, 153 (1971) (to *"bear arms"* means *"to serve in the armed forces of the state"*); Garry Wills, *To Keep and Bear Arms*, N.Y. Rev. Books, Sept. 21, 1995, at 62 (the Second Amendment's *"bearing arms"* phrase only has meaning in the militia context given that *"one does not bear arms against a rabbit"*).

On the other hand are the individual right*ists*, who say it's all about "*the right of the People to keep and bear Arms*" and "*that militia stuff is just what we call our gun club!*"[1] Gun rights groups have long wished that the Framers had used different language to make their right more explicit. If courts would just give the Second Amendment its "*original intent*," they argue, their right would be secure and so would their homes.

But gun rights advocates do not usually take the Second Amendment to its absolute conclusion of allowing any person to have any weapon at any time. If it says that the right "*shall not be infringed*" then, for example, no federal or state statute should punish the crime of being a felon in possession of a firearm.[2]

1. Under President George W. Bush and then Attorney General John Ashcroft, the Justice Department had the Office of Legal Counsel change positions to adopt the individual rights theory. MARK V. TUSHNET, OUT OF RANGE: WHY THE CONSTITUTION CAN'T END THE BATTLE OVER GUNS 1 (2007). On the politics of gun prosecution, *see, e.g.,* Margaret E. Sprunger, *D.C. as a Breeding Ground for the Next Second Amendment Test Case: The Conflict Within the U.S. Attorney's Office,* 53 CATH. U. L. REV. 577 (2004).

NRA headquarters, Washington, D.C.

2. Even the National Rifle Association (NRA) argues that the right to bear arms is absolute only for "law-abiding" citizens. See Brief for the National Rifle Association and the NRA Civil Rights Defense Fund as Amici Curiae Supporting Respondent, *District of Columbia v. Heller,* 128 S. Ct. 2783 (2008) (No. 07-290) *available at* http://www.nraila.org/heller/proamicusbriefs/nra_amicus_heller.pdf.

The nonprofit NRA dedicates itself to protecting its Second Amendment vision as well as marksmanship, firearm safety, hunting, and self-defense. William Conant Church (also a founder of the New York Metropolitan Museum of Art) and George Wood Wingate started the NRA as the American Rifle Association in New York in 1871. The NRA may be the single most powerful nonprofit organization in the United States and claims to be the oldest continuously operating U.S. civil

liberties organization with "more than four million members." NRA-ILA: Who We Are, And What We Do, http://www.nraila.org/About/ (last visited Aug. 4, 2008).

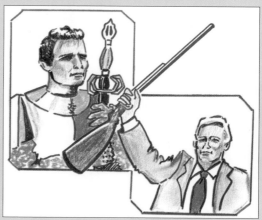

Image by Helen Koop

Charlton Heston bearing the arms in the movies and accepting a presentation rifle in 2000 at the NRA convention, exclaiming that presidential candidate Al Gore could only take it "*[f]rom my cold, dead hands!*" This statement was actually part of a NRA slogan and had no relation to Heston's famous line from PLANET OF THE APES (20th Century Fox 1968), "*Get your hands off me, you damn dirty ape.*"

3. Regarding what you get under the various Second Amendment absolutist arguments, see Tushnet at 31.

4. *See* John-Peter Lund, *Do Federal Firearms Laws Violate the Second Amendment by Disarming the Militia?* 10 TEX. REV. L. & POL. 469 (2006).

A single M1A2 Abrams tank in 2007 costed just over $23 million, not counting outfitting costs. U.S. Dep't of Defense, *Department of Defense Budget for Fiscal Year 2007: Program Acquisition Costs by Weapon System,* at 51 (2006), at http://www.defenselink.mil/comptroller/defbudget/fy2007/fy2007_weabook.pdf (last visited July 28, 2008).

Interestingly, the gun on the Abrams tank is smoothbore, i.e., not rifled. Thus it bears a remarkable similarity to the firearms at the time of the American Revolution, most of which were smoothbore muskets.

And it's not just about who gets to play with the guns but what specific toys you get.[3] If *"the right of the People to keep and bear Arms shall not be infringed,"* why should there be any limit on the type of weapon you can buy? If the Second Amendment's purpose is to make sure citizens can fight against a tyrannical government, why not allow them to buy an Abrams tank if they have a spare $23 million?[4] After all, a tank is just a tractor with a big gun on it![5]

The Second Amendment's history is complicated, not because we lack sources or contemporaneous accounts, but because contemporary politics dictates interpretation.[6] Much of this has to do with how we Americans feel about our heritage and a dichotomy in American mythology.

5. The Arms: The Tank. The tank gets its name from its origins in the Royal Navy, when Winston Churchill supported experiments on "land ships" in 1915. To keep the new weapon a secret, the English labeled the crates "tanks" when they shipped them to France. Tanks have "hatches," "hulls," "bows," and "ports," reflecting their naval origin. The basic idea of a tank traces back to the Renaissance, with even Leonardo da Vinci designing one.

6. The Second Amendment is the only one of the Bill of Rights with a preamble—"*[a] well regulated Militia, being necessary to the security of a free State ....*" — which raises the question of whether the amendment grants an individual right. It is also a grammatical mess.

As originally written the Second Amendment appears,

"A well regulated Militia, being necessary to the security of a free State, the right of the People to keep and bear Arms, shall not be infringed."

Modern editions of the Constitution often drop the capitals for the words "Militia," "State," "People," and "Arms" and drop the incorrect commas after "Militia" and "Arms":

"A well regulated militia being necessary to the security of a free state, the right of the people to keep and bear arms shall not be infringed."

What this gives is a complex sentence—meaning a sentence with one independent clause and one or more subordinate clauses—starting with the subordinate or dependent clause:

"A well regulated militia being necessary to the security of a free state, ..."

followed by the independent clause,

"the right of the people to keep and bear arms shall not be infringed."

See the classic WILLIAM STRUNK, JR. & E.B. WHITE, THE ELEMENTS OF STYLE 5–8 (Macmillan 3d ed. 1979). Also, any general grammar such as JOHN E. WARRINER, MARY E. WHITTEN & FRANCIS GRIFFITH, ENGLISH GRAMMAR AND COMPOSITION 107 (1973) or CELIA MILLWARD, HANDBOOK FOR WRITERS 41–43 (1950).

If you attribute meaning to grammatical convention, then it argues for the reading that the Second Amendment is about not infringing on the *"right of the people to keep and bear arms."* This is enough to make your average NRA member a grammarian!

But what did a comma mean to the Founders?! According to a popular eighteenth century grammar, CHARLES GILDON & JOHN BRIGHTLAND, A GRAMMAR OF THE ENGLISH TONGUE 149 (1711): "After a *Comma* always follows something else which depends upon that which is separated from it by a *Comma* . . . ." (emphasis in original). What follows the comma in the Second Amendment is

"the right of the people to keep and bear arms shall not be infringed."

Thus, in eighteenth century grammar, the second part of the Second Amendment was dependent on the first part,

"A well regulated militia being necessary to the security of a free state, ..."

This is enough to make your average gun control advocate not just a grammarian but an *historical* grammarian!

Leonardo da Vinci

Modern re-creation of a tank from da Vinci's drawings

On the one hand is Hawkeye who, as generations of American school children know, never misses with either rifle or tomahawk.[1] He is a fictionalization of the real-life, albeit legendary, Daniel Boone or Davy Crockett.[2] The Hawkeyes, Boones, and Crocketts bravely live on the frontier and fight *for* civilization but are not really part of it.[3]

1. *See* Tushnet at 27 (2007) (discussing Hawkeye's iconic nature). Hawkeye (also known as Natty Bumpo, Leatherstocking, the Pathfinder, the Trapper, the Deerslayer, and *La Longue Carabine* (or "Long Rifle") was James Fenimore Cooper's hero in the Leatherstocking Tales, which were, in order of the story's chronology, The Deerslayer (1841), The Last of the Mohicans (1826), The Pathfinder (1840), The Pioneers (1823), and The Prairie (1827).

James Fenimore Cooper 1822

2. James Fenimore Cooper used stories from Boone's life as the basis for parts of his Leatherstocking Tales.

Daniel Boone by Chester Harding (1820), when Boone was 85

Daniel Boone (20th Century Fox) aired on NBC for 165 episodes, from September 24, 1964 to September 10, 1970. Between this and Fess Parker playing Davy Crockett, King of the Wild Frontier (Buena Vista 1955), every kid in America wanted a coonskin cap! There is no record, however, that Daniel Boone ever wore a raccoon skin cap.

The Last of the Mohicans has led to various movie and television adaptations, including the 1932 serials starring Harry Carey, the 1957 TV series starring Lon Chaney and John Hart, and the 1992 movie starring Daniel Day Lewis as Hawkeye and Native American activist Russell Means as Chingachgook, which also has a really good soundtrack. The Last of the Mohicans (20th Century Fox 1992). From Cooper's Hawkeye comes Iowa as the "Hawkeye State." The U.S. Navy has a carrier-based tactical surveillance plane called the Hawkeye, that is, "the eyes of the fleet."

Davy Crockett by Henry Huddle (1889)

Fess Parker as Daniel Boone

Fess as Davy Crockett

3. *See* Carl T. Bogus, *The Hidden History of the Second Amendment*, 31 U.C. Davis L. Rev. 309, 387–88 (1998) (discussing sociologist James William Gibson's study on American cultural mythology, James William Gibson, Warrior Dreams: Violence and Manhood in Post-Vietnam America 17 (1995)).

Although Bogus does not discuss Hawkeye from M*A*S*H, in a way the character fights just as much for civilization on the frontier of war. M*A*S*H's Hawkeye is just as undomesticated, at least from the order of the army. His shots are punch lines, and his aim as sharp as Cooper's Hawkeye.

Alan Alda as Hawkeye

These books are loved world wide and there is a series of Soviet era stamps of the tales.

The Last of the Mohicans (Associated Producers Inc. 1920)

The Grumman E-2 Hawkeye

Hawkeyes fight alone; they are rugged and most certainly individual. In the end, though, they have to leave civilization for a new wilderness. Their continued presence threatens the community.[4] Still, with their individual guns, they are literally "straight shooters."[5] They exemplify the individual right to bear arms.

---

4. *See* Susan Ford Wiltshire, Greece, Rome, and the Bill of Rights 135 (1992), citing the classic western Shane (Paramount Pictures 1953) for the hero who must leave society after he has done what he has to do. Another example is John Wayne's character, Ethan Edwards, in John Ford's epic western classic The Searchers (Warner Brothers 1956). Another great western, Pale Rider (Warner Brothers 1985), is thematically similar to Shane, with the hero leaving for the wilderness at the end.

Alan Ladd enjoys a moment of civilization with Jean Arthur before his character, Shane, must leave.

John Wayne tries to come home in The Searchers.

"The Preacher" in Pale Rider. "Ethan Edwards" in The Searchers and "Shane" must live apart in the end. Image by Helen Koop.

The Long Rifle

The Brown Bess

The Three Musketeers—without muskets—1894 illustration

5. Hawkeye never misses, which is how we Americans think of ourselves (at least us guys). One reason Hawkeye hits is technology; he has a Long Rifle called *Killdeer*, and it is not a musket. The **Long Rifle**, aka the **Pennsylvania Rifle** or **Kentucky Rifle**, could be over four feet long. Pennsylvania German gunsmiths created the longer barrel for finer sighting and to give the gunpowder more time to burn, increasing muzzle velocity and accuracy. The gunsmiths would make the rifle the height of the customer's chin so he could see the muzzle while loading. Thus Hawkeye is accurate partly because he is tall. The Long Rifle was also the Kentucky Rifle from the song "The Hunters of Kentucky," about the Battle of New Orleans.

A **rifle** gets its name from the grooves ("rifling") cut into the walls of the barrel. The raised areas of the rifling are called "lands," which cause the ball (what we now call the bullet) to spin in flight. This improves accuracy and range, just like a properly thrown American football. Archers had long realized that a twist added to the tail feathers of their arrows caused them to spin in flight and gave them greater accuracy.

A **musket** is a smoothbore gun, meaning that it has no rifling in the barrel (though the original rifles were called "rifled muskets"). The musket gets its name from the French "*mousquette*," a male sparrow hawk, or from "*mousquet*," meaning "little fly" from the Italian "*mosca*" or "fly," which was the word for a crossbow arrow. When the gun arrived, the old crossbow arrow name became the gun's name. *See* Webster's Word Histories 313 (1989).

British Redcoats used a musket called the **Brown Bess** (nickname origin unknown) for over one hundred years during the British Empire's expansion. Despite the image of the independent American with his individual rifle, during the American Revolution, both sides used the Brown Bess because it was faster to load and fire than a rifle.

A soldier with a musket was a "musketeer," meaning that the main job of Alexander Dumas's heroes in The Three Musketeers (1844), Athos, Porthos, Aramis, and d'Artagnan, was supposed to be shooting, not fencing. Despite this, Dumas's books and the numerous movies, television shows, cartoons, and even the candy bar feature swords as they call out, "*All for one and one for all*." Muskets, after all, are heavy, cumbersome, and not what a gentleman would carry around for dueling. Early pistols were also cumbersome and had only one shot and thus less practical for self-defense than the dashing rapier or saber, which were also badges of social rank. Not until the nineteenth century's **Patterson Colt** did pistols start to posses the utility that justified their weight and bulk. The best and most complete adaptation of Dumas remains The Three Musketeers (20th Century Fox 1973), followed by The Four Musketeers (20th Century Fox 1974).

In 1932 the 3 Musketeers candy bar had three pieces: vanilla, chocolate, and strawberry (hence the name). In 1945 this changed to the chocolate and nougat bar we know.

Trailer image from the James Bond film, Dr. No. (United Artists, 1972) looking out from the gun's rifling.

British Redcoat with his Brown Bess

The Three Musketeers, (united Artists 1921).

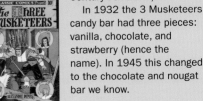

On the other hand, there are the sheriffs or soldiers defending America, as part of an official force. They either bring or maintain society's law and order. Though they are certainly strong individuals, they live in society, not outside it. Look at Gary Cooper as Sergeant York, a civilized Christian pacifist who soldiers to save democracy.[1] Cooper also brings civilization to the Wild West when he stands up to the bad guy, Frank Miller, in HIGH NOON.[2]

John Wayne helps win the Wild West as the soldier upholding the myth that Colonel Friday was an American hero in FORT APACHE.[3] He appears again as the consummate soldier in SANDS OF IWO JIMA.[4]

Although these heroes play with just as many guns as the Hawkeyes, they do it as officials.[5] They exemplify a collective right to bear arms within the context of a "*well regulated Militia.*"

---

1. SERGEANT YORK (Warner Brothers 1941). Gary Cooper won his first Oscar for his performance. *See Bogus, Hidden History,* at 388–89 for a discussion of this theme.

2. HIGH NOON (United Artists 1952). Cooper won his second Oscar for this movie. A pretty good science fiction remake of HIGH NOON was OUTLAND (Warner Brothers 1981), even though it lacked HIGH NOON's theme song.

3. FORT APACHE (RKO 1948). An older but still cute Shirley Temple is part of the cast.

4. SANDS OF IWO JIMA (Republic Pictures 1949). This film contains the first recorded use of the phrase "*lock and load.*"

5. And the guns they played with were the **Winchester '73**, the **Colt Peacemaker**, and the **shotgun**, the first modern firearms as well as Hollywood standard issue.

The **Winchester Model 1873** was a lever action rifle from the Winchester Repeating Arms Company and the beginning of a series of similar models. "Winchester" became synonymous with lever-action repeating firearms. Because of its popularity and association with western movies, such as WINCHESTER '73 (Universal Pictures 1950) with Jimmy Stewart, this is the

Jimmy Stewart in Winchester '73

John Wayne shoots a Winchester in The Searchers

Chuck Connors in The Rifleman

"gun that won the West." Chuck Connor's Winchester in *The Rifleman* (television broadcast on ABC from 1958 to 1963) had a trick feature of a screw pin and large loop lever that tripped the trigger allowing the gun to fire like a modern semi-automatic. During the opening credits, Connors fires twelve shots even though the Winchester only held eleven rounds.

In *Wanted: Dead or Alive* (Four Star Productions 1958–61) Steve McQueen was too cool for cool as bounty hunter Josh Randall, packing a sawed-off Winchester model 1892 called Mare's Leg in the show. Any shortened rifle, or a lengthened pistol, is often called a "**carbine.**"

The **Colt Single Action Army** handgun (SAA) was a single action (meaning that pulling the trigger also cocked the hammer) revolver (meaning that it had a cylinder with five or six rounds that "revolved" with each shot readying the next round for fire). The U.S. government chose it as the standard military service revolver from 1873 until 1892. Colt also made the **Peacemaker**, a SAA with the barrel etched with "Peacemaker." But more important for the Wild West, the Peacemaker became the Hollywood standard.

A **shotgun** shoots a large "slug" or small pellets of

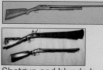
Shotgun and blunderbuss

"shot" in a pattern. A shotgun is smoothbore, meaning it has no rifling. The Boy Scouts of America still offer a merit badge for shotgun mastery. The shotgun's ancestor is the **blunderbuss**, a short, large-caliber muzzle-loader flared at the end, which was supposedly a Pilgrim favorite, probably because it fired shot and thus is good for turkey hunting.

The shotgun featured in the February 11, 2006, **Dick Cheney hunting incident**. The Vice President accidentally

More recently, the mythical rugged individual has metaphorically married the soldier/sheriff to create a paramilitary dude or righteous vigilante taking "the law" into his own hands. He is hostile to other government officials because they are part of the problem that faces civilization and "true" American values. He is not a Hawkeye because he is in society and he does not "soldier" on. He has the badge or uniform but still protects society on his own.

In the military context, these characters are born of the disillusionment displayed in films like PLATOON and FULL METAL JACKET.[6] This leads, at least thematically if not chronologically, to RAMBO.[7]

In the civilian context, films like SERPICO[8] display the disillusionment that leads to DEATH WISH[9] and DIRTY HARRY.[10]

---

shot Harry Whittington, a seventy-eight-year-old lawyer. Whittington suffered a nonfatal heart attack from one of the lead shots near his heart. Jon Stewart of *The Daily Show* noted that Cheney's shooting Whittington was the first time a sitting vice president shot someone since Aaron Burr mortally shot Alexander Hamilton in a duel in 1804. *See Dick Cheney Shooting Jokes*, ABOUT.COM, http://politicalhumor.about.com/od/cheneyshooting/a/cheneyshooting.htm (last visited Sept. 11, 2010).

January 2007's *Texas Monthly*, composite photograph (used with permission)

Image by Helen Koop. FIRST BLOOD, PLATOON (Orion Pictures 1986) and FULL METAL JACKET (Warner Brothers 1987).

6. The title FULL METAL JACKET refers to a bullet used in a barracks scene early in the movie. A full metal jacket bullet (FMJ) is encased in a copper alloy extending around the bullet. The jacket allows for higher muzzle velocities and increases accuracy and reliability in re-peating firearms. FMJs are actually less lethal than a standard soft lead bullet. The lead bullet tends to expand in the body, causing more deaths. Conversely, FMJs pass through the body, causing a greater chance of wounds. In war this is advantageous because killing an enemy soldier only removes one from the field, whereas wounding an enemy can remove three or more as soldiers carry their wounded comrades out of the fighting.

Common FMJ bullets

7. FIRST BLOOD (1982), followed by the rest of the franchise: RAMBO: FIRST BLOOD PART II (1985), RAMBO III (1988), RAMBO (2008), and maybe even an upcoming RAMBO V.

Image by Helen Koop

8. SERPICO (Paramount Pictures 1973). Al Pacino is a cop who will not take a bribe "set up" by those that do.

9. DEATH WISH (Paramount Pictures 1974). Charles Bronson plays a nice "liberal" whose wife and daughter get raped and killed. He then goes out and murders every mugger he can.

10. DIRTY HARRY (Warner Brothers 1971). The final scene, in which Callahan throws his badge in the water, is homage to the end of HIGH NOON. Of course, the drama of this ending did not stop Clint Eastwood and Warner Brothers from coming back to make Dirty Harry into a very profitable franchise with MAGNUM FORCE (1973), THE ENFORCER (1976), SUDDEN IMPACT (1983), and THE DEAD POOL (1988).

July 11, 1804—The Burr-Hamilton duel

These guys probably do not represent much, if anything, about the legalities of the Second Amendment. They just have big guns.[1] Despite their putative claims to upholding "the law," one thing the John James Rambos and Dirty Harry Callahans could care less about is legal structure.

So what protects us from them?

Law versus guns and how to protect society plays out in the film and play A Few Good Men when Lieutenant Daniel Kaffee (Tom Cruise) cross-examines Colonel Jessep (Jack Nicholson), the soldier gone amok. Following the famous exchange:

Kaffee: *I want the truth!*

Jessep: *You can't handle the truth!*[2]

Jessep goes on:

"*Son, we live in a world that has walls, and those walls have to be guarded by men with guns. Whose gonna do it? You? You, Lt. Weinburg?*"

Continuing, Jessep shows his utter contempt for any law but his own:

"*I have a greater responsibility than you could possibly fathom . . . . You don't want the truth because deep down in places you don't talk about at parties, you want me on that wall, you need me on that wall . . . . I have neither the time nor the inclination to explain myself to a man who rises and sleeps under the blanket of the very freedom that I provide, and then questions the manner in which I provide it. I would rather you just said thank you, and went on your way. Otherwise, I suggest you pick up a weapon, and stand a post. Either way, I don't give a damn what you think you are entitled to.*"[3]

---

1. Dirty Harry claims his ".*44 Magnum, [is] the most powerful handgun in the world and would blow your head clean off.*" But the term "magnum" refers to the bullet, not necessarily the gun. The .44 Remington Magnum is a large-bore cartridge originally for revolvers but now also for carbines and rifles with a lengthened .44 special case, loaded to higher pressures for greater energy. Different hand guns are made to shot this magnum bullet in the .44 caliber, such as the **Smith & Wesson Model 29**, and thus gained the name "Magnum 44s." By the time of Dirty Harry in 1971, other guns and bullets packed triple the power.

Dirty Harry continued his association with the .44 Magnum in all the movies, including Sudden Impact (Warner Brothers 1983), where he held the gun on a bad guy and said, "*Go ahead, make my day.*"

Smith & Wesson Model 29

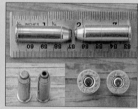
Magnum bullets

2. The *ABA Journal* ranked A Few Good Men (Columbia Pictures 1992) No. 14 on its list of the twenty-five greatest legal movies. Richard Brust, *The 25 Greatest Legal Movies: Tales of Lawyers We've Loved and Loathed*, ABA Journal, Aug. 2008, at 38–53. The oft-quoted line, "*You can't handle the truth,*" is now part of American culture. See, e.g., Tooth Fairy's (20th Century Fox 2010) promotional poster spoofing the line with "*You can't handle the tooth.*"

Image by Helen Koop

3. The full exchange follows:
Kaffee: *Colonel Jessep, did you order the Code Red?*
Judge Randolph: *You don't have to answer that question!*
Col. Jessep: *I'll answer the question!* [to Kaffee]
Col. Jessep: *You want answers?*
Kaffee: *I think I'm entitled.*
Col. Jessep: *You want answers?*
Kaffee: *I want the truth!*
Col. Jessep: *You can't handle the truth!* [pauses]
Col. Jessep: *Son, we live in a world that has walls, and those walls have to be guarded by men with guns. Whose gonna do it? You? You, Lt. Weinburg?*
I have a greater responsibility than you could possibly fathom. You weep for Santiago, and you curse the marines. You have that luxury. You have the luxury of not knowing what I know. That Santiago's death, while tragic, probably saved lives. And my existence, while grotesque and incomprehensible to you, saves lives. You don't want the truth because deep down in places you don't talk about at parties, you want me on that wall, you need me on that wall. We use words like honor, code, loyalty. We use these words as the backbone of

John James Rambo and Dirty Harry Callahan are fun, with exciting action scenes and exaggerated lines like Dirty Harry's

"Go ahead, make my day!"[4]

Coronel Jessep is not fun. In fact, when he ordered an extrajudicial (illegal) punishment, a "Code Red," on a young marine, he was deadly:

Kaffee: *Did you order the Code Red?!*

Jessep: *You're goddamned right I did!*

The law prevails in A FEW GOOD MEN, with Jessep's arrest and Kaffee gaining self-worth as both officer and lawyer. Sure Coronel Jessep protected the wall, but only law protects us from Coronel Jessep.

Law, and not guns, ultimately protects society.

These American myths are the prism through which we view guns and the Second Amendment. They give the Second Amendment, like the First Amendment, a personal quality, different from other parts of the Bill of Rights. For most

Americans the rights that relate to trial and criminal procedure are an abstraction, including the Fourth, most of the Fifth, the Sixth, and the Eighth Amendments. They are not personally relevant because police do not search most homes, and prosecutors do not charge most people.

But guns we pick up and shoot. We see them every day on television and in movies. As children we aspire to them.[5] The Second Amendment itself bleeds into popular culture.[6]

---

a life spent defending something. You use them as a punch-line. I have neither the time nor the inclination to explain myself to a man who rises and sleeps under the blanket of the very freedom that I provide, and then questions the manner in which I provide it. I would rather you just said thank you, and went on your way. Otherwise, I suggest you pick up a weapon, and stand a post. Either way, I don't give a damn what you think you are entitled to.
Kaffee: *Did you order the Code Red?*
Col. Jessep: *I did the job I . . .*
Kaffee: *Did you order the Code Red?*
Col. Jessep: *You're goddamned right I did!*
....

4. Dirty Harry is great for the macho monologue: *"I know what you're thinking. 'Did he fire six shots or only five?' Well, to tell you the truth, in all this excitement I've kind of lost track myself. But being this is a .44 Magnum, the most powerful handgun in the world and would blow your head clean off, you've got to ask yourself one question. 'Do I feel lucky?' Well do ya, punk?"*

Image by Helen Koop

Who needs legal structures with Harry around? He gets to be cop, judge, jury, and executioner. And he gets to do it with the biggest gun. Again, a high percentage of Harry's bad guys seem to be nonwhite inner city males despite the fact that whites commit most crimes.

5. Certainly we boys do!
Who didn't want *"an official Red Ryder carbine-action 200-shot range model air rifle with a compass in the stock, and this thing which tells time"* like nine-year-old Ralphie Parker in A CHRISTMAS STORY (MGM 1983). Like him, most of us had our hopes dashed by well-meaning adults saying, *"No, you'll shoot your eye out!"*

Ralphie Parker shooting his Red Rider - Image by Helen Koop

The Red Rider BB gun

....

6. One of America's favorite dysfunctional families discussed gun control. In the "The Cartridge Family" episode of the *Simpsons*, Homer and Lisa discuss the Second Amendment's individual versus. collective rights conflict:
Homer: But I have to have a gun! It's in the Constitution!
Lisa: Dad! The Second Amendment is just a remnant from revolutionary days. It has no meaning today!
Homer: You couldn't be more wrong, Lisa. If I didn't have this gun, the king of England could just walk in here anytime he wants and start shoving you around.

Photo by Dong Passon "Homer Bearing Arms"

Photo by Dong Pas- son "Homer Bearing All"

"The Cartridge Family," *The Simpsons* (Fox television broadcast, November 2, 1997), *quoted in* Saul Cornell & Nathan DeDino, *A Well Regulated Right: The Early American Origins of Gun Control*, 73 FORDHAM L. REV. 487, 489 (2004) (also citing Jonah Goldberg, *Homer Never Nods: The Importance of The Simpsons*, NAT'L REV., May 1, 2000, at 36, 37).

But the modern popularity of guns and gun rights misses the fact that *"the People"* at the time of the Second Amendment were mostly white males who owned property.[1] What then did the Framers intend by a *"right . . . to bear Arms"* in 1789, in a society with no standing armies or police?[2]

And what did the *"right . . . to bear Arms"* mean before 1789?

ARMS BEFORE GUNS

Coming Out of Egypt Armed to the Teeth!

When the ancient Jews following Moses left Egypt they left armed:

"God took the people toward the way of the Wilderness to the Sea of Reeds. And the Children of Israel were armed when they went up from Egypt."[3]

Justice Scalia, author of *Heller*

1. The Second Amendment Cases. The Second Amendment has become more pertinent because of *District of Columbia v. Heller*, 128 S. Ct. 2783 (2008), where the Supreme Court for the first time recognized the individual's limited right to bear arms. This caused quite a stir in academia. *See, e.g.,* Douglas G. Smith, *The Second Amendment and the Supreme Court*, 6 Geo. J. L. & Pub. Pol'y 591 (2008) (supporting the Court's individual right reading); Jonathan D. Marshall, *Symposium Introduction: District of Columbia v. Heller*, 59 Syracuse L. Rev. 165 (2008); Maxine Burkett, *Much Ado About . . . Something Else: D.C. v. Heller, the Racialized Mythology of the Second Amendment, and Gun Policy Reform*, 12 J. Gender Race & Just. 57 (2008).

Before *Heller*, only the Fifth Circuit had done so, in *United States v. Emerson*, 270 F.3d 203, 218–20 (5th Cir. 2001). In *Silveira v. Lockyer*, 312 F.3d 1052, 1060 (9th Cir. 2002), the Ninth Circuit divided Second Amendment scholarship into the collective rights view, the individual rights view, and the limited individual rights view. For an argument that the legal standard of reviewing Second Amendment cases should be strict scrutiny and that even under this highest standard of review most gun regulations would survive judicial review, *see* Adam Winkler, *Scrutinizing the Second Amendment*, 105 Mich. L. Rev. 683 (2007).

The Supreme Court had addressed the Second Amendment three times before, upholding the right to bear arms only in the context of a *"well regulated Militia"*: *United States v. Cruikshank*, 92 U.S. 542 (1876); *Presser v. Illinois*, 116 U.S. 252 (1886); *United States v. Miller*, 307 U.S. 174 (1939). *Heller*, however, was the NRA's hoped-for change. *See* John Gibeaut, *A Shot at the Second Amendment*, ABA Journal, Nov. 2007, at 50. The academic proponents of the individual right to guns are called the "insurrectionists." Much of their work has been done with healthy grants from the NRA. Bogus, *Hidden History*, at 318 and n.37 (noting that Stephen P. Halbrook received $38,569.45 during 1991–92 from the NRA to support his work writing books and articles advancing the concept that the Second Amendment provides an individual right).

2. The Second Amendment Scholarship. Much of the Second Amendment scholarship is about the scholarship itself. *See, e.g.,* Carl T. Bogus, *The History and Politics of Second Amendment Scholarship: A Primer*, 76 Chi.-Kent L. Rev. 3 (2000). "The scholarship is full of broad claims, factoids, and counterpunching," but "[t]he payoff for following the details of the argument rapidly diminishes." Tushnet at 25. Thus, "[i]t may well be that history has little to contribute to this debate." Cornell & DeDino at 491. *See also* Christopher Keleher, *The Impending Storm: The Supreme Court's Foray Into The Second Amendment Debate*, 69 Mont. L. Rev. 113 (2008) ("Pontificating on the Second Amendment has become a cottage industry.").

For even a small sampling of the Second Amendment academic debate, *compare* H. Richard Uviller & William G. Merkel, The Militia and the Right to Arms, or, How the Second Amendment Fell Silent (2002), *with* Randy E. Barnett, *Book Review Essay: Was the Right to Keep and Bear Arms Conditioned on Service in an Organized Militia?* 83 Tex. L. Rev. 237 (2004). *See also Forum: Rethinking the Second Amendment*, 25 Law & Hist. Rev. 139 (2007) (displaying the points and counterpoints of the historical argument). (The forum included Robert H. Churchill, *Gun Regulation, the Police Power, and the Right to Keep Arms in Early America: The Legal Context of the Second Amendment*, 25 Law & Hist. Rev. 139 (2007), with responses by David Thomas Konig, *Arms and the Man: What Did the Right to "Keep" Arms Mean in the Early Republic?* 25 Law & Hist. Rev. 177 (2007); William G. Merkel, *Mandatory Gun Ownership, the Militia Census of 1806, and Background Assumptions Concerning the Early American Right to Arms: A Cautious Response to Robert Churchill*, 25 Law & Hist. Rev. 187 (2007); Saul Cornell, *Early American Gun Regulation and the Second Amendment: A Closer*

These articles and books were the NRA's groundwork for *Heller*. After *Heller*, Smith & Wesson produced a commemorative model 442 .38 caliber snub-nose. You can buy one for around $600. Smith and Wesson plans to use the proceeds to fund further gun rights litigation. *See* http://www.smith-wesson.com/webapp/wcs/stores/servlet/ProductDisplay?catalogId=11101&storeId=10001&productId=78445&langId=-1&parent_category_rn=15704&isFirearm=Y.

Presumably the children of Israel "liberated" their arms from their former masters, the Egyptians. After generations of slavery they certainly would have had the right to them, as well as any number of other items, for services rendered in building the pyramids!

The key, though, is that slaves do not bear arms, only free men do.[4] For the ancient Hebrews, bearing arms out of Egypt manifested their change in status.

As we will see, guns and slavery are connected

both at the Founding and today. The message for the Second Amendment's interpretation is clear. If free men can bear arms, the Second Amendment must give the right to do so.

Look at the Evidence, 25 LAW & HIST. REV. 197 (2007), and Churchill's response at Robert H. Churchill, *Once More Unto the Breach, Dear Friends*, 25 LAW & HIST. REV. 205 (2007).) *See also* George A. Mocsary, Note, *Explaining Away the Obvious: The Infeasibility of Characterizing the Second Amendment as a Nonindividual Right*, 76 FORDHAM L. REV. 2113 (2008) (for a twist on the debate, this article examines how many historical points each side must explain away, concluding that the individual right prevails). *But see* Wills (critiquing work of the five most prolific "insurrectionists"—Robert J. Cottrol, Stephen P. Halbrook, Don B. Kates, Joyce Lee Malcom, and Robert Shalhope—and arguing that "*it is the quality of their arguments that makes them hard to take seriously*"). More recently, *see* Paul Finkelman, *It Really Was About a Well Regulated Militia*, 59 SYRACUSE L. REV. 267 (2008).

For an early exposition of the insurrectionist theory, *see* Stephen P. Halbrook, *To Keep and Bear Their Private Arms: The Adoption of the Second Amendment, 1787–1791*, 10 N. KY. L. REV. 13 (1982); Stephen P. Halbrook, *The Right of the People or the Power of the State: Bearing Arms, Arming Militias, and the Second Amendment*, 26 VAL. U. L. REV. 131 (1991); Sanford Levinson, *The Embarrassing Second Amendment*, 99 YALE L.J. 637 (1989). Levinson calls the Second Amendment "*embarrassing*" because many who espouse an expanded concept of individual rights from other parts of the Bill of Rights also believe in gun control. For an early critique of insurrectionist theory, *see* Dennis A. Henigan, *Arms, Anarchy and the Second Amendment*, 26 VAL. U. L. REV. 107 (1991).

---

4. "*For most of human history, a distinctive feature of a free man is that he possesses arms, and a distinctive feature of a slave is that he does not . . . .*" Kopel at 24.

Paul Newman's character, Captain Ari Ben Canaan, in EXODUS (United Artists 1960), a movie about the beginning of modern Israel, knew this.

See Stephen P. Halbrook, "*Arms in the Hands of Jews Are a Danger to Public Safety*": *Nazism, Firearm Registration, and the Night of the Broken Glass*, 21 ST. THOMAS L. REV. 109 (2009), arguing that the gun registration laws of the "liberal" Weimar Republic in Germany made it easier for the Nazi to later disarm German Jews.

Exodus refugee ship in 1947

3. *Exodus* 13:18, *quoted in* David B. Kopel, *The Torah and Self-Defense*, 109 PENN. ST. L. REV. 17, 24 (2004). Kopel also notes other translations that convey the same meaning, including the American Standard Version "*and the children of Israel went up armed.*" Kopel at 24 n.32.

Exodus (Greek for "departure"), the second book of the Jewish Torah and Christian Old Testament, tells how Moses led the Israelites out of Egypt. Moses gave the Israelites the Ten Commandments. According to tradition, Moses wrote *Exodus* and the other four books of the Torah, which consists of *Genesis*, *Exodus*, *Leviticus*, *Numbers*, and *Deuteronomy*.

THE TEN COMMANDMENTS (Paramount Pictures 1956), directed by Cecil B. DeMille, starred Yul Brynner and Charlton Heston before his PLANET OF THE APES and NRA days.

The Ancient World: Hoplites, Legionnaires, and Democracy: The Roman poet Virgil began THE AENEID (or, in Latin, *Aeneis*) with "*Arma virumque cano*" "*I sing of arms and the man.*"[1]

For the ancient Greeks and Romans of the republic, bearing arms in defense of the city was central to citizenship.[2]

Arms and armor defined the man. The Greeks had the ILIAD's heroic images of bearing arms. When Achilles killed Hector, he stripped him of his arms and thus his symbolic identity.[3]

For Aristotle, possessing arms was the mark of a free citizen:

"*[T]he defense forces are the most sovereign body under this constitution,*

---

1. VIRGIL, THE AENEID, line 1, *quoted in* WILTSHIRE at 138. Virgil made up the "legend" of Aeneas on a commission from Caesar Augustus, who wanted to "class up" Rome's origins. The Mediterranean Greco-Roman culture already had a legend about Aeneas, a character in Homer's ILIAD. Virgil forged the disconnected tales of Aeneas's wanderings into Rome's foundation myth, linking it to the Trojan legend while also glorifying Roman virtues and legitimizing Augustus's Julio-Claudian dynasty. Several centuries later, Dante, in THE INFERNO, has Virgil do duty as tour guide of hell.

Aeneas flees the burning Troy, with his father on his back, to eventually found Rome

Virgil guiding Dante through Hell

4. ARISTOTLE, POLITICS, *quoted in* WILTSHIRE at 136.

Plato and Aristotle from Raphael's *The School of Athens*

5. WILTSHIRE at 135. The Framers of the Constitution shared Plato's fears, which is why we today do not live in a direct democracy but a republic.

Two and a half millennia after Plato, Roscoe Pound (1870–1964), legal scholar and dean of Harvard Law School (1916–36), voiced the similar concern that "*[i]n the urban industrial society of today a general right to bear efficient arms so as to be enabled to resist oppression by the government would mean that gangs could exercise an extralegal rule which would defeat the whole Bill of Rights.*" ROSCOE POUND, THE DEVELOPMENT OF CONSTITUTIONAL GUARANTEES OF LIBERTY 91 (1957).

2. Our very word "citizenship" derives from "city." WEBSTER'S NEW INTERNATIONAL DICTIONARY OF THE ENGLISH LANGUAGE 491 (2d ed. 1942); WILTSHIRE at 134.

3. Achilles's triumph over Hector and the display of his armor and stripped body before the walls of Troy. Brad Pitt was Achilles in TROY (Warner Brothers 2004)

6. Hoplites were primarily spear men fighting in a phalanx (plural is "phalanxes" or "phalanges"), a rectangular formation of heavy infantry. "Phalanx" derives from the Greek "*phalangos*" ("finger"), which is where we get phalanx bones in the hands and feet. Each man in a phalanx was like a finger in the hand to hit the enemy.
The Arms: The Roman Sword. Roman legions also generally fought in a phalanx but used the sword ("*gladius*") as their main weapon, which came from Spain ("*gladius Hispaniensis*"). A gladiator is named for the *gladius* he wielded.

Greek hoplite

Greek phalanx

and those who possess arms are the persons who enjoy constitutional rights."[4]

Plato, conversely, had a much more conservative, and undemocratic, view of bearing arms. He feared the power of the rabble. For him an armed citizenry was a threat to the oligarchic government he preferred.[5]

The Greek citizen-soldier was a "hoplite" (from his shield, the "*hoplon*"), meaning an armored and armed man.[6]

The citizen equipped himself. By definition, a hoplite was one who could afford the armor, accepted the duty of risking his life to defend his state, and thus had a political voice.[7]

The Greeks and Romans lacked our concept of individual and inalienable rights.[8]

Poster for SPARTACUS (Universal Pictures, 1960) showing the Roman gladius

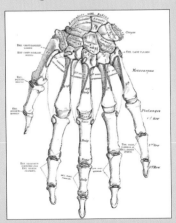

A Roman *gladius*

7. The word "politics" derives from "*polis*," the Greek word for "city," "city-state," "citizenship," or "citizens." Other English derivations include "policy," "polity," and "police." WEBSTER'S at 1909. This concept of accepting the duties of citizenship in return for a political voice reaches well into our time and, for instance, is a key theme of the film GLORY (Tri-Star Pictures 1989). The film depicts the 54th Massachusetts regiment, with its commander, Robert Gould Shaw, and its assault on Fort Wagner, South Carolina, in 1863. One of the key scenes has Morgan Freeman's character, John Rawlings, slapping Denzel Washington's character, Trip, and stating, "*There ain't no niggers here!*" Rather, they are men with rights and a voice earned on the battlefield. As the very racist Union General William Tecumseh Sherman noted, "*when the fight is over, the hand that drops the musket cannot be denied the ballot.*" *Quoted in* Pamela S. Karlan, *Ballots and Bullets: The Exceptional History of the Right to Vote*, 71 U. CIN. L. REV. 1345, 1349 (2003), *citing* ALEXANDER KEYSSAR, THE RIGHT TO VOTE: THE CONTESTED HISTORY OF DEMOCRACY IN THE UNITED STATES 88 (2000).

Indeed, Lincoln's Emancipation Proclamation both proclaimed Southern slaves' freedom and issued a call to arms. "*I do order and declare that all persons held as slaves . . . are, and henceforward shall be free . . . [a]nd I further declare and make known, that such persons of suitable condition will be received into the armed service of the United States to garrison forts, positions, stations, and other places, and to man vessels of all sorts in said service.*" President Abraham Lincoln, The Emancipation Proclamation (Jan. 1, 1863), *available at* http://avalon.law.yale.edu/19th_century/emancipa.asp.

Blacks, however, fought in the Revolution in units, including the 1st Rhode Island Regiment. In 1775 Washington came north and wrote another general, "*We have some Negroes, but I look upon them in general [as] equally serviceable with other men . . . . [M]any of them have proved themselves brave.*" *Quoted in* RICHARD BROOKHISER, WHAT WOULD THE FOUNDERS DO?: OUR QUESTIONS, THEIR ANSWERS 171 (2006).

Assault on Fort Wagner and Robert Gould Shaw's death

The Shaw/54th Memorial, Boston Commons

A 1780 drawing of American soldiers from the Yorktown campaign shows (*far left*) **a black infantryman from the 1st Rhode Island Regiment**

8. *See generally* WILTSHIRE ch. 1.

The Greeks especially viewed their rights not as inherent to themselves but as arising from the context of their *polis* (city-state).[1] For this reason, the institution of slavery, widespread in "democratic" Athens and "republican" Rome, was not an intellectual problem. If your rights came from your status in the *polis* (or later from Roman citizenship), then too bad if you happened to be a slave![2]

Thus our modern debate on whether we have an individual or collective right to bear arms would not have had much meaning to an ancient Greek or Roman. A rich Roman, for instance, would have had no restriction on the arms he could buy and, indeed, could raise his own legion if he could afford it.[3] Indeed, Romans had a much broader concept than we do of what was private law, the *res privada*, in which the state or government had no interest, as opposed to subjects of public law or regulation, the *res publica*.[4]

Under this legal framework, a Greek or Roman could have any weapon he could afford without regulation, but his concept of bearing arms was decidedly collective, in the context of his city—be it Athens, Sparta, or Rome.[5]

---

1. The Athenian practice of ostracism exemplifies that individual rights had context for Greeks only in the *polis*. Ostracism occurred when the assembly voted to expel a citizen from the city for ten years. (This would have been the ancient Greek version of a "time-out"). This often defused confrontations between political rivals or expelled anyone who had the potential to become a tyrant. Although technically not a criminal punishment, ostracism stripped a  man of his political identity. Moreover, if the person returned before his ten years without having been recalled, the penalty was death. "Ostracism" comes from "*ostraka*," the pieces of broken pottery used as voting tokens. Voters would write the name of the person on the pottery, and 6,000 pieces meant ostracism. Paper in the form of papyrus from Egypt was far too expensive for such a use. Of course, this practice is the basis for our modern verb "ostracize."

2. *See* Wiltshire at 114, 122, 166 (discussing slavery in both Greece and Rome). War captives became slaves, like the mythical Andromache, Hector's wife, after the Trojan War.

Our word "slave" comes from the Middle English "*sclave*," from the Old French "*esclave*," from Medieval Latin "*sclavus*" and ultimately from the Byzantine Greek "*sklabos*" (from "*sklabenoi*") meaning "Slavic people." This is because the Vikings had enslaved many Slavic peoples from Eastern and Central Europe and sold them to the Byzantine Empire. Before the tenth century other words meant slave, such as the old Latin word "*servus*," the basis of the word "serf."

3. Marcus Licinius Crassus was one of the wealthiest men to ever live and raised his own legion to defeat Spartacus. One of the ways he got wealthy was by owning the only fire department in Rome. He would send it to a burning building but would only have his men put out the fire if the owner sold it to him cheap. Crassus is where we get the English word "crass" for a tasteless display of wealth, from the Latin "*crassus*" ("thick," "solid," "fat," or physical and peasant-like). WEBSTER'S at 619. Marcus Licinius probably descended from prosperous farm folk.

6. *See* Konig, *Arms and the Man*. The iconic Minuteman with his hand on the plow but ready to stand his ground at Concord in 1775.

4. Our word "republic" actually comes from the Latin "*res publica*" ("public thing" or "public matter").

Laurence Olivier as Crassus

5. The word "militia" comes from the Latin "*miles*" ("soldier"), which is also the origin of the word "mile" for the standard distance to measure a Roman soldier's (legionary) march.

Like the AENEID'S linking "*arms and the man*" to Rome's national origins, we Americans also link bearing arms with our national origins.[6] But, ironically, the Roman example was the Founders' greatest fear. The legions of standing armies and their generals destroyed the Roman Republic and constitution.[7] Men like James Madison, Thomas Jefferson, John Adams, and even George Washington feared this. They put faith in the militia as a check on standing armies.[8]

But as for a "*right*" to bear arms, only centuries after the Greeks and Romans would individuals claim such a right.

Arms in Medieval England: The Anglo-Saxons were a militia society; the "*fyrd*" referred to all able-bodied men providing for defense. These men provided their own weapons and provisions but only had to serve locally for a short period, to allow them to plant in the spring and harvest in the fall. The *fyrd* goes back to at least the seventh century, when Alfred the Great developed the system.[9]

---

7. See Wiltshire at 139. On January 10, 49 BC Julius Caesar crossed the Rubicon River in northern Italy with a legion. The Rubicon was the Roman Constitution's boundary that a general could not legally cross with an army. When he crossed the river he reportedly quoted the Athenian playwright Menander, saying "*alea iacta est,*" "the die is cast." This began the Roman civil war that Julius eventually won. But in 40 BC, senators, including Brutus, who wanted to restore the Constitution, assassinated Caesar in the senate chamber. This started another civil war that Caesar's nephew Augustus eventually won, making himself the first Roman emperor. For a brief discussion of the Roman Constitution, *see* Scott D. Gerber, *The Court, the Constitution, and the History of Ideas*, 61 VAND. L. REV. 1067, 1094–99 (2008).

Although Julius was assassinated, the "Caesar cut" hairstyle is named for him, which is odd because Julius Caesar was bald by age 30. The Caesar cut is also known as the "Clooney cut" after George Clooney. Although the Caesar cut was named for Julius Caesar, the Caesar salad was not. An Italian born Mexican named Cesare Cardini had a restaurant in Tijuana, Mexico, during prohibition. He supposedly invented the salad on July 4, 1924, when he was running out of food and used what was at hand to make the Caesar salad. He added the dramatic flair of the table-side tossing "by the chef." The Caesar salad is romaine lettuce and croutons dressed with Parmesan cheese, lemon juice, olive oil, egg, Worcestershire sauce, anchovies, and black pepper.

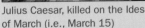
Julius Caesar, killed on the Ides of March (i.e., March 15)

Caesar salad

8. James Madison in THE FEDERALIST No. 46 wrote:

"*Let a regular army, fully equal to the resources of the country, be formed; and let it be entirely at the devotion of the federal government; still it would not be going too far to say, that the State governments, with the people on their side, would be able to repel the danger. The highest number to which, according to the best computation, a standing army can be carried in any country, does not exceed one hundredth part of the whole number of souls; or one twenty-fifth part of the number able to bear arms. This proportion would not yield, in the United States, an army of more than twenty-five or thirty thousand men. To these would be opposed a militia amounting to near half a million of citizens with arms in their hands, officered by men chosen from among themselves, fighting for their common liberties, and united and conducted by governments possessing their affections and confidence. It may well be doubted, whether a militia thus circumstanced could ever be conquered by such a proportion of regular troops. Those who are best acquainted with the last successful resistance of this country against the British arms, will be most inclined to deny the possibility of it. Besides the advantage of being armed, which the Americans possess over the people of almost every other nation, the existence of subordinate governments, to which the people are attached, and by which the militia officers are appointed, forms a barrier against the enterprises of ambition, more insurmountable than any which a simple government of any form can admit of.*"

For a further discussion of the Framers' fear of standing armies, *see* **Chapter 3: The Third Amendment: Don't Count It Out Yet!** *See also* WILTSHIRE at 132.

9. As William Blackstone noted, "*[i]t seems universally agreed by historians, that King Alfred first settled a national militia in this kingdom, and by his prudent discipline made all the subjects of his dominion soldiers . . . .*" 1 WILLIAM BLACKSTONE, COMMENTARIES *409, *quoted in* William S. Fields & David T. Hardy, *The Third Amendment and the Issue of the Maintenance of Standing Armies: A Legal History*, 35 AM. J. LEGAL HIST. 393, 396 (1991).

The only professional soldiers were the *"housecarls"* who the kings or great lords equipped and supported.[1] They took an individual oath to the lord.

In 1066 William the Bastard (later William the Conqueror) invaded England and won the kingdom. William brought with him two weapon systems that the Anglo-Saxons lacked: mounted knights and archers. The Anglo-Saxons did not allow common people to have bows and arrows. They were only for nobles (called *"thanes"*) for sport hunting.[2] This was one of William's advantages at Hastings, and he won the battle after Harold got an arrow in the eye.[3]

With William came Norman feudalism, a very different system of military organization from the Anglo-Saxon *fyrd* and *housecarls*.[4] Rather than the personal oath, which was the basis of the Anglo-Saxon system, feudalism was a system of land tenure where everyone got land with strings attached. The landlord, called a *"knight,"* had to provide military service to the next landlord higher up. This service eventually reached the king.[5] Under feudalism everyone but the king is a renter!

---

1. *Housecarls* were household troops, personal warriors, and the bodyguard of Scandinavian lords and kings. The anglicized term comes from the Old Norse *"huskarl"* or *"huscarl"* (literally, "house man," i.e., armed man (*"churl"*) in the service of a specific house). The term later covered the lord's armed soldiers. The word entered English when Canute the Great occupied a big chunk of Anglo-Saxon England. Other variations of the word are *"ceorle,"* which is also the basis of the British place and surnames of Carlton and Charlton, meaning "the farm of the churl." The names Carl and Charles are derived from *churl* or *ceorle*. In Tolkien's fictional Middle Earth, a *"ceorl"* is a rider of Rohan.

2. DAVID HOWARTH, 1066: THE YEAR OF THE CONQUEST 105 (1977).

3. Harold gets an arrow in the eye on the Bayeux Tapestry. A modern gun rights advocate could say that it serves Harold right for agreeing to bow and arrow control.

4. William Sutton Fields, *The Third Amendment: Constitutional Protection from the Involuntary Quartering of Soldiers*, 124 MIL. L. REV. 195, 196 n.4 (1989). The *fryd* made up most of King Harold's army at the Battle of Hastings in 1066, in contrast to William's feudal army. The Battle of Hastings marked the demise of the *housecarls*. Harold's surviving *housecarls* went to Europe as mercenaries, with many arriving in Byzantium, where they joined the Varangian Guard. By the twelfth century, the Varangian Guard had so many Saxons that it was sometimes called the "English Guard."

Hagia Sofia, the jewel of Byzantine architecture

The Arms: The Danish Battle-Axe. The main weapon of the Anglo-Saxon *housecarl* was the "Danish" two-handed battle-axe. About the height of a man, it could easily cut though the chain mail armor of the day.

5. *See* **Chapter 3: The Third Amendment: Don't Count it Out Yet!** (discussing feudalism). In 1156 Henry II introduced the system of *"scutage"* (Latin for "shield"), where knights and lords bought out of military service. The king used the money, basically a tax, to hire professional soldiers. Tom W.

Modern reproduction of the battle-axe

Bell, *The Third Amendment: Forgotten but Not Gone*, 2 WM. & MARY BILL RTS. J. 117, 118–19 (1993).

6. For this reason, trial by battle in England was a Norman practice. See **Chapter 7: Trial by Jury or . . . by God!** regarding trial by battle as an antecedent of trial by jury. After trial by battle lost its validity, the practice of dueling continued among the noble class, that is, those who could bear arms. Eventually this led to the dueling code, or *"code duello,"* requiring that only "gentlemen" could kill each other in a civilized manner. *See generally* ROBERT BALDICK, THE DUEL: A HISTORY (1965). A key part of the dueling code ritual was that the challenged party chose the weapon.

The Normans sought to take arms away from the Anglo-Saxons.[6] Although this conqueror's expedient contributed to the success of Norman rule in England,[7] it also planted the seeds of future arguments for the right to bear arms. Many of the Framers, including Jefferson, believed in *"the ancient constitution,"* the notion that Anglo-Saxons lived in a sort of primitive democracy.[8] This, presumably, was the source of the *"rights of Englishmen"* in the face of despotic "Norman" kings. As modern gun enthusiasts assert, the right to bear arms is a big part of the Anglo-Saxon package.

About a century later, England's Norman rulers had changed. Or perhaps they just recognized a few things they could not stamp out.

In the 1181 Assize of Arms, King Henry II required all free male subjects to bear arms and serve in an early militia system.[9] These early militias not only defended England, they maintained domestic order.[10] The men kept night watch to confront and capture suspicious persons. Every subject had to protect the king's peace, which meant responding to the "hue and cry."[11]

The Arms: The Dueling Pistol. One special firearm was the dueling pistol, which was never a weapon of self-defense but of honor. The pistols came in a set of two, identical in reliability and accuracy. Generally they were either single-shot flintlock or percussion cap pistols using black powder and firing lead balls. Usually "the seconds" loaded the guns, and the duelists fired from between twenty and forty feet. With modern pistols, such short distances would normally assure fatality for both duelists. But dueling pistols were smoothbore, meaning they were not rifled to increase accuracy. Some guns had a secret form of rifling, called "scratch rifling," that was difficult to see with the naked eye. This is why the *code duello* allowed duelists and seconds to inspect the guns and why the party that did not supply the guns got to choose his weapon.

7. The Robin Hood stories reflect this. Robin is a Saxon, and the bad guys—the Sheriff of Nottingham and Guy of Gisbon—are Normans. Ironically, in most of the modern stories Robin and the "Merry Men" are fighting to restore King Richard I, the Lion Hearted (1157–99) to the throne, who was just as Norman as his brother the "evil" King John "Lackland." Robin Hood remains a Hollywood perennial. *See, e.g., Douglas Fairbanks as* ROBIN HOOD *(United Artists 1922).* THE ADVENTURES OF ROBIN HOOD (Warner Brothers 1938) with Errol Flynn; ROBIN HOOD: PRINCE OF THIEVES (Warner Brothers 1991) with Kevin Costner; Disney's ROBIN HOOD (Buena Vista 1973); or even Mel Brooks, who got

Little John knocking Robin off the bridge with his staff

into the act with the spoof ROBIN HOOD: MEN IN TIGHTS (20th Century Fox 1993). ROBIN HOOD (Universal Pictures 2010) reworked the story yet again.

The Arms: The Bow and Staff. Robin and the Merry Men use the bow and quarterstaff made from the trees of Sherwood Forest (usually the yew and oak, respectively). As for the bow, see note below. The **staff** or the **quarterstaff** was Little John's weapon. It may have gotten its name from the way the fighter holds it by placing his hands a "quarter" of the way on the staff. Or, because it can be a nonlethal weapon, the user can "give quarter," i.e., mercy. See **Chapter 3: The Third Amendment: Don't Count It Out Yet!** with a note on giving quarter. The fact that the wielder can use the quarterstaff nonlethally made it the weapon of choice for Xena's sidekick (and perhaps girlfriend/significant other) Gabrielle in *Xena: Warrior Princess*, an American television series (Pacific Renaissance Pictures Ltd., from September 15, 1995 to June 18, 2001) (a spinoff from *Hercules: The Legendary Journeys*). Lucy Lawless played Xena, and Renee O'Connor was Gabrielle, who spent her time helping Xena be good. The show achieved a cult following among the lesbian community despite, or perhaps because of, Xena and Gabrielle's ambiguous relationship.

8. *See* Mark DeWolfe Howe, *Juries as Judges of Criminal Law*, 52 HARV. L. REV. 582, 584 (1938–39); **Chapter 7: Trial by Jury or ... by God!**

9. On the medieval militia system, *see* Fields & Hardy at 400–01.

10. Fields & Hardy at 400 n.30; LEONARD W. LEVY, ORIGINS OF THE BILL OF RIGHTS 136 (1999).

11. LEVY at 136. The *hue and cry* (Latin *hutesium et clamor*, "a horn and shouting") was when anyone who witnessed a crime called upon all able-bodied men to help catch a criminal. The Statute of Winchester, 13 Edw. I, cc. 1, 4 (1285) (Eng.) provided that the hue and cry continued against the fugitive from town to town and county to county until the felon was caught and delivered to the sheriff. Falsely raising the hue and cry was itself a crime.

This was the precursor to the "posse."[1] The militias were much closer to police than a national guard.

Each soldier bought and maintained his own armor and weapons, which the crown periodically inspected. King Henry III, for instance, specifically required every able-bodied man between fifteen and fifty to own a weapon other than a knife,[2] and the weapon that the kings most wanted men to have was the longbow.[3]

In addition to being Robin Hood's weapon of choice, the longbow was a mainstay of English armies, especially during the Hundred Years' War.[4] The English won the battles of Crecy (1346),[5] Poitiers (1356), and most famously

1. "*Posse comitatus*" (Latin for "the power of the county") referred to the county sheriff's authority to conscript any able-bodied man over the age of fifteen to help him keep the peace or pursue a felon. The sheriff's specific power to conscript men into an ad hoc militia distinguishes the *posse comitatus* from the older "hue and cry." In the earlier medieval period the term was "*pro toto posse suo*" invoking the power of every able-bodied man to apprehend the accused. *See* Danny Danziger & John Gillingham, 1215: The Year of Magna Carta 176 (2003). This is the posse in Western books and movies. *See e.g.*, Posse (Paramount Pictures 1975).

2. Levy at 136.

4. Robin Hood shooting his longbow.
 The Hundred Years' War (in French, *Guerre de Cent Ans*) lasted from 1337 to 1453 between the Houses of Valois and Plantagenet (Anjou) for the French throne. The conflict lasted 116 years, but taking into account periods of peace, the actual duration of the war was 81 years. The Plantagenets eventually lost, but still claimed the French throne, which is why the Royal coat of arms of the English monarchs such as Henry V had the French fleur-de-lis.

3. After all, it was a lucky shot from a Norman archer that got Anglo-Saxon Harold in the eye to end the Battle of Hastings in William's favor.
 The **English longbow**, or the Welsh longbow, was about 6 feet 6 inches (2.0 meters) long and made from the English yew tree. *See generally* Robert Hardy, Longbow: A Social and Military History (1976). Although rightly famous as a weapon in English armies and for hunting, it was not as powerful for its size as the Asian composite bow, generally made from horn, sinew, and wood. Sinew and horn store more energy than wood for the same length of bow, making the composite bow particularly good for mounted archery. The relative merits of each type of bow remain a subject of controversy among archers.

Harold gets it in the eye at Hastings

Composite bow

English longbow

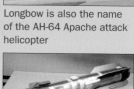

Mounted Mongol archers

Longbow is also the name of the AH-64 Apache attack helicopter

There is also the AGM-114L Longbow Hellfire, an air-to-ground missile

A Dakota Longbow T-76 sniper rifle

5. The Battle of Crécy, with English longbowmen driving away French crossbowmen. Note the French fleur-de-lis standards on the left and the English lions and fleur-de-lis standard on the right.

Agincourt (1415) because of their archers.

Agincourt took on legendary status in English history. It was the focal point of Shakespeare's HENRY V.[6]

The myth of the common man with his common longbow (like Robin Hood) winning at Agincourt is a precursor for the common man's right to bear arms.[7]

Agincourt was only one

battle in the Hundred Years' War, a dynastic struggle for the French throne—hardly a centerpiece of democracy![8] But the image of the bow as the common Englishman's weapon remained fixed.[9]

---

6. The Battle of Agincourt, on Friday October 25, 1415 (Saint Crispin's Day), complete with archers. This was Henry V's great victory. Shakespeare's play HENRY V always had propaganda value. Written in 1599 during Queen Elizabeth Tudor's reign, its hero is her ancestor King Henry (a Lancaster and Tudor ancestor). Laurence Olivier's HENRY V (Eagle-Lion Distributors Ltd. 1944) version was a rouser for Britons fighting World War II. Kenneth Branagh's 1989 HENRY V (Renaissance Films 1989) version showed a darker Henry. Henry's Saint Crispin's Day speech is probably the best male bonding fest of all time:

"We few, we happy few, we band of brothers;
For he today that sheds his blood with me
Shall be my brother; be he ne'er so vile,
This day shall gentle his condition:
And gentlemen in England now a-bed
Shall think themselves accursed they were not here,
And hold their manhoods cheap whiles any speaks
That fought with us upon Saint Crispin's day."

The line, "We band of brothers ..." provides the title for Stephen Ambrose's book BAND OF BROTHERS (1992) and the HBO miniseries (2001) of the same name.

7. Not to mention that it allowed the common Englishman to give French nobility the "bowfinger"! The end of the arrow is the "fletching" or bird feathers, which stabilizes the arrow in flight, with the third feather being the "cock" feather. This led to the gesture of the "bird," "flipping the bird," "flipping someone off," "shooting a bird," "flying the bird," the "two-fingered salute," or "bowfinger," commonly performed in England by flicking the "V" upwards from wrist or elbow. The legend (that many historians dispute but is too good to pass up here!) is that this "V" sign was the English bowmen's gesture at Agincourt after hearing that the French planned to cut off their arrow-shooting fingers. JULIET BARKER, AGINCOURT: HENRY V AND THE BATTLE THAT MADE ENGLAND 284 (2006) (attributing the story to King Henry V's inventing this before the Battle of Agincourt to motivate his archers). The English instead won against the odds, showing off their intact "two-fingered salute." The movie BOWFINGER (Universal Pictures 1999) was a spoof of Hollywood with the insult worked into the title.

Arrow fletching with a green "cock" feather

Churchill giving the traditional English obscenity. But turning it around, it became his "V for victory" sign. The connection between the two shows his message of defiance.

The "V for victory" sign eventually became the ubiquitous "peace" sign displayed by the diverse likes of John Lennon and Richard Nixon (who may have been giving America the bowfinger!). The American "**flipping** the bird" is a simplified version of the English "two-fingered salute."

8. Joan of Arc at the Siege of Orléans. The French also claimed the common touch. Joan was a common girl (supposedly) who in 1429 convinced the heir to the French throne to send her to fight, saying God told her to drive out the English. The English had her killed  as a heretic, but the French made her a saint. Joan is the story behind the movie THE MESSENGER: THE STORY OF JOAN OF ARC (Columbia Pictures 1999).

9. As have many common expressions related to archery, such as being "straight as an arrow" from the sixteenth century, "bolt upright" from the fourteenth century (another name for an arrow is a "bolt," though it usually refers to a crossbow projectile), "point blank," "high strung," and "to brace oneself." E.G. HEATH, A HISTORY OF TARGET ARCHERY 25 (1973). To miss the mark in archery is to "sin," from the Old English "synn."

Although a common man can make a bow, it takes practice to master. King Edward I (1272–1307) banned all sports but archery, to make the English effective longbowmen.[1] And though the bow was relatively easy to make, arrow making was its own special craft called "fletching" and the artisans who made the arrows were "fletchers."[2]

In fact, there was so much archery practice going on that it changed homicide law. For the early medieval period, a person's intent in killing someone did not matter. The killer owed the victim's family the "*wergild*" ("man price"), regardless of whether the death was an accident or murder.

Archery accidents were among the most common causes of unintentional slaying in Medieval England.[3] It would have been unseemly for the king to encourage archery and then hold men responsible for the arrow deflecting off a tree and killing someone.[4] Thus, by the thirteenth century, the king's courts started to recognize that

1. This was in the Assize of Arms of 1252. Edward I is the "father of the military longbow," HARDY at 41, and is the king in BRAVEHEART (Paramount Pictures 1995), played by Patrick McGoohan.

Edward I

Edward I's successors followed the same policy. Edward II in his ban singled out soccer, ordering that, "*We command and forbid on behalf of the King, on pain of imprisonment, such game to be used.*" RICK BEYER, THE GREATEST STORIES NEVER TOLD 14–15 (2003). In 1366, King Edward III allegedly outlawed bowling because his troops were skipping archery practice. *See* Mort Luby, Jr., *The History of Bowling*, BOWLERS JOURNAL 70 (1983). An archer practices archery, but an expert is a "toxophilite," from the Greek "*toxon*" for bow.

W.F. PATERSON, NCYCLOPAEDIA OF ARCHERY 106 (1984). The Boy Scouts still offer a merit badge in archery. *See* http://www.scouting.org/ (last visited Oct. 8, 2008).

2. "Fletching" is related to the French "*flèche*" ("arrow") from Old French and ultimately the Frankish "*fliukka*." WEBSTER'S at 966. The English surnames Fletch and Fletcher derive from this term, meaning "one who fletches," that is, makes arrows.

The *Fletcher* class destroyers (named for Admiral Frank F. Fletcher) were built between 1942 and 1944

The movie FLETCH (Universal Pictures 1985) is about a wisecracking investigative newspaper reporter, Irwin M. Fletcher (Chevy Chase), and was followed by the sequel FLETCH LIVES (1989).

Other English surnames related to archery include Archer, Arrowsmith, Bowman, Bowyer, Stringer, and even Abbott, an abbreviated form of "at the butts" ("butts" were originally the earth mounds behind the archery practice target but now also refer to the straw targets themselves). HEATH at 25; PATERSON at 33–35. Bowman is the character in 2001: A SPACE ODYSSEY (MGM 1968) that beats Hal, the homicidal computer. There is also Arrowsmith, with its alternative spelling "Aerosmith," the American rock band. Aerosmith's front man is Steven Tyler (sometimes known as the Demon of Screamin') who fathered Liv Tyler, who went on to play in INVENTING THE ABBOTTS (20th Century Fox 1997). It all goes back to archery!

3. Thomas A. Green, *The Jury and the English Law of Homicide, 1200–1600*, 74 MICH. L. REV. 414, 446 (1976). This gave us the origins of degrees of homicide, such as first and second degree murder and voluntary and involuntary manslaughter.

Of course, some archery "accidents" were not accidents at all. King William II, known as Rufus (for his red completion), was William the Conqueror's second son. He died "by accident" from a stray arrow while hunting in the forest. His younger brother, Henry, conveniently became king.

Death of King William II (Rufus)

not all homicides were the same, and that the killer's intent mattered (i.e., the "*mens rea*").

In many ways, the kings' support of archery reflected the attitude toward bearing arms in general. Each able-bodied man was expected to arm himself for the common defense in militia service or to be a source of recruits for military service.[5] The kings wanted men they could mold into an army, not the old feudal levy or Anglo-Saxon *fyrd*.[6] Thus, bearing arms was as much a tax as a privilege.

But a modern analogy to the Second Amendment's right to bear arms would be a strain. Today the government does not require every able-bodied person to keep and maintain an effective military weapon, such as an M16 rifle.[7] In fact, the government makes it illegal,[8] and even the National Rifle Association does not object.[9]

What caused this change in government attitude to arms and citizens?

---

4. Henry I (1100–35) passed a law that absolved an archer of homicide if he accidentally killed someone while practicing. This was the first official sign of kings encouraging archery. HEATH at 20–21.

5. By the Tudor period, government expected all men to meet in the churchyard after the Sunday service to practice archery and drill. COLIN RHYS LOVELL, ENGLISH CONSTITUTIONAL AND LEGAL HISTORY 271 (1962).

6. See HARDY at 44.

8. See generally STEPHEN P. HALBROOK, FIREARMS LAW DESKBOOK: FEDERAL AND STATE CRIMINAL PRACTICE (2008 ed.).

 **7.** The **M16** rifle, including the pictured M16/A1/A2/A3/A4 versions, has been the United States military's primary rifle since 1964. It followed the **M14**.

One can still buy the semi-automatic **AR-15** (Armalite Model 15), patterned after the fully automatic M16. In fact, the AR-15 was the original name for what became the military's M16. Also, black market conversion kits can turn the AR-15 into a full automatic assault rifle.

AR-15 with accessories

The **Springfield M1903**, formally the **United States Rifle, Caliber .30, Model 1903**, was an American magazine-fed, bolt-action rifle used primarily during the first half of the twentieth century.

9. But there is still the Civilian Marksmanship Program (CMP) promoting firearm safety training and rifle practice for all qualified U.S. citizens. Congress created the CMP in 1903 to provide civilians the chance to practice marksmanship so they would be ready to later

 serve in the military—the same purpose of the English kings with archery. From 1916 until 1996 the Army administered the CMP. The National Defense Authorization Act for Fiscal Year 1996 (36 U.S.C. §§ 40701–40733) created the Corporation for the Promotion of Rifle Practice & Firearms Safety, Inc. (CPRPFS) to take over the CMP. See the CMP website, http://www.odcmp.com/ (last visited Oct. 8, 2008).

The **M1 Garand**, formally the **United States Rifle, Caliber .30, M1**, in 1936 replaced the M1903 and was the first semi-automatic rifle generally issued to the infantry of any nation. (The military still used the M1903 as a sniper rifle.) This was the main rifle of World War II and Korea. The M1 Garand was Clint Eastwood's rifle in GRAN TORINO (Warner Brothers 2008)

In 1957 the **M14** in turn replaced the M1.

EARLY MODERN ARMS AND CHANGES IN THE MILITIA

Guns. Guns changed everything.[1]

Throughout medieval times, the kings wanted people to shoot the longbow. But the gun signaled the end of the bow as a military weapon.[2]

A gun is a relatively easy thing to use and train a man to fire.[3]

And a gun does not have to be very good by modern standards to be a more effective weapon than the bow and arrow.[4] With a bit of inventiveness, an unskilled shooter with even an early gun can be very deadly.[5]

The advent of guns also coincided with changes in the English militia system.

---

1. "Point blank" used to mean a shot by archers in the sixteenth century who aimed the arrow at the small white, or blank, bull's-eye in the center of the target. Indeed, the Spanish word for "target" and "white" is *blanco.* Firearms have considerably more destructive power than arrows and thus the term "point blank" is now synonymous for direct and uncompromising rejection or blunt frankness as in "point-blank" refusal or "point-blank denial." Robert Hendrickson, QPB Encyclopedia of Word and Phrase Origins 574 (2d ed. 2004).

2. Unless, of course, you are John James Rambo, a troubled Vietnam vet and Green Beret skilled in survival and combat. With slogans like *"Heroes never die . . . They just reload,"* Rambo again made the bow one cool way to kill people. His name alone does it, "Ram-Bow." Along with his personal missile launcher, the bow is a complete part of the action figure!
The bow was also the weapon of choice for Burt Reynolds and Jon Voight in the movie Deliverance (Warner Brothers 1972), based on the James Dickey novel of the same name. In 2008, the Library of Congress selected Deliverance for preservation in the U.S. National Film Registry for being *"culturally, historically, or aesthetically significant."*

Image by Helen Koop

3. Whether the Chinese get the credit for inventing guns and gunpowder is still a subject of debate. See, e.g., Dudley Pope, Guns 17 (1965) (*"We do not know for certain who first discovered gunpowder; who invented the first gun; and when and where it was first used."*). The academic consensus, though, is that Chinese alchemists searching for an elixir of immortality discovered gunpowder in the ninth century AD. But instead of an elixir of immortality, they found an elixir of death.
   Gunpowder is sulfur, charcoal, and potassium nitrate (saltpetre or saltpeter), which burns rapidly, producing volumes of hot solids and gases that can propel projectiles. This formula is also called "**black powder**" and is different from modern **smokeless powder**, the name given to a number of propellants used in firearms and artillery that are more powerful and produce negligible smoke. They also leave fewer residues in the gun, allowing for modern semi- and fully automatic firearms, which would otherwise jam from the particles of older black powder.
   For those of us who grew up "Trekkie," "Arena" (NBC television broadcast January 19, 1967) is the *Star Trek* classic episode where Kirk beats the Gorn by blasting him with a bit of homemade gunpowder in a palm tree trunk cannon. Although the Gorn is one of the cheesier Star Trek monsters, it still scared the heck out me when I was a little kid.

A gun from the Yuan (Mongol) Dynasty (1271–1368)

4. The earliest guns were simple barrels with a small hole at the end to place a lit match to shoot (called the flash pan), much like a cannon. This led to the **Matchlock**, the first mechanism or "lock," allowing the shooter to pull a lever or trigger while holding onto the gun with both hands and to keep both eyes on the target. A variation of the Matchlock was the **arquebus**, from Dutch "*haakbus,*" ("hook gun").
   Wheel-lock (c. 1500) was a firing mechanism of a rotating steel wheel to provide ignition. A wheel lock uses the same principle as a Bic lighter.
   The **Snaphance** (1560s), a variation of the **Snaplock**, used a flint to hit metal, causing hot metal shavings to ignite the powder. This led to the **Flintlock** (c. 1600), which worked generally the same as the snaplock but with safety and reliability features. Flintlocks continued in common use for over two centuries, until the mid nineteenth century. "**Lock**

A Wheel-lock pistol

From the end of the 1500s, the English divided the militia into the "general muster" of all able-bodied men from sixteen to sixty and a smaller "trained band" of the most reliable men (socially, politically, and religiously) for actual military training. The men of property in the community had the duty to arm the small group of reliable men.[6] Thus, unlike the Second Amendment's articulation of a "*right . . . to keep and bear Arms,*" those trusted few who bore the arms were not the ones who necessarily kept them.

This relationship infused the whole system with issues of social class and power. In 1671, for example, Parliament drastically raised the property qualifications for legally possessing firearms, which disarmed all but the very wealthy.[7]

---

time" is the time it takes for the gun to fire after the trigger is pulled. Hawkeye's long rifle was a flintlock.

The flintlock's long use has left us several expressions:

"*Lock, stock, and barrel*" refers to the flintlock's three main parts. During the American Revolution, the French shipped muskets to America in three parts—lock, stock, and barrel—to be assembled in America.

"*Going off half-cocked*" comes from the half-cock position of the hammer to open up the flash pan to put in priming gunpowder. After that the shooter "cocked" the hammer full for firing.

"*Flash in the pan*" happened when the gunpowder in the priming pan went off, causing noise and smoke without igniting the main charge in the gun barrel and launching the ball.

Matchlock

Flintlock

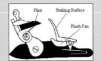

Flintlock diagram

6. Robert H. Churchill, *Gun Regulation* at 144–45 (2007) (outlining the differences between the militia traditions of England and America).

5. And a sniper is murderous. "Sniper" gets its name from the snipe, a wary, quick bird that hunters could not kill with a bow and arrow. In the sixteenth century hunters began to use guns. The bird was still hard to kill unless the hunter hid and patiently waited for a good shot. Thus, "sniper" is a hidden marksman. HENDRICKSON at 671. See SNIPER (TriStar Pictures 1993), followed by SNIPER 2 (2002) and SNIPER 3 (2004).

7. LEVY at 136.

Parliament granted the crown the power to disarm any person "*dangerous to the peace of the Kingdom.*" Parliament also enacted permanent game laws restricting gun ownership on the basis of wealth. Finally, in 1688 Parliament prohibited any Catholic "*from keeping arms unless they publicly renounced the doctrine of transubstantiation.*" Churchill, *Gun Regulation*, at 155–56 (citing An Act for Ordering the Forces in the Several Counties of this Kingdom, 13 & 14 Car. I, c. 3 (1662) (Eng.)); see also An Act for the More Effectual Preserving the Kings Person and Government, 30 Charles II, stat. 2, c. 1 (1677) (Eng.); Bogus, *Hidden History*, at 377–78. Similar prior laws limiting firearm possession included the following:

- A 1541 law prohibiting persons with incomes of less than £100 a year from owning handguns.
- In 1655 instructions issued to the militia to confiscate all arms and ammunition from strangers and to store all weapons, including those belonging to militia members themselves, in safe places.
- Measures enacted in 1659 requiring the inventorying of all arms and ammunition in private hands and the disarming of anyone of "*suspected or known disaffection*" to the government.
- The adoption of a firearm registration system in 1660.

See JOYCE LEE MALCOLM, TO KEEP AND BEAR ARMS: THE ORIGINS OF AN ANGLO-AMERICAN RIGHT 162 (1994).

Thus guns themselves became an issue, not just a weapon in an army or a hunting implement.[1]

Under the last Stuart king, James II, the question of who had the right to have the guns came to a head.

ARMS AGAINST CATHOLICS AND THEIR STUARTS

As the previous chapter outlined, the Stuarts were out of place and eventually out of time.[2]

The last of them, James II, ruled less than four years, 1685–88, and in addition to being stupid was unforgivably Catholic.[3]

Changes in technology and manufacture had increased the tension between Protestant and Catholic England. By James II's 1685 accession, guns had become more than a rich man's curiosity.[4] England was on the verge of the Industrial Revolution.[5]

The flintlock musket (or later the rifle) began to be mass produced, with interchangeable parts. Unlike a sword or bow, which takes time to learn to use effectively, a gun is relatively easy to use. Although becoming a

---

1. The Puckle Gun. The flintlock approached modern efficiency with the "**Puckle gun.**" In 1718, Puckle demonstrated his multishot gun with a preloaded revolving "cylinder" of eleven charges. A flint still ignited the charges, but it could fire sixty-three shots in seven minutes when the standard soldier's musket could at best fire three times per minute. Puckle provided two cylinders; one, intended for use against Christian enemies, fired conventional round bullets, while the second fired square bullets, for "*the Muslim Turks.*" Somehow the more damaging square bullets would convince the Turks of the "benefits of Christian civilization."

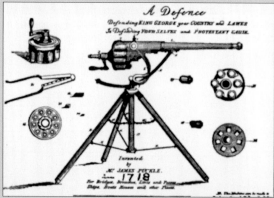

4. These pistols are beautiful and not mass produced. Only a rich man could afford such craftsmanship. This contrasts to the stark efficiency of a modern gun, such as a **Glock 29**, which despite its testosterone-inducing impressiveness is not beautiful.

2. See **Chapter 1: Of Dogma and Desire: Saying What You Believe about the First Amendment** (discussing the Stuarts and their fall).

Regarding the militia and Charles I, William Blackstone noted that the question of whether the king controlled the militia was a catalyst for the 1642 English civil war and "*the immediate cause of the fatal rupture between the king and his parliament.*" 1 WILLIAM BLACKSTONE, COMMENTARIES *412, quoted in Field & Hardy at 403 n.43.

James II

3. LOVELL at 389–90 (stating that James II "*was stupid and egocentric*").

5. The Industrial Revolution happened in the late eighteenth and early nineteenth centuries, bringing major changes in agriculture, manufacturing, and transportation. The Watt steam engine, for example, propelled the manufacture of any number of commodities, including arms. It created a

very different world from that which produced the sword. Making a sword takes time, which is part of the reason a sword can have mythic status. Guns, especially modern guns, do not have this quality.

marksman takes time and practice, in an afternoon a person could learn to effectively fire a musket.[6]

But at this very time of manufactured firearms, King James II was working to reduce all weapons in private hands, which meant mostly Protestant hands. He did so by using loyal militias to suppress and disarm political dissidents. Using the 1671 Game Act, for example, James II systematically disarmed parts of England where his Protestant enemies lived.[7]

Eventually, the Glorious Revolution of 1688 deposed James II, replacing him with his daughter, Mary Stuart, and son-in-law, William of Orange.[8] During the change of monarchy, London crowds stormed Catholic churches, and the mayor ordered the disarming of all Catholics.

When William arrived in London on December 28, 1688, and called a "convention" to work out his taking the throne as co-ruler with Mary.[9] This convention provided the basis for the English Bill of Rights, one provision of which guaranteed the right to bear arms—but only to Protestants.

Sir Bedivere casting the sword Excalibur back to the Lady of the Lake. Excalibur was King Arthur's legendary sword with magical powers.

7. *See* MALCOLM at 31–53, 103–06, *cited in* District of Columbia v. Heller, 128 S. Ct. at 2798.

9. Bogus, *Hidden History*, at 381. William technically could not call a Parliament because James II, on his way out of England, burned the writs convening Parliament in December. Parliament could not lawfully be convened unless summoned by writs impressed with the Great Seal, which James threw into the Thames River. This calling of a "convention" to work out the outlines of constitutional government set the precedent for America, culminating in the Constitutional Convention of 1789.

8. William of Orange

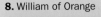

Mary Stuart

6. Indeed, gun technology has increased to the point where today any fool can load and fire a gun with devastating effect. A drive-by shooting, for instance, requires no skill at all. This reality is the main impetus for modern gun control laws.

Several video games revolve around drive-by shootings, including the *Grand Theft Auto* series, which allows the player to shoot his submachine gun out his car window.

THE DECLARATION OF RIGHTS OF 1689

As part of the deal, William recognized that Parliament made law and that he and Mary were under the law.[1] And in reaction to James's efforts to disarm Protestants, Parliament insisted on a right to bear arms:

"That the subjects which are Protestants may have arms for their defence suitable to their condition and as allowed by law."

Under this provision, Parliament defined the right to bear arms and specifically excluded Catholics. The wording makes it a poor precursor to any notion of a universal individual right to bear arms.[2] In fact, this right to bear arms was not really an individual's right but one that Parliament dispensed.[3]

Parliament then guaranteed the right of Protestants to bear arms in the context of militias.[4] Also, Parliament only guaranteed the right to bear arms *"suitable to their conditions, and as allowed by law."*[5] Parliament, thus, could (and still can) exclude all manner of persons from keeping arms and implement all manner of gun control.

The Second Amendment lacks these restrictions.

---

1. On the English Bill of Rights and Arms, see TUSHNET at 16–17.

The Declaration of Rights provided, for example, that "[t]he pretended power of suspending of laws or the execution of laws by regal authority without consent of Parliament is illegal" and that "levying money for or to the use of the crown by pretense of prerogative without grant of Parliament for longer time or in other manner than the same is or shall be granted is illegal." Quoted in Bogus, *Hidden History*, at 382–84.

2. Parliament proceeded this provision with An Act for the Better Securing the Government by Disarming Papists and Reputed Papists, 1 W. & M., c. 15 (1688) (Eng.).

American was not nearly as restrictive of the rights of Catholics to bear arms. In 1756 Virginia ordered the disarmament of all those refusing the test of allegiance set out in Parliament's 1714 Act for the Further Security of His Majesty's Person and Government, which required an oath of allegiance to the Hanoverian dynasty, Protestant succession, and against the Pope's ecclesiastical authority. However, the 1756 Virginia act exempted "*such necessary weapons as shall be allowed him by order of the justices of the peace at their court, for the defense of his house and person.*" Also, any Catholic willing to swear undivided allegiance to the sovereign still had the right to keep arms. See Churchill, *Gun Regulation*, at 157 (discussing the various acts).

3. Bogus, *Hidden History*, at 377–78 (arguing that the English Declaration of Rights did not confer an individual right to bear arms). Bogus notes that English historians emphasize that Parliament and William and Mary did not agree to any new rights but that they recognized preexisting principles. Bogus, *Hidden History*, at 379. *But see* MALCOLM at 162 (arguing that the English Bill of Rights conferred an individual right).

4. William Blackstone, writing just under one hundred years later, was to expand the right to bear arms to include Catholics: "*The fifth and last auxiliary right of the subject, that I shall at present mention, is that of having arms for their defence, suitable to their condition and degree, and such as are allowed by law. Which is also declared by the same statute I W. & M. st.2. c.2. and is indeed a public allowance, under due restrictions, of the natural right of resistance and self-preservation, when the sanctions of society and laws are found insufficient to restrain the violence of oppression.*" 1 WILLIAM BLACKSTONE, COMMENTARIES *136. Blackstone is saying that subjects have a right to own weapons as Parliament authorizes, as a check on a tyrannical king. Because the relationship has to do with protecting Parliament as the representatives of the people against the king, then this would allow all manner of gun control. Blackstone in context is tracking the 1689 DECLARATION OF RIGHTS but substituting "subjects" for "Protestants" to include Catholics. Bogus, *Hidden History*, at 398–99. Regarding Blackstone and arms, *see also* TUSHNET at 17–18; LEVY at 135.

5. See Steve Bachmann, *Starting Again with the Mayflower . . . England's Civil War and America's Bill of Rights*, 20 QUINNIPIAC L. REV. 193, 228, 229–30 (2000) (discussing the various types of persons the English intended to exclude from the right to bear arms).

ENGLISH VERSUS COLONIAL MILITIAS

At the same time the Stuarts and Protestants were struggling in England, the dynamic played out in America, though to what degree is a matter of debate.

The English brought the militia tradition to America.[6] But unlike England, most of the colonial militias consisted of all able-bodied white guys between sixteen and sixty.[7] Thus nearly every white man in America had some form of military training in a relatively large and universal militia system. Though the militia declined in England, it did not in America.[8]

Additionally, the colonial laws, unlike English laws, required every man to own his arms unless he was too poor.[9] There was little distinction, therefore, between "keeping" and "bearing" arms because a colonial militiaman usually brought his own gun to the muster.[10]

It may well have been that the average colonial militiaman did not view his gun as a right but rather as a tax.[11] Given that a colonial American did

---

6. In fact, the militia still exists, and if you are an American male reading this book you may be part of it. The United States still has a national "general" militia of all able-bodied men between seventeen and forty-five who are not members of the National Guard or Naval Militia, but it has no role in defense today. 10 U.S.C. § 311 (2006) provides:

Militia: composition and classes
(a) The militia of the United States consists of all able-bodied males at least 17 years of age and, except as provided in section 313 of title 32 [related to appointment of members in the National Guard], under 45 years of age who are, or who have made a declaration of intention to become, citizens of the United States and of female citizens of the United States who are members of the National Guard.
(b) The classes of the militia are—
(1) the organized militia, which consists of the National Guard and the Naval Militia; and
(2) the unorganized militia, which consists of the members of the militia who are not members of the National Guard or the Naval Militia.

See Fields & Hardy at 428 n.168.

8. Field & Hardy at 413–14.
The English practice at the time of the American Revolution was different. When England modernized its militia during the Seven Years' War (or what Americans call the French and Indian War) with the Militia Act of 1757, it ordered the listing of all men from eighteen to fifty to report, except public officers, teachers, clergy, mariners, and apprentices. This was probably over a million men, but only 30,000 were chosen by lot to serve in the militia for three years, and those that could provide substitutes, usually paid. This militia trained eighteen days a year and the crown provided the arms and uniforms, which the militiamen drew from central stores for training days only. Churchill, *Gun Regulation*, at 145 (citing 30 George II, c. 25 (1757) (Eng.)).
The American militias, however, were still the heirs to Cromwell's New Model Army, and this model led to the force that stood at Lexington and Concord. *See* Bachmann at 231.

7. Churchill, *Gun Regulation*, at 145–46. Generally, public officers, clergy, and certain key professionals were exempted,

but they still had to turn out for service during an alarm. The only colony that did not have a compulsory militia until the Revolution was Pennsylvania with its pacifistic Quakers. *See* **Chapter 1: Of Dogma and Desire: Saying What You Believe about the First Amendment.**

9. Churchill, *Gun Regulation*, at 147.

10. "Muster" means, in the military sense, to assemble troops or soldiers or sign them up for service. The word comes from the Latin "*monstrare*," meaning to show or display, as in the English words "demonstrate" or "remonstrate." WEBSTER'S at 1616. It is also related to the Latin word "*monstrum*," for a divine omen indicating misfortune, which is the origin of the word "monster." WEBSTER'S at 1589.

Boris Karloff as the monster in FRANKENSTEIN (Universal Pictures 1931)

11. *See* Churchill, *Gun Regulation*, at 147 (on requirements that every colonial American provide his own guns). This tax carried through to the early republic. For example, the Uniform Militia Act of 1792 provided that *"every free able-bodied male citizen of the respective states"* between eighteen and forty-five had to provide his own arms and *"[t]hat every citizen so enrolled . . . shall . . . provide himself with a good musket or firelock, a sufficient bayonet, belt, two spare flints, and a knapsack, a pouch with a box therein to contain not less than twenty-four cartridges . . . each cartridge to contain a proper quantity of powder and ball."* Quoted in LEVY at 143.

not pay taxes to maintain a police force, and Great Britain picked up the tab for the military, such requirements were not revolutionary. Thus the state could compel a man to serve in the militia, outfit himself with a weapon, and expend ammunition while bearing absolutely no legal obligation to compensate him for his expenses. This was taxation.[1]

Many an American colonial and early citizen would have been all too happy to have less of a *"right . . . to keep and bear Arms."*[2]

GUNS AND COLONIAL SLAVERY

What was the true purpose of the colonial militia?

Fighting the French and Native Americans during the French and Indian War would have been a use for them. And because there were no police except for maybe a county sheriff or constable, the militia would have had a role in assuring civil order from "insurrections." In the North there were not many insurrections, but the Southern militias'

---

1. See Saul Cornell & Nathan DeDino, *A Well Regulated Right: The Early American Origins of Gun Control*, 73 FORDHAM L. REV. 487, 496 (2004) (citing the Pennsylvania Constitution of 1776 as an example; PA. CONST. OF 1776, declaration of rights, § VIII). In addition to federal militia requirements, several state militia statutes had fairly universal requirements, such as to turn out for regular musters and be armed with certain equipment. New York, for instance, required every militia member to *"furnish and provide himself at his own expense with a good musket or firelock fit for service[,] a sufficient bayonet with a good belt, a pouch or cartouch box containing not less than sixteen cartridges . . . of powder and ball . . . and two spare flints[,] a blanket and a knapsack."* In Massachusetts, every six months, the clerk of each company made *"an exact List of [each man in the] Company, and of each Man's Equipments"* and sent it to the commanding officer of the company and regiment. *Quoted in id.* at 509–10.

2. Back to Hawkeye and the Gun Myth. It could be that most militiamen were not very good shots. See Bogus, *Hidden History*, at 341–42. Most colonial Americans lived in cites or well-settled rural farming communities. They would not have needed to be good shots. An academic debate exists on whether most colonial

Americans even had many guns outside of the militia's public magazines. *See, e.g.*, Churchill, *Gun Regulation*, at 147 n.23 outlining the scholarship. The fact remains that although Hawkeye never misses, the rest of us do.

3. Bogus, *Hidden History*, at 321 (arguing that *"[t]he Second Amendment was not enacted to provide a check on government tyranny; rather, it was written to assure the Southern states that Congress would not undermine the slave system by using its newly acquired constitutional authority over the militia to disarm the state militia and thereby destroy the South's principal instrument of slave control."*)

4. RUSSELL F. WEIGLEY, HISTORY OF THE UNITED STATES ARMY 202 (1984).
Part of this would have been to check a British war aim. During the war, a loyalist officer of the South Carolina militia urged the British to attack the Southern states because *"the instant that The Kings Troops are put in motion in those Colonies, these poor Slaves would be ready to rise upon their Rebel Masters."* Randall M. Miller, *A Backcountry Loyalist Plan to Retake Georgia and the Carolinas, 1778*, 75 S.C. HIST. MAG. 207, 213 (1974) (*quoting* letter of Moses Kirkland).

5. Virginia, South Carolina, and Georgia all had regulated slave patrols whose work had passed to the militia. Bogus, *Hidden History*, at 335. The fear of slave uprisings was ever present in the South, as the example below demonstrates.

"The Scenes which the above Plate represents are—Fig 1. A Mother entreating for the lives of her children.—2. Mr. Travis, cruelly murdered by his own Slaves.—3. Mr. Barrow, who bravely defended himself with his wife escaped.—4. A comp. of mounted Dragoons in pursuit of the Blacks."

6. North Carolina's 1741 slave code, for example, ordered that *"no slave shall go armed with gun, sword, club, or other weapon, or shall keep any such weapon."* Quoted in Churchill, *Gun Regulation*, at 148.

Putting down the Stono Rebellion

7. One such uprising was the Stono Rebellion in British South Carolina on September 9, 1739. Bogus, *Hidden History*, at 332–34. Under a literate African named Jemmy, about twenty slaves gathered at the Stono River to march to the sanctuary of Spanish Florida. Their timing may have been to avoid the September 29 effective date of the South Carolina Security Act of 1739 (which required all white males to carry arms on Sundays). They marched chanting "Liberty" and carrying a

job was to prevent slave uprisings.[3]

During the Revolutionary War, in fact, Southern states often refused to send their militias to support the war because they had to stay home for slave control.[4] Nor would the Southern colonies send arms to the Revolutionary Army because they needed their scarce guns against possible slave uprisings.[5]

This went along with disarming blacks in general, all part of enslaving them.[6] The recorded uprisings were relatively few but vivid in the minds of white Southerners.[7] Given the demographic realities, white hatred born of fear is no surprise.[8] The last thing Southern colonies wanted were armed black people or the loss of their militias as a means to control them. After all, John Locke noted that slavery

"is nothing else but the state of war continued between a lawful conqueror and a captive . . . ."[9]

"Liberty!" banner. They seized weapons and ammunition from a store at the Stono River Bridge, killing the two storekeepers. On the way, they gathered recruits, swelling their numbers to eighty. A mob of plantation owners and the mounted militia caught up with them the next day—twenty whites and forty-four slaves died in the suppression. The whites decapitated most of their prisoners and spiked their heads on every mile post from there to Charlestown. After Stono and other uprisings, South Carolina moved to penalize masters for imposing excessive work or brutal punishments and started a school to teach slaves Christianity (not, however, to learn to read and write). The Assembly also imposed a prohibitive duty on African slave importation and passed a law requiring a ratio of one white for every ten blacks on any plantation. Additionally, the Negro Act of 1740 prohibited slaves from growing their own food, assembling in groups, earning money, and learning to read.

The Southern slavers methods of putting down Stono and other rebellions were hardly original. In putting down the Spartacus revolt in 71 BC, the Romans lined the Appian Way—the main highway to Rome—with the crucified bodies of the slaves. Even earlier in antiquity, the Greek Spartans had their "helots," a slave population tied to the land to support Spartan citizens. The Spartans ritually mistreated, humiliated, and slaughtered them. Every autumn during a festival called "*crypteia*," the Spartans officially declared war on the helots, allowing any Spartan to legally kill them. A specific militia/death squad called the "*kryptes*" (recent graduates of the difficult Spartan manhood training system called the "*agoge*") did the dirty work. Generally they would pick out the strongest helots to kill to give themselves more honor—and to suppress leadership and dissent. Thucydides reports that in 425 BC the Spartans massacred two thousand helots in a carefully staged event:

"*The helots were invited by a proclamation to pick out those of their number who claimed to have most distinguished*

The Thrilling Adventure that Electrified the World!

themselves against the enemy, in order that they might receive their freedom; the object being to test them, as it was thought that the first to claim their freedom would be the most high spirited and the most apt to rebel. As many as two thousand were selected accordingly, who crowned themselves and went round the temples, rejoicing in their new freedom. The Spartans, however, soon afterwards did away with them, and no one ever knew how each of them perished."

THUCYDIDES, THE PELOPONNESIAN WAR 265 (T.E. Wick ed., 1982).

8. For example, 44 percent of Virginia's population was black. Bogus, *Hidden History*, at 326 n.73, 332 n.106, *citing* 1 BUREAU OF THE CENSUS, HISTORICAL STATISTICS OF THE UNITED STATES, COLONIAL TIMES TO 1970, at 22–36 (1976) (stating that in 1790, Virginia had total population of 692,000 people, consisting of 442,000 whites and 306,000 blacks; compared to Pennsylvania, the second largest state, with a total population of 434,000).

John Locke

9. Slavery Is War. Locke discussed slavery in *An Essay Concerning the True Original, Extent and End of Civil Government,* beginning with the observation:
"*The natural liberty of man is to be free from any superior power on earth, and not to be under the will or legislative authority of man, but to have only the law of nature for his rule.*"
Locke went on:
"*This is the perfect condition of slavery, which is nothing else but the state of war continued between a lawful conqueror and a captive, for if once compact enter between them, and make an agreement for a limited power on the one side, and obedience on the other, the state of war and slaver ceases as long as the compact endures; for, as has been said, no man can by agreement pass over to another that which he hath not in himself—a power over his own life.*"
Locke at 70. Colonial America read Locke but certainly did not need him to understand "*the state of war*" they perpetuated with slavery.

This role of the militias in slave control was very clear in the later debates on whether Southern states should ratify the Constitution. Patrick Henry, at the Richmond ratifying convention, focused on the militia as the people's only protection against federal control, and thus

"the great object is that every man be armed. . . . Every one who is able may have a gun."[1]

Lest there be any doubt about Henry's subject, he thundered on about slavery and security, suggesting that under the Constitution Congress could *"provide for the general defense"* by enlisting blacks in

1. LEVY at 147–48. Individual gun rights advocates often take Henry's statement out of context. He was talking about the militia. On the other hand, what was a militia for men like Henry but nothing more than free white men? See LEVY at 148, *quoting* a Charleston, South Carolina, newspaper.

A century earlier, in 1689, Parliament addressed the fear that Protestants might be disarmed and left defenseless against Catholics. In 1789 Madison responded with the Second Amendment to the analogous white fear that the militia might be disarmed, leaving whites defenseless against blacks. Bogus, *Hidden History*, at 386.

2. Bogus, *Hidden History*, at 352, *citing* 3 DEBATES OF THE SEVERAL STATE CONVENTIONS, ON THE ADOPTION OF THE FEDERAL CONSTITUTION at 590 (Jonathan Elliot ed., 2d ed. 1891).

The Supreme Court would later underscore the Framers' intent to exclude Southern blacks from bearing arms in *Dred Scott v. Sandford*, 60 U.S. 393 (1856). In *Dred Scott*, the Supreme Court held that a slave who traveled to a free state did not become free.

Part of the reason he or she must stay a slave is that the Southern delegates of the Constitutional Convention did not consent to *"the negro race, who were recognized as citizens in any one State of the Union [having] . . . the full liberty . . . to keep and carry arms wherever they went."* Moreover, blacks could not have had *"the full liberty of speech in public and in private upon all subjects upon which its own citizens might speak; to hold public meetings upon political affairs, and to keep and carry arms wherever they went."* See Carole Emberton, *The Limits of Incorporation: Violence, Gun Rights, and Gun Regulation in the Reconstruction South*, 17 STAN. L. & POL'Y REV. 615 (2006).

Dred Scott

3. Bogus, *Hidden History*, at 345–47.

History would eventually prove Henry's fear well founded—fortunately! On September 23, 1957, nine black high school students faced an angry mob of over one thousand whites protesting integration in front of Central High School in Little Rock, Arkansas. The next day, President Dwight D. Eisenhower ordered the U.S. Army's 101st Airborne Division to escort the nine students into the school and also federalized the entire 10,000-man Arkansas National Guard to take them out of Arkansas Governor Faubus' hands. The incident was the first important test for the U.S. Supreme Court's historic *Brown v. Board of Education*, 347 U.S. 483 (1954).

Soldiers from the 101st Airborne Division escort black students into the all-white Central High School in Little Rock, Arkansas

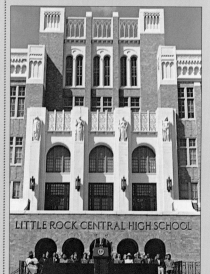

President Bill Clinton leading the fortieth anniversary of desegregation at Little Rock Central High School

the army and then emancipating them.[2] Moreover, Henry feared that the federal government could use Article I, Section 8, to subvert slavery by marching the state militia away or taking it over, leaving the South open to slave insurrection.[3]

The point then of the "*right . . . to bear . . . Arms*" in the "*well regulated*" militias of the South was to protect slavery as an institution and slaveholders as a class.[4]

The slaveholders' descendants would commit themselves to the same goal,[5] using any number of legal mechanisms to do it.[6]

---

4. Again, similar to the Southern attitudes toward blacks was the ancient Spartan hatred of the helots. Both originated in fear given the relatively small number of Spartans or Southern whites in comparison to slaves. Thucydides sums it up in a celebrated phrase: "*Spartan policy with regard to the helots had always been based almost entirely on the idea of security.*" THUCYDIDES, THE PELOPONNESIAN WAR 313 (Rex Warner trans., 1954). For a brief discussion of the Spartan slave system, see PAUL CARTLEDGE, THE SPARTANS: THE WORLD OF THE WARRIOR-HEROES OF ANCIENT GREECE 70, 73, 228–29 (2002). The same was true of the South's "*peculiar institution*" of slavery.

6. Ironically the Thirteenth Amendment of December 6, 1865, which officially abolished slavery, allowed the South to continue to oppress black Americans. It actually allows slavery for "*punishment of crime*" after "*conviction*":

"*Section 1. Neither slavery nor involuntary servitude, except as a punishment for crime where of the party shall have been duly convicted, shall exist within the United States, or any place subject to their jurisdiction.*"

Thus Southern legal institutions convicted a lot of black people, which then took away their civil right to own guns.

5. In the aftermath of the Civil War, the Ku Klux Klan devoted itself to maintaining the plantation system and the servitude status of blacks. To that end they worked to curb black education, economic advancement, voting rights, and the right to keep and bear arms. For a discussion of the Ku Klux Klan and depriving blacks of guns, see Cornell & DeDino at 523–24; see also Emberton at 615. Again, in a tie to ancient Greece, the name Ku Klux Klan (KKK) comes from combining the Greek "*kyklos*" ("circle") with the English word "clan" (misspelled with a "K").

Interestingly, D. W. Griffith's silent film THE BIRTH OF A NATION, also known as THE CLANSMAN (Epoch Film Co. 1915), ends with the disenfranchisement and disarming of blacks. The film remains one of America's most influential and controversial. Set during and after the Civil War, the film favorably presents white supremacy and the rise of  the KKK using innovative technical and narrative techniques and counts as a first Hollywood "blockbuster." Even today the Klan uses it as a recruitment tool "classic." This piece of Hollywood history puts into context the importance of a great film like GLORY (Tri-Star Pictures 1989).

The KKK and THE BIRTH OF A NATION also put into context Robert Franklin Williams's book NEGROES WITH GUNS (1961), which influenced the  Black Panther Party. Williams (1925–96) was president of the Monroe, North Carolina, NAACP in the 1950s and early 1960s when racial tensions were high and both official and KKK abuses against blacks rampant. Williams promoted both integration and armed black self-defense, disagreeing with Martian Luther King on this point.

The Thirteenth Amendment

Robert Franklin Williams

MILITIAS AND THE MINUTEMAN MYTH

With the Southern militias occupied with slave control, it left the militias often unavailable for the Revolutionary War. But despite the icon of the Minuteman, the fact was that militias from either the North or South were practically useless against a professional army.[1]

In the Revolution's early days, several of the colonial leaders believed militias could beat the British. But militias proved utterly inadequate to take on British Regulars.[2] After repeated pleas from George Washington explaining the inadequacies of militias, the Continental Congress authorized a regular army.[3]

Although the state militias were inadequate to beat

1. Lexington and Concord. In 1774 the British government ordered General Thomas Gage to disarm the colonies, and he went to Lexington and Concord to seize powder stores. At the same time, the British raided the powder magazine at Williamsburg, Virginia. The Virginia militia confronted the British officers and seized two hundred muskets from the royal governor's mansion. The timing of the two raids brought Massachusetts and Virginia together. *See Fields and Hardy at 417 n.112.* On April 19, 1775, the Concord militia drove the British back from the North Bridge. The action at Lexington and Concord was hardly a set battle—it was more like a badly planned British police action.

Commonative U.S. Postage Stamp

2. One possible exception was Daniel Morgan's brilliant victory at the Battle of Cowpens, but that did not happen until January 17, 1781. Good leadership and a smart battle plan made the militia's weakness into a strength and beat the British under Banastre Tarleton. What Morgan did was to ask his militia to fire *"two shots"* and then retreat like they were afraid. Tarleton took the bait, gave chase, and lost the battle. Cowpens was a turning point in the reconquest of South Carolina from the British, and an American tactical masterpiece. It was also the basis, more or less, of the last battle in the movie, THE PATRIOT (Columbia Pictures 2000). The real history of the Battle of Cowpens is actually far more interesting than the movie's presentation. But Jason Isaacs is well cast as Tarleton and Mel Gibson's nemesis, even though in real life Tarleton did not die in the battle and went on to serve in the British Parliament making his money in the slave trade.

Daniel Morgan

Tarleton

3. George Washington on the militia: they *"come in you cannot tell how, go you cannot tell when, and act you cannot tell where, consume your provisions, exhaust your stores, and leave you at last at a critical moment."* Quoted in Fields & Hardy at 420. For example, at the Battle of Guilford Courthouse the Virginia and North Carolina the militia ran before receiving even one casualty. Their commander noted, *"[t]hey had the most advantageous position I ever saw, and left without making scarcely the shadow of opposition."* Washington once rejected an offer from Virginia Governor Patrick Henry to send volunteer militia, stating that they were *"ungovernable."* Quoted in id. at 420.

Perhaps this history of militias being essentially ineffective against a regular army is one of the reasons that courts read the militia of yesterday to be the National Guard of today. *See, e.g., Maryland v. United States,* 381 U.S. 41, 46 (1965) (*"The National Guard is the modern Militia . . ."*). Indeed, as the experience of the Iraq War has shown, a modern American National Guard of any state is part of the overall military assets of the regular army.

Battle of Cowpens by William Ranney (1845), showing an unnamed black soldier firing his pistol to save Colonel William Washington (on the white horse in the center)

the British, the Minuteman myth remains—mostly because of the victory at Lexington and Concord.[4] Thus the Minuteman name is nearly synonymous with independence and lends itself to all manner of both military and paramilitary associations.[5]

But what happened at Lexington and Concord also shows the prevalence of gun regulation. It was, after all, the public powder stores and magazines of the militia that the British wanted to seize.[6]

Thus, perhaps the important question is not really whether the Second Amendment's Framers believed in the individual's right to bear arms but rather what they saw fit to regulate and control.

---

4. A Minuteman. Ralph Waldo Emerson's poem, "Concord Hymn" (1837) helped make the Minuteman an American icon. It commemorates the Battle of Lexington and Concord (April 19, 1775), the first fight of the American Revolution. The statue by Daniel Chester French has Emerson's first stanza inscribed at its base: *"By the rude bridge that arched the flood,*
Their flag to April's breeze unfurled,
Here once the embattled farmers stood,
And fired the shot heard round the world."
The *"shot heard round the world"* became the description of the beginning of the American Revolution.
The poem goes on:
"The foe long since in silence slept;
Alike the conqueror silent sleeps;
And Time the ruined bridge has swept
Down the dark stream that seaward creeps.
On this green bank, by this soft stream,
We set to-day a votive stone;
That memory may their deeds redeem,
When, like our sires, our sons are gone.
Spirit, that made those heroes dare
To die, and leave their children free,
Bid Time and Nature gently spare
The shaft we raise to them and thee."

Ralph Waldo Emerson (1803–82) was an American essayist, philosopher, poet, and leader of the Transcendentalist movement in the early nineteenth century. Emerson gave a public lecture in Washington, D.C., on January 31, 1862, and declared: *"The South calls slavery an institution . . . I call it destitution . . . Emancipation is the demand of civilization."*

5. The Minuteman is also a U.S. nuclear missile. As of 2008, it is the only land-based intercontinental ballistic missile in service in the United States. Again, not even the NRA argues that an individual

Minuteman as Americana

Minuteman vigilantes guarding their notion of the border

can own one of these, but would it not be the logical extension of the Second Amendment?

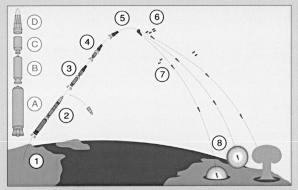

Minuteman as agent of death

6. The wife of Nathan Barrett, captain of one of Concord's militia companies, spotted one of her husband's men going home before the fight was over, stating he was *"feeling ill."* She told him to leave his gun. He would not give it up and ran away when she tried to get it. *Discussed in* Robert A. Gross, The Minutemen and Their World 126 (1976), *cited in* Churchill, *Gun Regulation*, at 139. This story shows that the gun was valuable property. *See* Konig, *Arms and the Man* (challenging Churchill's Minuteman story as a basis for the individual rights argument).

GUN REGULATION AT THE FOUNDING

Gun control is hardly a modern invention.

The Second Amendment itself articulates a *"well regulated"* right within the context of the existing militia system. This included requiring citizens to muster or face stiff penalties. All of this militia regulation allowed government to track who had the guns.[1]

States also commonly prohibited the use of firearms on occasions and in certain locations.[2] Additionally, during the early republic, just because a man owned his firearm and had the right to bear it did not necessarily mean that he had an unfettered right to *"keep"* it in his house.

Numerous states and cities had regulations on how to store firearms, and especially gun powder, most of which a man had to store in a safe public magazine.[3] These gun regulations made sense given the inherently unstable nature of firearms at the time. Gunpowder, which we today call "black powder" to distinguish it from the modern "smokeless" and more stable powder, could

1. See generally Cornell & DeDino at 502–05, noting that *"a variety of gun regulations were on the books when individual states adopted their arms-bearing provisions and when the Second Amendment was adopted. In the years after the Second Amendment, the individual states adopted even more stringent types of regulations."* See also SAUL CORNELL, A WELL-REGULATED MILITIA: THE FOUNDING FATHERS AND THE ORIGINS OF GUN CONTROL IN EARLY AMERICA (2006), noting that the right to bear arms was tied to military service, and that the Second Amendment was born of the Founders' fear of a standing army.

2. *"In reality, the decades after ratification of the Second Amendment saw increased, not decreased, levels of regulation."* Cornell & DeDino at 505.

4. This had to do as much with class as it did with race. The royalist and landed class of Virginia made it illegal for both black and white servants to bear arms. Also, the Massachusetts Puritans sought to deprive King Philip, a Native American war leader of his arms. Examples cited in Bachmann at 228. *See also* Nathan Kozuskanich, *Originalism, History, and the Second Amendment: What Did Bearing Arms Really Mean to the Founders?* 10 U. PA. J. CONST. L. 413, 418 (2008) (discussing contemporary usage of terms in the context of regulations barring blacks from *"bearing"* arms.)

3. Storing Powder. The statutes provide for the safe storage and transport of gunpowder by limiting the amount of gunpowder a person could possess, usually to around twenty to thirty pounds. Ordinances like that of Carlisle, Pennsylvania, proscribed keeping gunpowder *"in any house, shop, cellar, store or other place within the said borough."* The powder was to be kept *"in the highest story of the house . . . unless it be at least fifty yards from any dwelling house."* New York law required separating gunpowder *"into four stone jugs or tin canisters, which shall not contain more than seven pounds each."* Cornell & DeDino at 511. The early American regulations allowed people to own quantities of gunpowder but they could only *"keep"* a small amount in their homes. The owner had to pay to keep the rest in a public magazine and regulations specified the manner of transportation and storage. *Id.* at 511–12.

Given this history, the Supreme Court's striking down the requirements that guns have trigger locks seems out of line.

A powder keg

Revolver with a trigger lock

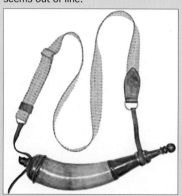

A powder horn. For small amounts of gunpowder, a gunman would use a powder horn. The horn is naturally hollow and waterproof to keep the powder dry.

The "Powder Horn" is also a Boy Scott badge for passing a high adventure resource course

blow up with a spark or even static electricity.

Although one could argue that the Second Amendment's Framers wanted to specify that the individual also had the right to "*keep*" as well as "*bear*" arms without control, regulation of guns was prevalent both before and after the Second Amendment. Any number of laws defined who could own guns, with the usual intent of barring slaves and even free blacks and white servants.[4] There were also laws prohibiting carrying concealed weapons.[5]

And these regulations went well beyond safety concerns; they sought to regulate guns and politics through loyalty oaths. Well before the Second Amendment, the Continental Congress encouraged states to pass laws to disarm loyalists who would not swear an oath to America.[6] This practice continued well after the Revolution and the Second Amendment.[7] After Shays' Rebellion in 1787, for example, the Massachusetts legislature allowed pardons only if the rebels swore allegiance to the state after delivering up their arms for three years.[8]

5. Regulation shifted dramatically after the Second Amendment and the War of 1812, when several states enacted laws against carrying concealed weapons. Cornell & DeDino at 505–06; *see also* Clayton E. Cramer & Joseph Edward Olson, *Pistols, Crime, and Public Safety in Early America*, 44 Willamette L. Rev. 699, 702–06 (2008) (discussing various pistol regulations both before and after the Second Amendment).

7. Regarding prevalence of nineteenth century antebellum gun regulation, *see* Cornell & DeDino at 512–15. A Pennsylvania law, for example, took all guns away from any person who "*refuse[d] or neglect[ed] to take the oath or affirmation*" to the state, and the person could not even borrow another's firearm. *Id.* at 506.

6. Cornell & DeDino at 506. For example, in 1776 Massachusetts passed, at the behest of the Continental Congress, an act that disarmed "*such Persons as are notoriously disaffected to the Cause of America, or who refuse to associate to defend by Arms the United American Colonies . . . .*" Moreover, "*every Male Person above sixteen Years of Age*" had to subscribe to a "*test*" of allegiance to the "*United American Colonies*." One who failed the test was "*disarmed . . . [of] all such Arms, Ammunition and Warlike Implements, as by the strictest Search can be found in his Possession or belonging to him.*"

This practice violates not only any notion of the Second Amendment but also the Fourth Amendment. See **Chapter 4: Molasses and the Sticky Origins of the Fourth Amendment.**

Engraving of Daniel Shays and Job Shattuck, the leaders of Shays' Rebellion

8. Cornell & DeDino at 508–09. Also, the rebel could not serve as a juror, hold government office, or vote "*for any officer, civil or military.*"

Shays' Rebellion was an uprising in Massachusetts from 1786 to 1787. Led by Daniel Shays and known as "Shaysites" (or "Regulators"), the rebels were mostly poor farmers under crushing debt and taxes who would often end up in prison or lose their land for failure to pay taxes. The state militia easily put down the rebellion by early 1787. But the rebels had much sympathy, and the rebellion energized calls to reevaluate the Articles of Confederation and gave strong impetus to the Constitutional Convention, which began in May 1787.

To the Founders' generation, the one that drafted, debated, and passed the Second Amendment, what we would call "gun control" was nothing new. This in many ways supersedes whether the Second Amendment provides an individual right to bear arms outside the military context. The generation of the Founders accepted the idea that government needed to regulate guns, and the Second Amendment did not change this.

The only question then (and now) was the extent of the regulation.[1]

THE SELF-DEFENSE MYTH

Ah, the iconic image of the frontiersman grabbing his flintlock off the fireplace mantle to defend hearth and home!

But yet again, reality challenges the image. Even if the gun was above the

1. A somewhat farcical gun control argument to get around the Second Amendment is to say that anyone can "*keep and bear*" any gun but bullets should cost $100,000 each! Aside from being an obvious sidestep of the gun policy debate, this argument ignores that unless you use the gun as a club, it is the bullet that kills.

A **bullet** is the hard projectile (usually lead) that a firearm or air gun propels. Technically the "bullet" (during the age of muskets it was called the "ball") is just the top part of the cartridge, which is made up of bullet, casing or shell, gunpowder, and primer. The technical advancement making bullets more effective killers at longer range was the change in shape from the round "ball" to "conical" (or cone shaped). The 1823 "Norton" bullet (for British Army Captain John Norton), the 1836 "Greener" bullet (for English gunsmith William Greener), and finally the 1847 soft lead "minie ball" (for French Captain Claude Étienne Minié) all led to our modern cartridge and conical bullet.

Of these nineteenth century bullets, the minie ball was the most successful. It was more effective for two reasons. First, the shape was more aerodynamic. (This is same reason that one can throw a football farther and more accurately than a basketball.) Second, and more important, the minie ball was of soft lead with a diameter that would not engage the rifled gun barrel when the shooter "rammed it home." Although the bullet did not engage the rifling on the way down, at the moment of firing the exploding gunpowder's propellant gases caused the skirt of the bullet's hollow base to expand, which would then engage the rifling as the bullet traveled out the gun barrel. This allowed for great rapidity of fire as well as accuracy.

The conical bullet came just in time to kill soldiers during the American Civil War

fireplace (gumming up the finely crafted gun works with soot), only a fool would have it loaded. The heat or spark from the fireplace could set it off at any time and, if not, humidity from cooking would have dampened the powder, making the gun useless.[2]

Although one could argue the modern right to use a gun in self-defense is part of the right to privacy, the Second Amendment's history does not support this argument.[3] The Framers of the Second Amendment would not have thought of guns as providing an individual right, rather than a collective right, of self-defense.[4] Guns at the time were an impractical means of defending the home from an intruder, though they could be used for collective self-defense against slaves, French, and Indians.

The better argument for this position, however, may be the Ninth Amendment's reservation of "*retained*" rights.[5] This would encompass a fundamental natural right of self-protection that predates the Constitution and the Second Amendment.

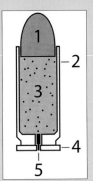

The modern cartridge:
1. the projectile bullet;
2. the case holding the parts;
3. the propellant, usually gunpowder or cordite;
4. the rim that hold the case in place during firing;
5. the primer that ignites the propellant.

A flying conical bullet and the flying conical football

The term "**silver bullet**" to describe an effective solution is supposedly the only type of bullet that can kill a werewolf.

"**Biting the bullet**" describes preparing for an unpleasant job or experience and comes from before anesthesia when a patient would brace himself before an operation, such as an amputation, by biting on something such as the soft lead of a bullet. Given that most people would have died after the operation anyway, lead poisoning was probably not a problem!

2. The Musket over the Fireplace. Even broken or obsolete guns were fine works of metalworking and wood, and often family heirlooms. So why not display them over the fireplace?

3. The NRA and any number of gun enthusiasts argue that the Second Amendment protects the right to have a gun for "self-defense." *See e.g.*, Brief for the NRA Supporting Respondent, *District of Columbia v. Heller*, 128 S. Ct. 2783 (2008) (No. 07-290). For an analysis of the self-defense right and firearms under international law, see David B. Kopel, Paul Gallant & Joanne D. Eisen, *The Human Right of Self-Defense*, 22 B.Y.U. J. PUB. L. 43 (2007).

4. Cornell & DiDino at 499 ("*Another anachronism in contemporary Second Amendment scholarship is the tendency to read modern notions of self-defense into the Founding Era. The linkage between firearms and self-defense in the Founding Era and the early Republic was much more tenuous.*") (citing Don B. Kates, Jr., *The Second Amendment and the Ideology of Self-Protection*, 9 CONST. COMMENT. 87 (1992); Nelson Lund, *The Second Amendment, Political Liberty, and the Right to Self-Preservation*, 39 ALA. L. REV. 103 (1987)). *See also* Kozuskanich at 424–25 ("*The surviving print material from the Revolution reveals that the American colonists were not concerned about arming themselves for personal self-defense; they were preoccupied with mobilizing communities so that they could defend themselves.*") On the "right of revolution" theme in connections with the Second Amendment and the ultimate futility of relying on the gun for security from crime, *see* David C. Williams, *Civic Constitutionalism, The Second Amendment, and the Right of Revolution*, 79 IND. L.J. 379 (2004).

5. *See* **Chapter 9: The Ninth Amendment: Still a Mystery after All These Years.**
   For example, in *United States v. Lopez*, 514 U.S. 549 (1995), the Supreme Court held that while Congress has broad lawmaking authority under the Commerce Clause, it is not unlimited and does not apply to carrying handguns.

Even a man well-schooled in loading and firing a flintlock would need some time to prepare his gun. By then his home would have been burglarized, with his wife and daughter ravaged![1] Far more expedient was a club or sword.[2] In fact, firearms accounted for only a small percentage of homicides before the Civil War, which demonstrates the general impracticality of using the guns of that time for individual defense.[3]

PREVENTING TYRANNY

Though history does not readily support the modern argument that the Second Amendment provides an individual right to self-defense, the history does

---

1. Loading a Muzzleloader.
   a. Measure powder charge.
   b. Pour measured powder down barrel.
   c. Place patch and ball on muzzle.
   d. Tap ball into barrel with starter.
   e. Take out ramrod.
   f. Ram ball down barrel.
   g. Be sure ball is completely seated.
   h. Clear vent hole with pick if necessary.
   i. On flintlock muzzleloader, pour powder into pan and close frizzen.
   j. On percussion lock muzzleloader, place cap on nipple.
From the South Carolina Hunter Safety Course, http://www.hunter-ed.com/sc/course/index.htm (under Chapter Five follow "Loading a Muzzleloader" hyperlink) (last visited Mar. 17, 2008).

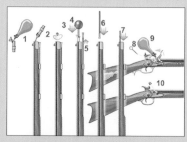

Cramer & Olson at 719–20 argue that "[a]s a practical matter, the often decisive first shot [of an eighteenth century pistol] can be discharged in virtually equal time [as a modern pistol]." Even if they are correct, Cramer & Olson do not account for loading time—a modern clip takes seconds at most!
A **clip** stores multiple rounds of ammunition together as a unit, ready to fit into the gun's magazine. A **magazine** is anywhere ammunition is stored, such as on a ship or inside the gun itself. Also, because magazines may be integral to the

2. Interestingly, Blackstone demonstrated the law of self-defense with the example of a sword, not a firearm: "*The law says, if a man attack you by a sword, you have no right to kill him, till you have made every attempt to escape.*" *Quoted in* Kozuskanich at 445.

3. Cornell & DiDino at 499, *citing* Eric H. Monkkonen, Murder in New York City 32 (2001). *See also* Cramer & Olson at 699 for an in-depth discussion of gun regulation and the contemporary definitions of "pistols" and "firearms" in colonial America and the early republic.

M1 rifle clip

firearm (fixed) or removable (detachable), the clip and magazine are often confused for each other.

A staggered-column 9 × 19 mm pistol magazine

4. Noah Webster, a leading Federalist, wrote that tyranny is the exercise of some power over a man which is not warranted by law or necessary for the public safety. Before a standing army can rule, the people must be disarmed; as they are in almost every kingdom in Europe.
   Also, John Adams argued that arms in the hands of citizens allow them to defend themselves at their discretion. Levy at 143. As Henry Neville, an Enlightenment political thinker influential with the American Founding generation, wrote: "*democracy is much more powerful than aristocracy, because the latter cannot arm the*

people for fear they could seize upon the government." *Quoted in* Field & Hardy at 408. *See also generally* Williams.

5. Levison at 657 ("*[A] state facing a totally disarmed population is in a far better position, for good or for ill, to suppress popular demonstrations and uprisings than one that must calculate the possibilities of its soldiers and officials being injured or killed.*").
   The NRA made a compelling case about the citizen's right to bear arms with its ad campaign featuring this image from Tiananmen Square.

Tiananmen Square, China, June 1989
Image by Helen Koop

show that the Framers intended the Second Amendment to be part of the protection against tyranny.[4] They knew all too well the history of the Stuart monarchs. They also knew the role guns played in starting the Revolution.[5]

Again, however, this leads to the same debate as to whether the protection against tyranny was an individual or a collective one. Madison's THE FEDERALIST No. 46 extols the virtues of the militia as the protection against a national tyrant using the army.[6] This would indicate a collective reading of the Second Amendment. But the fact was that militias were usually made up of individuals with individual guns, which would indicate an individual right.

6. Although both sides of the gun debate selectively quote from Associate Justice Joseph Story's COMMENTARIES ON THE U.S. CONSTITUTION (1833) describing the Second Amendment, his reasoning appears very much to echo Madison's FEDERALIST No. 46 arguments:

"The importance of this article will scarcely be doubted by any persons, who have duly reflected upon the subject. The militia is the natural defence of a free country against sudden foreign invasions, domestic insurrections, and domestic usurpations of power by rulers. It is against sound policy for a free people to keep up large military establishments and standing armies in time of peace, both from the enormous expenses, with which they are attended, and the facile means, which they afford to ambitious and unprincipled rulers, to subvert the government, or trample upon the rights of the people. The right of the citizens to keep and bear arms has justly been considered, as the palladium of the liberties of a republic; since it offers a strong moral check against the usurpation and arbitrary power of rulers; and will generally, even if these are successful in the first instance, enable the people to resist and triumph over them. And yet, though this truth would seem so clear, and the importance of a well regulated militia would seem so undeniable, it cannot be disguised, that among the American people there is a growing indifference to any system of militia discipline, and a strong disposition, from a sense of its burdens, to be rid of all regulations. How it is practicable to keep the people duly armed without some organization, it is difficult to see. There is certainly no small danger, that indifference may lead to disgust, and disgust to contempt; and thus gradually undermine all the protection intended by this clause of our national bill of rights."

Joseph Story

JOSEPH STORY, COMMENTARIES ON THE U.S. CONSTITUTION § 1897 (5th ed., Melville M. Bigelow 1891). Justice Story also described the Second Amendment's original meaning as a response to moderate Anti-Federalists who feared federal control over the militia: "It is difficult fully to comprehend the influence of such objections, urged with much apparent sincerity and earnestness at such an eventful period. The answers then given seem to have been, in their structure and reasoning, satisfactory and conclusive. But the amendments proposed to the constitution (some of which have been since adopted) show that the objections were extensively felt and sedulously cherished. The power of Congress over the militia (it was urged) was limited, and concurrent with that of the states. The right of governing them was confined to the single case of their being in the actual service of the United States, in some of the cases pointed out in the Constitution. It was then, and then only, that they could be subjected by the general government to martial law. If Congress did not choose to arm, organize, or discipline the militia, there would be an inherent right in the states to do it. All, that the Constitution intended, was, to give a power to Congress to ensure uniformity, and thereby efficiency. But if Congress refused, or neglected to perform the duty, the States had a perfect concurrent right, and might act upon it to the utmost extent of sovereignty. As little pretence was there to say, that Congress possessed the exclusive power to suppress insurrections and repel invasions. Their power was merely competent to reach these objects; but did not, and could not, in regard to the militia, supersede the ordinary rights of the States. It was, indeed, made a duty of Congress to provide for such cases; but this did not exclude the co-operation of the States. The idea of Congress inflicting severe and ignominious punishments upon the militia in times of peace was absurd. It presupposed, that the representatives had an interest, and would intentionally take measures to oppress them, and alienate their affections. The appointment of the officers of the militia was exclusively in the States; and how could it be presumed, that such men would ever consent to the destruction of the rights or privileges of their fellow-citizens. The power to discipline and train the militia, except when in the actual service of the United States, was also exclusively vested in the States; and under such circumstances, it was secure against any serious abuses. It was added, that any project of disciplining the whole militia of the United States would be so utterly impracticable and mischievous, that it would probably never be attempted. The most that could be done would be to organize and discipline select corps; and these for all general purposes, either of the States, or of the Union, would be found to combine all, that was useful or desirable in militia services."
Id. § 1207.
Regarding Justice Joseph Story and the Second Amendment, see TUSHNET at 20–22; Henigan at 119–20 (noting that the individual rights proponents usually fail to fully quote Justice Story).

But yet again, the question comes down to what this means today. In 1789 Madison could make the plausible argument, as he did in THE FEDERALIST No. 46, that armed citizens could stand against their government. Today, though, the notion that even the best armed of private citizens can effectively stand against the military is not realistic.[1] And with the type of paramilitary organizations around, there is a real question of whether this is desirable.

But the point remains that the Framers wrote the Second Amendment, and the rest of the Bill of Rights, with a clear belief in its value as a guarantee against a tyrannical national government.[2]

The only question is whether they saw this protection as an individual holding his gun alone or with his comrades.

MAKING THE SECOND AMENDMENT

In 1786, a decade after the Declaration of Independence, the United States was a loose government under the Articles of Confederation. A year later, in 1787, the Philadelphia Convention was charged to amend the Articles. But rather than only amend the Articles, the Convention created a whole new constitution.

Two camps emerged after the convention: the Federalists (who supported ratification of the Constitution) and the Anti-Federalists (who opposed it).[3] As discussed

---

1. On this point, Lenard Levy, a proponent of the interpretation that the Second Amendment protects an individual right to bear arms, notes that although "[t]he right to keep and bear arms still enables citizens to protect themselves against law breakers . . . . it is a feckless means of opposing a legitimate government." Levy at 149. See also Tushnet at 29 (the Second Amendment is "not realistic these days to think of an armed citizenry defending us against an oppressive government").

2. St. George Tucker also published a Second Amendment commentary. Tucker annotated Sir William Blackstone's Commentaries on the Laws of England and was the leading Jeffersonian constitutional theorist of his day. In footnotes 40 and 41 he distinguished the difference between the English right that Blackstone had described and the more extensive American right to bear arms: "The right of the people to keep and bear arms shall not be infringed. Amendments to C. U. S. Art. 4, and this without any qualification as to their condition or degree, as is the case in the British government." Further, he wrote: "Whoever examines the forest, and game laws in the British code, will readily perceive that the right of keeping arms is effectually taken away from the people of England." Tucker notes that "[i]n America we may reasonably hope that the people will never cease to regard the right of keeping and bearing arms as the surest pledge of their liberty." At 414 n.3.

3. This conflict was accentuated by the recent news of violent revolution in France with similar antifederal tensions.

....

4. See **Prequel and Preamble: Did They Forget to Pay the Bill?** Regarding the Bill of Rights and the Second Amendment as a limit on federal government rather than a grant of individual rights, see Bogus, *Hidden History,* at 369.

....

5. Madison intended his Bill of Rights to be inserted into the existing Constitution. The right to keep and bear arms was not to be inserted into Article I, Section 8, which specifies Congress's power over the militia. Rather, it was to fit in Article I, Section 9, between clauses 3 and 4, following the existing prohibitions on suspension of habeas corpus, bills of attainder, and ex post facto laws. This may show that the Second amendment is an individual right such as habeas corpus, etc.

James Madison

....

6. *Quoted in* Bogus, *Hidden History*, at 366. Bogus argues that this allowed Quakers out of military service in the militias.

Precursors to Madison's proposal included the Pennsylvania Constitution, which had the phrase "the right to bear arms" but not a militia clause. Levy at 135, 142. John Adams's Massachusetts Declaration of Rights of 1780 also used the phrase "to keep and bear arms." Id. at 143.

....

7. Regarding the redrafting of this amendment to its present form, see Bogus, *Hidden History*, at 369–71.

On July 21, 1789, Madison's draft

above in relation to slavery and guns, much of the Anti-Federalist opposition to the proposed Constitution had to do with its lack of listed rights. Only by listing protected rights, the Anti-Federalists argued, could the national government not encroach on them.[4]

In answer to these arguments, James Madison on June 8, 1789, presented to Congress what ultimately became the Bill of Rights, including the Second Amendment.[5] His proposal for the latter was worded thusly:

The right of the people to keep and bear arms shall not be infringed; a well armed, and well regulated militia being the best security of a free country: but no person religiously scrupulous of bearing arms, shall be compelled to render military service in person.[6]

Madison's proposal went through various modifications during the legislative process, and partisans of the modern gun control debate argue the meaning of each legislative point and counterpoint.[7] In September 1789 what became the Second Amendment went to the states:[8]

A well regulated Militia being necessary to the security of a free State, the right of the People to keep and bear Arms shall not be infringed.

This is the wording we argue about.[9]

---

amendments went to a select committee for review. On July 28, the committee returned a reworded Second Amendment, which was read,
"*A well regulated militia, composed of the body of the people, being the best security of a free State, the right of the people to keep and bear arms shall not be infringed; but no person religiously scrupulous shall be compelled to bear arms.*"
Quoted in Levy at 144–45.

On August 24, the House sent the following for the Senate's review:
"*A well regulated militia, composed of the body of the people, being the best security of a free state, the right of the people to keep and bear arms shall not be infringed; but no one religiously scrupulous of bearing arms shall be compelled to render military service in person.*"

The Senate changed the semicolon in the religious exemption portion to a comma and then removed the militia definition and the conscientious objector clause:
"*A well regulated militia, being the best security of a free state, the right of the people to keep and bear arms, shall not be infringed.*"

On September 9, the Senate sent its final version to the House:
"*A well regulated militia being the security of a free state, the right of the people to keep and bear arms shall not be infringed.*"

On September 21, the House accepted the changes but added the words "*necessary to*":
"*A well regulated militia being necessary to the security of a free State, the right of the People to keep and bear arms shall not be infringed.*"

This version went to the states to become the Second Amendment.

Academic careers are made arguing the relative meaning of these different versions to the modern gun control debate.

8. The Right in the State Courts. States did not receive the Second Amendment in a vacuum; most had their own constitutional provisions on the topic, and state courts decided cases under their own constitutions. For a survey of state constitutional provisions guaranteeing the right to bear arms in various forms, see Eugene Volokh, *State Constitutional Rights to Keep and Bear Arms*, 11 Tex. Rev. L. & Pol. 191 (2006).

Regarding the Second Amendment's application to the states today, see Michael Anthony Lawrence, *Second Amendment Incorporation Through the Fourteenth Amendment Privileges or Immunities and Due Process Clauses*, 72 Mo. L. Rev. 1 (2007) (arguing that the Supreme Court should recognize the Second Amendment as applying to the several states through the Fourteenth Amendment Privileges or Immunities Clause or, alternatively, through the Due Process Clause). For a counter view, see David A. Lieber, *The Cruikshank Redemption: The Enduring Rationale for Excluding the Second Amendment from the Court's Modern Incorporation Doctrine*, 95 J. Crim. L. & Criminology 1079 (2005).

9. And perhaps fruitlessly. See, e.g., Robert A. Creamer, *History Is Not Enough: Using Contemporary Justifications for the Right to Keep and Bear Arms in Interpreting the Second Amendment*, 45 B.C. L. Rev. 905 (2004) (arguing the limits of any historical approach to the questions of whether the Second Amendment protects an individual or collective right to bear arms and instead that contemporary justifications should determine the question). For an argument using an empirical study of contemporary word usage in the press on what the Second Amendment's words meant at the time, see Kozuskanich at 413 (asserting that the meaning of "*bear arms*" was military, not individual).

WHAT TO MAKE OF THE GUN HISTORY MESS

Guns are a great equalizer. With relatively little training a person with even a halfway decent gun is more powerful as any fighter alive—even Bruce Lee or Muhammad Ali![1] Make the gun a modern, easy-to-use Glock 17, and Bruce doesn't stand a chance.[2]

Maybe this fact is the essence of the NRA argument that only the gun rights of "law-abiding" people should not "*be infringed.*" Perhaps this approach conforms to the Framers' original intent. After all, they never intended people without property to have much of a say, and, as we have seen, in many states slaves and even free blacks could not legally touch a gun.

But historical arguments, no matter how well founded or presented, will convince no one in the gun debate. Indeed, given the state of the scholarship, with point *versus* counterpoint, factoid *versus* factoid, the debate is circular and never-ending.[3] Remember academic careers are made on this subject!

Regardless of whether you believe the Second

1. Bruce Lee as sidekick (literally) of the Gun toting Green Hornet.

Armed Gays
Don't Get
Bashed

Equalizing people in society is what this poster is about. The Pink Pistols also have the slogan, "Pick on someone your own caliber."

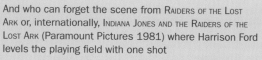

And who can forget the scene from RAIDERS OF THE LOST ARK or, internationally, INDIANA JONES AND THE RAIDERS OF THE LOST ARK (Paramount Pictures 1981) where Harrison Ford levels the playing field with one shot

Image by Helen Koop

Muhammad Ali

2. A Glock 17.

Amendment is about an individual right or not, it remains a creature of civilization. If the right to bear arms is "*inalienable,*" meaning it is a right in the "*state of nature*" or inherent in being a person, just like with other rights, only law gives it effect.[4] The real issue is not whether the Second Amendment guarantees an individual right, but that guns have always been subject to regulation, that is, gun control.

And in reality nearly everyone agrees with some form of gun control. As stated, even the NRA states that only law-abiding people should have the right to bear arms and does not advocate that a person can buy his own battle tank. Laws that prohibit a felon from possessing a firearm and that prevent us from owning a battle tank are gun control.[5]

And why not? Even First Amendment free speech is regulated.[6] If true for the First Amendment, so also for the Second. The only question then is the extent of the regulation, not its existence.

All constitutional niceties aside, in the end, law, and not guns, secures society's boundaries.

---

3. *See generally* TUSHNET.

4. As John Locke explained, in "*the state of nature*" a man is "*constantly exposed to the invasions of others . . . the greater part no strict observers of equity and justice.*" This makes man "*willing to quit this condition . . . to join in society with others . . . for the mutual preservation of their lives, liberties, and estates.*" John Locke, *An Essay Concerning the True Original, Extent and End of Civil Government, in* THE WORLD'S GREAT THINKERS: MAN AND THE STATE: THE POLITICAL PHILOSOPHERS 129 (1947).

5. As Associate Justice Scalia wrote in *Heller*, the right of self-defense is "*not a right to keep and carry any weapon whatsoever in any manner whatsoever for whatever purpose.*" Moreover, government can prohibit weapons in "*sensitive places such as schools and government buildings.*" 128 S. Ct. at 2816–17. What this really means is a lot of work for lawyers for a long time. *See, e.g.,* Cameron Desmond, Comment, *From Cities to Schoolyards: The Implications of an Individual Right to Bear Arms on the Constitutionality of Gun-Free Zones*, 39 McGEORGE L. REV. 1043 (2008); Glenn H. Reynolds & Brannon P. Denning, *Heller's Future in the Lower Courts*, 102 Nw. U. L. REV. 2035 (2008).

6. Justice Oliver Wendell Holmes's classic dictum that it is not protected free speech to falsely yell "fire!" in a crowded movie theater (assuming, of course, there is no fire) shows that even the right to free speech is not absolute. See **Chapter 1: Of Dogma and Desire: Saying What You Believe about the First Amendment.**

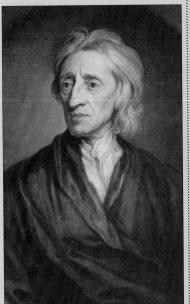

CHAPTER 3

The Third Amendment:

Don't Count It Out Yet!

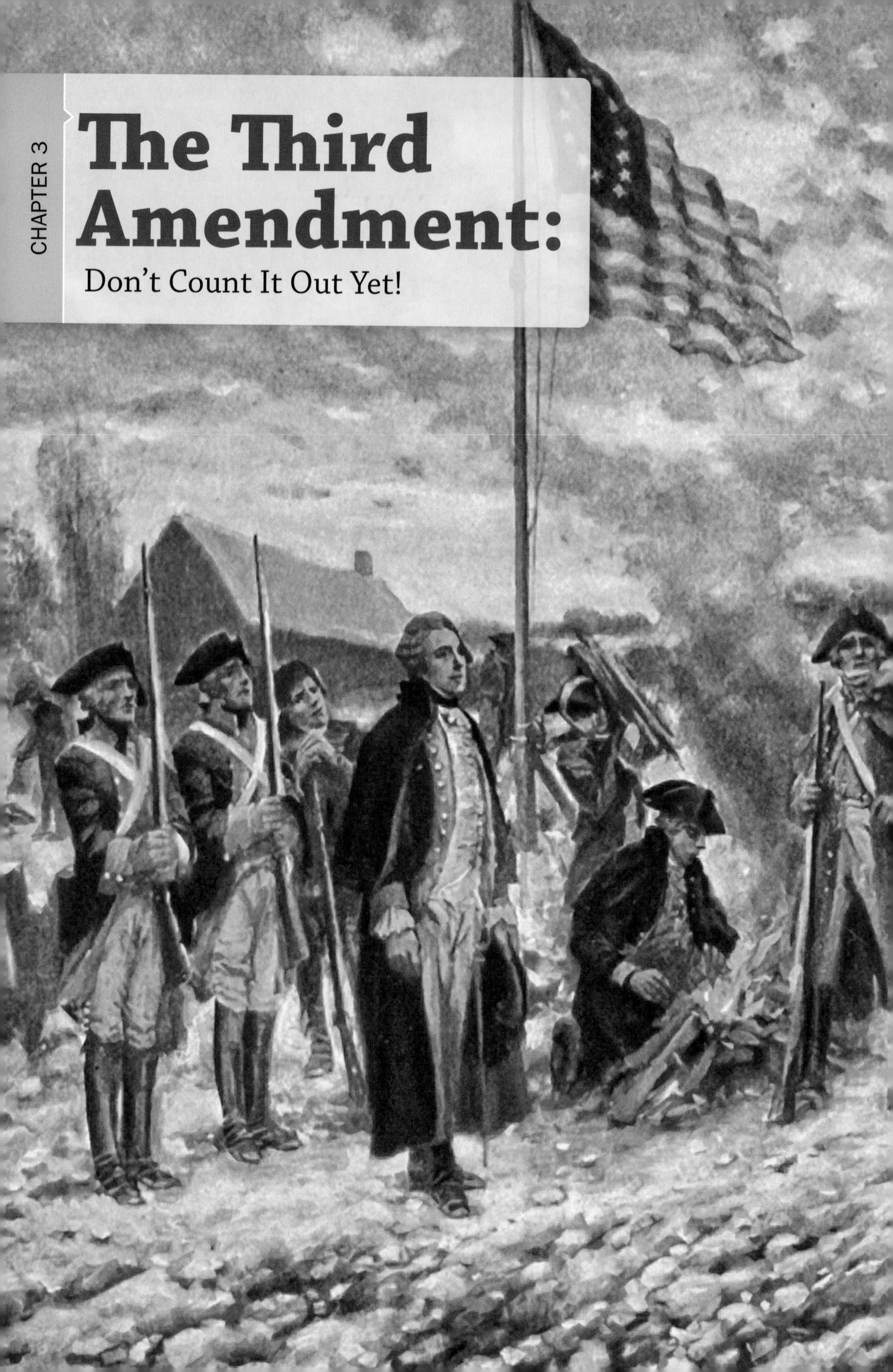

> *"No Soldier shall, in time of peace be quartered in any house, without the consent of the Owner, nor in time of war, but in a manner to be prescribed by law."*

—The Third Amendment

Who the heck cares about this one?

Pretty much nobody[1]—but we should.

Although today we don't worry about having an uninvited troop as a houseguest, the Founding Fathers thought this a biggie![2] So maybe we should consider the

1. *"In an Andy Warhol version of eighteenth-century constitutional history, the quartering issue got its fifteen minutes of fame in American life."* Robert A. Gross, *Public and Private in the Third Amendment*, 26 VAL. U. L. REV. 215, 218 (1992).

2. When arguing that Virginia should not ratify the U.S. Constitution, Patrick Henry noted that *"[o]ne of our first complaints, under the former government, was the quartering of troops upon us. This was one of the principal reasons for dissolving the connection with Great Britain. Here we have troops in time of peace. They may be billeted in any manner—to tyrannize, oppress, and crush us."* Quoted in William S. Fields & David T. Hardy, *The Third Amendment and the Issue of the Maintenance of Standing Armies: A Legal History*, 35 AM. J. LEGAL HIST. 393, 423 (1991).

Patrick Henry and the "Give me liberty or give me death" speech

Founders' concerns about quartering[1] and give the Third Amendment more acknowledgment.

One of the indictments of King George III in the Declaration of Independence was that he

"*has kept among us, in times of peace, Standing Armies without the consent of our legislatures [and][f]or quar-tering large bodies of armed troops among us . . . .*"[2]

Although five of the eight original states had constitutional prohibitions on the quartering of

---

1. Quartering is the placing of soldiers in lodgings. WEBSTER'S NEW INTERNATIONAL DICTIONARY OF THE ENGLISH LANGUAGE 2034 (2d ed. 1942). "Quarter" comes from the Latin "*quattuor,*" meaning "four," as in a division of four. JOHN AYTO, DICTIONARY OF WORD ORIGINS 425 (1990). It came to mean a place in a divided area or city where groups live, such as the "French Quarter" of New Orleans or the "Jewish Quarter" in many pre–World War II cities. The word used in this sense of lodging is where the military term presumably comes from as in the Third Amendment's reference to "*quartered.*"

This leads to the phrase "*giving no quarter,*" meaning that the battle's winner will take no prisoners, literally refusing to house the captured. Modern laws of war prohibit this, however. *See "IV Convention—The Laws and Customs of War on Land"* of the Hague Conventions of 1907, Article 23 ("*it is especially forbidden . . . to declare that no quarter will be given*"); *see also* The Nuremberg Trials, Oct. 1946 (declaring the 1907 Hague Conventions the customary law of war, binding on all parties in an international armed conflict). Thus John Belushi's cry of "*No prisoners!*" during the final mayhem

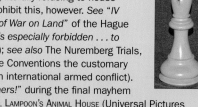

scene in NATIONAL LAMPOON'S ANIMAL HOUSE (Universal Pictures 1978) is totally contrary to the laws of war! He does, however, follow the long tradition of the jester, which is what the French call our bishop from the game of chess. The Bishop's deep groove symbolizes a bishop's or abbot's hat, called a "mitre." The original Indian piece was an elephant, and the groove represented the tusks, which the French interpreted as a jester's cap, hence the bishop is called "*fou*" ("crazy man").

The Latin *quattuor* is also the basis for the English "quarantine," "quarrel," and even "cadre." From it also comes square and thus "squad" and "squadron," originally meaning men in a square military formation. WEBSTER'S at 2444. "Squad" usually refers to a cavalry or navy unit, while "squadron" refers to an airplane unit. The infantry square, however, if it held, was the most effective way for infantry to beat back a cavalry charge because cavalry cannot outflank a square, and horses will not charge bristling bayonets. Perhaps the most famous use of the infantry square formation was against Napoleon at the Battle of Waterloo.

A squad also is an organizational unit in police departments (at least in Hollywood) such as *Police Squad!*, a 1982 television spoof of police dramas leading to the movies THE NAKED GUN: FROM THE FILES OF POLICE SQUAD! (Paramount Pictures 1988) and two sequels: THE NAKED GUN 2½: THE SMELL OF FEAR (Paramount Pictures 1991) and NAKED GUN 33⅓: THE FINAL INSULT (Paramount Pictures 1994), all staring Leslie Nielsen, Priscilla Presley, George Kennedy, and O. J. Simpson, which, before his very public trial, were Simpson's main acting credits.

2. THE DECLARATION OF INDEPENDENCE para. 15 (U.S. 1776). The Declaration of Independence had followed the Declarations and Resolves of October 14, 1774, which also condemned the keeping of standing armies and not providing "*suitable quarters*" for soldiers. *See* Seymour W. Wurfel, *Quartering of Troops: The Unlitigated Third Amendment*, 21 TENN. L. REV. 723, 726 (1951); *see also* MARK V. TUSHNET, OUT OF RANGE: WHY THE CONSTITUTION CAN'T END THE BATTLE OVER GUNS 13 (2007).

3. Fields & Hardy at 424. **State Constitutions.** A majority of the state constitutions, thirty-three in all, include a quartering amendment nearly identical to the U.S. Constitution's Third Amendment. Bell at 144. Most state quartering amendments differ from the Third Amendment only in matters of punctuation or capitalization, if at all. Connecticut's constitution, for example, stipulates that "*No soldier shall, in time of peace, be quartered in any house, without the consent of the owner; nor in time of war, but in a manner to be prescribed by law.*" CONN. CONST. art. I, § 17. California captures the substance of the Third Amendment in a somewhat different form: "*Soldiers may not be quartered in any house in wartime except as prescribed by law, or in peacetime without the owner's consent.*" CAL. CONST. art. I, § 5.

4. For the argument that the Third Amendment is obsolete, see Morton J. Horwitz, *Is the Third Amendment Obsolete?* 26 VAL. U. L. REV. 209 (1992). Horwitz notes that the Second Amendment is also an anachronism but that "*it has the good fortune to have its own special lobby, the National Rifle Association, prepared to spend a fortune to remind us that the very integrity of constitutional government is at stake in allowing us to own guns. But no one cares about the Third Amendment; no one even has any interest in perpetuating its memory.*" *Id.* at 209. For a counter to Horwitz, *see generally* Gross (arguing the Third Amendment's relevancy to the right of privacy).

British cavalry squadron at Waterloo

British infantry squares beat back French cavalry at Waterloo

troops,[3] today the Third Amendment remains the least cited of the Bill of Rights.[4] Only one federal court has bothered to deal with it,[5] and most of the measly Third Amendment scholarship centers on whether it is relevant at all.[6]

We have the protections of the Third Amendment not because the amendment grants it or because courts enforce it, but because modern armies find quartering troops in homes impractical.[7]

5. *Engblom v. Carey*, 677 F.2d 957 (2d Cir. 1982) addressed the 1979 New York prison guard strike. During the strike, the state evicted prison guards from their prison housing and reassigned the housing to the National Guard temporarily guarding the prisons. Using Fourth Amendment analogies, the Second Circuit Court of Appeals, before rejecting the plaintiffs' Third Amendment claim, ruled the Third extended to the states through the Fourteenth Amendment, and that National Guard troops are "soldiers" under the Third Amendment. *Id.* at 961. The court also ruled that *"one who owns or lawfully possesses or controls property will in all likelihood have a legitimate expectation of privacy."* See William S. Fields, *The Third Amendment: Constitutional Protection from the Involuntary Quartering of Soldiers*, 124 MIL. L. REV. 195, 204–10 (1989); Bell at 141–43; *see also* Ann Marie C. Petrey, *The Third Amendment's Protection against Unwanted Military Intrusion:* Engblom v. Carey, 49 BROOKLYN L. REV. 857 (1983). The prison guards still lost.

6. The Third Amendment is still connected to other amendments. Regarding the connection between the Third and Fourth Amendments, Justice Joseph Story, who wrote the first treatise on the Constitution in 1833, in one small paragraph regarding the Third Amendment stated that,

Justice Joseph Story

"[It] speaks for itself. Its plain objective is to secure the perfect enjoyment of that great right of common law, that a man's house shall be his own castle, privileged against all civil and military intrusion." 3 JOSEPH STORY, COMMENTARIES ON THE CONSTITUTION § 1892 (1833), *quoted in* Wurfel at 729. Also, the Third Amendment relates to the part of the Fifth Amendment that prohibits taking property without just compensation. See Bell at 145–47.

Supreme Court justices occasionally invoke the Third Amendment as a base for the right to privacy, as in William O. Douglas's concurrence in *Griswold v. Connecticut*, 381 U.S. 479, 484 (1965) (establishing the right to contraceptives).

Justice William O. Douglas

7. The word "troop" means a group of people or animals and has a specific military connotation as in a group of soldiers or even a Scout Troop, the fundamental unit of Boy Scouts. "Troop" comes from late Latin *"tropus"* ("herd") WEBSTER'S at 2720, and the Teutonic *"thorp"* or *"torp,"* meaning a crowd or village, found in modern place names such as Mablethorp and Althorp. *Id.* at 2630. This sense of the word relates to the beam of a house or roofs in the village, and thus the English word "tavern"—a place where modern troops of military persons and college students spend as much time as possible.

In most military nomenclature, a cavalry unit is a "troop," and an infantry unit is a "company." This often gets mixed, and a synonym for troop is "platoon," a military unit typically composed of two to four squads (thirty to fifty soldiers) that a commissioned officer, usually a lieutenant, and a noncommissioned officer, usually a platoon sergeant, lead. The word "platoon" comes from the seventeenth century French *"peloton,"* meaning a small ball or small detachment of men, which came from *"pelote"* (originally from Latin *"pillula,"* or "little ball"). The word *"peloton"* still means a pack of racing bicycle riders.

PLATOON (Orion Pictures 1986) is a Vietnam War film written and directed by Oliver Stone, starring Charlie Sheen, Tom Berenger, and Willem Dafoe.

F Troop was a TV sitcom from 1965 to 1967 on ABC

But in our modern comfort with huge standing armies, navies, and air forces, we should keep in mind that most of the Founders feared a standing army.[1] They knew of history, both ancient and, to them, recent, of the armies of democracy going amok.[2]

That history can tell us a lot about the Third Amendment's relevance for today.

THE ROMANS

Unlike the eighteenth century British Army, when the Stuart kings routinely placed their soldiers in the residences of the British people, the Roman Army of two thousand years earlier generally did not house its legionnaires with civilians.[3] Rather, the Romans only quartered legionnaires with civilians as a tool of political suppression.[4]

1. In 2007, the U.S. defense budget rose to $439.3 billion. Office of the Undersecretary of Defense, National Defense Budget Estimates for Fiscal Year 2007 (2006), *available at* http://www.defenselink.mil/comptroller/defbudget/fy2007/. This does not include many military-related items outside of the Defense Department budget, such as nuclear weapons research, maintenance, and production (approximately $9.3 billion, which is in the Department of Energy budget), Veterans Affairs ($33.2 billion), or the wars in Iraq and Afghanistan, largely funded through extrabudgetary supplements ($170 billion in 2007). Altogether, military-related expenses totaled approximately $626.1 billion.

About 43 percent of all U.S. taxes goes to military spending. This comes out to 48 percent of the military spending in the entire world. For allocation of U.S. 2007 taxes, see http://www.globalissues.org/article/75/world-military-spending#USMilitary Spending (last visited July 4, 2008).

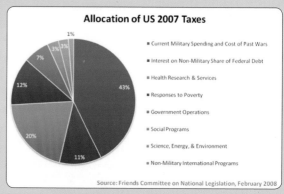

Allocation of US 2007 Taxes

- Current Military Spending and Cost of Past Wars
- Interest on Non-Military Share of Federal Debt
- Health Research & Services
- Responses to Poverty
- Government Operations
- Social Programs
- Science, Energy, & Environment
- Non-Military International Programs

Source: Friends Committee on National Legislation, February 2008

From: **http://www.globalissues.org/Geopolitics/ArmsTrade/Spending.asp#USMilitarySpending** (last visited July 4, 2008)

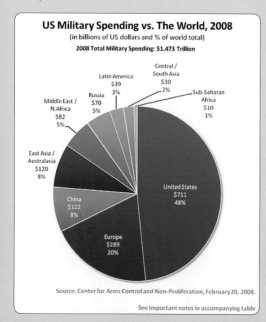

US Military Spending vs. The World, 2008
(in billions of US dollars and % of world total)
2008 Total Military Spending: $1.473 Trillion

Central / South Asia $30 2%
Latin America $39 3%
Russia $70 5%
Middle East / N.Africa $82 5%
Sub-Saharan Africa $10 1%
East Asia / Australasia $120 8%
China $122 8%
Europe $289 20%
United States $711 48%

Source: Center for Arms Control and Non-Proliferation, February 20, 2008.

See Important notes in accompanying table

World Military Spending, http://www.globalissues.org/article/75/world-military-spending#USMilitarySpending (Sept. 13, 2009) (citing U.S. Military Spending vs. the World, 2008, Center for Arms Control and Non-Proliferation).

2. Napoleon Bonaparte had risen to prominence as a general during the French Revolution. He converted democracy to become ruler of France as *First Consul of the French Republic* and then *Emperor of the French, King of Italy, Mediator of the Swiss Confederation*

Abigail Adams

Alexander Hamilton

and *Protector of the Confederation of the Rhine*. Although the full flowering of Napoleon's ambitions occurred after 1800, the drafters of the Third Amendment feared just such a man as him. Indeed, Alexander Hamilton could have been the very man they feared. At one point Hamilton controlled the entire United States Army. Abigail Adams referred to Hamilton as *"little Mars"* and *"a second Bona-party."* RONALD CHERNOW, ALEXANDER HAMILTON 566 (2004) *citing* RICHARD NORTON SMITH, PATRIARCH: GEORGE WASHINGTON AND THE NEW AMERICAN NATION 340 (1993).

Napoleon on His Imperial Throne by Jean Auguste Dominique Ingres (1806)

The Romans knew that a professional army was about discipline, which is much easier to achieve in barracks, or, as the Romans would call them, "*castras*" (singular "*castrum*"), meaning forts or camps.[5] Special Roman military units with officers called "*architecti*," ("chief engineers") built the camps, which they could build in a few hours even under enemy attack. They generally organized the camps on a set pattern[6] that, as the camps developed, had various amenities.[7]

Any number of English towns started out as Roman camps and several retain forms of the word "*castra*" in their names, usually in the suffix "-caster or "-chester", take, for example, Lancaster, Tadcaster, Chester, Manchester, and Ribchester.[8] European cities as well originated as Roman camps, such as Castres, France.

---

3. The legionnaire was a heavy infantryman and the basic military unit of the ancient Roman army. A legionnaire belonged to a legion ("*legio*" or "military levy or conscript," from "*legere*," "to choose"). WEBSTER'S at 1421. (This is the origin of the English word "levy," to refer to military conscription or raising of troops.) During the Roman Empire, a legion had several "cohorts" of these heavy infantry, with attached units of auxiliaries, who were not Roman citizens and provided cavalry and skirmishers. The size of a typical legion varied widely throughout Roman history but generally was around 5000 men.

4. For example, a city that rose up against Rome might see Roman troops quartered there. *See generally* SUSAN FORD WILTSHIRE, GREECE, ROME, AND THE BILL OF RIGHTS 142–43 (1992).

5. *Castras* is the origin of the English "castle." The castle is the basis of the rook in chess, which moves vertically or horizontally. The rook also can move in a special way called "castling," which is unique in chess because two pieces, the king and the rook, both move as the king is "castled." The word "rook" derives from the Persian "*rokh*" or "*rukh*," meaning a chariot. WEBSTER'S at 2166. In the Persian game of chess the rook is a chariot.

Castling move in chess

6. This is the origin of the English word "architect." WEBSTER'S at 141. Roman field armies also built *castras* each night, no matter how long they had marched that day. This protected them from night attack, and the discipline it took intimidated enemies. *See* ADRIAN GOLDSWORTHY, ROMAN WARFARE 23 (2000).

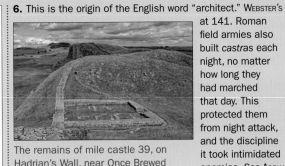

The remains of mile castle 39, on Hadrian's Wall, near Once Brewed National Park, England, showing Roman camp organization

7. The Canteen. A Roman camp in peacetime supported a marketplace where natives could enter as far as the units numbered 5, which was half-way to the headquarters ("*praetorium*"). In a typical Roman camp the street that crossed at right angles to the *via praetoria* was the *via quintana* ("5th street"), which is where the market sat, where legionnaires could buy amenities, food, and drink. The English word "canteen" comes from "*quintana*," as in a military cafeteria or a local bar or even the water bottle.

Castra at Masada, Palestine, in the Roman "playing card" layout

The reconstructed west gate at Arbeia Roman Fort in South Shields, England

8. KURT VON S. KYNELL, SAXON AND MEDIEVAL ANTECEDENTS OF THE ENGLISH COMMON LAW 4 (2000).

Roman legionnaires were paid professional soldiers.[1] But it was the very professionalism of Roman armies that underscored the Founders'fears of standing armies.

As the Roman military became more professional and permanent, it became more independent of civilian control. Although the Roman legionnaire took an oath to serve the people ("*populus Romanus*"), his benefits, livelihood, and pension came from his commanding general.[2]

The Framers structured our constitution to avoid this problem.

THE ANGLO-SAXONS IN THE MEAD HALL[3]

The sentiment, if not the exact words, "*a man's home is his castle*" goes back over one thousand years to the Anglo-Saxons.[4] For them, law was mostly private, and their law protected the home above all else.[5] They called this the "*frith*," or peace, over each home, and trespassers paid for invading the household enclosure, a value we still reflect in our modern crimes of trespass and burglary. Those who committed offenses against persons within a home's "*mund*" ("protection") faced additional fines.[6]

---

1. Our modern word "soldier" comes from the Latin "*solidus*" (Latin for "solid"), which was a Roman gold coin. WEBSTER'S at 2392. Romans paid legionnaires with the *solidus*, leading to the word "soldier." Constantine I introduced the *solidus* in 309–10 AD to replace the "*aureus*." The Eastern Roman (i.e., Byzantine) Empire used it until the tenth century. The modern Spanish word "*sueldo*" ("salary") also comes from *solidus* and also the French word "*sou*," a small coin of little value, as in "*sans le sou*"—"I'm broke," "without money." In English, this is where the word "cent" comes from.

2. WILTSHIRE at 138.

3. Mead hall, or moot hall, is where the Anglo-Saxons held their courts, called "*moots*." See **Chapter 6: How the Sixth Amendment Guarantees You a Court, a Lawyer, and a Chamber Pot.** After

court was done, or maybe even before or during, the moothall reverted to its normal function of being a meadhall for the drinking of mead.

Mead, or honey wine, is fermented from honey, water, and yeast. The English word comes from Old English "*medu*," from Proto-Germanic "*meduz*." Slavic "*miod*"/"*med*," which means "honey," and Baltic "*midus*," which means "mead," derive from the same Proto-Indo-European root. (Cf. Welsh "*medd*"; Old Irish "*mid*"; Sanskrit "*madhu*"). WEBSTER'S at 1519. (The modern Spanish word for honey, for instance, is "*miel*.") Traditionally, mead could preserve fruit and was warmed with a hot poker plunged in the mug from the fireplace. Mead was used in early India and during the "golden age" of Ancient Greece. Aristotle (384–322 BC) discussed mead in his *Meteorologica*. The Roman Pliny the Elder (23–79 AD) called mead "*militates*" in his *Naturalis Historia*.

The Anglo-Saxon epic BEOWULF features mead, where the main

character fights the evil Grendel at the mead hall. The movie THE 13TH WARRIOR (Touchstone Pictures 1999) also features mead, with Antonio Banderas's character, a Muslim who cannot drink the fermentation of "*wheat or grape*" taking a good swig of mead because "*honey, it's made from honey.*" Mead is also the favorite beverage of the skin-changer Beorn in J.R.R. Tolkien's THE HOBBIT (1937).

4. For more on the English reverence for the home, see **Chapter 4: Molasses and the Sticky Origins of the Fourth Amendment.** This focus on the privacy of the home is the thematic bridge between the Third and Fourth Amendments.

5. For example, they had no such thing as what we would call "criminal law"; it was all private, or what we would call "tort law."If you harmed someone, for whatever reason, be it malice or accident, you owed them or their family recompense. See Bell at 118. See also **Chapter 8: "Baby, Don't Be Cruel": What's So Cruel and Unusual about the Eighth Amendment?** for more on Anglo-Saxons and punishment.

6. Bell at 118. The Anglo-Saxon word "*mund*" is akin to the Latin, French, and later English words for "*manual*," or "of the hand" (as in "manual labor"). WEBSTER'S at 1499. In the Anglo-Saxon sense, it is a hand or palm, and thus the protection of the hand over the home. *Id.* at 1611.

Anglo-Saxon homeowners never had to quarter soldiers because for the most part they *were* the soldiers; there was no standing army. Instead, the "*fyrd*" or "*fierd*," a militia of all able-bodied men, was the army. They served locally for short durations with their own weapons and provisions. The only professional soldiers were the small contingents of "*housecarls*" that kings and earls maintained.[7]

NORMANS CRASHING THE PARTY!

After the Norman conquest in 1066, quartering became a problem.[8] Unlike the Anglo-Saxons who took an oath to fight for the king during the campaign season, the Normans brought with them feudalism, a system where nobody really owned any land outright but had to pay duties to the next lord, all the way up the chain to the king.[9] These Norman kings were ambitious, with holdings in France and elsewhere to defend. What they wanted was a regular supply of armed men called "knights."[10]

Knights were the mounted professional soldiers of their day, and the king compensated them with land and serfs.[11] Along with the land and serfs, however, went the duty to fight for the king.[12]

---

7. See **Chapter-2: Shooting Your Mouth Off about the Second Amendment**, discussing the *fyrd* as the origin of English and colonial militias and discussing *housecarls*.

8. The Battle of Hastings.

9. Hence our modern term "landlord" for someone to whom you owe rent.

10. Bell at 118–19; Fields & Hardy at 395–96; Fields at 196 n.4. "Knight" is the English term for the mounted fighter of the Middle Ages that originally referred to a boy, follower, or attendant. Other European names include the Spanish "*caballero*" (meaning "horseman" or "gentleman," and related to the word "chivalry"), the

Knights Dueling by Eugène Delacroix

Italian "*cavaliere*," the German "*ritter*" (related to the English word "rider"). WEBSTER'S at 1370.

A knight is also a crafty chess piece that can only move in a letter "L" pattern: either two squares horizontally and one square vertically or two squares vertically and one square horizontally. And, unlike other pieces, the knight can jump over pieces.

The tank is the knight of the modern battle field. Indeed, some tank regiments are still called "cavalry."

11. "Serf" comes from Latin "*servus*" ("servant" or "slave"). WEBSTER'S at 2284. Serfdom was the socio-economic status of unfree peasants under feudalism consisting

A re-creation of mid-seventeenth century pikemen looking "pawnish"

of the forced labor of serfs on the landowner's fields in return for protection and the right to work on the serf's own leased fields. A "villein" was the most common serf in the Middle Ages. Villeins generally rented small homes, with or without land. Villeins newly arrived in the city in some cases took to crime, which gives the modern "villain." Others words for serf were "peon" and "pawn," which came to English from the Spanish "*peon*." The pawn is a bit player or someone under a pledge of servitude. Both the words "peon" and "pawn" derive from the Latin "*pignus*" ("pledge") and the items having been pawned to the broker are "pledges" or "pawns." In chess, the pawn is the weakest and most numerous piece (some books do not call it a "piece" at all but just a "pawn") and represents infantry such as pikemen.

After the Civil War, the Thirteenth Amendment prohibited involuntary servitude such as "peonage" for all but convicted criminals. Congress also passed an antipeonage law on March 2, 1867, now codified at 42 U.S.C. § 1994 (2006): "*Peonage abolished— The holding of any person to service or labor under the system known as peonage is abolished and forever prohibited in any Territory or State of the United States; and all acts, laws, resolutions, orders, regulations, or usages of any Territory or State, which have heretofore established, maintained, or enforced, or by virtue of which any attempt shall hereafter be made to establish, maintain, or enforce, directly or indirectly, the voluntary or involuntary service or labor of any persons as peons, in liquidation of any debt or obligation, or otherwise, are declared null and void.*"

12. In fact, most of our words for military things are Norman French in origin: "army," "navy," "battle," "combat," "skirmish," "stratagem," "ambush" and the ranks of "sergeant," "captain," "lieutenant," "colonel," and "general." KYNELL at 51. So are the words "beef," "pork," and "lamb," all eaten at Norman tables, while the oppressed Saxons tended their "cows," "cattle," "pigs," and "sheep" out in the yard.

The Anglo-Saxon freemen were none too happy about becoming serfs and did not particularly warm up to the idea of supporting their local Norman knight. This resistance was the beginning of the Third Amendment.[1]

In 1156, Henry II wanted money to pay for soldiers rather than having to always deal with temperamental knights on campaign. He therefore introduced "*scutage*," a system where the knights did not have to be on call if they provided the king revenue for hiring professional soldiers.[2] This was the beginning of a modern army.

PARTY CRASHING IN MERRY OLDE ENGLAND

Compared to today, even the biggest medieval army was modest in size.[3] Even so, kings and lords still faced the problem of where to put their soldiers. Kings moved from castle to castle not only to spread the expense of their entourage but to assert control over the kingdom.[4]

With any increase in the number of professional soldiers, this castle-to-castle housing proved inadequate. Kings tried placing the men in local inns and taverns, but this

---

1. "*It was in the centralization of Norman rule, the militarization of the country, the abuse of the Saxon inhabitants, and the involvement in continental wars that the grievance against the involuntary quartering of soldiers first took root.*" Bell at 119.

2. Bell at 118–19; *see also* Fields & Hardy at 397.

    Scutage translates as "shield money," i.e., a sort of tax to the king so he could pay for his own troops. It comes from the Latin word for shield, "*scutum*." *See* GOLDSWORTHY at 125.

Trajan's Column: Legionnaires using their *scutum* in the "*testudo*" ("turtle formation")

4. *See* William Shakespeare's KING LEAR. King Lear divided his kingdom among his daughters who, by Act I, Scene 4, objected to his rowdy company of knights and retainers sucking up the hospitality.

 A modern chess board and the king

3. "**Army**" derives from the Latin "*armata*" ("act of arming," via Old French "*armée*"). WEBSTER'S at 151. Army can mean a nation's armed forces or a field army. Armies are divided into corps and divisions.

    A "**corps**" (pronounced as "core," derived from the Latin "*corpus*" or "body") is an organizational grouping of troops. It can also be a branch of service, such as the U.S. Marine Corps. In the nonmilitary context it can refer to humanitarian

    organizations such as the Peace Corps, Ameri Corps, Mercy Corps, or Job Corps.

5. A "*tally*"(Latin for "stick") was a piece of wood with marks or notches to record numbers. WEBSTER'S at 2573–74. Merchants used these to record sales. The buyer and seller would cut the wood lengthwise and each would take half. The Court of Exchequer used tallies as part of its accounting system on a big checkered table, which relates to the origin of the game checkers and the English term "check" in chess. Indeed, the expression in checkers, "king me," when the checker piece (or chit) makes it to the back rank, as well as that one "checks" the king in chess indicates the relationship to the King's Court of Exchequer.

Tally marks in Europe and North America are most commonly written as groups of five lines with the first four lines vertical and every fifth line diagonally across the previous vertical lines, making a "five-bar gate." In modern American English one hears the word "tally" for voting, as in "*the vote tally*." There is also "*keeping

could not accommodate the ranks. Kings thus turned to private farms and homes.

In private homes, soldiers paid with IOUs called "*chits*," "*tallies*," or "*billets*,"[5] which the recipient could then redeem or use to pay taxes.[6] By tax time, however, they may have had no value.[7]

Magna Carta of 1215 shows the problem of disbanded soldiers:

"*Immediately after concluding a peace, we will remove from the kingdom all alien knights, crossbowmen, sergeants and mercenary soldiers who have come with horses and arms to the hurt of the realm.*"[8]

Reacting to soldiers hanging around as unwelcome houseguests, the cities and towns objected. Across England, towns and boroughs began enacting charters that prohibited the forced billeting of soldiers in homes. In 1131 Henry I granted London such protection.[9] King Henry II, his sons Kings Richard I and John,[10] and King Henry III also granted London the same protection. The right to be free from quartering spread from London throughout England, Ireland, and Scotland.[11]

---

the tally" for game scores. The Latin "*talionis*" means "equivalent to" or "equal," which forms part of the term "*lex talionis*," or the law of proportionality in punishment. *See* **Chapter 8: "Baby, Don't Be Cruel": What's So Cruel and Unusual about the Eighth Amendment?**

"*Chit*" originally referred to a voucher for food or drink and now refers to a marker in board games or checkers. WEBSTER'S at 470.

....

6. Fields & Hardy at 400; Bell at 122–23; Hardy at 69.

Court of Exchequer c. 1460; Inner Temple Library, England

7. Because these receipts often proved worthless, "billeting" came to signify free room and board. Hardy at 127; Fields & Hardy at 400. *See also* COLIN RHYS LOVELL, ENGLISH CONSTITUTIONAL AND LEGAL HISTORY 169 (1962) (noting that when financial demands became acute, Edward I would seize merchants' wool and give Exchequer tallies in return).

"*Billet*" comes from the written order or ticket for the quartering of a military person. WEBSTER'S at 268. It is related to the word "bill," as in a "restaurant bill" or "bill of sale" or even a "bill" before Congress or Parliament. Both "bill" and "billet" derive from the Latin "*bulla*," meaning a seal, as in a sealed document. WEBSTER'S at 267. This is where the name "papal bull" comes from, pronouncing decrees from the Pope.

Papal bull of Pope Urban VIII, 1637, sealed with a leaden *bulla*

....

8. *Magna Carta*, cl. 51, *quoted in* DANNY DANZIGER & JOHN GILLINGHAM, 1215: THE YEAR OF MAGNA CARTA 95 (2003).

....

9. The charter stated that "*within the walls of the city no one is to be billeted; neither for one of my household nor for one of any other is lodging to be exacted by force.*" Quoted in Bell at 119.

10. King John's grant became special because it was in *Magna Carta* of 1215:

"*London shall have all its ancient liberties and free customs. Besides we will and grant that all the other cities, boroughs, and ports shall have all their liberties and free customs.*"

Magna Carta has taken on a mythic status as the origin of liberty. But at the time it was no big deal to anyone other than the barons and lords. Most of *Magna Carta* did not apply to the common folk. *See generally* DANZIGER & GILLINGHAM.

Magna Carta—not the original that King John signed, which has been lost (though four copies survive), but the 1225 version by Henry III

....

11. Bell at 119. For example, Oxford impliedly got the right when the crown granted it the same liberties as London. *Id.*

THE GROWTH OF ARMIES

For most of the Middle Ages, soldiers either lived off the land or plunder.[1] Their commanders, such as they were, gave little attention to the men's lodging and feeding. Men-at-arms, retainers of the great knights, and lords may have received more care, but they still lacked the uniformity that we associate with modern soldiers.[2]

The quality of the soldiery exacerbated the problem. Kings recruited men however they could, and thus tramps, beggars, and criminals filled their armies.[3] By the fourteenth century, soldiers traveling to and from the French wars often demanded free lodging from whomever they came into contact.[4] And the problem was not just the free lodging but that the soldiers often

---

1. Bell at 123.

"Uniformed" Hospitalers

Marine Corps enlisted blue dress uniform

The British infantry uniform, 1750–1835.

2. In fact, the uniform is relatively new in history. Generally, ancient soldiers did not have uniforms, with the exception of perhaps the Spartan hoplites, who all wore the same red cloak and carried a shield with the Greek letter *lamda* (λ). Some ancient soldiers may have looked uniformed but that had more to do with wearing the same ethnic dress.

Some Roman legions adopted the Spartans' red cloak to hide blood from wounds. Also, they wore similar armor and probably a white or off-white tunic. *See* Goldsworthy at 43, 171. But this probably had more to do with availability then any attempt to create a uniform.

The terracotta army of the first emperor of Chin (c. 200 BC) appears uniformed, but actually their dress is not standardized.

In the Middle Ages, retainers of a great lord or king may have worn his distinctive badge or coat of arms, but this was far from creating a standard dress for a whole army. An exception was the habits of the orders of military monks, such as the Knights Templar or Hospitaler, with mantles respectively of white (with red crosses on the shoulder) or black (with white crosses). As national armies started to form with the levies of the fifteenth and sixteen centuries, the only uniformity would have been a distinctive scarf. This is one explanation of the origin of today's necktie. Even royal guards would only be issued with distinctive coats to wear over ordinary clothing. But with the growth of the regimental system in the French Army in the mid-seventeenth century, uniforms started to be distinctive to various regiments. For one thing, this helped a commander see his units on the battlefield. But it was still some time before there would be a national uniform such as the British Redcoats.

The terracotta army

3. For example, Edward I one year pardoned 450 murderers and lesser criminals in exchange for their army service. Fields & Hardy at 399.

4. Bell at 122–23; Hardy at 69–70.

demanded a lot more.[5]

Neither kings nor Parliament really ever responded to the problem. In 1339, however, Parliament tried to put the burden on Scotland by ordering that *"the Captains and others being together, shall lie and forage upon Scotland, and not upon the Marches of England."*[6]

But armies were small, and the number of soldiers needing forced hospitality was relatively few.[7] Plus, the fighting of the Hundred Years' War was done in France. So with limited soldiers actually in England where *chits*, *tallies*, or *billets* were honored, the problem did not come to a head.

Things were to change, though, when England's wars got bigger, and even kings started to overstay their welcome.

---

5. Parliament repeatedly heard protests such as that described in William Langland's fourteenthcentury poem, *Piers Plowman*, where a man complained of having lost his wife, barn, livestock, home, and the maidenhood of his daughter to soldiers. Fields & Hardy at 399. English soldiers committed still worse abuses once they landed in Normandy. *Id.* at 399 n.22.

6. 13 Edw. 3, rot. 35 (1340).

7. Spain started a trend to bigger armies. Queen Isabella of Castile (as in Ferdinand and Isabella, of Columbus fame) was an exceptional woman and perhaps one of the great quartermaster generals of her day. She organized the supply to Ferdinand's soldiers during the conquest of Granada in southern Spain ending in 1492.

The queen in modern chess may have been patterned after Isabella. In chess's Indian and Persian historical ancestors, "*shatranj*," the queen, was a weak piece called a "*fers*"("vizier" or "minister"), only able to move or capture one square diagonally. The modern queen's move arose in fifteenth century Europe, and she became the most powerful and valuable piece on the board. *See* Marilyn Yalom, Birth of the Chess Queen (2004).

Isabella and Ferdinand were also the parents of Catherine of Aragon, who became the first divorced wife of England's King Henry VIII.

Isabella at the Conquest of Granada

Catherine of Aragon

Isabella of Castile

THE STUARTS TO THE ENGLISH BILL OF RIGHTS

Looking at the Stuart kings you are tempted to think that they actually wanted to lose the throne. But as discussed in Chapter 1, it was probably just stupidity in their gene pool.[1]

Under the Stuarts a lot of problems grew worse; not just with quartering troops, but with the monarchy itself.[2] By the seventeenth century, kings did not go to war—nations did. And, as such, nations began to field larger and more complicated armies. Armies had to train year-round and in peacetime.[3] But military logistics were inadequate to supply year-round facilities.[4]

In addition, who should pay the cost of the army became part of the power struggle between the Stuart kings and Parliament. The House of Commons, for instance, refused to provide King Charles I with enough money to house his troops, which forced him to quarter them in private homes.[5] Parliament then turned around and protested in the PETITION OF RIGHT of 1628:[6]

"Whereas of late, great companies of soldiers and mariners have been dispersed into diverse countries of the realm, and the inhabitants, against their wills have been compelled to receive them into their houses, and there to suffer them to sojourn, against the laws and customs of this realm, and to the great grievance and vexation of the people . . ."[7]

The petition went on to demand (in nice language)

"that your Majesty would be pleased to remove the said soldiers and mariners, and that your people may not be so burdened in time to come . . ."[8]

Charles I, however, ignored the PETITION OF RIGHT, which set the stage for the English Civil War.[9]

After having argued in the PETITION OF RIGHT against quartering troops in homes,

---

1. James I (James VI of Scotland) Charles I, Charles II, James II.

For more on the Stuarts, see **Chapter 1: Of Dogma and Desire: Saying What You Believe about the First Amendment.**

2. Hardy at 127.

3. Fields & Hardy at 408–09.

4. Bell at 123.
"Logistics" derives from the ancient Greek "λόγος" or "logos," meaning "ratio," "word," "calculation," "reason," "speech," and "oration." Ancient Greek, Roman, and Byzantine armies had "logistikas" ("officers") responsible for acquiring and organizing the army's supplies and quarters. This leads to the modern definition of "logistics" as the branch of military science regarding procuring, maintaining, and transporting material, personnel, and facilities. WEBSTER'S at 1453. In both military and civilian contexts, logistics is a branch of engineering regarding "people systems" rather than "machine systems."
   There is an old saying that "*Amateurs study strategy [or tactics]; professionals study logistics.*" The quote has been attributed to several people, including General Omar Bradley, General Robert H. Barrow, Napoleon, Helmuth von Moltke, and Carl von Clausewitz.

5. Gross at 217.

6. Bell at 124. This was one of many examples of Parliament outmaneuvering Charles I.

7. PETITION OF RIGHT, 1628, 3 Car. 1, cap. 1, § VI (Eng.), *reproduced at* http://www.constitution.org/eng/petright.htm (last visited July 12, 2008).

8. PETITION OF RIGHT, § VIII, *quoted in* Field & Hardy at 403. *See also* Wurfel at 723 (noting that the PETITION OF RIGHT was the "*first statutory limitation on quartering...*").

9. The movie CROMWELL (Columbia Pictures 1970) dramatizes (with several historical inaccuracies) Charles I's demise and execution.

the parliamentary forces might have avoided doing so during the ensuing English Civil War (1642–51). But principle bowed to necessity, and both Royalists (King Charles I's forces) and Roundheads (Parliament's forces) resorted to quartering soldiers in homes despite official disavowals, the extensive use of tents, and attempts to repay the civilian hosts.[10]

In the end Charles I lost the English Civil War and his crown (both literally and figuratively),[11] which lead to Cromwell's dictatorship. After Cromwell, Charles I's son, King Charles II, ascended to the throne in 1660.

But despite all these changes in government, the practice of quartering troops in homes did not wane. During the Third Anglo-Dutch War of l672–74, for example, conflicts broke out between civilians and soldiers on the issue of quartering.[12] Again, the problem was a lack of barracks for soldiers.[13]

After Charles II died, his brother King James II exacerbated this issue. Among many miscalculations, James II used quartering not just as an expedient but as repression. In 1678 he brought the "Highland host" of about ten thousand soldiers to winter in Scotland to repress the nonconformist Presbyterian Covenanters.[14] In reaction, Parliament passed the Anti-Quartering Act of 1679:

"Noe officer military or civill nor any other person whatever shall from henceforth presume to place quarter or billet any souldier or souldiers upon any subject or inhabitant of this realme . . . without his consent . . . ."[15]

Thus, in 1679 and beyond, English homeowners, theoretically, now had powerful protections against forced quartering because this act applied to town and country, not only in peace but also during war. But James II ignored this act to his peril and ultimately lost the throne.[16]

---

10. Bell at 124.

11. Given that a "crown" can refer to both your kingship and your head, Charles I lost both!

Charles I's execution

13. Fields at 197–98.

14. Bell at 124.

King James II

The Battle of Texel, 11–21 August 1673, during the Third Anglo-Dutch War

12. Fields at 198. Charles I's *"dredged up from the scum of society"* his troops. *See also* Lovell at 305–06.

The **Anglo-Dutch Wars** were four to six wars (depending on how historians count them) between England and the Netherlands fought in the seventeenth and eighteenth centuries for control over sea and trade routes. They are known as the **Dutch Wars** in England and the **English Wars** in the Netherlands.

15. Anti-Quartering Act of 1679, 31 Car. 2, ch. 1, *quoted in* Bell at 124.

16. Hardy at 128; Fields & Hardy at 405.

THE GLORIOUS REVOLUTION AND THE BILL OF RIGHTS

Many things triggered James II's demise: anti-Catholicism, his insolence, political miscalculation, and popular dissatisfaction over billeting.[1] All of this brought about the Glorious Revolution of 1688. Parliament invited James's son-in-law, William of Orange, and his daughter, Mary Stuart, to depose him. When William landed in England, James lost his nerve and fled to France.[2]

To get the throne, William and Mary made a deal with Parliament to accept, among other things, what eventually became the English Bill of Rights of 1689. One of these accused James II of subverting English liberties by "*quartering soldiers contrary to law . . . ,*" and of raising and keeping a standing army in time of peace.

Parliament did not address the quartering issue in the Bill of Rights.[3] It did not need to because, at the time, there were no standing armies in England.[4]

Very soon, however, Parliament realized this error and passed the Mutiny Act, forbidding quartering soldiers in private homes without the consent of the owners.[5] The act did not, however, appropriate any money for barracks, but it did direct authorities to billet soldiers in alehouses, inns, and stables. This provided homeowners some protection. Parliament also went on to declare it illegal to raise or keep a standing army without Parliament's consent.

But the Mutiny Act did not extend to the colonies.[6] For American colonists, the issue became but another example of England's disrespect of their rights as Englishmen.

---

1. Bell at 122–23.

2. The two political parties in Parliament at the time, the Whigs and Tories, had different theories about the legality of James II's overthrow. For the Whigs, James had abdicated by violating popular rights in what became the Declaration of Rights and the English Bill of Rights. For the Tories, James simply abandoned the throne. Fields & Hardy at 405.

William of Orange

Mary Stuart

3. Fields & Hardy at 406.

4. Another possible explanation, of course, is that William III was also quartering troops in private homes and Parliament did not want to blame him for the same sin of James II. *See* Lois G. Schwoerer, The Declaration of Rights, 1689, at 71 (1981). But if this were the case, then surely the standing army prohibition would have affected William too.

5. Fields & Hardy at 406, *citing* Mutiny Act, 1689, 1 W. & M., sess. 2, cap. 4 (Eng.). *See* Lovell at 397–98 (noting that the Mutiny Act was to raise an army to challenge James II's attempts to regain the throne).

6. Hardy at 73.

7. Bell at 125; Fields & Hardy at 414; Fields at 199.
  King Philip's War was an armed conflict between Native Americans and New England colonists from 1675–76. The conflict was one of the bloodiest in American history relative to the size

King Philip

of the population. *See generally* Eric Schultz & Michael J. Touglas, King Philip's War: The History and Legacy of America's Forgotten Conflict (2000).

Joseph Dudley   Sir Edmund Andros

The Dominion of New England (1686–89) was a short-lived administrative union of the New England colonies under a decree from James II to enforce the Navigation Acts and to coordinate colonial defense. The Dominion was very unpopular in New England, which resisted England's centralized authority and the curtailment of various colonial rights by Dominion governors Joseph Dudley and Sir Edmund Andros, as well as their quartering of troops. James II's overthrow in England caused the Dominion's collapse.

THE COLONIAL EXPERIENCE AND THE ROAD TO REVOLUTION

As early as King Philip's War (1675–76), Massachusetts and Connecticut colonists complained about the English quartering soldiers in their private homes. New Yorkers likewise complained in 1688 during the Dominion of New England.[7]

At different times the colonies passed their own versions of the Mutiny Act, including the New York Assembly's 1683 Charter of Liberties and Privileges:

"Noe Freeman shall be compelled to receive any Marriners or Souldiers into his house and there suffer them to Sojourne, against their willes provided Always it be not in time of Actuall Warr within this province."[8]

But the final catalyst for this issue, as well as many others, was the Seven Years' War, or, as Americans know it, the French and Indian War.

THE FRENCH AND INDIAN WAR

During the French and Indian War (1754–63), thousands of British regulars came to North America. Surely British Redcoats must have felt frustrated as they "protected" the colonies while receiving inadequate support for their maintenance.[9] Conversely, colonists had to question how much of Britain's military effort protected them, as opposed to the interests of her empire.

But though the colonists protested, the British forced troops on them.[10] The quartering continued through Pontiac's War of 1763.[11]

---

8. Bell at 125, *quoting* 1 THE ROOTS OF THE BILL OF RIGHTS 166 (B. Schwartz ed., 1980). Other colonial legislatures passed similar laws with exceptions for *"innholders or other houses of entertainment."* Hardy at 130.

....

9. Bell at 125; Fields & Hardy at 415; Fields at 200.
   American colonists repeatedly denied General Edward Braddock's requests for quarters and provisions. His successor, John Campbell, Earl of London, complained in 1756 that Americans opposed his efforts at every turn. Bell at 125.

British soldier in 1742

....

10. Bell at 125.

"**Redcoat,**" refers to British army soldiers because of the color of their uniforms during the late seventeenth to nineteenth centuries. The Tudor Yeoman of the Guard and Yeomen Warders, formed in 1485, traditionally wore Tudor red and gold, which, coupled with the idea that the red would conceal blood, may have been the origin of the tradition. The colonists in Boston called them *"lobsters"* or *"lobsterbacks." See generally* RICHARD HOLMES, REDCOAT: THE BRITISH SOLDIER IN THE AGE OF HORSE AND MUSKET (2001).

11. Pontiac's Rebellion was a 1763 Native American uprising against the British in the Great Lakes region after the British had won the French and Indian War/Seven Years' War (1754–63). Numerous tribes joined the uprising, but Pontiac was the most prominent of many native leaders. The policies of General Jeffrey Amherst of limiting the distribution of gunpowder to Native Americans provoked the conflict. The British negotiated with the Native Americans, and Pontiac won several concessions.
Amherst, Massachusetts; Amherst, New Hampshire; Amherst, Nova Scotia; Amherst, New York; Amherst County, Virginia; Amherstburg, Ontario; Amherst Island, Ontario, and Amherst College in Massachusetts are all named for the general. As for Pontiac, there are no known contemporary paintings, but General Motors did name a car after him.

Pontiac as imagined by John Mix Stanley in the nineteenth century

General Jeffery Amherst   Pontiac Hood Ornament

The British won the French and Indian War, but it left them with a huge American frontier to defend. Confronted with a burdensome war debt, the British government thought the colonists should help pay part of the bill for their own defense.[1]

Thus in 1765, Parliament passed the Quartering Act, requiring the colonists to pay for the British soldiers' barracks and succor. If the barracks were insufficient, quartering was to be in inns, livery stables, alehouses and, if all else failed, private buildings. The colonists resented this last alternative the most.[2]

A modern army is a hungry thing. To feed, clothe, and house the British Army in America, Parliament coupled the Quartering Act with the notorious 1765 Stamp Act to generate the revenue to support British troops.[3] Thus quartering became mixed with a hated tax on all business and commerce and part of the slogan *"no taxation without representation."*[4]

THE INTOLERABLE ACTS AND THE BOSTON TEA PARTY

Resistance grew throughout North America against the Quartering and Stamp Acts.[5] Parliament suspended the New York Assembly until it implemented the Quartering Act.[6] In October 1768, the Massachusetts

---

1. Bell at 126; Fields at 200.
See generally BARBARA W. TUCHMAN, THE MARCH OF FOLLY: FROM TROY TO VIETNAM, "Chapter 4: The British Lose America" (1984) (*"a phenomenon noticeable throughout history regardless of place or period is the pursuit by governments of policies contrary to their own interests"*). Tuchman notes the examples of the Trojans bringing in the horse, British policy in colonial America, and U.S. policy in Vietnam.

2. Bell at 126.
  For example, Samuel Adam's in the *Boston Gazette* of Oct. 17, 1768, wrote as follows:
  "Where Law ends, (says Mr. Locke) tyranny begins, if the Law be transgress'd to another's harm: No one I believe will deny the truth of the observation, and therefore I again appeal to common sense, whether the act which provides for the quartering and billeting the King's troops, was not transgress'd, when the barracks at the Castle which are sufficient to contain more than the whole number of soldiers now in this town, were absolutely rufus'd: This I presume cannot be contested."
  Reprinted in 5 THE FOUNDERS' CONSTITUTION 215 (Philip B. Kurland & Ralph Lerner eds., 1987). Adams also cited the abuses of quartering in his 1772 List of Infringements and Violations of Rights. *Reprinted in* Hardy at 134.
  Samuel Adams was one of the Founding Fathers instrumental in forming the rebellion against Great Britain that became the American Revolution. He was also John Adams's second cousin. Although Samuel Adams made his living as a brewer, he did not brew Samuel Adams Beer, a brand the Boston Beer Company named for him.

Samuel Adams

3. The Stamp Act of 1765 was not just a tax on stamps as we know it in the modern sense of a postage stamp. Rather, it applied to all legal documents, permits, commercial contracts, newspapers, wills, pamphlets, and even playing cards. You could not live and breathe in the colonies without having to pay for a stamp on your documents.

4. Bell at 126; Fields at 200.

5. Bell at 126; *see also* Hardy at 132 (noting resistance to quartering in Quebec, Montreal, Massachusetts, Connecticut, New York, Maryland, east Florida, and Georgia).

6. Bell at 126.

royal governor had to house troops in the statehouse after Boston refused to provide quarters.[7]

After the Boston Tea Party of December 16, 1773, Parliament passed five laws, including a new Quartering Act in June 1774.[8] General Thomas Gage, commander-in-chief of British forces in America, specifically requested that Parliament pass this Quartering Act because the colonies were not providing sufficient barracks for his men.[9] This new act allowed British commanders to quarter troops in private *homes*, not just private *buildings*, making it one of the so-called Intolerable Acts.[10]

The First Continental Congress in 1774 called for the Quartering Act's repeal in its Declaration and Resolves.[11] In 1775 the Declaration of the Causes and Necessity of Taking Up Arms also decried *"quartering soldiers upon the colonists in time of profound peace."*[12] Finally, *"[f]or quartering large bodies of armed troops among us . . . "* the DECLARATION OF INDEPENDENCE justified breaking the *"political bands"* with England.[13]

Thus, if the British had not asserted that they could forcibly quarter troops in American homes, there might not have been an American Revolution.

7. Bell at 126; Wurfel at 726.

8. Bell at 126.

9. Wurfel at 724. For a full quote of the Quartering Act of 1774, see Wurfel at 724–25 n.8.

11. *"Resolved, N. C. D. That the following acts of Parliament are infringements and violations of the rights of the colonists; and that the repeal of them is essentially necessary in order to restore harmony between Great Britain and the American colonies, viz . . . the act passed in the same session for the better providing suitable quarters for officers and soldiers in his Majesty's service in North-America."* Reprinted in Bell at 125–26.

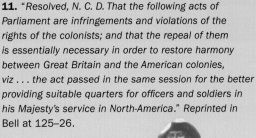

Thomas Gage (1719–87), British commander-in-chief in North American from 1763 to 1775, during the early days of the American Revolution. Gage was the one who ordered the march on Lexington and Concord to which the Minutemen responded.

A Minuteman, an icon of Americana

10. Bell at 126; Fields & Hardy at 416; Fields at 201.

12. Bell at 127; SOURCES OF OUR LIBERTIES 296 (R. Perry ed., 1952).

13. Bell at 127; THE DECLARATION OF INDEPENDENCE para. 15 (U.S. 1776).

DURING THE REVOLUTION

Britain's decision to quarter troops in American homes was not worth the effort. Indeed, perhaps this entire issue was more about publicity then any real wrong. Most of the quartering went on in inns and taverns, not private homes. In fact, very few examples exist of British soldiery invading homes.

But any real wrong was not the point; it was the perception of this wrong that mattered. Britain's assertion that it could quarter troops in the Quartering Act of 1775 and the fact that the English Mutiny Act did not apply in America gave offense to the colonists. This perception of unfairness gave prominence to the issue that became the Third Amendment.

Thus, with quartering troops such a big issue on the road to revolution, one would think that the American revolutionary commanders would have been more careful. But the American Army, just as the British Army, quartered troops with civilians during the Revolutionary War.[1] This, of course, cuts against the image that the American revolutionary soldier lived at Valley Forge the entire time, with its log huts, the ancestor of modern army bases.[2]

Military necessity ruled, even with a republican army.

QUARTERING IN THE BILL OF RIGHTS

When the Framers set about making a republic, they initially did not

---

1. Bell at 127; Hardy at 79–80.

2. Gross at 220.
  On December 19, 1777, Washington's poor army stumbled into Valley Forge, Pennsylvania, for its winter quarters. Although Valley Forge was a good choice strategically, the British had outmaneuvered Washington and thus got to spend the winter in warm Philadelphia.

Washington at Valley Forge

The U.S. Navy has had at least two ships named *Valley Forge*.

The Essex class aircraft carrier *Valley Forge* (CV/CVA/CVS-45/LPH-8)

The Ticonderoga class cruiser USS *Valley Forge* (CG-50)

3. *See generally* **Prequel and Preamble: Did They Forget to Pay the Bill?**

4. *See* Bell at 128–29.

5. *See* Fields at 202. Regarding the quartering issue, eight of the states sent proposals for a Bill of Rights to Congress. Five of these proposals contained protections against quartering.

6. *See e.g.,* **Chapter 8: "*Baby, Don't Be Cruel*": What's So Cruel *and* Unusual about the Eighth Amendment?** (noting that the entire discussion of the Eighth Amendment in Congress was a few sentences from two representatives).
  Regarding Madison's proposal, Thomas Sumter of South Carolina objected to what became the Third Amendment and moved that *"No soldier shall be quartered in any house without the consent of the owner."* Elbridge Gerry of Massachusetts moved that *"No soldier shall, in time of peace, be quartered in any house, without the consent of the owner, nor in time of war but by a civil magistrate in a manner prescribed by law."* But Roger Sherman of Connecticut and Thomas Hartley of Pennsylvania agreed with the Third Amendment as written and this prevailed. *Quoted in* Fields at 203.
  Thomas Sumter was a Revolutionary Militia general, later a U.S. congressman from South Carolina, and a source of the fictional Benjamin Martin in the movie THE PATRIOT

GENERAL THOMAS SUMTER

include a Bill of Rights in the Constitution.[3] Thus the quartering issue became a big arrow in the quiver of those opposing the Constitution's ratification.[4] Although their arguments did not defeat the Constitution, their concerns lead to the Bill of Rights.[5]

The House of Representatives extensively debated the Third Amendment, in contrast to other parts of the Bill of Rights, many of which we today consider far more relevant.[6]

The states had offered variations of a quartering amendment for congressional consideration.[7] The debate centered on whether the prohibition against quartering troops in homes should be allowed in *"time of war."*[8] This lead to the Third Amendment's final version, with the qualifier that *"in time of war"* quartering could occur in homes *"in a manner to be prescribed by law."*

This qualifier in any given political climate easily swallows the Third Amendment. The Constitution gives Congress several powers over the military,[9] which already seem broad enough to allow quartering troops in homes. But the president alone could not do so because to quarter troops in homes requires at least congressional acquiesce, if not action.

But the debate in Congress at the Third Amendment's passing underscores the Framers' real concern: the fear of a standing army.

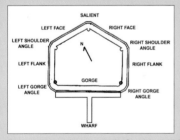

(Columbia Pictures 2000). During the war a British general said he *"fought like a Gamecock,"* earning Sumter the nickname of "The Carolina Gamecock." The "Gamecock City" of Sumter, South Carolina, was named for him, and "Gamecock" is a nickname for a South Carolina native. University of South Carolina students are Fighting Gamecocks or the Gamecocks. Fort Sumter was also named after him, which is where the South started the Civil War on April 12, 1861. Also, the design of Ft. Sumter was a basis, more or less, for the layout of the baseball field.

....

7. Bell at 129–30.
- Maryland—*"That soldiers be not quartered, in time of peace, upon private houses, without the consent of the owners."*
- New Hampshire — The same article restricting standing armies, followed up with *"nor shall Soldiers in Time of Peace be quartered upon private Houses without the consent of the Owners."*
- Virginia — *"That no Soldier in time of peace ought to be quartered in any house without the consent of the owner, and in time of war in such manner only as the laws direct."*
- New York—*"That in time of Peace no Soldier ought to be quartered in any House without the consent of the Owner, and in time of War only by the Civil Magistrate in such manner as the Laws may direct."*
- North Carolina—*"That no soldier in time of peace ought to be quartered in any house without the consent of the owner, and in time of war in such manner only as the Laws direct."*
Id.

8. What Is "War"? The War of 1812 and the Civil War. Depending on what *"nor in time of war, but in a manner to be prescribed by law"* means, the U.S. military regularly violated the Third Amendment during the War of 1812 and the Civil War. Congress did declare war against Britain in 1812 but not against the Confederacy. In both cases, however, Congress did not pass any law allowing for the quartering of soldiers in homes even though the military was regularly doing so. Bell at 135–36. Of course, the British did so during the War of 1812, as well as the Confederacy, despite the fact that it prohibited the practice in its own Confederate Constitution, which has the same Third Amendment as the U.S. Constitution. C.S. Const. art. I, § 9, cl. 14.

....

9. For example, Congress has the power to call the militia during unrest *"to execute the Laws of the Union, suppress Insurrections, and repel Invasions,"* *"[t]o raise and support Armies,"* and *"[t]o make rules for the Government and Regulation of the land and naval Forces."* U.S. Const. art. I, § 8, cl. 15, 12, and 14. Also, Congress may hold a power to quarter troops as *"necessary and proper"* to fulfill its constitutional duties to support armies.

THE FEAR OF A STANDING ARMY

Quartering troops in homes invaded privacy and it could be inconvenient, expensive (at least temporarily and maybe permanently depending on whether you could someday redeem the vouchers), and even destructive. But it does keep soldiers in contact with the people they are supposed to serve.[1] And, of itself, the practice is not necessarily a threat to democracy.

Conversely, a standing army always has the potential to derail democracy, which the Founders knew and feared.[2] These men had read Niccolo Machiavelli's THE PRINCE, and they were aware of his warnings against standing armies of paid troops.[3]

Machiavelli recognized the need for security forces:

"The chief foundations of all states," wrote Machiavelli, *"are good laws and arms. And . . . there cannot be good laws where there are not good arms . . . ."*[4] But a full-time, paid standing army, which Machiavelli called *"mercenaries,"* would destroy freedom:

"The mercenaries . . . are useless and dangerous, and if any one supports his state by the arms of mercenaries, he

1. Blackstone, for instance, wrote that "[n]othing ought to be more guarded against in a free state, than making the military power, when such a one is necessary to be kept on foot, a body too distinct from the people. Like ours, it should wholly be composed of natural subjects; it ought only to be enlisted for a short and limited time; the soldiers also should live intermixed with the people; no separate camp, no barracks, or inland fortresses should be allowed. And perhaps it might be still better if, by dismissing a stated number, and enlisting others at every renewal of their term, a circulation could be kept up between the army and the people, and the citizen and the soldier be more intimately connected together.

"To keep this body of troops in order, an annual act of parliament likewise passes, 'to punish mutiny and desertion, and for the better payment of the army and their quarters.' This regulates the manner in which they are to be dispersed among the several innkeepers and victuallers throughout the kingdom; and establishes a law martial for their government."
1 BLACKSTONE, COMMENTARIES *414–15, *quoted in* Wufel at 725–26.

William Blackstone

2. *United States v. Miller*, 307 U.S. 174, 178 (1939) ("The sentiment of the time strongly disfavored standing armies; the common view was that adequate defense of country and laws could be secured through the Militia—civilians primarily, soldiers on occasion.").

3. Niccolo Machiavelli (1469–1527) was an Italian diplomat, politician, and political philosopher during the Renaissance. He wrote several books on politics including THE PRINCE (1513). Because of his realist political philosophy his surname passed into common speech as a synonym for any devious political move or motive. See MAURIZIO VIROLI, NICCOLO'S SMILE, A BIOGRAPHY OF MACHIAVELLI (2000). The rapper Tupac Shakur, for example, used the pseudonym Makaveli, derived from Machiavelli.

Tupac Shakur (1971–96)

will never stand firm or sure, as they are disunited, ambitious, without discipline, faithless, bold amongst friends, cowardly amongst enemies, they have no fear of God, and keep no faith with men."[5]

The Founding generation did not want Machiavelli's standing army of "*mercenaries.*"

During the Revolution, George Washington had to repeatedly plead for Congress to create an army. Washington knew that militias could not beat the British Army.[6]

After the Revolution, though, Congress quickly disbanded the army.[7] The Framers then wrote the Constitution to defuse military power and to do everything possible to keep it under civilian control.[8] Later, the young United States realized that it still needed an effective military force.[9] So America accepted a standing army but only reluctantly.[10]

The Anti-Federalists continued to fear that the Constitution gave the national government the power to create a standing army and potentially quarter it amongst the people.[11] A standing army not under civilian control could eventually endanger democracy and civil liberties.[12]

---

4. NICCOLO MACHIAVELLI, THE PRINCE AND THE DISCOURSES 44 (Mod. Library ed., 1950) (1513). Machiavelli's reference to "*good arms*" also applied to what we would today call a police force and the National Guard in times of emergency.

For Machiavelli on standing armies and security against attack, see TUSHNET at 11; Field & Hardy at 406-07, *citing* both THE PRINCE AND THE ART OF WAR.

5. MACHIAVELLI at 45.

6. *See* TUSHNET at 13 for Washington's call for an army during the Revolution.

7. Surrender of Lord Cornwallis at Yorktown. One could even debate whether the American army can trace its descent from the army of the Revolution. After the Revolutionary War, the entire army was disbanded. Thus the modern American army descends from Congress's reauthorization of it years later. When George Mason and Elbridge Gerry's proposed to limit the army to only several thousand men, Charles Cotesworth Pinckney responded that the proposal was acceptable as long as any invading force agrees to the same number. Fields & Hardy at 421–22.

American Revolutionary regulars

8. The U.S. Constitution divides war powers between Congress and the president:

- The president is commander-in-chief; art. II, § 2, cl. 1.
- The president appoints officers but only with advice and consent of the Senate; art. I, § 2, cl. 2.
- Congress declares war; art. I, § 8, cl. 11.
- Congress raises and supports armies; art. I, § 8, cl. 12.
- Congress makes rules governing and regulating armed forces; art. I, § 8, cl. 14.
- A two-year limitation is placed on military appropriations; art. I, § 8, cl. 12.
- Congress shares authority over the militia with the states; art. I, § 8, cl. 15 and 16.

9. On the militia not being up to task of the Indian wars, *see* Fields & Hardy at 421.

10. "*As in post-1689 England, the standing army would be denounced, derided, and retained.*" Fields & Hardy at 421. *See also id.* at 426 ("*By 1789 Americans had crossed the line the English Whigs had passed a century before: a standing army might be a nuisance, but now it was an American nuisance.*").

11. Dennis A. Henigan, *Arms, Anarchy and the Second Amendment*, 26 VAL. U. L. REV. 107, 116–19 (1991).

12. Fields & Hardy at 422–23.

Patrick Henry, at the Virginia ratifying convention, stated that "[t]he great object is that every man be armed . . . Everyone who is able may have a gun." Though this is an oft-quoted statement for the individual interpretation of the Second Amendment, Henry was speaking in the context of militias. LEONARD W. LEVY, ORIGINS OF THE BILL OF RIGHTS 147–48 (1999).

In response to Anti-Federalist arguments about a standing army, James Madison in THE FEDERALIST No. 46 argued that anything like the Third Amendment was unnecessary. The federal government, he argued, could never raise an army powerful enough to overcome the militias.[1]

History did not vindicate Madison's belief in the militia. Perhaps he knew it would not, and this was part of the reason, in addition to his fear of standing armies and war, that he later presented the Third Amendment to Congress.[2]

THE THIRD AMENDMENT FOR TODAY

Even the best army is a two-edged sword. Even if the Framers might have imagined that the United States would someday be a power like France or Britain, they never would have dreamed of the superpower it is today.

In 2007 the United States military budget and military-related expenses were $626.1 billion,

1. THE FEDERALIST No. 46:
"Let a regular army, fully equal to the resources of the country, be formed; and let it be entirely at the devotion of the federal government; still it would not be going too far to say, that the State governments, with the people on their side, would be able to repel the danger. The highest number to which, according to the best computation, a standing army can be carried in any country, does not exceed one hundredth of the whole number of souls; or one twenty-fifth part of the number able to bear arms. This proportion would not yield, in the United States, an army of more than twenty-five or thirty thousand men. To these would be opposed a militia amounting to near half a million of citizens with arms in their hands, officered by men chosen from among themselves, fighting for their common liberties, and united and conducted by governments possessing their affections and confidence. It may well be doubted, whether a militia thus circumstanced could ever be conquered by such a proportion of regular troops."

2. "Of all the enemies to public liberty war is, perhaps, the most to be dreaded because it comprises and develops the germ [beginning] of every other. War is the parent of armies; from these proceed debts and taxes . . . known instruments for bringing the many under the domination of the few. . . . No nation could preserve its freedom in the midst of continual warfare." JAMES MADISON, POLITICAL OBSERVATIONS (1795).

3. Office of the Undersecretary of Defense, National Defense Budget Estimates for Fiscal Year 2007 (2006), http://www.defenselink.mil/comptroller/defbudget/fy2007/ (last visited July 4 2008). This does not account for costs of maintaining state based national guards.

4. Department of Housing and Urban Development, http://www.nhl.gov/about/budget/fy07/fy07budget.pdf (last visited July 28 2008).

accounting for 43 percent of all national taxes.[3] In contrast, the 2007 Department of Housing and Urban Development's budget was $33.6 billion.[4] Thus what we spent on housing and related programs in 2007 could fit over eighteen times into the military budget. This is a lot of *tallies*, *chits*, and *billets*.

Is it such a metaphorical stretch to suggest that the discrepancy in spending between housing and the military violates the Third Amendment's spirit if not its letter?[5]

The Founders knew that a "democratic army" is a contradiction.[6] Although armies may defend democracy, and American armies have an admirable history of defending our democracy, they are not democratic institutions. Of all the Bill of Rights, the Third Amendment best reminds us of this.

Keeping in mind the Framers' original intent, the Third Amendment may be relevant after all.

---

5. But the courts easily dispatched other metaphorical Third Amendment claims, such as a party claiming that subpoenas violated the Third Amendment, *Securities Investor Protection Corp. v. Executive Securities Corp.*, 433 F. Supp. 470, 473 n.2 (S.D.N.Y. 1977); Army reservists claiming that orders to march in a parade violated the Third Amendment, *Jones v. United States Secretary of Defense*, 346 F. Supp. 97 (D. Minn. 1972); and that *"[t]he 1947 House and Rent Act . . . is and always was the incubator and hatchery of swarms of bureaucrats to be quartered as storm troopers upon the people in violation of Amendment III . . . ,"* *United States v. Valenzuala*, 95 F. Supp. 363, 366 (S.D. Cal. 1951). For a brief survey of Third Amendment litigation, see Frank B. Lewis, *Whatever Happened to the 3rd Amendment?* N.Y.L.J., Feb. 26, 1979, at 1.

6. The **Selective Service System** still administers military conscription, i.e., the "draft." All males between eighteen and twenty-five must register so the U.S. government has a list of potential soldiers. Despite the objection to the draft during the Vietnam War, it does have a democratizing effect on the military. It could ensure a cross-section of America in military service. Such, however, was not the case during the Vietnam War, where the sons of the rich and powerful got deferments.

Burning a draft card during the Vietnam War

Molasses and the Sticky Origins of the Fourth Amendment

"The right of the people to be secure in their persons, houses, papers, and effects, against unreasonable searches and seizures, shall not be violated, and no Warrants shall issue, but upon probable cause, supported by Oath or affirmation, and particularly describing the place to be searched, and the persons or things to be seized."

—The Fourth Amendment

Molasses.[1] Molasses gave us the Fourth Amendment.

Yes, that sticky, dark brown stuff, practically a food group in Southern cooking, is why we have the Fourth Amendment, with all the case law, statutes, and arguments related to search and seizure. Take away this uniquely American ingredient and we would have a different Constitution.[2] Take molasses out of the mix and we would have a different nation.

Sure America inherited legal notions of protecting a person's house and papers from England, embodied in the saying *"a man's home is his castle."* This English source is especially reflected in the Fourth Amendment's first clause: the reasonableness clause. But it is the American ingredient (i.e., molasses) that was the crucial American foundation of the Fourth Amendment's second clause: the warrants clause.

So what was the big deal about molasses? Surely colonial Americans could not have consumed or sold sufficient quantities of Boston Baked Beans or sugar cookies to make an economic difference. No, they did not. The answer is that molasses was New England's commercial lifeblood in the eighteenth and nineteenth centuries. As the more "spirited" of you know, molasses is rum![3]

1. Molasses is a thick syrup produced by boiling down juice from sugar cane, ranging from light to dark brown in color. In Portuguese it is *"melaços"* (plural of *"melaço"*); in Spanish *"melaza,"* from Late Latin *"mellaceum"* ("honey").
See also "melit-" in various Indo-European roots, which leads to Spanish *"miel"* ("honey"). WEBSTER'S NEW INTERNATIONAL DICTIONARY OF THE ENGLISH LANGUAGE 1579 (2d ed. 1942).

2. *See, e.g.,* William J. Stuntz, *The Substantive Origins of Criminal Procedure,* 105 YALE L.J. 393 (1995) (noting that history produced many of the curiosities and inconstancies of modern criminal procedure).

3. Rum is an alcoholic liquor distilled from fermented molasses or sugar cane. From the Latin *"sacarhrum"* ("sugar"). WEBSTER'S at 2183.

And rum fueled the commerce of the Atlantic Basin because it was the currency of the slave trade.[1]

"A MAN'S HOME IS HIS CASTLE": THE ENGLISH SOURCE OF OUR FOURTH AMENDMENT

Mesopotamia and the Bible: The idea of a person's home being sacrosanct did not originate in England. The Code of Hammurabi, from eighteenth century BC Mesopotamia (modern Iraq), speaks to this issue:

"If a man makes a breach into a house, one shall kill him in front of the breach and bury him in it."[2]

The Hebrews also believed in the sanctity of the home, providing that when a householder kills a burglar at night

"there shall be no blood guilt," but *"if the sun has risen upon the intruder, there shall be blood guilt for him."[3]*

The sanctity of the home applied to civil as well as criminal law:

"When you make a loan to another man, do not enter his house to take a pledge from him. Wait outside, and the man whose creditor you are shall bring the pledge out to you."[4]

Rome: A Roman home was under the household gods'

special protection. Cicero exclaimed,

"what is more inviolate, what better defended by religion than the house of a citizen . . . . This place of refuge is so sacred to all men, that to be dragged from thence is unlawful."[5]

As with the Hebrews, Roman law justified killing a burglar as self-defense but required the victim to cry for help before using deadly force.[6]

Roman law provided for search warrants but only under very specific procedures:

- an accuser had to describe in court the goods he was seeking and provide

---

1. Molasses to rum to slaves.

2. Code of Hammurabi, art. 21, 1750–1700 BC, *quoted in* Nelson B. Lasson, The History and Development of the Fourth Amendment to the United States Constitution 14–15, n.5 (1937). Lasson also outlines biblical, Roman, and other ancient sources. This quote begs the question of why anyone would want a dead body in his wall during a Mesopotamian summer?

Hammurabi

3. *Exodus* 22:2–3. Later Jewish law reasoned the thief in the night intends to kill. David B. Kopel, *The Torah and Self-Defense,* 109 Penn. St. L. Rev. 17, 33 (2004). "The act of breaking in is the burglar's death warrant." Kopel at 36.

4. *Deuteronomy* 24:10–11, *quoted in* Samuel Dash, The Intruders: Unreasonable Searches and Seizures from King John to John Ashcroft 153 n.8 (2004).

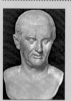

5. *Quoted in* Dash at 9.
Marcus Tullius Cicero (106–43 BC) was a Roman philosopher, statesman, lawyer, political theorist, and constitutionalist who greatly influenced the American Founding Fathers. He was one of Rome's greatest orators until Mark Anthony had him assassinated.

6. Kopel at 27.

7. Susan Ford Wiltshire, Greece, Rome, and the Bill of Rights 147–48 (1992). Tarzan could do a search in Ancient Rome. Roman laws came from "the Senate and the people of Rome," or, in Latin, "*Senatus Populusque Romanus*"— at least in theory—with the initials "SPQR" becoming a common symbol and official signature of the government. Rome offered law to the diverse peoples of the empire. The symbol of Rome's traditional founders,

Tarzan of the Apes, (First National, 1918) was the first Tarzan movie.

sealed documents in front of the witness;

- during the search the searcher could only wear a loincloth (*"licium"*) and had to carry a platter (*"lanx"*) to prevent planting contraband in the accused's home.[7]

Thus the Romans had an early version of the Fourth Amendment's requirements that

"no Warrants shall issue, but upon probable cause, supported by Oath or affirmation, and particularly describing the place to be searched, and the persons or things to be seized."

The actual phrase *"a man's home is his castle"* comes from Justinian's Code and was a well-established cliché by the American Revolution.[8]

THE RIGHTS OF ENGLISHMEN:

The sanctity of the homestead was one of the oldest principles of Teutonic law.[9] Later, both Anglo-Saxon and Norman law recognized the right to protect one's home. The right passed into the common law as early as 1505.[10]

Indeed, the concept of "the king's peace," the basis of modern sovereignty, comes out of the notion of the sanctity of the home, in this case the king's. Over time, the king's judges extended his "court" to the whole realm; his protection and government eventually covered the whole country.[11]

Skipping ahead a few centuries (about four millennia from Hammurabi), takes us to William Pitt the Elder's 1766 speech in the English House of Commons proclaiming the home's sanctity:

"The poorest man may, in his cottage, bid defiance to all the forces of the Crown. It may be frail; its roof may shake; the wind may blow through it; the storm may enter; the rain may enter; but the King of England may not enter; all his force dares not cross the threshold of the ruined tenement."[12]

Romulus and Remus suckled by a she wolf, shows Rome's militant side. The twins were sons of the war god Mars. Romulus became king after he killed Remus with a shovel.

8. Justinian, Roman emperor (sixth century AD). The Code of Justinian (in Latin, *"Codex Justinianeus,"* formally *"Corpus Juris Civilis"* ("Body of Civil Law") was the collection of laws and legal interpretations developed under Byzantine emperor Justinian I from 529 to 565. *Code of Justinian*, Encyclopedia Britannica, http://www.britannica.com/EBchecked/topic/308835/Code-of-Justinian.

Justinian I

9. Frederick Pollock, *English Law before the Norman Conquest*, 14 L. Q. Rev. 301, 301 (1898).

10. Lasson at 14–15. *See also Semayne's Case*, (1604), 77 Eng. Rep. 194, 195 (K.B.), *cited in* Benjamin D. Barros, *Home as a Legal Concept*, 46 Santa Clara L. Rev. 255 (2006). For a comprehensive treatment of this history, *see* William J. Cuddihy, The Fourth Amendment: Origins and Original Meaning 602–1791 (2009).

11. *See* **Chapter 6: How the Sixth Amendment Guarantees You a Court, a Lawyer, and a Chamber Pot.**

12. William Pitt the Elder, *quoted in* Leonard W. Levy, Origins of the Bill of Rights 151 (1999). Despite Pitt's speech, the general search warrant was Britain's routine method of search. A general warrant allowed the official who had it to search any place, at any time, without getting prior permission from a court. But the British also originated ideas that culminated in the Fourth Amendment. William Cuddihy, *From General to Specific Warrants: The Origins of the Fourth Amendment, in* The Bill of Rights: A Lively Heritage 88 (Jon Kukla ed., 1987). Plus, Pitt got the city of Pittsburgh named for him.

Even though lawyers still quote Pitt today, his terrific statement of the right to privacy in one's home may have been honored more in the breach than the practice. Some believe Pitt asserted a myth.[1]

Pitt, though, was responding to the case of John Wilkes, a milestone in the assertion of the right to be free from unreasonable searches.[2] The case, as well as the slogan *"Wilkes and Liberty,"* became famous on both sides of the Atlantic.

So who was this John Wilkes that scarcely anyone today remembers?

JOHN WILKES AND THE NORTH BRITON NO. 45:

John Wilkes was a member of Parliament and publisher of *The North Briton*, a political magazine mocking the government's pubic relations pamphlet called *The Briton*.[3] After honorably fighting a duel, he took a break from frolicking with women of ill-repute in the London slums to frolicking with women of ill-repute in the Paris slums. While in France, Madame de Pompadour asked Wilkes how far freedom of the press went in England, to which

he responded, *"I don't know. I am trying to find out."*[4]

One particular edition, *The North Briton* No. 45, harshly criticized King George III's speech to Parliament lauding the Treaty of Paris, which ended the Seven Years' War, as *"honorable to my crown and beneficial to my people."*[5] Mockingly, No. 45's "anonymous author"— everyone guessed it was Wilkes—wrote that *"it must be a peace from God for it passes all human understanding."* No. 45 went on to state, with dripping sarcasm:

---

1. DASH at 3. Myth or not, the concept has resonance. During the Watergate hearings, Senator Herman Talmadge responded to John Ehrlichman's assertions that the executive has the authority to order unwarranted searches by quoting Pitt. Ehrlichman's response was, "*I am afraid that has been considerably eroded over the years, has it not?*" However, this availed him nothing after Talmadge drew applause upon retorting, "*Down in my country we still think it is a pretty legitimate principle of law.*" Records of the Select Committee on Presidential Campaign Activities 1973, 1974, *Senate Watergate Hearings*, National Archives, *reprinted in* DASH at 2.

John Ehrlichman

Herman was married to Betty. In 1976 she learned from TV news that Herman was divorcing her. Three years later Betty testified before the Senate Ethics Committee that Herman kept thousands in cash in an overcoat stuffed in the closet. The Senate censured Herman, and he lost the next election.

Betty operated a restaurant out of her home and wrote two cookbooks. The *New York Times* asked Betty how she found the nerve to slaughter her first pig. "*Real easy, honey, I just thought, 'You little male chauvinist, you,' and I went to it.*" Herman should have known that this was not the type of woman you divorce!

Herman Talmadge

2. DASH at 31.

3. Quite the libertine, **John Wilkes** rejected his boring Calvinist upbringing and boring Calvinist wife in favor of sex, food, and drink. He did, however, keep his Calvinist antimonarchism and truly enjoyed being King George III's nemesis. DASH at 26–27. *See also* COLIN RHYS LOVELL, ENGLISH CONSTITUTIONAL AND LEGAL HISTORY 446–47, 454–55 (1962).

4. LASSON at 43 n.108, *citing* RAYMOND POSTGATE, THAT DEVIL WILKES 53 (1930). Wilkes's statement shows that his case is not just a precursor to the Fourth Amendment but also the First Amendment.

As for **Madame de Pompadour**, she tangentially enters this story in another way. As Louis XV's mistress and one of the women known to history as "*Les Grande Horizontales,*" for the influence they had on Louis from the horizontal

position, she encouraged him to ally with Austria, which lead to the Seven Years' War. As outlined in the next section, the Seven Years' War, also known as the French and Indian War, prompted the Boston writs of assistance case.

"every friend of his country must lament that a prince of so many great and amiable qualities, whom England truly reveres, can be brought to give the sanction of his sacred name to the most odious measure and to the must [sic] unjustifiable public declarations, from a throne ever renowned for truth, honor, and unsullied virtue."[6]

The king's speech had also defended the unpopular cider tax and responded to the riots in the cider districts of England by calling for *"a spirit of concord"* and *"obedience to law"* essential for *"good order."* To this No. 45 rhetorically asked,

"Is the spirit of concord to go hand in hand with the Peace and Excise, through this nation? Is it to be expected between an insolent Exciseman, and a peer, gentleman, free holder, or farmer, whose private houses are now made liable to be entered and searched at pleasure?"[7]

THE DUNK WARRANT:

Predictably, Wilkes raised the ire of George III, who sent his minions to do something about it. On April 30, 1763, secretary of state George Montagu-Dunk, the Earl of Halifax, wrote what is known to history as the Dunk Warrant.[8] This general warrant sent crown officials to search and seize all papers and presses of the authors, printers, and publishers of Wilkes's paper and to arrest anyone they could get their hands on—forty-nine people in all.[9] It did not take them long to find Wilkes, who refused to obey the warrant, declaring it *"a ridiculous warrant against the whole English nation."*[10]

France lost that war, and Madame Pompadour was blamed. But to her credit, she popularized champagne in France, stating, *"Champagne is the only wine that leaves a woman beautiful after drinking it."* Quoted in IAN LENDLER, ALCOHOLICA ESOTERICA: A COLLECTION OF USEFUL AND USELESS INFORMATION AS IT RELATES TO THE HISTORY AND CONSUMPTION OF ALL MANNER OF BOOZE 63 (2003). (The statement is ambiguous as to whether it is the man or woman doing the drinking.) And the Pompadour  haircut is named after her. What would Elvis have done without it?

5. DASH at 27. George III was actually accurate. The Treaty of Paris was very favorable, giving Britain all of Canada and monopolistic control over the North Atlantic.

George III

6. DASH at 27, *quoting* JOHN WILKES, A COMPLETE COLLECTION OF THE GENUINE PAPERS, LETTERS, ETC. IN THE CASE OF JOHN WILKES, ESQ. 2 (1769). No. 45 started by stating, *"[t]he King's speech has always been considered by the legislature and by the public at large as the speech of the minister."* This protected the author from a charge of insulting the king. Wilkes was to later abandon this precaution, to his undoing. *Id.* at 5 n.6.

7. LASSON at 43 n.108, *quoting THE NORTH BRITON NO.* 45. Thus, the issue was in part searches and seizures to regulate commerce and taxation of alcohol, which is an interesting parallel to the rum and molasses dispute in the American colonies discussed below.

8. The Dunk Warrant is known as *"the most important warrant in history."* Actually, George Dunk, the Duke of Halifax, was not so bad. He was born George Montagu but added his wife's last name of Dunk, though given that his wife was vastly richer than he, it may not have been an indication he was ahead of his time in gender relationships.

History remembers him as the "Father of the Colonies," who helped found Nova Scotia. The following are named after him: Halifax, Massachusetts; Halifax, North Carolina; Halifax, Pennsylvania; Halifax, Vermont; Halifax, Virginia; Halifax County, North Carolina; Halifax County, Virginia; and Halifax, Nova Scotia.

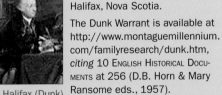

The Dunk Warrant is available at http://www.montaguemillennium.com/familyresearch/dunk.htm, *citing* 10 ENGLISH HISTORICAL DOCUMENTS at 256 (D.B. Horn & Mary Ransome eds., 1957).

Lord Halifax (Dunk)

9. *See* Stuntz at 399.

10. LASSON at 44. They had to carry Wilkes out of his house sitting in his chair for his appearance before Dunk. For not answering questions, Dunk put him in the Tower but had to release him a few days later upon a writ of habeas corpus because of Wilkes's parliamentary privilege. When executing the warrant they took all of Wilkes's personal papers, including his will. *See* DASH at 29–30 for the interesting Dunk/Wilkes correspondence regarding his property.

Wilkes and his gang sued the crown officials for trespass.[1]

THE WILKES CASES:

As the cases that eventually became *Wilkes v. Wood* and *Entick v. Carrington* went through the court system,[2] juries found in favor of the plaintiffs—Wilkes and the other editors and publishers.

On appeal, the cases ended up before Chief Justice Pratt, who later became Lord Camden.[3] His opinion for the first time condemned general warrants:

"To enter a man's house by virtue of a nameless warrant in order to procure evidence, is worse than the Spanish Inquisition; a law under which no Englishman would wish to live an hour."[4]

An important point is that the *Wilkes* searches were under a general warrant from the secretary of state that, until then, was legal. Lord Camden's opinion thus set an important legal principle:

A search can be illegal even with a warrant.[5]

The *Wilkes* cases made privacy in one's papers central:

"Papers are the owner's goods and chattels: they are his dearest property; and are so far from enduring a seizure, that they will hardly bear an inspection; and though the eye cannot by the laws of England be guilty of a trespass, yet where private papers are removed and carried away, the secret nature of those goods will be an aggravation of the trespass, and demand more considerable damages in that respect."[6]

---

1. At one point, Wilkes went before Secretary of State John Montagu, 4th Earl of Sandwich, an old drinking buddy. Montagu, from the vantage of his position of respectability, said to Wilkes,

"Wilkes, you will die of the pox [syphilis] or on the gallows." To which Wilkes responded, "[t]hat depends, my lord, on whether I embrace your principles or your mistress." RAYMOND POSTGATE, THAT DEVIL WILKES 39 (rev. ed., Dobson Books Ltd. 1956).

Montagu does have another historical achievement. A gambling addict, he at one time did not want to leave his game and told his servant to "bring my meat to me between two slices of bread." Thus, John Montagu, 4th Earl of Sandwich, gave us the "sandwich."

Sandwich was a great supporter of Captain James Cook's Pacific exploration, which is why Cook named the

Sandwich Islands (now Hawaii) after him in 1778, as well as the South Sandwich Islands at the tip of South America, one of which is Montagu Island.

Earl of Sandwich

2. See *Wilkes v. Wood*, 98 Eng. Rep. 489 (C.P. 1763), 19 Howell's State Trials 1153; *Entick v. Carrington*, 19 Howell's State Trials 1029 (C.P. 1765).

3. Lord Camden (Chief Justice Pratt). As you can see, he was a "bigwig." Several websites have the complete *Entick* opinion; see, e.g., http://www.constitution.org/trials/entick/entick_v_carrington.htm.

4. LASSON at 44.

England had a long history of warrantless searches of homes related to religious disputes. See **Chapter 1: Of Dogma and Desire: Saying What You Believe about the First Amendment.** The English Reformation caused a massive escalation of general searches and seizures. Cuddihy, *Warrants*, at 87. For example, the king's government searched Catholic homes with abandon after the Gunpowder Plot to kill King James I. *Id.* at 89.

5. See Stuntz at 398.

6. *Entick*, 19 Howell's State Trials at 1066, *quoted in* Stuntz at 398.

7. LEVY at 153. This was especially true in the colonies, where justices of the peace and magistrates had no power to deny them. *Id.* at 154–56. These were general warrants allowing press gangs to invade homes as well as taverns to kidnap men for service in the Royal Navy. *Id.* at 156.

8. DASH at 31–32. Dash argues that Camden's opinion was purely a jurisdictional ruling that the secretary of state lacked the power to issue the warrant. Camden did not challenge that the *king* could still issue a general warrant. Indeed, Camden was generally pro-government as the last line of his opinion shows: "When licentiousness is tolerated, liberty is in the utmost danger; because tyranny, bad as it is, is better than anarchy, and the worst of governments is more tolerable than no government at all." *Entick,* http://www.constitution.org/trials/entick/entick_v_carrington. htm. Wilkes would certainly not have agreed, given that he dedicated a good portion of his adult life to licentiousness.

Though Dash may be right, the opinion's broad language and the fact that on appeal the Court of Kings Bench powerfully upheld Camden could signal a broader right. See LASSON at 46–47 (reporting the justices' opinion on

Although a warrant can fulfill all the forms of legality, it must still be reasonable to be legal.

In his ruling, Camden broke from long precedent. From 1700 to 1763, in a collection of the 108 known warrants, all but two were general warrants. This use of general warrants only increased over time.[7] Indeed, Camden held that just because the secretary of state always issued general warrants, it did not make the practice legal, and "[i]t is high time to put an end to them."[8]

SO WHAT HAPPENED TO WILKES AND COMPANY?

Wilkes and his associates won big. After various jury trials and appeals the case cost the crown over £100,000.[9] This would be roughly equivalent to $24,692,320 in today's dollars—a staggering sum by any measure.[10]

In Britain and America, Wilkes became a folk hero, with the slogan "*Wilkes and Liberty*" reverberating.[11] When the British imprisoned

the leader of the New York chapter of the Sons of Liberty, Alexander McDougall, his partisans used the number "45," after *The North Briton* No. 45, as the symbol of their cause.[12] Wilkes-Barre, Pennsylvania, as well as Wilkes Counties in North Carolina and Georgia, are named after this intrepid publisher.[13]

Wilkes republished No. 45 under his own name. The king's attorney general wasted no time charging him criminally with seditious libel and for obscenity for an indecent poem, *Essay on Women.*[14]

---

appeal). And as with many legal opinions, what it said is less important than what it meant. As Pitt argued, "*the King of England may not enter.*"

Both sides of the Atlantic hailed the victory against arbitrary power (King George's power), not just freedom from the jurisdiction of the English secretary of state.

......

9. Lasson at 45.

......

10. According to the website How Much Is That?, http://eh.net/hmit/, a 1760 pound (£) would be worth £127.28 pounds in 2004. The exchange rate for 2004 was $1.94.

......

11. Lasson at 45–46.

......

12. Levy at 160. On the forty-fifth day of the year, forty-five Sons of Liberty ate forty-five pounds of beef from a forty-five-month-old bull, drank forty-five toasts to liberty, and after dinner went to the jail to cheer Mc-Dougall forty-five times. On another day they had forty-five virgins who were forty-five years old sing forty-five songs to McDougall. *Id.* The claim of forty-five virgins forty-five years old must have involved some literary license!

Booth as Mark Anthony

the other hand, he was probably just going for the drama. See James L. Swanson, Manhunt: The 12-Day Chase for Lincoln's Killer (2007).

......

14. Dash at 32–35. The *Essay on Woman* was a parody of Alexander Pope's *Essay on Man*.

Using the obscenity charge, the king succeeded in getting Parliament

13. *See generally John Wilkes*, The New Encyclopedia Britannica 661–62 (15th ed. 2002).

See also John Wilkes Booth, who shot President Lincoln at the Ford Theatre in 1865. Booth may have been trying to emulate his namesake when he yelled, "*Sic semper tyrannis*" ("*Death to tyrants*"), from the Virginia state seal as he jumped off the balcony and broke his leg. On

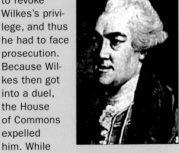

to revoke Wilkes's privilege, and thus he had to face prosecution. Because Wilkes then got into a duel, the House of Commons expelled him. While recuperating from his dueling injury in France, he was tried in absentia and convicted. Undaunted by being an outlaw, he ran for Parliament again and won another seat. Wilkes eventually beat the rap for the outlawry charge but not for the sedition and obscenity convictions. With no rule to exclude the illegal evidence in the criminal case, as would happen in a modern criminal case, the crown used the evidence from the illegal warrant to convict him. For the complete story, *see* Postgate; Arthur H. Cash, John Wilkes: The Scandalous Father of Civil Liberty (2006). Thus, although Wilkes won big in the civil case, he did not win his criminal case. In fact he probably never would have thought of asking for an enforceable right to suppress the evidence in his criminal case. *See* Stuntz at 400.

He eventually served twenty-two months in prison.[1]

Lord Camden scored better: Camden New Jersey, South Carolina, and Maine are all named for him, as is Camden Yards, home of the Baltimore Orioles.[2] He became one of the most popular men in Britain. The city of London had his portrait painted and hung in the Guildhall with an inscription by Dr. Samuel Johnson reading, "zealous supporter of English liberty by law."[3] Reprints of his portrait ended up in pubs and alehouses all over the realm.[4] That is a lot better acclaim than King George III ever got.[5]

MOLASSES: THE AMERICAN INGREDIENT OF THE FOURTH AMENDMENT

"I know not why we should blush to confess that molasses was an essential ingredient in American Independence," said John Adams.[6]

In modern cooking with refined sugar, fructose, saccharine, and aspartame, molasses is something of a curiosity. Few people today are even aware that it comes in different forms for different purposes.[7] An eighteenth century American, however, would have known this as a matter of course, as well as the fact that from molasses you get rum.

John Wilkes in Fetter Lane, London

See Nathaniel Philbrick, Sea of Glory: America's Voyage of Discovery, The U.S. Exploring Expedition 1838–1842 (2003).

1. It was not hard time and more of a vacation for him. Wilkes went on to become the Lord Mayor of London and a great court reformer.

Wilkes's great nephew, Lieutenant Charles Wilkes, U.S. Navy, lead the

1838–42 U.S. Exploring Expedition to Antarctica that, among other things, proved Antarctica was a continent. For this a big chunk is named "Wilkes Land."

Lt. Wilkes

2. Camden Yards in Baltimore.

3. Lasson at 46.

4. Dash at 32. All this popularity for Camden is interesting given that he may not have received it had it any of his new fans actually read his opinion. To be sure, he handed Wilkes and crew a big win. But he was a pro-government guy, a "bigwig," stating in the opinion, "*[b]efore I conclude, I desire not to be understood as an advocate for libels.*" Entick, http://www.constitution.org/trials/entick/entick_v_carrington.htm.

5. Actually, George had a sad end. He had porphyria, a maddening disease depicted in the movie The Madness of King George (Samuel Goldwyn Company 1994), based on the play by Alan Bennett, The Madness of George III (1991). He died blind, deaf, and mad at Windsor Castle in 1820.

King George in 1762 and in late life.

6. John Adams in a letter to George Washington, *quoted in* Lendler at 107. Alcohol, in fact, was the Founding generation's drug of choice. Richard Brookhiser, What Would the Founders Do?: Our Questions, Their Answers 41 (2006).

THE MOLASSES ACT OF 1733

With the Molasses Act of 1733, Parliament provided that the American colonies could only get molasses from the British West Indies, namely, Jamaica, Barbados, and a few other islands.[8] But the British West Indies could not come anywhere close to meeting the demand. For example, just the tiny colony of Rhode Island during the mid-1700s needed 14,000 hogsheads of molasses annually for its distilleries. The British West Indies could only produce 2,500 hogsheads.[9] In the mid-1760s, Rhode Island had twenty-two rum distilleries and Massachusetts had more than sixty-three, mostly in Salem and Boston.[10] By 1770 around 140 rum distilleries operated in the colonies, most in northern port towns, importing 6.5 million gallons of molasses and producing almost 5 million gallons of rum.[11]

The colonies, of course, met the supply deficit by buying from the French and Spanish West Indies.[12] The French and Spanish also were an excellent market for American fish and lumber, providing capital for American ventures and making up the trade imbalance with Britain. This was directly contrary to the interests of the British crown.

---

7. The quality of molasses depends on the maturity of the sugar cane, the amount of sugar extracted, and the method of extraction. There are three major types: **unsulfured, sulfured, and blackstrap.**

Unsulfured molasses is the finest quality made from the juice of sun-ripened cane, clarified and concentrated.

Sulfured molasses is from immature green sugar cane treated with sulfur fumes during the sugar-extracting process. Molasses from the first boiling is the best grade because only a small amount of sugar has been removed. The second boil molasses takes on a darker color, is less sweet, and has a heavier flavor.

Blackstrap molasses is from the third boil and has value as cattle feed and for industrial uses.

8. In 1773, Jamaica's exports to Britain were worth five times the exports of all thirteen colonies. BROOKHISER at 81–82.

9. LASSON at 51–52.

So what is a hogshead?

It is a large keg or barrel containing 63 to 140 gallons. The legal standard was set in 1423 at 63 gallons (or 52½ imperial gallons).

So how big is that? Well, a beer keg is 15½ gallons and a pony keg is 7¾ gallons (6½ cases or 165 cans). Thus a hogshead equals 4 kegs or 8 pony kegs or 1,320 cans.

Now, nearly any major British or American city can boast a Hogshead bar, tavern, alehouse, or pub.

10. The play and movie 1776 (Columbia Pictures 1972) got the history right. "Molasses to rum to slaves" sings Edward Rutledge of South Carolina to underscore that if slavery was a Southern sin, the North was its procurator:

"Who sails the ships out of Boston laden with bibles and rum? Who drinks the toast to the ivory coast? Hail Africa the slavers have come! New England with bibles and rum.! . . . 'Tisn't morals, 'tis money that saves . . . 'Tis Boston can boast to the West Indies coast, 'Jamaica we brung what ye crave.'"

For another popular history source, see IAN WILLIAMS, RUM: A SOCIAL AND SOCIABLE HISTORY OF THE REAL SPIRIT OF 1776 (2005).

The real Edward Rutledge, the youngest signer of the DECLARATION OF INDEPENDENCE, succeeded in getting Jefferson's condemnation of slavery taken out. After the Convention, though, he went home and freed his slaves.

Edward Rutledge

11. JOHN J. MCCUSKER & RUSSELL R. MENARD, THE ECONOMY OF BRITISH AMERICA 1607–1789, at 290 (1985) see also 1 JOHN J. MCCUSKER, RUM AND THE AMERICAN REVOLUTION: THE RUM TRADE AND THE BALANCE OF PAYMENTS OF THE THIRTEEN CONTINENTAL COLONIES (1989).

12. LASSON at 52.

MERCANTILISM VERSUS CAPITALISM:

What Britain was trying to do was to maintain its mercantilist economy in the face of emerging capitalism. Under mercantilism, colonies were part of the economic structure of the mother country.[1]

Thus Britain expected her American colonies to be a source of raw materials for British (mostly English) industry and to be the market for the manufactured goods. Colonies were not supposed to have large factories or manufacturing plants, or, in the case of molasses, large distillation facilities to compete with

those in Britain. According to this policy, colonial distilleries should not have even existed or at the most should have only had the capacity to process the molasses from the British West Indies.

But most Americans and many British viewed the Molasses Act as unfair.

---

1. Blake's print illustrates mercantilism and is a subtle social commentary. Although the three sisters appear harmoniously bound, only white Europe has a necklace, with black Africa and red America wearing slave bands. Europe holds America across the shoulders and grips Africa.

Europe Supported by Africa & America by William Blake (c. 1796)

3. Okay, as far as we know he never said this. But then he probably did not utter the famous, "*Sir, I have not yet begun to fight!*" line either. In his official report, Jones wrote that he answered British Captain Pearson's question regarding whether he had surrendered "*in the most determined negative.*" Jones later reported to Louis XVI that he said, "*I haven't as yet thought of surrendering, but I am determined to make you ask for quarter.*" This seems a lot to say as poor *Bonhomme Richard* was sinking under him. A contemporary account is that Jones said, "*I may sink, but I'll be damned if I strike.*" Though this one is pretty good, it still does not hit the nail like "*Sir, I have not yet begun to fight,*" which came from one of Jones's lieutenants, Richard Dale, writing forty-five years later. *See* EVAN THOMAS, JOHN PAUL JONES: SAILOR, HERO, FATHER OF THE AMERICAN NAVY 344 n.192 (2003).

John Paul Jones

John Paul Jones was actually born John Paul in Scotland. Before the Revolutionary War, during a dispute aboard ship, Jones ran a sailor through with a sword. To beat the rap in Tobago he skipped out of port and changed his name to John Paul Jones. *See id.* at 33–34; SAMUEL ELIOT MORISON, JOHN PAUL JONES: A SAILOR'S BIOGRAPHY 24–25 (1959).

2. Adam Smith. Sources state that the quality of this rum was quite high. *See* CLIFFORD LINDSEY ALDERMAN, RUM, SLAVES AND MOLASSES: THE STORY OF NEW ENGLAND'S TRIANGULAR TRADE 74–75 (1972).

4. Or, as Captain Jack Sparrow often asked in PIRATES OF THE CARIBBEAN: DEAD MAN'S CHEST (Buena Vista Pictures 2006), "*Why is the rum always gone?*" followed by standing up with a hangover, and "*Oh, that's why.*"

Actor Johnny Depp also stars in THE RUM DIARY, a film based on Hunter S. Thompson's novel THE RUM DIARY (1999).

Other names for rum are Kill-Devil, Demon Water, Pirate's Drink, Navy Neaters, Barbados Water, Screech, and a low-grade type called "tafia."

The following terms frequently describe various rums.

Light rums, aka silver, white, or Brazilian *cachaca*, have very little flavor aside from sweetness and thus are good for cocktails. **Gold rums**, aka amber rums, are medium-bodied rums aged in charred white oak barrels after bourbon has been produced in them. **Spiced rums** have additives like spices and caramel for flavor. **Dark rum**, aka black or red rum, is generally aged longer, giving them a stronger flavor, with hints of molasses or caramel. **Flavored rums** are infused with fruit flavorings like mango, orange, citrus, coconut, or lime. **Overproof rum** has a much higher than the standard 40 percent alcohol. **Premium rum** is treated as a sipping spirit, such as cognac or scotch.

So Captain Jack Sparrow, as well as the rest of us, has plenty to choose from.

Dark, spiced, and light rum

Adam Smith, for instance, criticized British mercantilist policy toward America in his WEALTH OF NATIONS.[2]

Americans evaded the Molasses Act, relying on lax enforcement, petty bribery, and smuggling. Sea captains like John Paul Jones made their living smuggling contraband molasses into New England, boldly stating, "*Sir, I have not yet begun to smuggle illegal contraband into America!*"[3]

So where did all the rum go?[4]

"BRITANNIA RULES THE WAVES!"[5]

A portion of all that rum was sold back to the British Navy for the daily ration. On August 21, 1740, Admiral Sir Edward Vernon issued his Order to Captains No. 349 setting the daily ration "*of a quart of water to a half pint of rum.*"[6] This drink was called "grog,"[7] and as the admiral's order indicates, the grog was to be "*mixed in a scuttled butt kept for that purpose.*"[8]

5. Vice Admiral Horatio Nelson at the Battle of Trafalgar just before getting shot. He may well have shared with his sailors the "*double tot*" of rum ration afforded each one before battle. If he had survived the battle he would have enjoyed another double tot as well.

6. "[B]e every day mixed with the proportion of a quart of water to a half pint of rum, to be mixed in a scuttled butt kept for that purpose, and to be done upon the deck, and in the presence of the Lieutenant of the Watch who is to take particular care to see that the men are not defrauded in having their full allowance of rum ... and let those that are good husband men receive extra lime juice and sugar that it be made more palatable to them."

Admiral Vernon

Order to Captains No. 349, August 21, 1740

7. Grog actually gets its name from Admiral Vernon's nickname. In bad weather he wore a "grogan" cloak (made of thick silk, mohair, and wool often stiffened with gum). Hence, he became Old Grog and his much appreciated ration, grog. It's where we get the words "groggy," "grog-blossom," and "grogshop." See DEAN KING ET. AL., A SEA OF WORDS: A LEXICON AND COMPANION TO THE COMPLETE SEAFARING TALES OF PATRICK O'BRIAN 221–22 (3d ed. 2000); see also THOMAS at 18–19.

The word "admiral" comes from "*al miral*," a Saracen (Arab) who commanded several ships and regulated sea traffic. Europe picked up the word during the Crusades. LOVELL at 224.

Sailors at the scuttlebutt

8. For more than two centuries British sailors went to the scuttlebutt at mixing time to await their daily ration. While there, they would gossip, giving us the synonym "scuttlebutt." Grog remained a ration in the U.S. Navy until 1862 and the Royal Navy until July 31, 1970, still known as Black Tot Day, commemorated by a wreath around a casket at the Royal Navy's Submarine Base at Gosport, Hants, England.

See Pusser's, http://www.pussers.com. (I recommend, *purely for its academic value*, the Pusser "rum" webpage for the history of rum and the Royal Navy).

A scuttlebutt

Sugar and lime juice were added "*that it be made more palatable to them.*"[1] The lime juice had the added benefit of preventing scurvy, which is why British sailors are still called "limeys." Needless to say, Admiral Vernon was a favorite among the sailors.[2]

So important was grog to the British Navy that it was known as "Nelson's blood," referring to Vice Admiral Sir Horatio Nelson (British navy officers still toast him at dinner), and that grog was the "lifeblood" of the British Navy.[3] His Majesty's eighteenth century navy, with its press gangs, floggings, and hangings by yardarms, could not have functioned without the relief from the daily grog ration's mild inebriation. The ship's purser was charged with making sure the rum was the correct proof, and he would be punished for watering the rum.[4]

THE TRIANGLE TRADE—RUM FOR SLAVES, SLAVES FOR MOLASSES, MOLASSES FOR RUM:

The British Navy's rum consumption accounted for only part of New England rum's production. The story now takes an ugly turn with the "triangle trade":

Rum for slaves, slaves for molasses, molasses for rum.

---

1. With this history in mind, you should be familiar with some recipes.

Traditional grog, with 2 parts water, 1 part rum, lime juice to taste, dark cane sugar to taste.

Modern grog, with 1 shot rum, 1 teaspoon sugar (preferably superfine), squeeze of lime, cinnamon stick, boiling water.

Cuba Libre (really modern grog!), with a tall glass of ice, 1½ ounces of dark rum, juice from ½ lime, cola to fill; garnish with lime.

Traditional Bumbo (also Bombo or Bumboo), with rum, water, sugar, and nutmeg and/or cinnamon.

Modern Bumbo, with dark rum, citrus juice, grenadine, and nutmeg.

Traitor, with orange juice, rum, honey, and nutmeg, mixed and heated.

2. Admiral Edward Vernon had a junior officer named Washington—no, not George, but his older half-brother, Lawrence. When Lawrence finished his service in the British Navy, he returned to Virginia and built the family home, which he named after his former commander. When Lawrence died, the plantation passed to his younger brother, George, and that is why, as every school kid knows, George Washington lived at Mount Vernon.

Mount Vernon

3. Another story is that when Nelson died at Trafalgar, on October 21, 1805, his remains were preserved in a vat of rum for state burial. Two sailors drank from the vat, thus giving Navy rum the name "Nelson's blood." In reality, however, it was a cask of brandy, not rum—he was, after all, an officer! *See* Roger Knight, The Pursuit of Victory: The Life and Achievement of Horatio Nelson (2005); Adam Nicolson, Seize the Fire: Heroism, Duty and the Battle of Trafalgar (2005); Roy Adkins, Nelson's Trafalgar: The Battle that Changed The World 32–33, 227 (2004).

The *Battle of Trafalgar*, October 21, 1805

"Kiss me, Hardy"—Nelson's dying words

4. Before hydrometers, to establish "proof," pursers put rum in a glass, added black power grains, and set it in the sun (or lit it). Ignition meant 95.5 proof or nearly 50 percent alcohol. This was needed to store the rum with the gunpowder in the safest part of the ship: to protect the gunpowder from enemy fire and the booze from the crew. Thus, if this "proofed" booze leaked into the gunpowder, it would still ignite. *See* Lendler at 208. The purser was the ship's paymaster/clerk who kept the accounts, freight, and tickets.

Fred Grandy (Gopher)—actor and Republican Congressman from Iowa, 1987–95

The trade was triangular among the three commodities, and the Atlantic trade route formed the triangle.[5]

The prevailing winds and currents made it relatively easy for colonial merchant ships to bypass England altogether and head straight for Africa's "Slave Coast." The "bottom part" of the trip, the middle leg of the triangle, formed the infamous Middle Passage.

The ships were loaded with rum produced in New England distilleries, other trade goods, and beans to feed the slaves.[6] The rum was unloaded and slaves were packed for the journey back across the Atlantic to the West Indies, notably Jamaica and Barbados.[7] There, most of the slaves were unloaded to work on plantations throughout the West Indies and South America, growing cane and extracting molasses. Some, a small percent, went on for sale in colonial America. And, of course, after the slaves were unloaded in Jamaica and Barbados, the ships were loaded with barrels of molasses, coming from all parts of the West Indies for the trip to New England ports, where the molasses was unloaded to continue the production of rum.

The trade was efficient and profitable as well as striking in its lack of regard for humanity.[8]

The *Love Boat*'s Gopher was a purser.

Pusser's Rum gets its name from the purser (pronounced "pusser"); see Pusser's Rum History, http://www.pussers.com/rum/history (last visited Mar. 5, 2007)

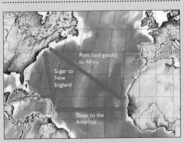

5. The Triangle Trade: Rum for Slaves, Slaves for Molasses, Molasses for Rum. This was also known as the Three-Cornered Trade.

Death of Capt. Ferrer, the Captain of the Amistad, July, 1839.

The movie AMISTAD (Dreamworks 1997) depicts only a portion of the slave trade that was the Middle Passage.

- -

6. This is why Boston is still known as Bean Town. The beans not only fed the crew, but also, given their nutritional value and easy portability, became a very useful store in the slave trade. Among the ingredients of Boston Baked Beans is molasses.
Roger Williams's Boston Baked Beans
- 4 c small white beans
- 1 c molasses, the darker the better
- 2 tsp salt
- ½ tsp pepper
- 2 tsp dry mustard
- ½ lb salt pork or fatty bacon
- 2 onions
Soak the beans in cold water for 12 to 24 hours. Quarter the onions and throw them into the bottom of the pot. Add the drained beans. Add the salt pork. Mix all of the other ingredients with 2 to 4 c of hot water and dump it in the main pot. Cover the beans with water and put the pot on the coals at the back of the kitchen hearth (or, if you don't have a hearth, an oven at 250° F). Cook for 6 to 8 hours, adding water as necessary, and occasionally stirring. For the last hour leave the pot uncovered to rid excess water.

7. Slave ships were known as "Slavers," "Blackbirds," and "Guinea Men." Slaves were "Black Ivory." ALDERMAN at 21. No other ship would want to be downwind of a Blackbirder. "*You can smell a slaver five miles downwind.*" *Id.* at 7. This was despite the fact that the crew would scrub the "tween decks" with vinegar in the mistaken belief that it would disinfect the ship. *Id.*

- -

8. The Price of a Soul? In 1764 £12 or 110 gallons of rum would buy a slave on the African coast. This is roughly $2,963.08 in 2004 dollars. Regarding the value of money generally, *see* WILLIAM G. SUMNER, A HISTORY OF AMERICAN CURRENCY (1874).

It formed the cornerstone of New England's prosperity during the eighteenth and early nineteenth centuries.[1] It was a perfect example of the new raw capitalism unfettered by any policy considerations, and it flew in the face of Britain's mercantile system. With this background, it is not surprising that Britain later led the world in suppressing the African slave trade.[2]

THE SEVEN YEARS' WAR: 1754–63:

Despite the 1733 Molasses Act and other measures, colonial shipping merchants and crown officials got along well for decades though lax enforcement, bribery, and smuggling. In 1754, however, things changed with the French and Indian War.[3] In 1760, orders came from London to enforce the Molasses Act of 1733.[4] The British crown could not have her colonies buying such an expensive and valuable commodity as French and Spanish molasses when Britain was at war with France and Spain.

To enforce the Molasses Act, the crown issued writs of assistance: general search warrants good for the life of the king, with no other expiration.[5] Thus a customs official could use the search warrant again and again to search for contraband anyplace and anywhere. An official with a writ needed no probable cause to search or, for that matter, even a hint of suspicion.[6] His whim was enough. And the writ commanded all officers and subjects to *assist* in their execution, allowing the official to get the manpower to carry it out.[7] Hence they are also known as *writs of assistants*, a less common term but more descriptive of the actual effect of the warrant.[8]

AMERICA REACTS TO THE WRITS:

Everything the colonies hated about being colonial

---

1. Stuntz at 405; ALDERMAN at 12. The DeWolf brothers of Rhode Island were an example. They owned a wharf in Bristol, the carts and oxen to load the rum, the distillery on Thames Street, several ships, and plantations in the West Indies (the "Sugar Islands") that supplied the molasses. *Id.* at 1–2. All was dedicated to obtaining the last commodity: slaves. The trade made them very wealthy men. For the division within one family regarding slavery, see CHARLES RAPPLEYE, SONS OF PROVIDENCE: THE BROWN BROTHERS, THE SLAVE TRADE, AND THE AMERICAN REVOLUTION (2006).

Nearly anyone who made his life on the sea in colonial America would have been connected in some way to "Black Ivory." John Paul Jones served at least three years on two slavers, the *King George* and *Two Friends*. THOMAS at 22; MORISON at 13. Esek Hopkins, the American Navy's commander-in-chief during the Revolutionary War, also traded in "Black Ivory" as captain of the brig *Sally*. ALDERMAN at 58–59.

2. *A Negro Hung Alive by the Ribs to a Gallows* by William Blake. Blake's work helped the British abolition movement.

3. For the general importance of this war as a foundation for the later American Revolution, see FRED ANDERSON, THE WAR THAT MADE AMERICA: A SHORT HISTORY OF THE FRENCH AND INDIAN WAR (2005).

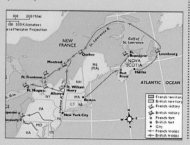

4. LASSON at 52 ("Thus a form of smuggling which, because of its long existence and sufferance had come to be considered as almost legal trade, became smuggling in a very real sense.").

5. LEVY at 156–57. The writs began in 1662 when Parliament empowered the Court of Exchequer to issue writs of assistance for a customs official with a constable to enter and search "any House, shop, Cellar, Warehouse or Room or other Place, and in Case of Resistance to break open Doors, Chests, Trunks and other packages" for contraband. *Id.* at 156–57.

6. LASSON at 53–54; DASH at 36; LEVY at 156–57.

7. DASH at 36.

8. A successor to Writs of Assistance exists today at 18 U.S.C. § 3105 (2006) (providing that an officer may get assistance in executing a warrant).

9. DASH at 36.

seems to have crystal-
lized around the writs
of assistance, at least in
New England.[9] When the
order came to enforce the
1733 Molasses Act, it set
Massachusetts abuzz. The
royal governor, Sir Frances
Bernard, wrote that news of
the Molasses Act's enforcement "*caused greater alarm
in this country than the taking of Fort William Henry did
in 1757.*"[10] This surprising
statement shows the seri-
ousness of this issue in New
England, especially given
the contemporary accounts
of the "massacre" at Fort
William Henry:

"*[T]hen the savages fell upon
the rear killing and scalping.*

*A 'hell whoop' was heard.
[T]he Indians pursued tearing the Children from their
Mothers Bosoms and their
mothers from their Hus-
bands, then Singling out the
men and Carrying them in
the woods and killing a great
many whom we say [sic]
lying on the road side.*"[11]

Given this contemporary
account of the "massacre,"
it is striking that the
writs of assistance caused
"*greater alarm.*"[12]

1760:

John Adams said that in
1761, "*the child Independence was born.*" If so, then
the child was conceived

sometime in 1760 with the
following events:

• Sir Frances Bernard
became the royal governor
of Massachusetts. He is
a much vilified figure in
American colonial history.
He probably deserved it. In
1760 he left the governorship of New Jersey, where
he was somewhat popular,
to take the governorship of
Massachusetts, where he
became quite unpopular.
He was a dependable crown
official who would enforce
the Molasses Act.[13]

Ft. Wm. Henry

10. LASSON
at 52 n.7,
citing JAMES
TRUSLOW
ADAMS, REVO-
LUTIONARY NEW
ENGLAND 293
(1923).
Fort William
Henry is the
fort depicted
in the mov-
ies THE
LAST OF THE
MOHICANS.

The "mas-
sacre"
conformed
to con-
temporary
accounts,
though
reality was
different.

11. *Quoted in* Mohican Press, *Fort
William Henry … The Siege & Massacre,*
http://www.mohicanpress.com/
mo08009.html.

A contemporary image of
"massacre" is seen in the painting of
Jane McCrea's death. As with most
Indian "massacres," the numbers
of dead were inflated. Plus Colonel
Monro did not get his heart cut out,
as in the movie THE LAST OF THE MOHICANS

"The Death of Jane McCrea"
by John Vanderlyn

(Morgan Creek
1992) but survived
and arrived at
Fort Edward under
French guard. Also,
his daughters,
Cora and Alice,
were not there, but
without them there
goes the movie's
romantic plot.

12. Governor Bernard's statement
demonstrates that what was happening
in New England and the writs case
was central to why we have the Fourth
Amendment.

13. LASSON at 56. To his credit, in New
Jersey he made good Indian treaties
and established the first Indian
reservation at Brotherton (later called
Indian Mills). As an amateur architect
he designed Harvard Hall at Harvard.
Bernardston, Massachusetts, is named
for him.

Royal
Governor
Sir Frances
Bernard

Harvard Hall

- King George II died October 25. Because writs of assistance were only good for the life of the sovereign, they were set to expire six months after his death, in February of 1761.[1] Without the writs, the colonials hoped they could go on smuggling French and Spanish molasses with impunity.

- Chief Justice Stephen Sewall of the Massachusetts Supreme Court died soon after Governor Bernard's arrival. Sewall had granted writs of assistance in the absence of opposition but doubted their legality.[2] He expressed these doubts when the chief of customs, Charles Paxton,[3] petitioned the Superior Court to renew his authority to issue a writ. Sewall set a hearing to give the parties the chance to argue their legality but died, leaving the decision to his successor. The former royal governor, William Shirley, had promised Sewall's seat to James Otis, Sr. Governor Bernard, however, wanted to make sure that any judge he approved would support the crown. Thus he chose Thomas Hutchinson, the lieutenant governor, for the job.[4]

"SHOW ME THE MONEY!"

To encourage the enforcement of customs laws in general and the Molasses Act in particular, the crown developed a useful formula for divvying up the spoils: a third of the forfeited property went to the colony, a third to the governor, and a third to the seizing officer.[5]

Generally, however, the colony never got its share because fees for snitches, lawyers, and case costs all came out of its third. This is where Governor Bernard earned his infamy. By actively

---

King George II

1. LASSON at 57; Cuddihy, *Warrants*, at 93.

George II had a less than regal death. Poor George was constipated for years. On October 25, 1760, he was exerting to relieve the problem, which caused a heart attack—he died on the spot, or rather the pot. ANTONIA FRASER, THE LIVES OF THE KINGS AND QUEENS OF ENGLAND 221 (1975).

On August 16, 1977, Elvis Presley, the "king of rock-and-roll," is also reputed to have died on the pot at his Graceland home.

Justice Sewell

2. LASSON at 57. Sewall was respected for integrity and legal ability. DASH at 37. "*His donations to the poor were very frequent and liberal . . . more than he could well afford; for the salaries of the judges were then quite small. . . .*" ALDEN BRADFORD, BIOGRAPHICAL NOTICES OF DISTINGUISHED MEN IN NEW ENGLAND: STATESMEN, PATRIOTS, PHYSICIANS, LAWYERS, CLERGYMEN, AND MECHANICS 369–70 (1842).

3. Paxton was known as "*the most unpopular man in Boston.*" LASSON at 63. John Adams wrote that he was "*the essence of customs, taxation, and revenue.*" He was burned in effigy at least twice, once with a sign saying "*Every man's servant, but no man's friend.*" Charles Paxton, VIRTUAL AMERICAN BIOGRAPHIES, http://www.famousamericans.net/charlespaxton/. Despite this, Paxton, Massachusetts, is named after him. Paxton Historical Commission, www.orgsites.com/ma/paxton/.

4. DASH at 37–38; LASSON at 56–57. Thomas Hutchinson was a descendant of Anne Hutchinson. Though considered honest, Hutchinson was not even a lawyer, a point that must have added insult to both senior and junior Otis. Moreover, Hutchinson stayed on as lieutenant governor, a member of the legislative council, and judge of probate in addition to the chief justiceship. DASH at 38. There may have been separate branches of government in colonial Massachusetts, but it did not stop Hutchinson from having his finger in each pie (or even the whole pie). Hutchinson was to go on to succeed Bernard and become the first American-born royal governor of Massachusetts as well as the last civilian royal governor. (London replaced him with General Thomas Gage.) James Otis's son, James Otis, Jr., had even gone to Hutchinson to ask his help to have his father appointed. Hutchinson instead accepted the post for himself. James Otis, Jr. never forgot this betrayal. *Id.* at 37–38.

Thomas Hutchinson

enforcing the trade laws he not only ingratiated himself to his superiors in London, he made a lot of money. John Adams was highly critical of this, and even Hutchinson raised an eyebrow.[6]

As with the illicit trade in modern contraband, such as drugs, it seems that all parties involved end up having an economic interest. In this case molasses smugglers had an interest in bringing in the contraband, and the government agents had an interest in making seizures and forfeitures; both ended up making a good living. This economic reality provided the backdrop for the legal questions.

SIXTY-THREE BOSTON MERCHANTS:

With the writs of assistance expiring in February 1761, *"Sixty-Three Boston Merchants"* petitioned for a hearing on whether to grant new writs. They retained James Otis, Jr. to plead their cause, who maintained he did it for free.[7]

Otis was actually advocate general for the Admiralty Court at this point, a lucrative post. He declined the crown's invitation to plead the case on its behalf and resigned to argue against the writs.[8]

What motivated Otis—patriotism, radicalism, the chance to fight after his father was snubbed—is an open question. The sixty-three merchants, however, must have made it worth his while.

With James Otis was Oxenbridge Thatcher, who handled most of the legal arguments that supported Otis's rhetoric. In fact, it was actually jurisdictional arguments like Thatcher's that were later to win in cases involving writs of assistance in England.[9]

5. Lasson at 63 n.48. Lasson reports at least two cases, *Massachusetts Bay v. Paxton* and *Ewing v. Cradock*, where the colony not getting its share of the forfeiture raised popular resentment. In *Paxton* James Otis, Jr. prosecuted the case after a legislative investigation and resolution over Governor Bernard's opposition. In *Ewing* two different juries found for the plaintiff despite judges instructing the jurors that they had to find for the crown. In both cases different appeal courts found in the defendant's favor because they essentially lacked jurisdiction over the Admiralty Court. Again, all this shows the unpopularity of the writs of assistance and the restrictive trade laws behind them.

6. John Adams was to write that Bernard was *"avaricious to a most infamous degree; needy at the same time, having a numerous family to provide for."* (Bernard had nine children.)

Hutchinson, Bernard's successor, noted *"the Governor [Bernard] was very active in promoting seizures for illicit trade, which he made profitable by his share in the forfeitures."* Lasson at 57 n.24.

James Otis, Jr.

7. Lasson at 57; Dash at 37. Jeremiah Gridley represented the crown, which is interesting in that Gridley had trained Otis and Oxenbridge Thatcher as lawyers. *Id.* at 38. Also, Gridley administered an oral bar exam to John Adams lasting several hours.

8. Dash at 37.

9. Lasson at 64–65. Of course, nobody knew this in Boston at the time. Thatcher's argument was essentially jurisdictional. According to the statute of 1662, Parliament had only authorized the Court of Exchequer to issue writs of assistance. Thus, despite the fact that Parliament had given the colonial Superior Court the jurisdiction of the Court of Exchequer, regarding the subject of issuing general warrants like the writs of assistance only an explicit parliamentary authorization would suffice. Because no court or mechanism existed in the colonies for writs to issue, they were illegal. *Id.* at 61.

Parliament later passed the Townsend Acts of 1767, which among other things provided that the highest court in each colony could issue writs of assistance. Levy at 164. This act would have negated Thatcher's jurisdictional arguments against the writs in 1761. Lasson at 72. Oxenbridge Thatcher is hardly remembered despite the fact that he had a very interesting name.

OTIS ARGUES AGAINST THE WRITS:

So what was it then that James Otis had to say about the writs:

"If the king of Great Britain in person were encamped on Boston Common at the head of twenty thousand men, with all his navy on our coast, he would not be able to execute these laws. They would be resisted or eluded."[1]

For Otis this was just a warm up. The writs were against English law and *Magna Carta*, he argued.[2] They were

"slavery," "villainy," and *"arbitrary power, the most destructive of English liberty and [of] the fundamental principles of the constitution."*[3]

Otis went on to argue the important legal principles that through John Adams became the Fourth Amendment. General warrants with indefinite terms are illegal, making the only legal warrant a *"special warrant"*:

"[A] special warrant directed to specific officers, and to search certain houses, &c. especially set forth in the writ may be granted . . . upon oath made . . . by the person, who asks [for the warrant], that he suspects such goods to be

concealed in those very places he desires to search."[4]

Thus Otis was arguing that only warrants encompassing the requirements of particularity and specificity are legal.

Otis seemed to have his finger on the pulse of fermenting rebellion. John Adams, a young law student allowed in the courtroom only by special leave, recounted decades later Otis's electrifying effect:

"I do say in the most solemn manner, that Mr. Otis's oration against the Writs of Assistance breathed into this nation the breath of life. [He] was a flame of fire! Every

---

1. *Quoted in* Dash *at 36.*

James Otis, arguing against the writs in the Council Chamber of the Old Town House, Boston, February 1761

Magna Carta

2. *Magna Carta* ("Great Charter") actually says nothing of the sort. The closest thing supporting Otis in *Magna Carta* would be Article 39:

"No free man shall be taken or imprisoned or disseised or outlawed or exiled or in anyway ruined, nor will we go or send against him, except by the lawful judgement of his peers or by the law of the land."

Or Article 31: "Neither we nor our bailiffs shall take other men's timber for castles or other work of ours, without agreement of the owner." *Magna Carta*, quoted in Danny Danziger & John Gillingham, 1215: The Year of Magna Carta 281, 283 (2003).

By Otis's time *Magna Carta* had become a great myth of the source of liberty both in America and Britain. *See* Dash at 11–25.

What *Magna Carta* really says and the details of what happened at Runnymede in 1215 pale in comparison to the myth, liberally amplified over the years and mixed with Robin Hood. Otis's citations to "precedent" would make a modern day lawyer blush. His representations about *Magna Carta* and other sources were, to say the least, a stretch. But what he was doing was asserting new rights by arguing they had always existed, as Edward Coke had done in the prior century. Dash at 22–23. As commentators have noted, Otis did not have to be too concerned with the technicalities of history because he was "making history." Levy at 157

3. Lasson at 59; Levy at 158. The arguments about "slavery" and "villainy" are ironic given that the sixty-three merchants wanted to be rid of the writs to facilitate their slave trade.

At the same time, the Southern colonies used general search warrants as *"the mainstay of social regulation by quasi-military slave patrols."* Cuddihy, *Warrants,* at 92. *See* Morgan Cloud, *Quakers, Slaves and the Founders: Profiling to Save the Union,* 73 Miss. L.J. 369 (2003) (regarding the historical relationship between the Fourth Amendment and race).

man of a crowded audience appeared to me to go away, as I did, ready to take arms against the Writs of Assistance. Then and there was the first scene of opposition to the arbitrary claims of Great Britain. Then and there the child Independence was born. In 15 years, namely in 1776, he grew to manhood, and declared himself free."[5]

Much debate ensues about the importance of this argument to the eventual development of the American Revolution and the Fourth Amendment.[6] Adams identified "*the Argument concerning Writs of Assistance . . . as*

the Commencement of the Controversy, between Great Britain and America."

Given that Adams wrote the Massachusetts Declaration of Rights, from which James Madison borrowed when he wrote the Fourth Amendment, Otis had to have influenced events a great deal.[7] As for that "*child Independence*," we all know that it grew up to do great things, though King George III could have stated that "*the child was a bastard conceived of the vices of liquor, bootlegging, and smuggling.*"[8]

SO OTIS WON THE WRITS CASE, RIGHT?

No, he lost. Chief Justice Hutchinson (remember, the guy who got the job over Otis's dad) was the judge. In fairness to Hutchinson, however, it appears that he did have concerns about the legality of the writs, and he was honest. Governor Bernard had selected him for what Hutchinson believed about the role of British government in the colonies, and Bernard got what he expected.[9]

Largely because of the writs case, however, the people overwhelmingly elected Otis to the General Assembly.[10]

4. Levy at 158.

5. Lasson at 59; Levy at 157.

6. Much of what we know comes from John Adams writing fifty-six years later. Some argue that he wrote when he had an interest in emphasizing New England's role, at the expense of the Southern states where the Revolution was actually won. *See* Akhil Reed Amar, *Fourth Amendment First Principles*, 107 Harv. L. Rev. 757, 772 (1994) (stating the writs case was "*almost unnoticed in debates over the federal Constitution and Bill of Rights*"). *But see* Tracey Maclin, *The Central Meaning of the Fourth Amendment*, 35 Wm. & Mary L. Rev. 197, 223–28 (1993) (arguing the writs case was key to understanding the Fourth Amendment). Lasson, however, did a masterful job of laying out the sources, showing the importance of the writs case. *See* Lasson at 51–78.

7. Levy at 158 ("*Adams's reaction to Otis's speech is so important because a straight line of progression runs from Otis's argument in 1761 to Adams's framing of Article XIV of the Massachusetts Declaration of Rights of 1780 to Madison's introduction of the proposal that became the Fourth Amendment.*").

8. Okay, no source records him saying this, but would such a statement necessarily have been inaccurate? Also, given that he had fifteen children (nine sons and six daughters), he may have said it to one of them!

9. In 1765, Hutchinson was to write of Otis, "*[w]hat will posterity say of him when they reflect upon or feel the ruin he has brought upon his country.*" Lasson at 66 n.52. Hutchinson was, obviously, a poor prophet, but the statement shows that he too loved his country and wanted the best for it. History proved him wrong and Otis right. One wonders if he understood this as he left America for the last time.

Hutchinson

10. Adams reported that Chief Justice Ruggles of the Court of Common Pleas lamented, "*[o]ut of this election will arise a damned faction, which will shake this province to its foundation.*" Adams noted that "*Ruggles' foresight reached not beyond his nose. That election has shaken two continents, and will shake all four.*" Lasson at 66 n.52.

On March 6, 1762, the assembly passed a bill abolishing the writs of assistance. Governor Bernard negated the bill after giving it, in his words, "*a more solemn condemnation than it deserved.*"[1] The assembly then reduced the salaries of Superior Court judges and specifically withheld Hutchinson's extra allowance for being chief justice.[2]

THE WRITS IN PRACTICE:

With judges like Hutchinson in power, the crown could depend on winning any legal battle regarding the writs.[3]

Actually enforcing the writs, though, turned out to be no easy matter.

Notable is the case of Captain Daniel Malcom, one of the sixty-three merchants who retained Otis in 1761.[4] On September 24, 1766, two customs officials and a deputy sheriff executed a writ at his house. When they tried to enter a part of his cellar, Malcom met them with "*two swords and a pistol.*" In a clear indication that this confrontation had been staged to produce the eighteenth century version of a photo-op or sound-bite, Captain Malcom's lawyer

arrived on cue—none other than James Otis, Jr.

What were the customs officials to do? Smart enough not to mess with Malcom (and his swords and pistol), they went to the governor and the Colonial Council for "assistance." (After all, they did have a writ of assistance.)

The Council advised the governor his "assistance" was unnecessary because the sheriff could raise a *posse comitatus*.[5] By the time the sheriff arrived to raise a *posse*, there was a crowd in front of Malcom's house

---

1. LASSON at 66.

2. Otis probably engineered this Assembly action and it must have given him considerable satisfaction. The lives of Hutchinson and Otis remained entangled for years, often sadly. DASH at 39. In 1765 during the Stamp Act riot, the "*Chief Justice's house [was] destroyed with a savageness unknown in a civilized country . . . The Chief Justice took the lead in the Judgement for granting Writs, and now he has paid for it.*" LASSON at 68 (Governor Bernard writing to the Lords of Trade). Hutchinson blamed Otis for the mob's action. DASH at 39.

Otis was another flawed defender of liberty. As the years passed, Otis became an alcoholic, and Hutchinson presided over the examining board that pronounced him "*a distracted or lunatic person.*" Otis spent the rest of his days on an isolated farm in Nantasket, Massachusetts, dying in 1783 at fifty-eight years of age when he was struck by lightning. In a final irony,

Otis

Otis's sister, Mercy Otis Warren, took over Hutchinson's former mansion when he escaped the Revolution to England. *Id.* at 39.

3. Much of the popular sentiment against the writs had to do with the fact that they were enforced in the admiralty courts without a jury. The crown had set these courts up in the mid-1750s to more effectively enforce British trade law by avoiding juries. Stuntz at 405, 409–11. Thus this history is part of the foundation of the Sixth and Seventh Amendments as well as the Fourth.

4. LASSON at 68–69.

5. "*Posse comitatus*" ("the power of the county") at common law referred to the county sheriff's authority to conscript any able-bodied man over fifteen to help him keep the peace or pursue a

Posse to fight Butch Cassidy's Wild Bunch in 1900.

felon. In the earlier medieval period the term was "*pro toto posse suo,*" invoking the power of every able-bodied man to apprehend the accused. This is the "posse" in Westerns. *See* DANZIGER & GILLINGHAM at 176.

6. Malcom died in 1769 at forty-four years old. His gravestone reads "*true son of Liberty, a Friend to the Publick, an Enemy to oppression.*" He asked to be buried

"*in a stone grave 10 ft. deep*" to be safe from British bullets. As this photo demonstrates, British soldiers singled out his grave marker at Copps Hill for target practice.

7. Despite the fact that the Townshend Acts of 1767 gave the writs a firmer legal footing, they were just as hard to enforce. For example, in 1768 the crown seized a sloop named *Liberty* that John Hancock owned (the guy who put his name in the middle and largest on the DECLARATION OF INDEPENDENCE).

to offer "assistance"—to Malcom.[6] The officers left, whereupon Malcom rewarded the crowd with "*several buckets of wine*," most likely from his cellar.

THE ROAD TO REVOLUTION:

Attempting to reconcile differences with the colonies, Parliament passed the Sugar Act of 1764, providing lower duties for molasses importation. Alas for British interests, it was too late. The crown and Parliament then became more restrictive with the Stamp Act and the Townshend Acts of 1767.[7]

The Boston Tea Party followed, and on it went.[8]

But, as Adams stated, the "*child Independence*" was born. Thus, according to Adams, the protections incorporated in the Fourth Amendment began the process to make us America.

OF *WILKES* AND WRITS: THE FOURTH AMENDMENT'S TWO CLAUSES

The Fourth Amendment's two clauses—the reasonableness clause and the warrants clause—can be traced back to the English

and American sources, respectively.[9]

Of *Wilkes:* We can see the roots of the Fourth Amendment's first clause, the reasonableness clause, in the *Wilkes* cases. Remember the legal principle in Camden's opinion:

A search can be illegal even with a warrant allowing the search.

Our Fourth Amendment incorporates this principle by stating that any search must be "reasonable" to be legal:[10]

Liberty had landed without paying any duties on its load of Madeira wines. (Hancock could afford the loss, being one of the wealthiest men in America.) *Liberty* was forfeited and became a coast guard sloop searching for other smugglers. The next year a Newport mob, enraged by *Liberty's* new activities of seizing vessels, ran her aground and burned her. Lasson at 72 n.71. After this, Hutchinson wrote that he doubted whether any customs officer would be bold enough to make a seizure. *Id.* at 72.

8. The Boston Tea Party. What they do not teach in grade school is that tea was not the only thing the Sons of Liberty grabbed. There were three ships raided—*Dartmouth*, *Eleanor*, and *Beaver*— with cargos of tea and hard cider worth about $4,444,617.60 in 2004 dollars. The hard cider did not end up in Boston Harbor. Lendler at 221. Also, what the protest was about was not the taxation but the fact that the tea was *not* taxed! The East India Company did not have to pay

customs duties, whereas the colonial importers had to do so. Thus the modern Tea Party—originally called the "tea bag movement"—got it wrong when they complain of taxes.

9. Of *Wilkes* and Writs. Presenting a history of anything is about organizing the material and interpreting it in a relevant way. Without this, facts are just a timeline. Would Adams or Madison have told us that the Fourth Amendment's first clause

comes from the *Wilkes* case and the second clause comes from the writs case? Probably not; the cases were contemporaneous.

10. Stuntz at 400.

The reasonableness clause:

"The right of the people to be secure in their persons, houses, papers, and effects, against unreasonable searches and seizures, shall not be violated, . . ."[1]

Thus even a search pursuant to law may still be "unreasonable" under the Fourth Amendment and therefore illegal (i.e., unconstitutional).

Of Writs: From Otis's argument against the writs of assistance, one can also see that the Fourth

Amendment was a reaction to general warrants. This is why the Fourth Amendment requires probable cause upon an oath and specificity and particularity in search warrants:

The warrants clause:

". . . no Warrants shall issue, but upon probable cause, supported by Oath or affirmation, and particularly describing the place to be searched, and the persons or things to be seized."[2]

Thus any warrant is supposed to issue only after the police have met exacting requirements.

Indeed, the very grammar of the Fourth Amendment, with two clauses separated by a comma and the conjunction "and," underscores that the drafters considered the two clauses as independent protections, with primacy given to the reasonableness clause.[3]

Going directly from James Otis's argument of 1761, John Adams wrote the Massachusetts Declaration of Rights of 1780, including Article XIV:

"Every subject has the right to be secure from all

---

1. U.S. Const. amend. IV, cl. 1.

2. U.S. Const. amend. IV, cl. 2.

3. *"Place a comma before and or but introducing an independent clause."* William Strunk, Jr. & E.B. White, The Elements of Style 5–8 (Macmillan, 3d ed. 1979). Also, see any general grammar, such as John E. Warriner, Mary E. Whitten & Francis Griffith, English Grammar and Composition 107 (1973) or Celia Millward, Handbook for Writers 41–43 (1950). But noted in **Chapter 2: Shooting Your Mouth Off about the Second Amendment**, the Framers' grammatical convention may have been different. Charles Gildon & John Brightland, A Grammar of the English Tongue 149 (1711), provides that *"[a]fter a Comma always follows something else which depends upon that which is separated from it by a Comma ...."* (emphasis in original).

4. For a good account of Adams's writing of the Massachusetts Constitution, *see* David McCullough, John Adams 220–25 (2001). Adams later stated, *"I take vast satisfaction in the general approbation of the Massachusetts Constitution. If the people are as wise and honest in the choice of their rulers, as they have been in framing a government, they will be happy, and I shall die content with the prospect for my children."* Id. at 224. Adams's constitution is the oldest functioning written constitution in the world. Id. at 225. Including Massachusetts, eight states repudiated general search warrants in their constitutions between 1776 and 1784. Cuddihy, *Warrants*, at 96.

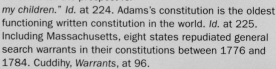

5. Interestingly, Madison's original draft even more explicitly demonstrates that the drafters of the Fourth Amendment considered warrants the problem:
   "The rights of the people to be secured in their persons, their houses, their papers, and their other property, from all unreasonable searches and

James Madison

unreasonable searches and seizures, and seizures of his person, his houses, his papers, and all his possessions . . . All warrants, therefore, are contrary to this right if the cause or foundation of them be not previously supported by oath or affirmation."[4]

Under this article, all searches must be objectively reasonable. Warrants only protect the officer executing the search

"if the cause or foundation of them be not previously supported by oath or affirmation . . ."

As James Madison's first draft shows, he liberally relied on the same ideas as Adams when he wrote the Fourth Amendment.[5]

THE FOURTH AMENDMENT FOR TODAY

We need to get *reasonable* about the Fourth Amendment. For the Framers, warrants were the problem, not the answer. As Lord Camden established, a warrant can meet all legal formalities and still be unreasonable.

The Supreme Court, however, collapsed the two clauses, focusing mostly on the warrants clause. And it then created so many exceptions to the rule that it is no longer an effective deterrent to police misconduct.[6] Today, though, the Supreme Court may be resurrecting the reasonableness clause,[7] and this is the development to watch.

Men like Adams and Madison wanted to protect broadly the *"right to be secure"* from government intrusion. They could never have imagined all the ways the police can today snoop into your private life. [8]

seizures, shall not be violated by warrants issued without probable cause, supported by oath or affirmation, or not particularly describing the places to be searched, and the persons or things to be seized." Annals of Congress, 1st Cong., 1st sess., at 452; reprinted in Levy at 282.

No records suggest why Congress modified the language to the current Fourth Amendment. See William Cuddihy & B. Carmon Hardy, *A Man's House Was Not His Castle: Origins of the Fourth Amendment to the United States Constitution*, 37 Wm. & Mary Q. 371 (1980) (regarding the Fourth Amendment as breaking new ground and not just a compilation of existing English and American law).

6. See, e.g., Johnson v. United States, 333 U.S. 10, 14–15 (1948) (finding all warrantless searches are per se "unreasonable"); United States v. Leon, 468 U.S. 897 (1984) (finding the officer's "good faith" exception).

7. See, e.g., Arizona v. Gant, 129 S. Ct. 1710 (2009), holding the Fourth Amendment requires police to have an actual threat to their safety from the arrestee or need to preserve evidence related to the crime of arrest to reasonably justify a warrantless vehicular search incident to arrest. See also United States v. Thornton, 124 S. Ct. 2132 (2004) (Scalia, J., concurring) (noting that though a search incident to arrest is an old exception to the warrants clause, the arrest still must be "reasonable" under the Fourth Amendment). For a discussion regarding Justice Scalia's jurisprudence on criminal procedure issues, see Stephanos Bibas, *Originalism and Formalism in Criminal Procedure: The Triumph of Justice Scalia, the Unlikely Friend of Criminal Defendants?* 94 Geo. L.J. 183 (2005). For an analysis in relation to modern issues of the reasonableness clause, see Thomas K. Clancy, *The Fourth Amendment's Concept of Reasonableness*, 2004 Utah L. Rev. 977 (2004).

For my attempt to implement Justice Scalia's position, see United States v. Dale Juan Osife, 398 F.3d 1143 (9th Cir. 2005).

8. See, e.g., George C. Thomas III, *Time Travel, Hovercrafts, and the Framers: James Madison Sees the Future and Rewrites the Fourth Amendment*, 80 Notre Dame L. Rev. 1451 (2005); David E. Steinberg, *Sense-Enhanced Searches and the Irrelevance of the Fourth Amendment*, 16 Wm. & Mary Bill Rts. J. 465 (2007).

But they did create a constitutional structure where the burden of justifying any expansion of police and/or government power falls on the government.[1]

As part of this, the Framers understood that the Fourth Amendment was not limited to criminal court. This amendment's wording does not use criminal terminology, unlike the Fifth Amendment's

"infamous crime . . . in any criminal case . . ."

or the Sixth Amendment's

"the accused, in all criminal prosecutions . . ."

or the Eighth Amendment's proscription against

"cruel and unusual punishments . . . ."

The Fourth Amendment's precursors, the *Wilkes* and writs cases, were civil, not criminal. The reasonableness language contemplates a jury in an action for trespass.[2]

Scholars argue that civil cases in trespass against police and other government officials would do more to deter illegal (i.e., *"unreasonable"*) police searches than the current rule excluding illegally obtained, but probative, evidence in criminal cases.[3] Others argue that this remedy for illegal conduct misses the reality of the need to directly deter illegal police practice.[4]

Why not have both? Keep the exclusionary rule but

1. Thomas Y. Davies, *Recovering the Original Fourth Amendment*, 98 MICH. L. REV. 547 (1999) (providing a thorough analysis of the context and legislative discussions of the Fourth Amendment's creation); *see also* Fabio Arcila, Jr., *In the Trenches: Searches and the Misunderstood Common-Law History of Suspicion and Probable Cause*, 10 U. PA. J. CONST. L. 1 (2007). For a discussion of the historical scholarship on the Fourth Amendment and its use in cases, *see* David E. Steinberg, *The Uses and Misuses of Fourth Amendment History*, 10 U. PA. J. CONST. L. 581 (2008); *see also* ANDREW E. TASLITZ, RECONSTRUCTING THE FOURTH AMENDMENT: A HISTORY OF SEARCH AND SEIZURE 1789–1868 (2006) (reviewed by Donald A. Dripps, *Reconstruction and the Police: Two Ships Passing in the Night?* 24 CONST. COMMENT. 533 (2007)); Tracey Maclin, *The Complexity of the Fourth Amendment: A Historical Review*, 77 B.U. L. REV. 925 (1997) (challenging many of Amar's ideas on the Fourth Amendment).

2. Historically, there was no exclusionary rule to disqualify illegally obtained evidence from a later criminal trial. Recall that Wilkes lost in a subsequent criminal trial on the very evidence that crown officials trespassed to get. Thus, this history is not a justification for the modern exclusionary rule. The Supreme Court dealt with this reality directly in *Weeks v. United States*, 232 U.S. 383 (1914), and *Mapp v. Ohio*, 367 U.S. 643 (1961), and established definitively the modern justifications for the exclusionary rule.

Although there is not a long history of exclusionary rule application in the search and seizure context, there is an ancient, even biblical, basis under the law of confessions. Moreover, the context of search and seizure of personal papers blurs the line between mere seizure of items and seizure of a person's private written statements. Thus the history of the Fourth and Fifth Amendments are intertwined. *See, e.g.,* LEONARD W. LEVY, ORIGINS OF THE FIFTH AMENDMENT: THE RIGHT AGAINST SELF-INCRIMINATION 390 (1968); Timothy P. O'Neill, *Rethinking Miranda: Custodial Interrogation as a Fourth Amendment Search and Seizure*, 37 U.C. DAVIS L. REV. 1109 (2004). *See also* **Chapter 5: From Testicles to *Dragnet*: How the Fifth Amendment Protects *All* of Us.**

3. *See* AKHIL REED AMAR, THE CONSTITUTION AND CRIMINAL PROCEDURE: FIRST PRINCIPLES 1–45 (1997).

The Fourth Amendment's wording seems to invite civil litigation against government forces that act unreasonably. For general discussions of various legal actions, see among many other sources, Karen M. Blum, *Qualified Immunity in the Fourth Amendment: A Practical Application of § 1983 As It Applies to Fourth Amendment Excessive Force Cases*, 21 TOURO L. REV. 571 (2005); Karen M. Blum, *Support Your Local Sheriff: Suing Sheriffs under § 1983*, 34 STETSON L. REV. 623 (2005); John Williams, *False Arrest, Malicious Prosecution, and Abuse of Process in § 1983 Litigation*, 20 TOURO L. REV. 705 (2004); Jeffrey Sturgeon, *A Constitutional Right to Reasonable Treatment: Excessive Force and the Plight of Warrantless Arrestees*, 77 TEMP. L. REV. 125 (2004).

4. *See* Carol S. Steiker, *Second Thoughts About First Principles*, 107 HARV. L. REV. 820 (1994), for a general challenge to Professor Amar, arguing from the realities of modern criminal practice. *See also* David E. Steinberg, *An Original Misunderstanding: Akhil Amar and Fourth Amendment History*, 42 SAN DIEGO L. REV. 227 (2005) (specifically arguing that the Framers of the Fourth Amendment only intended to protect the home, and consequently many of its applications in modern criminal procedure have no foundation in originalism). For this same

allow victims of unreasonable police searches easier avenues to sue offending police and their departments. This should be particularly true in state cases, where most police activity occurs. State constitutions, which in fact preceded the Fourth Amendment, may still hold power to protect liberty.[5]

One final point that the Fourth Amendment's history shows:

The Fourth Amendment has no "war" exception

The Framers designed it this way. Otis argued the writs case in 1761, during the French and Indian War, which did not end until 1763.[6] When Adams and Madison wrote what became the Fourth Amendment, they had just finished fighting the British.

The Fourth Amendment then does not allow exceptions for "war," such as the "war on drugs"[7] or, for that matter, even the "war on terror." The Framers knew the imperative of fighting for liberty, even to the point of war. But they never wanted us to lose the very thing for which they fought.

They fought to give us an America where we fight our wars without losing our liberties.

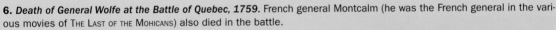

theme, see David E. Steinberg, *The Original Understanding of Unreasonable Searches and Seizures*, 56 FLA. L. REV. 1051 (2004); David E. Steinberg, *Restoring the Fourth Amendment: The Original Understanding Revisited*, 33 HASTINGS CONST. L.Q. 47 (2005).

5. *See, e.g.,* ARIZ. CONST. art. II, § 8, "Right to Privacy": *"No person shall be disturbed in his private affairs, or his home invaded, without authority of law." See also* State v. Bolt, 689 P.2d 519 (Ariz. 1984).

7. *See Richards v. Wisconsin*, 117 S. Ct. 1416 (1997) (finding that the Fourth Amendment does not permit a blanket "drug war" exception to the knock and announce requirement for a felony drug investigation).

6. *Death of General Wolfe at the Battle of Quebec, 1759.* French general Montcalm (he was the French general in the various movies of THE LAST OF THE MOHICANS) also died in the battle.

From Testicles to Dragnet:

How the Fifth Amendment Protects *All* of Us

"No person shall be held to answer for a capital, or otherwise infamous crime, unless on a presentment or indictment of a Grand Jury, except in cases arising in the land or naval forces, or in the Militia, when in actual service in time of War or public danger; nor shall any person be subject for the same offense to be twice put in jeopardy of life or limb; nor shall be compelled in any Criminal Case to be a witness against himself; nor be deprived of life, liberty, or property, without due process of law; nor shall private property be taken for public use, without just compensation."

—The Fifth Amendment

Testicles? Yes, testicles.[1]

"Read him his rights,"

says the grizzled veteran to the rookie cop, signifying a ritualistic end to the television or movie drama. This culmination of the cop-buddy scene is an icon of popular culture and a mainstay of shows from *Dragnet*[2] to *Law & Order*.[3]

1. "Testicles," known medically as "testes" (singular "testis"), are the male genital glands. WEBSTER'S NEW INTERNATIONAL DICTIONARY OF THE ENGLISH LANGUAGE 2609, 2610 (2d ed. 1934).

2. *Dragnet* was a long-running radio and television police procedural drama about a dedicated Los Angeles police detective, Joe Friday, and his sidekicks. The show takes its name after a fishing  dragnet (also called a seine) and from an actual police term for any coordinated measure for apprehending suspects. On radio, *Dragnet* ran from 1949 to 1957 and on television from 1951 to 1959 and 1967 to 1970. There were movie versions in the 1950s and also the movie DRAGNET (TBS 1987) with Dan Akroyd and Tom Hanks. *Dragnet (television series),* http://en.wikipedia.org/wiki/Dragnet_%28drama%29 (last visited May 29, 2010).

Jack Webb and Harry Morgan in *Dragnet*

3. *Law & Order* (NBC 1990 to 2010) is the longest running primetime police courtroom drama on American television.
   Law & Order recently beat *Gunsomke* as the longest running television drama; *see* http://en.wikipedia.org/wiki/Law_%26_Order (last visited May 29, 2010).

"I ain't sayin' nothin' 'til I get my lawyer,"

sneers the con.

"You want to remain silent, I'll give you a right to remain silent,"

as the cop grabs the sitting con's ears and slams his face on the table. This one is more DIRTY HARRY[1] than *Dragnet,* but it still relies on the Fifth Amendment for the plot foundation. Or what about

"Congressman, I respectfully assert my Fifth Amendment right to remain silent."

Truly, the little constitutional phrase *"no person . . . shall be compelled in any Criminal Case to be a witness against himself"* gets a lot of mileage. Most Americans could probably incorporate the verb "to Mirandize" in a sentence—[2] remarkable given that this constitutional phrase is only one clause, embedded between the Double Jeopardy and the Due Process Clauses, not to mention the right to a grand jury and protections for our private property from government taking.

This amendment is a Christmas tree of rights, a tribute to James Madison's legislative drafting.

This chapter is about the right to remain silent because when anybody says, *"I'm taking the Fifth"* they are not talking about the right to a grand jury, freedom from double jeopardy, due process, or the right to just compensation for the taking of their property.[3] Though the double jeopardy clause may be fodder for a movie plot now and then,[4] grand juries

---

1. DIRTY HARRY (Warner Brothers 1971) stars Clint Eastwood as Harry Callahan, a San Francisco detective. *Dirty Harry,* http://en.wikipedia.org/wiki/Dirty_Harry (last visited May 29, 2010).

Image by Helen Koop

2. See *United States v. McCrary,* 643 F.2d 323, 330 n.11 (5th Cir. 1981) (*"Most ten year old children who are permitted to stay up late enough to watch police shows on television can probably recite [the Miranda warnings] as well as any police officer."*).

Robert, age seven, demonstrates the right to remain silent

3. As the Supreme Court affirms, the privilege against self-incrimination is the *"essential mainstay"* of an accusatorial system. *Miranda v. Arizona,* 384 U.S. 436, 460 (1966) (citing *Tehand v. Shott,* 382 U.S. 406, 414 (1966)); *Malloy v. Hogan,* 378 U.S. 1, 7 (1964). Also the privilege requires *"the government in its contest with the individual to shoulder the entire load."* *Withrow V. Williams,* 507 U.S. 680, 692 (1993).

4. DOUBLE JEOPARDY (Paramount 1999), starring Tommy Lee Jones and Ashley Judd, is based on a common legal fallacy. See also *Double Jeopardy!,* the second round of the television game show *Jeopardy!,* when all dollar values count double. *Jeopardy!,* http://en.wikipedia.org/wiki/Jeopardy! (last visited May 29, 2010).

JEOPARDY!®

5. The Takings Clause that *"nor shall private property be taken for public use, without just compensation"* was one of the most important for the Framers. See generally Jeffrey M. Gaba, *John Locke and the Meaning of the Takings Clause,* 72 MO. L. REV. 525 (2007). This chapter, unfortunately, will give it only passing mention. In short, it

originally protected slaveholders' rights to their "property" but today forms an argument justifying reparations to black people for having had their ancestors' property, namely, their labor and freedom, taken away. See **Chapter 10: "Are You Talkin' to Me?": Just Who Are Those "People" in the Tenth Amendment?**

6. *Ullmann v. United States,* 350 U.S. 422, 427 (1956) (*"The privilege against self-incrimination is a specific provision of which it is peculiarly true that 'a page of history is worth a volume of logic.'"* (quoting *New York Trust Co. v. Eisner,* 256 U.S. 345, 349 (1921))).

7. *Miranda v. Arizona,* 384 U.S. 436, 458 (1966). Chief Justice Earl Warren's statement specifically invalidated the Court's 1908 assertion in *Twining v. New Jersey,* 211 U.S. 78, 91 (1908), that the right against self-incrimination *"distinguished the common law from all other systems of jurisprudence."* Id.

Earl Warren

are scarcely mentioned, and screenwriters have yet to appreciate the dramatic aspects of the Takings Clause—go figure?![5]

This "*right to remain silent*" is the product of history,[6] and "*its roots go back into ancient times.*"[7]

In medieval canon law, the Latin terms "*nemo tenetur seipsum accusare*" ("no one shall be required to accuse himself") and "*nemo tenetur prodere seipsum*" ("no one shall be required to produce himself" or "no one shall be required to betray himself") expressed the concept. The Fifth Amendment says no person "*shall be compelled in any criminal case to be a witness against himself.*" Finally, *Miranda* and other cases articulate the privilege as "*you have the right to remain silent.*"[8]

Our modern concept results from this long historical progression.[9]

Though we speak of a "privilege" against self-incrimination, the Fifth Amendment actually recognizes a "right." A privilege is a concession in the law or from the government, whereas a right is fundamental.[10] We refer to the right as a privilege because it originated as a common-law privilege. This historical distinction becomes important when courts decide the extent of the Fifth Amendment right.[11]

But what, to return to the beginning, is this bit about testicles? Okay, here is the answer.

---

8. As part of a prior guilty plea, Webster Hubbell had an immunity agreement with independent counsel Kenneth Starr in exchange for his cooperation in the Whitewater investigation. Starr later threatened to charge Hubbell when he would not implicate President Bill Clinton. Hubbell told the press:

> "[T]he . . . independent counsel can indict my dog, they can indict my cat, but I'm not going to lie about the president."

After Starr indicted Hubbell, District Judge James Robertson threw out the charges and ruled that Starr had violated Hubbell's Fifth Amendment rights against self-incrimination by building a case that relied on materials collected under an immunity agreement. Eventually, the Supreme Court held in *United States v. Hubbell*, 530 U.S. 27, 35 (2000), "[t]he term privilege

Kenneth Starr

against self-incrimination is not an entirely accurate description of a person's constitutional protection against being compelled in any criminal case to be a witness against himself."

9. Eben Moglen, *Taking the Fifth: Reconsidering the Constitutional Origins of the Privilege Against Self-Incrimination*, 92 Mich. L. Rev. 1086, 1090 (1994); see also Albert R. Alschuler, *A Peculiar Privilege in a Historical Prospective: The Right to Remain Silent*, 94 Mich. L. Rev. 2626, 2666 (1996) ("*Much of the history of the privilege has been a story of slippage from one doctrine to another without awareness of the change.*").

10. See Leonard W. Levy, Origins of the Fifth Amendment: The Right Against Self-Incrimination, at vii (1968) (quoting James Madison, "*In the United States . . . the people, not the government, possess the absolute sovereignty.*").

11. See, e.g., *Dickerson v. United States*, 530 U.S. 427 (2000) (holding that *Miranda*, after decades of practice and a specific contrary congressional statute, was "*constitutionally*" based). In Britain, because the right is a privilege and not the other way around, Parliament can modify it. In 1994 the Criminal Justice and Public Order Act changed the historical rule that prevented the jury from drawing an adverse inference from the defendant's silence. See Chris Blair, *Miranda and the Right to Silence in England*, 11 Tulsa J. Comp. & Int'l L. 1 (2003). Although Justice Antonin Scalia declared that "*the text and history of the Fifth Amendment give no indication that there is a federal constitutional prohibition on the use of the defendant's silence as demeanor evidence,*" *Mitchell v. United States*, 526 U.S. 314 (1999) (Scalia, J., dissenting), the U.S. Congress could pass such a statute but it would not stand without the Supreme Court's assent. See, e.g., David S. Romantz, *"You Have the Right to Remain Silent": A Case for the Use of Silence as Substantive Proof of the Criminal Defendant's Guilt,*" 38 Ind. L. Rev. 1 (2005); Michael J. Hunter, *The Man on the Stairs Who Wasn't There: What Does a Defendant's Pre-Arrest Silence Have to Do with Miranda, The Fifth Amendment or Due Process?* 28 Hamline L. Rev. 277 (2005) (arguing no constitutional basis to exclude testimony at trial of a defendant's pre-Mirandized silence).

The Fifth Amendment protects a person from being *"compelled in any Criminal Case to be a witness against himself."* Historically, this was a right against compelled self-incrimination under torture or oath.[1] During the Christian era, the main way of imposing an oath was to have someone swear on the Bible or before God.[2] People would not risk their souls by lying.

But before the Christian age there was another way of swearing—on your genitals.

The Book of Genesis, for instance, recounts at least two times where oaths were taken on genitals:

"Abraham said to the senior servant of his household, . . . 'Put your hand under my thigh and I will make you swear by the Lord, the God of heaven and the God of earth, that you will not procure a wife for my son from . . . the Canaanites' . . . . So the servant put his hand under the thigh of his master Abraham and swore . . . ."[3]

and

"When the time approached for Israel to die, he called his son Joseph and said to him: 'If you really wish to please me, put your hand under my thigh as a sign of your constant loyalty to me; do not let me be buried in Egypt.'"[4]

Indeed, the Latin root for "testimony" is "testicle."[5] Thus, by protecting us from compelled searing, the Fifth Amendment protects not

1. Taking an oath is not what it used to be. In societies without writing, oaths—that is, the oral pronouncement of a commitment, belief, or covenant—had far greater significance than today. Hammurabi's Code provided that false witnesses be punished as harshly as those properly convicted. Sadakat Kadri, The Trial: A History, from Socrates to O.J. Simpson xvii (2005). Accuser and accused in an Athenian murder trial would swear on their children's heads while standing atop the entrails of a boar, a ram, and a bull. Kadri at 19.

The Romans, like other ancient peoples, sacrificed and dismembered animals to give oaths greater significance. See Alschuler at 2642; see also Covenants, 17 The New Encyclopaedia Britaninica 421–25 (15th ed. 2002). Indeed, fifteen centuries before Christ, the Iranian god Mithra was the guardian of oaths, contracts, and friendships. The religion of Mithraism, allowing only men, became increasingly popular among Roman soldiers around 100 AD but fell into decline after Christianity became the dominant religion of the empire in 312 AD.

Mithra, god of oaths

2. See, e.g., Lyndon Johnson sworn in as president aboard Air Force One at Love Field after Kennedy's assassination. (Actually, Johnson swore on a Roman Missal.)

3. *Genesis* 24:2–9.

Abraham Sacrificing Isaac (1650)

4. *Genesis* 47:29–31. In this second example, though Joseph, the oath taker, swears on his father's genitalia, he is invoking the same lineage and sterility risks.

5. The word "testicles" comes from Latin *"testiculi"* or *"testis,"* meaning "little witnesses." All such "test" words, including "protest," "protestant," "testify," and "attest," have this "testicle" connection. Robert Hendrickson, Encyclopedia of Word and Phrase Origins 662 (1997). Under Roman law no man could testify unless his testicles were present as evidence

only our souls but also our genitalia.

Our modern profane age begs the question of whether going back to genitalia swearing would not be a better guarantee against perjury than the current "oath or affirmation." As President Lyndon Johnson said,

"I never trust a man 'til I have his pecker in my pocket."[6]

Or as the character Tony Montoya said in SCARFACE,

"All I got is my word and my balls & I don't break 'em for nobody!"[7]

But we would also have to go back to the system where women are not competent witnesses.

BIBLICAL SOURCES

Under the Talmud, the body of Jewish civil and religions law,[8] a person cannot be a witness against himself.[9] Ancient Jewish law, reading from Deuteronomy and Numbers, provided that before a person could be punished there had to be two competent witnesses against him.[10] A person could not testify against his close kin,[11] and the rabbis, scribes, and lawyers reasoned a man was a relative to himself. Thus, because an accused was his own kinsman, it precluded his confession.[12]

---

or "witnesses" of his virility. Thus, to "detest," at root, means "to bear witness against"; therefore, to curse, and implicitly, to hate to the bottom of your testicles. *See* THE BARNHART DICTIONARY OF ETYMOLOGY 1129 (Robert K. Barnhart et al. ed., 1988); *see also* WEBSTER'S at 2610.

6. *See* STEVEN J. RUBENZER & THOMAS R. FASCHINGBAUER, PERSONALITY, CHARACTER, AND LEADERSHIP IN THE WHITE HOUSE: PSYCHOLOGISTS ASSESS THE PRESIDENTS 101 (2004) (discussing Johnson's "pecker in my pocket" comment).

7. Al Pacino in SCARFACE (Universal Pictures 1983).

8. WEBSTER'S at 2574; *see also* Talmud, 11 THE NEW ENCYCLOPAEDIA BRITANINICA 525 (15th ed. 2002).

10. *Deuteronomy* 19:15: "One witness shall not rise up against a man for any iniquity, or for any sin, in any sin that he sin; at the mouth of two witnesses, or at the mouth of three witnesses, shall a matter be established."
   Numbers 35:30: "[W]ho soeth killeth any person, the murderer shall be slain at the mouth of the witnesses; but one witness shall not testify against any person that he die."
   Deuteronomy 17:6: "at the mouth of two witnesses, or three witnesses, shall he that is to die be put to death; at the mouth of one witness he shall not be put to death."
   As for the duties of a witness, *Ephesians* 4:29 admonishes, "*Let no corrupt communication proceed out of your mouth . . .*" and *Proverbs* 11:9 provides, "*A hypocrite with his mouth destroyeth his neighbor . . .*"
   See J. W. EHRLICH, THE HOLY BIBLE AND THE LAW 155 (1962).

9. Irene Merker Rosenberg & Yale L. Rosenberg, *In the Beginning: The Talmudic Rule against Self-Incrimination*, 63 N.Y.U. L. REV. 955 (1988). See also LEVY, "Appendix on Talmudic Law," at 433–41 (1996), noting the accusatorial nature of Talmudic criminal procedure, including the presumption of innocence. Levy takes issue with Wigmore's statement that the right to silence "*in other systems of the world it had had no place.*" *Id.* at 439.

11. *Deuteronomy* 24:16 provided that "*the father shall not be put to death for the children, nor shall the children be put to death for the father; every man shall be put to death for his own sin.*" See Rosenberg & Rosenberg at 976 n.77, 1000.

12. "*Ein adam maysem atzmo rasha*" ("No man may render himself an evil person") is the basic Talmudic rule. See Rosenberg & Rosenberg at 1048. In a capital case, Talmudic law considered a confession as suicide and thus a sin. LEVY at 439.

Under Jewish law then, nobody wasted time deciding whether a criminal defendant made a "voluntary" statement. Jewish law succeeded in eliminating the need to inquire whether a statement came from torture or whether the defendant simply had a sick mind or falsely accused himself.[1]

The idea was to affirm the sanctity of each person's life no matter how evil his conduct might appear. This rule also recognizes the role of kinship in ancient Jewish society—a role much more powerful than in ours.[2]

CHRISTIANITY AND THE MIDDLE AGES

Something much closer to the privilege we now understand emerged as a limitation on the religious duty to confess. By the third century, public confession and penance for wrongdoing was an obligation of Christian faith. By the fourth century, however, Saint John Chrysostom[3] preached against public confession:

"I do not say that you should betray yourself in public nor accuse yourself before others, but that you obey the prophet when he said, 'reveal your ways to the Lord.'"[4]

Keeping confessions private became the norm to encourage what was good for the soul without fear of secular prosecution.[5] Although private confession remains the practice in the

---

1. Rosenberg & Rosenberg at 1041. American jurisprudence reflects concern with the reliability of confessions both in the prohibition against admitting involuntary statements and in the *corpus delicti* rule disallowing convictions for crimes when the only evidence is the defendant's own statement. *Id.* at 1034.

2. *See generally* Rosenberg & Rosenberg at 1028. These two witnesses had to be qualified, meaning among other things they were adult men with no interest in the outcome. They had to be competent, of good character, and not related to each other. Also, the witnesses had to give the suspect advance warning that he was about to commit a punishable offense, and then observe the defendant commit the *corpus delicti* of the crime. Circumstantial evidence was not probative of guilt. Accomplice liability was virtually nonexistent, and there was no culpability for attempt.

3. Saint John Chrysostom ("*Chrysostomos,*" "golden mouthed," for his eloquence). Saint John was a doctor of the Church, born at Antioch, c. 347 AD, and died at Commana in Pontus, in 407. John, whose surname Chrysostom occurs for the first time in the "Constitution" of Pope Vigilius (cf. P.L., LX, 217) in the year 553, is generally considered the most prominent doctor of the Greek Church and the greatest preacher ever. *St. John Chrysostom,* THE NEW ENCYCLOPAEDIA BRITANINICA 291–92 (15th ed. 2002).

Saint John in a one thousand-year-old Byzantine mosaic in Constantinople's (Istanbul) Hagia Sophia

4. *Quoted in* Alschuler at 2626–39, 40 nn. 52–57; *see also* R.H. Helmholz, *Origins of the Privilege against Self-Incrimination: The Role of the European Ius Commune,* 65 N.Y.U. L. REV. 962, 982 (1990); Charles P. Sherman, *A Brief History of Imperial Roman Canon Law,* 7 CAL. L. REV. 93 (1918) (noting that the western church's gain of temporal power in the fourth century led to private confession).

5. LEVY at 21. Theologically, not only Saint Chrysostom but also Saint Augustine spoke against the death penalty, torture, and forcing men to accuse themselves.

Augustine's CONFESSIONS, an autobiography, also showed a different sense of a confession. For him and medieval people a "confession" was a purging of guilt as a step toward purification.

Saint Augustine

Catholic Church today,[6] our society seems to have gone back to public confession![7]

From this evolution away from public confession in the Middle Ages comes the idea of *nemo tenetur prodere seipsum* ("no one is bound to reveal his own shame"). This went hand in hand with the proposition that *nemo punitur sine accusatorie* ("no one should be condemned without an accuser"), originating from Jesus not condemning the woman accused of adultery.[8]

Thus ecclesiastical courts through the Middle Ages would not force a person to accuse himself because the wrongdoer would eventually answer to God for any crime or sin. The courts would, however, force answers if the person was already accused.[9]

THE *IUS COMMUNE* AND TRIAL BY COMPURGATION

The *ius commune* was a combination of Roman and canon law in medieval Europe and was originally accusatorial in nature. For most of the Middle Ages, both church and secular courts used procedures that we would recognize, though in a very primitive form. Private accusation led to an open trial by ordeal (*purgatio vulgaris*). Even trial by combat was accusatorial, with a known complainant or plaintiff and open confrontation.[10]

6. A confessional. Even our modern secular law recognizes the priest-penitent privilege and will not compel a priest to reveal a confession. See BLACK'S LAW DICTIONARY 1071 (5th ed. 1979).

8. *John* 8:10–11: *"Woman, where are thine accusers? Hath no one condemned thee?"* The woman replied, *"No one, Lord."* And Jesus said to her, *"Neither do I condemn thee."* Helmholz at 975.

Christ and the Woman Taken in Adultery (1621)

7. From *Oprah* to *Dr. Phil* to *Jerry Springer* to *Montel Williams* and any number of others, public confession has become a mainstay of daytime television.

Image by Helen Koop

9. See Leonard W. Levy, *Origins of the Fifth Amendment and Its Critics*, 19 CARDOZO L. REV. 821, 846 (1997) (*"The right was not a canon law invention because the canon law merely protected the revelation of an unsuspected crime but required a suspected person to incriminate himself."*).

10. LEVY at 22; also at 7, 21 (noting that the earlier European procedure was accusatorial). *See also* Alschuler at 2646. See **Chapter 7: Trial by Jury or … by God!** for more on trial by ordeal.

Heaven, the Mass, and Purgatory

The main form of accusatorial procedure at this time was compugation (*purgatio canonica*).[1] If a defendant could swear his innocence and produce the required number of "compurgators"[2] or "oath helpers" to swear they believed the defendant's oath, he was acquitted. The specific oath that the compurgators swore was known as the "oath *ex officio*."[3] This form of oath originally allowed for compurgators and clergy charged with crimes to swear innocence.

As we will see, the "oath *ex officio*" later became the center of controversy in England, and its abolition is the Fifth Amendment's foundation.

Trial by compurgation worked for two reasons.

First, the belief system of the accused and court regarding the power of oaths allowed it.[4] An oath's mystical power was great, enough in church courts, and in the early king's courts, to be conclusive proof of innocence. Damnation was serious stuff for these people![5]

Second, the accused, having no obligation to accuse himself, allowed it. The *nemo tenetur prodere seipsum* and *nemo punitur sine accusatorie*

---

1. See **Chapter 7: Trial by Jury or . . . by God!** for more on trial by compurgation.

   "**Compurgation**—to purify wholly, to make pure. 1. Vindication from a charge; also, testimony or evidence that vindicates. 2. Law. The exculpation of a defendant by oaths of persons who swear to his veracity or innocence." The practice of compurgation trials probably came from the Germans, who got it from India either directly or indirectly. KADRI at 25.

   Compurgation was long a regular form of trial in the ecclesiastical courts, and in the civil courts it was used in many forms of civil and criminal proceedings until gradually superseded by the jury system. WEBSTER'S at 551. In the sense of purification, compurgation is synonymous with "purgation," which leads directly to the church's evolving teachings on purgatory throughout the Middle Ages. *Id*. In England, trial by compurgation was also known as "wager of law." 3 THE NEW ENCYCLOPEDIA BRITANNICA 507 (15th ed. 2002).

   Purgatory is an intermediate state after death for expiatory purification. The Roman Catholic Church teaches, as defined by the Councils of Florence and Trent, that purgatory is a place or state of punishment wherein the souls of those who die in God's grace may expiate venial sins or satisfy divine justice for the temporal punishment still due to remitted mortal sin.

2. "**Compurgator**—1. Law. A witness to the veracity or innocence of an accused person, with whom he swears, and originally applied to such witnesses in the trials in the ecclesiastical courts, and later to the oath helpers employed in early English and Germanic law, and to those acting in the wager of law. 2. Any witness or testifier to the innocence or freedom from blame of another." WEBSTER'S at 551; see also BLACK'S LAW DICTIONARY 261 (5th ed. 1979). Judges in England made jurors out of the old conjurors. KADRI at 37.

3. BLACK'S LAW DICTIONARY 967 (5th ed. 1979).

4. Alschuler at 2642–43. Medieval canon law not only accepted oaths but listed 474 ways in which they had special significance in the *ius commune*.

   For an explanation of compurgation and ordeals in practice among the Anglo-Saxons, see COLIN RHYS LOVELL, ENGLISH CONSTITUTIONAL AND LEGAL HISTORY 43–49 (1962); see also R.H. Helmholz, *Crime, Compurgation and the Courts of the Medieval Church*, 1 LAW & HIST. REV. 1 (1983) (describing church jurisdiction and procedures, including compurgation during the Middle Ages).

5. **Medieval Cathedral Last Judgment Scene.** To make a false oath put you on the wrong side of this picture.

   Note Gustave Dore's illustration of Dante's *Inferno*, with the oath-breaking fallen angel Lucifer gnawing upon the great traitors/oath breakers Judas, Brutus, and Cassius, in the very heart of hell.

6. See Helmholz at 962–90; see also Michael R.T. MacNair, *The Early Development of the Privilege against Self-Incrimination*, 10 OXFORD J. LEGAL STUD. 66 (1990) (arguing that the privilege "*came into English law from the common family of European laws and particularly the canon law*").

   Compurgation and ordeal did not allow for a man to testify for himself. This led to the fundamental common-law dictum before the end of the Middle Ages that a man could not be forced to testify against himself. LOVELL at 4. It also led to the rule in England that a defendant could not testify, that is, until 1898. *Id*. at 49.

7. JOHN HENRY WIGMORE, EVIDENCE IN TRIALS AT COMMON LAW 273 (John T. McNaughton ed., 1961). For Wigmore's earlier work, see John H. Wigmore, *Nemo Tenetur Seipsum Prodere*, 5 HARV. L. REV. 71 (1891–92); John H. Wigmore, *The Privilege against Self-Crimination; Its History*, 15 HARV. L. REV. 610 (1901–02).

   The compurgation trial in criminal cases at common law did not survive

Dante's Inferno by Gustave Dore (1890)

concepts encompassing the early privilege against self-accusation and incrimination were thus a key component.[6]

Compared to trial by ordeal or battle, compurgation was not so bad. But there was the big problem that even jurists at the time recognized: shameless liars go free.[7] Moreover, the church felt the need to deal more and more with the worst of all crimes:

heresy. This set the stage for the reform of criminal procedure.[8]

ENTER THE INQUISITION

By the mid-thirteenth century, the church perceived the need to defend itself from new ideas. Part of its answer was the Inquisition. The imperious Pope Innocent III came to the papal throne in 1198.[9] In 1215

he convened the Fourth Lateran Council to chart the church's course in the face of new heresies.[10] Under Innocent III, the church hardened its position regarding heretics and obliged secular authorities to exterminate them.[11] This included reforming the criminal procedure of the ecclesiastical courts.[12]

---

the Assize of Clarendon but persisted in ecclesiastical courts and some civil cases until 1602. Alschuler at 2643 n.70.

For a modern descendant of the compurgator oath, see Federal Rule of Evidence 608: "RULE 608. EVIDENCE OF CHARACTER AND CONDUCT OF WITNESSES. *(a) Opinion and reputation evidence of character. The credibility of a witness may be attacked or supported by evidence in the form of opinion or reputation, but subject to these limitations: (1) the evidence may refer only to character for truthfulness or untruthfulness, and (2) evidence of truthful character is admissible only after the character of the witness for truthfulness has been attacked by opinion or reputation evidence or otherwise."*

See also Rule 405, "Method of Proving Character."

8. Oaths and Defendants Going Full Circle. Given the deep religious significance of oaths, and perhaps in reaction to the old compurgation trials, common-law courts, in England and America, disqualified criminal defendants and other interested parties from providing sworn testimony. Alschuler at 2645 and n.77; WIGMORE at 285. This gave prosecutors a great advantage because their witnesses were under oath and thus more credible. Defendants did not gain the

right to testify in America until the mid-nineteenth century. See Joel N. Bodansky, *The Abolition of the Party Witness Disqualification: A Historical Survey,* 70 KY. L.J. 91 (1982). Now a defendant enjoys an unconditional Sixth Amendment right to testify under oath. See *Rock v. Arkansas,* 483 U.S. 44, 51–53 (1987). Massachusetts may still allow defendants to decide whether to offer unsworn statements. Alschuler at 2663 (citing *Commonwealth v. Stewart,* 151 N.E. 74 (Mass. 1926)). See also Federal Rule of Evidence 603, requiring an *"oath or affirmation"* of *"every witness."*

9. At different times, Pope Innocent put both England and France under interdict, which included excommunicating the kings and freeing their subjects from the religious duty to obey them. Innocent eventually absolved King John for agreeing to *Magna Carta*, which he thought shameful and detrimental. LEVY at 20.

10. *The Dream of Innocent III* by Giotto di Bondone. The dream, according to the Legend of Saint Francis, was that the Franciscans, by their reforms and life of poverty, would prop up the church. The specific image of the church here is the Lateran

Cathedral, which is where the Council gets it name.

The movie BROTHER SUN, SISTER MOON (Paramount 1972) also depicts the Franciscans' relationship with Innocent III, culminating in the meeting of Francis and the pope (Sir Alec Guinness).

---

11. Innocent III in 1199 established *per inquisitionem.* KADRI at 34.

According to Innocent III, faithfulness to a heretic was faithlessness to God; living heretics must die and heretics already dead must be dug up from consecrated ground and burned. *Reported in* LEVY at 22. Saint Thomas Aquinas also supported death for heretics and reasoned that though a person need not accuse himself, if an inquisitor asked, the accused was bound to answer: *"Now it is to the glory of God that the accused confess that which is alleged against him ... Therefore it is a mortal sin to lie in order to cover one's guilt."* Quoted in LEVY at 446 n.26.

---

12. The Fourth Lateran Council also prohibited clergy from administering oaths in trials by ordeal, divesting the procedure of its rationale as a judgment of God, causing trial by ordeal to die out. LEVY at 15.

The new code of ecclesiastical criminal procedure incorporated *inquisitio*, precursor of the Holy Inquisition. With our modern view of the Inquisition we sometime forget that the inquisitorial model was a great leap forward in criminal procedure from trial by ordeal or oath.[1]

Still, the procedures were secretive, with unknown accusers, no lawyers, and no right to challenge proof. Worse, a new form of oath, *de veritate dicenda*, required the suspect to swear to tell the truth to all questions. This oath was the great trap of the Inquisition and a departure from the earlier ecclesiastical procedure that protected the right not to accuse oneself.[2] The reason for this is that the confession of guilt was the central objective to fulfill the sacred mission of saving a soul.[3]

On the other hand, the church's new procedure incorporated a highly sophisticated evidence system meant to protect the innocent.[4] Under Innocent III the charge had to have been brought under the conditions of common report or notorious suspicion (*clamosa insinuatio*) or open public actions (*fama publica*).[5] Complete proof consisted, ideally, of the testimony of two unimpeachable eyewitnesses. "Proximate indications" or "half-proofs," such as hearsay and presumptions or conjectural proofs, could not support the conviction.

Complete proof was hard enough to produce when the crime was an overt act. Heresy is what we would today call a "thought crime." In the Middle Ages documentary evidence was rare.[6] The accused needed to confess. This was because there were only two ways to prove a heresy offense: get the perpetrators to confess or get their confederates to snitch.[7]

---

1. Wigmore at 273. For a general history, see Edward Peters, Inquisition (1988).

2. Levy, MacNair, and Helmholz all seem to agree on this point. *See generally* Levy.

3. The **auto-de-fe** was a feature of the later Spanish Inquisition, but the inquisitor's purpose was the same thought history. It was the culmination of the inquisitorial process, which was a religious act. Through it the heretic was brought back into the church. Despite the painting, torture and burning did not happen at the auto-de-fe. 1 *Auto de fe*, The New Encyclopaedia Britannica 722–23 (15th ed. 2002). Back in 1232 Pope Gregory IX, however, did convince Emperor Frederick II of Germany to burn heretics. Kadri at 40.

Saint Dominic Presiding over an Auto-da-Fe by Pedro Berruguete (1475)

4. Even **Innocent III** cautioned inquisitors against heresy convictions based just on "*violent presumptions.*" Levy at 27.

5. Wigmore at 275–76 (noting that Elizabeth I's and James I's English courts would drop these requirements in favor of using the *ex officio* oath for the investigation and charge).

6. Regarding the problem of heresy being a thought crime and needing a confession, see Kadri at 49. Remember, few could write, and what they did write was not printed. Johann Gutenberg did not invent European printing with his Bible until 1450–55. Today there are only twenty-two known copies.

Johann Gutenberg

7. Stuntz at 414. Because of this, confession became the *regina probationum* ("queen of proofs"). Kadri at 50.

As a leading inquisitor of the early 1300s, Bernard Gui stated: "The accused are not to be condemned unless they confess or are convicted by witnesses, though not according to the ordinary laws, as in other crimes, but according to the private laws or privileges conceded to the inquisitors by the Holy See, for there is much that is peculiar to the Inquisition." *Quoted in* Levy at 27.

Bernard Gui is the bad guy in the movie and book, The Name of the Rose (20th Century Fox 1986). The book is a very enjoyable murder mystery and primer on medieval theology.

8. Modern law calls this the "cruel trilemma," *Murphy v. Waterfront Commission*, 378 U.S. 53, 55 (1964), including the unhappy choice among perjury for lying under oath, contempt for refusing to respond, or conviction. To avoid this problem, the privilege against self-incrimination exists. The *Oxford English Dictionary* notes usage of the word "trilema" in 1672, 1690, 1725, 1860, and 1887. *Cited in* Alschuler n.76.

That is where the oath came in handy for the inquisitor, putting the accused between a rock and a hard place:

- If he did not take the oath he was held in contempt in a dungeon until he did.

- If he took the oath he exposed himself to the nearly certain risk of punishment for perjury if he lied, not to mention eternal damnation.

- If he admitted heresy he was condemned.[8]

What the inquisitors did was to borrow and adapt the old compurgation oath and turn it into the inquisitional oath. Given that the judge inquisitor sat as indictor, prosecutor, and fact finder in his official capacity, i.e. *ex officio*, the oath became known as the *ex officio* oath.[9] The oath *ex officio* was a creature of necessity.[10]

But despite the Inquisition's fearsome reputation, it actually led to relatively few executions. Anyone who repudiated heresy could return to the community at least once.[11] It was much more lenient than the "justice" in the secular courts. Conversely, though, there were also very few real acquittals because its procedures, including torture and oaths, assured convictions.

OATHS AND TORTURE

To our modern thinking it is hard to understand that torture was only the second arrow in the inquisitor's quiver. Indeed, commentators at the time believed that oaths were worse and even defined them as a more cruel torture because oaths tormented your soul. Torture gave you physical pain, but an oath subjected you to eternal pain.[12]

---

9. LEVY at 24.

10. Plea Bargaining: The Modern Inquisition? Although we take great pride in our "adversarial system," plea bargaining begs the question of whether it is just another form of inquisition.

See Alschuler at 2635–37 (noting that the legal system is substantially less accusatorial than the rhetoric suggests); see generally GEORGE FISHER, PLEA BARGAINING'S TRIUMPH (2004). By any conservative counting, well over 90 percent of criminal cases end in a guilty plea, making "pleading" the pragmatic reality. See, e.g., Santobello v. New York, 404 U.S. 257, 260 (1971). The right to remain silent is *the* crucial component of this system because it is the defendant's incriminating statement that the prosecutor "buys." Losing the right to silence would crush the system.

11. KADRI at 45 (noting the relatively low number of actual executions under inquisitorial procedures).

12. As many critics both in and out of the church recognized for centuries, coerced confessions are inherently unreliable. In 1725 the Council of Rome abolished the oath and declared null and void all confessions so extracted. LEVY at 24. Perhaps this too was a precursor of the Fifth Amendment's protection from being *"compelled in any Criminal Case to be a witness against himself."*

Modern canon law also recognizes a privilege against self-incrimination, providing that *"[t]he accused is not bound to confess the offense and cannot be constrained to take an oath." Codex Iuris Canonici,* 1983 CODE ch.1728, § 2. Also, there is an exclusionary rule: *"A confession or any other declaration of a party lacks all probative force if it is proved that it was made through an error of fact or it was extorted by force or grave fear." Id.* at ch.1538. The 1917 Code of Canon law also recognized the privilege. See WIGMORE at 291 n.107.

For the modern Catholic Church's teaching on confession, see CATECHISM OF THE CATHOLIC CHURCH 357–73 (1994). For an explanation of the Catholic Church penal process, see WILLIAM H. WOESTMAN, O.M.I., ECCLESIASTICAL SANCTIONS AND THE PENAL PROCESS: A COMMENTARY ON THE CODE OF CANON LAW (2003). For an outline of the rights of accused in canon law, see PATRICIA M. DUGAN, THE PENAL PROCESS AND THE PROTECTION OF RIGHTS IN CANON LAW (2005).

Moreover, the Inquisition had very specific rules on torture, though at times honored by the letter rather than the spirit of the law.[1] For example, the inquisitor could only torture the accused once, and the accused had to repeat his confession "freely" in court.[2]

But many an inquisitor, zealous to save the soul, would get around this procedural protection by just granting a "continuance" of the torture to avoid the repetition.[3] Thus, if the accused retracted his confession, he went back to the rack for a continuance or would starve in a solitary dungeon.

Also strange (and fascinating) to our modern thinking is that medieval jurists believed that torture could cause a person to speak but not to lie.[4]

For medieval theologians and legal moralists both the *will* and *reason* (the ability to distinguish good from evil) were the agents of human action.[5] Reason showed good or evil, and the will allowed the person to choose to act one way or the other.[6] The idea was that torture could make you speak involuntarily only to tell the truth but could not overcome your free will to make you lie.[7] Thus tortured confessions were legally reliable.[8]

CHURCH COURTS IN ENGLAND AND DOUBLE JEOPARDY

With the ecclesiastical courts came inquisitorial

1. There were whole classes of people the Inquisition did not torture. Conversely, old Roman law provided that slaves could be tortured because they were so lowly or were unable to tell the truth without the aid of torture. WILTSHIRE at 166; KADRI at 8.

2. The Exclusionary Rule. Canon law shows the historical roots of our modern exclusionary rule. While courts have only in the last one hundred years or so began to suppress the evidence from illegal searches, they have for centuries suppressed involuntary or tainted confessions. Alschuler at 2658 n.128 (quoting a judge from a 1742 trial: "*If the examination is upon oath, it cannot be read, for persons are not to swear against themselves: All examinations ought to be taken freely and voluntarily, and not upon oath. And then we can read them.*"). *See also* Edward Peters, *Destruction of the Flesh—Salvation of the Spirit: The Paradox of Torture in Medieval Christian Society, in* THE DEVIL, HERESY AND WITCHCRAFT IN THE MIDDLE AGES: ESSAYS IN HONOR OF JEFFREY B. RUSSELL 131, 144–45 (Alberto Ferreiro ed., 1998) ("*Especially in the case of torture, jurists of both laws worked out meticulous and detailed rules of procedure that required, among other things, restrictions on the kinds and frequency of torture that could be employed, and a voluntary repetition of a confession originally made under torture, but the repetition was to be made later, and away from the scene of the torture.*").

3. LEVY at 27–28.
For a brief outline of torture procedures, see JOHN H. LANGBEIN, TORTURE AND THE LAW OF PROOF 12–16 (1976).

4. Peters at 138–39. Also personal e-mail from Dr. Peters on file with the author.

5. *See* Peters at 138 (regarding the importance for medieval scholastics of the relation between sin, guilt, confession, free will, and ethics).

6. For relationship between of sin and crime, see Peters at 140–40. Criminal sins were grave offenses and mortal sins of a particular character manifested in an external act and that act could cause *scandlum*. *Id.* at 141. All of this is a precursor to the modern notion in criminal law that for there to be a crime there must be both a criminal act, *actus reus*, and the correct mental state, *mens rea* (the defendant's will).

7. James Franklin, *Evidence Gained from Torture: Wishful Thinking, Checkability, and Extreme Circumstances,* 17 CARDOZO J. INT'L & COMP. L. 281 (2009) (evaluating whether torture produces the truth both today and historically).

Beccaria

8. During the Enlightenment, the Marquis Beccaria wholly rejected this ideal on the reliability of torture confessions. "*The torture of a criminal, during the course of his trial, is a cruelty, consecrated by custom in most nations. It is used with an intent either to make him confess a crime, or explain some contradictions, into which he has been led during his examination; or discover his accomplices; or for some kind of metaphysical and incomprehensible purgation of infamy; or, finally, in order to discover other crimes, of which he is not accused, but of which he may be guilty.*" MARQUIS BECCARIA OF MILAN, AN ESSAY ON CRIMES AND PUNISHMENTS WITH A COMMENTARY BY M. DE VOLTAIRE 58 (new ed., 1872), *quoted in* Mitchell Franklin, *The Encyclopediste Origin and Meaning of the Fifth Amendment,* 15 LAW. GUILD REV. 41, 46 (1956). As Beccaria went on: *There is another ridiculous motive for torture, namely, to purge a man from infamy. Ought such an abuse to be tolerated in the eighteenth century? . . . It is not difficult to trace this senseless law to its origin . . . This custom seems to be the off-spring of religion, by which mankind, in all nations and in all ages, are so generally influenced. We are taught by*

procedures,[9] including the *ex officio* oath. This whole procedure was contrary to England's emerging common law, and the struggle between king and church played out as the common law developed. Henry II described the oath as

"*repugnant to the ancient Customs of his Realm, his peoples Liberties, and hurtful to their fames.*"[10]

The fact that there were both church and king's

courts in England led to another part of the Fifth Amendment, the Double Jeopardy Clause:

. . . nor shall any person be subject for the same offense to be twice put in jeopardy of life or limb . . . .[11]

We take the concept of a prohibition against double jeopardy for granted.[12]

At the time of King Henry II, however, the protection against facing the same charge or punishment

twice was not defined. Henry wanted to retry "*crimonius clerks*" in the king's courts after they had claimed benefit of clergy to avoid the king's justice. Archbishop of Canterbury Thomas Becket resisted.[13]

Becket asserted, for the first time in England, a long-standing principle of canon law.[14] The double jeopardy prohibition means that the same sovereign cannot try or punish you twice for the same crime.[15]

---

our infallible church, that those stains of sin . . . are to be purged away in another life, by an incomprehensible fire. Now infamy is a stain, and if the punishments and fire of purgatory can take away all spiritual stains, why should not the pain of torture take away those of a civil nature? I imagine that the confession of a criminal, which in some tribunals is required as being essential to his condemnation, has a similar origin, and has been taken from the mysterious tribunal of penitence, where the confession of sins is a necessary part of the sacrament. BECCARIA at 60. See also *Ullmann v. United States*, 350 U.S. 422, 450–53 (1956) (Douglas, J., dissenting) (discussing Beccaria's influence on the Founding generation).

9. LEVY at 46.

10. LEVY at 48. You have to wonder, however, if Henry was truly interested in good judicial procedure or just against the church's prerogatives.

11. U.S. CONST. amend. V.

12. Aside from the mention of the movie DOUBLE JEOPARDY (Paramount 1999) at the start, this chapter does not extensively treat the Double Jeopardy Clause. However, see

Chapter 8: "*Baby, Don't Be Cruel*": Just What's So Cruel *and* Unusual about the Eight Amendment? (discussing double jeopardy as part of the concept of proportionality in punishment).

13. Henry II disputing with Thomas Becket.

14. The Catholic Church preserved the concept through the Dark Ages, starting in 391 AD when Saint Jerome interpreted the Bible's *Book of Nahum* text as promising that God would not punish the same offense twice. By 847, this interpretation formally entered canon law. *See* Creekpaum at n.17, *citing Bartkus v. Illinois*, 359 U.S. 121, 152 n.4 (Black, J., dissenting).
   Church courts got the concept from old Roman law, which had a double jeopardy rule. WILTSHIRE at 152. *See also* David S. Rudstein, *A Brief History of the Fifth Amendment Guarantee against Double Jeopardy*, 14 WM. & MARY BILL RTS. J. 193 (2005); Justin W. Curtis, *The*

Meaning of Life (or Limb): An Originalist Proposal for Double Jeopardy Reform, 41 U. RICH. L. REV. 991 (2007); Kyden Creekpaum, *What's Wrong with a Little More Double Jeopardy? A 21st Century Recalibration of an Ancient Individual Right*, 44 AM. CRIM. L. REV. 1179 (2007); JAY A. SIGLER, DOUBLE JEOPARDY: THE DEVELOPMENT OF A LEGAL AND SOCIAL POLICY ch. 1 (1969). For the history of the Double Jeopardy Clause and King Henry II and Thomas Becket, see Rudstein, *Brief History*, at 207–08.

15. *See, e.g.,* Ronald J. Allen, Bard Ferrall & John Rathaswamy, *The Double Jeopardy Clause, Constitutional Interpretation and the Limits of Formal Logic*, 26 VAL. U. L. REV. 281 (1992) ("*Without the double jeopardy prohibition, the state would possess almost limitless power to disrupt the lives and fortune of the citizenry*."). Despite its ancient pedigree, voices do call for exceptions to the rule. See David S. Rudstein, *Retrying the Acquitted in England, Part I: The Exceptions to the Rule against Double Jeopardy for "New and Compelling Evidence*," 8 SAN DIEGO INT'L L.J. 387 (2007).

Saint Jerome by Ghirlandaio (1480)

Thus it limits the state's power to try and retry a person until conviction. In this it is a key concept of the rule of law.[1]

Henry II allegedly had Becket murdered in 1170.[2] After Becket's canonization, English judges saw the wisdom in prohibiting double jeopardy.[3]

By 1300, the common law recognized *autrefois acquit* ("formerly acquitted") and *autrefois convict* ("formerly convicted") as a bar to future prosecution.[4] From this point on, the prohibition of double jeopardy was a mainstay of the common law.[5]

COMMON LAW VERSUS CHURCH AND PREROGATIVE COURTS

The common-law and ecclesiastical courts, however, were not the only modes of trial and criminal procedure in England. The king still had his prerogative courts—that is, courts exercising the king's "prerogatives" as opposed to the common-law courts—with an inquisitorial system of criminal procedure often at odds with the principles embodied in the common law courts.[6]

Torture, for example, was illegal in the common law

Noble chess players, Germany, c. 1320

1. "Jeopardy" (*"jocus paritus"*) is a chess term meaning a set problem. Baker at 77.

See Creekpaum at 1182 n.17 (2007) (noting that the double jeopardy prohibition goes back to 660 BC). The *Book of Nahum* 1:9 (King James) states that "*affliction shall not rise up the second time.*"

The Ancient Greeks adopted the concept by 355 BC. Also, criminal acquittals were final under Roman law. On Greek and Roman double jeopardy law, see Rudstein, *Brief History* at 199–202 (2005).

Jeopardy! is also an American quiz show featuring trivia and has been on the air almost continuously since 1964.

2. Earliest known portrayal of Becket's murder.

3. Creekpaum at 1182–83 and n.21. The double jeopardy concept could also have come into English law from canon law after the Norman Conquest in 1066, or directly from ancient Roman law. It could be that the concept is so fundamental that it evolved in England itself.

For more on the Becket theory of the Double Jeopardy Clause origins, as well as other sources, see Rudstein, *Brief History*, at 205–11.

4. Creekpaum at 1183. The word comes from the French *"autre"* ("another") and *"fois"* ("time"), forming the compound, *"autrefois,"* meaning "formerly."

5. By the 1760s, William Blackstone summarized English double jeopardy jurisprudence in a pithy "*universal maxim . . . that no man is to be brought into jeopardy of his life more than once for the same offence.*" William Blackstone, 4 Commentaries on the Laws of England 335–36, *quoted in* Creekpaum at 1183 and Rudstein, *Brief History*, at 204. American lawyers, the best of whom trained reading Blackstone, incorporated the rule into American law well before the Bill of Rights. See Rudstein, *Brief History*, at 221–26. During the debates before Congress on the Bill of Rights, the protection against double jeopardy was a given. *See id.* at 226–32.

The first U.S. Congress passed the prohibition on double jeopardy without

courts. However, with special warrant from the king, the privy council[7] could use torture through its judicial arm, the Court of Star Chamber.[8] The prerogative courts also used the inquisitorial oath, that is, the *ex officio* oath.[9]

Starting with Henry VIII, the Tudor and Stuart monarchs continued to use and abuse the power of these courts to stamp out any challenge to their authority. The reaction against the Stuarts led to the common law's recognition of the right against self-incrimination.

HENRY VIII: THE GUY WOULD LEAVE YOU SPEECHLESS

Why do you need the right to remain silent if you do not have something you want to remain silent about?

Well, Henry VIII and his immediate successors gave everyone a reason to stay silent.[10] Chapter One featured Henry and his friend Sir Thomas More, who along with many others, paid the price for Henry's quest for a male heir. In such an environment, who didn't need the right to remain silent?

---

objection. See Steve Bachmann, *Starting Again with the Mayflower . . . England's Civil War and America's Bill of Rights*, 20 Q. L. REV. 193, 240 (2001).

Thus Blackstone's *"universal maxim"* passed right through to the Fifth Amendment: *"nor shall any person be subject for the same offense to be twice put in jeopardy of life or limb."*

Blackstone

6. LEVY at 42.

....

7. Privy Council. In England this started out as the king's council of close advisors, thus the name "privy" for private. Later, powerful sovereigns would use the Privy Council to circumvent the courts and Parliament. For example, a committee of the council, which later became the Court of the Star Chamber, could inflict any punishment except death without regard to evidence rules or the burden

of proof. Henry VIII, *"on the advice of the Council,"* enacted laws by mere proclamation and Parliament did not regain prominence until after his death. In 1553 the council had forty members, making it ineffective as an advisory body. Smaller committees developed that evolved into the modern cabinet. *Privy Council,* 9 THE NEW ENCYCLOPEDIA BRITANNICA 713 (15th ed. 2002).

....

8. The Star Chamber was no more than a committee of the Privy Council exercising the king's judicial powers. LEVY at 100–01; *see generally* Frank Riebli, *The Spectre of Star Chamber: The Rule of an Ancient English Tribunal and the Supreme Court's Self-Incrimination Jurisprudence,* 21 HASTINGS CONST. L.Q. 807 (2002). References to the "Starred Chamber" go back to 1348. The Star Chamber would have probably fallen into historical obscurity had not the Supreme Court alluded to it over seventy-five times as an example of arbitrary power. *See, e.g., Watts v. Indiana,* 338 U.S. 49, 54 (1949) ("Ours is the accusatorial as opposed to the inquisitorial system. Such has been the characteristic of Anglo-American criminal justice since it freed itself from practices borrowed by Star Chamber from the Continent whereby an accused was interrogated in secret for hours on end."). *Star Chamber, Court of,* 11 THE NEW ENCYCLOPEDIA BRITANNICA 218 (15th ed. 2002). Relatively speaking though, its procedures were not that bad for its day.

The Star Chamber gets its name, in one version, from the room preserved in Westminster Abbey where the court sat. Another version is that it gets its name from the metaphor of the king being the sun and his judges the stars reflecting the king's light (what royal suck-up thought of this one?).

The Star Chamber today

....

9. The infamy of the Star Chamber is still evocative, as in the movie THE STAR CHAMBER (20th Century Fox 1983).

....

10. Henry VIII was already fat in this painting, and he got fatter!

Sir Thomas More

As it turns out, More became the first Catholic in Tudor England to go on record as refusing to incriminate himself as he became one of Henry VIII's earliest and most distinguished victims in his trial of 1535.[1] Thus More's trial is a milestone in the development of the right to remain silent.[2]

During various interrogations, More ardently asserted the right to remain silent:

"I nothing doinge nor nothinge sayenge againste the statut it were a very harde thing to compel me to saye either precisely with it

againste my conscience to the losse of my soule, or precisely againste it to the destruction of my bodye."[3]

In this he relied on the old canon law principles of *nemo tenetur prodere seipsum* ("no one is bound to reveal his own shame") and *nemo punitur sine accusatorie* ("no one should be condemned without an accuser").[4]

More could assert this even though he had used the canon law's inquisitorial procedures with *ex officio* oaths.[5] For More the difference was between the law of God and the law of the realm, which *"was the difference between heaven*

and hell." In More's legal mind, common-law treason was the charge, not heresy, and thus he had the right not to accuse himself.

Though More was right, it did not save him—at least not in this life![6] But though More lost his head, the fact remains that it was not from his own statements.

Had there been the *Miranda* rule, requiring the police to warn a suspect of the right to remain silent, the perjured testimony they used to convict More would have been inadmissible. Of course, Henry had slated More for execution regardless, and

---

1. Levy at 94.

2. More needed the Fifth Amendment: *"nor shall [the accused] be compelled in any Criminal Case to be a witness against himself . . . ."*

3. *Quoted in* Levy at 70.

4. Levy at 70, *citing* William J. Kenealy, S.J., *Fifth Amendment Morals,* The Catholic Lawyer, Autumn 1957, at 341.

5. More was one of the defenders of the *ex officio* oath before the procedure was turned on him. His reasoning was theological: that if the oath were abandoned, *"the stretys were likely to swarme full of heretyks."* Thomas More, *Apology of Syr Thomas More Knight,* 219a–227b (1533), *quoted in* Levy at 65. Again, the key distinction in More's mind was the difference between ecclesiastical courts and a political prosecution.

6. Again, see **Chapter 1: Of Dogma and Desire: Saying What You Believe about the First Amendment,** noting Solicitor General Richard Rich's perjury.

Richard Rich

7. Given the criminal procedures that existed at the time, poor Thomas More did not have a chance. *"The most distinctive feature of the emergent criminal trial in Tudor England (1485–1603) was the imbalance of advantage between the state and the accused."* Peter Westen, *The Compulsory Process Clause,* 73 Mich. L. Rev. 71, 81 (1974). The prosecution could interrogate the accused, sometimes under torture, take witness statements and bind witnesses over for trial, and have them testify under oath. *Id.* at 82.

A defendant like More had no right to a lawyer (though More did not need one) and had no protection against self- incrimination or cruel and unusual punishments. *Id.* Indeed, he was generally not even informed of the charges until the day of trial and if incarcerated could not collect evidence or witnesses. He had no right to confront the witnesses against him in person or to summon witnesses in his favor or even to present witnesses if he had them. He could make a statement in his defense but it could not be under oath and therefore lacked weight. *Id.* More's trial happened at the mid-point in the history of common-law criminal procedure. The old system had self-informed juries who were the witnesses in the case with few lawyers and much less prosecutors. Thus, there was little need to afford the accused many of the procedural protections we today take for granted. By Tudor time, however, the crown employed professional prosecutors, and jurors did not know about the case beforehand. Thus the accused

they would have lied about Mirandizing him.[7]

MARY AND ELIZABETH TUDOR

As we saw in Chapter 1, when Henry VIII died in 1547 his sickly son, Edward VI, became king for six years. In 1553, Henry's daughter by Catharine of Aragon, Mary, became queen and wanted everyone to go back to being Catholic.

Mary's Inquisition was a commission *"for a severer way of proceeding against heretics."*[8] It eventually became the Court of High Commission, the ecclesiastical arm of the Privy Council, just as the Star

Chamber was the judicial arm. Mary's commission had the sovereign's discretionary power to invent its own procedures, with one exception: it was expressly commanded to use the oath *ex officio*.[9]

In response, defendants began to refuse to take the oath, a refusal that itself could get you burned. But like More, they borrowed from the old canon law and argued that you should have a right to remain silent in the face of accusation.[10]

Despite Mary's best efforts, English Protestantism lived on after her death in 1558.

When Mary's half-sister, Elizabeth I, took over she declared that she had no desire *"to make windows into men's souls."* But Elizabeth's tenuous political situation made religious nonconformity more treasonous than even under Henry; and Catholics and Puritans were the nonconformers.[11]

Because of this, Elizabeth was crucial to the Fifth Amendment's development.

Her government made a special project of persecuting Catholic priests.[12]

---

had all the disadvantages at trial without any of the protections now written in our Fifth and Sixth Amendments. See **Chapter 6: How the Sixth Amendment Guarantees You a Court, a Lawyer, and a Chamber Pot.** Thus even a lawyer of More's stature did not stand a chance when his king wanted a judicial murder.

8. LEVY at 76.

Mary Tudor

9. LEVY at 77.

10. See MacNair at 67.

During this time John Foxe published FOXE'S BOOK OF MARTYRS, giving accounts of the religious persecutions and the defenses raised. It became a primer on the values of freedom of religion and speech as well as procedural rights of an accused, including the right to remain silent. See LEVY at 79–82.

11. Again, see **Chapter 1: Of Dogma and Desire: Saying What You Believe about the First Amendment.**

Elizabeth Tudor

12. In 1585 Parliament banished all Catholic priests as traitors. Parliament required any person suspected of being a *"Jesuit, seminary or massing priest"* to be imprisoned without bail until he answered whether he was one. LEVY at 108; see also WIGMORE at 285 n.79.

In fact, the great common-law jurist, Sir Edward Coke, complained that Catholic priests justified giving elusive answers under oath by trickery and "*an implacable disagreement about what language is.*" For example, a priest would respond to

"*I am a judge that has the right to ask whether you are a priest*"

by saying

"*no*" (meaning "*You are not a judge that has the right to ask me whether I am a priest.*").[1]

And of all the Catholic priests, those crafty Jesuits were the worst for Elizabeth. They trained

abroad and kept coming back to England. And they started to have real success in converting souls.[2]

Edmund Campion started out as a young cleric with a bright future in the Church of England. But then he converted to Catholicism, became a Jesuit priest, and returned to England.

In 1580 Elizabeth's government caught Father Campion. Under torture he supposedly incriminated himself, which formed the basis of a claim against him that he sought to disaffect Catholics from allegiance to the queen. At his sham trial he asserted, like More, a right not to answer

"*bloody questions . . . undermining of my life; whereunto I answered as Christ did to the dilemma, Give unto Caesar that is due to Caesar, and to God that to God belongeth.*"[3]

Asserting a right to silence did not save Campion any more than it saved Father Alexander Briant. Briant responded to the question whether he should obey the queen if the pope commanded otherwise, that the

"*question is too high and dangerous for him to answer . . . .*"

Likewise, Father Ralph Sherwin declared that

---

1. SIR EDWARD COKE, A TREATISE AGAINST LYING AND FRAUDULENT DISSIMULATION, discussed in James Oldham, *Truth-Telling in the Eighteenth-Century English Courtroom*, 12 LAW & HIST. REV. 95, 119 n.112 (1994).

In 1995 President Bill Clinton famously testified before a grand jury about whether he "is" involved in a sexual relationship with Monica Lewinsky that "*[i]t depends on what the meaning of the word 'is' is.*" With Jesuit logic, though hardly the same motivation, Clinton testified as follows:

"*It depends on what the meaning of the word 'is' is. If the—if he—if 'is' means is and never has been, that is not—that is*

Sir Edward Coke

one thing. If it means there is none, that was a completely true statement . . . . Now, if someone had asked me on that day, are you having any kind of sexual relations with Ms. Lewinsky, that is, asked me a question in the present tense, I would have said no. And it would have been completely true.*"

Timothy Noah, *Bill Clinton and the Meaning of "Is"* SLATE, posted Sunday, Sept. 13, 1998, at 9:14 PM ET, http://www.slate.com/id/1000162/ (last visited July 30, 2010).

2. See LEVY ch. III.

3. See LEVY at 91–94, quoted at 93. See also St. Edmund Campion, THE CATHOLIC ENCYCLOPEDIA, http://www.newadvent.org/cathen/05293c.htm (last visited Aug. 8, 2005).

Father Edmund Campion

4. Quoted in LEVY at 99.

5. He was scrupulous (his critics would have said "unscrupulous") in protecting Elizabeth in religious matters. He was incorruptly loyal to her, and she always backed him and called him her "*little black husband.*" LEVY at 120.

Bill Clinton commenting on the scandal

"he prayeth to be asked no such question, as may touch his life."[4]

Fathers Campion, Briant, and Sherwin all died together. But their statements are the very essence of the Fifth Amendment:

"nor shall [the accused] be compelled in any Criminal Case to be a witness against himself . . . ."

Catholics were not Elizabeth's only problem, there were also the Puritans.

Elizabeth's bishops in her Church of England were there to impose her view. The first among these was John Whitgift, whom Elizabeth made archbishop of Canterbury in 1583.[5] He took Queen Mary's "commission" and made it into the infamy that we know today as the High Commission.[6] Whitgift, with the queen's support, made the *ex officio* oath a matter of common practice and challenged any member of the Privy Council who interceded for the Puritans.[7]

The High Commission's jurisdiction, as with all the ecclesiastical courts, was generally only over clergy.[8] Thus the issues related to this part of the history of the right to remain silent played out in a religious context.

The Puritans objected to the High Commission's inquisitorial procedures and the *ex officio* oath because they were guilty of not believing in many of the Church of England's teaching. Their specific objections, however, were that the procedures, especially the oaths, were inquisitorial and *"popish."* Several objected that the oath formed both accusation and proof.

Their specific theological argument against taking any oath was the Third Commandment:

"Thou shall not take the name of the Lord, thy God in vain."[9]

---

6. Its full name was the Court of High Commission for Ecclesiastical Causes. Levy at 125. The term "high commission" refers to the fact that it came directly from the monarch. The only higher you could get would be God, which Whitgift viewed as the same thing.

7. Whitgift wrote the twenty-four "articles" for the commission to use against Puritans. Levy at 134. As to procedure, the old rules applied: if the accused refused to take the oath he was convicted or in the legal terminology of the time "*pro confesso*" and "*convicto.*" If he refused to answer he was imprisoned for as long the commission wanted. As with the Roman canon law, unlike the common

law, complete proof in the form of two witnesses or a confession was needed. *Id.* at 132–33. Taking the oath and lying, which today most of us would say was a "white lie" or a "fib," was not an option for these people.

8. Wigmore at 277–78. Only in matrimonial and testamentary cases did they have jurisdiction over laymen.

9. *See Exodus* 20:7; *see also Deuteronomy* 5:11; *Leviticus* 19:12. The Puritans also disseminated information concerning the Talmudic confession rule to assert the right to silence in heresy prosecutions. *See* Horowitz, *The Privilege against Self-Incrimination—How Did It Originate?* 31 Temple L.Q. 121 (1958). **The Ten Commandments (or Decalogue):** A list of religious and moral imperatives spoken by God to Moses on Mount Sinai engraved on two stone tablets. They are prominent in Judaism and Christianity.

The Ten Commandments (Paramount Studios 1956) is also a Cecil B. DeMille classic staring Charlton Heston as Moses and Yul Brynner as Ramses II. For a discussion of the Ten Commandments, see **Chapter 1: Of Dogma and Desire: Saying What You Believe about the First Amendment.**

John Whitgift

According to the Puritans, Jesus reaffirmed this prohibition in the Sermon on the Mount:[1]

"*Again, you have heard that it was said to the people long ago, 'do not break your oath, but keep the oaths you have made to the Lord.' But I tell you, do not swear at all: either by heaven, for it is God's throne; of by the earth, for it is his footstool; or by Jerusalem, for it is the city of the great king. And do not swear by your head, for you cannot make even one hair white or black. Simply let your 'yes' be 'yes,' and your 'no,' 'no'; anything beyond this comes from the evil one.*"[2]

In 1591 the Puritan clergyman Thomas Cartwright and eight colleagues protested against the oath *ex officio*, arguing that under the Third Commandment and Sermon on the Mount that no man should be compelled "*to sweare to accuse him selfe.*" Moreover, the *ex officio* oath "*put the conscious upon the racke.*"[3] Again, for these people, this was serious stuff. The real rack would break your body. The oath would break your soul.[4]

When Cartwright and colleagues refused the "*oath of inquisition*," it stymied the High Commission. The court's own roots from ancient canon law and even Whitgift's procedures made it impossible to proceed. Without a confession the commission could not secure the conviction. All it could do was put the defendant in a dungeon for contempt.

So what was Whitgift to do? The answer, or so he thought, was to switch to another court: the Star Chamber.

---

1. *Sermon on the Mount* by Carl Heinrich Bloch (nineteenth century).

2. *Matthew* 5:33–37.

Catholics did not have this argument because early on the church ignored this teaching, noting that Abraham (*Genesis* 21:23–24), Saint Paul (2 *Corinthians* 1:23), and even God (*Isaiah* 62:8) had taken oaths. Indeed, as shown above, the church started the oath practice and continued it during this time in other countries. The Puritans, however, argued that both Catholicism and Anglicanism got it wrong. Today's Jehovah's Witnesses will not take oaths. Federal Rule of Evidence 603 now allows for oath "*or affirmation.*"

Thomas Cartwright

3. *See* Alschuler at n.89, *citing* Thomas Cartwright, Treatise on the Oath Ex Officio 33 (R. Albert Peal & Wheelan H. Carlson eds., 1951); *see also* Levy at 177.

4. The Rack. The rack was the favorite device of English torturers. The word comes from the German "*recken*" ("to stretch or draw out"). The device came from machines used in leather factories.

Obviously, most people have no idea what they are saying when they declare, "*I have 'racked my brain' to find the car keys!*"

Torture rack in the Tower of London

THE STAR CHAMBER'S ROAD TO INFAMY

The Star Chamber's job was to try cases of disobedience to royal orders and the related crimes of riot, contempt, libel, forgery, counterfeiting, and fraud.[5] To do this it had much more flexible procedures not bound by ecclesiastical tradition or the common law.[6] Moreover, because the Star Chamber was technically not an ecclesiastical court, it could put laymen under the oath *ex officio*,[7] and the court could use any means to trap an accused into confessing, including torture.

As it turned out, however, Cartwright and others could defeat even this procedure because a defendant still had to repeat any confession in court without compulsion. All they needed to do was to remain silent, which they did. They were already in prison for contempt, so what more could the judges do? And because Cartwright was a prominent clergyman, torturing him would have just made matters worse for the crown. Besides, torture appears to have been reserved for Catholics.[8]

Cartwright and colleagues eventually agreed to live in peace with the Church of England and were released from prison. They had won by remaining silent.[9]

But by using the law courts to enforce religious conformity, the English crown allowed the religious objections to the *ex officio* oaths to take on legal weight.[10]

---

5. LEVY at 100. If one looks, the prosecution of these crimes has something to do with keeping the king's peace or stability in the realm. Thus it was not a difficult jump for Whitgift to extend the Star Chamber's work to heresy and treason, as had been done in the past.

6. The Star Chamber versus the High Commission? In short, both are the king's prerogative courts, i.e., an extension of his God-given royal power and an outgrowth of his legislative, executive, and judicial functions. The Star Chamber punished crimes against the state while the High Commission punished crimes against the church. Given that denying the king's role as head of the church was both heresy and treason, it is easy to see how the two got mixed. Historically, though, the Star Chamber was just the judicial arm of the king's Privy Council, while the High Commission has its origins in the law courts of the Catholic Church, which did not belong to the king until Henry VIII.

7. WIGMORE at 281.
  The Star Chamber by this time actually had two modes of procedure. The normal procedure was long and paper driven, taking up to three years. It was inquisitorial in that it gathered facts from the defendant and the parties' witnesses, but it also allowed elements of adversarial proceedings such as formal complaints, answers, and the chance for the accused to consult counsel. *See* Riebli at 813–15 (2002). Whitgift did not bother with this and instead sought the Star Chamber process called "*ore tenus*." LEVY at 184; Reibli at 815. See also BAKER at 118 for a discussion of the Star Chamber.

8. LEVY at 187.

9. In the 1950s, what a man believed again became a crime. Supreme Court Justice Abe Fortas in a 1954 speech compared the government's attempts to eradicate communists to seventeenth century England's attempts to eradicate heretics:

> [T]he clock has come full circle: That the battleground is again the question whether a man should be compelled to answer as to his beliefs and affiliations. In the days when the privilege was born, it was a crime to be a heretic. Deviation and dissent were considered dangerous to the state, then as now.

Abe Fortas, *The Fifth Amendment: Nemo Tenure Prodere Seipsum*, 25 CLEVELAND B. ASS'N. J. 95, 101 (1954).

Abe Fortas

10. The Supreme Court stated, "*the privilege [against self-incrimination] [is] necessary to prevent any reoccurrence of the inquisition and the star chamber, even if not in their stark brutality.*" *Couch v. United States*, 409 U.S. 322, 327 (1973), *quoting Ullman v. United States*, 350 U.S. 422, 428, 446 (1956). Also, the Court views the Star Chamber as historically important to the protection against self-incrimination and returns to the Star Chamber to describe the privilege's scale. *See, e.g., Pennsylvania v. Muniz*, 496 U.S. 582, 595–97 (1990).

THE LEGAL ARGUMENTS AGAINST THE OATH

Robert Beale was clerk of the Privy Council. From 1588 through 1590 he advanced the then novel argument that *Magna Carta* limited the commission's oath power.[1] Beale found old common-law court orders that prohibited the ecclesiastical courts from extending jurisdiction, and thus ecclesiastical procedures such as the *ex officio* oath, to temporal matters.[2] Beale also quoted *Magna Carta* Chapters 28 and 29 as prohibiting oaths *ex officio*.[3]

Beale's reading of history and the words of *Magna Carta* were, to say the least, creative. *Magna Carta* actually proscribed compurgation oaths, not the *ex officio* oath. Beale also read the word "bailiff" in *Magna Carta* to cover ecclesiastical judges, which by implication meant the High Commission.[4]

This argument was dangerous to royal prerogative: the High Commission had power purely because the monarch had it to give.[5]

Invoking *Magna Carta* suggests that the king has limited power and is under the law of the land.[6] If the monarch did not have the power to give, the Inquisition had no authority. The High Commission (i.e., the Court of High Commission for Ecclesiastical Causes) was so named because its "commission" came from the sovereign.

The Tudors had power and prestige, and under them the High Commission flourished. But the commission's procedures came to be seen as at odds with the common law, which had incorporated the legal principle of *nemo*

---

1. Beale never published his work himself. Whitgift got a copy of it and gave it to another member of the High Commission, Dr. Richard Cosin, to write a reply. The quotations in Cosin's work gave Beale's ideas public attention, and this is why we know of them today. Levy at 172.

The Puritan lawyer James Morice, in *A briefe treatise of Oathes exacted by Ordinaries and Ecclesiasticall Judges* (1598), expanded Beale's arguments. He also used *Magna Carta* Chapter 29 to decry the "*ungodlye and intolerable Inquisition.*" Levy at 193–98. Morice, even more than Beale, made his argument on the legal ground of liberty rather than on issues of religious conscience or reform. Morice also advanced these arguments as a member of Parliament.

Nicholas Fuller, lawyer for any Puritan *cause célèbre*, had been Cartwright's lawyer and expanded on the idea of the right to silence as a basic liberty as well as a religious imperative. See *id.* at 186; see also *id.* at 232–36 (detailing Fuller's arguments). Fuller got the common-law judges to hear petitions for writs of prohibition and habeas corpus against the ecclesiastical courts.

Magna Carta

2. Levy at 171. Thus *ex officio* oaths were only allowed in cases of wills and marriage.

3. Reading the actual text of *Magna Carta* shows Beale's stretch:

"*Chapter 28. No constable or other royal bailiff shall take corn or other provisions from any man without an immediate cash payment, unless the seller permits postponement of this. Chapter 29. No constable shall compel any knight to give money instead of castle-guard, if the knight is willing to undertake the guard himself, or to supply another responsible man to do it, if he cannot do it himself for any reasonable cause. Further, a knight taken or sent on military service shall be excused castle-guard in proportion to the time he was on this service.*"

For the text of *Magna Carta*, see Danny Danziger & John Gillingham, 1215: The Year of Magna Carta 275–90 (2003).

4. See Levy at 171. Beale also found in Chapter 29 a bar to general search warrants. See *id.* at 172.

In this Beale was a precursor to James Otis, Jr. and his argument against the writs of assistance in colonial Boston in 1761. See **Chapter 4: Molasses and the Sticky Origins of the Fourth Amendment.**

5. Why was *Magna Carta* So Important? The actual text of Magna Carta gives scant support to the arguments of the common-law lawyers against the *ex officio* oath. But the importance of it was the principle that kings ruled by agreement of the subjects. Granted, in 1215 it was a pretty one-sided agreement in the king's favor. The point is, however, that the barons at Runnymede got King John to agree that he had to govern according to a set of rules limiting his power. From then on, everything else is a matter of interpretation and expansion. Indeed, *Magna Carta* Chapter 1 shows that King John "*and [his] heirs*" rule not by divine right but by some type of contract:

tenetur seipsum prodere from the *ius comune* and the old canon law granting the accused the right to remain silent.[7]

The Stuarts, who followed the Tudors, lost prestige and then power, setting the groundwork for the common law's triumph, and eventually the Fifth Amendment.[8]

JAMES I

King James I took the throne of England upon Elizabeth's death in 1603. Although you did not want to be a Catholic or Puritan in Elizabeth's England, she did have the finesse and balance that inspired loyalty. James lacked much of this and quickly used up any goodwill Elizabeth had earned. But despite his arbitrary quirks, James would probably have had an uneventful reign, at least concerning the Fifth Amendment's history, but for the Puritans.

The Puritans turned to the common law for protection. The common-law courts had long issued writs (lawyer speak for "orders") of prohibition against ecclesiastical courts to block their jurisdiction. James had to have marveled on the strangeness of the king's common-law courts limiting the power of the king's ecclesiastical courts.

But the writs of prohibition flew, as did the writs of habeas corpus,[9] to release the Puritans held in contempt for not taking the *ex officio* oath. Parliament also got into the act and began to directly challenge the king with bills supporting the common-law courts' power to issue the writs of prohibition.[10]

"Chapter 1. In the first place we have conceded to God, and by this our present charter confirmed for us and our heirs for ever that the English church shall be free, and shall have her rights entire, and her liberties inviolate; and we wish that it be thus observed. This is apparent from the fact that we, of our pure and unconstrained will, did grant the freedom of elections, which is reckoned most important and very essential to the English church, and did by our charter confirm and did obtain the ratification of the same from our lord, Pope Innocent III, before the quarrel arose between us and our barons. This freedom we will observe, and our will is that it be observed in good faith by our heirs for ever.

We have also granted to all freemen of our kingdom, for us and our heirs for ever, all the underwritten liberties, to be had and held by them and their heirs, of us and our heirs for ever . . ."

6. This brings up another connection between the Fifth Amendment's right to remain silent and *Magna Carta*, namely, the Due Process Clause. *See* WILTSHIRE at 57 (comparing *Magna Carta* Chapter 39 and the Fifth Amendment Due Process Clause). *Magna Carta* Chapter 39 states that no one shall be deprived of liberty except "*under the law of the land.*" This is the same "*due process*"

As in the Fifth Amendment's statement that no person shall, "*be deprived of life, liberty, or property, without due process of law . . . .*"

For a discussion of some of your due process rights, see **Chapter 6: How the Sixth Amendment Guarantees You a Court, a Lawyer, and a Chamber Pot.**

....

7. Helmholz at 65.

....

8. Alschuler at 2647.

....

9. "*Habeas corpus*" is Latin for "you have the body." This was an order commanding a person detaining another to produce the prisoner. Thus the issue is the legality of the detention, not guilt or innocence. Habeas corpus is "*the great writ of liberty*" issuing from the common-law courts. BLACK'S LAW DICTIONARY 638–39 (5th ed. 1979). See U.S. CONST. art. I, § 9.

10. LEVY at 227–28. The judges of other courts also got into the act supporting Parliament and the common-law courts, including the King's Bench, Common Pleas, and Exchequer.

Sir Henry Montague, chief justice of the King's Bench in 1616, advocated that ecclesiastical courts should follow common-law court procedures and do away with the *ex officio* oath. *Id.* at 228.

James I

Even those who had no particular affinity for the Puritans, like Sir Francis Bacon, jumped in against *ex officio* oaths.[1]

And in the center of this controversy, was Edward Coke, lord chief justice of England.

King James made Edward Coke (pronounced "Cook") chief justice of the Court of Common Pleas in 1606.[2] Given Coke's history of defending royal prerogative under Elizabeth, James had reason to believe he made a good choice.[3] James was wrong.

Coke instead entered the fray as the great defender— indeed the expander—of the common law over the ecclesiastical courts.[4] The conflict with King James came about because James needed to check any challenge to the ecclesiastical structure because he depended on his ecclesiastical courts to not only say he was above the law but that God wanted you to believe it.[5]

Despite this, Coke continued to issue writs of prohibition against the ecclesiastical courts' use of the *ex officio* oath.[6] Coke persisted in citing *Magna Carta* Chapter 29 to argue

not only that the common-law courts were superior to the other courts in England but that even the king was under the common law.[7]

The final straw for James was Coke's decision in *Burrowes and Others v. The High Commission* in 1616. In this case, eight Puritan ministers, imprisoned for not taking the *ex officio* oath, petitioned for a writ of habeas corpus from the King's Bench. Coke ruled that the High Commission could not imprison the defendants for failing to take the oath.[8]

Shortly after this, King James dismissed Coke for good. But Coke's work, as

---

1. According to Bacon, ecclesiastical court procedure was "*contrary to the laws and customs of this land and state . . . [specifically] the oath 'ex officio'*"

Sir Francis Bacon

Quoted LEVY at 215. Bacon recognized that no man is bound to accuse himself because common-law procedure allows for the grand jury to do so.

2. Coke had been speaker of the house in Parliament as well as Queen Elizabeth's solicitor general at the same time. In this dual role he used any number of delaying tactics to defend royal prerogative. LEVY at 199–200. Having such dual roles in what we would now call the executive and legislative branches did not bother such officials in the seventeenth century.

Sir Edward Coke

3. See, for example, Coke's service to King James in the prosecution of Sir Walter Raleigh, outlined in **Chapter 6: How the Sixth Amendment Guarantees You a Court, a Lawyer, and a Chamber Pot.**

4. *See generally* Charles H. Randall, Jr., *Sir Edward Coke and the Privilege against Self-Incrimination*, 8 S.C. L.Q. 417 (1955–56) (discussing Coke's lead of the common-law lawyers and courts in making the oath *ex officio* illegal). For a more general discussion of the sources of Cokes jurisprudence, see Paul Raffield, *Contract, Classicism, and the Common-Weal: Coke's Reports and the Foundations of the Modern English Constitution*, 17 LAW & LITERATURE 69 (2005). For a standard biography, see CATHERINE DRINKER BOWEN, THE LION AND THE THRONE (1956).

5. LEVY at 242–43.

What played out between Coke and King James regarding royal power was much like what occurred between Becket/Henry II and More/Henry VIII but with an interesting progression.

• Becket defended the church's power, including ecclesiastical court jurisdiction, against Henry II's royal courts (i.e., the early version of the common-law courts).

• More also defended the church against Henry VIII's desire to take it over and use the ecclesiastical courts as instruments of state policy.

• Coke went full circle, back to Henry II, to expand the king's common-law courts at the expense of the ecclesiastical courts. King James knew that because of the legal standards of procedure protecting even defendants charged with political crimes, which at this point included heresy, and emerging independence of the common-law courts, such a diminution of the ecclesiastical courts directly challenged his power. Remember James's motto: "*No bishops, no king.*"

6. A **writ of prohibition** is an order from a superior court limiting an inferior court's actions, often defining jurisdiction. The counterpart is the **writ of** *mandamus* ordering an inferior court to do something. At this point, the common-law courts defined ecclesiastical court jurisdiction. This was the result of the long struggle between the king's common-law courts and the Catholic Church's ecclesiastical courts. The irony here is that kings from Henry II pushed for the supremacy of the various king's courts as they fought for control with Rome. Now the "king's" common-law courts were limiting what were now the king's ecclesiastical courts. No wonder James was miffed!

Burrowes exemplified, is the basis for the abolition of the oath and the creation of our right to remain silent.

Coke became a hero for those who believed in rights and liberties under the rule of law, one of whom was John Lilburne.

ENTER JOHN LILBURNE: HOW A GUY WHO TALKED A LOT GAVE US THE RIGHT TO BE SILENT

For sheer pugnacity, one would be hard pressed to find John Lilburne's equal.

Four times he stood trial for his life on treason charges and passed most of his adulthood in prison, a good portion of which was for refusing the take the *ex officio* oath.[9] Both in and out of prison he expounded his ideas in political pamphlets.

In Tudor times the High Commission maintained the pretense that it was all about theology.[10] By Lilburne's time, prosecutions using the *ex officio* procedure gave up the pretense that they were rooting out heresy, at least the religious kind.

Rather, it was about political ideas, like democracy, dangerous to the king. Lilburne was not a Carthwright, but instead a popular government critic.[11] He also represents an evolution in Puritanism from religious egalitarianism to democracy: if you do not need the king (or his church) to get to God, why do you need him to get to good government?

In 1637 Lilburne was twenty-three years old and arrested for importing *"libelous and seditious books."* His trial was before the Court of Star Chamber, with no jury. He refused the *ex officio* oath because

"no man's conscious [sic] ought to be racked by oaths and imposed."[12]

If you are interested in an extensive academic debate (or just have insomnia) on the use of the writ of prohibition and its role in the development of the privilege against self-incrimination, see Charles M. Gray, *Prohibitions and the Privilege against Self-Incrimination*, in TUDOR RULE AND REVOLUTION: ESSAYS FOR G.R. ELTON FROM HIS AMERICAN FRIENDS 345 (Delloyd J. Guth & John W. McKenna eds., 1982) (taking shots at Levy, and for Levy's response, see Levy's article).

....

7. Again, see **Chapter 6: How the Sixth Amendment Guarantees You a Court, a Lawyer, and a Chamber Pot** for an account of Coke's main confrontation with King James.

8. Burrowes and the others actually did not win their case because Coke also ruled that even though the High Commission could not imprison them for refusing the oath, it could for obstinate heresy and great schism. Thus, what Coke did was to allow the High Commission to win the specific case but only after Coke established in the basis of the win that the *ex officio* oath was not legal and affirmed that a common-law court could say so.

John Marshall

Chief Justice John Marshall of the U.S. Supreme Court was to do much the same almost two hundred years later in *Marbury v. Madison*, 5 U.S. 137 (1803), where he gave the Jefferson administration a win but only after ruling that the Supreme Court had the power of judicial review over acts of Congress. For more on this, see **Chapter 10: "Are You Talkin' to Me?": Just Who Are Those "People" in the Tenth Amendment?** Marshall would have read Coke avidly and was probably conversant on *Burrowes*.

....

9. His nickname became Freeborn John. See Harold W. Wolfram, *John Lilburne: Democracy's Pillar of Fire*, 3 SYRACUSE L. REV. 213 (1952); WIGMORE at 282 (describing him as a man "*constituted somewhere between a patriot and a demagogue . . . .*"

Lilburne led the Levellers, one of many Puritan sects. They were an informal alliance of agitators and pamphleteers during the English Civil War (1642–48) pushing for constitutional reform and equal rights. To them, all men possessed natural rights that resided in the individual. "Leveller" was actually a derogatory term that Lilburne did not like. Wolfram at 226 n.45. It was like being called a communist in the 1950s.

10. Of course, the king was vested in the theology, making him the head of the church and thus the country.

....

11. Stuntz at 415.

....

12. *Miranda*, 384 U.S. at 459. *See also* Alschuler at 2649 n.90, *citing* JOHN LILBURNE, THE JUST OFFENSE OF JOHN LILBURNE IN THE LEVELER TRACKS 450, 454 (William Haller & Godfrey Davies eds., 1944) (containing Lilburne's description of his Star Chamber prosecution, written at the time of his 1653 treason trial).

Lilburne also asserted,

"I am unwilling to answer to any impertinent questions, for fear that with my answer I may do myself harm."[1]

What Lilburne asserted was the right to silence in the Star Chamber court.[2] Unfortunately for him, this defense did not work. The Star Chamber ordered him publicly whipped, pilloried,[3] fined, and sent to Fleet Prison.[4]

Lilburne spent the next three years in prison until he acted *"in obedience to the orders."* Politically, though, this made him famous.[5]

CHARLES AND PARLIAMENT

Charles I tried to enforce Anglican reforms on Presbyterian Scotland, which led to war. This and other ineptitudes forced him in 1640 to call his

first Parliament in eleven years.

The common-law lawyers and Puritans drove the agenda of parliamentary supremacy.[6]

Parliament immediately sided with the Puritans, abolished the High Commission and Star Chamber in 1641, and forbade the remaining ecclesiastical courts from issuing *ex officio*

---

1. *Quoted in* Wolfram at 217. As any trial lawyer will attest, judges do not take kindly to a litigant who tells them a question is *"impertinent."*

2. Lilburne maintained it was the first time someone had refused the *ex officio* oath before the Star Chamber. *See* LEVY at 275.

3. From the pillory Lilburne continued to argue against the *"inquisition oath."* He kept this up despite receiving at least five hundred lashes. With his back bleeding, Lilburne was able to pull out of his pocket three of the seditious books for which he was charged and threw them to the crowd. (The Star Chamber could have convicted Lilburne just by searching him.) The court ordered that Lilburne *"be laid alone, with irons on his hands and legs, in the Wards of the Fleet, with the basest and meanest sort of prisoners are used to be put."* To avoid someone else repeating Lilburne's performance, the court ordered that prisoners to receive corporal punishment be bound and *"have their garments searched before they be brought fourth, and neither writing, nor other thing suffer to be about them."* Wolfram at 218 n.21.

The pillory (stocks)

4. Wolfram at 217. Fleet Prison was notorious. Built in 1197 off Farringdon Street on the Fleet River's east bank, it became a prison for the Star Chamber's victims. Afterward it was the prison for debtors and persons imprisoned for contempt of court by the Court of Chancery. Fleet and King's Bench prisons were also where racket sports developed. During the eighteenth century "gentlemen" imprisoned until they could repay their creditors amused themselves by hitting balls against the walls with rackets.

Fleet Prison Racquet Ground by Stadler (1808)

5. Freeborn John was his nickname despite the fact that he spent most of his adult life in prison.

6. *See* Wolfram at 220–21 n.29, citing Maguire, *Attack of the Common Lawyers on the Oath Ex Officio as Administered in the Ecclesiastical Courts, in* ENGLAND IN ESSAYS IN HISTORY AND POLITICAL THEORY IN HONOR OF CHARLES HOWARD MCILWAIN 199, 204–05 (1936), for the argument that Coke and the common-law lawyers had already succeeded in abolishing the *ex officio* oath by writs of prohibition and judicial decision.

7. R. Carter Pittman, *The Colonial and Constitutional History of the Privilege against Self-Incrimination in America*, 21 VA. L. REV. 763, 772 (1934–35). The act abolishing the Star Chamber cited *Magna Carta* chapter 29 as its basis and endorsed the common-law procedure whenever life, liberty, or property was at stake. LEVY at 281–82. This was the **Long Parliament** the king summoned in November 1640, as distinguished from the **Short Parliament** of April to May 1640. Resistant to King Charles's demands, Parliament also caused the king's advisers to resign and passed an act forbidding its own dissolution without its members' consent. Tension between the king and Parliament increased until the English Civil War in 1642. After the king's defeat in 1646, the army, led by Thomas Pride, exercised political power and in 1648

oaths.[7] Parliament also freed political prisoners, starting with Lilburne.[8] He was free to fight another day.[9]

Charles I did not do so well. In 1642 the English Civil Wars began, and Parliament eventually defeated the Royalist forces for good in 1648. Kings had been deposed before, but Parliament specifically tried Charles for high treason.[10] At his trial Charles refused to enter a plea, claiming no court had jurisdiction over a monarch and that the court's power grew only out of a barrel of gunpowder. This defense sealed his fate.[11]

FREEBORN JOHN WINS THE PRIVILEGE AT COMMON LAW

Charles's passing did not end Lilburne's struggle. By 1649, Lilburne succeeded in incurring the wrath of the new government under the Long Parliament and Oliver Cromwell's control.[12] At four o'clock one morning toward the end of March 1649, two hundred armed men arrested Lilburne at his home.[13]

---

expelled all but sixty members of the Long Parliament. The remaining group, called the Rump Parliament, brought Charles to trial and execution in 1649. Cromwell forcibly ejected it in 1653.

After Oliver Cromwell's protectorate, the Parliament was reestablished in 1659 and, with those excluded in 1648 restored to membership, it dissolved itself in 1660.

Cromwell dissolving the Long Parliament in 1653

8. He was the first prisoner released. Wolfram at 220 n.26. Parliament declared his Star Chamber sentence *"illegal, and against the Liberty of the subject"* as well as *"bloody, cruel, wicked, barbarous, and tyrannical." Id.* at 220. Just after Parliament opened, a new member, Oliver Cromwell, made his first speech demanding Lilburne's liberty. LEVY at 279. As we will see in the next chapters, Cromwell later put a lot of energy into trying to return Lilburne to prison or having him executed.

9. And fight he did. He entered the parliamentary army during the English Civil Wars (1642–48), rising to the rank of lieutenant colonel and commanding a regiment of dragoons. While the war raged, he disputed with the House of Lords. The lords imprisoned him and wanted to prosecute him with *"great rigour."* Cromwell directly intervened because of Lilburne's popularity with the troops. Wolfram at 226. After battle wounds and ideological disagreements, he left the army but continued his political fights for what we would now call civil rights.

10. This was a first. Lilburne, although believing Charles deserved execution, refused to participate in his trial, arguing that he should have a jury instead of a special court. He also did not think the monarchy should be abolished before a new constitution and government were formed. Wolfram at 226 n.45. Lilburne was right; the result of Charles's execution was Cromwell's dictatorship.

11. The trial of Charles I.

12. But one example was the Levellers 1647 *Humble Petition of Many Thousands to Parliament.* Among other agitations, the Levellers demanded a privilege against self-incrimination:

"*Thirdly, that you permit no authority whatsoever to compel any person or persons, to answer to any questions against themselves or nearest relations except in cases of private interest between party and party in a legall way, and to release such as suffered by imprisonment, or otherwise, for refusing to answer to such interrogatories.*"

Pittman at 773.

13. Wolfram at 228.

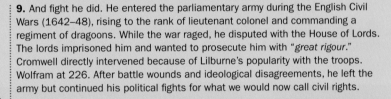

Cromwell thought that this would neutralize Lilburne's popularity; Cromwell was wrong.[1]

Gone was the Star Chamber, so Cromwell had to rely on the common-law courts. He stacked a court with his judges[2] and had Lilburne charged with the crime of publishing seditious material that denounced Cromwell and Parliament, some of which had Lilburne's name on it.

Previously in 1637 before the Star Chamber, Lilburne asserted he that did not have to incriminate himself. He lost. At his arraignment this time, Lilburne again declared, *"by the laws of England, I am not to answer questions against or concerning myself."* To answer would be *"un-Englishmanlike."*[3] As a sign of how the legal culture had changed, or how much the privilege was part of the common law, the presiding judge replied, *"you shall not be compelled."*[4] Thus, at the start, Lilburne won the victory denied him in 1637.

Lilburne's victory on this point is significant because he asserted a full right to remain silent, not just freedom from compulsion to incriminate by oaths or torture. This is significant because the common-law criminal procedure at the time needed self-incrimination to operate. Generally, a justice of the peace would examine the accused felon and save the testimony for the defendant's later trial.[5] At trial the defendant, though not put under oath, was examined and usually bullied into self-incrimination.[6]

Lilburne now asserted that no man is bound to incriminate himself even if legally charged.[7] This is beyond anything Coke ever

---

1. Cromwell usually won, as in CROMWELL (Columbia Pictures, 1970), with Richard Harris in the title role and Alec Guinness as Charles I. It is a good movie dramatically but with factual flaws, like the fact that the roundheads and cavaliers did not have distinctive dress.
Besides the movie, several cities and places are named for Cromwell as well as the WWII *Cromwell* tank.
   As good as any summation of Cromwell's career is Monty Python's 1989 song "Oliver Cromwell" from the 1991 MONTY PYTHON SINGS to the tune of Frederic Chopin's Polonaise op. 53 in A flat major. One should also compare the Irish perspective in *Young Ned of the Hill* by the Pogues, from the 1989 album

PEACE AND LOVE: *"A curse upon you Oliver Cromwell, You who raped our Motherland, I hope you're rotting down in hell, For the horrors that you sent, To our misfortunate forefathers . . ."*

2. Cromwell issued an "extraordinary commission" of judges to get Lilburne's treason conviction, stating *"the Kingdom could never be settled so long as Lilburne was alive."* LEVY at 300.

Oliver Cromwell

3. Wolfram at 228. In the 1760 and 1770s Americans would argue for these same rights as "Englishmen."

4. Alschuler at n.98 (quoting 4 How. St. Tr. at 1292–93); LEVY at 304. Lilburne argued that the *"fundamental laws of England"* gave him this right, even though neither *Magna Carta* nor the Petition of Right mention it. Wolfram at 224.

5. WIGMORE at 286. Some scholars argue the Framers never intended the modern privilege because it is against *"common morality,"* as any normal person would always give a suspected person a chance to give his side of the story. See Alschuler at 2666 (*quoting* WALTER B. SCHAEFER, THE SUSPECT IN SOCIETY 59 (1967)); *see also* Charles T. McCormick, *Law and the Future: Evidence*, 51 N.W. U. L. REV. 218, 222 (1956). If this is true, then the law should be open to allowing juries to hear evidence the defendant made an "exculpatory no," which it currently does not allow absent some extraordinary circumstance. See Alexandra Natapoff, *Speechless: The Silencing of Criminal Defendants*, 80 N.Y.U. L. REV. 1449 (2005).

6. WIGMORE at 286 (citing, among cases in note 85, Sir Thomas More's trial, 1 How. St. Tr. 386, 389 (1535)). This was to be known as the "French system" of criminal procedure after the practice in France of continuing to use the *ex officio* oath in criminal procedure. Reaction to this was one of the factors leading to the French Revolution. *Id.* at 291–95.

7. WIGMORE at 289.

asserted. Coke's focus was mainly on the coercive *ex officio* oath and procedures. The right had moved from a struggle against the *ex officio* oath in the ecclesiastical courts to opposing incriminating questions in common-law courts.[8]

We now take for granted that Lilburne's statement, "*I am not to answer questions against or concerning myself,*" asserts a right that would apply to both an accused and a witness. Thus the right Lilburne asserts goes beyond just the defendant's right to silence in the face of accusation and merges with the privilege of a witness not to self-incriminate.[9]

The judges in Lilburne's trial thus had to proceed without his confession. Yet, even without a confession, it should have been an easy prosecution case. What neither they nor Cromwell accounted for, though, was the jury.

LILBURNE'S TRIAL

Lilburne's trial revolved around his claims that he had the right to a lawyer and other procedural protections we now take for granted.[10] Most relevant on the emergence of the right to remain silent is that a lawyer allows a criminal defendant to remain silent while the lawyer speaks for him.[11] But given that Lilburne could out-talk anyone in the courtroom, he really did not need a lawyer. He relied on the defense that the prosecutor had the burden of proving his guilt. Lilburne's own popularity, or perhaps the popularity of the ideas in his publications, protected him.[12] During trial, the judges and prosecutor tried to get him to make incriminating statements, but Lilburne was too smart:

8. John H. Langbein, *The Historical Origins of the Privilege Against Self-Incrimination at Common Law*, 92 Mich. L. Rev. 1047 (1994). He argues that the origin of the right to remain silent arose from adversarial procedure and the emergence of criminal defense lawyers at the end of the eighteenth century.

9. This is often called the witness privilege and, for the accused, the confession privilege. *See generally* McCormick at 283–84 (outlining the two branches in the history of the privilege—the privilege of the accused and the privilege of a witness). *See also* Katharine B. Hazlett, *The Nineteenth Century Origins of the Fifth Amendment Privilege against Self-Incrimination*, 42 Am. J. Legal Hist. 235 (1998) (an extensive analysis of the two branches of the privilege in American jurisprudence and distinguishing it from English common law).

10. The next chapter treats Lilburne's trial in greater detail. *See generally* Wolfram at 233–52; Levy at 305–09.
His trial was at the London Guild Hall. *Id.* at 301.

11. Levy, following Wigmore, placed much of the origin of the modern privilege with Lilburne's trial, making the privilege well established by the late seventeenth century. Wigmore at 298–99. Langbien deemphasizes this history, maintaining that the modern privilege did not result until the mid-1800s with more available defense counsel. Langbien at 1071–84.

12. Lilburne was actually tried for what he wrote in prison *after* his arrest under statutes passed just for him. Levy at 303. Lilburne's *Agreement of the People* (1647–49) really got him into trouble by articulating the following:
- the right for all to vote for their representatives;
- the right against self-incrimination;
- the freedom of religion and press;
- the equality of all persons before the law;
- the right of a jury for any judgment touching life, liberty, or property;
- the abolition of capital punishment except for murder;
- no military conscription of conscientious objectors;
- no monopolies, tithes, or excise taxes;
- that taxation be proportionate to real or personal property;
- the grading of punishments to fit the crime; and
- the abolition of imprisonment for debt.
Most of these rights are now in the U.S. Constitution.

Lord Keble: *Mr. Lilburne, you do acknowledge it to be your own handwriting?*

Lilburne: *I am too old with such simple gins [tricks] to be catched; I will cast mine eyes upon none of your papers, neither shall I answer to any questions that concern myself: I have learned more law out of the Petition of Right, and Christ pleading before Pilate, than so.*[1]

The prosecutor jumped in with a theological retort to again try to get Lilburne to incriminate himself:

Mr. Attorney: *Would you had learnt more gospel!*

Judge Jermin: *You may answer a question, whether it be true or false; and confess and glorify God.* [Picking up on the theological argument.]

Lilburne: *I have said, Sir; prove it: I am not to be catched with such fooleries.*

So much for beating Lilburne with theology! At this point, Lord Keble tried to solve the problem with a judicial finding, but Lilburne would have none of it:

Lord Keble: *You see the man, and the quality of the man, this is the paper that he delivered into his own hand, and that is sufficient, as well as if it was of his own handwriting.*

Lilburne: *Good Sir, your verbal bench-law is far short* of your written text in your own law-books.[2]

Lilburne's judges were out to kill him, and Lilburne knew it. For example, after hearing the prosecution's case, Keble told the jury they should convict:

Lord Keble: *I hope the jury hath seen the evidence so plain and so fully that it doth confirm to them to do their dirty duty and find the prisoner guilty of what is charged upon him.*

But even these judicial pronouncements were no match for Lilburne, who argued, implausibly, that the material might have been forged. During the entire trial the judges could not stop him from reading

---

1. This is a reference to the Gospel of John, where Pilate interrogated Jesus, who states that he *"came into the world . . . to bear witness to the truth; and all who are on the side of truth listen to my voice,"* to which Pilate replies, *"What is truth?"* Jesus did not answer. Lilburne thus asserts not only the same right to silence Jesus exercised but a martyr claim as well.

Agreement of the People (1647)

Christ before Pilate by Mihály Munkácsy (1881)

2. Wolfram at 241–42.

3. Levy at 308; *see also* Randall (showing Coke as Lilburne's foundation).

legal points from Coke to the jury.[3] This was despite the fact that the judges continually asserted they decided the law, not the jury.

In trying to stifle Lilburne, Lord Keble explained, for the jury's benefit, that he had more than one judge because with "*one judge, and no more . . . you would have outtalked them; but you cannot do so here.*" Keble fought a losing battle:

Lilburne: *Truly, Sir, I am not daunted at the multitude of my judges, neither at the glittering of your scarlet robes, nor the majesty of your presence, and harsh austere deportment towards me, I bless my good God for it, who gives me courage and boldness.*[4]

Lilburne had a knack for not letting anyone forget that he was the victim. In this he knew not only the value of speech, but of silence. The jury took only two hours to acquit him, and for a short while he was a free man.[5]

LILBURNE'S LEGACY

Lilburne only enjoyed his freedom until 1651, less than two years later, when Cromwell's House of Commons tried and convicted him without any semblance of a trial. He was fined and banished for life upon pain of death.

Lilburne, of course, returned and was tried again in 1653. This time he had another jury, Lilburne's strong suit. Using much the

same trial tactics as in his 1649 trial, he persuaded the jury to return a not guilty verdict.[6]

But Cromwell got Lilburne in the end with another manufactured charge and procedure. He sent Lilburne to prison on Jersey Island, where Lilburne could not publish pamphlets or other writings. Lilburne died there in 1657.

Lilburne was a pivotal figure in the history of many of our trial rights, including the right to remain silent.[7] He once said, "*I shall leave this Testimony behind me, that I died for the Laws and Liberties of this nation.*"[8]

4. LEVY at 308.

5. Regarding Lilburne winning his trial, see **Chapter 7: Trial by Jury or … by God!**

6. LEVY at 309–12. Upon examination, a juror claimed, implausibly, that he did not think that the Lilburne named in the indictment was the same Lilburne before the court.

7. As the Supreme Court stated in *Miranda v. Arizona*, 384 U.S. 455 (1966), "*Perhaps the critical historical event shedding light on its [privilege against self-incrimination] was the trial of one John Lilburne, a vocal anti-Stuart Leveller, who was made to take the Star Chamber Oath in 1637.*" *Id.* at 459 (*citing* The Trial of John Lilburne and John Warton, 3 How. St. Tr. 1315 (1637)).

8. LEVY at 312.

Despite Lilburne's assertions to the contrary, the privilege against self-incrimination is not explicit in any of the English fundamental laws, such as *Magna Carta*, and did not make it into the *Petition of Right*, or the *English Bill of Rights*. Pittman at 764. The closest actual written reference to the right is in the *Scottish Claim of Rights of 1689*, stating "*that the using of torture without evidence or in ordinary crimes, is contrary to law.*" Yet even this document authorizes torture in certain cases.

Perhaps a better illustration of Lilburne's impact on the right to remain silent comes from the statements of the jurors in his 1653 trial. Cromwell's Parliament ordered an investigation of this jury.[1] The foreman refused to answer questions, saying only that he followed his conscience. Another juror replied, *"What he can tell is one thing; but to accuse himself is another thing."*[2]

These jurors got the lesson, as did the rest of the country: Englishmen have the right against self-incrimination.[3] By the time of the English Bill of Rights of 1689, the privilege had become so well established and universally recognized that *"to have inserted it would have been very much like reaffirming the law of gravitation."*[4] Indeed, England recognized the privilege before there was freedom of religion, speech, or press, or protections against unreasonable searches.

As a trial right, the privilege existed before the rights against double jeopardy, to see the indictment, to adequate time to prepare a defense, to assistance of counsel, to compulsory process for witnesses, and to have defense witnesses sworn.[5]

1. Showing that among many other character flaws, Cromwell was a very bad loser.

2. LEVY at 311.

3. For various examples of the right secured, see LEVY ch. X. For example, even during the Popish Plot, a supposed conspiracy of Catholics and the Jesuits to overturn the government, the sham courts that convicted and sent at least fourteen innocent people to their deaths respected the right against self-accusation. *Id.* at 316.

4. Pittman at 774. The Supreme Court cited Pittman in *Miranda,* 384 U.S. at 459 n.29.

The standard explanation for why the right is not explicit in English constitutional sources such as the *English Bill of Rights of 1689* is that *"[i]n the early 1650's this privilege was so well established in the customary law of England that it was never even thought necessary by any English Parliament to pass an act or resolution touching the matter."* *Id.* at 774.

5. Wolfram at 243 n.102.

6. For example, in *Entik v. Carrington,* 19 How. St. Tr. 1029–73 (1765), **Lord Camden** based the rule against unreasonable searches as an extension of the right against compelled self-incrimination: *"It is very certain, that the law obligeth no man to accuse himself: because the necessary means of compelling self accusation falling upon the innocent as well as the guilty, will be both cruel and unjust; and it should seem, that search for evidence is disallowed upon the same principal."* The Supreme Court in *Boyd v. United States,* 116 U.S. 616, 633 (1886), recognized the Fourth and Fifth Amendments' *"intimate relationship."* See LEVY at 390–94. The Court has reiterated its recognition of the relationship on numerous occasions, including *Mapp v. Ohio,* 367 U.S. 655, 656–57 (1960) (applying the exclusionary rule for search and seizure violations to the states through the Fourteenth Amendment). This intimate relationship of the Fourth and Fifth Amendments still comes into play. Distinguishing *Boyd* in *Fisher v. United States,* 425 U.S. 391 (1976), the Supreme Court held that the Fifth Amendment did not protect documents created without government compulsion. More recently, though, in *United States v. Hubbell,* 530 U.S. 27 (2000), the Court dealt special prosecutor Kenneth Starr a blow and reaffirmed a person's Fifth Amendment right to protection from searches under subpoena of personal business papers. See Aaron M. Clemens, *The Pending Reinvigoration of Boyd: Personal Papers are Protected by the Privilege against Self-Incrimination,* 25 N. ILL. U. L. REV. 75 (2004).

7. The late Supreme Court Justice Hugo Black often cited Lilburne's work in his opinions and wrote in an ENCYCLOPEDIA BRITANNICA article that Lilburne's constitutional work of 1649 was the basis for the rights contained in the U.S. Constitution. In fact, Lilburne's nickname, Freeborn, originates from the Leveller idea that all men were born free and equal and possessed natural rights that resided in the individual, not the government. These ideas are the foundation of John Locke's TWO TREATISES OF GOVERNMENT that there can only be *"government with the consent of the governed"* and the natural rights of *"life, liberty, and property."* In turn, Locke is the foundation of Thomas Jefferson's DECLARATION OF INDEPENDENCE, which states that *"all Men are created equal, that they are endowed by their Creator with certain unalienable Rights, that among these are Life, Liberty, and the Pursuit of Happiness—That to secure these Rights, Governments are instituted among Men, deriving their just Powers from the Consent of the Governed . . . ."* Paralleling this descent of ideas is that John Lilburne's first cousin, William Lilburne, was Thomas Jefferson's great-great-grandfather.

Indeed, Lilburne's right to remain silent in many ways was the anchor for other rights.[6]

Englishmen in America believed they had the right as part of their heritage from England.[7] As the Supreme Court in *Miranda* summed up, *"These sentiments worked their way over to the Colonies and were implanted after great struggle into the Bill of Rights."*[8]

THE PURITANS IN AMERICA: ANNE HUTCHINSON AND THE SALEM WITCHES

The Puritans settled in North America when opposition to the *ex officio* oath was strongest.[9] These people were Lilburne's contemporaries, part of the same religious and political movement. They fought the wilderness

while their political kin fought the English Civil Wars. Lilburne's trials put all England's attention upon the Star Chamber, the High Commission, and the other courts using *ex officio* proceedings. The religious persecution these proceedings embodied drove the Puritans to America.[10] Indeed, it was not just the *ex officio* oath but the oaths of supremacy and allegiance that drove the Puritans.[11]

John Locke

8. *Miranda*, 384 U.S. at 459.

9. Pittman at 769, 775 ("*Before the storm of puritan revolution had passed in old England, the privilege against self-incrimination had become a cherished reality in New England.*").

10. Pittman at 770–71. Even crossing the Atlantic, the Puritans were forced to say the prayers in the Anglican prayer book twice a day.

Mayflower in Plymouth Harbor by William Halsall (1882)

On September 16, 1620, the May-flower set sail from Plymouth England with forty-eight crew and one hundred one settlers. During the three-month voyage two died and two were born.

One of the great American myths is that the Mayflower's nasty sailors dumped the Pilgrims off at Plymouth without enough food for the winter. Actually, it was beer. As one Pilgrim wrote, "[w]e could not take time for further search or consideration, our victuals being much spent, especially our beere." RICH BEYER, THE GREATEST STORIES NEVER TOLD: 100 TALES FROM HISTORY TO ASTONISH, BEWILDER & STUPEFY 34–35 (2003).

A Native American actually saved the Pilgrims. In March 1621, an Indian named Samoset walked into their colony and said in English "Welcome, Englishman, I

am Samoset. Do you have any beer?" Samoset came back a few days later with Squanto, who spoke English well and was the subject of the movie SQUANTO: A WARRIOR'S TALE (1994).

11. Moglen at 1100-01 (noting that Puritan America was even more sensitive to the spiritual power of oaths than their English contemporaries); *see also* Alschuler at 2649.

Oddly enough the old compurgation oath appeared in the colonies in only one situation. Dishonest fur traders would get Indians drunk and exchange liquor for many hides. *See* Pittman at 776 n.57. Massachusetts, Connecticut, and Plymouth all used the oaths of purgation to deal with this problem. LEVY at 355, 381. If one accused of selling liquor to Indians did not purge himself by compurgation oath, he would be taken confessed, and usually fined (the old *pro confesso* formula of the Inquisition). New York expanded use of compurgation oaths during the colonial period to included the crimes of selling liquor to Indians, taking seamen's notes for liquor or food, entertaining slaves, stealing furs from Indians, selling liquor to servants, failing to report imported copper money, trading with the Iroquois for certain articles, and giving credit to servants. *Id.* at 382. Refusing the oath subjected the person to double the penalty of the guilty. *Id.* By the Revolution, these purgative oath procedures no longer existed. *Id.*

In 1642 John Winthrop[1] reported the consensus on the law of self-incrimination in the colony:

"Where such an act is committed and one witness or strong presumptions do point out the offender, there the judge may examine him strictly and he is bound to answer directly, though to the peril of his life. But if there be only light suspicion, . . . then the judge is not to press him to answer nor is to be denied the benefit of law, but he may be silent, *and call for his accusers. But for examination by oath or torture in criminal cases, it was generally denied to be lawful."*[2]

Winthrop's survey shows the accused *"may be silent"* and that oaths and torture are unlawful.[3] Thus, the American Puritans (i.e., the Pilgrims) brought the right with them as it existed at the time. In this America started ahead of England, where it took centuries and a very creative reading of *Magna Carta* to get as far.

Despite this rule, the Pilgrims proved as capable as any English High Commission of ignoring the right when expedient. Clearly, no one, especially Winthrop, bothered with it in Anne Hutchinson's 1638 heresy trial.[4] Of course, it could be that Pilgrim courts respected the right in normal criminal cases but, as in Europe, heresy was the exception, especially when it challenged the religious and political power structure.[5]

1. John Winthrop (1587–1649) was first governor of Massachusetts Bay Colony. On April 8, 1630, Winthrop led the "Winthrop Fleet" of eleven

John Winthrop

vessels and seven hundred people to Massachusetts, the greatest fleet to ever carry Englishmen to a new land. Before leaving the ships, Winthrop gave his famous "city on a hill" sermon (from Matthew 5:14—*"A city set on a hill cannot be hid."*), preaching that the Puritans had a special pact with God to create a holy community in the New World. This had to have been news to King Charles I, if he heard of it, who approved the colony's charter as just another commercial venture.

2. Moglen at 1103–04, n.722, *citing* JOHN WINTHROP, HISTORY OF NEW ENGLAND 47 (J. Savage, ed., Boston, Phelps & Farnham 1826); *see also* LEVY at 347.

3. This articulation gets to the foundation of the Fifth Amendment's specific wording: *"nor shall [the accused] be compelled in any Criminal Case to be a witness against himself . . . ."* This Winthrop statement also supports *Miranda's* articulation that you have "the right to remain silent."

Anne Hutchinson on Trial by Edwin Austin Abbey

Hutchinson's Statue at Massachusetts's State House. The inscription reads: *"In Memory of Anne Marbury Hutchinson; Baptized at Alford Licolnshire England July 20, 1595; Killed by the Indians at East Chester New York 1643; Courageous Exponent of Civil Liberty and Religious Toleration."*

4. Anne Hutchinson (1591–1643) led a dissident group in Massachusetts as their preacher. Her heresy was called Antinomianism—the belief that faith rather than works and obedience lead to salvation. This was not really out of the mainstream of Puritan doctrine, at least in England. The real problem was that Hutchinson challenged the colony's authoritarian power structure, and since she was a smart, influential woman her sin was all the worse. Winthrop, desiring to nip the heresy in the bud, used a

heresy trial to get her. A court banished her as a heretic after a two-day trial in 1638. She led sixty followers to found Portsmouth, Rhode Island (Aquidneck Island) and later she moved to the Bronx in northern New York City. In 1643, Siwanoy Indians scalped her and five or six of her children. Several notables claim descent from her, including governor Thomas Hutchinson (from the last chapter), as well as Franklin D. Roosevelt, George H. W. Bush, and George W. Bush. The Hutchinson River, and thus the Hutchinson River Parkway, are named after her. It was not until 1987 that Governor Michael Dukakis pardoned Anne, finally revoking Governor Endicott's 350-year-old banishment order. *Anne Hutchinson*, 6 THE NEW ENCYCLOPEDIA BRITANNICA 175 (15th ed. 2002). *See also* EVE LAPLANTE, AMERICAN JEZEBEL: THE UNCOMMON LIFE OF ANNE HUTCHINSON, THE WOMAN WHO DEFIED THE PURITANS (2004).

5. The Supreme Court has used Hutchinson's trial as a historical argument to justify both limiting the right against self-incrimination and expanding it. In 1908, despite Lilburne's struggles to win recognition of the right under *Magna Carta*, the Supreme Court ruled that Hutchinson's trial showed that the privilege was *"not regarded as part of the law of the land of Magna Carta or the due process of law which has been deemed an equivalent expression . . . ."*

The privilege against self-incrimination also did not come into play in the Salem witch trials of the 1690s. These "trials," however, illustrate no principle of law; no lawyer participated, and the torture was not judicial torture.[6] In fact, they were really not judicial proceedings but a form of political tribunal officially named a "court of oyer and terminer" ("court to hear and determine").

In a regular trial, both then and today, a voluntary confession evidences guilt. In Salem, however, the confession was *not* evidence of guilt, that was already decided when a group of little girls had a vision that you were bewitching them or one of your neighbors, in his confession, named you an accomplice.[7]

If you confessed you were a witch, you got forgiven and lived. If you denied it, you died. All of the fifty or so persons who confessed to being witches were pardoned, whereas the nineteen who maintained innocence did so to the very end and met the noose.[8]

But, with the exception of the Hutchinson political trial and the Salem hysteria trials, it appears that the right against self-incrimination took hold in America with the Puritans.

Twining v. New Jersey, 211 U.S. 78, 105–06 (1908). As support, Justice William Henry Moody declared that Hutchinson's judges were "*not aware of any privilege against self-incrimination or conscious of any duty to respect it.*" Scholars roundly criticize *Twining's* poor use of history, with Levy stating the "*justices were unbelievably ignorant of the English backgrounds.*" LEVY at 334–35; *see also* Pitman at 242–43 n.102. Later, in *Adamson v. California*, 332 U.S. 46, 88–89 (1946), four justices rejected the *Twining* rule, with Justice Hugo Black writing: "*The lamentable experience of Mrs. Hutchinson and others, contributed to the overwhelming sentiment that demanded adoption of a Constitutional Bill of Rights. The Founders of this Government wanted no more such "trials" and punishments as Mrs. Hutchinson had to undergo. They wanted to erect barriers that would bar legislators from passing laws that encroached on the domain of belief, and that would, among other things, strip courts and all public officers of a power to compel people to testify against themselves.*" Black's more expansive view won in *Miranda*.

Justice Moody

Justice Black

6. *See* Pittman at 782. Indeed, Cotton Mather, one of the principal clerics involved, instructed judges against using torture and instead advocated "*crosse and swift questions*" to bring about confessions. His advice was not followed. *See* LEVY at 363.

Cotton Mather

The Salem witch trials

7. *See generally* PETER CHARLES HOFFER, THE SALEM WITCHCRAFT TRIALS: A LEGAL HISTORY (1997) (putting the witchcraft allegations and "legal" proceedings in the context of village power struggles and exterior threats from Indians and French). For the basic modern psychiatric study of the events, see MARION L. STARKEY, THE DEVIL IN MASSACHUSETTS (1949).

One of the magistrates during the "trials" was **John Hathorne** (1641–1717), notable for the fact that he was the only one later not to repent. His great-great-grandson was Nathaniel Hawthorne, author of THE SCARLET LETTER (1850). Anne Hutchinson may have been the model for THE SCARLET LETTER's Hester Prynne.

8. LEVY at 363.

A more recent literary adaptation of the Salem witch trials is Arthur Miller's 1953 play THE CRUCIBLE, an allegory for 1950s McCarthyism. (McCarthy's House Committee on Un-American Activities questioned Miller in 1956.) Jean-Paul Sartre adapted the play for his 1957 film LES SORCIÈRES DE SALEM,

Nathaniel Hawthorne, 1860s

and Miller himself did the same for THE CRUCIBLE (20th Century Fox 1996), starring Daniel Day-Lewis, who happens to be Miller's son-in-law.

COLONIAL GOVERNORS AND INQUISITORIAL PROCEEDINGS

The colonies' relative independence from England allowed precursors to our Fifth Amendment to appear in various colonial charters and statutes.[1] When a colony became a royal province, however, it tended to lose control of the administration of justice. Royal governors, some with overbearing personalities, often implemented inquisitorial practices, especially when the governors sat outside the normal court structure and acted as a special court of inquiry.[2]

For example, in the aftermath of Bacon's Rebellion,[3] Royal Governor Sir William Berkley took harsh measures of pacification and retaliation, including using inquisitorial procedures of investigation, which led to summary trials and executions.[4] In response the Virginia House of Burgesses[5] in 1677 passed the following resolution:

"It is answered and clear that the law has provided that a person summoned as a witness against another, ought to answer upon oath, but no law can compel a man to swear against himself in any manner wherein

he is liable to corporal punishment."[6]

The House of Burgesses articulated the common-law right in a statutory resolution. About one hundred years later Virginia became the first state to constitutionally recognize the right against self-incrimination, leading directly to the Fifth Amendment.[7]

SILENCE ON THE ROAD TO REVOLUTION

In colonial America the right against self-incrimination existed much the same as in England.[8]

---

1. For example, the *Massachusetts Body of Liberties* of 1641, No. 45, gave colonists protection against compulsion either by torture or by an oath to confess their own delinquency:

> *"No man shall be forced by torture to confess any crime against himself nor any other unless it be in some capital case where he is first fullie convicted by clear and sufficient evidence to be guilty, after which if the cause be of that nature that it is very apparent there be other conspirators or confederates with him, then he may be tortured, yet not with such torture as be barberious and inhumane."*

Cited in Pittman at 776.

The Body of Liberties, written by Puritan minister **Nathaniel Ward** (1578–1652), was the first American constitution. Based on the common law, *Magna Carta*, and the Old Testament, the *Body of Liberties* was advanced for its day. It was a precursor to John Adam's MASSACHUSETTS DECLARATION OF RIGHTS OF 1780, still the oldest functioning written constitution in the world. *See* DAVID McCULLOUGH, JOHN ADAMS 220–25 (2001).

2. *See* Pittman at 783–84.

3. Bacon's Rebellion, also known as the **Virginia Rebellion**, was an uprising in 1676 in the Virginia Colony led by Nathaniel Bacon. Many of the issues had to do with opposition to Governor Berkley's favorable policies toward Indians. Specifically, Berkley refused to allow Bacon and the frontiersmen to take action against all tribes, including peaceful ones. These actions made Berkley unpopular. Berkley eventually regained control of the colony, and Bacon died suddenly before being captured. *Bacon, Nathanial*, 1 THE NEW ENCYCLOPEDIA BRITANNICA 777 (15th ed. 2002). Berkeley granted Bacon's land to William Randolph, who founded the influential Virginia family.

Berkeley

4. He hanged thirty-eight of Bacon's followers, causing King Charles II to comment that *"[t]hat old fool has put to death more people in that naked country than I did here for the murder of my father." See* Nathaniel Bacon (died 1622), http://en.wikipedia.org/wiki/Nathaniel_Bacon (last visited Jan. 6, 2006).

Charles II

5. Not counting prior Native American claims, such as the Iroquois Confederacy, the House of Burgesses was the first elected legislative assembly in the New World.

6. LEVY at 358; *quoted in* Alschuler at 2651 (with seventeenth century spelling).

Indeed, the colonists clambered for their rights as "Englishmen."[9] Among these was the right not to be dragged into an "inquisitorial court" for examination.[10] Indeed, many hoped that if England would consent to a colonial Bill of Rights on the English model, it would avoid the Revolution. Parliament never provided this, and history took its course.

Despite this, in America the right to silence existed in normal criminal procedure during the late colonial period and early republic.[11] But what did this really mean?

In the run-of-the-mill criminal case, probably not a whole lot. The privilege was a trial right and did not affect pretrial questioning because at the time such questioning was not under oath.[12] In fact, the routine pretrial procedure in America, even after the ratification of the Bill of Rights, involved a magistrate interrogating the accused, which resolved the majority of criminal cases.[13]

This may have been very much akin to modern plea bargaining, a summary proceeding that saved courts and prosecutors time and energy, with the accused having some benefit. If the accused did

not answer, the jury in a later trial could consider the failure to answer.

THE PRIVILEGE IN AMERICAN CONSTITUTIONS

The reaction to royal governors, as well as the Lilburne/Puritan legacy, led seven states to insert a privilege against self-incrimination in their constitutions or bills of rights before 1789.[14] The states, and eventually the Fifth Amendment, focused on the privilege against torture[15] and compulsion from oaths.

---

7. Levy at 358, 405. *See* Section 8 of the *Virginia Declaration of Rights* (1776) by **George Mason:**

"*That in all capital or criminal prosecutions a man hath the right to demand the cause and nature of his accusation, to be confronted with the accusers and witnesses to call for evidence in his favor and to a speedy trial and a partial jury of 12 men of his vicinage, without whose unanimous consent he cannot be found guilty; nor can he be compelled to give evidence against himself; that no man may be deprived of his liberty except by law of the land or the judgment of his peers.*"

George Mason (1725–92) was a patriot, statesman, and Virginia delegate to the Constitutional Convention. His *Virginia Declaration* was Madison's model for the Bill of Rights. George Mason University is named for him, as well as Mason Counties in Kentucky, West Virginia, and Illinois.

8. Levy at 404.

9. Coke would not have supported this view. For him the common law did not apply overseas. But Americans transported his thoughts anyway, and the common law spread with the English language. *See* Daniel J. Hulsebosch, *The Ancient Constitution and the Expanding Empire: Sir Edward Coke's British Jurisprudence*, 21 Law & Hist. Rev. 439 (2003).

10. Pittman at 787.

11. Alschuler at 2649 (reporting the legal manuals generally in use by judges and magistrates stated that "*the offender should not be examined on oath*").

12. Langbein at 1059–62; E.M. Morgan, *The Privilege against Self-Incrimination*, 34 Min. L. Rev. 1, 14–22 (1949).

13. Langbein at 1066–71. Moglen at 1187 identifies two different procedures of criminal justice in colonial America, with the summary procedure affecting lower class defendants rather than taxpayers. By threatening to deprive Americans of the criminal procedure reforms of the Treason Act of 1698, Parliament proposed to do to American higher classes what the

American higher classes did to their own vagrant strangers, slaves, and indentured servants. *See id.* at 1118, 1120–29 (suggesting that the privilege's scope was limited to only criminal prosecutions at common law and noting that several state constitutions excluded the privilege in summary proceedings). For a contrary view, see Levy at 849.

With this history we should consider that much of the modern tension related to the extent of the privilege against self-incrimination may be more a question of how the federal courts over time, but especially in the 1960s through *Miranda*, have extended the privilege to the marginalized.

14. Pittman at 764–65 (Virginia, Pennsylvania, Maryland, and North Carolina in 1776; Vermont in 1777; Massachusetts in 1780; and New Hampshire in 1784).

15. Pittman at 788. The colonial courts in New England had expressly approved torture in certain circumstances. *Id.* at 776. This brutality inspired the Fifth Amendment, as reflected in its wording that "*no person … shall be compelled in any criminal case to be a witness against himself …*." Alschuler at 2651–52.

But in "constitutionalizing" the right, the Framers expanded it from what the English courts had enforced against the High Commission.[1] The Fifth Amendment refers not just to the initiation of criminal proceedings or to the first accusation but also to the criminal trial itself. Thus the Fifth Amendment privilege is not just to guarantee an adequate evidentiary basis for interrogation but is an absolute privilege that no evidentiary showing can overcome.[2]

True, the Framers did not write that a defendant has the "*right to remain silent*." But they wrote the Fifth Amendment before police existed as we know them today.[3] The Framers' experience was with royal governors. Yet our modern *Miranda* privilege against self-incrimination in the face of police interrogation may well conform to the Framers' original intent. As Patrick Henry declared when objecting to the Constitution because it lacked a Bill of Rights, Congress might

"*introduce the practice of France, Spain, and Germany—of torturing, to extort a confession of crime.*"[4]

MADISON SAVES THE DAY!

When James Madison wrote the Bill of Rights, he went well beyond the old *nemo tenetur seipsum prodere* rule.[5] Madison wrote it expansively to apply to criminal cases, civil cases, and any kind of government inquiries, such as congressional hearings.[6]

THE RIGHT, RIGHT FROM THE BEGINNING

American jurisprudence started with a judicial culture that took the right to remain silent for granted.

---

1. The privilege in England stayed much more based in evidence law. *See* Hazlett (outlining how the original English privilege arose from a series of criminal cases that fused the two common-law rules of evidence: the witness privilege and the confession rule).

2. Alschuler at 2647.

3. The modern Supreme Court's reading of the Fifth Amendment has drawn criticism on several fronts. For one thing, the reading that a person has a "*right to remain silent*" is broader than the Fifth's language that no person shall be "*compelled in any Criminal Case to be a witness against himself . . . .*" This results in a defendant not getting testimony from a guilty witness because the guilty witness can invoke the right to silence. This violates the Framer's explicit intent, written into the Sixth Amendment, of the right "*to have compulsory process for obtaining witnesses in his favor . . . .*" *See* Akhil Reed Amar, The Constitution and Criminal Procedure: First Principals 49–51 (1997).

4. Henry did not go to the Constitutional Convention because he "*smelt a rat.*" Levy at 418; Pittman at 789.

Patrick Henry before the House of Burgesses by Peter F. Rothermel (1851)

5. Levy at 427. Though the Fifth Amendment does state that no one "*shall be compelled* in any Criminal Case *to be a witness against himself,*" Levy argues that the first Congress

did this for other reasons having to do with pending legislation and did not intend to limit the right to just criminal cases. *See id.* at 423–29. Otherwise the government could use a civil case or other investigation as a ruse to compel a person to incriminate himself. The wording "*in any Criminal Case*" was not in Madison's original draft. *Id.* at 422. Indeed, Madison's original draft would have protected a privilege against self-infamy as well as self-incrimination. Thus it would have protected a person from having to make statements that exposed him to public disgrace or loss of reputation. *Id.* at 423–24. State courts at this time followed this reading of the privilege, but this is not the modern practice. *Id.* at 429.

James Madison

A notable example of the right in the early republic occurred in *Marbury v. Madison*, where Charles Lee (an ancestor of Robert E. Lee) argued that Attorney General Levi Lincoln did not have to answer incriminating questions about what happened to Marbury's judicial commission. (Lincoln probably burned it.) The Supreme Court agreed.

Later, in Aaron Burr's treason trial, the court upheld the right of a witness not to incriminate himself.[7] Thus, from the earliest days of our Constitution, the Supreme Court accepted a legacy that led it to *Miranda* and the "*right to remain silent.*"[8] And despite many calls to overturn *Miranda*, the case has withstood the test of time.[9]

Perhaps no one summed up the Fifth Amendment's history and legacy better than later Supreme Court Justice Abe Fortas:

"The principle that a man is not obliged to furnish the state with ammunition to use against him is basic to this conception . . . [the state] has no right to compel the sovereign individual to surrender or impair his right to self-defense. . . . [The Fifth Amendment's fundamental value] is intangible, it is true; but so is liberty, and so is man's immortal soul. A man may be punished, even put to death, by the state; but . . . he should not be made to prostrate himself before its majesty. Mea culpa belongs to a man and his God. It is a plea that cannot be exacted from free men by human authority. To require it is to insist that the state is the superior of the individuals who compose it, instead of their instrument."[10]

Because of history, we can talk about the right to silence.

---

6. Remember the example at the start of this chapter: "*Congressman, I respectfully assert my Fifth Amendment right to remain silent.*"

7. Levy at 429.

8. For background on the *Miranda* case, with interviews of the still living participants, see GARY L. STUART, MIRANDA: THE STORY OF AMERICA'S RIGHT TO REMAIN SILENT (2004). For an early experiment in *Miranda*-like warnings in nineteenth century New York, see Wesley MacNeil Oliver, *Magistrates' Examinations, Police Interrogations, and Miranda-Like Warnings in the Nineteenth Century*, 81 TUL. L. REV. 777 (2007); *see also* Alan Hirsch, *Threats, Promises, and False Confessions: Lessons of Slavery*, 49 HOW. L.J. 31 (2005) (arguing that the nineteenth century experience of dealing with coerced confessions of slaves informs the current debate in coercive interrogation).

William Rehnquist

9. See *Dickerson v. United States*, 530 U.S. 428 (2000) (holding that *Miranda* is constitutionally based and that Congress cannot overrule it by statute), with *Chavez v. Martinez*, 123 S. Ct. 1994 (2003) (holding that the Fifth Amendment right is a "trial right"). *See generally* Thomas Y. Davies, *Farther and Farther from the Original Fifth Amendment: The Recharacterization of the Right against Self-Incrimination as a "Trial Right" in Chavez v. Martinez*, 70 TENN. L. REV. 987 (2003).

10. Fortas at 98–100. In 1962 Fortas later represented Clarence Earl Gideon before the Supreme Court in *Gideon v. Wainwright*, 372 U.S. 335 (1963).

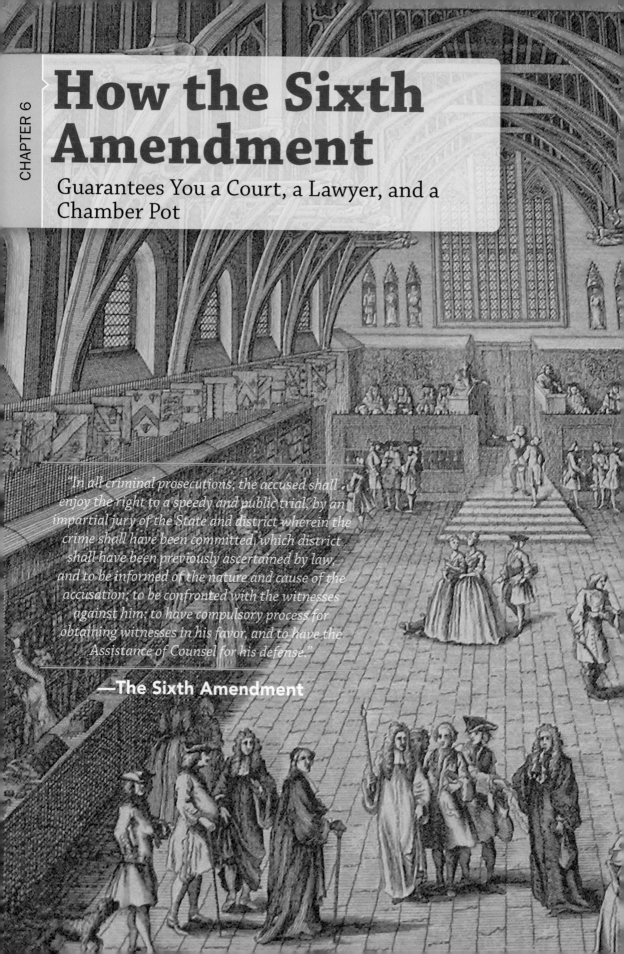

How the Sixth Amendment

Guarantees You a Court, a Lawyer, and a
Chamber Pot

*"In all criminal prosecutions, the accused shall
enjoy the right to a speedy and public trial, by an
impartial jury of the State and district wherein the
crime shall have been committed, which district
shall have been previously ascertained by law,
and to be informed of the nature and cause of the
accusation; to be confronted with the witnesses
against him; to have compulsory process for
obtaining witnesses in his favor, and to have the
Assistance of Counsel for his defense."*

—The Sixth Amendment

In 1649, John Lilburne needed to urinate.

He also needed a lawyer, notice of the charges, the right to subpoena witnesses, time to prepare his case, and the right to testify:

"I earnestly entreat you, that now you will pleased to give me a copy of my indictment, or so much of it, as you expect a plea from me upon, and an answer unto, and counsel assigned me, and time to debate with my counsel, and subpoena for witnesses."[1]

Lilburne got none of these rights. But, with persistence, he did get to pee:

"Sir, if you will be so cruel as not to give me leave to withdraw to ease and refresh my body, I pray you let me do it in the Court. Officer, I entreat you to help me to a chamber pot."[2]

1. 4 St. Tr. 1296, *quoted in* Harold W. Wolfram, *John Lilburne: Democracy's Pillar of Fire*, 3 Syracuse L. Rev. 213, 235 (1952).

John Lilburne, otherwise known as Freeborn John, was "[a]n honest and true-bred, free Englishman; that never in his life feared a Tyrant, nor loved an Appressor [sic]." Diane Parkin-Speer, *John Lilburne: A Revolutionary Interprets Statutes and Common Law Due Process*, 1 Law & Hist. Rev. 276, 296 (1983) (quoting William Haller & Godfrey Davies, The Leveller Tracts, 1647 to 1653, n.449 (1944). Another description was that Lilburne was "an obstreperous and forward opponent . . . constituted somewhere between a patriot and a demagogue . . . ." 8 John H. Wigmore, Evidence 291 (3d ed. 1940).

2. Wolfram at 245. A chamber pot is a bowl-shaped container, usually ceramic with lids, kept in the bedroom as a toilet, in common use until the nineteenth century. Webster's New International Dictionary of the English Language 446 (2d ed. 1942).

The chamber pot is the origin of the words "potty" and "potty training."

Contemplating the Zen of potty training

"[Whilst it was fetching, Mr. Lilburne followeth his papers and books close; and when the pot came, he made water, and gave it to the foreman.]"[1]

To be fair, judges had to complete trials in one sitting.[2]

But these judges had a special commission from Lord Protector Cromwell: kill Lilburne,[3] and Lilburne knew it.[4]

Lilburne's fight for his life helped us get the trial rights we take for granted. He laid the foundation for the list of trial rights that is the Sixth Amendment—the entitlements of the accused. Further, to make sure the accused gets all these rights, the Sixth Amendment finishes the list with the right *"to have the Assistance of Counsel for his defense."*[5]

"COUNSEL FOR HIS DEFENSE" IN HISTORY

Where there are courts, there are lawyers.[6]

Ancient Athenians defended themselves in court, but they could hire a *"logographos"* to write a speech for them to memorize.[7]

The Romans would appoint a *"procurator"* to handle legal business, especially when the party could not attend court. His function was like our modern attorney or agent for legal matters. Over time the Roman

---

1. Wolfram at 245 to 46.

2. Wolfram at 239 n.9. Not until 1794 did some criminal courts have the right to adjourn, that is, take a break.

3. Wolfram at 229. Cromwell issued an "extraordinary commission" of judges to get Lilburne's treason conviction, declaring that *"the Kingdome could never be settled so long as Lilburne was alive."* Quoted in LEONARD W. LEVY, ORIGINS OF THE FIFTH AMENDMENT: THE RIGHT AGAINST SELF-INCRIMINATION 300 (1968).

Oliver Cromwell

4. What Lilburne faced was like the "Double Secret Probation" that Dean Vernon Wormer put on Delta House in NATIONAL LAMPOON'S ANIMAL HOUSE (Universal Pictures 1978). So, from John Lilburne we get John Belushi!

Image by Helen Koop

5. U.S. CONST. amend. VI, cl. 3. The lawyer we all want to be is Atticus Finch from TO KILL A MOCKINGBIRD (Universal Pictures 1962), the film adaptation of Harper Lee's Pultzer Prize–winning novel (1960). Gregory Peck was tailor made for the role of a dignified Southern lawyer defending an innocent black man in the pre–civil rights South.

6. Regarding lawyers and the ancients, see R. BLAIN ANDRUS, LAWYER: A BRIEF 5,000 YEAR HISTORY (2009).

7. ROSCOE POUND, THE LAWYER FROM ANTIQUITY TO MODERN TIMES 32 (1953). *"Logographos"* derives from *"logos"* as in the modern "logo," like "team logo," but literally translated as "persuasive word" and *"graphos,"* as in the modern "graph" or "graphic," but refers literally to "writing."

Socrates in his trial famously did not employ a *logographos*. THE WORKS OF PLATO, *Apology*, at 59 to 60 (Irwin Edman ed., Benjamin Jowett trans., Random House 1956).

8. POUND at 37.
Our word "attorney" comes from the Indo-European *"ter,"* meaning "to turn," still seen in the English word "turn." The later Latin *"attorn"* meant "to turn over to another." The earliest attorneys were thus not necessarily lawyers but anyone designated to take the place of another in a transaction. We still see this when a person signs a "power of attorney" over to another who may be, but usually is not, an attorney. WEBSTER'S at 179.
Technically, an "attorney at law" is someone licensed to practice law, whereas a "lawyer" is someone "learned in the law" but not necessarily licensed. BLACK'S LAW DICTIONARY 118, 799 (5th ed. 1979).

9. POUND at 44 to 45.
For an example of the patron–client relationship, see Marlon Brando in Francis Ford Coppola's THE GODFATHER (Paramount Pictures 1972). The American Film Institute ranks THE GODFATHER No. 2 in its best movies list.

Empire's size made this more common.[8]

A Roman citizen who came to court to argue for others was a "*patronus causarum*" ("patron of the cause").[9] This term came from the great men of Rome, the patrons or patricians, who had many dependant client families and slaves. These were reciprocal relationships, and the patron would defend his "client" in court. Patrons who were good lawyers would get other people wanting to attach themselves to him to handle specific cases (or causes), hence *patronus causarum*. This is also the source of the modern reference of a lawyer "taking on a client."[10]

The Romans systematically taught rhetoric, and men like Cicero were great trial attorneys and cross-examiners.[11] Cicero defined "advocacy" as advancing "*points which look like the truth, even if they do not correspond with it exactly.*"[12]

Perhaps it was statements such as Cicero's that prompted Jesus, who was born just over a generation after Cicero, to say

"*Woe unto you also, ye lawyers! For ye lade men with burdens grievous to be borne, and ye yourselves touch not the burden with one of your fingers.*"[13]

---

10. Pound at 46.

11. Cicero Denouncing Cataline by Cesare Maccari (1888).
    See C.A. Morrison, *Some Features of the Roman and the English Law of Evidence*, 33 Tul. L. Rev. 577, 582 (1958). In the later empire, trials became inquisitorial and the art of cross-examination and other trial skills declined. *Id.* at 589; Pound at 50.
    Marcus Tullius Cicero (106–43 BC) was a Roman statesman, lawyer, political theorist, philosopher, and one of Rome's greatest orators and prose stylists. *Cicero*, Oxford Classical Dictionary 234 to 38 (1970); Columbia Encyclopedia 558 to 59 (4th ed. 1975). Classical learning and history had great influence on America's Founding Fathers. *See, e.g.,* Louis J. Sirico, Jr., *The Federalist and the Lessons of Rome*, 75 Miss. L.J. 431 (2006).

12. *Quoted in* Sadakat Kadri, The Trial: A History, from Socrates to O.J. Simpson 15 (2005).

13. *Luke* 11:46 (King James). For the trial of Jesus before the Sanhedrin, see J.W. Ehrlich, The Holy Bible and the Law 146 (1962), noting that the Sanhedrin was the highest court of ancient Judea.

Just after Jesus's death, though, the Roman lawyer Quintilian wrote his text on rhetoric and cross-examination.[1] The Romans also gave us the first bar license and attempts to prohibit the unauthorized practice of law.[2] Because the lawyers were patrons, and thus leaders of great houses, they shunned getting paid as an advocate—at least officially. Emperor Claudius set the fee for lawyers at 10,000 *sesterces* or 100 *aurei*.[3]

In early medieval England, around the king's courts in Westminster, advocates began to congregate, working for a fee. Over two centuries after the Norman Conquest, Edward I issued an edict in 1292 directing the Court of Common Pleas to choose *"attorneys and learners"* to follow the courts and monopolize the legal profession.[4]

1. POUND at 48 to 49. **Marcus Fabius Quintilianus** (c. 35 to c. 100 AD) was a Roman rhetorician from Spain. Medieval and Renaissance schools of rhetoric widely used his writings. See http://www.thelatinlibrary.com/quintilian.html (last visited July 7, 2007) for a Latin text, and http://www.public.iastate.edu/~honeyl/quintilian/index.html (last visited July 7, 2007) for an English translation.

2. A law of 468 AD prohibited advocacy by those not admitted to practice in Roman courts. POUND at 51.

Saint Ives

3. This is about $475. POUND at 53. This 10,000 *sesterces* fee remained the standard, at least officially, throughout the Middle Ages. Saint Ives, canonized in 1347, was famous for being such a great lawyer that he always commanded the maximum fee, but so honest that he would accept no more. Thus depictions show him with the bag of exactly 10,000 *sesterces*. On his tomb was inscribed ("*Sanctus Ivo erat Brito / Advocatus et non latro / Res miranda populo*"). "St Ives was Breton / A lawyer and not a thief / Marvelous thing to the people." ST. IVES CATHOLIC ENCYCLOPEDIA, http://www.newadvent.org/cathen/08256b.htm (last visited July 7, 2007). *See also* POUND at 5 to 54. Saint Ives is the patron saint of lawyers, not Saint Thomas More, who is the patron saint of statesman.

5. From the thirteenth century, the Inns of Court in London have been hostels and schools for training English lawyers. They were literally inns where students lived, ate, and learned. Today every English barrister belongs to an Inn, which supervises and disciplines its members, as well as providing libraries, dining facilities, and professional accommodation. Each also has a church or chapel. Over the centuries the number of active Inns of Court was reduced to four: Lincoln's Inn from 1422, Gray's Inn from 1569, Inner Temple from 1505, and Middle Temple from 1501. *See* A.W.B. Simpson, *The Early Constitution of the Inns of Court,* 28 CAMBRIDGE L.J. 241 (1970); Simpson at 241; Paul Brand, *Courtroom and Schoolroom: The Education of Lawyers in England Prior to 1400,* 60 BULL. INST. OF HIST. RESEARCH 147 (1987); S.E. THORNE, *The Early History of the Inns of Court with Special Reference to Gray's Inn*, ESSAYS IN ENGLISH LEGAL HISTORY 137–54 (1985). ROBERT R. PEARCE, A HISTORY OF THE INNS OF COURT AND CHANCERY (1848).

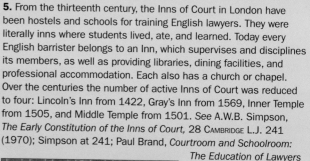

Combined arms of the four Inns of Court

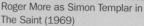

Roger More as Simon Templar in *The Saint* (1969)

Saint Thomas More

4. By the 1200, lawyers would hang out at Westminster and follow the court, cashing in on the fee-for-justice system. DANNY DANZIGER & JOHN GILLINGHAM, 1215: THE YEAR OF MAGNA CARTA 183 (2003); J.H. BAKER, AN INTRODUCTION TO ENGLISH LEGAL HISTORY 20 (2002); COLIN RHYS LOVELL, ENGLISH CONSTITUTIONAL AND LEGAL HISTORY 136 (1962).

The Middle and Inner Temple Inns get their name because they stand on the old English headquarters of the Knights Templar.

The Templars were the zealots yelling "*God wills it!*" in the movie KINGDOM OF HEAVEN (20th Century Fox 2005). Simon Templar, otherwise known as "The Saint," acts the modern day Knight Templar in Leslie Charteris's books, television show, and 1997 movie, THE SAINT (Paramount Pictures 1997).

This meant that unlike the rest of Europe the English courts, and not the great universities, trained new lawyers. This led to the Inns of Court system.[5]

Because of the Inns of Court,English lawyers did not follow the pattern of the rest of Europe with lawyers trained in Roman and canon law.[6] Rather, English law became its own insular tradition, to which we in America are heirs.[7] A key part of that training, in addition to attending lectures and taking notes in court, involved the "moots" or practice arguments.[8]

Later we will talk more about lawyers, but we are ahead of the story. Lawyers need a place to practice law— and that place is a court.

---

6. BAKER at 28. For the outline of the medieval history of continental lawyers and their education in the great universities, see James A. Brundage, *The Medieval Advocate's Profession*, 6 LAW & HIST. REV. 439 (1988).

The Lawyers by Honoré Daumier (c. 1855), depicting lawyers from the Continental (i.e., non-English) tradition

7. Modern American lawyers are members of "the bar." The term comes from the Inns of Court, which, being inns, had bars. Later the bar was a railing that divided the hall in the Inns of Court, with students on one side and the readers or "benchers" on the other. Graduating students crossed the symbolic physical barrier and were "admitted to the bar." This is the origin of the word "barrister."

The drama of legal training formed the backdrop of John Jay Osborn, Jr.'s THE PAPER CHASE (1970) as well as *The Paper Chase* (20th Century Fox 1973) television show (CBS, 1978 to 79). The fictional Professor Charles Kingsfield uttered the now famous lines of clichéd pomposity, *"You teach yourselves the law. I train your minds. You come in here with a skull full of mush, and if you survive, you'll leave thinking like a lawyer."*

Professor Kingsfied – Image by Helen Koop

8. POUND at 89 to 90. By the end of the Middle Ages, the legal profession had three categories: (1) judges and serjeants, (2) apprentices in the Inns of Court, and (3) attorneys. *Id.* at 82. This is the origin of our modern notions of "lawyer" and "attorney."

The serjeants are what we today think of as courtroom lawyers, or the English "barrister," a lawyer who speaks for an accused. As early as 1259 the serjeants wore a coif, that is, a headdress. POUND at 81. But the modern wigs of English barristers and justices entered only with the Restoration, as part of French custom under Charles II. LOVELL at 151 n.26.

Conversely, an attorney is one who stands in for you as your agent. Anyone can give someone, not just a lawyer, a "power of attorney" to act in one's stead. *See generally* POUND at 77 to 93 ("Organization of Lawyers in Medieval England"); George C. Thomas III, *History's Lesson for the Right to Counsel*, 2004 U. ILL. L. REV. 543, 561 to 73 (2004) (noting historical distinction between pleaders as "sergeants" versus "attorneys" as agents); J.H. Baker, *Cousellors and Barristers: An Historical Study*, 27 CAMBRIDGE L.J. 205 (1969). England maintains the historical distinction between solicitors and barristers. Thomas at 572. The Sixth Amendment, however, more generally incorporates the "right to assistance of counsel," encompassing both functions.

The title *"serjeant-at-law"* comes from the Knights Templar whose senior Knights were *"freres sergens"* or *"fraters servientes."* KURT VON S. KYNELL, SAXON AND MEDIEVAL ANTECEDENTS OF THE ENGLISH COMMON LAW, 147–63 (2000).

The Order of the Coif is an honorary society for law students with good grades.

GOING COURTING

Where there are lawyers, there are courts.[1]

We "court."[2] A "suitor" goes "courting."[3] We can be "courteous," or a "courtesan," or just "curtsey"—all may be part of "courtship."[4] Dating is part of courtship, and, with a tennis date, we play on a "court."[5] If we play the game well, it "suits" us.

1. The U.S. CONSTITUTION provides for courts:

"*The judicial Power of the United States, shall be vested in one supreme Court, and in such inferior Courts as the Congress may from time to time ordain and establish. The Judges, both of the supreme and inferior Courts, shall hold their Offices during good Behavior, and shall, at stated Times, receive for their Services a Compensation, which shall not be diminished during their Continuance in Office.*"

U.S. CONST., art. III, § 1.

2. The word "court" comes from the Latin "*cohors,*" an enclosed farmyard (as in "horticulture" or as in a tennis or basketball court, or the modern word "cartilage" for a surrounding space or yard. WEBSTER'S at 611. The Latin word "*cohort*" for a tactical unit of one-tenth of a legion (one hundred men) in the Roman army passed into English to refer to any group of people (usually bonded by friendship). *Id.*

"Court," as a legal term, comes from "*cortem*" (Latin), "*cort*" (Old French), and "*curt*" (Anglo-Norman), combined with the word "*curia.*"

At least one account of the connection between the court, as an enclosed yard, and a court as a place of law is that "court" referred to the inner courtyard of a castle. After the Norman Conquest, the castle courtyard was where the Anglo-Saxon commoners were allowed to call upon the local lord to settle disputes, hence the expression "going to court."

3. The verb "to court," as in "courtly love," is the basis of the words "courtesy," "courtesan," "curtsey" and the song *"Going Courting"* from SEVEN BRIDES FOR SEVEN BROTHERS (Metro-Goldwyn-Mayer 1954). Indeed, the term, "romance" and "romantic" come from the stories of courtly love written in the Latin vernacular of France, a Romance language (i.e., written in the language "of Rome"). *See* WEBSTER'S WORD HISTORIES 114, 400 to 01 (1989); JOHN AYTO, DICTIONARY OF WORD ORIGINS 141, 448 (1990).

4. Courtship is traditionally the wooing of a female by a male with dating, flowers, songs, chocolates, and other gifts. If a woman woos the man, she is a "suitoress." Scientists often compare the human activity of courtship with mating rituals of other animals. Today the term has an anachronistic quality compared to the more modern "hanging out" or "hooking up." American literary references include Henry Wadsworth Longfellow's THE COURTSHIP OF MILES STANDISH (1858) as well as THE COURTSHIP OF EDDIE'S FATHER (Metro-Goldwyn-Mayer 1963) and the TV spin–off (ABC 1969 to 72).

5. "Real tennis" is the original racquet sport from which modern tennis descends. The original game is closer to modern "court tennis" in the United States or "royal tennis" in the United Kingdom. The term "real" may be a corruption of "royal" and related to the game's connection with royalty in England and France in the sixteenth and seventeenth centuries.

Henry VIII was an avid tennis player and built several tennis courts, including one at his palace of Hampton Court, which is still the home to an active tennis club. Henry played there from 1528 until he got too fat.

A young, tennis-playing Henry VIII

A fat, non–tennis-playing Henry VIII

Hampton Court Palace

We go to court. In court, we argue as "suitors."[6] Our lawyers usually wear a "suit"—indeed, they are "suits."[7] A lawyer can assess his suit, which either means he is evaluating his case or looking at his clothes. He can also use a particular ability or fact and thus "play to his strong suit."[8] If he plays it wrong, he "courts" disaster.

From whence did all these courts and suitors come?

---

6. "Suitor" as far back as Anglo-Saxon times was a party in a dispute in the county courts (*shire moots*). BLACK'S LAW DICTIONARY 1286 (5th ed.). Today the word "suit" has several meanings, including a lawsuit, a business suit, swim suit, space suit, environmental suit, jumpsuit, etc. "*Suit*," comes from the Latin "*sequita*" and "*sequere*" and means "something that follows," as in the English "sequence," the root of the words "sect" and "set." It also referred to uniformed followers or retinue who wore the same suit. AYTO at 510. There is also "suite," as in a set or grouping in music or offices.

---

7. The suit as formalwear has gone through an evolution from the frock coat to the morning coat, which got its name for the fact that the coat's cut allowed gentlemen to get their morning exercise by horse riding. The morning coat was a more casual form of half-dress from the traditional frock coat. The once extremely casual "lounge suit" is now our business and formal suit. The slang "suit" to refer to professionals, establishment management, or government employees came first from Hollywood, referring to movie executives. Now artists, working people, and hackers use the term pejoratively for anyone in authority.

U.S. Department of Justice seal

A solicitor general's morning coat

◄ Stylized dudes from the 1920s, one with a double-breasted coat and the other sporting a morning coat

A "suit"

A formal frock, the morning suit or "cutaway," and President John Kennedy wearing the once very casual "lounge suit." The U.S. solicitor general and his assistants still wear the morning coat to argue before the Supreme Court. The movie TOMBSTONE (Hollywood Pictures 1993) has Kurt Russell's Wyatt Earp in a full frock coat, with Virgil and Morgan Earp in morning coats. Doc Holiday wears a "coachman's cloak," making it easier to hide the shotgun. In the movie MY COUSIN VINNY (20th Century Fox 1992), Vinny wears the "ridiculous" suit at the start of the trial but it is actually a more formal morning coat.

TOMBSTONE – Image by Helen Koop

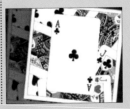

8. A suit in cards is one of four categories dividing a deck: spades, diamonds, clubs, and hearts. Thus playing to your "strong suit" is playing your best cards.

THE ANGLO-SAXON COURTS

The Anglo-Saxon judges and ministers were *"witans,"* their courts *"moots,"* and their laws *"dooms."*[1]

For the Anglo-Saxons, justice was communal, a matter of custom, and connected with governance in general. The local court called the *"hundred"* met every month and dispensed justice to *"suitors."*

There were no lawyers or professional judges. Anglo-Saxon justice lacked executive power and was more akin to a modern arbitration. Indeed, at this time the "king's peace" was something special, an extension of the peace of his own house—i.e., his *"court"*—which only later became his courts.[2]

The *witans* were wise men, counselors, or ministers.[3] The *witan* met as the king's counselors in the *"Witenagemot"* (from *"witan"* and the Old English *"gemot,"* meaning "meeting" or "assembly").[4] *Gemot* is also the root word for *moot,* meaning an assembly or law court.[5]

The *Witenagemot* declared *dooms,* and the Anglo-Saxon county courts (*"shire moots"*) passed *"witena doms,"* which encompass our modern concepts of not just laws but also decrees, judgments, and statutes. The shire moots met twice a year.[6]

---

1. *See generally* BLACK'S at 909, 1436. Even before the Anglo-Saxons, Julius Caesar wrote of Celtic priest-judges called "druids" enforcing law and custom. BAKER at 2.

2. Sir Fredrick Pollock, *English Law Before the Norman Conquest,* 14 LAW Q. REV. 291, 292, 296, 301 (1898).

3. BAKER at 9. Our modern words *"wit"* and witness comes from the old English *"witan"* ("to know"). It is also the source of *"witless"*—destitute of wit or understanding; *"whittling"*—a person of little wit or understanding, a pretender to wit, one given to smart sayings but inferior in wit; *"witmonger"*—one who passes on smart or witty sayings; *"witship"*—a witty person; *"witsnapper"*—a maker of witty quips; *"witted"*—having wit or understanding; *"witticism"*—a witty saying, a sentence, or phrase, a clever or amusing expressed conceit formerly, a jeer or jibe; *"wittisize"*—to express oneself wittily or indulge in witticisms; *"witified"*—having wit; *"witting"*—knowledge, intelligence, judgment; *"wittingly"*—knowingly, knowledge of, by design; *"witty"*—possessed of wit; *"witwanton"*—using wit wantonly; *"wittooth"*—a wisdom tooth; *"witess"*—a female wit. WEBSTER'S at 2940, 2942.

WITNESS (Paramount Pictures 1985) stars Harrison Ford and Kelly McGillis, with the feature film debut of Viggo Mortensen. WITNESS FOR THE PROSECUTION (United Artists 1957) stars Tyrone Power, Marlene Dietrich, Charles Laughton, and Elsa Lanchester, and it is based on Agatha Christie's play about a master barrister defending a man for murder. When the defendant's wife unexpectedly appears for the prosecution, it tests the lawyer's skill to the limit.

Tyrone Power: WITNESS FOR THE PROSECUTION

4. George Jarvis Thompson, *The Development of the Anglo-American Judicial System,* 17 CORNELL L.Q. 9, 11 to 13 (1932) (hereafter Thompson I). R.C. VAN CAENEGEM, THE BIRTH OF THE ENGLISH COMMON LAW 13 (2d ed. 1988); A.K.R. KIRALFY, POTTER'S HISTORICAL INTRODUCTION TO ENGLISH LAW 11 (4th ed. 1958). *See also* Pollock at 292 n.2. *Witans* would have included senior clergy, the leading *"thegns,"* and *"ealdormen"* (from which we get our modern term *"alderman"*). All of the Anglo-Saxon kingdoms in England had a *Witenagemot.* At various times, especially in Wessex, the *witan* would elect the king. THE COLUMBIA ENCYCLOPEDIA 2996 (4th ed. 1963).

The British Isles circa 802

5. In various parts of England one can still find "moot halls" as meeting places, the remnant of the old *"folkmoot"* of the tribal Angles, Saxons, and Jutes. The Scandinavian people of Jämtland have the *"jamtamót"* or assmbly. As for modern references, the wizard court in the *Harry Potter* books and movies meets in the *"Wizengamot."* J. R. R. Tolkien's THE LORD OF THE RINGS' Ents meet in an *"Entmoot."* Tolkien was an expert in Old English literature and the epic BEOWULF.

Beowulf fights the dragon

A *doom* generally just meant an accounting or reckoning.[7] But it also implicated divine judgment or fate, and thus punishment from God, giving us our modern usage of the word.[8]

As a great council, the *Witenagemot* had what we would call today legislative and judicial functions.[9] As such it was the precursor of both Parliament and high courts. Thus, when Parliament tries a high public official or when the U.S. Senate tries a president or federal judge after the House of Representatives impeaches him, it exercises the function from its predecessor, the *Witenagemot*.[10]

Although the Normans replaced the *Witanagemot* with the *"Curia Regis,"* or King's court, the *moots* continued to function in the counties or, as the Anglo-Saxons would say, the *shires*.[11] They continued in the context of Norman law and custom as well as the king's emerging royal courts and an entire system of church courts that the Normans brought over with them to England.[12]

By 1278, the *moots* had lost all jurisdiction over criminal prosecution, but the courts limped on until 1846.[13] And as we noted, the Inns of Courts still use the word "moots" to refer to law school practice arguments. This history gives us the modern word and concept of something that new facts and events make "moot."[14]

---

6. Pollock at 292.

7. *The Doomsday Book*, William the Conqueror's survey of England in 1086, was an accounting of what England was worth. After William took over, he wanted to know the value of everything. In so doing, he gave history a window into the life of England at the time.

8. From Old English *"dōm,"* Proto–Germanic *"domaz,"* means "judgment," "law" (compare Sanskrit *"dhaman,"* "law"). WEBSTER'S at 770.

Doom (id Software 1993) is a fun and gory first person "shooter" computer game invoking the modern understanding of the word.

9. *See* Pollock at 292. Regarding the powers of the *witan*, see LOVELL at 15 to 16 (1962); ROSCOE POUND, THE DEVELOPMENT OF CONSTITUTIONAL GUARANTEES OF LIBERTY 12 (1957) (noting that the "national council," which under Anglo-Saxon kings had been an assembly of wise men, became the Norman kings' court of his feudal vassals).

10. Thompson I at 13, *citing* the High Court of Parliament in England and the General Court of Massachusetts (consisting of the governor and both legislative houses) as examples.

A king and his *witan* from an eleventh century Old English hexateuch [British Library]

The 1999 U.S. Senate trial of President Bill Clinton after the House of Representatives impeached him

11. BAKER at 6. The Shire is also the home of the Hobbits in J. R. R. Tolkien's fictional Middle-earth in THE LORD OF THE RINGS.
The word *"shire"* is still found in a great number of place and regional names in England and even in the state name New Hamp*shire*. New Hampshire was the ninth state to ratify the U.S. Constitution, the minimum number for it to take effect.

12. VAN CAENEGEM at 12 to 13; *see also* Thompson I at 10 and n.3.

13. The County Court Act of 1846. *See also* The County Courts Amendment Act, ending the *hundred* courts. *Cited in* Thompson I at 13.

14. *See* BLACK'S at 909.

THE NORMANS TAKE OVER

In 1066 AD, William the Bastard conquered England and thus became William the Conqueror.[1] (Getting your name changed for all of history from "the Bastard" to "the Conqueror" is at least one way to treat an inferiority complex.)

William did not replace the *Witenagemot*.[2] Rather, he rolled it into the *Curia Regis* but allowed the Anglo-Saxons to keep their laws, swearing upon his coronation to preserve *"the good ancient laws of the Anglo-Saxon kings."*[3]

William claimed his advisers were like the old *Witenagemot,* but in reality they were just a rubber stamp. He almost immediately sent his sheriffs to collect all the revenue they could get their hands on.

William brought to England feudalism: a system of social organization where everyone is a tenant to someone else, with the king being the ultimate landlord. William, however, accepted the concept that the king was *"first among equals" (primus inter pares)* among the barons.[4]

In this new mix of Anglo-Saxons, and Normans, the king became a unifying source of justice for both.[5] As time went on, more and more subjects would seek redress and justice from the king's

1. The Bayeux Tapestry depicting the Battle of Hastings.

2. Under the Anglo-Saxons, the *witan* elected, more or less, the king. When the *witan* "elected" William, it turned out to be its last act. Lovell at 11.

3. Kynell at 36; Van Caenegem at 12; Baker at 12.

4. Lovell at 53, 60 to 61.

5. Van Caenegem at 18.
   This process began under the Anglo-Saxons, who believed that if *"the law was too heavy"* the king could give relief. Pound, Development of Guarantees, at 52.

6. In ancient Rome, a *"curia"* was a tribe or clan and came to mean the tribe's meeting place. The *Curia Romana*, or just the *Curia*, was the highest ecclesiastical court with jurisdiction over Europe, including England. *See* George Jarvis Thompson, *The Development of the Anglo-American Judicial System*, 17 Cornell L.Q. 395, 399 (1932) (hereafter Thompson III). It is still the government of the Vatican State.

7. Baker at 17. Thompson I at 18 n.49 (citing Sir William S. Holdsworth, History of English Law 32 (3d ed.1922)) (noting that the *Curia Regis* was a feudal institution with membership based on land tenure, which the *Witenagemot* was not).
   Over two centuries later, Edward I saw an advantage of bringing the new middle class into the *Curia Regis*. He called the Great Curiae in 1295 and 1305, which included many "common" knights and middle class. This was the beginning of Britain's House of Commons. Thompson I at 20. Edward I's *Curia Regis* moved from being just the king's advisers to the core of the later House of Lords. Lovell at 132. For this reason his portrait hangs in the U.S. Congress.
   Edward I was the king in the movie Braveheart (Paramount Pictures 1995), played by Patrick McGoohan.

House of Commons

EDWARD I·

Edward I in U.S. House

"Norman" courts, rather than from the church, the local lord, or the old *shire moots*.

THE NORMAN COURTS

Norman courts start with the *Curia Regis,* or the King's Court.[6] William the Conqueror's successors developed the *Curia Regis* as a government institution.[7] Indeed, for centuries the entire government of England consisted of the "king in council," with authority delegated from him.[8]

With the many courts that existed in England (we today call these "forums"), church courts, manor courts, Anglo-Saxon *shire* and *hundreds* courts, the king's justice was sometimes hard to get.[9] This was especially true because his justice and court originally traveled with him.

Slowly, though, the idea that a court was something independent of the direct person of the king started to appear.

Although the *Curia Regis* would travel with the king over his dominions for centuries, William the Conqueror's son, King William Rufus, made Westminster Hall in London its center.[10] Thus a place existed where the courts and the common law would develop. Later, King Henry I started delegating judges to go to counties to hear pleas as if they were the king.[11] These judges were eventually called "*justiciae*" or "*justiciarius.*"[12]

---

8. Thompson I at 22. The judicial function of Parliament's House of Lords came from this part of the *Curia Regis*. Until the Constitutional Reform Act of 2005 and the new Supreme Court of the United Kingdom, the House of Lords was the U.K.'s court of last resort and the precursor of the U.S. Supreme Court. Historically, the House of Lords also functioned as a court of first instance for the trials of peers and for impeachment cases. This is the precedent for the American system where the Senate sits as a court for impeachment trials. Technically, the Lords sit as "the king in Council in Parliament," harkening back to the old role of the *Curia Regis* as being directly from the king's person. *See generally* Thompson III at 432 ("*[Lords] are vested with the entire judicial function of the High Court of Parliament . . .*"). *See also* FREDERICK G. KEMPIN, JR., HISTORICAL INTRODUCTION TO ANGLO-AMERICAN LAW 42 (3d ed. 1990).

9. The word "forum" comes from Roman trials. POUND at 44. Roman trials, *in judicio*, originally happened in the marketplace of Rome, called the "*forum*," which later became the place of government and judicial proceedings. This is why we still call a court a forum to resolve legal questions, though today the statement tends to refer to jurisdiction or venue as in the statement, "this court is not the correct forum for this issue." Forum is also related to the Latin "*foris*" meaning "out of doors," which is where we get "forensic" as well as "forest." Later, Roman trials moved indoors to a large public building called a "*basilica*." After the Roman Empire became Christian, the word "basilica" referred to a large and/or important church with special ceremonial status from the pope. Saint Peter's in Rome, for instance, is a basilica and not the cathedral of Rome.

A FUNNY THING HAPPENED ON THE WAY TO THE FORUM (United Artists 1966) starring Zero Mostel, from the stage musical with lyrics by Stephen Sondheim, is a comedic farce supposedly inspired by on the ancient Roman playwright Plautus. It is about Pseudolus, a bawdy slave who tries to win his freedom by helping his young master woo the girl next door.

Plautus (Titus Maccius Plautus (c. 254 to 184 BC))

Ruins of the Roman Forum

10. BAKER at 37; Thompson I at 19.

William Rufus (William II) was William the Conqueror's second son. The first son, Robert, got Normandy, the more valuable of dad's possessions. Henry, the next son, got squat from dad but by being smart and ruthless ended up with the whole realm. ANTONIA FRASER, THE LIVES OF THE KINGS AND QUEENS OF ENGLAND 27 to 31 (1975).

William Rufus (William II)   Henry I

11. VAN CAENEGEM at 20. These were "*curiales*" sent on "*eyres*," "*itinera*" or journeys. *Eyres* is the root of our modern word "itinerary." BAKER at 16 n.15.

12. BAKER at 15. This gives us our modern title "justice," usually for the judges on a state or federal supreme court.

THE KING'S JUDGES

These traveling justices expanded the king's "court."

Although these justices had only the power the king delegated to them, for the first time a "court" became something more than attached to a person, as in "the king's court" where

he "held court." (This could also be a bishop or baron's court.)[1] With the judges having the king's delegated authority to "hold court," the word "court" broadened to encompass our modern notion of a separate place for resolving legal disputes.

In 1166, a century after the Norman Conquest,

King Henry II, William's great grandson, periodically sent *Curia Regis* judges to every county, taking over much of the work of the old Anglo-Saxon courts.[2] These judges had the king's commission under the great seal to supervise the justice system. Their job was to conduct an early form of investigative inquest called

---

1. Lovell at 88.

2. In 1166, Henry II by statute transferred the jurisdiction from the shire courts to the king's courts. From 1154 to 1189, the shire courts also lost jurisdiction over land disputes. Kempin at 25.

3. Baker at 17.
The word *"oyer"* ("to hear") is related to the word *"oyez"* (pronounced "O, yez" and meaning *"hear ye"*; Black's at 997). Oyez is the pronouncement many modern court bailiffs still use to commence a session such as the U.S. Supreme Court: "Oyez!

Oyez! Oyez! All persons having business before the Honorable, the Supreme Court of the United States, are admonished to draw near and give their attention, for the Court is now sitting. God save the United States and this Honorable Court!" "Oyez" is Law French, a form of Norman French that evolved over centuries in the English law courts. Town criers traditionally yelled "Oyez" to attract attention before a proclamation.

4. Baker at 18; Thompson I at 24; Roger D. Groot, *The Jury in Private Criminal Prosecutions Before 1215*, 27 Am. J. Legal Hist. 113, 114

(1983). The justices of the U.S. Supreme Court used to ride circuit and still have individual responsibility over the circuit courts of appeal. *See* David R. Stras, *Why Supreme Court Justices Should Ride Circuit Again*, 91 Minn. L. Rev. 1710, 1711 (2007) (arguing that having justices return to circuit riding would help keep justices in tune with the country and help citizens know the court).

An assize judge riding circuit

5. Thompson I at 25. The assize replaced the ancient *eyres*. The term "assize" comes from the Old French *"assises"* or "sessions" and is still the name of criminal courts in several countries, e.g., France, Belgium, and Italy. This is the source of the modern phrase, *"the court is now in session." See* Webster's at 612.

6. Danziger & Gillingham at 179; Baker at 13. Later, *Magna Carta* stated *"common pleas should not follow the king but should be held in some central place." Id.* at 19 (citing *Magna Carta* 1215, cl. 17). *See also* A.E. Dick Howard, Magna Carta: Text and Commentary 12 (1964). Westminster Hall continued

Westminster Hall on the first day of term, 1797
for centuries housing, at various times, the Courts of Chancery, Common Pleas, King's Bench, and Exchequer. Baker at 37.

"oyer and terminer" ("to hear and determine") or to try prisoners already charged with crimes, called *"gaol [jail] dilivery."*[3]

King Henry II's court was "the bench" and eventually became the Court of Common Pleas. Judges of this central court in Westminster had responsibility for a circuit.[4] When the judges went out on circuit, they held an "assize."[5] They applied the same law and returned to Westminster to compare notes. Thus Henry II gets credit for starting the "common law."[6]

Forget our modern notion of judicial independence.

Justices in medieval England were the king's men, well paid for implementing the king's justice.[7] Because any modern idea of police or prosecutors was centuries away,[8] these justices were, in part, de facto prosecutors and not the neutral referees we envision today.[9]

7. J.G. BELLAMY, THE CRIMINAL TRIAL IN LATER MEDIEVAL ENGLAND: FELONY BEFORE THE COURTS FROM EDWARD I TO THE SIXTEENTH CENTURY 10 to 11 (1998); KEMPIN at 88 to 91; LOVELL at 110.

Not until the Act of Settlement of 1701 were the king's justices guaranteed secure salaries and life tenure. KEMPIN at 91 to 93; George Fisher, *The Jury's Rise as Lie Detector*, 107 YALE L.J. 575, 617 (1997). The U.S. Constitution protects judges in this regard at Article III, Section 1: *"The Judges, both of the supreme and inferior Courts, shall hold their Offices during good Behavior, and shall, at stated Times, receive for their Services a Compensation which shall not be diminished during their Continuance in Office."*

9. Forget *Law & Order*, where every program begins: *"In the criminal justice system, the people are represented by two separate yet equally important groups: the police, who investigate crime, and the district attorneys, who prosecute the offenders. These are their stories."*
At this time there was no "criminal justice system," much less police or "district attorneys." *Law & Order* (NBC, from 1990 to 2010).

8. But who knows what we think of as a judge after *Rowan & Martin's Laugh-In* classic skit with Flip Wilson, *"Here come da judge."* Originally, British comic Roddy Maude-Roxby played a stuffy magistrate with black robe and powdered wig. The "judge" sketch would feature an unfortunate defendant brought before the court and guest star Flip Wilson introduced the sketch with *"Here come da judge!"* The catchphrase came from nightclub comedian Pigmeat Markham who later played the judge on the show. Later, Sammy Davis, Jr., donned the judicial robe and wig, adding such lines to the skit as *"If your lawyer's sleepin', better give him a nudge! Everybody look alive, 'cause here come da judge! Here come da judge!"*

Sammy Davis, Jr.

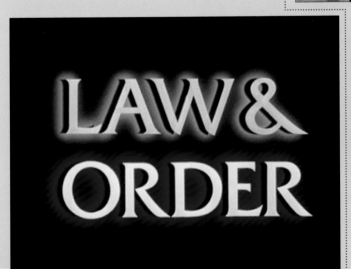

Rowan & Martin's Laugh-In (NBC, from January 22, 1968 to May 14, 1973) was an American sketch comedy television program that ran for 140 episodes. Comedians Dan Rowan and Dick Martin hosted it.

HENRY II GETS TOUGH ON CRIME!

Henry II also decided it was time to launch a "tough on crime" campaign.[1] The fact that getting tough on crime increased his power and revenues probably had nothing to do with it!

The nature of justice was changing. Since Anglo-Saxon times, justice had been a private matter but now was becoming a public concern. This was a slow process, spanning the reigns of several monarchs.[2] But the trend had begun, and Henry II played to it.

Getting tough on crime in twelfth century England meant challenging the church's jurisdiction. Before the Norman Conquest, England had no separate ecclesiastical courts or independent ecclesiastical law. The Norman kings created a dual system of courts and law.[3] Thus, in criminal matters, the church had a big chunk of jurisdiction that Henry II thought should be his.

Most of the early judges were clerics of one kind or another because generally only clerics could read or write.[4] Henry II began to change this. In 1179, he sent out twenty-one justices, most of whom were not churchmen and thus loyal only to him.[5]

Ten years later, in 1189, Henry introduced the Grand Assize, giving precedence to the king's courts over the local baronial courts. Thus the common law could develop into a universal system throughout the kingdom. Theoretically, under this system no one was above the law, not even the king.[6]

Motivating Henry was that justice was a moneymaker; enforcing criminal law meant

---

1. Lovell at 101 (noting that under Henry II crime became a government matter). Henry was a busy guy. In addition to justice reform, he started the Plantagenet (aka Angevin) dynasty by becoming king of England, being duke of Normandy and count of Anjou, and marrying Eleanor of Aquitaine (by accounts a hottie with a big chunk of land). By his death, his dominions looked like the map shown here, and his relationship with Eleanor was scintillating enough for a movie, The Lion in Winter (Universal Pictures 1968).

3. Levy at 43. This was part of William the Conqueror's deal for the pope's blessing his English invasion. Under the Anglo-Saxons, bishops sat as judges. John H. Wigmore, Evidence in Trials at Common Law § 2250, 270 (McNaughton ed. 1961). For the split of king's and church courts, see Thompson III at 395 to 965, 400 to 02. See also Charles Donahue, Jr., Ius Commune, Canon Law, and Common Law in England, 66 Tul. L. Rev. 1745 (1992). See also **Chapter 1: Of Dogma and Desire: Saying What You Believe about the First Amendment.**

The Ghent Altarpiece: The Just Judges (1427 to 30), showing Continental judges riding circuit

2. See generally Daniel Klerman, Was the Jury Ever Self-Informing? 77 S. Cal. L. Rev. 123, 130 to 32 and n.44 (2003 to 04), citing J.G. Bellamy, The Criminal Trial in Later Medieval England 103 (1998). In Europe getting tough on crime spurred the Inquisition. Richard M. Fraher, The Theoretical Justification for the New Criminal Law of the High Middle Ages: "Rei Publicae Interest, Ne Crimina Remaneant Impunita," 1984 U. Ill. L. Rev. 577 (1984). All of this was part of criminal law becoming a public concern rather than a private matter. See also Laura Ikins Stern, Inquisition Procedure and Crime in Early Fifteenth-Century Florence, 8 Law & Hist. Rev. 297 (1990).

4. Kempin at 89.

5. Danziger & Gillingham at 179.
Regarding the power of early judges in Europe and England, see Walter Ullmann, Medieval Principles of Evidence, 62 Law Q. Rev. 77 (1946).

6. Kynellat 52, 54.

fees, fines, and revenues for the enforcer. The king's judges collected more than enough revenue to both pay for themselves and to dump a lot into the king's coffers. Getting tough on crime was profitable, refuting the maxim that "crime doesn't pay"—it did for the king![7]

Regarding the church, Henry II's actions planted the seeds of a power struggle that was to play out over centuries.[8] This struggle involved the legal questions of what we today would call "subject matter jurisdiction" and "forum shopping."[9] As Henry knew, and modern lawyers know, the outcome of a case often depended on who heard it—the king, the archbishop, or the local baron.[10]

Henry's grant of primacy for the royal courts over the church courts stymied the growth of inquisitorial procedures in England. Thus Henry gets credit for England's developing the common law rather than inquisitorial procedure.

But English law did not develop independently from the rest of Europe. Both the church's and continental Europe's inquisitorial procedures influenced the common law.

The Inquisition always gets a bad rap. But the Latin "inquisito" actually translates as either "inquest" or the pejorative "inquisition." Inquisito originally meant nothing more than a judicial inquiry based upon a report.[11] In fact, many procedural protections now part of the common law actually came from the church's Inquisition—for example, the concept that a person is innocent until proven guilty.[12]

---

7. See BAKER at 502 to 03.

For example, coming back from the Third Crusade, King Richard the Lionheart was captured in Germany and held for ransom. His brother, John (later King John), used the law courts to raise the ransom. See KYNELL at 69.

In another example, justices from 1218 to 1219 raised £4,000 for King Edward I, who needed "great treasure" for the war on Scotland and raised it by "causing justice to be done on malefactors." Quoted in BAKER at 14. Thus, because justice was a moneymaker, Patrick McGoohan's Edward I got to beat up on Mel Gibson's William Wallace in BRAVEHEART.

8. During most of the medieval period, if a suspect made it to the church altar, he received sanctuary and a secular officer could not arrest him. KIRALFY at 363 to 64; BAKER at 512 to 13. Regarding "criminous clerks" and Henry II's struggle with Thomas Becket, see KYNELL at 56 to 58.

9. See generally Thompson III at 395 to 411 (the ecclesiastical courts); KIRALFY at 16 to 17; KEMPIN at 42.

Earliest known portrayal of Becket's murder

10. Henry II's assertion of royal jurisdiction brought him to his fateful conflict with Archbishop Thomas Becket. See **Chapter 1: Of Dogma and Desire: Saying What You Believe about the First Amendment.** The English church/state power struggle did not resolve itself until

Henry VIII effectively made himself Pope of England. See **Chapter 1: Of Dogma and Desire: Saying What You Believe about the First Amendment.**

King Henry VIII

11. Walter Ullmann, Some Medieval Principles of Criminal Procedure, in JURISPRUDENCE IN THE MIDDLE AGES 1 (1980).

12. Kenneth Pennington, Innocent until Proven Guilty: The Origins of a Legal Maxim cited in PATRICIA M. DUGAN, THE PENAL PROCESS AND THE PROTECTION OF RIGHTS IN CANON LAW (2005); see also Walter Ullmann, The Defense of the Accused in the Medieval Inquisition, 481, 486 in LAW AND JURISDICTION IN THE MIDDLE AGES (George Garnett ed., 1988). See the discussion of the presumption of innocence later in this chapter.

The church also provided the concept that a person must intend to commit a crime before the act is a crime (i.e., a sin).[1] The common law eventually incorporated this as *mens rea,* or mental state.[2] This is why a child or an insane person who is unable to intend to commit a crime is innocent. This was a drastic change from the law before, which had provided that if a person was killed, it did not matter whether it was an accident or murder.[3]

Even in heresy trials, where the church relaxed many procedural protections,[4] the accused still had an absolute right to his own advocate. The advocate was under oath to defend the accused fully under the law and to make any legal "exceptions" (i.e., objections).[5] If the accused could not pay for his own lawyer, canon law allowed appointed counsel an honorarium from public funds.

Thus, under church law, a defendant would not have had to fight on his own.[6] European criminal procedure, based in the *inquisito,* allowed for these procedural protections, including

---

1. Anselm, Archbishop of Canterbury in the 1090s wrote: "*Had they known it, they would never have crucified the Lord . . . a sin knowingly committed and a sin done ignorantly are so different that an evil . . . may be pardonable when done in ignorance.*" KADRI at 36 to 37.

2. For a general discussion of *mens rea* history, see Martin R. Gardner, *The* Mens Rea *Enigma: Observations on the Role of Motive in the Criminal Law Past and Present,* 1993 UTAH L. REV. 635.

3. Trial of Animals. Without a *mens rea* requirement, why not make an animal responsible for a criminal act? Even the Greeks prosecuted nonhuman killers such as dogs. PLATO, LAWS bk. IX (873D to 874A), *cited in* SADAKAT KADRI, THE TRIAL: A HISTORY, FROM SOCRATES TO O.J. SIMPSON 9, 146 to 77 (2005). During medieval times, animals got the right to confront their accusers and due process. Often this involved cases of sex with animals, i.e., buggery. Kadri recounts the interesting case of a Jacques Ferron in Vanvres, France, as late as 1750. The villagers came to court to testify as to the defendant's good character. Unfortunately for Ferron it was for the donkey, and he burned. *Id.* at 149 to 50. See a movie entitled THE ADVOCATE (European title: THE HOUR OF THE PIG) (1993) regarding the trial of a pig accused of killing a boy, set in fifteenth century France. Colin Firth represents the pig but more is involved than just the swine's culpability.

Execution of a sow

Underlying much of this was belief in witchcraft, because witches could always turn into animals. *See* **Chapter 7: Trial by Jury or ... by God!** (briefly discussing witch trials). As for inanimate objects that kill, such as an axe, the law conceived of the "deodand" ("gift of God"). KADRI at 171. The object was forfeited to the king for distribution to the poor.

4. See **Chapter 5: From Testicles to *Dragnet*: How the Fifth Amendment Protects *All* of Us** for more on heresy trials.

5. Ullmann, *The Defense of the Accused,* at 482 to 83. The advocate did, however, have to promise to "desert" the cause as soon as he felt his position was irreconcilable with justice.

6. Counsel for the Defense by Honoré Daumier (c. 1860).

7. But in the end, even a lawyer is on his own, trial as Hamlet noted when looking at a lawyer's skull:

"*There's another: why may he be the skull of a lawyer? Where be his quiddits now, his quillets, his cases, his tenures, and his tricks? Why does he suffer this rude knave now to knock him about the sconce with a dirty shovel, and will not tell him of his action of battery?*" WILLIAM SHAKESPERE, HAMLET, act V, sc. 1.

"*Quiddits*" and "*quillets*" refer to hair-splitting arguments and trivial objections and relate to our more modern word "quibble."

A witch with her animals, casting a spell

Edwin Booth playing Hamlet. Booth was the most famous actor of his day but will be remembered as the brother of John Wilkes Booth

the right to a lawyer, centuries before the English common law.[7]

THE KING'S PEACE:

Most people wanted the king's peace, and they were willing to pay for it.

To get a case heard in the king's court, a person had to buy a "writ" (i.e., an order) from the king to his justices, directing them to hear the case, which was a considerable source of royal income.[8] And what the people got for their money were the king's professional judges, an inquest, and a jury of witnesses to find the facts, all backed up with royal muscle.

The people in fact demanded more of the king's peace from Henry II's fourth son, John, in *Magna Carta* Chapter 18. Generally, *Magna Carta* recognizes limits to the king's power, but this clause requires *more* rather than less of the king's power.[9] King John promised to send two justices to each county four times a year to hold assizes (or sessions).[10]

---

8. Thompson I at 22; KIRALFY at 21. For discussion of the writ system, see BAKER at 54. A writ (*"breve"* in Latin and *"brief"* in French) was a thin parchment strip with a letter in the king's name sealed with the tip of the great seal. *Id.* at 57.

10. *"To no one will we sell, to no one will we deny or delay right or justice."* Magna Carta, cl. 31, quoted in DANZIGER & GILLINGHAM at 175; *see also* HOWARD at 15. Five of *Magna Carta's* clauses limit a sheriff's powers (4, 24, 26, 30, and 48).

9. DANZIGER & GILLINGHAM at 176 to 78. BAKER at 20. Historians recognize King John's reign as a near total failure. He succeeded in losing nearly all dad Henry II's empire with the exception of England and the Channel Isles, winning him the nicknames Lackland (*Sans Terre* in French) and Soft Sword. No other English king or queen has since named their son John. For whatever reason, John was the first king to take the title *Rex Angliae* (King of England) instead of *Rex Anglorum* (King of the English). LOVELL at 10 to 11.

King John is the bad guy in the Robin Hood movies, including Claude Rain's depiction in THE ADVENTURES OF ROBIN HOOD (Warner Brothers 1938), with Errol Flynn as Robin. Even Disney's animated ROBIN HOOD (Buena Vista Pictures 1973) picks on King John, having him suck his thumb and cry for *"Mommy"* whenever Robin steals his gold, which is an amusing reference to his mother Eleanor of Aquitaine. He also says *"Mommy always liked Richard best,"* a reference to his brother King Richard the Lionheart who no one would have dared called Soft Sword.

King John had to have had a serious inferiority complex. After all, his dad was the hyperactive, overachieving King Henry

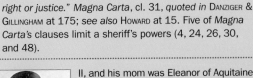
Winston Churchill

II, and his mom was Eleanor of Aquitaine, a ruler in her own right. John was a twerp who couldn't cut it.

But his weakness led to *Magna Carta*. As Winston Churchill wrote, "[w]hen the long tally is added, it will be seen that the British nation and the English-speaking world owe far more to the vices of John than to the labours of virtuous sovereigns." 1 WINSTON CHURCHILL, A HISTORY OF THE ENGLISH-SPEAKING PEOPLES, 190 (1958).

John's mom: Eleanor of Aquitaine

John's dad: Henry II

King John

Richard the Lionheart

King John

Katherine Hepburn and Peter O'Toole sparring as Eleanor and Henry in THE LION IN WINTER

John signs *Magna Carta*

It was "the *king's* peace," rather than just "the peace," because there were originally several "peaces" from which to choose.[1] The church or a local baron or lord offered peace within his own lands. *Magna Carta* shows the early stages of the "king's peace" growing from being one of several "peaces" in England to eventually the only one over the whole realm.

In America today, when a state or the federal government exercises its sovereignty (akin to the power of the sovereign king) to impose penalties under criminal law or civil regulation and uphold law and order, it imposes a type of king's peace. The English,

in fact, still call it the king's (or queen's) peace.

Eventually, the "king's peace" arrived at a point where crime was not just against an individual victim but against the king's peace, *contra pacem regis,* and a personal affront to the sovereign. The English still caption a criminal case as *Rex (Regina) v. The Accused,* which in republics like the United States became *State, People,* or *Commonwealth v. The Accused.*[2]

If you had the king's writ, you could travel the realm and not be subject to anyone else's jurisdiction. School children, when playing a game, still shout for time out with "*Pax*" in England

or "*King's X*" in America, reflecting this older notion.[3]

BRINGING THE KING'S PEACE WITH THE KING'S COURTS

Over time the king's courts expanded. As mentioned, a complete system of ecclesiastical courts already existed with very broad jurisdiction and ultimate appeal to Rome.[4] Courts also developed around the king's "*justiciar.*" Because the early Norman kings were often in France, the *justiciar* became a viceroy in the king's stead. As the kings spent more time in England—especially after John lost most of France—the *justiciar* became less necessary. After 1234

---

1. Justices of the peace used to be referred to as "justice of peace." Pollock at 184.

2. LOVELL at 12; BAKER at 60.

3. LOVELL at 12. Modern English statute citation still recalls the king's role in establishing law and order through his peace. For example, the English statute "I Eliz. II, cap.3"

Elizabeth II presiding over the queen's peace

indicates the third law to receive royal assent during the first year of Queen Elizabeth II. *Id.* at 140.

4. Church courts had different procedures than the common-law courts with sworn testimony, proof by paper (sworn depositions), and pleadings. LOVELL at 95.

The "*Roman Rota*" often heard these cases and exists today. Since the Middle Ages the case would go

to "auditors" who would hear the evidence (Latin "*audire,*" "to hear or listen". The "*rota*" referred to the round table (Latin "*rota*") or the round room where they sat. Auditor, THE CATHOLIC ENCYCLOPEDIA, http://www.newadvent.org/cathen/02070c.htm (last visited May 15, 2007). *See also* BAKER at 126 to 27. The Roman Catholic Church's legal system is the oldest and one of the most advanced still in use today. In 1534 England abolished appeals to Rome. *Id.* at 130.

5. BAKER at 15. Hugh le Despenser was a greedy man who wormed his way into Edward II's affections through a probable homosexual relationship. This did not sit well with Edward II's wife, Isabella, who eventually deposed Edward II. In a

Execution of **Hugh Le Despenser**

variation of the normal execution of traitors by hanging, drawing, and quartering, Hugh also had his penis and testicles cut off and burnt in front of him as punishment for his relationship with Edward.

Queen Isabella (also known as the She-Wolf of France) was by accounts as good looking as Sophie Marceau, who played her in BRAVEHEART. *See* ALISON WEIR, QUEEN ISABELLA (2005).

6. See **Chapter 1: Of Dogma and Desire: Saying What You Believe about the First Amendment** regarding the office of chancellor.

justiciars were not regularly appointed and the last one, Hugh le Despenser, had a very bad end in 1265.[5]

With the abolition of the office of *justiciar,* much of his governing powers passed to the "chancellor," who became second to the monarch in dignity, power, and influence.[6] As for the *justiciar's* judicial powers, they were divided among what became the **Courts of Chancellery** and the three common-law courts of **Common Pleas, King's (or Queen's) Bench**, and **Exchequer**.

The **Courts of Chancellery** grew up around the chancellor, developing and applying the law of equity, often the great rival of the common law.[7] In chancellery court, if justice was on your side, you would win regardless of legal formalities, and the motto was "*nullus recedat a curia cancellariae sine remedio*" ("no one should leave the Chancery in despair").[8]

The **Court of Common Pleas** was the second oldest common-law court (after Exchequer), established during the late twelfth century. It generally dealt with civil cases between private parties. *Magna Carta* provided that there should be a court,the Common Bench (later the Court of Common Pleas) that met in a fixed place, Westminster Hall in London.[9]

The **Court of King's Bench** grew out of the king's court or *Curia Regis* and was not originally a law court but the center of the king's administration. Generally, its cases were criminal and civil cases where the government (i.e., the king) had an interest. It also supervised jurisdiction of all the courts by issuing writs of error, *mandamus,* and *certiorari.*[10]

The **Court of Exchequer** had by 1190 exercised a judicial role, with judges known as **barons**. Originally, this court dealt with actions by the crown for monies owed to it and actions by private citizens regarding financial matters with the king.[11]

Isabella and a young Edward III

7. Equity according to Aristotle was a way to correct general laws that could not cover every situation. It required decisions based on the law's intent rather than its wording. BAKER, at 106, *citing* ARISTOTLE, ETHICA NICOMACHEA, bk. 10 (W. David Ross trans., (Oxford Univ. Press, 1925).

8. BAKER at 102. Although equity grew to rival the common law, the Court of Chancellery worked in conjunction with the King's Bench. *Id.* at 101. Chancellery offered swift and inexpensive justice, especially for the poor, *id.* at 104, as opposed to the common-law courts that used an inflexible system of writs to do business. Writs were orders to the king's officials to take action. They were expensive and claims would fail just because a writ was incorrect. *See* George Jarvis Thompson, *The Development of the Anglo-American Judicial System*, 203, 209, *et seq.* (1932) (hereafter Thompson II); KEMPIN at 37 to 40. The king's chancellor could provide relief to injustice by issuing an injunction to stop the writ's execution. *See* Justin C. Barnes, *Lessons from England's "Great Guardian of Liberty": A Comparative Study of English and American Civil Juries*, 3 U. ST. THOMAS L. J. 345, 352 to 354 (2005). The Court of Chancery emerged soon after Edward I's death in 1307. LOVELL at 147.

9. *See* Thompson I at 36 to 38; KEMPIN at 33; BAKER at 44 to 47.

10. *See* Thompson I; at 38 to 41, KEMPIN at 34 to 35; G.R. ELTON, THE TUDOR CONSTITUTION (2d ed. 1982). *See also* BAKER at 41 to 44, 49 to 50.

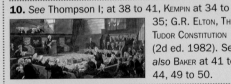

11. *See* Thompson I at 35; BAKER at 47 to 49. Over time through legal fictions the Exchequer court's jurisdiction grew until, by 1290, it had become a regular common-law court on a par with King's Bench and Common Pleas. The Exchequer court got its name from the large table with squares. In ages before calculators and computers, or before Europe knew of the Chinese abacus, the table kept accounts straight by markers placed on the table to represent sums.

As mentioned in **Chapter 3: The Third Amendment: Don't Count It Out Yet!**, our term for "checks" as well as the game checkers and the terminology of chess ("check" and "checkmate") refer to the same type of table. BAKER at 18 and n.22; KEMPIN at 35 to 36. It was the Court of Exchequer that issued the writs of assistants that started the Boston writs cases, the precursor to the Fourth Amendment. *See* **Chapter 4: Molasses and the Sticky Origins of the Fourth Amendment.**

The jurisdiction between these courts waxed and waned over the centuries.[1] And there were other courts as well, exercising jurisdiction over subject matter or place.[2]

TUDOR AND STUART TRIALS

A defendant in Tudor England had the deck stacked against him.[3]

Trials during this time were unfair for the defendant because criminal procedure had changed greatly from the early system where jurors were the witnesses. The older system assured a form of rough community justice and balance. But this system had passed into history by Tudor times, and other procedural protections for the defendant had not yet developed.[4]

A defendant had no counsel, no evidence rules, no right to compel witnesses, and no right to see the indictment beforehand. The prosecution could interrogate him, sometimes under torture, because he had no protection against self-incrimination. The prosecution could present its case through summoned witnesses under oath.[5] Or, as we will see in the next section, the prosecution could present statements without having to even produce the witness because the defendant had no right to confront his accusers.

Although the defendant had a public trial by jury,[6] he was not informed of the charges against him until the day of

---

1. For a description of the original jurisdiction of the courts, see Baker at 38. In 1880, the various courts were reorganized with Common Pleas, the King's (then the Queen's) Bench, and Chancellery combined into the High Court of Justice. The jurisdiction of American courts has from the start included all the common-law subjects as well as equity. See Thompson I at 42. Regarding early colonial courts, see Kempin at 44 to 47. Today most U.S. courts are courts of law and equity. See Fed. R. Civ. P. 2 (1938).

Four illuminations on vellum from around 1460 showing the four courts at Westminster Hall—Chancery, Common Pleas, King's Bench, and Exchequer. They are part of the Inner Temple Library's collections and provide the earliest known depictions of the English courts and court dress. Inner Temple Library, http://www.innertemplelibrary.org.uk/welcome.htm (last visited May 15, 2007).

Court of Chancellery

Court of King's Bench

Court of Common Pleas   Court of Exchequer

As one scholar has stated, "[t]he most distinctive feature of the emergent criminal trial in Tudor England (1485 to 1603) was the imbalance of advantage between the state and the accused." Peter Westen, *The Compulsory Process Clause*, 73 Mich. L. Rev. 71, 81 (1974).

2. Other courts included Admiralty, Thompson III at 414, and the Courts of the Lord High Constable and Earl Marshal of England, *id.* at 421 to 24 (the latter was charged with marshalling the king's forces and is where we get the modern term "court marshal," which also is spelled "court-martial," showing the association with the military). See *also* Baker at 122 to 24. There were also the king's prerogative courts such as the Star Chamber and the High Commission. See Thompson II at 203 to 29; Kempin at 40 to 41; Baker at 117 to 19. The abuses in these courts helped bring about the English Revolution and their abolition. Thompson II at 240 to 43; Kempin at 75. Finally, the House of Lords, as part of the High Court of Parliament, is the precursor to the U.S. Supreme Court. Thompson III at 432; Kempin at 42.

3. The Tudors: Henry VII, Henry VIII, Edward VI

Mary, and Elizabeth

trial. He thus had no time or right to collect his own evidence or witnesses.

A defendant could make a statement in his defense but not under oath.[7] He lived or died depending on what he said. An "altercation" is how Sir Thomas Smith, a scholar and official of Queen Elizabeth I, described the trial.[8]

The altercation began as soon as the defendant pleaded not guilty and the sheriff called the local jury. Although the defendant could challenge a juror if he had cause, this rarely happened. The jury was sworn and began to hear evidence, usually from a justice of the peace who read to the court and jury his written record of the defendant's and witnesses' statements. If there were live witnesses, only the judge interrogated them.[9]

After this altercation, the judge told the jury what he thought of the evidence and how they should vote. The jury would probably hear several cases and then deliberate. The whole trial lasted less than an hour; a model of brevity and efficiency. To top it off, there was no appeal—they could convict and hang you the same day.

But criminal procedure was starting to change, and men were fighting for the right to defend themselves.[10] Sir Walter Raleigh argued for the right to confront his accuser. He didn't get it, but because of him, we do.

---

4. "*In short, while changes were under way that would soon transform the criminal trial into a truly adversary proceeding, criminal trials in the sixteenth century were primarily one-sided inquests into the truth of the prosecution's charges.*" Westen at 82.

5. Westen at 82.

6. Westen at 82.

7. Westen at 84 argues convincingly that "*the rule arose at a time when the jurors themselves were considered the sole 'witnesses' to the facts, and simply failed to adjust to reflect the new role of the jury as a trier of evidence presented by others.*"

9. See Landsman, *Contentious Spirit*, at 513 to 14, describing judicial interrogation from the inquisitorial model. Tudor and Stuart trials were "*nasty, brutish, and essentially short.*" *Id.* at 498 (quoting J. S. Cockburn, A History of the English Assizes 1558 to 1714, at 109 (1972)).

10. Sir Nicholas Throckmorton's treason trial of 1554 lasted one day from 7:00 A.M. to 5:00 P.M. *See generally* P.R. Glazebrook, *The Making of English Criminal Law: The Reign of Mary Tudor*, 1977 Crim. L. Rev. 582, 586 to 88. He had no lawyer, no time to prepare, no right to call witnesses. The judges and prosecution engaged in "*one continuous onslaught on the defendant.*" *Id.* at 587; Fisher at 603. But he stood his ground, defended himself well, and the jury acquitted him. The judges were so angry they sent the jurors to prison! (Judges could do this until 1670.) The Supreme Court referred to Throckmorton in *Miranda v. Arizona*, 384 U.S. 436, 443 (1966). Throckmorton was imprisoned, released, and fled to France but by 1557 was back in favor with Queen Mary and later rose rapidly in the service of Queen Elizabeth. His daughter Elizabeth married Sir Walter Raleigh. London's Throgmorton Street is named for him.

8. Sir Thomas Smith (1513 to 77), an English scholar and diplomat, was one of Elizabeth's most trusted Protestant counselors, appointed in 1572 as chancellor of the Order of the Garter and a secretary of state. Smith's book, *De Republica Anglorum—the Manner of Government or Policie of the Realme of England,* was written between 1562 and 1565, and published in 1583. *See* http://www.constitution.org/eng/repang.htm (last visited May 31, 2007). *See* Stephan Landsman, *The Rise of the Contentious Spirit: Adversary Procedure in Eighteenth Century England,* 75 Cornell L. Rev. 497, 504 to 05 (1990) (summarizing Smith's description).

The most prolific modern scholar on this subject, John Langbein, coined the phrase "*the accused speaks*" model of trial, which describes the main aspect of trial—the defendant's statement. *See, e.g.,* John Langbein, *The Criminal Trial before the Lawyers,* 45 U. Chi. L. Rev. 263 (1978) I, however, have chosen to use Smith's phrase of the "*altercation*" trial because it better describes the courtroom dynamic and because Smith wrote before Langbein.

SIR WALTER RALEIGH AND THE HISTORY OF THE CONFRONTATION CLAUSE

The right to confront your accusers is over two thousand years old, coming

"to us on faded parchment, . . . with a lineage that traces back to the beginnings of Western legal culture."[1]

As William Shakespeare knew, it is dramatic:

King Richard: "*Then call them to our presence, face to face and frowning brow to brow, ourselves will hear the accuser and the accused freely speak.*"[2]

The essence of cross-examination is the right to confront any witness. Thus, from Vinny to Kaffee, it's a Hollywood mainstay![3]

As we will see, despite history and Shakespeare, Sir Walter Raleigh in 1603 didn't get the right to confront.[4]

1. *Coy v. Iowa*, 487 U. S. 1012, 1015 (1988). See Fred O. Smith, Jr., *Crawford's Aftershock: Aligning the Regulation of Nontestimonial Hearsay with the History and Purposes of the Confrontation Clause*, 60 STAN. L. REV. 1497, 1506 (2008).

2. WILLIAM SHAKESPEARE, RICHARD II, act 1, sc. 1, *quoted in Coy* 487 U.S. at 1014. See also DANIEL J. KORNSTEIN, KILL ALL THE LAWYERS?: SHAKESPEARE'S LEGAL APPEAL 194 (1994) (citing RICHARD II at act 1, sc. 1, ll. 15 to 17); *see also* Graham at 213 (citing *Richard II* and *Much Ado About Nothing*).

4. *Crawford v. Washington*, 541 U.S. 36, 44 to 45 (2004) provides a standard history. *But see* Thomas Davis, *What Did the Framers Know, and When Did They Know It? Fictional Originalism in Crawford v. Washington*, 71 BROOK. L. REV. 105 (2005); Robert Kry, *Confrontation under the Marian Statutes: A Response to Professor Davies*, 72 BROOK. L. REV. 493 (2007).
Regarding the leading historical theories on the Confrontation Clause, see Daniel Shaviro, *The Confrontation Clause Today in Light of Its Common Law Background*, 26 VAL. U. L. REV. 337 (1991).

Richard II

3. Movies like MY COUSIN VINNY and A FEW GOOD MEN depend on the dramatic value of confrontation through cross-examination.

MY COUSIN VINNY (20th Century Fox 1992) Image by Helen Koop

A FEW GOOD MEN (Columbia Pictures 1992) Image by Helen Koop

Confronting with the Greeks and Romans:

Socrates argued during his 499 BC trial about the lack of confrontation:

"And the hardest of all, I do not know and cannot tell the names of my accusers . . . for I cannot have them up here, and cross-examine them; and therefore I must simply fight with shadows in my own defense, and argue when there is no one who answers."[5]

Socrates's "shadow boxing" in his own defense remains one of the best metaphors for the right to confront your accusers.

Although "confrontation" is a modern legal term, the concept is old, with Romans requiring proceedings *viva voce* ("live voiced").[6]

The Catholic Church later incorporated the Roman rule in canon law.[7] Indeed, at times the church could be extremely technical about its application.[8] Part of the reason for the church's exactitude, though, was the Bible.

---

5. THE WORKS OF PLATO, *Apology* 60 (Irwin Edman ed., Benjamin Jowett trans., Random House 1956). An Athenian trial consisted of the parties making a speech during which they called and cross-examined witnesses. POUND at 33.

Socrates

6. As the Supreme Court noted: "*[s]imply as a matter of Latin the word "confront" ultimately derives from the prefix "con-" (from "contra" meaning "against" or "opposed") and the noun "frons" (forehead)."* Crawford v. Washington, 541 U.S. 36, 44 to 45 (2004).

Emperor Hadrian   Pope Gregory I

7. Frank R. Herrmann & Brownlow M. Speer, *Facing the Accuser: Ancient and Medieval Precursors of*

the *Confrontation Clause*, 34 VA. J. INT'L. 481, 511 (1994). For example, the Emperor Hadrian while sitting as a judge rejected written testimony against an accused. *Id.* at 489. Justinian's Code later incorporated this rule assuming that the witness will testify before the adverse party. *Id.* at 490 to 93. Pope Gregory I (also known as Pope Gregory the Great) adopted this rule for the Catholic Church, *Id.* at 493–99, which remained the rule until excepted for heresy prosecutions. *Id.* at 535 to 37.

8. The Cadaver Synod. Pope Stephen VI hated his predecessor Pope Formosus so much he put his dead body on trial in February 897 AD. But because Formosus still had the right to confrontation, they unsealed his vault at Saint Peter's and brought his eight-month-old corpse to court. KADRI at 160. They put him in papal robes, condemned him, hacked off the three fingers of his right hand he used for blessings, and had him buried in a potter's field. Grave robbers dug him up but found nothing valuable and threw him into the Tiber River. *Id.* at 160 to 61. Later Stephen was dethroned and strangled in prison, and his successor Theodore II rehabilitated poor Formosus. A monk "miraculously" found the body after a year and a half out of the grave and ten months in the Tiber. His "body" got a new set of papal robes and a third reburial.

Despite the right of confrontation, the church from then on prohibited any future trials of dead bodies.

Pope Formosus and Stephen VII (now Stephen VI) by Laurens (1870)

Confronting in the Bible:
Susanna was a hottie of biblical proportions.[1]

Two old guys saw her in the garden and wanted sex. If she didn't, they would say they saw her commit adultery. (How's that for psychological projection!)[2]

What was she to do?

Susanna stayed virtuous and true, so the scorned elders accused her of adultery.

At trial, the prophet Daniel volunteered as her lawyer and saved her by confronting the accusers:

"Daniel said to them, 'Separate these men and keep them at a distance from each other, and I will examine them.'"

Daniel showed their accusations to be inconsistent.[3]

Because Susanna got a lawyer and the right of confrontation, virtue triumphed and she was acquitted.[4]

As the Susanna story shows, the right of confrontation provided a check to keep oaths and testimony valid, a key biblical theme:

"With his mouth the godless destroys his neighbor, but through knowledge the righteous escape."[5]

The right of confrontation gave Daniel the knowledge to let *"the righteous escape."* As the Ninth Commandment states:

"Thou shalt not bear false witness against thy neighbor."[6]

Indeed,

"the thief is better than a man that is accustomed to lie."[7]

And to guarantee truth, the Bible prescribed questioning and confrontation:

1. *Susanna and the Elders* by Artemisia Gentileschi (1610).
　For a nice account of this story identifying Daniel as an early "public defender," see Andrus at 35 to 41.

4. Virtue triumphed every week for Perry Mason but without the right to confrontation you get no Perry Mason. The key to every case was Perry's (actor Raymond Burr's) incisive cross-examination of the real bad guy (or sometimes gal) who breaks down on the witness stand. Of course, Perry did one better than Daniel and actually got the bad guys to admit guilt on the stand.
　Perry Mason ran on radio from 1943 to 1955 and on television from September 1957 to May 1966. There were later television versions with Raymond Burr reprising the role. The title character is a fictional Los Angeles defense attorney who originally appeared in detective fiction by Erle Stanley Gardner.
　Matlock (NBC, from September 23, 1986, to May 8, 1992) had basically the same confrontation formula as *Perry Mason* but with Andy Griffith providing a homespun quality.

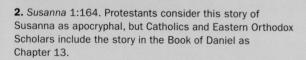

2. *Susanna* 1:164. Protestants consider this story of Susanna as apocryphal, but Catholics and Eastern Orthodox Scholars include the story in the Book of Daniel as Chapter 13.

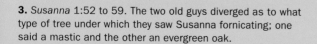

3. *Susanna* 1:52 to 59. The two old guys diverged as to what type of tree under which they saw Susanna fornicating; one said a mastic and the other an evergreen oak.

Raymond Burr

"And the judges shall make diligent inquisition: and, behold, if the witness be a false witness, and hath testified falsely against his brother, then shall ye do unto him, as he had thought to have done unto his brother . . . ."[8]

Jesus had a variation on the confrontation and adultery theme.

Jesus's enemies brought a woman before him accused of adultery.[9] The penalty would have been her death by stoning.[10] The real issue, though, was that they wanted to catch Jesus condoning disobedience to the law by showing compassion. But using the right of confrontation, he avoided the problem with a legal nicety:

"Hath no man condemned thee? Neither do I condemn thee: go and avoid this sin."[11]

Because no one was around to confront, and perhaps implicate himself, Jesus beat his enemies at their own game.[12]

Later Saint Paul stood accused before the Roman governor Festus and demanded his right as a Roman citizen to confront his accusers:

"To whom I answered, that it is not the manner of the Romans for favor to deliver any man to the death before he which is accused, have the accusers before him, and have place to defend himself, concerning the crime."[13]

When King James I charged Sir Walter Raleigh with high treason in 1603, Raleigh could rely on Socrates, the Romans, Susanna, and Saint Paul to demand and plead for the right to confront his accuser.

Daniel, from Michelangelo's Sistine ceiling

5. *Proverbs* 11:9. Regarding oaths in the ancient world, see **Chapter 5: From Testicles to** *Dragnet:* **How the Fifth Amendment Protects** *All* **of Us**

6. *Exodus* 20:16.

7. *Ecclesiastics* 20:25; Ehrlich at 199.

8. *Deuteronomy* 19:18, 19; Ehrlich at 172. For the penalty for false witness, see *Deuteronomy* 19:18.

Old Testament prophet/judge Joel, from the Sistine ceiling

9. *Christ and the Woman Taken in Adultery* **(1621).**

10. *See* **Chapter 8: "***Baby, Don't Be Cruel***": Just What's So Cruel** *and* **Unusual about the Eighth Amendment?**

11. *John* 8:3 to 7.

12. *See* Kenneth Graham, *Confrontation Stories: Raleigh on the Mayflower,* 3 Ohio St. J. Crim. L. 209, 214 (2005) (criticizing Justice Scalia's view of history and arguing that the right to confrontation was not in the common law but in the colonies from the Puritan's reading of the Bible, such as the woman taken in adultery without an accuser).

13. *See Coy v. Iowa,* 487 U.S. 1012 (1988) (quoting this passage from *Acts* 25:16).

Saint-Paul before Governor Festus

Festus was one of Matt Dillon's deputies and a sidekick in the television show *Gunsmoke,* which originated on radio (1952 to 61) and ran on TV from 1955 to 1975.

Confronting with Sir Walter Raleigh: Raleigh was a poet, courtier, explorer,[1] and one of Queen Elizabeth I's favorites.[2] He looked good in a good-looking court. But Elizabeth's successor, James I, didn't like him at all.

In November 1603, James had him tried for treason, charging him with conspiring with Lord Cobham and others on behalf of Spain. The basis of the charge was pure hearsay: a sailor named Dyer testified that *"someone in Lisbon"* told him that James would never be king because Raleigh and Cobham would slit his throat.[3]

At one point in the trial, Raleigh let loose:

"Do you bring the words of these hellish spiders against me? . . . I find not myself touched, scarce named; and the course of proof is strange; if witnesses are to speak by relation to one another, by this means you may have any man's life in a week; and I may be massacred by mere hearsay."[4]

But upon interrogation (and perhaps torture) in the Tower of London, Cobham implicated Raleigh.[5]

Although Cobham later recanted, at Raleigh's trial the prosecution read his statements to the jury. Every man, Raleigh insisted, had the right to confront his accuser.

Cobham, Raleigh logically argued, lied to save himself:

"Cobham is absolutely in the King's mercy; to excuse me cannot avail him; by accusing me he may hope for favour."[6]

Raleigh called for his common-law right to confront his accuser:

"The Proof of the Common Law is by witness and jury: let Cobham be here, let him speak it. Call my accuser before my face . . . ."[7]

---

1. Sir Walter Raleigh (1552 or 1554 to 1618) established the first, though unsuccessful, English colony in America (June 4, 1584) at Roanoke Island, North Carolina. Raleigh counties in North Carolina and West Virginia, among other places, are named for him.

2. Raleigh is the guy who laid his cloak before Elizabeth's feet (one of the great suck-up feats in history!). His relationship with Elizabeth I is the subject of numerous depictions, including the movie THE VIRGIN QUEEN (20th Century Fox 1955) (Bette Davis and Richard Todd) and ELIZABETH: THE GOLDEN AGE (2008) (Clive Owen and Cate Blanchett), a sequel to ELIZABETH (Gramercy 1998). Elizabeth was called the Virgin Queen because she never married, probably to keep power, and is not a comment on her chastity. *See, e.g.,* CHRISTOPHER HIBBERT, THE VIRGIN QUEEN: ELIZABETH I, GENIUS OF THE GOLDEN AGE (1992).

Bette Davis as Elizabeth

King James I.

Sir Edward Coke, the prosecutor, argued this hearsay was good evidence, responding in court to Raleigh, *"Your treason had wings."*[8]

The judges refused his request, though Raleigh persisted; after all, even in trial by ordeal, the accused had the right to confront his accuser. But Raleigh's was truly an altercation with Attorney General Coke:

Coke: *Thou art the most vile and execrable traitor that ever lived.*

Raleigh: *You speak indiscreetly, barbarously and uncivilly.*

Coke: *I want[i.e., lack]words sufficient to express thy viperous treason.*

Raleigh: *I think you want words indeed, for you have spoken one thing half a dozen times.*

Coke: *Thou art an odious fellow, thy name is hateful to all the realm of England for thy pride.*

Raleigh: *It will go near to prove a measuring cast between you and me, Mr. Attorney.*[9]

Coke at the end of his case decided on a bit of showmanship. He pulled out of his pocket another Cobham letter, once again confessing the plot with

Raleigh and retracting his retractions with *"nothing but the truth . . . the whole truth before God and his angels."*

Matching the showmanship, Raleigh then pulled out from his pocket yet another Cobham letter exonerating Raleigh: *"I never practiced with Spain by your procurement; God so comfort me in this for my affliction, as you are a true subject, for any thing that I know . . . God have mercy upon my soul, as I know no treason by you."*[10]

Although Cobham probably wrote this "last" letter before Coke's, Raleigh got the last word.

---

3. Kadri at 83.   **4.** *Quoted in* Kadri at 83.   **5.** Kadri at 82.

6. *Crawford*, 541 U.S. at 44 (citing D. Jardine, Criminal Trials 435 (1832)). For an excerpt from Criminal Trials 389 to 520 (David Jardine ed., 1850), see http://www.wfu.edu/~chesner/Evidence/Linked%20Files/Additional%20Assigned%20Readings/TRIAL%20OF%20SIR%20WALTER%20RALEIGH.htm (last visited June 3, 2007).

7. Cobham.

rooke 1.ᵉ Cobham.

8. Kadri at 82.

9. Many consider Coke's conduct during this trial a blemish on his strong record in the development of the common law and judging. While on the King's Bench he stood against King James I at his life's peril. Perhaps, though, his conduct during the trial was not out of line for its day. For the quotations of Raleigh's cross-examination from the *State Trials*, see Allen D. Boyer, *The Trial of Sir Walter Ralegh: The Law of Treason, The Trial of Treason and the Origins of the Confrontation Clause*, 74 Miss. L.J. 869, 892 to 93 (2005).

10. Boyer at 893. Raleigh had contacted Cobham to get this "last" letter by putting a note in a hollowed out apple, which he threw in Cobham's cell. Given Cobham's numerous contradictory statements, he would have easily been impeached under today's Federal Rule of Evidence 801(d)(1).

Sir Edward Coke

Sir Walter Raleigh

In the end Raleigh never got the right to confront his accuser. And despite Raleigh's protestations that his trial was "*the Spanish Inquisition*," the jury convicted him and the court gave him the death sentence.[1]

By any standard, the procedure in Raleigh's trial was unfair. As one of Raleigh's judges lamented, "*the justice of England has never been so degraded and injured as by the condemnation of Sir Walter Raleigh.*"[2]

But his trial led to various legal reforms guaranteeing the right to confrontation, such as the requirement in treason law of a face-to-face confrontation. Courts also created rules of unavailability, admitting out-of-court statements only if the witness could not testify in person. Courts also ruled that a suspect's statements could only incriminate himself, not another.[3] These reforms became part of the common law, which over 150 years later gave the context for the Sixth Amendment's Confrontation Clause.[4]

Despite these reforms, however, the altercation criminal trial was slow to change.[5]

LILBURNE STILL PLEADS FOR A LAWYER

And now we're back to John Lilburne needing to pee.

---

1. Because of complicated politics beyond the scope of this chapter, Raleigh was not executed until fifteen years later, on October 29, 1618. On that day, Raleigh put on his best clothes and declared, "*I have a long journey to go, and therefore will I take my leave.*" After putting off his gown and doublet, he asked the executioner to show him the axe. "*This is a sharp medicine but it is a physician for all diseases.*"

While mounting the scaffold he also famously smoked a pipe of tobacco. This was to annoy King James, who detested tobacco and had even written a book called A COUNTERBLASTE TO TOBACCO alleging that the devil had brought it to England. (Actually, Raleigh gets credit for having popularized tobacco and making the Virginia Colony profitable.)

Raleigh commemorated on a tobacco can

See RICH BEYER, THE GREATEST STORIES NEVER TOLD: 100 TALES FROM HISTORY TO ASTONISH, BEWILDER & STUPEFY 28 to 29 (2003) (noting that James I was an antismoking fanatic calling it "*a custom loathsome to the eye, hateful to the nose, harmful to the brain, dangerous to the lungs.*" In 1605, he increased tobacco taxes 4,000 percent to discourage its use.

About three centuries later, the Beatles in John Lennon's song "I'm So Tired" from *The White Album* also indicted Raleigh for tobacco: "*Although I'm so tired, I'll have another cigarette/And curse Sir Walter Raleigh, he was such a stupid get! [git].*" "Get" or "git" comes from Middle English and means an illegitimate offspring (bastard son of a bastard), related to "beget."

2. *Quoted in Crawford*, 541 U.S. at 45 (citations omitted).

3. *See Crawford*, 541 U.S. at 44 to 45 (citations omitted).

The BEATLES

The Beatles, better known as the *White Album* (1968) has no graphics or text other than the band's name and a serial number

4. "*In all criminal prosecutions, the accused shall enjoy the right to . . . be confronted with the witnesses against him . . . .*" U.S. CONST. amend. VI.

In addition, the Treason Clause protects these rights in the context of treason trials: "*No Person shall be convicted of Treason unless on the testimony of two Witnesses to the same overt Act, or on Confession in open court.*" U.S. CONST. art. III, § 3.

Just before the American Revolution, colonists such as Thomas Jefferson invoked Blackstone's third volume, identifying confrontation as incident to trial by jury. Graham at 218. Precursors to the Sixth Amendment were John Adams's Massachusetts and George Mason's Virginia constitutions. *Id.* at 216 to 17. Mason, over 150 years after Raleigh's execution, wrote the first American confrontation clause in 1776 in his room at Raleigh's Tavern in Williamsburg. *Id.* at 219.

Raleigh's Tavern in Williamsburg, Virginia   George Mason

Lilburne at every point outlined for the jury the unfairness of the process against him:

"My prosecutors have had time enough to consult with counsel of all sorts and kinds to destroy me, yea, and with yourselves; and I have not had any time at all, not knowing in the least what you would charge upon me, and therefore could provide no defense for that which I knew not what it would be."[6]

But despite his repeated requests for a lawyer, Lilburne was on his own.[7]

In 1649, an accused had no right to representation. As one of his judges told him, *"counsel lies in matter of law, not of fact."* The idea here was that a defendant did not need a lawyer because no lawyer could present the facts better than the defendant himself. If a legal issue arose, the judge would be the defendant's counsel.[8]

Judge Keble: *Hear me one word, and you shall have two . . . your life is by law as dear as our lives, and our souls are at stake if we do you any wrong.*

Lilburne would have none of it:

"If you will not allow me counsel. I have no more to say to you, you may murder me if you please."[9]

---

5. Our friend, John Lilburne, also argued for his confrontation rights in his Star Chamber trial of 1639, ten years before his 1649 trial featured in this chapter: *"produce them in the face of the open court, that we may see what they accuse me of; and I am ready here to answer for myself."* Quoted in Graham at 212 to 14 (arguing that Lilburne's experience had greater effect on the Puritan founders of America than Raleigh's trial).

6. Wolfram at 237. Lilburne's objects here to not getting the indictment before the trial in sufficient time to prepare a defense. Until the late nineteenth century in England, the defendant did not know the nature of the charge nor was he permitted to see the prosecution's depositions. J.M. Beattie, *Scales of Justice: Defense Counsel and the English Criminal Trial in the Eighteenth and Nineteenth Centuries*, 9 LAW & HIST. 221, 223 (1991). In America, the Sixth Amendment would guarantee defendants like Lilburne the right *"to be informed of the nature and cause of the accusation . . . ."* Coupled with the Fifth Amendment's guarantee of an indictment, Lilburne would have had no complaint. Even if Lilburne had gotten the indictment, he would probably not have been able to read it. Until 1362 indictments were written in French or Latin. During Cromwell's time indictments were in English but afterward went back to French or Latin. Not until 1751, under George II, were they written in English. *See* Wolfram at 229 n.58 (citing ORFIELD, CRIMINAL PROCEDURE FROM ARREST TO APPEAL 223 to 24 (1947)); *see also* POUND at 127.

7. Actually, not totally. Lilburne did have legal help present and spent a lot of time arguing that his solicitor, Mr. Sprat, be allowed to talk for him. *See, e.g.,* Wolfram at 240. Lilburne succeeded in getting the court to allow him to have Mr. Sprat *"hold your papers and books."* Id. Lilburne, however, could more than hold his own; not only could he argue better than judge and prosecutor, he was no slouch on trial objections:

    Attorney General: *What did lieutenant colonel Lilburne say to you concerning your pay? Did not he ask you . . .*

    Lilburne: *I pray, Sir, do not direct him what to say, but leave him to his own conscience and memory, and make him not for fear to swear more than his own conscience freely tells him is true.*

    Many trial lawyers today miss this objection, which in its modern form is *"objection, leading."* See Federal Rule of Evidence 611(c). Lawyers were excluded from most parts of the trial in 1539 and barred in all capital cases after 1670. KADRI at 58.

8. Lord Keble relied on the law at the time. **Lord Coke** had written that the accused only needed a lawyer if a legal issue presented: *"First, that the testimonies and the proofs of the offense ought to be so clear and manifest, as there can be no defense of it. Secondly, the court ought to be in stead of counsel for the prisoner, to see that nothing be urged against him contrary to law and right . . . ."* 3 COKE'S INSTITUTES fol. 29 (quoted in Wolfram at 236 n.81; also *The Third Part of the Institute of the Law of England: Concerning High Treason and Other Pleas of the Crown in Criminal Causes* at 29 (London M. Flesher, 1644)). In another context, Coke responded in 1613 to Jesuit jurists  that *"the law of England, is a law of mercy; . . . . and it is far better for a prisoner to have a Judges [sic] opinion for him, than many counselors at the Bar; the Judges to have a special care . . . to see . . . that justice be done to the party."* King v. Thomas, 80 Eng. Rep. 1022 (K.B. 1613), *quoted in* Westen at 86 n.59.

9. Wolfram at 236. Lilburne is playing to the jury. Also, he always had more to say.

John Lilburne faced a mode of trial far more stream-lined than today; not having defense counsel made everything go faster. In fact there normally was no prosecutor either.[1] But as Lilburne's trial illustrates, judges often found it impossible to be the defendant's lawyer:

Judge Keble: *I hope the jury hath seen the evidence so plain and so fully that it doth confirm to them to do their dirty duty and find the prisoner guilty of what is charged upon him.*[2]

Judge Keble declared this before Lilburne had presented his defense, belying his prior statement to Lilburne that *"your life is by law as dear as our lives."*[3]

Even after hearing Lilburne's defense, Keble cheered for the prosecution:

Judge Keble: *. . . you will clearly find the like treason hatched in England.*[4]

Tudor-Stuart judges, as their Norman predecessors, held office at the pleasure of the crown.[5] The judge's job was to help the accuser, usually the victim, establish the prosecution case as well as be *"counsel for the defendant."*[6] The accused had to speak for himself and to respond to prosecution evidence when presented. If he did not defend himself, no one would do it for him.[7] The thinking of the time was that *"everyone of common understanding may as properly speak to a matter*

---

1. One thing to keep in mind is that the Lilburne, Raleigh, and Sir Thomas More trials were state trials with prosecutors. Generally, prosecutors were a rarity in criminal procedure. John H. Langbein, *The Origins of Public Prosecution at Common Law*, 17 AM. J. LEGAL HIST. 313, 315 (1973). For the average criminal case the judge-as-counsel system may have worked well enough. An average judge would have been just trying to get through his caseload. The jury decided the case after an inquest-type trial. Every juror knew the penalty for most felonies was death, and many probably knew or had heard of the defendant. Juries had a tradition of deciding the defendant's fate with the verdict of guilty or not guilty regardless of the evidence. In a relatively homogenous community this was rough justice. See generally Langbein, *Before the Lawyers*, at 288 to 89, 308, for examples of the procedures in normal cases.

2. *Quoted in* Wolfram at 247. Lilburne's trial followed the abuses of the Tudors and Stuarts, leading eventually to the end of the judge-as-counsel idea. KIRALFY at 364.

3. From the start, the judicial bias was clear. During the reading of the indictment Lilburne saw the prosecutor and judge whispering together:

Lilburne: *Hold a while, hold a while, let there be no discourse, but openly; for my adversaries or prosecutors whispering with the Judges, is contrary to the law of England, and extremely foul and dishonest play: and therefore I pray let me have no more of that injustice.*
Mr. Attorney: *It is nothing concerning you (let me give him satisfaction), it is nothing concerning you, Mr. Lilburne.*
Lilburne: *By your favor, Mr. Prideaux, that is more than I do know; but whether it be or not, by the express law of England, it ought not to be; therefore I pray let me have no more of it.*

This should have been the end of the issue, but Lilburne's judges seem to have been unable to avoid taking the bait and as the reading of the indictment droned on, one of the judges felt he had to justify himself:
Judge Thorp: *Mr. Lilburne, I desire to correct a mistake of yours in the law: You were pleased to condemn it as unjust, for the attorney-general's speaking with me when your indictment was a reading; you are to know, he is the prosecutor for the state here against you, and he must confer with us upon several occasions, and we with him, and this is law.*
Lilburne: *Not upon the bench, Sir, by your favour, unless it be openly, audibly, and avowedly, and not in any clandestine and whispering way: And by your favour, for all you are a judge, this is law, or else sir Edward Coke, in his 3d part instit. cap. high treason, or petty treason, hath published falsehoods, and the parliament hath licensed them; for their stamp in a special manner is to that book.*
Judge Thorp: *Sir Edward Coke is law, and he says, The attorney-general, or any other prosecutor may speak with us in open court, to inform us about the business before us in open court.*
Judge Thorp: *I tell you, Sir, the attorney-general may talk with any in the court, by law, as he did with me.*
Lilburne: *I tell you, Sir, it is unjust, and not warrantable by law, for him to talk with the court, or any of the judges thereof, in my absence, or in hugger-mugger, or by private whisperings.*

of fact as if he were the best lawyer . . . ."[8]

If a defense attorney was even there, his only role was to speak as to matters of law, leaving the defendant to fend for himself on any matter of fact.[9]

Certainly, most defendants were not up to the task, but Lilburne was:

"Truly, Sir, I am not daunted at the multitude of my judges, neither at the glittering of your scarlet robes, nor the majesty of your presence, and harsh austere deportment towards me, I bless my good God for it, who gives me courage and boldness."[10]

JUDGES START TO BECOME JUDGES

Lilburne's judges had a commission to get him executed. Since medieval times, judges were the king's law enforcers. Largely this remained their role through the Tudor monarchs, and Cromwell expected the same consideration once he was in charge.

Over time, though, judges had started to become trained professionals. Customarily they did their job with little oversight from the king. To the dismay of monarchs, judges started to become independent. An example of this happened a generation before Lilburne, with Sir Edward Coke, Lord Chief Justice of England.

Of Coke and King: Coke is a biggie in common-law history.[11]

Lord Keble: *No, Sir; it is no hugger-mugger for him to do as he did; spare your words, and burst not out into passion; for thereby you will declare yourself to be within the compass of your indictment, without any further proof . . .*

Even at this stage, Lilburne played to the jury, evident in his use of the common term "hugger-mugger." WEBSTER'S at 1211 ("*1. To act or confer stealthily. 2. To blunder along.*"). Lilburne makes his point despite, or perhaps using, the judges' protestations. His judges and prosecutor never bother to say what they were discussing, a point the jury could not have missed. Wolfram at 233 to 34.

4. Wolfram at 250.

5. *See* POUND at 134 (noting how American royal colonial governors, like their Stuart king masters, removed judges who did not decide as dictated). *See also* John H. Langbein, *The Historical Origins of the Privilege against Self-Incrimination at Common Law*, 92 MICH. L. REV. 1047, 1050 (1994) (discussing the limitations of court-as-counsel and citing Lilburne's trial judges as examples).

6. Talk about a conflict of interest! For example, John Hawles, in his 1689 tract, recognized that judges "*generally have betrayed their poor client, to please, as they apprehend their better client, the king.*" Langbein, *The Privilege,* at n.13.

7. J.M. BEATTIE, CRIME AND THE COURTS IN ENGLAND: 1660 to 1800, at 223 (1986).

8. William Hawkins, *A Treatise of the Pleas of the Crown* (London 1721). As John Langbein stated when discussing the history of the right to remain silent, "*the right to remain silent when no one can speak for you is simply the right to slit your throat, and it is hardly a mystery that the defendant did not hasten to avail themselves of such a privilege.*" Langbein, *The Privilege,* at 1054.

9. *See,e.g.,* BEATTIE at 360 (citing to a trial from the Surrey Assizes in 1752, where the judge explained "*your counsel knows his duty very well, they may indeed speak for you in any matter of law that may arise on your trial, but cannot as to matter of fact, for you must manage your defense in the best manner you can yourself.*" Cited in Langbein, *The Privilege,* at n.34).

10. Wolfram at 245. Lilburne made this statement in the closing argument for the jury's benefit.

11. Edward Coke. Coke was a prosecutor, law teacher, writer, a legal historian, and eventually the Lord Chief Justice of England. His INSTITUTES ON THE COMMON LAW OF ENGLAND is our main source for much of the history and procedure of the common law. Coke had been Speaker of the House in Parliament as well as Queen Elizabeth I's solicitor general at the same time. In this dual role he used any number of delaying tactics to defend royal prerogative. LEONARD W. LEVY, ORIGINS OF THE FIFTH AMENDMENT: THE RIGHT AGAINST SELF-INCRIMINATION 199 to 200 (1968).

Having dual roles in the executive and legislative branches did not bother seventeenth centaury potentates.

As for Coke's influence, Lilburne, a Puritan, would go to the House of Commons with a Bible in one hand and Coke's INSTITUTES in the other. Harold J. Berman, *Religious Foundations of Law in the West: An Historical Perspective,* 1 J.L. & RELIGION 3, 33 (1983).

Lilburne with either the Bible or Coke in hand

We heard of Coke in the last chapter. King James I had made Edward Coke (pronounced "Cook") chief justice of the Court of Common Pleas in 1606, three years after Coke secured Walter Raleigh's conviction.

Once in this position, Coke led the judges of his day in asserting the supremacy of the common law over the other courts, both temporal and ecclesiastical. But even more than that, Coke fought for the supremacy of the rule of law over magnates, lords, and even the king.[1]

James I, however, was a big advocate of the divine right of kings—being one, it came easily to him.[2] In 1598 he wrote THE TRUE LAW OF FREE MONARCHIES, asserting among other things *rex est loquens* ("the king is the law speaking").[3]

Technically, James was not saying he was above the law but that he *was* the law—a debatable distinction.[4]

Coke did not buy the party line. In the Privy Council[5] in 1608, with the chief justices[6] and other potentates of the realm, Coke argued with Bishop Bancroft, who was acting as James's proxy. Relying on good old *Magna Carta* Chapter 29, Coke argued the king was not above the law.

Bancroft: "*All judges, temporal and ecclesiastical,*

---

1. Coke's tool of choice in these jurisdictional disputes was the writ of habeas corpus: "*it manifestly appeareth, that no man ought to be imprisoned but for some certain cause ….*" Quoted in William F. Duker, *English Origins of the Writ of Habeas Corpus: A Peculiar Path to Fame*, 53 N.Y.U. L. REV. 983, 984 (1978).

2. Among other arrogations, James thought himself the end all of criminal procedure. On his coronation trip from Edinburgh to London he had an alleged pickpocket hanged without trial. *Reported*

James I of England (and James VI of Scotland)

in LEVY at 206. The reaction of Sir John Harrington sums up the what Englishmen thought: "*I hear our new king has hanged one man before he was tried; it is strangely done: now if the wind bloweth thus, why may not a man be tried before he has offended?*" *Id.* at 473 n.1.

3. *See* LEVY at 243. During the reign of James's son, Charles I, in 1644 Samuel Rutherford would write *Lex, Rex ("The Law is King")*, expounding the theological arguments for the rule of law over the rule of men and kings. *See* The Liberty Library of Constitutional Classics, http://www.constitution.org/sr/lexrex.htm (last visited December 5, 2005).

4. Lest you think this concept is dead, look to President Richard Nixon's statement during his 1977 interviews with David Frost: "*When the President does it, that means it is not illegal.*" *See Frost/ NIXON* (Universal Studios 2008) (dramatizing the Frost-Nixon interviews of 1977).

5. Privy Council. In England this started out as the king's council of close advisors, thus the name "privy," for private. Later, powerful sovereigns would use the Privy Council to circumvent the courts and Parliament. For example, a committee of the council, which later became the Court of the Star Chamber, could inflict any punishment except death without regard to evidence rules or the burden of proof. Henry VIII, "*on the advice of the Council,*" enacted laws by mere proclamation, and Parliament did not regain prominence until after Henry VIII's death. In 1553 the council had forty members, making it ineffective as an advisory body. Smaller committees developed that evolved into the modern cabinet. *Privy Council* 9 THE NEW ENCYCLOPEDIA BRITANNICA 713 (15th ed. 2002).

6. How Many Chief Justices Do You Need? At this point in history there was more than one "Chief Justice" in England. The three high common-law courts—the Court of Common Pleas, the Court of the King's (or Queen's) Bench, and the Court of the Exchequer—each had its own chief justice. That of the Exchequer Court was styled as the lord chief baron of the Exchequer, and that of the Common Pleas was Chief Justice of the Court of Common Pleas, leaving the head of the King's (or Queen's) Bench to be known simply as the Lord Chief Justice. The courts were combined in 1875, leaving a single Chief Justice. In this, the law went

Bishop Bancroft

are but delegates of the king who might repossess jurisdiction in whatever cases he pleased. This was clear in divinity that such authority belongs to the king . . ."

Coke: "But under Magna Carta Chapter 39, the king cannot personally decide any case nor remove any from his courts of justice; the judges alone decide this.[7]"

King James: "Common law judges are like papists who quote scripture and then put forth their interpretation to be unquestioned![8] I, the king, am the Supreme Judge and all courts are under me. If I choose, I may sit on the bench and decide cases.[9] The law is founded on reason, which I posses, and I, the king, protect the law."

Coke: "The king lacks legal knowledge and the law protects both the king and the subjects."

Now James was really angry. Rising, he shook his fist in Coke's face. Although Coke had used diplomatic phraseology in saying that the "law protects the king" rather than the king is under the law, James saw right through it.

"Yours is traitorous speech! The king protects the law, not the law the king!"

Coke, no dummy, fell on all fours begging the king's pardon, which James eventually gave.[10]

So ended the incident, for the time being.[11]

---

full circle. Before King Edward I's reign all these functions were under the office of *justiciar*, roughly equivalent to the modern prime minister.

7. LEVY at 243 (stating that Coke cited *Magna Carta* Chapter 39, but depending on the numbering system, this is also numbered Chapter 29):

"*No free man shall be taken or imprisoned or disseised or outlawed or exiled or in any way ruined, nor will we go or send against him, except by the lawful judgment of his peers or by the law of the land.*"

8. Being called a "papist" was not a good thing in post-Reformation England. Given the weakness of *Magna Carta* as precedent, James's statement may not have been so wrong. Yet in these arguments all the Stuarts (with the possible exception of James's grandson Charles II) seem to miss the big picture: the era of "divine right" legitimating power was passing.

9. Actually, James was historically correct. *See* BAKER LEGAL HISTORY, at 98. The Norman kings did just this. Also, Coke's argument that *Magna Carta* limited the king's power on this point is unconvincing. In fact *Magna Carta* Chapter 18 requires the king to be more active in justice administration. What the barons extracted from a weak King John in 1215 was not a limitation on the king's power to hear a case but the exact opposite: a demand that the king, or the king's proxies (i.e., his judges), come more often to hear cases. *See* DANZIGER & GILLINGHAM at 177 ("*As a rule Magna Carta set limits to what the king could do; but in this one clause he was required to give more, rather than less, government.*").

King James I

10. What we have of the meeting comes from various sources including Coke's own account. In these sources, especially Coke's, it is hard to tell what is a verbatim transcription and what he added later.

See generally CATHERINE DRINKER BOWEN, THE LION AND THE THRONE: THE LIFE AND TIMES OF SIR EDWARD COKE 302 to 06 (1956); LEVY at 243 to 44. This Coke history was well known during colonial times in both America and Britain. *Id.* at 243.

11. This was a petty way for James to win the argument. James might have well just said, "*It's good to be the king!*" *See* HISTORY OF THE WORLD, PART I (20th Century Fox 1981).

Coke the Unrepentant:
Begging and receiving King James's pardon did not change Coke. He kept on with his *Magna Carta* Chapter 29 arguments and issuing writs of prohibition against the ecclesiastical courts' use of the *ex officio oath.*[1]

At this point, the common-law courts defined ecclesiastical court jurisdiction. This was the result of the long struggle between the king's common-law courts and the Catholic Church's ecclesiastical courts. The irony here is that kings from Henry II and after pushed for the supremacy of the various king's courts as they fought for control with Rome. Now, the "king's" common-law courts were limiting what were now the king's ecclesiastical courts. No wonder James was miffed! James was to remark on the chief justice's *"perverseness"* and that *"[m]y spirit shall be no longer be vexed with this man."*[2]

So what was James to do? Coke had become popular with the people and the House of Commons. Besides, James had nothing for which he could punish Coke.

James decided to promote Coke out of his problematical position of Chief Justice of Common Pleas and make him Chief Justice of the King's Bench, that is, Chief Justice of England. James also made Coke a member of the Privy Council to seduce him even more.[3] It did not work. Coke continued standing up for the ideal of the common law, and, in 1616, James finally dismissed him.[4]

Judges were becoming judges, not just the king's men or law enforcement. They were beginning to view themselves under the law, not just under the king, and the king was under the law as well. And the main tool these judges used to advance the rule of law was the writ of habeas corpus.

THE WRIT OF HABEAS CORPUS

"The privilege of the Writ of Habeas Corpus shall not be suspended, unless when in Cases of Rebellion or Invasion, the public Safety may require it."

—U.S Const. art. I, § 9

---

1. A *Writ of Prohibition* is an order from a superior court limiting an inferior court's actions, often defining jurisdiction. The counterpart is the *Writ of Mandamus,* ordering an inferior court to do something.

If you are interested in an extensive academic debate (or just have insomnia) on the use of the Writ of Prohibition and its role in the development of the privilege against self-incrimination, see Charles M. Gray, *Prohibitions and the Privilege against Self-Incrimination, in* Tudor Rule and Revolution: Essays for G.R. Elton from His American Friends 345 (Delloyd J. Guth & John W. McKenna eds., 1982).

2. Levy at 249. Unlike with King Henry II back in 1170, and his comment that led to the murder of Thomas Becket, discussed in Chapter 1, James's statement did not appear to have inspired anyone to snuff out the Chief Justice.

James I

3. Levy at 252 to 54. James got the idea from Frances Bacon, his solicitor general, who defended royal prerogative by arguing that the common law was just the crown's servant and the twelve common-law judges were the twelve lions supporting Solomon's throne. *Id.* at 254. (This argument had to have appealed to James's vanity and shows Bacon to be a toady of the first order.) Though Coke was busy advancing the common law and Bacon was busy becoming the first real scientist in modern history, they found time to detest each other.

4. Levy 254.
Coke outlived James by nine years. Consequently, James never got around to getting back at Coke. James's son, Charles, did. In 1634 Charles's lackeys searched Coke's house while Coke was on his deathbed for *"seditious and dangerous papers."* They stole everything they could get their hands on, nearly all his writings, including manuscripts of his legal works, jewelry, money, and valuables. They even took his will. It took his heirs seven years to get any of it back, and they never got the will. *See* Nelson B. Lasson, The History and Development of the Fourth Amendment to the United States Constitution 31 to 32 (1937); Samuel Dash, The Intruders: Unreasonable Searches and Seizures from King John to John Ashcroft 21 to 22 (2004).

We know habeas corpus today as "the great writ" for its role in securing individual liberty.[5] But habeas corpus did not start as a tool to guard individual liberty.[6]

Originally, the king's traveling judges used it to get jurisdiction over a defendant who was otherwise not present. It was a way of securing a party's appearance after other more lenient ways did not work.[7] Thus it functioned more like a modern summons, arrest warrant, or extradition order, or for a person in custody.[8]

Later judges of one court would use the writ of habeas corpus to get jurisdiction over individuals and their cases *("causa")* from other courts. This is a function like the modern use of the writ to secure the rights of individuals or their causes, known then as the *habeas corpus cum causa.*

The "king's judges" would use habeas corpus against the ecclesiastical court to limit their jurisdiction in favor of "the king's" (i.e., common-law) courts. This is what the kings wanted when the church courts belonged to Rome. But since Henry VIII, the ecclesiastical courts were the king's ecclesiastical courts.[9]

The king's judges, like Edward Coke, turned the writ of habeas corpus back on the king by using it to limit the jurisdiction of the ecclesiastical courts.[10] This challenged the very notion that justice flowed from the king to the subjects.

Courts, through habeas corpus, were emancipating themselves from the king's rule to follow the rule of law. The proponents of this view created a history that the writ of habeas corpus sprang somehow from *Magna Carta* as a basic right.[11]

As we have seen, Oliver Cromwell was no more a supporter of judicial independence than the Stuarts. But the Habeas Corpus Act of 1679 came from this period and is the precursor to the habeas corpus rights in the American Constitution.[12]

This is the role of the writ of habeas corpus today: to limit the executive branch's prerogatives, whether kings or American presidents.[13]

---

5. A writ is just lawyer-speak for "order."

6. Habeas corpus. Latin for "you have the body," commands a person detaining another to produce the prisoner. The issue is the legality of the detention, not guilt or innocence. Habeas corpus is *"the great writ of liberty"* issuing from the common-law courts of Chancery, King's Bench, Common Pleas, and Exchequer. BLACK'S at 638 to 39. *See* U.S. CONST. art. I, § 9.

7. *See* Duker at 1000.

Coke

8. This is still the purpose of the modern *writ of habeas corpus ad prosecundum*. The original habeas corpus writ was the *habeas corpus ad respondendum*, directing a sheriff or other official to produce the body (the *"corpus"*) of a party to respond (*"ad respondendum"*) in court. Duker at 992, 996 and 1007.

9. Duker at 1018 to 23.

10. Duker at 1031 to 36.

11. Duker at 1031.

12. The U.S. CONSTITUTION, Article I, Section 9, states that *"[t]he privilege of the Writ of Habeas Corpus shall not be suspended, unless when in Cases of Rebellion or Invasion, the public Safety may require it.* For a copy of Habeas Corpus Act of 1679....", see http://press-pubs.uchicago.edu/founders/documents/a1_9_2s2.html (last visited Feb. 26, 2008).

13. *See, e.g., Hamdi v. Rumsfeld,* 542 U.S. 507 (2004) (holding that Yaser Esam Hamdi, a U.S. citizen being detained indefinitely as an "illegal enemy combatant" must have the ability to challenge this detention before an impartial judge). For a good, brief outline of the history of habeas corpus and its modern application, see James Robertson, *Quo Vadis, Habeas Corpus?* 55 BUFF. L. REV. 1063 (2008).

JUDICIAL INDEPENDENCE

One of the great grievances against the Stuarts was their lack of respect for judicial independence.[1] In 1688, the Glorious Revolution removed the final Stuart king, James II. Parliament gave the realm to William III and Mary but only under the condition that they recognize various civil rights, which eventually culminated in the Act of Settlement of 1701, the Act of Succession, and the English Bill of Rights.

Among many rights, it provided that only both houses of Parliament in agreement could remove a judge.[2] Moreover, judges would keep their job *quamdiu se bene gesserint* ("during good behavior").

Judges at last were free to follow the law, not just the whim of a monarch, as William Blackstone noted some decades later:

"[T]he court must pronounce that judgment [sentence] which the law has annexed to the crime, and which has been constantly mentioned,

together with the crime itself, in some or other of the former chapters."[3]

When judges were the king's men, they had considerable discretionary power to exercise "the king's" prerogative pardon powers.[4] Now, despite the fact that English courts are still "the King's (or Queen's) Bench,"[5] Parliament appoints the judges and is the only entity that can remove a judge for cause.[6]

Any modern court views the "rule of law" as ultimate

James II

1. *See* Fisher at 617 to 18 and n. 163.

2. **Act of Settlement** (12 & 13 Will., 3 c.2 (Eng.)) also settled succession to the English throne on the Electress Sophia of Hanover, a granddaughter of James I, and her Protestant heirs. It remains the main Act of Parliament governing succession to the throne.

Blackstone

3. 4 BLACKSTONE, COMMENTARIES ON THE LAWS OF ENGLAND 369 to 72 (1st ed. 1769).

4. On judges gaining the king's discretionary power over pardons, see Thomas A. Green, *The Jury and the English Law of Homicide, 1200 to 1600*, 74 MICH L. REV. 414, 425 (1976). During the Middle Ages this had much to do with practicality. A convict was hanged within hours of conviction. Thus, for the king's pardoning power to work, the king's representative (the judge) in conjunction with the jury had to decide without delay whether the defendant deserved pardon.

5. The **Queen's Bench** (or **King's Bench**, for a male monarch) is now a division of the High Court of Justice of England and Wales. Subdivisions include the Commercial Court, the Admiralty Court, and the Administrative Court. It is also the name of the superior court in the Canadian provinces of Saskatchewan, Alberta, New Brunswick, and Manitoba. The *Law Reports* use the abbreviation QB (or KB) in legal citations.

6. The Act of Settlement of 1701 gave judicial appointments to Parliament. This had the effect of subordinating the common law to statute law. LOVELL at 412. As discussed above, the Framers did not intend this subordination for America. *See Marbury v. Madison*, 5 U.S. (1 Cranch) 137 (1803).

authority. Certainly, law comes from Parliament or Congress, but judges must be free to apply the law. This idea goes far back to Aristotle and his requirement that judges apply the law

"to redress the inequality which is this kind of justice identified with injustice."[7]

To Aristotle, an equitable or just decision is what the legislator would have decided in the particular circumstances if he had been present. For this reason judges and juries had to have separate powers from legislators.[8]

As discussed, judges in England started out as law enforcement and as the "king's judges," to affect his rule and laws, or the "king's peace." Parliament took them over and became supreme over the king and his courts.

America was different.

The Framers of the American Constitution specifically rejected the notion of parliamentary supremacy as the exclusive basis of government.

The Declaration of Independence's indictment of King George III, for instance, was a legal fiction; it was really an indictment of Parliament's actions, such as the Stamp Act, the Intolerable Acts, etc.

Thus, for America, the Framers created a government with separation of powers where judges are supposed to have power and independence to apply the law and Constitution.[9]

This was how the Framers ensured the rule of law.

7. The following is **Aristotle** in context: *"The law never looks beyond the question, what damage was done? And it treats the parties involved as equals. All it asks is whether an injustice has been done or an injury by one party on the other. Consequently, what the judge seeks to do is to redress the inequality, which is this kind of justice identified with injustice. Thus in a case of assault or homicide the action and the consequences of the action may be represented as a line divided into equal parts . . . What the judge aims at doing is to make the parts equal by the penalty he imposes . . ."* ARISTOTLE, ETHICS 148 to 49 (Penguin Classics ed. 1955).

8. Lawmakers pass general laws prospectively, *"while . . . the juror [is] actually judging present and specific cases."* ARISTOTLE, RHETORIC 32 (George A. Kennedy trans., 2d ed. 2007), *quoted in* Robert Stein, *Rule of Law: What Does It Mean?* 18 MINN. J. INT'L L. 293, 297 (2009).

9. See **Chapter 10: "Are You Talkin' to Me?": Just Who Are Those "People" in the Tenth Amendment?** regarding judicial discretion. For the cautionary tale of what happens when judicial independence is lost, see JUDGMENT AT NUREMBERG (United Artists 1961), a fictionalized film account of the Nuremberg Trials after WWII. Stanley Kramer directed Spencer Tracy as the American judge trying to understand how German judges could have condoned Nazi crimes against humanity.

THE FRAMERS AND THE RULE OF LAW

The Framers believed in the rule of law.[1] Indeed, the entire premise of the American Revolution was to "re-establish" the rule of law from a despotic king.[2]

Or as Thomas Paine forcefully extolled in COMMON SENSE in 1776,

"the world may know, that so far as we approve of monarchy, that in America THE LAW IS KING. For as in absolute governments the King is law, so in free countries the law OUGHT to be King; and there ought to be no other."

The Declaration of Independence, in addition to declaring *"inalienable rights,"* indicted King

---

1. The world "legal" has Indo-European roots and comes to English from Latin, as Thomas Aquinas wrote:

"Law is a rule and measure of acts whereby man is induced to act or is restrained from acting: For lex (law) is derived from ligare (to bind), because it binds one to act."

Thus, the Latin *"ligare"* is also in the English *"ligature"* because what is "legal" is what binds. It is also the root of the Latin *"legere"* (*"to read"*) as in to "bind with the written word." Modern Spanish has *"leer"* (*"to read"*), which is seen in the English verb *"leer,"* as in to stare at someone.

The Roman/Latin for "law"(*"ius"*) had two meanings: objective rules of actions and subjective rights to act. Thus, although the Romans had a limited concept of individual rights, they did have the framework of rule of law. SUSAN FORD WILTSHIRE, GREECE, ROME AND THE BILL OF RIGHTS 86 (1992).

2. Jacob Reynolds, *The Rule of Law and the Origins of the Bill of Attainder Clause*, 18 ST. THOMAS L. REV. 177, 187 (2006).

The concept of the rule of law connected to democracy is old in European tradition. Iceland boasts the oldest democratic assembly with the lawspeaker, the "skapti thoroddsson", speaking from the "law rock", "the althing". KADRI at 22.

The "**Alþingi,**" Anglicized variously as *"althing"* or *"althingi"* (literally the "all-thing"), is still Iceland's national parliament, founded in 930 AD.

The word "parliament" comes from the French *"parler,"* KYNELL at 108, still evident in the English word "parlor" and "parley."

An Icelandic stamp with the LOGSOGUMATHAR ALTHING ("lawspeaker at the althing").

3. THE DECLARATION OF INDEPENDENCE shows the import of the rule of law. After the Preamble, the Declaration indicts King George III for not following the rule of law:

"He has refused his Assent to Laws, the most wholesome and necessary for the public good.

He has forbidden his Governors to pass Laws of immediate and pressing importance, unless suspended in their operation till his Assent should be obtained; and when so suspended, he has utterly neglected to attend to them.

He has refused to pass other Laws for the accommodation of large districts of people, unless those people would relinquish the right of Representation in the Legislature, a right inestimable to them and formidable to tyrants only.

He has called together legislative bodies at places unusual, uncomfortable, and distant from the depository of their Public Records, for the sole purpose of fatiguing them into compliance with his measures.

He has dissolved Representative Houses repeatedly, for opposing with manly firmness his invasions on the rights of the people.

He has refused for a long time, after such dissolutions, to cause others to be elected, whereby the Legislative Powers, incapable of Annihilation, have returned to the People at large for their exercise; the State remaining in the mean time

George III for failing to uphold the law.[3]

The Framers read Aristotle:

"It is more proper that the law should govern than any of the citizens [and] persons holding supreme power should

be appointed only guardians and servants of the law."[4]

They read the Enlightenment thinkers, including John Locke:

"Freedom of men under government is to have a standing rule to live by,

common to every one of that society, and made by the legislative power erected in it; a liberty to follow my own will in all things, where that rule prescribes not: and not to be subject to the inconstant, uncertain, arbitrary will of another man."[5]

---

exposed to all the dangers of invasion from without, and convulsions within.

He has endeavoured to prevent the population of these States; for that purpose obstructing the Laws for Naturalization of Foreigners; refusing to pass others to encourage their migrations hither, and raising the conditions of new Appropriations of Lands.

He has obstructed the Administration of Justice by refusing his Assent to Laws for establishing Judiciary Powers. He has made Judges dependent on his Will alone for the tenure of their offices, and the amount and payment of their salaries."

4. *Quoted in* Reynolds at 185 and n.45. "Anyone," Aristotle wrote, "who bids the law to rule seems to bid god and intellect alone to rule, but anyone who bids a human being to rule adds on also the wild beast." ARISTOTLE, POLITICS bk. III, ch. 16, at 111 (Peter L.P. Simpson trans., Univ. of North Carolina Press 1997), *quoted in* Stein at 297. For Aristotle, the rule of law trumps majority rule.

Locke

Rutherford

Montesquieu

5. Locke, quoted in Reynolds at 179.

In addition to Locke, the Founders read Samuel Rutherford's *Lex, Rex* ("*The Law is King*") (1644), giving the theoretical foundation of the rule of law. Rutherford in turn influenced Charles Montesquieu's THE SPIRIT OF THE LAWS (1748). From there came the U.S. Constitution, which provided the subject of Alexis de Tocqueville's study, DEMOCRACY IN AMERICA.

Grotius

de Tocqueville

God thinking about what Grotius wrote

For the Enlightenment even God is subject to the rule of law. Hugo Grotius's LAWS OF WAR AND PEACE I, i, x (1625), the origin of all international law, states that: "Measureless as is the power of God, nevertheless it can be said that there are certain things over which that power does not extend .... Just as even God cannot cause that two times two should not make four, so He cannot cause that which is intrinsically evil be not evil." Quoted in WILTSHIRE at 68.

"Even the will of an omnipotent being cannot change or abrogate" natural law, which "would maintain its objective validity even if we should assume the impossible, that there is no God or that he does not care for human affairs."

Much later, Sigmund Freud would offer another explanation of the source of the rule of law:

"Civilization obtains mastery over the individual's dangerous desire for aggression by weakening and disarming it and by setting up an agency within him to watch over it, like a garrison in a conquered city."

Freud, *quoted in* KADRI at 14. One of the things garrisoning that aggression is the rule of law.

Freud

And they went to the movies!

Well, not really; they went to the theater to see Joseph Addison's play *Cato, A Tragedy* (1712) about the ancient Roman Cato fighting to save the Roman Republic from Julius Caesar.[1] The play underscored the Founders' fear of those who would subvert the republic and the rule of law.

Cato lost.[2] But the play may have given us some of the American Revolution's best lines:

Patrick Henry, for instance, may have got

"Give me Liberty or give me death!"[3]

from *Cato* Act II, Scene 4:

"It is not now time to talk of aught/But chains or conquest, liberty or death."

Also, Nathan Hale's valediction,

"I regret that I have but one life to lose for my country"[4]

may have come from Act IV, Scene 4:

"What a pity it is/That we can die but once to serve our country."

---

1. RICHARD BROOKHISER, WHAT WOULD THE FOUNDERS DO?: OUR QUESTIONS, THEIR ANSWERS 24 to 25 (2006). Washington had the play performed for his men at Valley Forge during the winter of 1777 to 78.

Mʳ JOHN KEMBLE as CATO.

It must be so plato thou reasonest we

London Published by T. Hughes & Ludgate 30 March 1813

John Kemblein playing the Roman Cato in Addison's play

2. *Cato the Younger* (95–46 BC), was a politician and statesman in the late Roman Republic, remembered for his lengthy conflict against Julius Caesar and his moral integrity. When Caesar finally defeated him, Cato refused to surrender and took his own life. WILTSHIRE at 29.

Cato the Younger

3. Henry, though, may never have said, *"Give me liberty orgive me death!"* The speech did not appear in print until William Wirt's LIFE AND CHARACTER OF PATRICK HENRY (1817), and historians speculate that Wirt invented it after the fact.

Patrick Henry before the House of Burgesses by Peter F. Rothermel (1851)

4. Nathan Hale (1755–1776) was a Continental Army soldier during the American Revolution and America's first spy. The British captured and hanged him. Although he was only twenty-one when he died, he made it on a postage stamp in 1925 and 1929.

5. *"Loyalty,"* echoed Justice Hugo Black in 1960, *"comes from love of good government, not fear of a bad one."* BLACK'S at 881.

6. How about STAR WARS (20th Century Fox 1977), with the virtuous Jedi knights fighting the evil empire to bring back the old republic? The empire's admirals, generals, and evil emperor Palpatine even have British accents!

For the Framers a republic was the best government and the way to achieve true civic virtue.[5] They, like Cato, were set to fight against an empire: the British Empire. A virtuous republic fighting against an evil empire is an American archetype.[6]

The Framers put it all together to make a democratic republic

"to the end that it may be a government of laws and not of men"

as John Adams provided in the Massachusetts Constitution of 1780.[7] James Madison's FEDERALIST No. 51 noted:

"If men were angels, no government would be necessary. If angels were to govern men, neither external nor internal controls on government would be necessary. In framing a government which is to be administered by men over men, the great difficulty lies in this: you must first enable the government to control the governed; and in the next place oblige it to control itself."[8]

With the possible exception to Madison's reference to angels, Adams, Madison, Locke, and Aristotle could have written each other's sentences.

---

7. John Adams's Massachusetts constitution stands as the famous exposition of separation of powers as the basis for the rule of law:
"*In the government of this commonwealth, the legislative department shall never exercise the executive and judicial powers or either of them: the executive shall never exercise the legislative and judicial powers, or either of them: the judicial shall never exercise the legislative and executive powers, or either of them:* **to the end it may be a government of laws and not of men.**"
MASSACHUSETTS CONSTITUTION, Part the First, art. XXX (1780) (emphasis added).

Ronald Reagan at Berlin's Brandenburg Gate, challenging Gorbachev to *"Tear down this wall!"* on June 12, 1987

And don't forget Ronald Regan decrying the Soviet Union as an *"evil empire"* to the National Association of Evangelicals in Orlando, Florida, on March 8, 1983.

Reagan giving the *"evil empire"* speech

8. For a discussion of antecedents to the American rule of law tradition, see Steven G. Calabresi, *The Historical Origins of the Rule of Law in the American Constitutional Order*, 28 HARV. J.L. & PUB. POL'Y 273 (2005). Regarding law in the early colonies, see, for example, William E. Nelson, *Authority and the Rule of Law in Early Virginia*, 29 OHIO N.U. L. REV. 305 (2003); William E. Nelson, *The Utopian Legal Order of the Massachusetts Bay Colony, 1630 to 1686*, 47 AM. J. LEGAL HIST. 183 (2005).

Thus the Framers not only knew the value of the rule of law but also the difficulty in structuring a democratic republic to give it effect. As Aristotle warned,

"now, anyone who bids the law to rule seems to bid god and intellect alone to rule, but anyone who bids a human being to rule adds on also the wild beast. For desire is such a beast, and spiritedness perverts rulers even when they are the best of men. Hence law is intellect without appetite."[1]

Roger Sherman followed in 1787 when he wrote that

"[n]o bill of rights ever yet bound the supreme power longer than the honeymoon of a new married couple, unless the rulers were interested in preserving the rights."[2]

With this problem in mind, the Framers sought a way to structure their new republic so it would last.

To make it last, they divided the power among three branches of government with a system of checks and balances.[3] This gave the rulers, exercising political power in conjunction with and in opposition to the other branches of government, an interest in preserving individual rights.

The power of judicial review is part of this system to assure individual rights, such as the right to a lawyer.

THE DEFENDANT GETS LILBURNE'S LAWYER

Again back to Lilburne pleading for counsel:

"I am sure by common equity and justice that I may have counsel and solicitors also assigned me."[4]

---

1. THE POLITICS OF ARISTOTLE (350 B.C.), *quoted in* Scott D. Gerber, *The Court, the Constitution, and the History of Ideas,* 61 VAND. L. REV. 1067 (2008).

2. Roger Sherman, writing in the New Haven Gazette *quoted in* Seymour W. Warfel, *Quartering of Troops: The Unlitigated Third Amendment,* 21 TENN. L. REV. 723, 727 (1951).

Roger Sherman (1721 to 93) served on the Committee of Five that drafted the DECLARATION OF INDEPENDENCE and became a representative and senator. He was the only person to sign the four great American state papers: THE CONTINENTAL ASSOCIATION, the DECLARATION OF INDEPENDENCE, the ARTICLES OF CONFEDERATION, and the CONSTITUTION.

Civil War general William Tecumseh Sherman was a distant descendant, and Watergate-era prosecutor Archibald Cox was a direct descendant of Sherman.

Roger Sherman

William Tecumseh Sherman

Archibald Cox

3. Because British merchants had the largest amount of liquid capital, there was little reason not to have them present at Parliament for money matters. Because they were commoners, it made sense that all bills relating to money or taxation start in the House of Commons. Following this, the U.S. CONSTITUTION provides that all money bills begin in the House of Representatives. U.S. CONST. art. I, § 7. LOVELL at 185 n.11, 196.

4. Wolfram at 236.

5. Cromwell proved himself no more principled than the Stuarts in this use of "trials" for utilitarian ends. Cromwell, as the monarchs before him, used the law of "high treason," which had its roots in the ancient Germanic relationship of faith between a lord and his men. This is why even in modern times the murder of a husband by the wife, or the master by the servant, was not just murder but "petit treason."

Lilburne's trial followed a long line of state cases where the crown had used the legal form of the trial to affect the ruler's wishes.[5] Generally, that meant killing somebody for high treason.

By no means was Lilburne's trial of 1649 the end of it. Less than twenty years later the Popish Plot trials occurred.

The Popish Plot: The Popish Plot (1678–81) was a conspiracy to discredit English Catholics hatched by two corrupt English clergymen, Titus Oates and Israel Tonge. They fabricated that a "popish plot" existed to murder King Charles II and replace him with his Roman Catholic brother James. Charles II did not believe Oates, but the conspiracy took a life of its own, fueled by anti-Catholicism.[6] King Charles, who already had problems appearing too Catholic because he had a Catholic wife, could stop neither Oates nor the hysteria.[7]

Oates initially made forty-three allegations against various members of Catholic religious orders, including Jesuits and numerous Catholic nobles.[8] At one point Charles personally interrogated Oates, catching him in a number of lies, and ordered his arrest. But Parliament later forced Oates's release.

The trials before Lord Chief Justice Sir William Scroggs were notorious because the defendants did not have lawyers and could not testify on their own behalf.[9] Oates had his victims at a disadvantage. He testified against them under oath, whereas they could only defend with their own unsworn statements.

---

6. Oates was a bad person. He had been an Anglican priest but the church dismissed him from various posts for *"drunken blasphemy,"* theft, and allegations of sodomy. In 1677 he became a chaplain aboard HMS *Adventurer* but was soon accused of buggery (a capital offense) and spared only because he was clergy. Oates fled England and joined the Catholic Order of the Jesuits, later claiming it was just to learn their secrets. When he returned to London he befriended the rabid anti-Catholic clergyman Israel Tonge and the two hatched the alleged "plot." Oates's Plot, THE CATHOLIC ENCYCLOPEDIA, http://www.newadvent.org/cathen/11173c.htm (last visited July 11, 2007).

7. As part of the hysteria, Parliament passed a bill excluding all Catholics from Parliament. In the streets people played with Popish Plot playing cards lauding Oates, including *"Oates uncovers the plot"* and *"The executions of the 5 Jesuits."*

Set of common tiles at the time illustrating the so called "Popish Plot."

8. Sixteen innocent men were executed in direct connection with the plot, and eight others executed for being Catholic priests in the persecution that followed. The names of the executed are: in 1678 Edward Coleman (December 3); in 1679, John Grove, William Ireland, S.J. (January 24) Robert Green, Lawrence Hill (February 21), Henry Berry (February 28), Thomas Pickering, O.S.B. (May 14), Richard Langhorn (June 14), John Gavan, S.J., William Harcourt, S.J., Anthony Turner, S.J., Thomas Whitebread, S.J., John Fenwick, S.J. (June 20); in 1680, Thomas Thwing (October 23), William Howard, Viscount Stafford (December 29); and in 1681, Oliver Plunkett, Archbishop of Armagh (July 1). Those executed as priests were in 1679, William Plessington (July 19), Philip Evans, John Lloyd (July 22), Nicholas Postgate (August 7), Charles Mahony (August 12), John Wall (aka, Francis Johnson), O.S.F., John Kemble (August 22), and Charles Baker (aka David Lewis), S.J. (August 27). Oates's Plot, The CATHOLIC ENCYCLOPEDIA, http://www.newadvent.org/cathen/11173c.htm (last visited July 11, 2007).

9. As Fisher at 618 to 23 argues, the oath was still the basis of the criminal justice system's legitimacy, which could not tolerate conflicting oaths.

Oates got a state apartment and a £1,200 allowance from Parliament. Purges of Catholics spread, as did rumors of plots and French Catholic invasions. At least fifteen innocent "popish plotters" died the horrible traitor's death.[1]

As King Charles moved against him, Oates grew even bolder. He eventually denounced the king, which was strange because the supposed original plot was to kill Charles.

Oates eventually was punished but only for a while. Charles arrested and tried Oates for sedition and sentenced him to prison and a fine of £100,000.[2] When James II became king, he had Oates retried and sentenced to pillory, public whippings, and prison—and had him defrocked.[3] Ironically, some of the same Jesuits who had been at the mercy of Oates's sworn testimony could now testify against him and Oates, as a defendant, could not.

But the injustices of the law as applied, including Lilburne's trial and Oates's Popish Plot, lead to reform. This reform was the foundation of our Sixth Amendment.

THE TREASON ACT OF 1696

Just over ten years after the Popish Plot, Parliament passed the Treason Act of 1696.[4] One of the main reforms was guaranteeing the accused the right to counsel in treason cases—about fifty years too late for Lilburne but his legacy nonetheless.[5]

But this created a strange anomaly in the law: an accused had the right to a lawyer in a treason case, and in a misdemeanor case, but not with a felony charge.[6] Thus a person could still face the death penalty without the right to any legal help.

Much of this had to do with social class. Treason defendants tended to be powerful people or, at least, powerful at one time. They could afford a lawyer.[7] But in addition to social class, there were other reasons unique to treason trials that argued for a lawyer for the defendant.

---

1. For example, Edward Coleman, sentenced to death on December 3, 1678, was hanged, drawn, and quartered.

2. Judge George Jeffreys declared that Oates was a *"Shame to mankind."* Following James II, King William of Orange and Queen Mary pardoned Oates in 1688, and Parliament gave him a pension. Oates died in 1705.

Judge Jeffries himself was no gem. He was *"the most consummate bully ever known in his profession"* and took *"a delight in misery merely as misery."* See LORD MACAULAY, THE HISTORY OF ENGLAND 73 to 75 (1979) (describing Judge Jeffreys).

3. Oates's punishment became a precursor to the Eighth Amendment because at the time it was "unusual" for a common law court to defrock a clergyman. See **Chapter 8: "Baby, Don't Be Cruel"**: What's So Cruel *and* Unusual about the Eighth Amendment?

Coleman drawn to his execution.

Judge George Jeffreys

For one thing, the Tudors, Stuarts, and Cromwell did not pick treason trial judges for their impartiality. Defendants like Sir Thomas More and John Lilburne knew this all too well. Treason law was complex. The government always managed to have its lawyer there to prosecute.[8] Thus treason trials were different in character from the short, simple trial of the average guy.

The Treason Act, at least, recognized that a lawyer makes one's other rights possible.

THE RIGHT TO DEFEND

Two of the rights we take for granted are the right to compel (i.e., subpoena) witnesses to come to court and the right to testify on our own behalf. A lawyer makes these rights a reality.

The power to ask for a subpoena assumes enough legal knowledge to use court procedures well before a trial. Likewise the defendant having the right to testify assumes that he will have a lawyer to question him. Both of these rights, however, were relatively late in coming.

Compulsion of Witnesses: In 1649 Lilburne wanted to subpoena witnesses:

"Subpoenas . . . [some of my witnesses] are parliament men, and some of them officers of the army, and they will not come in without compulsion."[9]

As with his other pleas, Lilburne did not prevail.[10]

Although Lilburne could call witnesses, he could not subpoena them. Not until the end of the seventeenth-century, with Parliament passing acts in 1696 and 1702, could a defendant compel witnesses to appear and have them sworn.[11]

This meant the prosecutor's sworn witnesses had more credibility than the defendant's. The antipathy of courts to allowing the defendant to subpoena witnesses had the same source as the rules preventing the defendant from testifying.

Titus Oates in the pillory

4. Langbein, *The Privilege*, at 1067 to 68, Langbein, *Before the Lawyers*, at 309; Fisher at 617 to 18.

5. The Treason Act of 1696 placed the accused and the crown on the same level. Lovell at 411.

6. *See* Kiralfy at 360 to 61.

7. Langbein, *Before the Lawyers*, at 309. As Langbein puts it, *"they legislated safeguards for themselves and left the underlings to suffer as before."*

8. Langbein, *Before the Lawyers*, at 309 to 10.

9. *Quoted in* Langbein, *The Privilege*, at 1056 (citing 4 State Trials at 1312). *See also* Wolfram at 238.

10. "Subpoena" is a noun from Latin meaning "under penalty," the first words of the writ (order) commanding the presence of someone under penalty of failure, from "*sub*" meaning "under" and "*poena*" meaning "penalty."

11. Fisher at 583, 597, 616. *See also* Langbein, *The Privilege*, at 1056. The reasoning behind the rule precluding not only defendants from testifying but also his witnesses was that felonies were capital and the system could not allow conflicting oaths with the death penalty. Thus not only could the defendant not testify under oath, Fisher at 598, his witnesses could not as well because of their bias to try to save him. *Id.* at 598 to 99 (citing Gilbert).
    Westen cites Parliamentary acts in 1589 and 1606 giving the accused a limited right to call witnesses to testify but notes the accused still did not have the right to compel witnesses or to have them sworn. *See* Westen at 84 to 85, 87, 90 (noting that this was a key goal of Lilburne's Levellers).

Defendants Testifying:
During medieval compurgation trials, the defendant took an oath. A compurgation trial, however, is about the oath, not the testimony, because the oath was the evidence.[1] Thus, before the sixteenth century the defendant could give his oath. But from the sixteenth to the nineteenth centuries, courts precluded the defendant from doing so, although he could give the jury his statement.[2]

The reason for the change was that the oath had become not just the evidence but instead the foundation for testimony. This created the potential for conflict because, unlike a medieval compurgation trial, there could now be conflicting testimony, meaning conflicting oaths. Both society and the criminal justice system could not accept the possibility of conflicting oaths because the oath legitimated the system.

Thus a rule developed in evidence law precluding a party from testifying on his own behalf. The party's interest in the outcome was a temptation for perjury and would therefore undermine the old system of oaths.[3]

This "party witness rule" was to protect the oath;[4] making classes of witnesses not competent to testify and prevented them from facing the temptation to lie. This was a product of the fact that juries did not yet have their modern role of detecting lies.[5]

In addition, there was a more practical necessity for prosecutors. If the oath is the evidence rather than

---

1. When the oath itself is qualitative evidence a natural tendency arises to play a numbers game counting multiple oaths as multiple proofs. See John H. Wigmore, *Required Numbers of Witnesses; A Brief History of the Numerical System in England*, 15 HARV. L. REV. 83, 85 (1901 to 02); *See also* Fisher at 652 to 55. The origins for this concept are biblical. Wigmore at 85 n.1 (quoting *Deuteronomy* 17:6, 19:15; *Numbers* 35:30; *Matthew* 18:16; *2 Corinthians* 13:1; *1 Timothy* 5:19; *Hebrews* 10:28; *John* 8:17). From there, the notion moved into Roman and canon law, Wigmore at 84, and the English chancery courts. *Id.* at 99. Thus matters such as wills, originally subject to ecclesiastical or chancery court jurisdiction, have required numbers of witnesses even today. In the common law, however, the jurors themselves were the witnesses, accounting for why jurors still take oaths. Thus numerology never came into practice in the common-law courts with the exception of cases involving treason or perjury. In treason cases it was because of the politics involved, where the sovereign could all too easily justify executions on little or no evidence. *Id.* at 100. As for perjury, more than one witness is needed as a practical matter to overcome the defendant's false testimony. *Id.* at 106; Fisher at 701.

2. Robert Popper, *History and Development of the Accused's Right to Testify*, 1962 WASH. U. L.Q. 454; 464 to 65. *See also* Fisher at 596 to 97 (noting the oddity that a defendant could testify in misdemeanor and in civil cases at the time).
    We call it a witness "stand" because in England the witness

 actually stands in a box to testify. In America the witness sits in the "stand."

3. For Blackstone's views on the exclusion of the infamous or interested witnesses, including defendants, see Popper at 456. The modern reaction to this rule can be seen in Federal Rule of Evidence 601, which provides that *"[e]very person is competent to be a witness except as otherwise provided in these rules or by statue."* Moreover, Federal Rule of Evidence 603 requires a witness to take an *"oath or affirmation"* before testifying. These modern rules react to the older system protecting the oath itself. *See* Fisher at 591. Indeed, Roman and canon law barred testimony of any potential perjurers, including women (in some cases), slaves, and those below age fourteen. *Id.* at 642. Additionally, rules barred testimony from the insane, the infamous, paupers, infidels, criminals, and children. *Id.* at 590, 606, 625; Morrison at 585. Because Quakers would not take oaths, the system disqualified their testimony, Fisher at 643, 657, and Edward Coke stated that only Christians could testify because the oath had meaning only to them. *Id.* at 657.

---

4. James Oldham, *Truth-Telling in the Eighteenth-Century English Courtroom*, 12 LAW & HIST. REV. 95, 96, 107 (1994). Wigmore traced the party disqualification rule to the distinction between the common-law jury trial and the wager of law (i.e., compurgation). *See* Joel N. Bodansky, *The Abolition of the Party-Witness Disqualification: An Historical Survey*, 70 KY. L.J. 91, 92 n.3 (1981 to 82). On the disqualification of interested parties, see Fisher at 657 and Q. Ullmann, *Medieval Principles of Evidence*, at 80 to 82. *See also* Westen at 86 (noting that the rationale was to avoid a "swearing match" because contradictory witnesses meant that someone committed perjury and the oath lost legitimacy).

the testimony, conflicting oaths would cancel each other, and the presumption of innocence would always mean no conviction.[6]

The party witness rule was rife with abuse, as Oates demonstrated. For one, it became clear that informants could testify under oath because they were not "parties" to the prosecution, despite the fact that they were paid for a conviction. Another anomaly of the party-witness disqualification rule was that codefendants tried

separately could testify under oath for each other. But in a joint trial they could not do so unless they testified for the prosecution.[7]

Thus, the party-witness disqualification rule put the defendant at an unfair disadvantage.[8] The Stuart monarchs in particular were infamous for their use of perjurers to achieve state ends. The Treason Act of 1696, allowing defendants to testify under oath, came from this experience. Finally, conflicts between trial witnesses started

to become a question of credibility rather than competence, and something for the jury to decide.[9]

In the context of the normal felony trial, however, the right of the defendant to testify under oath was a long time coming.[10] In the U.S., the first statute explicitly giving defendants this right was in 1864 in Maine.[11] In England, an 1898 statute gave the right.[12] Finally, the U.S. Supreme Court ruled in 1961 against any bar on the defendant testifying under oath.[13]

5. Fisher at 625 to 26.

6. Oldham at 103 (quoting Gilbert and noting that the lack of oath rendered the defendant's testimony the equivalent of hearsay and thus to be given less weight).

7. Popper at 457. Indeed the rule on codefendants not being allowed to testify in a joint trial lasted in England until the Statute of 1869. *Id.* at 469.

8. As Gilbert was to write, "*By the now Law in Cases of Treason the Witness against the King are admitted to their Oaths, because this [party disqualification rule] was abused in the late Reigns to derive a Credibility on the King's Witnesses as being upon Oath, tho' contradicted by Men of better Credit upon their Words only.*" *Quoted in* Fisher at 617.
See also Id. at 602 to 04 (stating how reforms were also a reaction to the Throckmorton trial of 1554). *See also* Popper at 456 to 57; Fisher at 617 to 18 (on reaction to Stuart perjurers); *Id.* at 607 to 08 (for the development of the two-witness rule for perjury and treason prosecutions). Regarding the Treason Act of 1696, see Langbein, The Privilage, at 1056. Of particular notoriety were the trials of Algeron Sydney and William Lord Russell.

9. Oldham at 98.
The law still gave presumptions to avoid direct conflicts between oaths. For instance, the so-called "rule of Bethel's case" determined that affirmative testimony was more credible than negative testimony. A basic rhetorical principle is that one cannot prove a negative, only a positive. The extension of this idea was that affirmative testimony was more truthful than negative testimony. For a complete accounting and survey of sources, see Fisher at 584, 597, 631 to 38.
Despite the best attempts of evidence experts and judges, the law could not avoid direct conflicts such as in the case of alibi defenses where one witness testifies the defendant was there and another that he was not. *Id.* at 648.

10. *See* Fisher at 581 n.9 (regarding secularization and democratization breaking down the oath system).

11. Fisher at 584.

12. Fisher at 662 (citing an Act to Amend the Law of Evidence, 61 & 62 Vict. Ch. 36 (1898)).

13. *Ferguson v. Georgia*, 365 U.S. 570, 593 (1961). Justice William J. Brennan gives an extensive historical account of the rule excluding defendants from testifying. *See also Rock v. Arkansas*, 483 U.S. 44, 51 to 53 (1987) (recognizing that defendants have an unconditional Sixth Amendment right to testify under oath).
But allowing testimony under oath breeds ethical dilemmas. Anatomy of a Murder (Columbia Pictures 1959) is a realistic trial court drama directed by Otto Preminger and starring Jimmy Stewart as a small town lawyer and George C. Scott as the prosecutor, with Ben Gazzara as the defendant and Lee Remick as his wife. Real life lawyer Joseph Welch, who represented the U.S. Army in the McCarthy hearings, does a good turn as the judge. As the lawyers battle, Stewart's character is smart and works hard to keep the lines of his ethical conduct clear. *See* Richard Burst, *The 25 Greatest Legal Movies: Tales of Lawyers We've Loved and Loathed*, ABA Journal Aug. 2008, at 41 (ranking *Anatomy of a Murder* as No. 4 on the list).

PROSECUTORS, REASONABLE DOUBT, AND THE PRESUMPTION OF INNOCENCE

Prosecutors: Though Lilburne complained of the injustice of not having a lawyer, the problem for most criminal defendants was that they did not have a prosecutor. If you have a prosecutor, the judge can leave the inquisitorial role. Plus, professional prosecutors, by definition, adhere to professional standards.[1]

From before Norman times, all prosecution was private.[2] The self-informed juror generally did not need a prosecutor.

For special cases, however, the king did have his own attorneys. The king had the "*praerogative*" (prerogative) of not having to appear himself in court. Thus, he sent an attorney, at first for specific cases in specific courts, but then generally to appear at any time in any court,that is, an "attorney general." By the

seventeenth century these had become the offices of attorney general and solicitor general, and these were the first professional prosecutors.[3]

At the same time, the king's justices still had a prosecutorial function; remember, the king picked them to be law enforcement.[4] By Tudor times, the king's Justices of the Peace took over the pretrial case investigation for later presentation to the traveling justices

---

1. Hamilton Burger was the prosecutor in Perry Mason, who Perry dutifully beat every week.You have to wonder whether his character went home saying, *"Just once, I want to beat Perry Mason!"*

2. DANZIGER & GILLINGHAM at 180.

3. POUND at 111 to 13.

These are offices today in the government of the United States. The **Attorney General** heads the Department of Justice and is the only member of the President's Cabinet who does not have the title of "secretary". The **Solicitor General** argues before the Supreme Court when the U.S. government is a party and answers to the Attorney General. As mentioned, he and his assistants argue Supreme Court cases wearing a morning coat.

U.S. Department of Justice Seal. Regarding the history of the Department of Justice seal and its meaning, see Rafael Alberto Madan, *The Sign and Seal of Justice*, 7 AVE MARIA L. REV. 123 (2008).

4. Glazebrook, at 583; Langbein, *Origins*, at 314 to 18.

5. The Office of Justice of the Peace grew out of the practice from the early 1200s where the king would appoint local knights to *"keep the king's peace."* "Justices of peace" started to get royal commissions under Edward II. KYNELLat 156. Under Edward III these knights became regular officials with the name "justices of the peace." They could arrest and jail suspects and impose an early form of bond. BAKER at 24 to 25. Early justices of the peace tried felonies but over time, they began to have a much more defined role in purely pretrial procedure. By the sixteenth century, they presided over only misdemeanor trials and the duties of arrest and detention. Langbein, *Origins*, at 319.

6. Langbein, *Origins*, at 320 to 23; Glazebrook at 584.

7. *See generally* Glazebrook; Langbein, *Origins*, at 313; Thompson I at 28 to 31. Justices of the Peace conducted an early form of the preliminary hearing. *Id.* at 319.

Justices of the Peace still exist today in many states, conducting preliminary hearings. Though modern criminal procedure and law constrains these Justices of the peace, the form is similar to the medieval period and they still "bind over" defendants for trial. Glazebrook at 584.

Judge Roy Bean (c. 1825 to 1903) is the most famous American Justice of the Peace. Although known as the "Hangin' Judge," there is no evidence he ever ordered an execution. Instead, he was an eccentric saloon keeper who posted signs proclaiming "ICE COLD BEER" and "LAW WEST OF THE PECOS." He was first elected to office in 1884.

See THE LIFE AND TIMES OF JUDGE ROY BEAN (Cinerama Releasing 1972), directed by John Huston and staring Paul Newman.

from Westminster.[5] These Justices of the Peace had a specific role in bail decisions and an early type of subpoena power to investigate crime. This backed up private victims in their prosecutions.[6]

Under Queen Mary, Parliament passed several statutes from 1554 to 1555 defining the role of Justices of the Peace and in essence making them England's first prosecutor corps.[7] The Justices of the Peace served in this prosecutorial/ inquisitorial role as an alternative to paid professional prosecutors well into the eighteenth century.[8] This prosecutorial function fit well with the Justices of the Peace's traditional role to keep the king's peace and make bail determinations.[9]

By the 1730s, things in England, especially London, began to change. Urbanization and population density pressured the older system of justice. Before professional police, *"thief takers"*, who gained rewards for convictions, began to dominate criminal justice.[10] In various cases such as high treason, the crown employed attorneys. Now, different agencies of the government began to employ lawyers for prosecution.[11] The crown could no longer rely on the victim to prosecute crime.[12]

Prosecutors now had to prove the case with "reason" and evidence, overcoming "reasonable doubt."

THE WESTERNER (Samuel Goldwyn 1940), directed by William Wyler, starred Gary Cooper and Walter Brennan, who won his record-setting third Best-Supporting Actor Oscar playing Judge Roy Bean.

8. Langbein, *Before the Lawyers*, at 282. *See* Bruce P. Smith, *The Emergence of Public Prosecution in London, 1790 to 1850*, 18 YALE J.L. & HUMAN. 29, 33 (2006) (discussing the summary proceedings in police offices that dispensed with the need for victim participation in prosecution).

9. Glazebrook at 585.

10. *See* Beattie at 234; Fisher at 647; Landsman, *Contentious Spirit* at 572. We would call these *"thief takers"* "bounty hunters." But unlike modern bounty hunters who chase known felons and give them to the

police, *thief takers* notoriously hauled anyone, usually the poor, to court and secured their conviction (and reward) with their own perjured testimony. There were no police forces, prosecutors, or defense attorneys to check them. And no *thief taker* could have been as cool

as Steve McQueen in *Wanted: Dead or Alive* (CBS, from 1958 to 1961). *See also Dog the Bounty Hunter* (A&E, from August 31, 2004 to the present).

Walter Brennan as Roy Bean, with Gary Cooper

11. *See* Beattie at 221 to 22, 225 (noting the appearance of lawyers in court records in the 1720s and 1730s and specifically under the reign of George I).

12. *See generally* John H. Langbein, *The Prosecutorial Origins of Defense Counsel in the Eighteenth Century: The Appearance of Solicitors*, 58 CAMBRIDGE L.J. 314 (1999). Langbein, *The Privilege*, at 1070 describes the growth of professional prosecution through the 1770s and 1780s.

Reasonable Doubt:

Lilburne complained bitterly and often about his lack of trial rights. But somewhat offsetting this was a very high burden of proof. Judges held themselves and the prosecution, whether victims or lawyers, to the standard of proof "*clearer than noon day*," which Lilburne's prosecutor argued:

Attorney General: "*You have heard the several charges proved unto you; for my part, I think it as clear as noon day.*"[1]

This high standard of proof is part of the justification for denying the accused a lawyer.[2]

This "*clear as the light of noon day*" standard was a mainstay of medieval law, with origins from canon and Roman law.[3] It was also articulated as the "*any doubt*" standard. Thus jurors were to acquit if they had any doubts. Under medieval law an oath in a compurgation trial or trial by ordeal could defeat reason under the "any doubt" standard.

For prosecution, the balance was this: though the accused did not have

the right to representation, subpoena power, the indictment, or to testify under oath, the prosecutor had the entire burden of proof "*beyond any doubt*"— not just the modern standard of proof "*beyond a reasonable doubt.*"[4]

But just as professional prosecutors came on the scene, the intellectual foundation of England was changing. The seventeenth century was the Age of Reason.[5] Part of this was the "scientific revolution," stressing a rational approach to observation

1. *Quoted in* Wolfram at 243

The burden of proof was solely on the crown, thus eliminating the need, theoretically, for the defendant to provide any evidence to rebut the prosecution. Lovell at 150. As discussed above, the defendant was supposed to rely on the court to safeguard his legal interests. Westen at 86.

2. For example, **Chief Justice Sir William Scroggs** said to the Popish Plot defendants that "*the proof belongs to [the crown] to make out these intrigues of yours; therefore you need not have counsel, because the proof must be plain upon you, and then it will be in vain to deny the conclusion.*" *Quoted in* Langbein, *Before the Lawyers*, at 308.

3. Richard M. Fraher, *Conviction According to Conscience: The Medieval Jurists' Debate Concerning Judicial Discretion and the Law of Proof*, 7 Law & Hist. Rev. 23, 23 to 24, 42 (1989); Anthony Morano, *A Reexamination of the Development of the Reasonable Doubt Rule*, 55 B.U. L. Rev. 507, 509 (1975) (outlining Roman and canon law origins).

To meet this standard, Roman and canon law (the *ius commune*) require proof by two unimpeachable witnesses or by confession.

Thus because of the exacting standard of proof, the confession became all-important. To get it, torture became a practice.

The rules for torture, however, were exacting. Also, the defendant had to repeat the confession freely in open court. If not, the court suppressed the statement.

4. Coke articulated "*the testimonies and the proofs of the offense ought to be so clear and manifest, as there can be no defense of it . . .*" Edward Coke, The Third Part of the Institute of the Law of England: Concerning High Treason and Other Pleas of the Crown in Criminal Causes 29 (London M. Flesher 1644). *See* Moreno at 512 (for discussion of Coke and the any doubt standard).

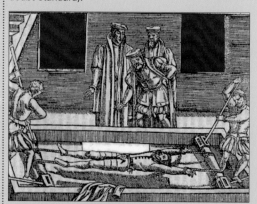

5. The **Age of Reason** was a period of seventeenth century Western history in which modern philosophy emerged and departed significantly from medieval scholasticism. The Age of Reason was after the Renaissance and before of the Enlightenment (or it was the earlier part of the Enlightenment). It marked a return to classical logic and the scientific method began in the classical era (ancient Greece and Rome) and reborn in the Renaissance.

and a logical/reasonable method for determining and explaining nature. This thinking influenced criminal procedure.[6] Methodology and reason became the standard for decision making rather than "irrational proofs."[7]

In 1756, Geoffrey Gilbert published one of the earliest works on evidence. He started it by discussing the nature of human reasoning and abstracting John Locke's *An Essay Concerning Human Understanding*,[8] marking the first effort to connect the law of proof with a methodology for decisionmaking. In this, Locke and Gilbert depart from medieval thought and jumped back to Aristotle's discussion of proof:

"[I]t is evidently equally foolish to accept probable reasoning from a mathematician and to demand from a rhetorician scientific proofs."[9]

Aristotle's point, which Locke and Gilbert echo, is that the nature of proof in science is different than other human endeavors. For the rhetorician, including the players in a system of criminal justice, a rational approach is to accept *"probable reasoning,"* not absolute proof *"beyond all doubt."* Proof *"beyond a reasonable doubt,"* the modern standard, must do.[10]

To establish this proof the best evidence is necessary but not absolute evidence, which is rarely present.[11] This freed the common-law jury system from the inquisitorial obsession with extraction of confessions to prove a criminal case.

The School of Athens by Raphael (1509 to 10)

Although created in the Renaissance, the painting shows the dawn of the Age of Reason.

6. See Barbara J. Shapiro, "Beyond Reasonable Doubt" and "Probable Cause" 7 (1991).

7. Anti-Catholicism drove much of this change in thinking. Theodore Waldman, *Origins of the Legal Doctrine of Reasonable Doubt*, 20 J. Hist. Ideas 299, 300 to 01 (1959). *"Moral certainty"* became the standard that scientists, philosophers, and religious thinkers used to distinguish themselves from *"irrational"* Catholics. Waldman at 303, 310; Shapiro at 7, 19.

John Locke

8. Waldman at 305 to 06, 311; Morano at 513 to 14. *See also* Shapiro at 8, 11, 17, 18, 25, 26; Michael MacNair, *Sir Jeffrey Gilbert and His Treatises*, 15 Legal Hist. 252, 256 (1994).

9. Waldman at 306, *quoting* Aristotle, Ethica Nicomachea bk. 10, Ch. 3, (W. David Ross trans., Oxford Univ. Press, 1925).
   Aristotle, a detail of Rafael's *The School of Athens*. Aristotle gestures to the earth and his belief in knowledge through empirical observation and experience, while holding a copy of his *Nicomachean Ethics*.

10. In tort and civil law, this leads to the "reasonable man" standard. Waldman at 311, 315 to 16.

11. Waldman at 313. Evidence law does, of course, employ the higher standard of *"scientific proof,"* especially relating to expert testimony. Federal Rules of Evidence 702 and 703. However, it is still the jury using Aristotle's *"probable reasoning"* that decides the case.

Professional prosecutors, who arrived just as beliefs about the nature of proof were changing, pushed for the "*reasonable doubt*" standard. The prosecutor had to introduce only certain kinds of logical proof but no longer proof "*clear as the noon day*" or "*beyond any doubt*."[1] Thus the push for the "*beyond a reasonable doubt*" standard decreased the prosecutor's burden.

But despite the decrease from "*beyond all doubt*" to "*beyond a reasonable doubt*," one thing never changed in the common law: the prosecutor had the burden of proof because the defendant was presumed innocent.[2]

The Presumption of Innocence: About the same time courts were figuring out "*beyond a reasonable doubt*," Justice William Blackstone in 1769 wrote that

"*the law holds that it is better that ten guilty persons escape than that one innocent suffer.*"[3]

This statement to describe the presumption of innocence is called "*Blackstone's formulation*" or the "*Blackstone ratio*." But though Blackstone gets the credit, the idea was hardly original to him.[4]

In *Genesis,* Abraham reminds God of the presumption of

innocence when God was going to destroy Sodom and Gomorrah for their "*wickedness*":

"*Will you sweep away the righteous with the wicked?*"

Certainly God, Abraham beseeches, would not ignore the presumption of innocence:

"*Far be it for you to do such a thing—to kill the righteous with the wicked, treating the righteous and the wicked alike. Far be it for you! Will not the Judge of all the earth do right?*"[5]

God agrees that if there are fifty good people he will spare the cities. Abraham

---

1. Morano at 508, 514. See SHAPIRO at 21 for a contrary view and the prosecutorial origins of the "*reasonable doubt*" standard. Shapiro argues that the older standard incorporating the term "*moral certainty*" encompassed the "*reasonable doubt*" standard.

Blackstone

2. *Coffin v. United States,* 156 U.S. 432, 453 (1895) ("*The principle that there is a presumption of innocence in favor of the accused is the undoubted law, axiomatic and elementary, and its enforcement lies at the foundation of the administration of our criminal law.*").

3. 4 BLACKSTONE, COMMENTARIES ON THE LAWS OF ENGLAND *358 (1st ed. 1769).

4. Coffin at 456, quoting from Lord Gillies in the English *McKinley's* case (1817), 33 St. Tr. 275, 596, that "*this presumption [of innocence] is to be found in every code of law which has reason, and religion, and humanity, for a foundation. It is a maxim which ought to be inscribed in indelible characters in the heart of every judge and juryman.*"

Despite this nice pronouncement, all governments have not universally followed it. German chancellor Otto von Bismarck, for example, supposedly remarked that "*it is better that ten innocent men suffer than one guilty man escape.*" Quoted in Alexander Volokh, n Guilty Men, 146 U. PENN. L. REV. 173, 195 (1997), available at http://www.law.ucla.edu/volokh/guilty.htm (last visited

Otto von Bismarck (1815 to 1898) was a Prussian/German statesman of the late nineteenth century.

Oct. 8, 2010). But if Otto is correct, and the presumption of innocence is not universal, then out the door goes PRESUMED INNOCENT (Warner Brothers 1990) from Scott Turow's novel of the same name (1987).

5. *Genesis* 18:20 to 32.

6. See Volokh at 173 to 74 (discussing God and Abraham and tracing the concept of the ratio of guilty to innocent from ancient times through the present).

The Destruction of Sodom.

eventually plea bargains this down to ten *"righteous"* people:

"And he said, Oh let not the Lord be angry, and I will speak yet but this once: Peradventure ten shall be found there. And God said, I will not destroy it for ten's sake."

Presumably Sodom and Gomorrah had many hundred wicked inhabitants who were all going to "beat the rap" to save just ten—much better than Blackstone's ratio of ten to one.[6] Of course, Abraham may not have made a very good deal because God, being God, already knew there would not be ten good people in the cities and smote them anyway.[7]

Ancient Greek law in both Athens and Sparta incorporated the presumption of innocence.[8] It also was a key part of Roman law

"that no man should be condemned on a criminal charge in his absence, because it was better to let the crime of a guilty person go unpunished than to condemn the innocent."[9]

The Emperor Julian once sat as a judge where a prosecutor who could not beat the presumption of innocence declared

"Oh, illustrious Caesar! if it is sufficient to deny, what hereafter will become of the guilty?"

Julian replied:

"If it suffices to accuse, what will become of the innocent?"[10]

Roman law combined with the biblical precedent for the presumption of innocence and passed into the church's canon law.[11] It remained the standard of church court procedure throughout the Middle Ages and even applied in heresy trials, although other heresy inquisition procedures, such as torture, negated it.[12]

---

7. But God did save Abraham's nephew, Lot. The homosexual practices of Sodom give us our modern term "sodomy."

As for playing God with the presumption of innocence, see MINORITY REPORT (DreamWorks and 20th Century Fox 2002), which shows a science fiction world of 2054 were police, with the help of clairvoyants, arrest criminals *before* they commit the crime.

10. *Quoted in Coffin*, 156 U.S. at 455 (citing Rerum Gestarum, L. XVIII, c. 1).

Julian (331/332 A.D.–363 A.D.)

Fragment of *The Justice of Trajan* by Delacroix (1840) showing Trajan taking time out from the Dacian Wars to hear the case of a mother whose son was murdered.

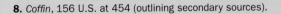

8. *Coffin*, 156 U.S. at 454 (outlining secondary sources).

9. *Quoted in Coffin*, 156 U.S. at 454 (citing letter from Trajan to Julius Frontonus; Dig. L. XLVIII, tit. 19, 1. 5). The Supreme Court in *Coffin* went on to quote from Roman law as follows: *"In all cases of doubt, the most merciful construction of facts should be preferred."* Dig. L. L, Tit. XVII, 1. 56.

In criminal cases the milder construction shall always be preserved." Dig. L. L, Tit. XVII, 1. 155, s. 2.

"In cases of doubt it is no less just than it is safe to adopt the milder construction." Dig. L. L, Tit. XVII, 1. 192, s. 1.

Emperor Trajan

11. *Coffin*, 156 U.S. at 455 (citing Decretum Gratiani de Presumptionibus, L. II, T. XXIII, c. 14, AD 1198; [***492] Corpus Juris Canonici Hispani et Indici, R.P. Murillo Velarde, Tom. 1, L. II, n.140; Kenneth Pennington, *Innocent until Proven Guilty: The Origins of a Legal Maxim*, cited in PATRICIA M. DUGAN, THE PENAL PROCESS AND THE PROTECTION OF RIGHTS IN CANON LAW (2005); see also Ullmann, *The Defense of the Accused* at 486.

12. See **Chapter 5: From Testicles to Dragnet: How the Fifth Amendment Protects *All* of Us.**

The presumption of innocence then passed from canon and Roman law to England.[1] In the ninth century, King Alfred hanged a judge who had executed a defendant

"*when the jurors were in doubt about their verdict, for in cases of doubt one should rather save than condemn.*"[2]

By 1471, English Chief Justice John Fortescue declared that

"*one would much rather that twenty guilty persons should escape the punishment of death than that one innocent person should be condemned and suffer capitally.*"[3]

Fortescue provides double Blackstone's ratio: twenty to one rather than ten to one.

Two hundred years later in 1678, however, Lord Chief Justice Matthew Hale defined the presumption of innocence as follows:

"*In some cases presumptive evidence goes far to prove a person guilty, though there be no express proof of the fact to be committed by him, but then it must be very warily pressed, for it is better five guilty persons should escape unpunished than one innocent person should die.*"[4]

Thus Hale's ratio is five to one, only half of Blackstone's.

Maybe Blackstone took

---

1. *Coffin*, 156 U.S. at 455. *See also* Ullmann, *Some Medieval Principles of Criminal Procedure*; Anthony Morano, *A Reexamination of the Development of the Reasonable Doubt Rule*, 55 B.U. L. Rev. 507, 509 (1975).

2. *Discussed in* Volokh at 182. Volokh also mentions King Æthelred the Unready providing that twelve *thanes* (knights) and a representative of the king would swear upon a relic that they would "*accuse no innocent man, nor conceal any guilty one.*"

3. *Coffin*, 156 U.S. 432 at 455, *quoting* Fortescue and *citing* DE LAUDIBUS LEGUM Angliae, (Amos trans, Cambridge Univ. Press, 1825). For Fortescue's comment on the jury's role in the presumption of innocence, see **Chapter 7: Trial by Jury or . . . by God!**

4. *Coffin*, 156 U.S. at 456 *quoting* Matthew Hale and *citing* 1 Hale P.C. 24 and 2 Hale P.C. 290.

5. *Quoted in* Volokh at 186. Despite this, Increase could never bring himself to decry what happened during the Salem witch trials.

6. *Quoted in* Volokh at 175.

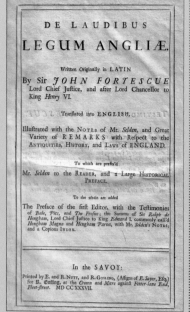

Increase Mather

Benjamin Franklin

the writings of his two illustrious predecessors and just split the difference to come up with his famous ten to one ratio.

In America, just under eighty years before Blackstone, Increase Mather on October 3, 1692, wrote that even with witches

"it were better that Ten Suspected Witches should escape, than that the Innocent Person should be Condemned."[5]

Although Benjamin Franklin was Blackstone's contemporary and certainly read him, he articulated the ratio in much grander terms: better that one hundred guilty persons *"escape than that one innocent Person should suffer."*[6] Thus Franklin advocated ten times Blackstone's ratio.

However we express the ratio—5:1, 10:1, 20:1, or 100:1—it still raises the question of how much

people, that is, modern jurors, actually believe that a defendant is innocent at the start of a trial.[7] In hundreds of courtrooms every day judges tell juries that defendants are *"presumed innocent"* and that prosecutors must prove their case *"beyond a reasonable doubt."*

But although we take this law for granted, the first time it all came together was in the Boston Massacre trial.

Carl Bett as Judd

Barry Newman as Petrocelli

Arthur Will as Owen Marshall

7. Who Killed Perry Mason? Every week for decades Perry Mason defended innocent clients. Later, *Matlock* carried on the formula with a folksy twist. In *Judd, for the Defense* (ABC, 1967 to 69), Clinton Judd defend innocent people and the social issues of the day. In the 1970's, *Owen Marshall: Counselor at Law* (ABC, 1971 to 74) defended the innocent along with his assistant Lee Majors, who became television's *The Six Million Dollar Man*. *The Bold Ones: The Lawyers* (NBC, 1968 to 72) featured Burl Ives as respected attorney Walter Nichols who hired two young brothers (Joseph Campanella and James Farentino) to defend the innocent. In *Petrocelli* (NBC, 1974 to 76), the client was certain to be convicted until Petrocelli would get evidence suggesting, but not necessarily proving, an alternative possibility, which the jury would accept as a reasonable doubt under the presumption of innocence.

But these shows are decades old. Today, the few television shows about criminal defense attorneys are edgy, such as *The Practice* (20 Century Fox TV, 1997 to 2004), with, more often than not, guilty clients providing the drama. Prosecutors now rule the television legal drama. *Law and Order* and its numerous spin-offs present the prosecutor putting away the guilty against the odds. Forget Blackstone's ratio; there are no innocents in the *Law and Order* world, and acquittals are miscarriages of justice. The *Law and Order* franchise, as well as semi-news shows like *Nancy Grace* (HLN, February 21, 2005 to present), represent an entire industry based on the presumption of *guilt*. Although not about lawyers, the reality show *COPS* (Fox, 1989 to present), which follows police officers around with cameras as they arrest suspects red handed, starts with the statement *"COPS is filmed on location as it happens. All suspects are considered innocent until proven guilty in a court of law."* The message: all defendants are guilty, and the presumption of innocence just gets in the way.

Image by Helen Koop

THE BOSTON MASSACRE TRIAL

The Boston Massacre trial of 1770 is our first record of the prosecution arguing for the *"beyond a reasonable doubt"* standard.[1]

On March 5, 1770, British soldiers in Boston faced an unruly crowd. After provocation, or without any reason at all (depending on whose side you read), the soldiers fired into the crowd, killing five people.[2]

At the murder trials in late 1770, Captain Thomas Preston and eight soldiers were represented by John Adams, a future signer of the Declaration of Independence and second American president.[3] Prosecuting the case for the crown was Robert Treat Paine, another future signer of the Declaration.[4]

Adams gave a passionate closing argument that the jury should acquit if they had *"any doubt"*:

"[T]he best rule in doubtful cases, is, rather to incline to acquittal than conviction: and . . . [w]here you are doubtful never act; that is, if you doubt of the prisoner's guilt, never declare him guilty; this is always the rule, especially in cases of life."[5]

Adams articulated the presumption of innocence.

Paine argued from the perspective of the Age of Reason:

"Our law in General that it is Ultima Ratio the last improvement of Reason which in the nature of it will not admit any Proposition to be true of which it has not Evidence . . ."[6]

A medieval lawyer or judge would never have made such a statement. But Paine builds on Locke and

---

1. Morano at 508. The somewhat later Irish Treason trials of 1798 are another possible source. *See id.* J.W. May, *Some Rules of Evidence: Reasonable Doubt in Civil and Criminal Cases,* 10 Am. L. Rev. 642 (1876); 9 J. Wigmore, Evidence § 2497 (3d ed. 1940); C. McCormick, Law of Evidence § 341 (2d ed. 1972). Langbein, *Before the Lawyers,* at 266 (citing McCormick, states that the "reasonable doubt" standard did not develop until the nineteenth century). Shapiro at 22 to 23, however, agrees with the Morano view that the Boston Massacre trials were first.

Crispus Attucks

2. This included Crispus Attucks, the first black man to die for American Independence.

For the record of the Boston Massacre trial with speeches and testimony, *see* the Boston Historical Society site, http://www.bostonmassacre.net/trial/index.htm (last visited June 13, 2007).

For the propaganda effect of the massacre and trial, *see* Arthur Schlesinger, Prelude to Independence: The Newspaper War on Britain, 1764 to 1776 (1958).

Paul Revere's illustration of the Boston Massacre

The Boston Massacre

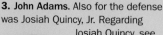
Boston Massacre trial bill

3. John Adams. Also for the defense was Josiah Quincy, Jr. Regarding Josiah Quincy, see Daniel R. Coquillette, The *Legal Education of a Patriot: Josiah Quincy Jr.'s Law Commonplace* (1763), 39 Ariz. St. L.J. 317 (2007).

4. Robert Treat Paine later served as Massachusetts's first attorney general (1777 to 90) and as a state supreme court judge (1790 to 1804).

Paine was assisted by Samuel Quincy, see Morano at 516 to 17, who was Josiah Quincy's brother. The Revolutionary War separated the two. Samuel Quincy was a Loyalist and left America forever in 1776.

Robert Treat Paine

Samuel Quincy

Gilbert's foundation to argue that doubts had to be reasonable:

"[I]f therefore in the examination of this Cause the Evidence is not sufficient to Convince you beyond a reasonable Doubt of the Guilt of all . . . you will acquit them, but if the Evidence be sufficient to convince you of their Guilt beyond a reasonable Doubt the Justice of the Law will require you to declare them Guilty . . . ."[7]

The judges were split on jury instructions. Senior Judge Edmund Trowbridge charged the jury with the *"any doubt"* standard.[8]

In the end, Adams won. Captain Preston was acquitted, and the jury found only two of his men, Hugh Montgomery and Mathew Kilroy, guilty of manslaughter. Their punishment was branding on the thumb with a hot iron after receiving *"benefit of clergy."*[9]

But despite Adams's successful assertion of the *"any doubt"* standard, it was the "reasonable doubt" standard that became our standard today. Perhaps this was in some part a reaction to the perceived leniency of the Boston Massacre trials. Thus what was the prosecutor's innovation to lessen the *"any doubt"* standard became the defendant's primary protection from an erroneous conviction.[10]

As the Boston Massacre trials illustrate, prosecutors were now facing defendants with trial rights, including the right to defense counsel, like John Adams.[11] But how did the process get from Lilburne, who did not get a lawyer despite his pleas, to Adams, and on to the Sixth Amendment guarantee of the defendant's right to the *"Assistance of Counsel for his defense"*?

5. *Quoted in* Morano at 517.

6. *Quoted in* Morano at 517.

7. *Quoted in* Morano at 517.

8. Morano at 517 to 18. In addition to Trowbridge and Oliver, Supreme Court Justice John Cushing and Superior Court Judge Benjamin Lynde presided over the trials. *Id.* at 517.
   Interestingly, Justice Peter Oliver agreed with the crown, telling the jury *"if upon the whole, ye are in any reasonable doubt of their guilt, ye must then, agreeable to the rule of law, declare them innocent."* He was a Loyalist, and his family were bitter business and political rivals of James Otis and Samuel Adams. He served as Chief Justice of Massachusetts from 1772 until deposed by Revolutionists in 1775. After leaving America during the Revolution, he never returned.

Peter Oliver

9. **"Benefit of clergy"** had passed into the common law as a basis for granting leniency. For example, instead of being hanged, a first-time offender convicted of manslaughter would receive the "burnt in the hand" punishment of a branded "M" for "manslayer." Originally this was to stop clerics from invoking the benefit more than once. Congress abolished benefit of clergy in 1790 though it survived in some states and may even remain technically available today. The British Parliament did not abolish benefit of clergy until 1827. *See* Jeffrey K. Sawyer, *Benefit of Clergy in Maryland and Virginia*, 34 Am. J. Legal Hist. 49 (1990).

10. Morano at 519. *See In re* Winship, 397 U.S. 358, 361 to 64, and 369 to 72 (1970) (Harlan, J., concurring).

11. John Adams argued during the trial, *"if I can but be the instrument of preserving one life, his blessing and tears of transport shall be a sufficient consolation to me for the contempt of all mankind."* Quoted in Deborah A. Schwartz & Jay Wishingard, *The Eighth Amendment, Beccaria, and the Enlightenment: An Historical Justification for Weems v. United States Excessive Punishment Doctrine*, 24 Buff. L. Rev. 781, 814 (1975).

John Adams

THE AVERAGE GUY'S TRIAL IN ENGLAND AND AMERICA

We Americans have the idea that all our great rights came from England and our job is to "preserve" the ancient customs and liberties. The American Revolution perpetuated this idea that we just wanted our *"rights as Englishmen."*

But America was the product of progressive Enlightenment thought. In many areas the colonists were more advanced in the concept of rights than the English. As the Boston Massacre trials demonstrated, this was especially true regarding the rights of the accused.[1]

The American Bill of Rights reflected a broader concept of liberty, giving status to a defendant's criminal and procedural rights unavailable in Britain.[2]

England versus America: The trial of the average Englishman, especially if he was poor, would have been much like the *"altercation"* of Queen Elizabeth's time. Existing records show a trial that lasted about half an hour, with the judge doing the direct and cross-examination.[3] The accused defended himself and was expected to tell his side of the events. His statement could exonerate or hang him.[4]

His trial was adversarial in that it was public, with witnesses and direct confrontation. The main adversaries were the judge and/or witnesses. Not until the eighteenth century did the trial became adversarial in the sense of a contest between a prosecutor and defense attorney.[5]

As discussed, by the mid-1700s, professional prosecutors started to appear as a matter of course. In response, any defendant who could sought counsel. Counsels' advocacy, by modern standards, was limited, as the following statement from a judge to a defendant in a trial at the Old Bailey in 1777 demonstrates:

"Your counsel are not at liberty to state any matter of fact;

---

1. Randolph N. Jonakait, *The Rise of the American Adversary System: America before England,* 14 WIDENER L. REV. 323 (2009) (noting that *"America moved to a full adversary system before England."*).

2. The English Bill of Rights only has statutory status, and the English wrote in using the phrase *"ought not"* instead of the "American Bill of Rights" *"shall not."* WILTSHIRE at 98.

3. BAKER at 510; Beattie at 221 to 22. *See also* Klerman at 135, 145 (regarding the judge's quasi-prosecutorial role). Regarding judicial power in the colonies, see William E. Nelson, *Government by Judiciary: The Growth of Judicial Power in Colonial Pennsylvania,* 59 SMU L. REV. 3 (2006).

4. Langbein, *The Privilege,* at 1053 to 54. Langbein notes that any real right to silence would not occur until much later with the advent of defense lawyers in the late 1800s.

5. *See generally* Langbein, *Before the Lawyers,* and John H. Langbein, *Shaping the Eighteenth-Century Criminal Trial: A View from the Ryder Sources,* 50 U. CHI. L. REV. 1 (1983). For Langbein's definition of the phrase *"the accused speaks trial,"* see Langbein, *Before the Laweyrs,* at 283. *See also* Landsman at 1 (extensively documented demonstration from the Old Bailey session papers of the development during the 1700s of the adversary trial and the transfer of the adversarial parts from judges to lawyers). *See also* Stephan Landsman, *From Gilbert to Bentham: The Reconceptualization of Evidence Theory,* 36 WAYNE L. REV. 1149 (1990) (outlining this same change by analyzing evidence scholars from Gilbert to Bentham).

6. Langbein, *The Privilege,* at 1054. *See also* Beattie at 226, 231 to 32. The Old Bailey is the central criminal court in London (a *"bailey"* is part of a castle), dealing with major criminal cases. It stands on the site of the medieval Newgate Gaol. For records, see http://www.oldbaileyonline.org.

The Old Bailey is often a feature in literature and film: Charles Dickens, in A TALE OF TWO CITIES, has Charles Darnay's treason trial at the Old Bailey. Sir John Mortimer used his own experience at the Old Bailey to create the fictional character Horace Rumpole, alias *Rumpole of the Bailey* (BBC, 1975 to 92). *V* in the graphic novel V FOR VENDETTA (Quality Comics (U.K.) and Vertigo/DC Comics (U.S.A.) 1982 to 88) and its film adaptation, V FOR VENDETTA (Warner Brothers 2006), blows up the Old Bailey.

An Old Bailey trial around 1808

they are permitted to examine your witnesses; and they are here to speak to any matters of law that may arise; but if your defense arises out of a matter of fact, you must yourself state it to me and the jury."[6]

Thus the defendant had to speak for himself, and defense counsel could not even give the jury a closing argument.[7] The lawyer could examine defense witnesses and argue points of law, but little else.[8]

But defense lawyers were at least there. Although they could not cross-examine witnesses, they did object to evidence. Over time these objections developed into arguments, questioning witnesses, and a form of cross-examination.[9]

In America, however, it appears that defense counsel were not just at the trial but participating in a fully developed adversarial system. This was certainly true by the Boston Massacre trial, where Adams argued to the jury after having cross-examined prosecution witnesses.

Thus the Sixth Amendment does not reflect the *"rights of Englishmen"* but of Americans. The First Congress, while arguing the Bill of Rights, passed the Sixth Amendment with almost no debate.[10] Americans knew well the history of Throckmorton and Raleigh, the Star Chamber cases against the Puritans, and the abusive prosecution of the "popish plotters."[11]

The Aaron Burr treason trial reflects the broad scope of the trial rights the Sixth Amendment articulates. Chief Justice John Marshall was prepared to allow Burr to subpoena President Thomas Jefferson or Jefferson's letter to his attorney general.[12] A defendant had no such right in England at the time.

The Sixth Amendment shows that by the end of the eighteenth century, America did not simply adopt England's adversary system but instead developed trial procedures independently and in advance of England.[13]

---

7. Langbein, *Before the Lawyers*, at 313. Part of this older type of trial lives on today in the defendant's allocution rights at sentencing. Also, under the U.S. military's procedure the accused may at sentencing make a sworn or unsworn statement. R.C.M. 1001(c)(2). The same is true at a pretrial investigation (the equivalent of a bind-over hearing). *See* R.C.M. 405 (f)(7), (11), and (12). Manual for Courts-Martial, United States (2008).

William Garrow

8. In America, though, the defendant shall *"have the Assistance of Counsel for his defense."* as guaranteed in the Sixth Amendment. In England these rights were not formally guaranteed until the Prisoner's Counsel Act of 1836. Beattie at 250.

9. Beattie at 233; Langbein, *Before the Lawyers*, at 311. *See also* Landsman, *Contentions Spirit* at 512 (regarding the growth of lawyer cross-examination).
   For an interesting account of a criminal defense lawyer of that time named William Garrow, see Beattie at 236; *also* Beattie n.14 for an accounting of lawyer fees.

10. Westen at 74.

11. Westen at 94.

12. Westen at 101 to 08. Burr ended up dropping his request, went to trial without it, and was acquitted.

13. Jonakait at 323. Jonakait extensively reviewed court records of colonial and early republic New Jersey and New York to conduct a detailed statistical analysis. He then compared this with Langbein's work on trials in England to note the difference in procedure and rights of the accused. For a brief history of lawyers in the colonies before the American Revolution, see Pound at 130 to 74.

Garrow cross examining

Americans had fully developed systems of public prosecution. The defendant could compel witnesses to testify and could testify under oath.[1]

And he had the right to a lawyer, an especially

important right because with a lawyer the defendant can assert all his other trial rights.[2]

LILBURNE'S LAWYER

In the end, Lilburne never

got the lawyer that *"common equity and justice"* should have given him. But his legacy is our Sixth and Fifth Amendments' guarantee of a lawyer.[3]

Because a lawyer does the talking, you have the right

1. *See generally* Jonakait.

This means by the nineteenth century a young Abraham Lincoln could get his start as a lawyer in Springfield, Missouri, and go on to become president of the United States. Henry Fonda starred as Young Mr. Lincoln (20th Century Fox 1939), a fictionalized biography-drama directed by John Ford. It centers on the murder trial and Lincoln's famous *"light of the silvery moon"* cross-examination. In the movie, the key witness is a friend of the victim who claims to have seen the murder at some distance under the light of the moon. Using an almanac, Lincoln demonstrated that on the night in question the moon could not have provided the light. He then drives the witness – Perry Mason like – to confess.

Duff Armstrong's grave marker. Find a grave at http://image1.findagrave.com/photos/2008/206/28517102_12170105037 9.jpg (last visited Sept. 25, 2010).

Courtroom scene from Young Mr. Lincoln showing that in early nineteenth century America, a defendant had his trial rights

Young Mr. Lincoln depicts the real life 1858 murder trial of William "Duff" Armstrong. In defending Armstrong, Lincoln cross-examined witness Charles Allen on how he could have seen Armstrong strike the victim. Allen testified that he was at a distance of 150 feet but could clearly see by the light of the full moon. Using an almanac, Lincoln showed Allen lied because the moon on that night could not have given off enough light. Armstrong was acquitted. He died in 1899 and is buried in Mason County, Illinois His grave plaque reads, "William Duff Armstrong, accused slayer of Preston Metzker, May 7, 1858 freed by Lincoln in almanac trial."

In 2003, the Library of Congress put Young Mr. Lincoln on the National Film Registry for being *"culturally, historically, or aesthetically significant."* The *ABA Journal* rates the film No. 23 in its Top 25 best lawyer films. *See* Richard Burst, *The 25 Greatest Legal Movies: Tales of Lawyers We've Loved and Loathed*, ABA Journal, Aug. 2008, at 45.

2. From Atticus Finch, the lawyer we all want to be, to *L.A. Law*, the lawyers with the sex lives we all want to have.

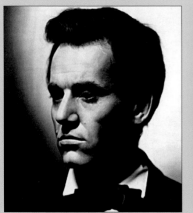

Fonda as Lincoln

A Young Abe Lincoln

to silence.[4] A lawyer can cross-examine witnesses and prepare the case. He knows procedures and the law.[5] He can call prosecutors and even judges to account.

The lawyer gives the defendant the chance to defend.

But even in America the universality of this right was a long time coming. It was not until 1963 that the Supreme Court ruled that every defendant in a serious case must have a lawyer, even if he can not afford one himself.[6]

Today the right is a given.

Although Lilburne never got his lawyer, he did have one thing going for him. As we will see in the next chapter, he had a jury.

L.A. Law was a television legal drama (NBC, 1986 to 1994). The fictional Los Angeles firm McKenzie, Brackman, Chaney, and Kuzak handled cases of abortion, racism, gay rights, homophobia, sexual harassment, AIDS, and domestic violence. And for law students of my generation, it was a must-see!

3. It never hurts to return to the actual words of the Sixth Amendment: *"and to have the Assistance of Counsel for his defense"*

The right to counsel from the Fifth Amendment comes in the context of the right to remain silent, which is meaningless without a lawyer to assert the defense. *But see* Berghuis v. Thompkins, 560 U.S. 370 (2010) (a suspect must expressly invoke his right to remain silent). Regarding the need of counsel for the right to remain silent, see Langbein, *The Privilege*, at 1048.

4. *See* **Chapter 5: From Testicles to** *Dragnet*: **How the Fifth Amendment Protects** *All* **of Us**

5. As the Supreme Court recognizes, the Sixth Amendment *"embodies a realistic recognition of the obvious truth that the average defendant does not have the professional legal skill to protect himself when brought before a tribunal with power to take his life or liberty. . ."* Johnson v. Zerbst, 304 U.S. 458, 462 to 63 (1938).

6. In June 1962, the Supreme Court agreed to review the felony conviction of a fifty-one-year-old drifter with an eighth grade education. Clarence Earl Gideon hand-wrote his petition from his Florida prison cell. *"The question is very simple. I requested the [trial] court to appoint me attorney and the court refused."* Future Justice Abe Fortas argued for Gideon.

Overturning precedent, the Court on March 18, 1963, unanimously reversed his conviction. *Gideon v. Wainwright*, 372 U.S. 335 (1963), remains the landmark case requiring that, under the Sixth Amendment, every defendant facing serious charges must have a lawyer. Five months after the Supreme Court ruling, Gideon was retried with a lawyer and acquitted.

Gideon died in 1972 and is buried in an unmarked grave in his hometown of Hannibal, Missouri George Hodak, ABA JOURNAL, Mar. 2009, at 72. The Florida Department of Corrections webpage features Gideon, ironic given that the case was against Florida. See http://www.dc.state.fl.us/oth/timeline/1963-1965.html (last visited July 8, 2007). *See* Paul M. Rashkind, *Gideon v. Wainwright: A 40th Birthday Celebration and the Threat of a Midlife Crisis*, FLA. B.D. 12 (Mar. 2003). *See* ANTHONY LEWIS, GIDEON'S TRUMPET (reissue ed. 1989), and the movie (1980) starring Henry Fonda as Clarence Earl Gideon. The title refers to the biblical Gideon, who ordered his small force to attack a larger enemy and won using trumpets as a trick. *Judges* 7:16 to 22.

Clarence Earl Gideon

Gideon's plea and handwritten petition to the Supreme Court

CHAPTER 7

Trial by Jury or . . . by God!

Why do we say "trial *by* jury"?

"In Suits at common law, where the value in controversy shall exceed twenty dollars, the right of trial by jury shall be preserved, and no fact tried by a jury, shall be otherwise re-examined in any Court of the United States, than according to the rules of the common law."

—The Seventh Amendment

The Declaration of Independence indicted King George III because he deprived us of "*trial **by** jury*."[1] The Seventh Amendment for civil cases, "*preserves*" "*the right of trial **by** jury*" if the parties are arguing about more than twenty bucks.[2] The Constitution at Article III, Section 2, mandates that "*Trials of all Crimes . . . shall be **by** jury*" and the Sixth Amendment orders that "*[i]n all criminal prosecutions*" trial shall be "*by an impartial jury . . . .*"

In the generation before the Constitution, the influential judge, Sir William Blackstone, extolled "*trial **by** jury*":

> *The trial by jury ever has been, and I trust ever will be, looked upon as the glory of the English law.*[3]

All of these pronouncements of "*trial **by** jury*" assume another choice.

There once was.

---

1. THE DECLARATION OF INDEPENDENCE para. 20 (U.S. 1776).

2. "Dollar" comes from the Low German "*taler*," which was a large silver coin from the sixteenth century. JOHN AYTO, DICTIONARY OF WORD ORIGINS 179 (1990). A "dollar" in colonial New England referred to the Spanish "piece of eight." Anyone could make change with that soft silver coin by cutting it in as many as eight parts. Hence our term "two bits" refers to a quarter (i.e., two bits of the piece of eight). The Continental Congress on July 6, 1785, adopted the "dollar" for U.S. currency on Gouverneur Morris and Thomas Jefferson's suggestion because the term was widely known but not British. Calling a dollar a "buck" is for "buckskin," referring to the price for a male deer hide. *Id.* at 82.

3. 3 BLACKSTONE, COMMENTARIES ON THE LAWS OF ENGLAND 379 (Univ. of Chicago Press 1979) (1765–69). Also, "*[t]he trial by jury . . . is also the trial by the peers of every Englishman, which as the grand bulwark of his liberties, is secured to him by the great charter.*" *Id.* at 342–43. As mentioned in other chapters, Sir William Blackstone (1723–80) was an English judge and professor who wrote COMMENTARIES ON THE LAWS OF ENGLAND, a historical and analytic treatise on the common law published from 1765 to 1769. It was extraordinarily influential in both England and colonial America and remains an important historical source on the common law. *See,* for example, Julian S. Waterman, *Thomas Jefferson and Blackstone's Commentaries*, 27 ILL. L. REV. 629 (1932–33), and for a brief discussion of Blackstone as a basis for the Seventh Amendment, *see* Steve Bachmann, *Starting Again with the Mayflower . . . England's Civil War and America's Bill of Rights*, 20 QUINNIPIAC L. REV. 194, 250–51 (2001).

William Blackstone

Blackstone knew of a time when the defendant had other choices for trial: compurgation, ordeal, or battle.[1] "*Trial by jury*" was a later addition that, over time, won out. But "*trial by jury*" owes something to the tradition of compurgation, ordeal, and battle, which were, after all, open and adversarial.[2] And like modern trials they often made for good entertainment.[3]

WHEN A TRIAL REALLY *WAS* A TRIAL: COMPURGATION, ORDEAL, AND BATTLE

Although we can hope that today's trials are more just, they are not nearly as much fun as the old types, at least for the spectators.[4] The main forms during medieval times were compurgation, ordeal, and battle. Given that the period of their use spans over one thousand years, the exact modes and manner of each varied. For most of the Middle Ages both church and secular courts used procedures we would recognize, though in a very primitive form: private accusation led to an open trial by compurgation ("*purgatio canonica*"), ordeal ("*purgatio vulgaris*"), or combat (which was actually another form of trial by ordeal or *purgatio vulgaris*).[5]

---

1. *United States v. Singer*, 380 U.S. 24, 27–28 (1965):

> *At its inception [trial by jury] was an alternative to one of the older methods of proof—trial by compurgation, ordeal or battle . . . Soon after the thirteenth century trial by jury had become the principle institution for criminal cases . . . yet, even after the older procedures of compurgation, ordeal and battle had passed into disuse, the defendant technically retained the right to be tried by one of them.*

Today the parties can choose a trial before a judge–a "bench" trial–but only after they formally waive trial by jury. *See* Fed. R. Crim. P. 23.

2. *See generally* James B. Thayer, *The Older Modes of Trial*, 5 Harv. L. Rev. 45 (1891–92).

Trial by Jury program (1875)

Scene from *Trial by Jury* (1875)

3. From light comedy to heavy drama, the jury is the platform.

Gilbert and Sullivan's comic opera *Trial by Jury* (1875) was a Victorian hit subjecting the legal system to satire.

Trial by Jury (Morgan Creek 1994) was a thriller/drama about a blackmailed juror during a mafia trial. *The Juror* (Sony 1996) had a similar premise and story line.

As for television, the jury appears countless times as a plot device or character. *Law & Order* usually ended with the jury. The *Law & Order* franchise's third spin-off was *Law & Order: Trial by Jury* (March 3, 2005– May 6, 2006), focusing on criminal trials in New York City.

Perry Mason, of course, never won his cases from the jury because his cross-examination left no doubt, much less a reasonable doubt, as to the defendant's innocence. *See* **Chapter 6: How the Sixth Amendment Guarantees You a Court, a Lawyer, and a Chamber Pot.**

However, for real drama nothing beats the classic 12 Angry Men (United Artists 1957). Henry Fonda and a cast of the best character actors of the day are riveting. Based on a very good stage play, 12 Angry Men was remade for television with a very good cast and adding a greater racial dynamic among the jurors. 12 Angry Men (MGM Television 1997). Though a good production, it will always be compared to the 1957 Fonda classic. An interesting script change would be to include women on the jury, but that is left for an enterprising screenwriter.

The classic 12 Angry Men (United Artists 1957)

4. But for sheer spectacle, it is hard to beat the O.J. Simpson farce.

O.J. Simpson in the famous white bronco with his police tail driving in formation

5. "*Purgatio*"—In English we get "purgation" or "purge." Just as a modern trial is to "clear one's name," the purgative effect of a medieval trial was to "clear one's soul."

Dante between purgatory and Florence by di Michelino (1465)

Thus these trials were closely related to the notion of purgatory, or clearing one's soul as part of the ultimate trial of final judgement. Dante's *Divine Comedy* is but one literary illustration.

These trials were accusatorial with a known complainant or plaintiff and open confrontation.[6] The inquisitorial procedure of medieval Roman and continental law (the "*ius commune*") was accusatorial and presumed the accuser's innocence.[7] All these modes of trial were part of an accusatory trial tradition, reflected in the religious and cultural notions of the person's final trial and judgment before God.[8] Our Anglo-American trial by jury is the heir of this tradition.

COMPURGATION, OTHERWISE KNOWN AS WAGER OF LAW OR TRIAL BY OATH

During most of the medieval period, compurgation was the main accusatorial procedure.[9] If a defendant could swear his innocence and produce the required number of "compurgators" or "oath helpers" to swear they believed the defendant's oath, he would win his civil suit or, if a criminal trial, his acquittal.[10] The English also called it "*wager of law*" because the "wage" was the defendant's promise or oath.[11]

6. A hanging and an early English illustration of trial by combat, an open and accusatorial mode of trial. *See* J.H. BAKER, AN INTRODUCTION TO ENGLISH LEGAL HISTORY 5–6 (4th ed. 2002) (regarding the older forms of trial).

7. Walter Ullmann, *Some Medieval Principles of Criminal Procedure*, 59 JURIDICAL REV. 1, 4 (1947), *reprinted in* WALTER ULLMANN, JURISPRUDENCE IN THE MIDDLE AGES (1980); Anthony Morano, *A Reexamination of the Development of the Reasonable Doubt Rule,* 55 B.U. L. REV. 507, 509 (1975) (arguing the presumption of innocence, a mainstay of modern criminal trial procedure, comes from canon law and Roman law).

Ma'at wearing feather of truth

Day of Judgment by Memling (1467–71)

9. Compurgation trials were important in the history of the right to remain silent. See **Chapter 5: From Testicles to *Dragnet:* How the Fifth Amendment Protects *All* of Us.**

10. George Jarvis Thompson, *The Development of the Anglo-American Judicial System: History of the English Court to the Judicature Acts,* 17 CORNELL L.Q. 9, 16–17 (1932). *See generally* R.H. Helmholz, *Crime, Compurgation and the Courts of the Medieval Church,* 1 LAW & HIST. REV. 1 (1983).

11. BLACK'S LAW DICTIONARY 1416 (5th ed. 1979). "Wager" has the same Germanic root ("*wathjam*" or "pledge") as "gage" and "engage," all of which preserve the original notion of "giving a pledge or security." It is also the root of "wedding." AYTO at 564.

8. Examining a last judgment scene reveals the elements of a modern criminal trial: a judge = Christ; a bailiff = Saint Michael; a half-way house = purgatory; souls huddled for judgment = a chain gang; a Department of Corrections = hell; souls on a scale = defendants in the trial courtroom; the graves = pretrial detention; pleading souls = sentencing allocution; angels pulling at the soul = public defenders; demons pulling the other way = prosecutors. (A prosecutor might be inclined to switch the last two.)

Christianity did not invent this idea of a last judgment. In Egypt, the goddess Ma'at measured out justice for the dead in the Hall of Two Truths. Ammit, a horrid hybrid of cat, crocodile, and hippopotamus, placed the hearts of the dead on a pan and dropped a feather of truth on the other. If the feather sank the scale, the departed gained entrance into the Kingdom of the Dead. But if it rose, outweighed by the heart's burden of deceit, Ammit would eat it, abandoning the owner to oblivion. SADAKAT KADRI, THE TRIAL: A HISTORY, FROM SOCRATES TO O.J. SIMPSON xvii (2005).

The chip or marker symbolizes the wager or promise to pay

The origins of the compurgation trials in England are Anglo-Saxon. Originally, the compurgators were probably the kinsmen of the accused or party.[1] Justice was communal; its enforcement involved clan and family relationships. It was this communitarian nature of justice that made the system work.

In small communities a false defendant would have a hard time rounding up eleven neighbors as oath helpers.[2] Rough justice prevailed; even an innocent defendant who was a jerk would have a hard time finding oath helpers, and perhaps that was the point.

Not just fear of damnation from perjury assured justice in compurgation trials, but also the process itself.[3] Obviously, though, damnation for breaking an oath had a lot more power in medieval society than in ours. If the accused could not get the required number of compurgators, he could elect to have trial by battle or ordeal.[4]

Different times and different types of cases required various numbers of compurgators. Eventually, however, the generally required number became twelve oaths, the defendant and his eleven oath helpers.[5] This shows compurgation trials as a basis for our modern twelve-member jury.

The word "compurgator" is synonymous with "conjuror" and "juror."[6]

The thing to remember with compurgation is that the oath *is* the evidence.[7] Today the oath is just part of the jury's credibility determination.

TRIAL BY ORDEAL- GOING THROUGH FIRE AND WATER:

We tend to view trial by ordeal as nothing more than primitive superstition contrasted with our supposed enlightenment.[8] This misses the point: the ordeal was about mercy!

From what we can glean from the records, a defendant had

---

1. Thayer, *Modes of Trial*, at 58.

2. R.C. VAN CAENEGEM, THE BIRTH OF THE ENGLISH COMMON LAW 66 (1988); FREDERICK G. KEMPIN, JR., HISTORICAL INTRODUCTION TO ANGLO-AMERICAN LAW 49 (3d ed. 1990); BAKER at 74.

    An example of this was Queen Uta of Germany, accused of adultery in 899 and acquitted only after eighty-two knights confirmed her chastity. KADRI at 20.

3. Dante puts the great traitors, or oath breakers, in hell's very heart. Brutus, Cassius, and Judas get munched on for eternity by Satan, the greatest oath breaker of all.

4. Helene E. Schwartz, *Demythologizing the Historic Role of the Grand Jury*, 10 AM. CRIM. L. REV. 701, 707 (1972).

5. VAN CAENEGEM at 66; KEMPIN at 49.

6. KADRI at 20.

The Conjurer by Hieronymus Bosch (sixteenth century) Note the character on the left stealing a money purse

    The synonym "conjuror" has come into modern English to refer to someone who performs magic tricks to amuse or trick an audience, that is, a magician. The original meaning from "conjuration" (from Latin "*conjure*," "*conjurare*," or to "swear together") can mean an invocation or evocation (the latter in the sense of binding by a vow). The original Latin, "*conjuration*" or "*conjurison*," formerly meant "conspiracy." WEBSTER'S NEW INT'L DICTIONARY 565 (2d ed. 1942).

7. The same is true for the other modes of trial of ordeal and battle. These supernatural proofs and the oaths upon which they rested were absolute proof. BAKER at 72.

8. See Thayer, *Modes of Trial*, at 63–64 ("*scholars discover it [the ordeal] everywhere among barbarous people . . .*").

9. "*Its actual effect was to save many people, about whom there was little human doubt of their guilt, from capital punishment and maiming.*" Margaret H. Kerr, Richard D. Forsyth & Michael J. Plyley, *Cold Water and Hot Iron: Trial by Ordeal in England*, 22 J. INTERDISCIPLINARY HIST. 573, 594 (1992). *See also* Pollock at 295 (noting high acquittal rate).

King William II

10. Kerr at 580 ("*The majority of people who underwent the ordeal passed and saved their lives.*"). See also Kerr at 578, 579, 581 tbl., and 586 (for examples and statistics).

a 68 percent success rate at ordeal.[9] Most people who faced ordeal passed.[10]

This is why the English kings saw it as a limitation of their authority, as the second Norman King, William II (William Rufus) commented:

"What is that? Is God a just judge? Damn whoever thinks it! He will answer for this by my good judgment and not by God's—which can be folded this way and that as anyone wants it."[11]

The kings didn't like the church's control. But the "withering of ordeal" was not judgment by God—God already knew if you were guilty! Rather

it was remitting the case *ad iudicium Dei* ("to the judgment of God").[12] As contemporary writers noted, the ordeal is a form of "grace" (we would say "commutation") for the guilty.[13] God could give you an earthly pardon, and the ordeal was your purge, not necessarily a trial of the facts.[14] In England, the Assize of Clarendon in 1166 specified that defendants would face the ordeal after a presentment jury, the precursor to our modern grand jury, had already determined guilt ("*malecrditus*").[15]

Ordeals involved elaborate rituals allowing all manner

of subjectivity.[16] In England the two main methods were of hot iron and water:

- **Hot iron:** In this ordeal, usually for women, the accused grabbed an iron bar, which a priest had blessed, and walked a certain number of paces.[17] Her hand was bandaged and three days later a "jury" unwrapped it to see if the wound was infected. If not, she was absolved.

- **Cold water:** In this ordeal, usually for men (unless the charge was witchcraft), a priest blessed a pool, making it holy water. The accused was tossed in tied up.[18]

---

14. *Quoted in* Peter Brown, *Society and the Supernatural: A Medieval Change*, 104 DAEDALUS 133, 140 (1975). *See also* Kerr at 575 (stating the quote as *"What is this? God is a just judge? May he perish who henceforth believes that."*). William was responding to the acquittal of fifty men for violating the forest laws. This quote also reflects the emerging church/state power struggle. Later Henry II would order an acquitted defendant from the ordeal to "adjure" the realm (i.e., banishment) but not forfeiture of his goods. Pollack at 180.

15. Brown at 138. Sir Frederick Pollock, *The King's Peace in the Middle Ages*, 13 HARV. L. REV. 177, 295 (1900) notes that the ordeal was originally an appeal to the local pagan god of water or fire.

16. VAN CAENEGEM at 69. Rebecca V. Colman, *Reason and Unreason in Early Medieval Law*, 4 J. INTERDISCIPLINARY HIST. 571, 582 and n.34 (1974) (clergy generally conducted ordeal trials).

17. BAKER at 72.

18. Roger D. Groot, *The Jury of Presentment before 1215*, 26 AM. J. LEGAL HIST. 1, 3 (1992). The ordeal was especially useful when the jury was unsure—*"leave it to God."* See Kerr at 577.

Modern grand juries find probable cause, and our trial or petit juries then find the defendant not guilty or guilty on the higher standard of proof beyond a reasonable doubt. This two-stage process came from the Middle Ages. In Europe, a form of inquest ("*inquisitio generalis*") developed to determine whether a *prima facie* case existed against the accused followed by the actual trial either by compurgation or inquisition ("*inquisitio specialis*"). *See* Ullmann, *Medieval Principles*, at 18. In England, the presentment jury developed from the inquest to send the case first to compurgation, or later ordeal, or later to jury trial. R.H. Helmholz, *The Early History of the Grand Jury and the Canon Law*, 50 U. CHI. L. REV. 613 (1983) (arguing canon law as the source of our modern grand jury).

1. *"God might be believed to speak in an ordeal, but the human group took an unconscionably long time letting Him get a word in edgewise."* Brown at 137. *See also* John W. Baldwin, *The Intellectual Preparation for the Canon of 1215 against Ordeals*, 36 SPECULUM 613, 629 (1961) (noting examples of the subjectivity in ordeal).

If the point was to really leave it all up to God, then why not just use dice or a coin to decide the question? *See* Fisher at 600–01.

2. *See* A.K.R. KIRALFY, POTTER'S HISTORICAL INTRODUCTION TO ENGLISH LAW, 4TH ED. 353 (1958). *See also* description in KEMPIN at 59–60; VAN CAENEGEM at 65.

See the illustration of a widow taking the ordeal for her dead husband by grasping a bar of red-hot iron. The bar does not burn her, thus proving his innocence.

3. KADRI at 27. *See also generally* DANNY DANZIGER & JOHN GILLINGHAM, 1215: THE YEAR OF MAGNA CARTA 183–85 (2003); VAN CAENEGEM at 64–65.

Ordeal of water

If he sank he was absolved because the holy water accepted him—or, conversely, the water repels the sin. They then fished him out (presumably before he drowned). The ordeal of cold water was akin to a rebaptism, where the soul came out of the water purged of sin.

It was the church, not the king, that controlled the process. If the defendant faced the king's justice, it most surely meant hanging or maiming. Thus it was much better to face an ordeal and the chance of God's "grace."[1] And a look at the procedures in detail shows how the defendant might get that grace.[2]

The ordeal of hot iron, for instance, involved a mass where the priest put the iron in the fire *"and sprinkle[d] it with holy water"* (of unspecified amount and temperature). After the priest took the iron out of the fire, he was to lay it on wood. (The wood absorbed some of the heat.) Then the priest was to read the Gospels (of unspecified length and reading speed) and then again *"sprinkle holy water over the iron"* (again, of unspecified amount or temperature). The accused then took the iron and carried it for *"nine paces."* (No mention of how fast the accused was to walk or, for that matter, run.)[3] Even at this point a few good calluses could assure God's mercy.[4] Then the priest or official bandaged the hand (unspecified as to how or with what) and waited three days, when the priest or a jury would decide if the wound had healed

---

1. Kerr at 573–74 asserts that the ordeal's mandatory use was only from the Assize of Clarendon in 1166 to the Fourth Lateran Council of 1215. Even Kerr, however, notes that the ordeal was mentioned *"in a number of [much earlier] Anglo-Saxon codes."* Id.

3. *See* Kerr at 588 (describing the ritual).

2. Other ordeals. Several other types of ordeals existed in Europe at different times.
◀ The one pictured at left is the ordeal of poison.

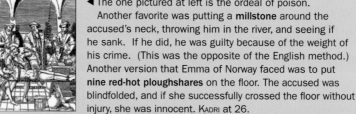

Another favorite was putting a **millstone** around the accused's neck, throwing him in the river, and seeing if he sank. If he did, he was guilty because of the weight of his crime. (This was the opposite of the English method.) Another version that Emma of Norway faced was to put **nine red-hot ploughshares** on the floor. The accused was blindfolded, and if she successfully crossed the floor without injury, she was innocent. KADRI at 26.

For others, usually clergy, there was the ordeal of a **coarse morsel** of bread. If, after fasting for a number of days, the accused choked, he was guilty.

An early form, called the **cauldron ordeal**, was to have the accused reach in a pot of boiling water for stones. If after a time the hand became infected, the accused was guilty.

In the **ordeal of bier**, the accused touched the victim's body and was condemned if the corpse bled anew. *Id.* at 37. Thus, in the trial of ordeal there was an early form of Crime Scene Investigation (CSI) with the belief that the dead could tell you who did it.

Edward the Confessor's mother, Emma of Norway, walked on nine red-hot ploughshares to prove she did not commit adultery with the Bishop of Winchester

---

4. Don't forget the Leidenfrost effect! *See* Kerr at 590. This is what causes water drops to skip off the frying pan's surface instead of immediately turning to steam. The heat causes the underside of the water drop to vaporize, making a buffer and the bounce.

Johann Gottlob Leidenfrost first described this effect in 1756.
◀ Modern Fijian fire walkers do not get burned because of this effect.
The holy water on the iron plus the accused's own perspiring palms would have given protection.

5. Brown at 139; Kerr at 594.

6. Kerr at 594 (noting modern studies show that infection before the fifth day is uncommon in burn cases).

7. Why not? There is no need to be cynical about everything! *"Ego te absolvo"* ("I give you absolution") is the statement a priest makes upon giving absolution-or, updated, *"You beat the rap!"*

Michelangelo's God on the Sistine ceiling

"normally."[5] If yes, that was the end of the ordeal.

Thus, in the ordeal of hot iron, the accused had at least four chances for success:

- the iron caused no injury because it was allowed to cool;

- the accused may have had a second- or third-degree burn, which would not have shown up as an infection on the third day;

- the bandage was ster-ile and no infection developed;[6] or

- God spoke and worked a miracle.[7]

All in all, it was a lenient test.[8]

The ordeal of cold water had similar subjectivities. In the tuck position, a person who expels air will likely sink and thus pass the ordeal.[9] Also, women did not usually face the ordeal of cold water. Their higher body fat would have caused them to float and thus fail.[10]

The available records show a pass rate of 82 percent.[11]

Women did face the ordeal of water in one class of cases: witch trials.[12] These trials killed 60,000 to 100,000 people over two centuries.[13] "*Swimming a witch*" became the trial norm for witchcraft persecutions.[14] Out of fear and superstition Europe relaxed criminal procedure to get after these servants of the devil.[15] But witch trials were a subversion of the normal process of mercy.[16] In the same way its modern equivalents subvert justice.[17]

---

8. Kerr at 593 ("*It would appear, therefore, that if the presence of infection on the third day after the ordeal was the test of guilt, it was a very lenient one.*").

9. Kerr at 587 (noting scientific studies showing that after maximum exhalation the floating rate falls to almost 0 percent in males over age fifteen).

10. Kerr at 582–83, 586–88.

A "Rubenesque" woman would not have stood a chance in the ordeal of cold water!

Venus at the Mirror by Rubens

Swimming a witch in Bedford. Sahe later hanged on March 30, 1613.

11. Kerr at 588.

12. English women were nine times more likely than men to be charged with witchcraft and twice as likely to be hanged. KADRI at 116.

Witchcraft defendant in the tucked position

13. KADRI at 105.

15. The Catholic Church originally taught that even believing in witches was a sin. Saint Augustine in the fifth century reasoned that only God could do magic and thus it was "*an error of the pagans*" to believe that "*some divine power other than the one God*" could do anything magical. Kadri at 106. Then after five centuries of teaching that it was blasphemous to believe in witchcraft, the church declared it a hearsay to deny witches existed. *Id*. at 109. But in places where the church was strong, the witch persecutions were both less frequent and milder. *Id*. at 111.

16. Without a strong central government or church, Germany was particularly bad. But in England, because of grand juries and petit juries, fewer than one in four defendants went to the gallows, a number far less than in any other country in Europe. KADRI at 117. "*Satan always got far less bang for his buck in England.*"*Id*. at 118.

Saint Augustine

17. Senator Joseph McCarthy and **Roy Cohn** at the McCarthy hearings' modern witch hunt for communists.
Arthur Miller's play THE CRUCIBLE (1953), ostensibly about the Salem witch trials, was really about McCarthyism.

14. The idea was that because witches partook of Satan's ethereal essence, they were unnaturally light and bobbed to the surface. KADRI at 112. This is the same reason they can fly on a broom.

This lead to the belief that water killed witches, which is why the Wicked Witch of the West melts in THE WIZARD OF OZ when Dorothy dumps water on her.

In a more satirical turn, Sir Bedevere from MONTY PYTHON AND THE HOLY GRAIL (Fox Video 1975) summed up the reasoning of witch trials: "*Witches burn, and so does wood, so witches are made of wood; wood floats on water, and so do ducks, therefore, if she weighs as much as a duck, she is a witch.*"

The Wicked Witch of the West

THE WIZARD OF OZ (MGM 1939)

But even if the accused failed the ordeal, the church's mercy could still extend to prevent hanging. The defendant could often take refuge in the church and buy his life by selling his freedom, that is, becoming a slave.[1] The kings resisted the practice. With the Assize of Clarendon of 1166, Henry II banished those who passed the ordeal, and denied the ordeal to those who confessed or those a presentment jury found to be of ill repute and who had taken stolen property.[2]

Henry II and the other English kings had several reasons for opposing ordeals. One, of course, was power. The kings wanted control over the church's jurisdiction. In addition the nature of justice was changing from private to public. The king had a role now in dispensing his justice and, as the source of justice, collected hefty fines in the process.

The church too moved away from ordeals as a way of resolving disputes. The church had always called the ordeal the "vulgar" mode of trial ("purgatio vulgaris"). Stories abounded of innocent people hanged after ordeals. Voices in the church warned that the ordeal immorally *"tempted God."*[3] Finally in 1215, with the Fourth Lateran Council, the church prohibited clergy from participating in ordeals, a restriction that effectively ended the practice.[4]

The ending of ordeal trials left an open niche in English criminal procedure. The church courts continued to use compurgation but, in the expanding king's courts, juries replaced ordeal.[5] Thus the Fourth Lateran Council of 1215 had more to do with the growth of jury trials in England than *Magna Carta* of the same year.[6]

---

1. Kerr at 589 n.30.

2. The term is *"adjournment of the realm."* Kerr at 575, 578 n.10; VAN CAENEGEM at 69–70; Groot, *Presentment*, at 22–23.

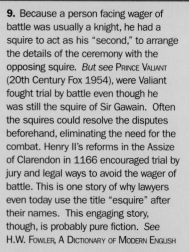

King Henry II

The Assize of Clarendon prohibited those accused of serious crime from purging (ordeal or compurgation) and required them to leave England within forty days. BLACK'S at 110. Clarendon began the transformation of English law from divinely ordained systems of trial by ordeal or battle toward what we now call the "evidentiary" model, beginning the common-law trial by jury.

3. Baldwin at 628–29 (recounting the many voices in the church on the immorality of ordeals). Men were studying both law and theology in the church's universities at this time, undermining belief in the ordeal. DANZIGER & GILLINGHAM at 186. See also Brown at 136; VAN CAENEGEM at 68–69.

4. Specifically, Canon 18, on ordeals. Baldwin at 613; KADRI at 35, 50.

5. DANZIGER & GILLINGHAM at 187; Helmholz, *Grand Jury*, at 617, 622. For details on the transition of trial by ordeal to trial by jury, *see also* Sir Frederick Pollock, *The King's Peace in the Middle Ages*, 13 HARV. L. REV. 177, 180–81 (1900).

6. Fisher at n.20 (citing Roger D Groot, *The Early Thirteenth Century Criminal Jury*, in TWELVE GOOD MEN AND TRUE: THE CRIMINAL TRIAL JURY IN ENGLAND, 1200–1800, at 3 (J.S. Cockburn & Thomas A. Green eds., 1988)); *see also* Pollack at 180.

For a detailed analysis of ordeal procedure and its place in medieval society, *see generally* Trisha Olson, *Of Enchantment: The Passing of the Ordeals and the Rise of the Jury Trial*, 50 SYRACUSE L. REV. 109 (2000).

7. Daniel Klerman, *Settlement and the Decline of Private Prosecution in Thirteenth-Century England*, 19 LAW & HIST. REV. 1, 11 (2001).

8. Thayer, *Modes of Trial*, at 45, 65–66; VAN CAENEGEM at 80; Pollock at 295. Actually, the source of trial by battle is subject to considerable scholarly debate. *See,* for example, Baldwin at 621, noting the source as the Lombards, VAN CAENEGEM at 65, noting the scholarship showing the Franks as the origin, and KIRALFY at 348, noting the relation to the Saxon blood feud. The Normans themselves may have gotten the custom from their own Scandinavian roots. Norsemen used the *"holmgång"* (or *"holmganga"*), a death duel, to settle disputes.

9. Because a person facing wager of battle was usually a knight, he had a squire to act as his "second," to arrange the details of the ceremony with the opposing squire. *But see* PRINCE VALIANT (20th Century Fox 1954), were Valiant fought trial by battle even though he was still the squire of Sir Gawain. Often the squires could resolve the disputes beforehand, eliminating the need for combat. Henry II's reforms in the Assize of Clarendon in 1166 encouraged trial by jury and legal ways to avoid the wager of battle. This is one story of why lawyers even today use the title "esquire" after their names. This engaging story, though, is probably pure fiction. *See* H.W. FOWLER, A DICTIONARY OF MODERN ENGLISH

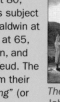

The Holmgång by Johannes Flintoe

TRIAL BY BATTLE, OTHERWISE KNOWN AS TRIAL BY COMBAT, JUDICIAL DUEL, WAGER OF BATTLE, TRIAL BY HIS BODY

No trial is more adversarial, confrontational, or open than trial by battle. Originally, the participants were the parties, and thus the term *"trial by his body."*[7]

Trial by battle probably came to England with the Norman Conquest.[8] It was a judicially sanctioned duel among nobles because only nobles, generally Normans, could bear arms.[9] Thus, even after the conquest, trial by battle never seemed

to gain much currency among the Anglo-Saxons, and it became the Norman (French) mode of trial.[10]

The Normans, though, did sanction trial by battle for Anglo-Saxons

"[i]f a Frenchman shall charge an Englishman with perjury, or murder or theft or homicide or [robbery], the Englishman may defend himself, as he shall prefer, either by the ordeal of hot iron or by wager of battle. But if the Englishman be infirm, let him find another who will take his place."[11]

A "Frenchman" had the option of acquitting himself *"by a valid oath."* Later

the person challenged would decide whether to have battle or jury.[12]

As time passed the law allowed a *"witness"* to stand in for some parties—in other words, a champion. Thus the English term for the procedure was *"wager of battel,"* from the oath or "wager" of the witness-champion.[13]

Originally, champions fought for women, the young, old, or sick.[14] The witness-champion was to speak from his own knowledge or that *"of his father"* and would thus defend his testimony. Before battle, the two champions would swear to the truth of what they said.[15]

USAGE 167 (2d ed. 1965) (noting that the term was just adopted by barristers but not solicitors in England, but that today could be had by any adult male).

But the most famous squire of all time is Sancho Panza, Don Quixote's sidekick. "*Panza*" means "belly" in Spanish.

Don Quixote and Sancho Panza by Pablo Picasso

Don Quixote and Sancho Panza by Gustave Doré (1863)

10. Thayer, *Modes of Trial*, at 66.

THE 13TH WARRIOR (Touchstone Pictures 1999) has a version of a *holmgång*. The movie and book are roughly

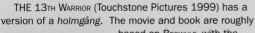

based on BEOWULF, with the movie's Viking leader called Buliwyf, with lines such as "*Luck, often enough, will save a man, if his courage hold,*" a paraphrase of "*Often, for undaunted courage, fate spares the man it has not already marked.*" See SEAMUS HEANEY, BEOWULF: A NEW VERSE TRANSLATION 39 (2000).

11. Laws of William ch. 6, *quoted in* George C. Thomas, III, *History's Lesson for the Right to Counsel*, 2004 U. ILL. L. REV. 543, 562 n.139 (2004).

12. BELLAMY at 36. *See* Roger D. Groot, *The Jury in Private Criminal Prosecutions before 1215*, 27 AM. J. LEGAL HIST. 116–25 (1983) (on how the appellee (i.e., the one challenged) could avoid trial by battle).

13. *See* BLACK'S at 1416. As with compurgation the oath *was* the evidence. KADRI at 20.

The witness-champions swearing their oaths before battle

14. DANZIGER & GILLINGHAM at 181; Groot, *Prosecutions*, at 116.

What to do with women was always a problem. A woman could offer to prove the appeal "*as the court adjudges.*" Klerman, *Settlement* at 11. The non–battle worthy or women were usually put to the ordeals of cold water or hot iron to prove innocence. *Id*. at 12.

IVANHOE (MGM 1952) had actor Robert Taylor's Ivanhoe fighting as the champion of Elizabeth Taylor's Rebecca. Rebecca is in love with Ivanhoe but he goes for Joan Fontaine's Lady Rowena instead (not the choice I would have made, but there it is!). The film is an adaptation of Sir Walter Scott's IVANHOE (1819).

But as this medieval drawing shows, women could fight with the male opponent handicapped in some way.

Classic Comics version of IVANHOE

15. Thayer, *Modes of Trial*, at 68.

Trial by battle was often used in land disputes, providing the basis for claiming that the "champion" would actually know who had the right claim. This allowed the champion to be a compurgator, or oath helper. In fact, compurgation trials eventually replaced trial by battle in most cases.[1]

In England it was supposed to be illegal to hire a champion. By 1275, however, the requirement (actually by then a legal fiction) that the champion be a witness was dropped.[2]

This practice of having champions was handy for English kings. It would have been unseemly as well as impractical for the king to have to fight in every dispute or, indeed, every time a crown official charged someone with a crime. Thus the king had his own champion.[3]

Fundamentally, trial by battle was another form of ordeal based on the notion that God would only let right prevail, *iudicium Dei*.[4] But the church discouraged the practice even more than other types of ordeals.[5] Such contests were expensive and thus unfair to the poor, most of whom had no training in the use of arms.[6]

Moreover, the church was adopting a more rational means of dispute resolution.[7] Trial by battle, as with other ordeals, tempted God by asking

---

1. Baldwin at 616–17.

2. Thayer, *Modes of Trial*, at 68. DANNY & GILLINGHAM at 181 (regarding the practiced of having "champions").

3. The champion of the King of England rode into Westminster Hall at the king's coronation, challenging "*if any person shall deny the king's title to the crown, he is to defend it!*" The Dymoke family has held this office since 1377. WEBSTER'S NEW INT'L DICTIONARY 447 (2d ed. 1942).

The king's champion figures into the Arthurian legend. *See* EXCALIBUR (Warner Brothers 1981) and CAMELOT (Warner Brothers 1967). It is also central to the movie EL CID (Allied Artists 1961), about the Spanish national hero El Cid Campeador, meaning "the king's champion" against the Moors in Spain.

In CAMELOT, Guinevere needed a champion because the king, Arthur, sat as judge over the court and thus could not defend her.

Julie Andrews and Richard Barton in the 1960 play CAMELOT

Charlton Heston, in his pre-NRA days, thinking "*swords don't kill people, people kill people.*"
Heston champions gun rights. *See* **Chapter 2: Shooting Your Mouth Off about the Second Amendment.**

4. The biblical story of David and Goliath formed the agrument for the procedure. Baldwin at 618. *See*

David and Goliath by Caravaggio (1600)

1 *Samuel* 17 describing how David killed the giant Goliath with a stone from his sling. Some medieval theologians compared trial by battle to the just war theory. Baldwin at 623.

5. Baldwin at 613.
Theologians argued the precedent of Constantine's prohibition of gladiatorial contests. *Id.* at 614 n.10.

Pollice Verso by Jean-Léon Gérôme (1872)

6. Thayer, *Modes of Trial*, at 67 n.1 (noting Saint Louis abolished the practice as unfair to the poor).

In England, however, the great monasteries were often involved in land disputes and thus had to retain champions. KEMPIN at 56.

7. In the late eleventh century, the church and European lawyers rediscovered Justinian's DIGEST, which showed that the Romans had differentiated between proof and verdict. KADRI at 49.

8. Baldwin at 618, 620, 628 (citing to the arguments of Saint Augustine). Still though,

trial by battle made for great spectacle.

9. William Shakespeare's *Richard II* has an example of trial by combat between Bolingbroke and Mowbray. But the combat ends up not being to the death when Richard banishes both parties. *See* KORNSTEIN, SHAKESPEARE'S LEGAL APPEAL

202–06 (1994). For the actual historical account, *see* Peter Earle, *Richard II,* in THE LIVES OF THE KINGS AND QUEENS OF ENGLAND 85 (Antonia Fraser ed., 1975); *see also* KURT VON S. KYNELL, SAXON AND

acceptance of something other than God's rational world.[8] Indeed, when selecting a champion, the parties hardly put full faith in God—no one picked the biggest wimp.[9]

In 1215, the church's Fourth Lateran Council also prohibited clergy from participation in trial by battle, which discouraged the procedure. Other modes of trial took over, such as compurgation. As time passed the inquest in ecclesiastical courts and European kingdoms replaced battle and the other ordeals. In England it was trial by jury.[10]

The emerging concept of the "king's peace" added to the demise of trial by battle.[11] In criminal cases the new king's courts extended and protected the king's peace by alleging that the defendant did a crime *"wickedly and in felony against the peace of our lord the king."* Because the king is now the accuser-as is still seen in the caption of criminal cases in Great Britain as *Rex (or Regina) v. The Accused*-the defendant cannot seek trial by battle *"since the king fights not, nor has none other champion than the country."*[12]

The English, however, did not formally abolish wager of battle until 1818.[13] Some, however, argue the practice continued throughout the nineteenth and even twentieth centuries in the duel code.[14]

MEDIEVAL ANTECEDENTS OF THE ENGLISH COMMON LAW 161 (2000).

See MONTY PYTHON AND THE HOLY GRAIL (1975), which has a version of trial by combat with the Black Knight getting his arms and legs cut off but famously yelling *"Okay, so we will call it a draw!"*

Both IVANHOE and MONTY PYTHON AND THE HOLY GRAIL were filmed on location at Doune Castle in Scotland. Since 2004 the castle hosts its annual Monty Python Day.

10. Baldwin 614; Thayer, *Modes of Trial*, at 67. *See also* Groot, *Presentment*, at 1, 24 (on the origins of the adversarial system from juries). Regarding the jury as substitute for trial by battle, ordeal, wager of law (compurgation), and inquisitorial procedures, see Morano at 509 and BARBARA J. SHAPIRO, "BEYOND REASONABLE DOUBT" AND "PROBABLE CAUSE" 3 (1991). For the view that early common-law trials had much in common with inquisitorial procedures, see Landsman II and Langbein, noting that up until the late eighteenth century trials were inquisitorial. *See also* Amalia D. Kessler, *Our Inquisitorial Tradition: Equity Procedure, Due Process, and the Search for an Alternative to the Adversarial*, 90 CORNELL L. REV. 1181 (2005) (noting the American tradition).

11. *See* **Chapter 6: How the Sixth Amendment Guarantees You a Court, a Lawyer, and a Chamber Pot** (regarding the growth of the king's peace).

12. Pollack at 179–80.

13. In 1818, a party threw a gauntlet into the Court of King's Bench, causing the court to rule that the system was abolished. BAKER at 74, n.12, *citing Ashford v. Thornton*, (1818) 1 B. & Ald. 405; Stat. 59 Geo. III, c. 46. In 1984 a Scottish defendant tried to wage battle, arguing that the 1818 rule only applied to England. *Id. See also* Alison L. LaCroix, *To Gain the Whole World and Lose His Own Soul: Nineteenth Centruy American Dueling as Public Law and Private Code*, 33 HOFSTRA L. REV. 501 (2004) (arguing that the duel code ("code duelo") came from trial by battle); Ellen E. Sward, *A History of the Civil Trial in the United States*, 51 U. KAN. L. REV. 347, 353 (2003) (noting that the duel was a "vestage" of trial by combat).

14. *See* ROBERT BALDICK, THE DUEL: A HISTORY (1965).

The Burr-Hamilton duel is the most famous in American history. The men meet at Weehawken, New Jersey, where the dueling laws were more lenient, hoping their duel would revive their respective political fortunes. Instead it ended Burr's political future and Hamilton's life. For the *code duello*, see the very good movie THE DUELISTS (Paramount Pictures 1977), Ridley Scott's first feature film, starring Keith Carradine and Harvey Keitel. Regarding defendants' attempts to assert the *code duello* as a defense in homicide cases, *see Griffin v. State*, 274 S.W. 611 (1925), and *Ward v. Commonwealth*, 116 S.W. 786 (1909).

Perhaps the longevity of trial by battle is due to the ideal it embodied: an open confrontation of two champions fighting for what is *right*. What courtroom lawyer sees him or herself in any other way?[1] And before we scoff at the notion that God will protect the *right*, don't we still believe in *iudicium Dei?* Name a classic Western where *right* does not win![2]

TO PLEAD OR NOT TO PLEAD-THAT WAS THE QUESTION

In the days of ordeal, battle, and compurgation the defendant could often choose not only his mode of trial but also his court: king, church, or local lord's. The accused needed to plead, in a sense accept jurisdiction, to start the case. Over time the effect of the Fourth Lateran Council was to leave but one form of trial: the jury.[3]

This raised a theological problem: having a party or defendant submit *"to God's judgment"* was allowed (after all, every soul would face it sooner or later), but, to the medieval mind, it was improper to require a person to submit to any form of *human* judgment (after all, people still had free will).[4] Specifically, medieval English courts could not bring themselves to compel a prisoner to *"put himself on the county,"* that is, submit to trial by jury.[5]

The problem then became how to get the accused to accept—that is, to "plead to," *de bono et malo* ("for good or ill")—the jury. If the accused pleaded *"not guilty,"* the judge would ask, *"How will you be tried?"* Answering the question meant that the accused accepted the court's jurisdiction and would not be pleading *"upon his clergy."*

---

1. Consider, for example, **Clarence Darrow** and **William Jennings Bryan** during the 1925 *Scopes* trial.

The movie and play Inherit the Wind (United Artists 1960) is a fictionalized account of the Scopes Monkey trial. The title comes from the King James Bible, *Proverbs* 11:29: *"He that troubleth his own house shall inherit the wind: and the fool shall be servant to the wise."*

2. From High Noon (United Artists 1952) to Tombstone (Hollywood Pictures 1993) to Star Wars (20th Century Fox 1977), the theme is *iudicium Dei: right* will triumph!

In the trial by battle, right wins, then ▼

and now. ▼ (Okay, so it's really *"A long, long time ago, in a galaxy far, far away,"* but you get the point!)

3. Baker at 508. *Also* Danziger & Gillingham at 189; Kiralfy at 247; Kempin at 63–64; Fisher at 588–89.

4. Pollock at 181–82.

5. From ordeal trials to jury *see* Pollack at 181; Klerman, *Settlement*, at 12.

6. Baker at 508; Black's at 621 (noting that the question would have been *"by God [an ordeal trial] or country [a jury trial]"*). *See also* Colin R. Lovell, English Constitutional and Legal History 149 (1962).

7. This is the origin in some jurisdictions of the rule that a defendant has thirty-five peremptory challenges, the thirty-sixth constituting a refusal to plead. Baker at 508 n.42.

8. *See* Pollack at 181–82.

9. Baker at 508 (citing an act of Parliament in 1275). *See also* Anthony Musson, *Twelve Good Men and True? The Character of Early Fourteenth-Century Juries*, 15 Law & Hist. Rev. 115, 134 (1997) (noting the procedure of a starvation diet to get the accused to submit to trial by jury).

If the accused was a lord he would answer "*by God and my peers*," which meant, up until 1948, he would get a trial in the House of Lords. If he was a commoner he pleaded "*by God and my country*" or "*by God and the country*" or to "*put himself on the country*," meaning trial by jury.[6] "*Country*" meant the petit jury of twelve. The clerk would respond, "*God send you a good deliverance*," a throwback to the older modes of trial of *iudicium Dei*.

If the accused would not plead, either by silence or by rejecting the customary three jury panels of twelve, he had "*refused the common law*" ("*tanquam refutans legem commune*").[7] This created a problem because without the prisoner's submission, the procedure could not go forward, though the refusal to submit was an independent offense of contempt against the king's power, that is, contempt of court.[8] All a judge or sherriff could do was put him in jail, a *prison forte et dure*, meaning under harsh conditions and meager diet, to force the accused to plead.[9]

Prison forte et dure, however, eventually took a deadlier turn, becoming *peine forte et dure*, a procedure where they pressed the accused under heavy weights until he pleaded or died.[10] Thus, when a defendant refused to plead and stood mute, he went to a "*press room*" until he submitted or suffocated.[11]

The reason some defendants endured pressing was because if they died before trial they died innocent and thus saved their estates.[12]

The simple expedient of entering a plea for the defendant eluded the common law until 1772, when Parliament made a mute plea the equivalent of a guilty plea.[13]

---

10. BAKER at 508–09. Andrea McKenzie, "*This Death Some Strong and Stout Hearted Man Doth Choose*": *The Practice of Peine Forte et Dure in Seventeen- and Eighteenth-Century England*, 23 LAW & HIST. REV. 279, 283 (2005).

11. See LEVY at 233.

Peine forte et dure is not the same as **execution by crushing**, which occurred after conviction. In ancient times, the Carthaginians executed people this way, and for over four thousand years of recorded history it was common in South and Southeast Asia using elephants.

Le Tour du Monde by Rousselet (1868)

12. If convicted the king got the condemned's property (i.e., it was "escheated" to the crown), leaving the defendant's heirs nothing. Mckenzie at 289 and n.12. Regarding bravado and class issues with jurors of a higher powered class, see *id.* at 304.

After Henry VIII, pleading in religious trials became very important. In 1586 Saint Margaret Clitherow refused to plead to the charge of harboring Catholic priests. She did this to avoid a trial where her children would have to testify. They laid her on a sharp rock, put a door on her, and loaded it with rocks and stones, killing her within fifteen minutes. This was March

Saint Margaret Clitherow

25, 1586, a Good Friday. *St. Margaret Clitherow*, THE CATHOLIC ENCYCLOPEDIA, http://www.newadvent.org/cathen/04059b.htm (last visited Feb. 28, 2008).

In America, the judges employed *peine forte et dure* during the Salem witch trials to kill those who would not plead to being a witch. Giles Corey died from *peine forte et dure* on September 19, 1692, after he refused to enter a plea. According to legend, his last words were "*more weight*," and he died as the weight was applied. Arthur Miller's political drama THE CRUCIBLE has Giles Corey refuse to answer "aye or nay" to witchcraft, but the movie version has him killed for refusing to reveal a source of information. The U.S. Constitution prohibits "*corruption of blood*" (i.e., preventing heirs for receiving the condemned's property and rights) in three prohibitions against bills of attainder: "*no Bill of Attainder . . . shall be passed . . . ,*" art. I, § 9, cl. 3; "*No State shall . . . pass any Bill of Attainder . . . ,*" art. I, § 10, cl. 1; and "*[t]he Congress shall have Power to declare*

Giles Cory pressed to death during the Salem witch trials

the Punishment of Treason, but no Attainder of Treason shall work Corruption of Blood, or Forfeiture except during the Life of the Person attainted," art. III, § 3, cl. 2. See Jacob Reynolds, *The Rule of Law and the Origins of the Bill of Attainder Clause*, 18 ST. THOMAS L. REV. 177 (2005).

13. Mckenzie at 282. As late as 1772 silence lead to an automatic contempt conviction rather than imposition of compulsory jury trial. BAKER at 509.

In 1827 Parliament changed a mute plea to not guilty, the modern practice.[1]

Given the state of pleading in 1649, John Lilburne, who we have seen in prior chapters, decided to play with his judges.

His judges had to try Lilburne because Cromwell wanted it but needed Lilburne to consent to the court's jurisdiction by pleading "*by God and by country*." Also, his case was too high-profile and political to press a plea out of him.

When asked to plead Lilburne stated:

"By the known laws of England, and a legal jury of my equals, constituted according to the law."

Lilburne was not following the formula.

His judges had to persuade him to say the "*by God and by country*" but Lilburne, being Lilburne, had to add,

". . . that is to say, by a jury of my equals, according to the good old laws of the land." [2]

What the heck, he knew they were there to kill him, so why not have some fun? Besides, Lilburne was playing to the jury.

THE JURY: THE JEWEL IN THE COMMON—LAW CROWN

Before there were police, prosecutors, defense attorneys, and professional judges, the jury was there! Sure, it was not exactly today's institution, but the basics of what a jury does and stands for existed: the conscience of the community.[3]

Although discussed, second-guessed, and often criticized, the trial jury is still with us after centuries.

JURIES IN ATHENS AND ROME

Athenians and Romans had

1. *See,* for example, Federal Rule of Criminal Procedure 11(a)(4), which states "**Failure to Enter a Plea.** *If a defendant refuses to enter a plea . . . the court must enter a plea of not guilty.*"

To plead or not to plead, that is the question! Nowhere does the Constitution provide a defendant the right to a plea agreement. Rather, both the original Constitution (at U.S. Const. art. 3, § 2) and the Bill of Rights (at U.S. Const. amends. VI, VII) guarantee the defendant a trial. But in any given jurisdiction some 95 to 99 percent of all cases end in a plea bargain. Without plea bargaining the American system of justice would collapse. Prosecutors clear their caseload and can put their resources toward other cases. Those standing for reelection can tout their high conviction rate even though it does not come from

trial victories. Despite belief that plea bargaining "lets criminals off," this is not necessarily true. Although each defendant acting rationally will try to get the best deal possible, defendants cannot collectively bargain (and their lawyers are prevented ethically from doing so). Through policy, the prosecutor can dictate the outcome of nearly all cases, saving his resources for the very few that go to trial.

What this means is that our American criminal procedure is not as adversarial as we tout. When the defendant accepts a plea bargain he has a "change of plea" hearing where he declares himself guilty. This is an inquisition.

History provides examples of famous plea agreements:
- Galileo in 1633 got house arrest from the Inquisition in exchange for reciting penitential psalms weekly and recanting Copernican heresies.
- Al Capone bragged about his light sentence for pleading guilty to tax evasion and Prohibition violations. The judge then declared that the bargain did not bind the court, and

Al Capone

Capone got seven and a half years in Alcatraz.

- To avoid execution, James Earl Ray pled guilty in 1969 to assassinating Martin Luther King Jr. and got ninety-nine years.

James Earl Ray
- In 1973 Spiro Agnew resigned as vice president and pled no contest to failing to report income and received three years' probation and a $10,000 fine (about one-third of the amount in issue).

Spiro Agnew

As for film, John Proctor was offered a plea to avoid hanging but has to confront honor and faith in THE CRUCIBLE (20th Century Fox 1996). AND JUSTICE FOR ALL (Columbia Pictures 1979) slams the criminal justice system and the ugliness of plea bargaining, ending with Al Pacino being dragged from the courtroom screaming *"Wanna make a deal!"*

Galileo facing the Roman Inquisition by Cristiano Banti (1857)

jury trials. For example, in the trial of Socrates, the central theme of Plato's *Euthyphro*, *Apology*, *Crito*, and *Phaedo*, Socrates had a jury of 500 Athenians to decide charges he had corrupted the youth and encouraged them to disbelieve in the ancestral gods. The jury voted to convict 280 to 220. The Athenians also had jury sentencing, with the jury voting 360 to 141 for death.[4]

Athenian juries were drawn at random from citizens. The Athenian playwright Aristophanes described the pharisaical jury practice in his comedy *The Wasps*. Athenian juries valued character evidence, often ignoring the formal law for equitable justice.[5] In most cases these jurors decided the punishment and, like in Socrates's case, they would hear the defendant's second speech regarding punishment.[6]

In ancient Athens you could actually make a modest living as a juror. Jurors got three *obols* per day, approximately one-third of a skilled artisan's daily wage, and the courts were open approximately 150 to 200 days a year.[7]

The Athenians also gave us the earliest known courtroom drama, Aeschylus's *The Oresteia*.[8]

Following a really bad family dynamic, Orestes kill his mother for killing his father for killing his sister (Clytemnestra, Agamemnon, and Iphigenia, respectively— that's a family that puts a capital "*D*" in *dysfunctional!*).

The Goddess Athena summoned ten Athenian citizens and bound them by oath to decide Orestes's fate for killing his mom. When they deadlocked, Athena broke the tie by voting not guilty.

The Furies, representing punitive vengeance rather than the rule of law, hiss at the verdict, which is common even today with a not guilty verdict.[9]

2. See Harold W. Wolfram, *John Lilburne: Democracy's Pillar of Fire*, 3 SYRACUSE L. REV. 213, 234–35 and n.79 (1952) (an excellent account of the Lilburne trial and its aftermath).

3. See, for example, *Ring v. Arizona*, 536 U.S. 584 (2002), deciding that juries, not judges, as the true conscience of the community, should decide on the death penalty.

4. The Death of Socrates. The higher number that voted for death shows that he should have had a mitigation lawyer under the American Bar Association standards, requiring two qualified counsel in every death case. For instance, a mitigation lawyer would have told him he should not have argued that instead of death he deserved meals at public expense for being a philosopher. *Apology*, THE WORKS OF PLATO 60 (Irwin Edman ed., Benjamin Jowett trans., Random House 1956). But Socrates did end up as a character in BILL & TED'S EXCELLENT ADVENTURE (Orion Pictures 1989).

5. Adriaan Lanni, "*Verdict Most Just*": The Modes of Classical Athenian Justice, 16 YALE J.L. & HUMAN. 277, 278 (2004) ("*The Athenians . . . thought giving juries unlimited discretion to reach verdicts based on the particular circumstances of each case was the most just way to resolve disputes.*"). Use of character evidence in modern trials is much more limited. See, e.g., FED. R. EVID. 608.
    See also Jeffrey Omar Usman, *Ancient and Modern Character Evidence: How Character Evidence Was Used in Ancient Athenian Trials, Its Uses in the United States, and What This Means for How These Democratic Societies Understood the Role of Jurors*, 33 OKLA. CITY U. L. REV. 1 (2008).

6. *Id*. This practice was known as *timesis*.

7. See Usman at n.5.

Murder of Agamemnon

8. KADRI at 4.

The goddess Athena, patroness of Athens

The Remorse of Orestes (1862), as he is pursued by the Furies

The Sacrifice of Iphigenia

9. KADRI at 5.
    For a modern hissing fury, see *Nancy Grace* (HLN Feb. 21, 2005–present), criticizing any defense verdict.

Nancy Grace

But despite the dissenting voices, *The Oresteia* reflects two important concepts about law:

1. That the rule of law ends the cycle of revenge murders, which went so far as Orestes's matricide of Clytemnestra.[1]

2. That ordinary men, rather than officials, have the power to judge.[2] Sure, they had an assist from Athena at the end, but those ordinary men coming together to resolve the cycle of violence was something special—a jury!

The ancient Romans had jury trials from the Roman Republic through the early Roman Empire. Juries ranged from 32 to 360 members, with 75 the most common size.[3]

The jurors were drawn from various social classes of free Romans. From the late Roman period into the Middle Ages, Roman courts switched to an early inquisitorial model, with public magistrates instead of juries deciding most issues. The courts would, however, call groups of *"vicini"* ("neighbors") for information on local facts or the reputations of the parties. As we will see, using locals as a form of proof extended from Roman Britain to the Anglo-Saxons and Normans.[4] In fact, some scholars argue that the Romans leaving Britain earlier than the rest of Europe, while Rome was still using this practice of calling *vicini*, is the origin of the later split between the English common-law jury system and the European inquisition.[5]

THE JURY'S SOURCE: FRANKISH, ENGLISH, SCANDINAVIAN, ANGLO—SAXON, OR NORMAN?

Taking the Roman *vicini* and adding various barbarian customs of tribal justice gives a number of possible sources for our jury. Scholars have argued that the jury's origin is Frankish, Scandinavian, Anglo-Saxon, Danish, or Norman.[6] The Swedes, Low Countries, and northern France, especially Normandy, used some type of jury from the twelfth century before Roman-canonical procedure took over.[7]

The jury's origin, from the Normans to England or from the English to Normandy, became an issue later in history.[8] During the seventeenth century, especially

---

1. Susan Ford Wiltshire, Greece, Rome, and the Bill of Rights 156 (1992).

2. Kadri at 6.

3. O.F. Robinson, The Criminal Law of Ancient Rome 4 (1995). *Also* Roscoe Pound, The Lawyer from Antiquity to Modern Times 42 (1951) (noting the size of Roman juries was from 32 to 75).

See also Wiltshire at 152, stating that Roman courts called *"iudicia publica"* or also *"quaestiones"* were, by Cicero's day, permanent courts presided over by *"praetors"* and having large juries that decided by majority vote.

4. *See* Mike MacNair, *Vicinage and the Antecedents of the Jury*, 17 Law & Hist. Rev. 537, 537–38 (1999). *Compare* Patrick Wormald, *Neighbors, Courts, and Kings: Reflections on Michael Macnair's Vicini*, 17 Law & Hist. Rev. 597 (1999).

5. *See* Bryce Lyon, A Constitutional and Legal History of Medieval England 14 (1960).

6. *See* Ralph V. Turner, *The Origins of the Medieval Jury: Frankish, English, or Scandinavian?* 7 J. Brit. Stud. 1 (1968) (outlining the debate and scholarship).

7. *See* Van Caenegem at 71 (regarding these antecedents), 73 (regarding the Franks and

the Carolingian monarchy as a source). Macnair outlines the scholarship, especially relating to the Norman claim as the jury source. *See also* Turner at 5–7; Charles H. Haskins, *The Early Norman Jury*, 8 Am. Hist. Rev. 613 (1903); James B. Thayer, *The Jury and Its Development*, 5 Harv. L. Rev. 249 (1891–92); Baker at 72; Barnes at 349 and n.26, (arguing that the king's court and the Norman inquest system eventually developed into the jury trial).

Norman 15th Century Jury of 12 with court officials

8. *See* MacNair at 539–40. *See generally* John Phillip Reid, The Ancient Constitution and the Origins of Anglo-American Liberty (2005).

9. But see Pollack at 189, attacking the myth of the "ancient" Anglo-Saxon constitution and arguing that most of the jury system came out of the Norman inquest procedures, not from King Alfred.

10. *Quoted in* Wolfram at 246.

11. Thomas Jefferson, for instance, adopted the theory that the English common law was the ancient pre-Norman law of Saxon England. Howe at 584.

12. The Sixth Amendment states:

"In all criminal prosecutions, the accused shall enjoy the right to a speedy and public trial, by an impartial jury..."

And the Seventh Amendment amplifies:

during the struggles with the Stuart monarchs and their notions of absolute monarchy, democratic proponents like the Puritans asserted "*Anglo-Saxon liberty*" and the "*ancient constitution*" as the legacy of all Englishmen against the "Norman" kingship.[9]

John Lilburne, for example, in his 1649 trial played to these themes with the jury, asserting his "*Anglo-Saxon liberty*."

When Lilburne argued the jury decided the law, one of his judges, Lord Keble, responded with indignation that the jury

> "*judges matter(s) of fact . . . not . . . law.*"

Lilburne responded that

> "*the jury by law are not only judges of fact, but of law also; and you call yourselves judges of the law, are no more but Norman intruders; and in deed and in truth, if the jury please, are no more but ciphers, to pronounce their verdict.*" (Emphasis added.)

Keble did not like being called a cipher, decrying,

> "*was there ever such a damnable blasphemous heresy as this is, to call the judges of the law, ciphers?*"[10]

But, as we will see, Lilburne knew that his audience was the jury.

The American Founding Fathers adopted Lilburne's ideal[11] and enshrined it in both the Sixth and Seventh Amendments.[12]

WHY TWELVE?

The Anglo-American trial settled on twelve jurors to unanimously decide the fate of criminal defendants. Sir Edward Coke explained that the "*number of twelve is much respected in holy writ, as 12 apostles, 12 stones, 12 tribes, etc.*"[13] Coke recognized that in our Judeo-Christian culture, twelve is an important number.[14]

The connection with the twelve apostles or the twelve tribes of Israel seems an obvious precedent.[15] Reflecting this biblical origin, trial by compurgation generally required the defendant's oath with eleven compurgators, totaling twelve oaths, which could have been the origin of the modern twelve-juror rule.[16] We do know, for instance, that in 879 AD King Alfred the Great signed a peace treaty with King Guthrum of Denmark establishing that a killer in both realms could cleanse himself of the blood guilt by producing twelve sworn men.[17]

"*In Suits at common law, where the value in controversy shall exceed twenty dollars, the right of trial by jury shall be preserved, and no fact tried by a jury, shall be otherwise re-examined in any Court of the United States, than according to the rules of the common law.*"

13. Quoted in WILTSHIRE at 162.

The Bill of Rights in the U.S. National Archives

14. "Twelve" is a native English word from the Germanic compound "*twa-lif*" ("two-leave," i.e., two is left after taking ten). Moreover, twelve is the last number before the formulaic thirteen, fourteen, etc. Twelve has its own name, a "dozen," reflected in the movies CHEAPER BY THE DOZEN (20th Century Fox 1950, and again in 2003) and THE DIRTY DOZEN (MGM 1967). There are twelve months in a year, twelve inches in a foot, twelve hours on a clock, and twelve days of Christmas. Twelve times twelve is a "gross," and twelve is between lucky eleven and unlucky thirteen. There are twelve signs in the zodiac (the Chinese zodiac as well) and twelve Olympian gods in Greek mythology. Although hardly a highbrow legal argument, all these twelves show that it is just not a good idea to have less than twelve jurors.

The twelve Olympian gods

The zodiac

15. The Twelve Apostles (thirteenth century). As G.K. Chesterton wrote, "*Our civilization has decided, and very justly decided that determining the guilt or innocence of men is a thing too important to be trusted to trained men. If it wishes for light upon that awful matter, it asks men who know no more law than I know, but who can feel the things I felt in the jury box. When it wants a library catalogued, or the solar system discovered, or a trifle of that kind, it uses up its specialists. But when it wishes anything done that is really serious, it collects twelve of the ordinary men standing about. The same thing was done, if I remember right, by the Founder of Christianity.*" G.K. CHESTERTON, TREMENDOUS TRIFLES 86 (1968), quoted in Phillip B. Scott, Jury Nullification: An Historical Perspective on a Modern Debate, 91 W. VA. L. REV. 389 (1988).

16. MacNair at 573; MacNair at 15. For the Supreme Court's acknowledgement of compurgation roots, see Apodaca v. Oregon, 406 U.S. 404, 408 nn. 2 & 3 (1972), discussed in Ethan J. Leib, Supermajoritarianism and the American Criminal Jury, 33 HASTINGS CONST. L.Q. 141–42 (2006).

12 ANGRY MEN (United Artists 1957), the classic jury drama

17. KADRI at 71.

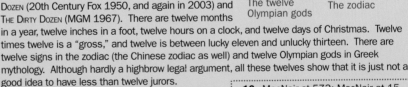

Also, the Anglo-Saxons and Danes had their twelve "*thegns*" ("*thanes*") sitting as a sort of early grand jury deciding whether a defendant would face trial by ordeal or battle.

But leaving aside historical arguments, it could just be that the English didn't like the decimal system, as shown by the fact that there used to be twelve pence to a shilling.[1]

THE EARLY ENGLISH JURY

The first recorded jury trial was in 1220 at Westminster. From there, the circuit judges took the procedure with them to the "*shires*" ("counties").[2] By the middle of the thirteenth century the trial by jury, at least in an early form, was standard.[3]

The Westminster trial of 1220, however, was probably not the first jury trial. The early jury system replaced the older form of accusation called an appeal, from the Latin verb "to name."[4] In England, private prosecutions were called "*appeals*," originally meaning an accusation. As the jury system emerged, the word "*appeal*" came to mean trial by jury without option of battle.[5]

The early jury was both our modern grand jury and trial jury. In modern practice the *grand* jury decides

---

1. WILTSHIRE at 161.

A shilling was an English unit of currency; it is still used in some former British Commonwealth countries. "Shilling" comes from "*schilling*," a term from Anglo-Saxon times relating to the value of a cow or sheep. Originally, twenty shillings made a British pound, and twelve pence made a shilling. Thus there were 240 pence in a pound.

The new five pence piece initially was of identical size and weight, had the same value, and inherited the shilling's slang name of a "bob."

A 1933 shilling

2. KADRI at 70.

3. Frederick Pollack, *The King's Peace in the Middle Ages*, 13 HARV. L. REV. 177, 187 (1899).

Magna Carta did not provide for criminal jury trials for everyone, only that barons would be tried by their peers. At the time only if a person was indicted by a grand jury could he have another jury. LOVELL at 116. Only later did *Magna Carta* become a symbol that the law is superior to men, including the king and his government. *Id.* at 118.

4. LOVELL at 109.

5. Klerman, *Settlement*, at 3; Pollack at 179.

6. The word "indictment" probably comes from the Latin "*indicare*," meaning "to point a finger," as in the more common modern English word "indicate." By the fourteenth century, it had come to mean a written accusation after formal inquiry. *See* BAKER at 505.

Of course, your "index" finger has the same origin.

Michelangelo's God uses his index finger to give Adam life

7. *See* SHAPIRO at 2. *Also* Kiralfy at 246; Groot, *Presentment*, at 1; BAKER at 73.

Raphael's Plato indicating up

Da Vinci's John the Baptist indicating God

whether a charge stands, called an "indictment,"[6] and the trial or *petit* jury decides guilt or innocence.

At least before Henry II, the early jury could exonerate an accused, condemn him, or send him to trial by ordeal.[7] Generally the early jury sent the accused to ordeal if it was unsure of guilt.[8] Thus it acted initially like a modern grand jury. The jury's opinion about guilt or innocence was still a verdict.

These jurors were essentially witnesses called to the "*eyre*," the periodic session of the royal county court.[9] They came from the "*hundred*" and "*vill*," each a smaller subdivision of the *shire*.[10] This truly was a jury "*of your peers*."[11] And these jurors testified; they came to court expecting to speak more than to listen.

Thus, from Norman times and perhaps even earlier, the jurors were self-

informed; they knew the parties and the facts. The judges knew less about the case than the jurors.[12] In fact several members of a trial jury may have been part of making the indictment or complaint, or were coroners, bailiffs, and constables.[13] "Witnesses," as we know them, only occasionally came to court.[14] The jury was therefore mainly a form of proof, not the decider of proof.[15]

---

8. Kerr at 577–78; *see also* VAN CAENEGEM at 62. Naomi D. Hurnard, *The Jury of Presentment and the Assize of Clarendon*, 56 ENG. HIST. REV. 374 (1941).

9. *See* Daniel Klerman, *Was the Jury Ever Self-Informing?* 77 S. CAL. L. REV. 123, n.29 (2003); Groot, *Prosecutions*, at 125–40 (describing the *eyre*). *See also* Justin C. Barnes, *Lessons Learned from England's "Great Guardian of Liberty": A Comparative Study of English and American Civil Juries*, 3 U. ST. THOMAS L.J. 345, 350 (2005); Margaret C. Klingelsmith, *New Readings of Old Law*, 66 U. PA. L. REV. 107 (1917–18).

10. Groot, *Presentment*, at 3 and n.9. The *hundred* was an Anglo-Saxon organization of "hundredors" (more or less ten "*tithing*" families) that paid the frankpledge (tax). The "*hundredarius*" (family head) would meet in the "*hundred gemote*" headed by the "*hundredary*." BLACK'S at 667. The *vill* was a smaller unit than the *hundred,* such as a parish, manor, or tithing. *See id.* at 1407. Both the words "village" and "villain" (referring to an unfree inhabitant of a *vill*) come from *vill*.

11. For more on jury composition, *see* Klerman, *Self-Informing Jury*, at 128. The Sixth Amendment reflects this in its requirement that the juries come from "*the State and district wherein the crime shall have been committed . . .*" This phrase is anachronistic, relating to *hundreds* and *vills*.

12. Klerman, *Self-Informing Jury*, at 127, 138; Shapiro at 4; Barnes at 350; Klingelsmith at 107; Kerr at 576–77. Through early modern times, the special jury remained a throwback to self-informed juries. *See* James C. Oldham, *The Origins of the Special Jury*, 50 U. CHI. L. REV. 137 (1983).

14. Klerman, *Self-Informing Jury*, at 136, 145 (demonstrating the relationship with compurgation).

15. MacNair at 548–49. The jury as a form of proof can still be seen in modern practice, where the jury renders the verdict but not the judgment, a function of the trial judge.

Klerman gives several examples of this from a thirteenth century treatise, THE PLACITA CORONE (c. 1274–75). Reproducing one example here shows both the nature of trials and the role of jurors and judges:

> Judge: *Thomas [the accused], you have greatly embroidered your tale and coloured your defense: for you are telling us only what you think will be to your advantage, and suppressing whatever you think may damage you, and I do not believe you have told the whole truth.*
>
> Thomas: *Sir, I have told the whole truth, and related the affair from the beginning to the end in every detail: and of this I trust myself to God and the country for both good and evil.*

13. Jurors were not passive note takers, like today, but more like witnesses. *See* Musson at 127–28, 142 (outlining the difficulty of getting jurors in the fourteenth century).

> To resolve this dispute, the judge called an "inquest" with a jury, which agreed with Thomas:
>
> Judge: *Thomas, these good people testify by their oaths to the truth of what you have said. So our judgment is that what you did to him, you did in self defense.*

Quoted in Klerman, *Settlement*, at 136. In Thomas's trial the judge rendered "*our judgment*" but only after the jury gave proof by "*their oaths*." It essentially appears as a form of compurgation. *See also* Morris S. Arnold, *Law and Fact in Medieval Jury Trials: Out of Sight, Out of Mind*, 18 AM. J. LEGAL HIST. 267, 279–80 (1974) (noting that law and fact for medieval jurors were essentially the same thing—*ex facto ius, ex jure factum*).

The jurors took an oath to give a true verdict.[1] Indeed, the very word "jury" comes from the Latin "*jurata*" ("an oath"), with "jurors" being "*juratores.*"[2] This oath had great weight and negated the fact that jurors customarily received "gifts" from both parties, probably more akin to what we would think of as a jury fee, for their service.[3]

The jurors also investigated the case, returning to testify as to what they had discovered and to make accusations.[4] In fact the oath of the early jurors, the antecedents of the oaths of today's petit and grand jurors, came from their oath to investigate crime and "present" it to the king for prosecution.[5] In this function the early jury was a precursor to police and prosecutors.[6]

Henry II and his successors saw one great advantage in the jury system—it was cheap.

The self-informed jury of unpaid laymen did all the hard and expensive work of what we today would call criminal investigation, civil discovery, and trial preparation.[7] The kings then collected the death taxes and court fees in civil cases and the hefty fines and forfeitures in criminal cases.

Justice was a moneymaker!

But the kings did have to provide for the procedure. At first they traveled around the realm directly dispensing justice. Later they sent judges to periodically exercise the king's authority in the counties, diminishing the authority of the local lord and church. All of this was the extension of the king's peace.[8]

This system of witness-jurors lasted into the fifteenth century.[9] The early English courts, in fact, frowned on our modern idea of a witness as an independent observer of events. In the 1470s Sir

---

1. Kerr at 575–76.

The word "verdict" comes from the Latin "*veredictum*" ("to tell the truth," that is, "*vere*," as in the English word "verify," and "*dictum*," as in the English word "dictate"), reflecting the duty of the jurors. BAKER at 72.

A jury oath from 1642 read as follows: "*You shall well and truly try, and true deliverance make between our Soveraign [sic] Lord the King, and the Prisoners at the Bar, whom you shall have in charge, and a true Verdict shall give according to your Evidence, so help you God.*"

Quoted in James Oldham, *Truth-Telling in the Eighteenth-Century English Courtroom*, 12 LAW & HIST. REV. 95, 106 n.58 (1994). Modern jury oaths are similar and even retain the "*so help you God,*" essentially *iusticium Dei*. Indeed, before the Elizabethan Perjury Statute of 1563, the only perjury punishable at common law was against jurors for giving dishonest verdicts (testimony). Michael D. Gordon, *The Perjury Statute of 1563: A Case History of Confusion*, 124 PROC. AM. PHIL. SOC'Y 438 (1980).

THE VERDICT (20th Century Fox 1982) is about a washed-up, alcoholic lawyer, played by Paul Newman, who gets one last case to save his career. The dramatic buildup is to the jury verdict.

THE VERDICT (Warner Brothers 1946) is a film noir, starring Sydney Greenstreet as a Scotland Yard detective investigating a murder with Peter Lorre as his friend.

The best movie showing a jury actually deliberating is 12 ANGRY MEN, though PHILADELPHIA (TriStar Pictures 1993) has a brief but informative jury deliberation scene.

2. BAKER at 72–73; Pollock at 188. For the comparison of the juror's oaths with the oaths taken by witnesses and compurgators, see BAKER at 75. See also Stephan Landsman, *The Civil Jury in America: Scenes from an Unappreciated History*, 44 HASTINGS L.J. 579, 584–85 (1993).

3. Musson at 132 and n.150. It was not until 1682 that it became punishable to contact or inform jurors outside court proceedings of any fact or law regarding a case before them. Landsman at 586.

4. Until Henry II became king in 1154, the jury was mostly an administrative institution in the king's governance. It was only after Henry II passed several statutes, called assizes, that the jury started to become an instrument of justice. Landsman at 583.

5. Pollack at 187.

6. Pollack at 181; Howard W. GOLDSTEIN, GRAND JURY PRACTICE 2-1 to 2-2 (2005); Groot, *Presentment*, at 4–5; Barnes at 350, 356. On Norman practices, see Thompson at 21.

John Fortescue wrote in *De Laudibus Legum Angliae* that witnesses were sinister because they could lie or be bribed to say anything, whereas twelve sworn "*good men and true*" could not. Because England relied on jurors and did not torture witnesses, he continued, its legal system was better than the Continental inquisition.[10] It was the jurors' specific oath to give a true verdict, rather than the judge, that served as the accused's main procedural protection.

These juror-witnesses implemented the social norms of their day. For instance, they would have known to whom a disputed cow belonged or, perhaps, to whom it *should* belong. For example, even if the cow technically belonged to Thomas, Hugh may have had a better right or need to it. Or maybe Hugh was just a nicer guy than Thomas. Juries could take this into account.

In a criminal case the juror-witness would have known before trial who killed whom. But the jury's verdict, the oath-bound duty to tell and implement the truth, accounted for all the complicated nuances of modern law, such as self-defense, accident, manslaughter, or first- and second-degree murder. If you were a defendant before a medieval jury you had a better chance than you have today of getting mercy. The jurors knew the punishments and thus effectively were the sentencers.[11]

Fortescue described

"who, then, in England can be put to death unjustly for any crime? Since he is allowed so many pleas and privileges in favor of life; none but his neighbors, men of honest and good repute, against whom he can have no probable cause of exception, can find the person accused guilty." [12]

In 12 ANGRY MEN Henry Fonda brings his own exhibit into the jury room, not admitted into evidence during the trial. The Norman jury system would have required this action. Today it is juror misconduct.

7. Landsman at 584; LOVELL at 86.

8. See **Chapter 6: How the Sixth Amendment Guarantees You a Court, a Lawyer, and a Chamber Pot.**

9. KADRI at 72; Klerman, *Settlement*, at 6 (noting that juries remained self-informed throughout the thirteenth and fourteenth centuries).

10. KADRI at 73.
The engraved frontispiece from *De Laudibus Legum Angliae* shows Fortescue with Prince Edward in France, and reads: "*Chancellor Fortescue following King Henry's Fortune, and attending his Son Edward into France, wrote this Book to recommend the Laws of England to the Esteem and Protection of that Young Prince.*" From the Boston College Law School website, http://images.google.com/imgres?imgurl=http://www.bc.edu/schools/law/library/meta-elements/jpg/FortescueTPfullsize.jpg&imgrefurl=http://www.bc.edu/schools/law/library/about/rarebook/exhibitions/newacq05.html&usg=__DykUvoTXBJDHIvQOAU59Pbcid28=&h=3504&w=2548&sz=1354&hl=en&start=15&tbnid=7EUBSgRbBH3sKM:&tbnh=150&tbnw=109&prev=/images%3Fq%3DJohn%2BFortescue%26gbv%3D2%26ndsp%3D21%26hl%3Den%26sa%3DN (last visited Dec. 5, 2009).

11. See **Chapter 8: "Baby, Don't Be Cruel": What's So Cruel and Unusual about the Eighth Amendment?** for more regarding the history of punishment and the role of jurors.

12. *Coffin v. United States*, 156 U.S. 432, 455 (1895), *quoting* Fortescue and *citing De Laudibus Legum Angliae* (Amos trans., Cambridge Univ. Press, 1825). What follows this quote is Fortescue's statement that "*one would much rather that twenty guilty persons should escape the punishment of death than that one innocent person should be condemned and suffer capitally.*"

Sir John Fortescue

It was rough justice, but justice nonetheless.

THE GRAND JURY AND PETIT JURY

In 1166, Henry II's Assize of Clarendon provided that after the jury of presentment, the case went to ordeal.[1] If Henry II wished by this reform to impose justice, this motive was secondary to asserting his power over church and barons, and making income from forfeited chattels of convicted felons.[2]

The Assize of Clarendon set up a purely accusatorial jury of twelve men to ferret out crime and "keep the peace."[3]

When this jury initiated a case it was a *"presentment"* to the king, as distinguished from an *"indictment,"* which came when the prosecutor gave the case to the jury.[4]

The language of this early grand jury showed its investigative role—it would issue a *"bulla vera"* ("a true bill") if it had a charge or a *"bulla ignoramus"* ("it was ignorant," meaning there was not enough evidence) if they had no charge.[5] The charges were organized in *"counts,"* from the French *"conte"* ("tale" or "story").[6]

If there was any doubt as to Henry II's purpose, he

heavily fined grand juries or their villages that failed to indict a suspect or to present a sufficient number of criminals.[7]

In 1215 a crisis in criminal procedure occurred. As noted, the church held the Fourth Lateran Council, prohibiting clergy participation in the ordeal, effectively ending it as a mode of trial. At this point the English presentment juries had to send the case somewhere. The answer was a smaller jury, namely, the *"petit"* (French for "small") jury, which we today call the "trial jury."[8] *Magna Carta* may have

---

1. Here the term "assize" has a meaning closer to the modern words "ordinance" or "decree" than a court session, though at this time they were all court sessions from the king's court. Henry II issued this decree after the Constitution of Clarendon and Northampton, which Archbishop Thomas Becket had repudiated because it infringed on church jurisdiction. GOLDSTEIN at 2-4. In this case the decree attempted to prevent the abusive practice of bringing laymen before the bishop after an anonymous accusation. *See* Schwartz at 707.

Henry II

2. Schwartz at 703–10 (noting various power struggles between Henry II and Becket, and Henry's attempts to wrest power from the English barons). *See also* GOLDSTEIN at 2-3 and 2-5; United States v. Navarro, 408 F.3d 1184, 1190 (9th Cir. 2005).

3. BAKER at 24; BELLAMY at 19. For the Assize of Clarendon and Constitution of Clarendon, *see* http://www.constitution.org/liberlib.htm (last visited June 1, 2007).

4. *Navarro*, 408 F.3d at 1190; BELLAMY at 23. The early grand jury, representatives from the *hundreds* and *vills*, presented the case to the traveling royal judges. BAKER at 24. This "presentment" to the king is why we still refer to an indictment as being "handed up." *See also* Thompson at 15. The first clause of the Fifth Amendment requires either an indictment or a presentment: *"No person shall be held to answer for a capital, or otherwise infamous crime, unless on a presentment or indictment of a Grand Jury . . ."*

5. Schwartz at 718; BELLAMY at 20, 46; BAKER at 505. *See also* David Crook, *Triers and the Origin of the Grand Jury*, 12 J. LEGAL HIST. 103 (1991) (tracing the evolution from available records of jurors from indictors to "*triatores*" or "trial juries").

6. As in the root of the English verb "to recount." BAKER at 76. The Latin is "*narratio*," as in the English word "narrative."

7. Schwartz at 709. Only much later did it become illegal to fine jurors. *See* GOLDSTEIN at 2-6.

Henry II's expansion of existing jury custom is why he gets credited with being the founder of the jury trial. KIRALFY at 241. *See also* BELLAMY at 33, noting that the Statute of Westminster of 1285 allowed the king to punish jurors or their villages for negligence or concealing felonies. Jury service could not have been popular given that in the fourteenth and fifteenth centuries an acquitted defendant could sue jurors who indicted him. *Id.* at 34.

8. *See* BAKER at 507–08; Shapiro at 4; Schwartz at 711 and n.47; Kiralfy at 248. On grand juries and petit juries forming a two-staged system, *see* Helmholz, *Grand Jury*, at 613. *See also* BAKER at 73 on the effect of the Fourth Lateran Council on the development of the petit jury.

been the foundation for this right to trial by jury.[9] *Vox populi* ("the people's voice") replaced *vox Dei* ("God's voice") as a mode of trial.[10]

This split developed a two-tiered system that Blackstone later noted

"wisely placed this strong and twofold barrier, of a presentment and a trial by jury between the liberties of the people and the prerogative of the crown."[11]

Blackstone's influence on law and lawyers in the colonies, firmly planted this concept of a jury trial in the minds of the Constitution's Framers.

THE CHANGING ROLE OF THE GRAND JURY

The trouble with Blackstone's view of the grand jury as *"a barrier"* for the *"liberties of the people"* is that the jury's early history belies it.

Henry II formalized the grand jury system because he wanted to gain power and money. Common people did not see the grand jury as a barrier to the king; rather, they feared it.[12] Not until the middle of the fourteenth century were grand jurors excluded from serving on trial juries for the same cases where they had just indicted a defendant.[13]

Henry II's successors carried on the grand jury practice. By the fourteenth century under Edward III, the grand jury became institutionalized with the number of grand jurors set at twenty-four and got the title *"le graunde inquest."*[14]

Over time, the grand jury became an instrument of governance rather than a barrier to it.[15]

9. "*No freeman shall be taken or imprisoned or disseised or exiled or in any way destroyed, nor will we go upon him nor send upon him, except by the lawful judgment of his peers or by the law of the land.*" *Magna Carta* of 1215.

(This clause could refer to either the grand or the petit jury.) *Cited in* Barnes at 348. *See also* GOLDSTEIN at 2-5 to 2-6. Fisher at 585 (noting record of first jury trial in 1220). For a general explanation of the *Magna Carta* in medieval law, *see* Paul R. Hyams, *The Charter as a Source for the Early Common Law*, 12 J. LEGAL HIST. 173 (1991).

Isabella and a young Edward III

10. VAN CAENEGEM at 71. From 1351 the trial jurors had to be different from the grand jurors. BAKER at 508. We extend this rule today to assure that evidence presented to a grand jury, not necessarily admissible at trial or perhaps illegally obtained, will not taint the trial.

11. Schwartz at 701.

12. Schwartz at 709 ("*Any thought that the grand juries were for the benefit of the people must be quickly dispelled by the historic fact that the grand jury was oppressive and much feared by the common people.*"). *See also* GOLDSTEIN at 2-1 to 2-2, noting that the grand jury has at different times been both the government's sword and the citizen's shield.

14. Roger A. Fairfax, Jr., *The Jurisdictional Heritage of the Grand Jury Clause*, 91 MINN. L. REV. 398, 408 n.39 (2006) (quoting GEORGE J. EDWARDS, THE GRAND JURY: AN ESSAY 2 (1906)); Pollack at 188 (noting that the grand jury came from "the grand inquest". From the reign of Edward III also came inquisitorial trial procedures, which could have ended the jury trial tradition. BELLAMY at 14–15. Edward III was a successful king who beat up on the French and Scots. His mother was Isabella (known as the She-Wolf of France), who was the princess in BRAVEHEART. *See* ALISON WEIR, QUEEN ISABELLA (2005). Edward's son, Edward, known as the Black Prince, died before becoming king but he was the prince in A KNIGHT'S TALE (Columbia Pictures 2001), played by James Purefoy.

William Blackstone

13. Pollack at 181.

Edward III and his son Edward, the Black Prince

15. From the seventeenth century the grand jury began to acquire powers beyond justice administration. It maintained roads and bridges, collected county cess and taxes, oversaw lunatic asylums, hospitals, and jails, and became an elected body. GOLDSTEIN at 2-8; *Navarro*, 408 F.3d at 1191. This was especially true in colonial America.

The grand jury of Blackstone's time that the Framers knew truly did stand against the power of the government. Today, though, the grand jury is totally under the prosecutor's control, who has sweeping powers of subpoena and investigation. The grand jury is not the shield for the people's liberties that it once was.[1]

JURIES AND THE KING'S COPS

Juries were now either grand or petit and, as the system formalized, they started to lose their character as bodies with independent knowledge of the facts. More and more the juries did not know directly about cases. Trials were starting to incorporate actual witnesses to give testimony, usually from what we would today call a "cop," a policeman.

Kings actually did not have cops in the modern sense of police officer; the concept of police and policing was centuries away.[2] There was a "constable," but during the Middle Ages this was a high military office.[3] Only later did the term become associated with policing.[4] What the king did have were sheriffs, coroners, and judges.

The Sheriff: The *"sheriff"* was the King's *"reeve"*

1. What's So Grand about the Grand Jury? The grand jury is a shell of what it was. The proponents of the American Revolution viewed the grand jury as a shield from government oppression, or in Blackstone's terms, the king's prerogative power. GOLDSTEIN at 2-6. Colonial grand juries refused to indict when the king infringed on the people's liberty. LEVY at 222. *See generally* Fairfax (demonstrating that the Framers intended a grand jury's indictment to be a prerequisite for federal court jurisdiction over a crime and thus should not be something a defendant can waive, as is common in modern plea practice and allowed by Federal Rule of Criminal Procedure 7). Today in America a prosecutor could indict *"a ham sandwich."* GOLDSTEIN at 2-14; Schwartz at 756–58 (on modern history and prosecutorial tactics). *See generally* Niki Kuckes, *The Democratic Prosecutor: Explaining the Constitutional Function of the Federal Grand Jury*, 94 GEO. L.J. 1265 (2006). England abolished the grand jury, KEMPIN at 54, as have many states of the United States, despite periodic calls for reform. *See, e.g.,* John F. Decker, *Legislating New Federalism: The Call for Grand Jury Reform in the States*, 58 OKLA. L. REV. 341 (2005); Kevin K. Washburn, *Restoring The Grand Jury*, 76 FORDHAM L. REV. 2333 (2008).

2. Sir Robert Peel, Britain's Conservative prime minister, helped create the modern police force in the 1860s while he served as home secretary. The father of modern policing, Peel developed the Peelian Principles, which defined police ethics. His most memorable principle was, *"the police are the public, and the public are the police."* English police are still called "bobbies" or "'peelers." For the history of the early police and the Bow Street Runners, *see* LOVELL at 509.

3. The constable originally was a stable boy keeping the lord's horses. The word comes from the Latin *"comes stabuli"* ("attendant of the stables"). Later it became a high military rank, the lord high constable of England, essentially the king's field marshal.

Constables also defended castles, and there is still a constable of the Tower of London. *Magna Carta* uses the term in this sense to denote a castellan with less power than the sheriff. *See* Irwin Langbien, *The Jury of Presentment and the Coroner*, 33 COLUM. L. REV. 1329, 1343 n.47 (1933).

4. The term "cop" could be short for "Constable On Patrol." Or it might come from Latin and Old French *"capere"* ("to capture"), hence a "copper," who "cops criminals," or to "cop a plea." "Cop" could also derive from the copper buttons on police uniforms.

"Cop" is now synonymous with "police officer," as in the television show *Cops* that follows police officers, constables, and sheriff's deputies as they police. *Cops* (Fox TV, Mar. 11, 1989–Mar. 21, 2009), http://www.cops.com/ (last visited Apr. 9, 2010). There is also the movie COP (1988) with James Woods.

The use of the phrase "cop a plea" or "cop out to a plea" could come from the fact that the hearing is officially called a "change of plea [to guilty] hearing," and shortened to "COP." The term "cop out" is also synonymous with doing something to avoid responsibility, as in "that's a cop out." The comedy COP OUT (Warner Brothers 2010), however, seems to use the term as a play on the buddy cop theme, as in the two buddies are going *out* on a date.

5. "The Reeve's Tale" is the third of Geoffrey Chaucer's THE CANTERBURY TALES. The reeve of the story, Oswald, is skinny and bad-tempered, and after the previous *Miller's Tale* annoys him, his story has a miller trying to swindle two "students." But they trick the miller's wife and daughter

("representative," "caretaker," or "overseer")[5] in the *shire*, thus his Anglo-Saxon name was "*shire-gerefa*," or in Norman French "*shire-reeve*" (evolving into *sheriff*).[6] It was an older Anglo-Saxon office that the Normans kept. The *sheriff* was supposed to collect the royal revenue.[7]

The only appeal from the *sheriff*, or his courts, was to the king.[8] However, the king was often overseas (and, in the early Norman period,

did not even speak English). Thus the "*justiciar*," "*regent*," or "*lieutenant*" heard the appeal.

As the king's interest in criminal cases grew, the *sheriff* started having a law enforcement role. He would direct the "*hue and cry*" to pursue criminals.[9] He would summon prosecuting victims to court and deliver defendants from jail. Over time he ran the jails, a role country sheriffs still play.

The Coroner: Offsetting some of the *sheriff*'s power was another crown official, the "*coroner*."[10] "*Coroner*" means "keeper of the pleas of the crown" or "crowner" or "coronator."[11] It was his duty to enforce the king's right to forfeited chattel.[12] He did this using an "*inquest*" (in Latin, "*inquisitio*") or coroner's court, often presiding over an early form of jury trial.[13]

Geoffrey Chaucer

"Students" drinking up a miller's wine in "The Reeve's Tale"

A seventeenth century depiction of Chaucer

into sex (perhaps willingly) and end up with a nice cake besides. (Who said medieval literature was boring?)

8. *See* Kynell at 47 (noting how the early jury functioned in the context of the *sheriff*'s inquests).

9. "**Follow that Car!**" The *hue and cry* to pursue criminals led centuries later to the sheriff swearing in a posse and declaring "*They went that 'a way!*" and later ordering a driver to "*Follow that car!*" Lovell at 41.

10. *See* Charles Gross, *The Early History and Influence of the Office of Coroner*, 7 Pol. Sci. Q. 656, 660, 665 (1892); Lovell at 101 (coroner established to check the *sheriffs*). The *coroners* were probably more popular than the *sheriffs* as they were popularly chosen and not just the king's representative. Conversely, *sheriffs* often bought their office intending private gain. Gross at 664.

11. Langbien at 1334. This role as "keeper of the pleas of the crown" used to be the *justiciar*'s. *Id.* at 1341.
   The term "*coroner*" comes from the Latin "*corona*" ("crown"), as in the English "coronation" for the crowning of a monarch. *See also* Corona brand beer for the crown on its label.

6. Van Caenegem at 13; Kynell at 86; Lovell at 33–35; W.A. Morris, *The Sheriff and the Justices of William Rufus and Henry I*, 7 Cal. L. Rev. 235, 240 (1910). *See also* Danziger & Gillingham at 175–76. Regarding the sheriff as the king's representative in the Anglo-Saxon *hundred* and *shire* courts, *see* Pollock at 293. For royal control of the sheriff, *see* Baker at 23.

7. This is the Sheriff of Nottingham of the Robin Hood stories, who takes from the poor to give to the rich.

12. "**Chattel**" means private movable property or goods, as opposed to "real property," i.e., real estate. The term included "*royal fish*," such as whales, sturgeon, and porpoises caught near or on the shore. *See* Thompson at 32. The word "cattle" derives from "chattel," as it originally referred to any domesticated quadruped livestock, including sheep, goats, swine, horses, mules, and asses, not just today's meaning of bovines, such as steers, cows, and bulls. Webster's at 425–26, 455.
   On the coroner's role in forfeitures to the crown, *see* Gross at 659, and in defending the king's interest against the local lords, *see* Gross at 667.

13. Gross at 663, 672. The inquest jury functioned more as the king's investigatory panel rather than a modern jury. Barnes at 349.

Where a death was involved he would make sure the king got his death tax. If it was a homicide or suicide the king fared even better because *all* the goods and chattels of the murderer or suicide went to him.[1]

This is where the modern understanding of the role of the coroner derives,[2] although most jurisdictions today use trained medical professionals in medical examiners' offices.

For most of the medieval period, the *sheriff* and *coroner* were the extent of law enforcement. But policing was a community matter, and the village had a greater role in ferreting out crime and seeking its prosecution.

The Judges: The king had another cop: the judge.[3] Judges from the Middle Ages had both executive and judicial powers. They were the king's men, and thus responsible for keeping the king's peace.

Not only would the judge examine the witnesses and comment on the evidence, he would often tell the jury what he thought its verdict should be. He could reject the verdict and send the jury to redeliberate or even put the jurors in jail or fine them.[4]

JURORS BECOME EVEN LESS INFORMED

Over time, as juries started coming from larger geographic areas and were

comprised of people with less personal knowledge of the parties and the dispute, the jury lost its investigatory role. Jurors did not know the parties, and the parties did not know them.

As William Shakespeare wrote,

> *"the jury passing on the prisoner's life / May in the sworn twelve have a thief or two / Guiltier than him they try."* [5]

Starting with crown officials like *sheriffs* and *coroners*, by the middle of the fifteenth century, jurors had become dependent on in-court testimony.[6] In 1523 Sir Thomas More argued that jurors should only have evidence from the trial.[7]

---

1. Thompson at 31–32. The *coroner*'s office probably started under Henry II and is mentioned in *Magna Carta* and the *eyre* of 1194.
    See Gross at 656; Langbien at 1334; Barnes at 348–49 (for the tie-in with inquest). In addition, see John H. Wigmore, *The History of the Hearsay Rule*, 17 HARV. L. REV. 437, 456 (1903–04), noting the coroner's inquest as an exception allowing hearsay before justices of the peace.

2. Some states maintain a variant of the old *coroner*'s inquest. ▼

3. By the fourteenth century, traveling justices and justices of the peace limited both the sheriff and *coroner*'s powers. LOVELL at 206–07.

4. John H. Langbein, *The Criminal Trial before the Lawyers*, 45 U. CHI. L. REV. 263, 291–95 (1977–78).

5. WILLIAM SHAKESPEARE, MEASURE FOR MEASURE act 2, sc. 1, ll. 19–21, *quoted in* KORNSTEIN at 52.

6. Klerman, *Settlement*, at 145–48; Westen at 80–81; Morano at 507.

7. Shapiro at 5. *Also see* Landsman at 587, noting that in the mid-1600s, jurors were isolated from outside influences and required to decide cases on in-court presentations.

Sir Thomas More

Many factors contributed to jurors becoming less self-informed. The courts were becoming more efficient after centralization at Westminster, with formal sessions and terms. The local townsfolk of the *vill* or *hundred* no longer showed up for jury duty whenever an *eyre* justice passed though.[8] The king started enforcing the criminal law with crown officials, ending the need for *le graunde inquest* to investigate and report crime.[9] The Black Death affected judicial institutions, as it did many other social organizations, by limiting the number of jurors but not the obligations of local communities.[10]

By this point another factor limited the self-informed jury. Legal decision making became a rational process.[11] Oaths as a form of proof became harder to justify, and *iudicium Dei* was on the wane. The king's judges now instructed the jurors on the law rather than jurors telling the judges the customary law of the community.

Juries also started to assume their modern role of lie detection.[12] Francis Bacon wrote in 1607 that

"the supply of testimony and the discerning and credit of testimony [were left to the] juries consciences and understanding."

Later in the century Sir Matthew Hale, the legal historian and most distinguished judge of his time, wrote that trial was

"the best method of searching and sifting out the truth [because juries] weigh the credibility of Witnesses, and the Force and Efficacy of their Testimonies."[13]

Thus the old system of relying on oaths as the basis for the criminal justice system was beginning to break down.[14] But this happened slowly, and portions of the old practices remained. By the beginning of the seventeenth century, for example, a defendant still could not subpoena witnesses and, even if the witnesses came to court, they could not testify under oath.[15]

---

8. Barnes at 349–50; Groot, *Prosecutions*, at 141. *See also* Klerman, *Settlement*, at 146, explaining how reforms in criminal law, such as the system of jail delivery or the periodic session of royal justice in the countryside that tried those in jail or on bail, made it more difficult to recruit local jurors. *Id.* at 125, noting that by the fifteenth century jurors did not come from the locality as before.

9. Waldman at 308; Barnes at 350.

10. Klerman, *Settlement*, at 147.

Illustration of the Black Death, from the Toggenburg Bible (1411). The Black Death killed between a third to two-thirds of Europe's population.

11. *See* Theodore Waldman, *Origins of the Legal Doctrine of Reasonable Doubt*, 20 J. Hist. Ideas 299, 314 (1959). *See also generally* Wigmore.

12. Shapiro at 13; Beattie at 235 (citing Shapiro).

13. *Quoted in* Shapiro at 11–12.

14. *See generally* Fisher; Beattie at 235.

Sir Matthew Hale   Sir Francis Bacon

15. Popper at 455–56; Langbein, *Historical Foundations*, at 1055–56 (seventeenth century defendants had no right to compel witness to come to court). *But see* Shapiro at 5–6 (noting Elizabethan legislation allowing for compulsion of witnesses and cross-examination by counsel).

This was in large part to protect from conflicting oaths in court, meaning that someone had committed perjury.

A system that relied on the power of oaths as proof could not suffer even the chance of perjury.

Slowly, though, trial by jury eliminated this problem. The jury's verdict conflicts with nothing because jurors can decide who lied or not.[1] By 1670 trials had advanced to the modern procedure of witnesses offering evidence and jurors making factual conclusions.[2]

All of these developments, however, were still a long way from our Sixth Amendment. The problem for the accused was that the old protections and rough justice of the self-informed jury gave way to a jury ignorant of the parties or dispute. And the process had not become formalized to provide the procedural protections-such as having a right to a lawyer, compulsory process, and confrontation-that the Sixth and Seventh Amendments to the U.S. Constitution guarantee.[3]

But judges were starting to change as well. With more passive jurors there had to be protections to assure the jury only considers valid proofs. These protections are the law of evidence.[4]

EVIDENCE AND THE HEARSAY RULE

With the expanded role of lawyers and the change in the jury from self-informed to ignorant, judges began to regulate the evidence. But evidence law did not start with the new adversarial trials of the nineteenth century. For example, the Romans had rules related to competency, summoning witnesses, privileges, leading questions, corroboration, and authentication of documents.[5]

---

1. See Fisher at 705–07, noting that the privacy of the jury room hides the shortcomings of the jury system just as the older competency rules hid the shortcomings of the oath system. For critiques of modern jury system and truth, see Oldham, *Truth Telling*, at 118 n.110.

2. Barnes at 356–57 (discussing *Bushell's Case*, Vaughan's Rep. 135 (1670)).

3. See generally Peter Westen, *The Compulsory Process Clause*, 73 Mich. L. Rev. 71 (1974). See also **Chapter 6: How the Sixth Amendment Guarantees You a Court, a Lawyer, and a Chamber Pot.**

4. Fisher at 708; John H. Langbein, *Historical Foundations of the Law of Evidence: A View from the Ryder Sources*, 96 Colum. L. Rev. 1168, 1194 (1996). See also Landsman at 595; Langbein, *Historical Foundations*, at 1170 (no reason for evidence law with the self-informing jury); Morrison at 591, citing 9 Holdsworth, History of English Law 126 (1926) (law of evidence did not grow until sixteenth century when juries were no longer self-informed).

5. See C.A. Morrison, *Some Features of the Roman and the English Law of Evidence*, 33 Tul. L. Rev. 577, 579–81 (1958–59) (for an extensive list). See also Pound at 47–48.

6. Hearsay is "a statement, other than one made by the declarant while testifying at the trial or hearing, offered in evidence to prove the truth of the matter asserted." Fed. R. Evid. 801(a)(c).

Moses with the Ten Commandments by Rembrandt (1659)

7. Exodus 20:16; see also Deuteronomy 5:20: "*Neither shall you bear false witness against your neighbor.*"

8. Frank R. Herrmann, S.J., *The Establishment of a Rule against Hearsay in Romano-Canonical Procedure*, 36 Va. J. Int'l L. 1, n.285 (1995).

Emperor Justinian I

9. Herrmann at 17–18; Morrison at 587.
    The Justinian Code, the *Corpus Juris Civilis* ("Body of Civil Law"), is the modern name for a collection of laws and written procedures from 529 to 534 AD under Justinian I, Byzantine Emperor. See also Wigmore at 437 (focusing on the Germanic and Anglos-Saxon roots of the hearsay rule). But see Morrison at 590 (noting that Wigmore "*more often than not*" writes of the Roman law of evidence).

The ancients also had an early hearsay rule.[6]

Ancient Jewish law, for instance, interpreted the Eighth (or Ninth) Commandment that

> "[t]hou shalt not bear false witness against thy neighbor"[7]

as a hearsay rule.[8] The reason was that one who bases his testimony on what others said is a false witness.

Ancient Roman law also had a highly developed hearsay rule. The courts of Cicero's day distrusted *testimonium ex auditu* ("testimony from hearing"). In the later Roman/ Byzantium period, the Justinian Code incorporated the same rule and generally excluded *ex auditu* testimony.[9]

Much of Roman law and the Justinian Code passed into the law of the Catholic Church. Saint Augustine cautioned that only eyewitness testimony was valid.[10] He used the biblical example of the soldiers guarding Christ's tomb. The Pharisees wanted to bribe the soldiers into saying that when they were asleep the Disciples took Christ's body. This would have been hearsay, according to Augustine, because if the soldiers were asleep, how could they see anything?[11]

Pope Gregory the Great was very concerned about defining the elements of a fair trial. Judges, according to Gregory, were to consider only live testimony under oath by witnesses with direct knowledge of the facts. Any reliance on hearsay, *testimonium ex auditu*, was not good judging.[12]

From the church, the hearsay rule passed into the *ius commune* and medieval law. Cases could move forward on the belief of the community or common fame ("*fama*"). But this was only sufficient to begin investigations.[13]

10. Hermmann at 30.

Saint Augustine

11. *Christ Risen from the Tomb* by Piero della Francesca.

Pope Gregory I, known as Gregory the Great

12. Herrmann at 21–26.

13. Herrmann at 27–29, 47.

From there, the inquest court had to produce actual witnesses who could testify to matters within their direct knowledge.

In the early days of the English common-law jury trial, a hearsay rule would not have made sense. The jurors were self-informed. They would have known who said what before the case went to court.[1] Because the jurors were the witnesses as well, a hearsay rule limiting witness testimony would have been inconsistent with the trial process.

As time when on, though, this began to change. In England the Constitutions of Clarendon of 1164 specified that "*laymen are not to be accused save by proper and legal accusers and witnesses in the presence of the bishop.*"[2] The reference to the bishop shows the direct source of the hearsay rule from canon law, which originated in old Roman law.

By the 1600s English courts started to exclude hearsay when the statement stood alone. It could, however, corroborate other testimony.[3] By the beginning of the 1700s, however, the rule against hearsay had become a fundamental principle of the common law.[4]

Much of the hearsay rule's growth in the common law came about because of the old reliance on the power of oaths as the basis for legitimizing the system. Today hearsay is not good evidence because it is not subject to cross-examination and violates the Sixth Amendment's Confrontation Clause. But for the lawyers and judges of the seventeenth and eighteenth centuries, hearsay was not reliable evidence because it was not under oath.[5]

The jury's role had changed. Rather than being self-informed, seventeenth century jurors came to

1. See Robert Popper, *History and Development of the Accused's Right to Testify*, 1962 Wash. U. L.Q. 454, 455 (1962) (noting jurors were the witnesses).

2. *Quoted in* Leonard W. Levy, Origins of the Fifth Amendment: The Right against Self-Incrimination 45 (1969).

3. Wigmore at 443.   4. Wigmore at 458.

5. For Baron Jeffrey Gilbert's evidence treatise, The Law of Evidence (1754), the importance of the oath as basis for hearsay rule rather than lack of cross-examination, see Langbein, *Historical Foundations*, at 1173–76, 1194; Landsman 592.

6. Waldman at 314.

7. William Blake's stylized Isaac Newton illustrates the Age of Reason, with an intellectual giant using his instruments and brain to pierce the darkness.

Newton by William Blake (1805)

8. Wigmore's famous statement is that cross-examination "*is beyond any doubt the greatest legal engine ever invented for the discovery of truth.*" *Quoted in* Langbein, *Historical Foundations*, at n.32, who argues that "*cross-examination in the hands of a skilled and determined advocate is often an engine of oppression and obfuscation, deliberately employed to defeat the truth.*" On cross-examination and lawyers as the basis for system legitimacy, see *id.* at 1197–98. For cross-examination replacing the oath as guarantor of truth, see Wigmore at 448. For more on hearsay in the eighteenth century, see Langbein, *Before the Lawyers*, at 301.

9. See **Chapter 6: How the Sixth Amendment Guarantees You a Court, a Lawyer, and a Chamber Pot** (regarding the recognition of the right to a lawyer).
    For how athe growth of cross-examination brings about the need for trained counsel, see Wigmore at 458 and Landsman at 569–72.

10. Mark DeWolfe Howe, *Juries as Judges of Criminal Law*, 52 Harv. L. Rev. 582, 583 (1938–39). See generally Klingelsmith at 107.
    Morano at 509 notes that the unchangeable nature of a jury verdict is because it replaced ordeals and the equally unchangeable *iusticium Dei.*

court to listen and decide the facts before them.[6] Evidence law, based on rational principles, now determined what the jury heard and the parameters of its decision. Thus the trial became like a closed Newtonian system where human reason could discern God's clockwork and find truth.[7]

Now the trained lawyer's cross-examination became the guarantor of truth and the basis for the system's legitimacy, not oaths.[8] But this guarantee assumes both the presence of trained lawyers and a system of procedure that gives them the freedom to exercise their skill.[9]

The early modern jury was only just beginning to see the changes in the system to allow many of the procedural rights we take for granted.

THE EARLY MODERN JURY

After the execution of King Charles I, Parliament abolished the Star Chamber and High Commission courts in 1641. Common-law courts and juries assumed the jurisdiction of these courts.

Jurors from the earliest times had the power of a general verdict, that is, they could declare someone guilty or not guilty without further explanation.[10] This raised the possibility of jury nullification: the jury could protect an accused from the king, reject a bad criminal law, or just give mercy to a guilty but worthy defendant.[11]

If jurors showed too much mercy, however, they ran the risk of imprisonment and fines.[12] Jurors were confined *"without meat, drink, fire or candle"* until they had a verdict.[13] Judges could also influence juries by telling them not only what they thought of the evidence but how the jurors should vote.

11. Fisher at 602 and n.83, *citing* Thomas Andrew Green, Verdict According to Conscience: Perspectives on the English Criminal Trial Jury, 1200–1800, at 28–64 (1985) (noting that medieval law did not provide for manslaughter, and juries would often twist facts to support a self-defense verdict); John H. Langbein, *Shaping the Eighteenth-Century Criminal Trial: A View from the Ryder Sources*, 50 U. Chi. L. Rev. 1, 52–55 (1983) (noting nineteenth century jury nullification to temper overly severe laws).

Later commentators connected this medieval history of jury power and *Magna Carta* to modern justifications of nullification. *See, e.g.*, Steve J. Shone, *Lysander Spooner, Jury Nullification, and Magna Carta*, 22 Q. L. Rev. 651, 658–59, 664–65, 666 (2004).

12. The Statute of Winchester of 1285 provided that the king could indict jurors for negligence or concealment of felonies. In 1528, the crown sent jurors that refused to indict in a case with *"pregnant and manifest"* evidence to Fleet Prison. A new jury indicted the defendant. J.G. Bellamy, The Criminal Trial in Later Medieval England 33 (1998). Regarding courts rejecting acquittals, *see* Langbein, *Before the Lawyers*, at 295.

13. Baker at 75, reporting that in Tudor times the court would fine a juror for eating sweets. This practice continued into the nineteenth century. *See, e.g.*, Glazebrook at 588 (jury sanctions in the context of Throckmorton's trial).

Again, the movie 12 Angry Men creates dynamic tension by having the jurors locked up together.

Modern American courts deal with deadlocked jurors with an "Allen charge," an additional instruction to motivate the jury to reach a verdict. The instruction gets it name from *Allen v. United States*, 164 U.S. 492, 501–02 (1896), where the Supreme Court upheld a supplemental instruction given to a deadlocked jury that urged jurors to reconsider their opinions and continue deliberating. *See also United States v. Wills*, 88 F.3d 704, 716 n.6 (9th Cir. 1996) (reviewing circuit case law on *Allen* instructions).

Later courts could also call a second jury, called a "jury of attaint," to review the first jury to decide whether it had willfully falsified its verdict and thus committed perjury. Penalties could include fines, forfeiture of goods, chattels, or lands to the king, and eviction of the jurors' wives and children from their homes.[1]

But it appears that after the overthrow of King Charles I, juries were getting more independent, which John Lilburne's 1649 treason trial shows.

LILBURNE'S JURY

As we have seen, John Lilburne's life was a trial. His 1637 sedition trial and 1649 treason trial were important to the history of the Fifth Amendment and a basis for most of the trial guarantees of the Sixth Amendment.

The record of his trial also informs us about the jury practice of his day.

In his 1649 trial, Lilburne had only two things going for him- the jury and a big mouth:

"[U]nto the jury, my countrymen, upon whose consciences, integrity and honesty, my life, and the lives and liberties of the honest men of this nation, now lies; who are in law judges of law as well as fact, and you only the pronouncers of their sentence . . . ." [2]

For Lilburne, everything was for the jury's ear.[3] And he could not resist challenging authority, whether king or Cromwell, judge or prosecutor, he made them all look bad:

"Sir, I entreat you give me leave to read the words of

the law, then; for to the jury I apply, as my judges, both in the law and fact." [4]

In response, one of Lilburne's judges, Jermin, tried lecturing the jury:

"Let all the hearers know, the jury ought to take notice of it. That the judges that are sworn . . . have ever been the judges of the law . . . and the jury are only judges, whether such a thing were done or no; they are only judges of matter of fact."

After further baiting from Lilburne, Jermin continued:

"That the jury are the judges of the law, which is enough to destroy all the law in the land; there was never such damnably heresy broached in this nation before." [5]

---

1. Eric G. Barber, *Judicial Discretion, Sentencing Guidelines, and Lessons from Medieval England, 1066–1215*, 27 W. New Eng. L. Rev. 1, 34 (2008).

John Lilburne, known as Freeborn John

2. *Quoted in* Wolfram at 246. For a briefer account of Lilburne's trials as the origins of the American jury rights, *see* Bachmann at 251–53 and Albert W. Alschuler & Andrew G. Deiss, *A Brief History of the Criminal Jury in the United States*, 61 U. Chi. L. Rev. 867, 902–03 (1994).

3. Wolfram at 251. For other background on the Lilburne trial, *see* Scott at 397–402. For Lilburne asserting confrontation rights, *see* Kenneth Graham, *Confrontation Stories: Raleigh on the Mayflower*, 3 Ohio St. J. Crim. L. 209, 212–14 (2005).

4. Wolfram at 246. Regarding Lilburne's self-training in law, *see* Diane Parkin-Speer, *John Lilburne: A Revolutionary Interprets Statutes and Common Law Due Process*, 1 Law & Hist. Rev. 276 (1983). As we have seen, Lilburne's argument about the tradition of juries defining the law has historical support. Lilburne expounded these ideas in this tract *The Legal Fundamental Liberties of the People of England* (1649). In many ways, Lilburne used his trial of 1649 as the oral presentation of *Fundamental Liberties*.

Lilburne's jurors must have enjoyed the show. They had sat all day with no break or meal. Just before deliberation, a juror asked for a drink:

> "[O]ne of the Jury desired to drink a cup of sack [wine], for they had sat long, and how much longer the debate of the business might last, he knew not; and therefore desired, that they might have amongst them a quart of sack to refresh them."**6**

Despite the long day, the judge denied the juror's request:

> "Gentlemen of the jury, I know, for my part, in ordinary juries that they have been permitted to drink before they went from the bar; but in case of Felony or Treason, I never so much as heard it so, or so much as

asked for; and therefore you cannot have it."

The judge did, however, allow that the jury "shall have a light" rather than deliberate in the dark.

The jury responded by taking less than two hours to acquit Lilburne.**7** The verdict was met with

> "a loud and unanimous shout . . . which lasted for about half an hour without intermission . . . .
> [An] infinitely enraged and perplexed Cromwell . . . looked upon it as a greater defeat than the loss of a battle would have been."**8**

Lilburne's trial shows a growing tradition of jury independence, which we inherited in the Sixth and Seventh Amendments. But it would be twenty years

before jurors had explicit protection from reprisal for acquitting a defendant.

BUSHELL'S CASE

The power of a judge to punish jurors continued until Bushell's Case in 1670, involving William Penn.**9**

Edward Bushell was a juror. In August 1670, he was on the jury that acquitted the Quaker William Penn and William Mead on a charge of unlawful assembly.**10** The judge ordered the jury "shall not be dismissed until we have a verdict that the court will accept." Furthermore, the judge denied the jury food, drink, fire, tobacco—and even a chamber pot!**11**

Despite this, the jury continued for acquittal. The judge would not accept the verdict, and he fined the jurors.

---

5. *Quoted in* Wolfram at 247. Given English history of the prior century with Henry VIII's break with Rome and the Puritan revolution, this statement had to have appeared to the jury exaggerated. *See* **Chapter 1: Of Dogma and Desire: Saying What You Believe about the First Amendment.**

6. *Quoted in* Wolfram at 251. **7.** Wolfram at 251.

William Penn

8. Wolfram at 252, *quoting* Lord Clarendon at 4 St. Tr. 1420.

9. William Penn (1644–1718), was the Quaker proprietor of Pennsylvania. His father, Admiral Sir William Penn, a hero of the Dutch War, had high hopes for his son. William disappointed dad by becoming a Quaker. But William, Jr., named Pennsylvania after dad. ▶

10. *See generally* Barnes at 356; SHAPIRO at 13; Kempin at 64; Shone at 654–55; Scott at 394, 406; LOVELL at 407.

For a modern discussion of jury nullification, *see* Simon Stern, *Between Local Knowledge and National Politics: Debating Rationales for Jury Nullification after Bushell's Case*, 111 YALE L.J. 1815 (2002).

11. KADRI at 91–92.

Bushell refused to pay. The judge threatened that

"[y]ou shall be locked up without meat, drink, fire, and tobacco. You shall not think thus to abuse the court; we will have a verdict, by the help of God, or you shall starve for it."[1]

Bushell applied for a writ of habeas corpus in the Court of Common Pleas, which held that the trial judge was wrong to override the jury's decision.[2] Lord Chief Justice John Vaughan drew a careful distinction between the respective role of a witness and a juror:

"*The Verdict of a Jury, and Evidence of a Witness are very different things . . . A witness swears but to what he hath heard or seen . . . but a jury-man swears to what he can infer and conclude from the testimony of such witnesses by the act and force of his understanding . . . .*"[3]

Never again would the law allow a judge to overtly coerce a jury.

The eighteenth century English jury, then, had a lot of discretion.[4] Trials went fast, with *voir dire* to help the defendant choose a jury.[5] The judge did little to instruct the jury, although

the judge did contol the evidence and attorneys.[6]

The jurors could ask witnesses questions directly,[7] a throwback to when they were the witnesses, and had free reign to assess a defendant's character.[8] Indeed, by finding defendants guilty of lesser charges, these eighteenth century juries decided punishment.[9]

Despite this power juries became even more separated from their communities. By the early 1700s, juries came from the whole county instead of the local vicinity and had changed from active neighborhood investigators to passive listeners.[10]

---

1. *Quoted in* LEVY at 218.

2. Nothing, of course, stops jurors from coercing each other.

3. *Quoted in* KADRI at 91–92.

Chief Justice of the Court of Common Pleas, Sir John Vaughan

4. *See generally* Langbein, *Before the Lawyers,* at 273–77.

5. Langbein, *Before the Lawyers,* at 279. Regarding the speed of eighteenth century English trials, see *id.* at 277–84.

6. Langbein, *Before the Lawyers,* at 284–91. See Langbein, *Historical Foundations,* at 1190 for an account of a judge rejecting the jury's acquittal three times before getting a guilty verdict.

7. Langbein, *Before the Lawyers,* at 288.

8. Langbein, *Before the Lawyers,* at 305.

9. Langbein, *Before the Lawyers,* at 304.

10. Langbein, *Historical Foundations,* at 1170–71.

11. KADRI at 93.

12. *See* Landsman at 592; Sward, *Civil Trial,* at 370–73.

13. *See* **Chapter 1: Of Dogma and Desire: Saying What You Believe about the First Amendment.** For accounts of the Zenger case, see GOLDSTEIN at 2–9, *Navarro,* 408 F.3d at 1192; Shone at 655; Scott at 408; Alschuler & Deiss at 871–74, 903 (giving a full account of the changing role of the jury in American history, especially how it has moved from a finder of both fact and law to its much more passive role today).

But what about the jury in America?

JURIES IN AMERICA

The colonists brought the jury with them to America.

Twelve years after his jury trial in England, William Penn guaranteed jury trials in Pennsylvania.[11] King James I guaranteed the jury in the Virginia Company Charter of 1606, and the Massachusetts Body of Liberties likewise incorporated trial by jury.[12]

In the colonial experience juries stood against the crown to protect the colonists' rights. In the case of John Peter Zenger, for instance, a jury of twelve New York colonists acquitted the publisher despite the crown's evidence.[13]

In the Boston writs cases, juries refused to find for the crown.[14] For this reason, the British moved cases involving forfeiture to admiralty courts, without juries.

Thus one of the bases for the American Revolution was King George taking away the jury, as noted in the Declaration of Independence:

"For depriving us, in many cases, of the benefits of Trial by Jury."

The Founders like Thomas Jefferson knew this:

"I consider trial by jury as the only anchor ever yet imagined by man, by which government can be held to the principles of its constitution."[15]

John Adams, often at odds with Jefferson on many ideological points, could not have agreed more:

"It would be an absurdity for jurors to be required to accept the judges' view of the law against their own opinion, judgment, and conscience."[16]

---

14. See **Chapter 4: Molasses and the Sticky Origins of the Fourth Amendment.** *See also* Nelson B. Lasson, The History and Development of the Fourth Amendment of the United States Constitution 51–78 (1937).

15. *Quoted in* Donald M. Middlebrooks, *Reviving Thomas Jefferson's Jury: Sparf and Hansen v. United States Reconsidered*, 46 Am. J. Legal Hist. 353, 353–54 (2004).

 Jefferson also wrote that: "Were I called upon to decide, whether the people had best be omitted in the legislative or judiciary department, I would say it is better to leave them out of the legislative. The execution of the laws is more important than the making of them." *Id. See* Howe at 582; Alschuler & Deiss at 876–77. *See also* Daniel D. Blinka, *Jefferson and Juries: The Problem of Law, Reason, and Politics in the New Republic*, 47 Am. J. Legal Hist. 35 (2005).

 In his *Notes on Virginia*, Jefferson touched on the relationship between jury and judge:

"[I]t is usual for the jurors to decide the fact, and to refer the law arising on it to the judges. But this division of the subject lies with their discretion only. And if the question relate to any point of public liberty, or if it be one of those in which the judges may be suspect of bias, the jury [may] undertake to decide both law and fact."

 Thomas Jefferson, Notes on the State of Virginia 140 (J.W. Randolph ed., 1853), *quoted in* Ian Ayres, *Pregnant with Embarrassments: An Incomplete Theory of the Seventh Amendment*, 26 Val. U. L. Rev. 385, 400 (1992). For more on the fact and law dichotomy in the jury and judge relationship, *see* Ellen E. Sward, *The Seventh Amendment and the Alchemy of Fact and Law*, 33 Seton Hall L. Rev. 573 (2003).

16. *Quoted in* Kempin at 69; Alschuler & Deiss at 906. **Adams** also wrote:

"It is not only his [the juror's] right, but his duty, in that case to find the verdict according to his own best understanding, judgment, and conscience, though in direct opposition to the direction of the court.

. . . The English law obliges no man . . . to put his faith on the sleeve of any mere man." *Quoted in* Howe at 605.

For these men, juries were the bulwark against the tyranny of government.[1] As such, juries had a role in defining and judging the law.[2] In fact, at the time most judges were laymen, not trained lawyers, and comparable to modern justices of the peace.[3]

Thus a colonial jury would have been in as good a position to decide the law as most judges.[4]

Although in colonial America and England jurors had lost their role as self-informed witnesses, they still

decided a defendant's sentence. Statutes existed that defined punishments, but the jurors knew the punishments and could deliberately find a defendant guilty of a lesser offense, despite clear evidence, to avoid the graver punishment.[5]

As in England, many trials

1. Barnes at 362–63. The debates on the Constitution's ratification discussed this issue; *see* THE FEDERALIST No. 83 as well as ANTI-FEDERALIST No. 83, both of which treat the issue of trial by jury. *See also* LEVY at 229–30; Barnes at 364; *Navarro,* 408 F.3d at 1193. Regarding the connection for the Framers between trial by jury and early American democracy, as well as an outline of various early state constitutional protections, *see* Paul D. Carrington, *The Civil Jury and American Democracy,* 13 DUKE J. COMP. & INT'L L. 79 (2003).

2. Howe at 586. On juries deciding both law and fact, *see* Barnes at 363–64. For the practice in state courts, *see* Howe at 595, 601.

3. Howe at 591.

4. In Rhode Island, for example, judges held office *"not for the purpose of deciding causes, for the jury decided all questions of law and fact; but merely to preserve order, and see that the parties had a fair chance with the jury."* Howe at 590–91.

5. On the jury's role in sentencing in England, *see* Langbein, *Before the Lawyers,* at 304 (also outlining early plea bargaining); BAKER at 517 (on jury mitigation and the so-called *"pious perjury"* of jury practice). Most crimes in England, many of which we would call minor, were punishable by death, making jury intervention more important. GREEN at 365.

In 1717, Parliament made many offenses *"clergyable,"* which meant a defendant could receive the common-law version of the medieval church's *"benefit of clergy."* Chris Kemmitt, *Function over Form: Reviving the Criminal Jury's Historical Role as a Sentencing Body,* 40 U. MICH. J.L. REFORM 93, 98–100 (2006) (a persuasive historical study on the role of original American juries as deciders of the sentence, and recommending that courts should advise modern juries of sentencing consequences to conform to the Framers' original intent). *See also* Langbein, *Ryder Sources,* at 40–41 (noting the example of finding the defendant guilty of a "clergyable" offense); KIRALFY at 368.

6. John Jay, the first chief justice of the Supreme Court, in a jury trial under the Supreme Court's original jurisdiction, instructed that the jury could judge both facts and law:
"It may not be amiss here, gentlemen, to remind you of the good old rule, that on questions of fact it is the province of the jury, on questions of law, it is the province of the court to decide. But it must be observed that by the same law, which recognized this reasonable distribution of jurisdiction, you have nevertheless a right to take upon yourselves to judge of both, and to determine the law as well as the fact in controversy." Georgia v. Brailsford, 3 U.S. (3 Dall.) at 4 (1794). *Discussed in* Alschuler & Deiss at 907.

John Jay

were basically sentencing hearings.

As Jefferson's and Adam's views show, the Founders viewed the jury as a bulwark against government oppression. They adopted the general verdict formula, allowing the jury to decide both the law and the facts.[6] A jury in the new U.S. republic was not just a "finder" of fact and law. Rather, the Founders considered the jury to be a mini-legislature.[7]

Alexis de Tocqueville observed that the jury was "*first and foremost a political institution*" and "*a form of popular sovereignty.*"[8] De Tocqueville went on;

"*[t]he jury is both the most effective way of establishing the people's rule and the most efficient way of teaching them how to rule.*"[9]

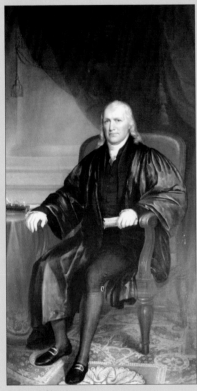

Samuel Chase

The impeachment of Justice Samuel Chase underscores the importance to the Framers of the idea that the jury should decide the law. One of the charges against Chase was that when sitting as a trial judge he tried "*to wrest from the jury their indisputable right to hear argument, and determine upon the question of law, as well as on the question of fact, involved in the verdict they are required to give.*" Quoted in Alschuler & Deiss at 908. On this and other counts, most senators, though not the two-thirds needed, voted to convict him after the House had impeached him. *Id.*

Although the Chase case was a great win for judicial independence in the new republic, it also shows that, for the Framers, juries deciding the law *was* the law. *See* WILLIAM H. REHNQUIST, GRAND INQUESTS: THE HISTORIC IMPEACHMENTS OF JUSTICE SAMUEL CHASE AND PRESIDENT ANDREW JOHNSON 595 (1992); Howe, at 588 n.20. For the Chase case and the relationship of judges and juries, see Landsman at 603–04.

de Tocqueville

7. Kemmitt at 103–04. The Framers looked to Aristotle for their ideal of a jury and its role. Equity demands that a jury must be a petit legislature. Aristotle understood that universal law is necessarily overbroad. To prevent injustice a jury or judge must act as the legislature would act if it dealt with this particular case. *See* Kemmitt at n.99, *citing* ARISTOTLE, ETHICA NICHOMACHEA, *reprinted in* 9 THE WORKS OF ARISTOTLE TRANSLATED INTO ENGLISH 1136–37 (W.D. Ross trans., Clarendon Press 1925). Another systemic manifestation of the exercise of equity was the much broader executive pardoning power in eighteenth century England and America. *See* **Chapter 8: "*Baby, Don't Be Cruel*": Just What Is So Cruel *and* Unusual about the Eighth Amendment?**

8. Kemmitt at 104, *citing* ALEXIS DE TOCQUEVILLE, DEMOCRACY IN AMERICA 313 (Arthur Goldhammer trans., Library of America 2004) (1835). De Tocqueville also described the jury as a "*gratuitous public school, ever open.*" Quoted in Carrington at 86. *See also* Landsman at 604–05; Aschuler & Deiss at 876.

9. Quoted in WILTSHIRE at 165 (*citing* ALEXIS DE TOCQUEVILLE, "*Trial by Jury in the United States Considered as a Political Institution,*" *in* DEMOCRACY IN AMERICA).

A tension existed in the early republic between the juries deciding law and the emergence of professional judges with an interest in orderly supervision of public affairs.[1] This tension plays out today in debates on jury nullification.

The question is not if the jury has the power to nullify a law or its application; *Bushell's Case* determined that affirmatively in 1670. Rather, the only question is whether the judge should tell jurors of their power and whether lawyers can argue it.[2]

The Supreme Court in 1895 determined this question against informing the jury about jury nullification.[3] The Supreme Court ignored Jefferson and Adams, who expressed the sense of the Founders regarding the jury's proper role.[4] Judges today specifically

---

1. Howe at 615; *see generally* Shone.

2. Howe at 584. *See* Andrew J. Parmenter, *Nullifying the Jury: "The Judicial Oligarchy" Declares War on Jury Nullification*, 46 WASHBURN L.J. 379 (2007) (discussing the history of jury nullification, including the Lilburne and Bushell trials, up to the modern debate).

The Jury by John Morgan (1861)

This English jury would have known its nullification power and in a system where most crimes were capital, with no plea bargaining, would have regularly exercised it.

For a satirical look at trial by jury in 1840 England, see *Trial by Jury, or Laying Down the Law*, with a French poodle as judge.

Trial by Jury, or Laying Down the Law by Sir Edwin Landseer

4. *But see* Stanton D. Krauss, *An Inquiry into the Right of Criminal Juries to Determine the Law in Colonial America*, 89 J. CRIM. L. & CRIMINOLOGY 111, 122, 214 (1998) (arguing there is not any real evidence that colonial juries had the nullification right).

3. *Sparf and Hansen v. United States*, 156 U.S. 51 (1895). For discussions of *Sparf*, see Howe at 588–89; Shone at 657; Alschuler & Deiss at 910–11; Middlebrooks *generally*.

Modern courts such as the Second Circuit explain that "*the power of juries to 'nullify'. . . is just that—a power; it is by no means a right . . . .*" *United States v. Thomas*, 116 F.3d 606, 615 (2d Cir. 1997). The District of Columbia Circuit Court of Appeals denounces jury nullification even more emphatically: "*A jury has no more 'right' to find a 'guilty' defendant 'not guilty' than it has to find a 'not guilty' defendant 'guilty,' and the fact that the former cannot be corrected by*

a court, while the latter can be, does not create a right out of the power to misapply the law. Such verdicts are lawless, a denial of due process and constitute an exercise of erroneously seized power." *United States v. Washington*, 705 F.2d 489, 494 (D.C. Cir. 1983).

Despite this, the Supreme Court continues to articulate that the jury's very purpose is to prevent government oppression. *See, e.g., United States v. Powell*, 469 U.S. 57, 65 (1984); *Williams v. Florida*, 399 U.S. 78, 100 (1970); *Duncan v. Louisiana*, 391 U.S. 145, 155 (1968) ("*the jury's historic function, in criminal trials, as a check against arbitrary or*

oppressive exercises of power by the Executive Branch"). The function of checking an arbitrary or oppressive power means jury nullification is not only a right but a duty. As Justice Oliver Wendell Holmes wrote: "*The jury has the power to bring in a verdict in the teeth of both law and facts.*" *Horning v. District of Columbia*, 249 U.S. 596 (1920).

For a thoughtful, and thought-provoking, discussion of instructions to modern criminal juries, see B. Michael Dann, "*Must Find the Defendant Guilty*": *Jury Instructions Violate the Sixth Amendment*, 91 JUDICATURE 12 (2007).

order modern jurors not to consider punishment. This is but one indication that our courts and government have not stayed true to the intent of the Framers and their beliefs on the jury's role.[5]

But despite this, the right to trial by jury is still alive.[6] Today we argue about the details of the right and, though important, even critical, the debate is not fundamental. No one questions a defendant's right to counsel, to compel witnesses, to confront an accuser, to testify under oath, to cross-exam, or to an open trial. Even in civil cases the Seventh Amendment is where the discussion starts.[7]

"By God!," you could exclaim, trial by jury has come a long way.

One of the modern arguments against jury nullification is what happened when Southern juries failed to convict whites accused of killing blacks during the Jim Crow era. *See* James Forman, Jr., *Juries and Race in the Nineteenth Century*, 113 Yale L.J. 895 (2004) (including an interesting outline of how race affected jury composition for most of American history). *See also Navarro*, 408 F.3d at 1194. The modern case of *Batson v. Kentucky*, 476 U.S. 79 (1986), affects jury composition to prevent exclusion of racial minorities from the jury. Even in the Middle Ages a defendant could disqualify a juror for having *"deadly enmities"* or *"greedy desire to get . . . land."* Klerman, *Settlement*, at 134; Levy at 216; Baker at 509.

5. The Queen of Hearts in Lewis Carroll's *Alice's Adventures in Wonderland* (1865) took away all chance for jury nullification. During the trial of the Knave of Hearts, when the King said the jurors should consider the verdict, the Queen declared: *"Sentence first, verdict afterwards."* Kadri at 35.

7. The Seventh Amendment states that it applies *"[i]n suits at common law."* Much modern debate interprets *"the common law"* of 1798 and 1791 to justify limiting the right to a jury. For example, when a federal judge exercises the powers of the old English Chancery courts in "suits in equity," there is no right to a jury. *See* Carrington at 84–85 (noting that the distinction *"is in [most] respects anachronistic because law and equity are seldom distinguished for any other purpose"*). For an insightful comparison of the power of 1791 common-law judges with modern federal judges' powers to deny a litigant the right to a jury through modern procedural devices, *see* Suja A. Thomas, *The Seventh Amendment, Modern Procedure, and the English Common Law*, 82 Wash. U. L.Q. 687 (2004). Thomas well demonstrates that modern judges exercise far greater powers to deny a jury trial than their common-law predecessors. *See also* Paul F. Kirgis, *The Right to a Jury Decision on Questions of Fact under the Seventh Amendment*, 64 Ohio St. L.J. 1125 (2003). For a contrary view, *see* Edith Guild Henderson, *The Background of the Seventh Amendment*, 80 Harv. L. Rev. 289 (1967) (arguing that colonial jury practice was variable and thus the Seventh Amendment did not intend to codify any specific practice). For a brief discussion of the range of colonial jury and trial practice, *see* Sward, *Civil Trial*, at 369–73, specifically noting that *"[e]quity was a hodgepodge, handled in many different ways, but often by the regular courts of the colonies using procedures drawn for English equity." Id.* at 373.

Regarding problems with the Seventh Amendment's language and grammatically flawed wording, *see* Ayers *generally* and at 386–89.

6. But Is the Jury Vanishing? For concerns, see Hon. William G. Young, *Vanishing Trials, Vanishing Juries, Vanishing Constitution*, 40 Suffolk U. L. Rev. 67 (2006); Hon. Sam Sparks & George Butts, *Disappearing Juries and Jury Verdicts*, 39 Tex. Tech. L. Rev. 289 (2007).

"Baby, Don't Be Cruel":

What's So Cruel *and* Unusual about the Eight Amendment? [1]

"Excessive bail shall not be required, nor excessive fines imposed, nor cruel and unusual punishments inflicted."

—The Eighth Amendment

Before his death in 1305, William Wallace saw his executioners pull out his intestines and burn them, and there was nothing *"cruel and unusual"* about it.

Wallace gets special attention because he was "Braveheart," and they made a block-buster movie about him. But he was only one of thousands during British history to receive the well-codified formula of a traitor's death.[2]

1. What would the Framers have thought of Elvis Presley singing "Don't Be Cruel" (1956) when they wrote the Eighth Amendment? Elvis released it as a single with "Hound Dog" on the other side. Written with Otis Black-well, it is the only record to have both sides reach No. 1 on the charts. *Don't Be Cruel by Elvis Presley,* SONGFACTS, http://www.songfacts.com/detail.php?id=1140

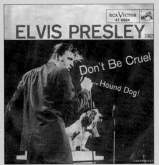

(last visited Jan. 13, 2008). *See* the lyrics at LyricsFreak, Don't Be Cruel Lyrics, http://www.lyricsfreak.com/e/elvis+presley/dont+be+cruel_20048329.html (last visited Jan. 13, 2008).

2. *BRAVEHEART* (20th Century Fox 1995).
Death by Hanging, Drawing, and Quartering. *"The victim, if male, was hanged but cut down while still alive [the hanging supposedly dulled the pain]; his genitals were cut off and burned before him; he was disemboweled, still alive, and then he was cut into four parts and beheaded. . . . Women convicted of treason were sentenced to being burned alive, although they were usually first strangled until unconscious."* LEONARD W. LEVY, ORIGINS OF THE BILL OF

RIGHTS 234–35 (1999). Parliament did not prohibit drawing and quartering for treason until 1870, but it was last inflicted in 1817, and burning of women ended in 1790. *Id.*
   See KURT VON S. KYNELL, SAXON AND MEDIEVAL ANTECED-ENTS OF THE ENGLISH COMMON LAW 134 (2000), for men-tion of William Wallace's revolt and execution.

Thus, even though his punishment was *"cruel,"* it was hardly *"unusual."*[1]

This strange coupling of *"cruel and unusual"* that the Eighth Amendment prohibits is the measuring rod for constitutional analysis of any punishment. Though people argue American punishment today is *"cruel,"* history provides many worse examples. Pulling out the tongue, slicing off the nose, cutting off genitals, and boiling to death were all common punishments throughout English history.[2]

But as we will see at the end of this chapter, the Eighth Amendment was part of punishment reform.[3] By the time it passed the traditional punishments of pillorying, disemboweling, decapitation, and drawing and quartering were out of style.[4]

The Constitution itself assumes the death penalty.

Guillotining of French nobility

The term **"capital punishment"** comes from decapitation (i.e., beheading). *capitation"* comes from the Latin *"caput," "capitis," "capitalis,"* ("head"), which is where we get the word *"capi-* of a column or a country. The neuter of adjective when describing punishment, i.e., *"capitale,"* meant death or loss of all civil rights, and banishment. *Capital Punishment,* THE CATHOLIC ENCYCLOPEDIA, http://www.newadvent.org/cathen/12565a.htm (last visited Feb. 28, 2008).

Decapitation: The cause of death is simple enough—after the chop no more blood flows to the brain, and without blood the brain gets no oxygen, destroying it within seconds or minutes.

The Classy Way to Go! Simple beheading, as opposed to hanging on the gallows, was a nobleman's prerogative. High nobles had the privilege of getting wacked by the sword instead of an axe.

But there were problems, especially with unskilled executioners. In late antiquity the Romans tried to martyr Saint Cecilia with beheading by unsuccessfully whacking her three times—this was after they tried to suffocate her with steam. She eventually died from her wounds.

During the French Revolution's egalitarian spirit, Dr. Joseph Guillotin was on a committee that recommended in 1791 a beheading device that made each person's execution equal to another. Guillotin did not invent the

Cigar cutter's curved blade versus the guillotine's blade

Execution of Louis XVI

guillotine; it just got his name. Older and less efficient devices were the Halifax Gibbet and Scottish Maiden. An apocryphal story claims that King Louis XVI (an amateur locksmith) recommended a triangular blade with a beveled edge be used instead of a curved blade. In 1793 the revolutionaries dispatched him with the beveled blade.

Saint Cecilia, who was wacked three times; her feast day is November 22

Saint Cecilia, with a cut neck

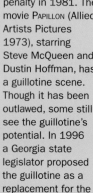
◄ Dr. Joseph Ignacio Guillotin (1814)

France used the guillotine from 1792 through "the Terror" of 1793 until it abolished the death penalty in 1981. The movie PAPILLON (Allied Artists Pictures 1973), starring Steve McQueen and Dustin Hoffman, has a guillotine scene. Though it has been outlawed, some still see the guillotine's potential. In 1996 a Georgia state legislator proposed the guillotine as a replacement for the electric chair so the condemned could be an organ donor. The proposal was not adopted.

A hapless, and later headless, Louis XVI

Halifax Gibbet

Scottish Maiden

A Corinthian capital

Washington, D.C., the U.S. capital

The Fifth Amendment, for instance, states that

"[n]o person shall be held to answer for a capital, or otherwise infamous crime . . ."

meaning that *"capital"* crimes existed aplenty.[5] Though scores of the Founders believed in the death penalty, others did not. Dr. Benjamin Rush, for example, a signer of the Declaration of Independence and one of the most influential Founding Fathers that most people have never heard of, opposed capital punishment:

"It is in my opinion murder to punish murder by death."[6]

As we will see, Rush was reflecting reformist Enlightenment thought.

The modern question that this history presents is, what does the Eighth Amendment's prohibition on *"cruel and unusual"* punishments mean? This is the central debate in the Supreme Court today.[7]

---

2. Levy at 234–35.

3. All the American colonies had capital punishment but generally for fewer crimes than England. Nicholas Levi, *Veil of Secrecy: Public Executions, Limitations on Reporting Capital P unishment, and the Content-Based Nature of Private Execution Laws*, 55 Fed. Comm. L.J. 131, 133–34 (2002).

4. All forms of corporal/physical punishment (except the death penalty) disappeared in the early years of the republic. See John Braithwaite, *A Future Where Punishment Is Marginalized: Realistic or Utopian?* 46 Ucla L. Rev. 1727, 1732 (1999). *Weems v. United States*, 217 U.S. 349, 389–400 (1910) (dissenting opinion), discusses the early attitudes toward the Eighth Amendment as forbidding the unusual cruelty in the method of punishment that the Framers condemned. As we shall see, the reaction to the punishment meted out to Titus Oates, including his pillorying, was a main source of the *"cruel and unusual"* clause.

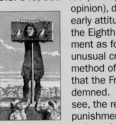

5. See Richard Brookhiser, What Would the Founders Do?: Our Questions, Their Answers 33 (2006). Justice Antonin Scalia specifically has stated, *"The death penalty, for example, was not cruel and unusual punishment because it is referred to in the Constitution itself . . . ."* Antonin Scalia, *Originalism: The Lesser Evil*, 57 U. Cin. L. Rev. 849, 863 (1989).

Justice Scalia

6. Benjamin Rush, Considerations of the Injustice and Impolicy of Punishing Murder by Death (1792); An Enquiry into the Effects of Public Punishments Upon Criminals and Upon Society (1787). For Dr. Rush and the movement to abolish the death penalty in early America, see Stuart Banner, The Death Penalty: An American History 103–09 (2002) and Louis P. Masur, Rites of Execution: Capital Punishment and the Transformation of American Culture, 1776–1865 (1989) (especially Chapter 3).

See also Levi at 135–36; Deborah A. Schwartz & Jay Wishingrad, *The Eighth Amendment, Beccaria, and the Enlightenment: A Historical Justification for the Weems v. United States Excessive Punishment Doctrine*, 24 Buff. L. Rev. 783, 823 (1975) (documenting Enlightenment thinkers as precursors, and showing the original intent of the Eighth Amendment's Framers).

Dr. Benjamin Rush (c. 1818)

For the abolition of capital punishment in England, see J.H. Baker, An Introduction to English Legal History 518 (4th ed. 2002), and in America see Levi at 136–38 (noting the first anti–death penalty movement in 1800–60 and the growth of prisons). See also Levi at 134, (noting that slaves received capital punishment more than whites). For death penalty reforms from the Civil War, see Levi at 138–39.

Conversely, for a presentation of literary support of the death penalty by William Wordsworth, see Gregg Mayer, *The Poet and Death: Literary Reflections on Capital Punishment through the Sonnets of William Wordsworth*, 21 St. John's J. Legal Comment. 727 (2007).

7. For example, a debated question is the extent to which the Eighth Amendment prohibits excessive punishments. See, e.g., *Roper v. Simmons*, 125 S. Ct. 1183, 1190 (2005) (*"[T]he Eighth Amendment guarantees individuals the right not to be subjected to excessive sanctions."*); *Atkins v. Virginia*, 536 U.S. 304, 311 (2002) (*"The Eighth Amendment succinctly prohibits 'excessive' sanctions."*); *Solem v. Helm*, 463 U.S. 277, 284 (1983) (*"The [Eighth Amendment] prohibits not only barbaric punishments, but also sentences that are disproportionate to the crime committed."*). See generally Samuel B. Lutz, *The Eighth Amendment Reconsidered: A Framework for Analyzing the Excessiveness Prohibition*, 80 N.Y.U. L. Rev. 1862 (2005) (citing Supreme Court cases prohibiting all *"excessive"* criminal sanctions). Conversely, others argue the Framers could not have intended the Eighth Amendment to restrict punishments like the death penalty prevalent when the Eighth Amendment was passed. See *Harmelin v. Michigan*, 501 U.S. 957, 975–83 (1991) (joint opinion) (Scalia, J.); *McGautha v. California*, 402 U.S. 183, 226 (1971); *Ewing v. California*, 538 U.S. 11, 31 (2003) (Scalia, J. concurring) (noting the Eighth Amendment prohibits *"only certain modes of punishment"*).

See generally Aimee Logan, Note, *Who Says So? Defining Cruel and Unusual Punishment by Science, Sentiment, and Consensus*, 35 Hastings Const. L.Q. 195–220 (2008).

"*Cruel and unusual*" are perhaps the most relative words in the Constitution. The words are relative to personal experience.[1] All punishment is *cruel* to somebody but not necessarily *unusual* to everyone.[2]

More pertinent to constitutional interpretation is that the words are also relative in history.[3] The word "cruel" had a slightly different meaning in the seventeenth century.[4] You could not imagine, for instance, John Adams saying to his wife Abigail, "*Baby, don't be cruel.*"[5]

And as we saw in Chapter 5, Puritans and others considered the ex *officio* oath "*cruel*," though few of us today would consider a compelled oath "*cruel.*"[6]

James Madison proposed what ultimately became the Eighth Amendment on June 12, 1789. Even at the time those voting on the Bill of

---

1. I once helped represent a battered woman convicted for killing her abusive spouse. She told us that "*[p]rison is the only safe place I have ever known.*"

2. **The Eighth Amendment's Perverse Boundaries:**
   Citizenship. Under the Constitution only Congress can confer citizenship, not the states. *Dred Scott v. Sandford*, 60 U.S. 393, 19 How. 393 (1856) (this wholly discredited case still stands for this proposition). The Supreme Court holds that taking away citizenship is "*cruel and unusual.*" Denaturalization is "*a form of punishment more punitive than torture, for it destroys for the individual the political existence that was centuries in the making.*" *Trop v. Dulles*, 356 U.S. 86, 101 (1958).
   But in *Rummel v. Estelle*, 100 S. Ct. 1133 (1980), the Supreme Court held that a life sentence for three minor felony thefts aggregating $229.11 was not a "*cruel and unusual*" punishment. By any measure this is an absurd result. Most of us would choose to lose citizenship (and spend life in the Cayman Islands) rather than have a life in prison. *But see* Charles Walter Schwartz, *Eighth Amendment Proportionality Analysis and the Compelling Case of William Rummel*, 71 J. CRIM. L. & CRIMINOLOGY 378 (1980) (arguing that *Rummel* was "*fundamentally sound*".

Dred Scott

3. *See* Harry F. Tepker, *Tradition and the Abolition of Capital Punishment for Juvenile Crime*, 59 OKLA. L. REV. 809, 814–15 (2006) (showing the historic relativity of the terms "*cruel and unusual*"). *See also* Margaret Jane Radin, *The Jurisprudence of Death: Evolving Standards of the Cruel and Unusual Punishments Clause*, 126 U. PA. L. REV. 989, 1030–32 (1978) (arguing that the Framers' use of a moral concept of "cruelty," rather than specifically enumerated list of prohibited punishments, demonstrates the validity of an evolving standard).

4. Anthony F. Granucci, "*Nor Cruel and Unusual Punishments Inflicted:*" *The Original Meaning*, 57 CAL. L. REV. 839, 860 (1969).

5. John and Abigail Adams.

6. The delegates discussed the Fifth Amendment just before the Eighth, showing these amendments' close thematic relationship. *See* Celia Rumann, *Tortured History: Finding Our Way Back to the Lost Origins of the Eighth Amendment*, 31 PEPP. L. REV. 661, 665–66, 668, 679 n.45 (2004) (noting the relationship between the Fifth and Eighth Amendments regarding prohibitions of "*barbarous interrogations*" and coercive interrogations). *See also* Laurence Claus, *The Antidiscrimination Eighth Amendment*, 28 HARV. J.L. & PUB. POL'Y 119, 131 (2005); Granucci at 848–50.

7. Tepker at 814. During the constitutional debates before ratification and the subsequent Bill of Rights, Noah Webster, an advocate of a national constitution and author of America's first great dictionary, stated the common sense of the problem: "*[U]nless you can, in every possible instance, previously define the words excessive and unusual—if you leave the discretion of Congress to define them on occasion, any restriction of their power by a general indefinite expression, is a nullity— mere formal nonsense.*" Id (quoting Noah Webster, Reply to the Pennsylvania Minority: "America," DAILY ADVERTISER (N.Y.), Dec. 31, 1787, reprinted in 1 THE DEBATE ON THE CONSTITUTION 553, 559 (Bernard Bailyn ed., 1993)).
   The relativity of terms even at the time creates a great problem for those arguing "*original intent*" in constitutional interpretation. For example, Justice David Brewer wrote that "*[t]he Constitution is a written instrument. As such its meaning does not alter. That which is meant when adopted it means now.*" *South Carolina v. United States*, 199 U.S. 437, 448 (1905). Given the clear relativity at the time of the Eighth Amendment's passage, advocating a meaning that "*does not alter*" appears to be a false altar indeed.

Noah Webster

Justice David Joseph Brewer

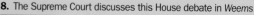

8. The Supreme Court discusses this House debate in *Weems v. United States*, 217 U.S. 349, 368–69 (1910), and *Furman v. Georgia*, 408 U.S. 238, 243–45, 262–63 (1972). This was quoted also in Tepker at 815 (citing 1 ANNALS OF CONG. 782 (Joseph Gales ed., 1834) and Granucci at 842).

Smith of South Carolina

Samuel Livermore of New Hampshire

Rights recognized the relativity of the terms.[7] Indeed, the sum total of legislative comment at the passing of the Eighth Amendment in Congress from Representatives Smith of South Carolina and Samuel Livermore of New Hampshire demonstrate this relativity:[8]

"Mr. Smith, of South Carolina, objected to the words 'nor cruel and unusual punishments'; the import of them being too indefinite."

Livermore offered the following analysis: *"The clause seems to express a great deal of humanity,* on which account I have no objection to it; but as it seems to have no meaning in it, I do not think it necessary. What is meant by the terms excessive bail?[9] Who are to be the judges? What is understood by excessive fines? It lies with the court to determine."*

9. The Bail Clause. Livermore refers to the Eighth Amendment's Bail Clause, that is: *"Excessive bail shall not be required . . ."* This clause is beyond this chapter's scope. In fact, a whole chapter could be devoted to it, starting with Elvis Presley's *JAILHOUSE ROCK!*

The Bail Clause further shows the Fifth and Eighth Amendments' link. The Eighth Amendment's *"[e]xcessive bail shall not be required"* of a person both thematically and historically connects to the Fifth Amendment's Due Process Clause that *"nor [shall a person] be deprived of life, liberty, or property, without due process of law . . . ."*

During Anglo-Saxon times a man could put up his land to assure appearance or a *"borh"* could act as a personal guarantor for a landless man. COLIN RHYS LOVELL, ENGLISH CONSTITUTIONAL AND LEGAL HISTORY 22 (1962); *see also* Caleb Foote, *The Coming Constitutional Crisis in Bail: I,* 113 U. PA. L. REV. 959, 965–79 (1965) (describing the history of bail in England and colonial America). Through the Middle Ages the bail practice was for an accused to have a surety but if he fled and was then caught and tried, the crown forfeited his goods even if he was acquitted. Thomas A. Green, *The Jury and the English Law of Homicide, 1200–1600,* 74 MICH. L. REV. 414, 425 (1976). *Magna Carta* Chapter 39 provided *"no freeman shall be warrested, or detained in prison . . . unless . . . by the law of the land."* Sheriffs originally had the king's authority to release or hold the accused but, because of exploitation, the Statute of Westminster (1275) limited their bail power and stipulated which crimes were bailable.

In the early seventeenth century, King Charles I ordered noblemen to loan him money and imprisoned those who refused. *See* Claus at 123 (regarding the high bonds of the 1670 and 1680s). In the PETITION OF RIGHT (1628), Parliament argued that Charles had flouted *Magna Carta* by imprisoning people without just cause or bail. Later, Parliament's Habeas Corpus Act of 1679 provided that *"[a] Magistrate shall discharge prisoners from their Imprisonment taking their Recognizance, with one or more Surety or Sureties, in any Sum according to the Magistrate's discretion, unless it shall appear that the Party is committed for such Matter or offences for which by law the Prisoner is not bailable."*

Subsequently the English Bill of Rights (1689) guaranteed that *"excessive bail hath been required of persons committed in criminal cases, to elude the benefit of the laws made for the liberty of the subjects. Excessive bail ought not to be required."*

Colonial America provided for bail, with some colonies simply copying British law. This carried through the American Revolution with, for example, VIRGINIA'S 1776 CONSTITUTION, Section 9 stating that *"excessive bail ought not to be required . . . ."* In 1785 Virginia added that *"[t]hose shall be let to bail who are apprehended for any crime not punishable in life or limb . . . . But if a crime be punishable by life or limb, or limb, if it be manslaughter and there be good cause to believe the party guilty thereof, he shall not be admitted to bail."*

The 1789 Judiciary Act, as well as the 1966 Bail Reform Act, guaranteed bail in noncapital, federal offenses. Currently the 1984 Bail Reform Act, 18 U.S.C. §§ 3141–3150, allows pretrial detention of the accused only if he is a danger to the community or risk of flight. Also, 18 U.S.C. § 3142(f) provides that a court can only deny bond for certain crimes: crimes of violence, an offense for which the maximum sentence is life imprisonment or death, certain drug offenses for which the maximum imprisonment is greater than ten years, repeat felony offenders, or if the defendant poses a serious risk of flight, obstruction of justice, or witness tampering. The Bail Reform Act seeks to deemphasize courts' need to rely on bonds.

Today in most states bail bondsmen finance bonds for a fee. On modern federal bond practice, *see* Ann M. Overbeck, Editorial Note, *Detention for the Dangerous: The Bail Reform Act of 1984,* 55 U. CIN. L. REV. 153, 193–97 (1986). The Supreme Court has yet to decide whether the constitutional prohibition on excessive bail applies to the states through the Fourteenth Amendment.

Jailhouse Rock album cover and a photo of Presley performing in "jail clothes" behind "bars."

Buster Keaton in JAIL BAIT (1937), where he agrees to pose as a murderer while a reporter searches for the real killer.

JAILHOUSE ROCK (MGM 1957). Presley plays Vince Everett, an ex-convict, analogous to Presley's then public image. After going to jail for a bar fight he meets Hunk Houghton, a washed-up country singer who teaches Everett to play an old guitar and to sing a few songs to become famous.

After this brief exchange the record states that "[t]he question was put on the clause, and it was agreed to by a considerable majority."[1] So, for Livermore and "a considerable majority," the clause that became our Eighth Amendment was not all that clear. If it reflected anything, it was "a great deal of humanity."[2]

The world of 1789 was, of course, a very different place, which the punishments reflect, as do Livermore's words:

"No cruel and unusual punishment is to be inflicted; it is sometimes necessary to hang a man, villains often deserve whipping, and perhaps having

---

1. 1 ANNALS OF CONG. 782–83 (1789).

2. With this history, the modern Supreme Court's reading of the Cruel and Unusual Punishments Clause is well founded. *See e.g.,* Weems, 217 U.S. at 378 ("the proscription of cruel and unusual punishments 'is not fastened to the obsolete, but may acquire meaning as public opinion becomes enlightened by a humane justice.'"). What is "cruel and unusual" must "draw its meaning from the evolving standards of decency that mark the progress of a maturing society" and punishment must accord with the "dignity of man." *Trop*, 356 U.S. at 100–01. *See also* William C. Heffernan, *Constitutional Historicism: An Examination of the Eighth Amendment Evolving Standards of Decency Test*, 54 AM. U. L. REV. 1355 (2005) (arguing that the jurisprudence on the Cruel and Unusual Punishments Clause conforms to the need to apply the Constitution to different issues). Regarding *Weems, see also* Rumann at 697; Granucci at 843; Bukowski at 423; Parr at 51–53; and Claus at 158–59. *See also* Pressly Millen, *Interpretation of the Eighth Amendment—Rummel, Solem, and the Venerable Case of Weems v. United States*, 1984 DUKE L.J. 789, 84–108 (1984) ("Weems would allow courts freely to decide what is "cruel and unusual," as the eighth amendment's adopters intended, without the scope of review being bound by narrow historical constraints."). Schwartz & Wishingrad at 793–800. On *Weems*'s break from earlier Eighth Amendment cases, *see* Claus at 152–53 and Granucci at 842.

3. Claus at 128–29; Granucci at 842. *See also* Claus at 129 (noting punishments under the original Federal Crimes Act). In all likelihood, Livermore would have known of William Blackstone's somewhat defensive catalogue of English punishments:

"Of these [crimes] some are capital, which extend to the life of the offender, and consist generally in being hanged by the neck till dead; though in very atrocious crimes other circumstances of terror, pain or disgrace are super-added: as, in treasons of all kinds, being drawn or dragged to the place of execution; in high treason affecting the king's person or government, emboweling alive, beheading and quartering; and in murder, a public dissection. And, in case of any treason committed by a female, the judgment is to be burned alive. But the humanity of the English nation has authorized, by a tacit consent, an almost general mitigation of such part of these judgments as savor of torture or cruelty: A sledge or hurdle being usually allowed to such traitors as are condemned to be drawn; and there being very few instances (and those accidental or by negligence) of any person's being emboweled or burned, till previously

Blackstone

deprived of sensation by strangling. Some punishments consist in exile or banishment, by abjurgation of the realm, or transportation to the American colonies: others in loss of liberty, by perpetual or temporary imprisonment. Some extend to confiscation, by forfeiture of lands, or movables, or both or of the profits of lands for life: others induce a disability, of holding offices or employments, being heirs, executors, and the like. Some, though rarely, occasion a mutilation or dismembering, by cutting off the hand or ears: others fix a lasting stigma on the offender, by slitting the nostrils, or branding in the hand or face. Some are merely pecuniary, by stated or discretionary fines: and lastly there are others, that consist primarily in their ignominy, though most of them are mixed with some degree of corporal pain; and these are inflicted chiefly for crimes, which arise from indigence, or which render even opulence disgraceful. Such as whipping, hard labor in the house of correction, the pillory, the stocks, and the duckingstool. Disgusting as this catalogue may seem it will afford pleasure to an English reader, and do honor to the English law, to compare it with that shocking apparatus of death and torment, to be met within the criminal codes of almost every other nation in Europe." Granucci at 862–63 (citing 4 W. BLACKSTONE, COMMENTARIES 377).

their ears cut off; but are we in the future to be prevented from inflicting these punishments because they are cruel?"[3]

Today we do not condone whipping or cutting off ears.[4] Livermore foresaw

that there would be other options less cruel to achieve the goals of criminal justice:

"If a more lenient mode of correcting vice and deterring others from the commission of it could be invented, it would

be very prudent in the Legislature to adopt it; but until we have some security that this will be done, we ought not to be restrained from making necessary laws by any declaration of this kind."' In 1789 there were virtually no prisons.[5]

---

4. Sterilization may be somewhat akin to cutting off ears and was held cruel and unusual in *Mickle v. Henrichs*, 262 Fed. 687 (D. Nev. 1918), but not in *State v. Feilen*, 70 Wash. 65, 126 Pac. 75 (1912).

Whipping was a punishment under federal law until 1839 and in some states long after. Claus at 143, 154. As late as 1963, Delaware's highest court upheld a whipping sentence. *State v. Cannon*, 1900 A.2d 514 (1963).

Whipping or **"flogging"** was a common form of discipline in the British Navy. The Latin *"flagellum"* (*"whip"*) is probably the source of the word *"flogging"* and *"flagellation."* Even Scalia, the most forceful proponent of originalism on the Supreme Court, would pause at imposing a whipping sentence. *"[I]n a crunch,"* he too might *"prove a faint-hearted originalist"*: *"I cannot imagine myself, any more than any other federal judge, upholding a statute that imposes the punishment of flogging."* Scalia at 861–62. (Presumably branding and the removing of body parts are out of bounds also, though as Livermore's statement shows, these were accepted punishments in 1789.) In light of *Rummel v. Estelle,* 100 S. Ct. 1133 (1980), upholding a life sentence for three minor felony thefts totaling $229.11, whipping would be preferable!

Whipping punishments are about humiliation, especially in the context of race. The film GLORY (Tri-Star 1989) has a whipping scene with actor Denzel Washington, underscoring the humiliating nature of the punishment. Regarding public punishments, see Chad Flanders, *Shame and the Meanings of Punishment,* 54 CLEV. ST. L. REV. 609 (2006), arguing that a government based on Enlightenment liberal principles is incompatible with punishments that inflict pain or suffering or humiliation; see also Jennifer Bellott, *To Humiliate or Not to Humiliate: Does the Sentencing Reform Act Permit Shaming as a Condition of Supervised Release?* 38 U. MEM. L. REV. 923 (2008).

The idea of humiliation by flogging was present in Christ's *"scourging,"* where the purpose was to humiliate Jesus and destroy him as a political threat. According to mainline Christianity, Christ suffered this humiliation as part of his redemption of humanity.

Delaware prison whipping post c. 1907, named Red Hannah

"Scourge" is the origin of the word "excoriate," ("to puncture or cut by mechanical means," usually involving only the epidermis). "Scourge" is also related to the word "scorn," which is to cause humiliation.

5. The prison reform movement did not succeed in creating the "penitentiary" system until the mid-1800s. See generally David J. Rothman, *Perfecting the Prison: United States, 1789–1865,* in MORRIS & ROTHMAN at Chapter 4. See also PENOLOGY: THE EVOLUTION OF CORRECTIONS IN AMERICA (George G. Killinger & Paul F. Cromwell, Jr., eds., 1973); James J. Beha II, *Redemption to Reform: The Intellectual Origins of the Prison Reform Movement,* 63 N.Y.U. ANN. SURV. AM. L. 773 (2008). KADRI at 99 notes that the penitentiary or reformatory started in the eastern United States.

Nathaniel Hawthorne's THE SCARLET LETTER (1850), takes place in Puritan New England but he wrote it at the start of the American prison movement, with insight into social realities:

"The founders of a new colony, whatever Utopia of human virtue and happiness they might originally project, have invariably recognized it among their earliest practical necessities to allot a portion of the virgin soil as a cemetery, and another portion as the site of a prison . . . The rust on the ponderous iron-work of its oaken door looked more antique than anything else in the New World . . . [the prison was] the black flower of civilized society." NATHANIEL HAWTHORNE, THE SCARLET LETTER 45–46 (Bantam Books 1986) (1850).

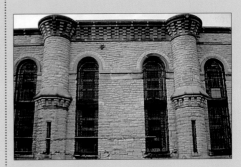

The prison from the film THE SHAWSHANK REDEMPTION (Columbia Pictures 1994)

Prisons would have been for Livermore the *"more lenient mode of correcting vice"* than the cruel punishments of his day.[1]

Livermore's statements underscore that the Eighth Amendment was for *"correcting vice and deterring others."* Notably, his statements leave out retribution as a goal of punishment. Although Livermore did say that *"villains"* often *"deserve whipping,"* the

main purpose of the Eighth Amendment was not to say what criminals *"deserve[d],"* but rather it was about *"a great deal of humanity."* The Eight Amendment reflects this humanity.

But Madison did not pull the words *"cruel and unusual"* out of the air. Rather, this wording is verbatim from the English Bill of Rights of 1689, Section 10, written exactly one hundred years earlier:

"That excessive bail ought not to be required, nor excessive fines imposed, nor cruel and unusual punishments inflicted."[2]

The only difference is that the Eighth Amendment states that excessive bail *"shall"*—rather than *"ought"*—not be required.

This language of the English Bill of Rights ended up in colonial legislation.[3] George Mason wrote it into Section 9 of the Virginia Declaration

---

1. This is not to say that prisons are easy places; in fact, they are well known for their cruelties. *See* country singer Johnny Cash, *At Folsom Prison* (Columbia 1968) and *At San Quentin* (Columbia 1969).

Johny Cash discussing prison reform with President Nixon.

2. LEVY at 231; Granucci at 840, 852–53 (noting that the 8th Amendment was taken verbatim from the English Bill of Rights of 1689). Note, *The Cruel and Unusual Punishment Clause and the Substantive Criminal Law,* 79 HARV. L. REV. 635, 636 (1965–66).

Granucci argues that *"[t]here is evidence that the provision of the English Bill of Rights of 1689, from which the language of the Eighth Amendment was taken, was concerned primarily with selective or irregular application of harsh penalties and that its aim was to forbid arbitrary and discriminatory penalties of a severe nature."* Granucci at 845–46; *cited also in Furman v. Georgia,* 408 U.S. 238, 243–44 (1972). *See also Gregg v. Georgia,* 428 U.S 153, 169 (1979) (noting the English Bill of Rights as source of the Eighth Amendment). COLIN DAYAN, THE STORY OF CRUEL AND UNUSUAL 18 (2007) (noting that *"cruel and unusual"* first appeared in the 1689 English Bill of Rights).

3. Predating the English Bill of Rights by almost fifty years was the Massachusetts Body of Liberties of 1641. Section 46 articulated that *"[f]or bodilie punishments we allow amounst us none that are inhumane Barbarous or cruel."* Claus at 130–31. *See also* Granucci at 850; Rumann at 667. The Reverend Nathaniel Ward (1578–1652), a Puritan clergyman and pamphleteer in England and Massachusetts, wrote the Body of Liberties, the first constitution in North America. The English Puritan Robert Beale was a great influence on Ward. *Id.* at 668–69; Granucci at 851. Indeed, Granucci argues that the intent of the cruel and unusual punishments clause in the English Bill of Rights was only to prevent courts from imposing punishments not in the statutes and disproportionate sentences. The American Framers, however, intended the meaning of Ward and Beal that torture, both before trial to obtain a confession as well as after trial as a punishment, is prohibited. Granucci, *passim,* and at 860.

LEVY at 237–38 notes that even after the Body of Liberties, Massachusetts branded robbers on the forehead and branded and flogged horse thieves. And the "scarlet letter" remained a favorite punishment as well as a future literary device in Nathaniel Hawthorne's THE SCARLET LETTER (1850), set in seventeenth century Puritanical Boston, about Hester Prynne, who gives birth after adultery, refuses to name the father, and struggles to create a new life of repentance and dignity. Several movie adaptations exist, including the THE SCARLET LETTER (Hollywood Pictures 1995), starring Demi Moore, Gary Oldman, and Robert Duvall.

Regarding the death penalty for moral offenses in Puritan New England justified by the *"pedagological"* function of the law, *see* Harold J. Berman, *Religious Foundations of Law in the West: An Historical Perspective,* 1 J.L. & RELIGION 3, 30 (1983).

4. Claus at 124–27; Tepker at 816. For passage in other states with variations on the formulation, *see* Claus at 133. For the Confederation Congress's ban on *"cruel and unusual"* punishments and in the Northwest Ordinance of 1787, *see* LEVY at 239 and Claus at 133.

See also Rumann at 673–74, 681 (arguing conclusively that the Framers intended a general ban on the use of torture in both the Eighth and Fifth Amendments). As Patrick Henry objected when arguing against the new Con-of Rights of 1776.[4] For the concepts of crime, punishment, and proportionality that the Eighth Amendment embodies, we begin with an earlier, even ancient, time.

"CRUEL AND UNUSUAL" FROM LEX TALIONIS

When we speak of punishment being "cruel" or "unusual," or even "cruel and unusual," we speak from a perspective; a "cruel" or "unusual" punishment is out of balance with a cultural norm. Or, to put it another way, the punishment is out of proportion

Proportionality is an ancient concept. The Bible speaks of "an eye for an eye."[5] Although often used today as an argument for retribution, this *"eye for an eye"* concept, also known as *lex talionis*,[6] is actually about proportionality in punishment.[7] *Lex talionis* avoids the potentially dis-

proportionate blood feud common in tribal societies.[8] The Eighth Amendment incorporates this ancient sense of proportionality.[9]

Ancient Greek myths incorporated a sense of proportionality and balance in punishment. Tantalus, who slaughtered his son and fed him to the gods, received the just retribution of spending eternity in Hades, forever parched and starved with drink and food always in view but out of reach.[10]

Patrick Henry before the House of Burgesses by Peter F. Rothermel (1851)

stitution because it lacked a Bill of Rights:

"In this business of legislation, your members of congress will loose the restriction of not imposing excessive fines, demanding excessive bail, and inflicting cruel and unusual punishments. These are prohibited by your declaration of rights. What has distinguished our ancestors?—That they would not admit of tortures, or cruel and barbarous punishment. But Congress may introduce the practice of the civil law, in preference to that of the common law. They may introduce the practice of France, Spain, and Germany—of torturing, to extort a confession of the crime. They will say that they might as well draw examples from those countries as from Great Britain, and they will tell you there is such a necessity of strengthening the arm of government, that they must have a criminal equity, and extort confession by torture, in order to punish with still more relentless severity. We are then lost and undone."

Quoted in Rumann at 677; Granucci at 841 n.10. See also Ingraham v. Wright, 430 U.S. 651, 664–66 (1977) (discussing the origins of the cruel and unusual punishments clause in the English Bill of Rights of 1679 and the Virginia Declaration of Rights of 1776).

5. "If a man injures his neighbor, what he has done must be done to him: broken limb for broken limb, eye for eye, tooth for tooth. As the injury inflicted, so must the injury suffered." Leviticus 24:19–20, in THE JERUSALEM BIBLE 162 (Jones ed. 1966). See LEVY at 231, 410; Tepker at 816.

6. The term "lex talionis" is Latin; "lex" ("law") and "talio" ("equivalent to" or "equal"), hence a law of proportionality. See Granucci at 844.

7. Irene Merker Rosenberg & Yale L. Rosenberg, *Lone Star Liberal Musings on "Eye for Eye" and the Death Penalty,* 1998 UTAH L. REV. 505, 509–10 (concluding the biblical verse "eye for eye" and lex talionis reflect not punitive or retaliatory values in ancient Jewish law but instead the standard of compensation or making the community whole); J.W. EHRLICH, THE HOLY BIBLE AND THE LAW 189–90 (1962) (noting that the "eye for eye" concept "established a fixed limit to retaliatory punishment"). See also Jack B. Weinstein, *Does Religion Have a Role in Criminal Sentencing?* 23 TOURO L. REV. 539, 542 (2007) (outlining historically the Jewish law against capital punishment); Alex Kozinski, *Sanhedrin II,* NEW REPUBLIC, Sept. 13, 1993, at 16 ("[T]he Talmud tells us, a Sanhedrin that upheld an execution in seven years or even in seventy years was scorned as a bloody court.").

Lex talionis is not a prohibition on cruelty. It allows heinous punishments for heinous crimes. Granucci at 848. But as Gandhi notes: "An eye for eye only ends up making the whole world blind." Mohandas Gandhi quotes, BRAINYQUOTE, http://www.brainyquote.com/quotes/quotes/m/mohandasga107039.html (last visited Jan. 20, 2008).

8. E.g., Ecclesiastics 8:5 "Reproach not a man that turneth from sin [crime], but remember that we are all worthy of punishment"; Deuteronomy 25:3 "If a person be adjudged wicked, order him beaten but no more than forty stripes, because above that number thy brother should seem vile unto thee."

9. Granucci at 844–46 (tracing the constitutional ban on excessive punishment to the Old Testament and other elements of Western tradition).

10. Tantalus is the origin of our word "tantalizing."

The Greeks are also the source of any number of philosophical arguments on proportionality in many aspects of life, including punishment. In fact the very first piece of prose we have from the Greeks (as opposed to Homer's poetry) comes from a fragment from the pre-Socratic philosopher Anaximander:

"From what source things arise, to that they return of necessity when they are destroyed . . . for they suffer punishment and make reparation to one another for their injustice according to the order of time."[1]

Thus the concept of proportionality keeps the universe in balance, both in the physical realm and the societal.

Aristotle later echoed this concept. He considered inequality in punishment an injustice, calling it *"the kind of justice indentified with injustice."* For Aristotle, *"what the judge aims at doing is to make the parts equal by the penalty he imposes."*[2]

Even Draco's law code, the source of our word "draconian" for its severity, protected the accused from retaliation and provided for

---

1. Anaximander (c. 610–546 BC) was the first of the known Greeks to publish a written document on nature. We only know of him from a fourth century AD Byzantine rhethorician named Themistius who saved the quoted fragment.

▼ Anaximander appears in Raphael's *School of Athens.*

2. *See* Granucci at 844 n.23. Aristotle in context reads as follows: *"The law never looks beyond the question, what damage was done? And it treats the parties involved as equals. All it asks is whether an injustice has been done or an injury by one party on other. Consequently, what the judge seeks to do is to redress the inequality which is this kind of justice identified with injustice. Thus in a case of assault or homicide the action and the consequences of the action may be represented as a line divided into equal parts . . . What the judge aims at doing is to make the parts equal by the penalty he imposes. . . ."* Aristotle, Ethics 148-49 (Penguin Classics ed., 1955).

The School of Athens (1509), showing Aristotle with the Ethics

·······················

3. Wiltshire at 155. According to tradition, Draco was Athens's first legislator. He lived in the seventh century BC. The Latin word *"draco"* means "dragon." Thus the name Draco Malfoy in the Harry Potter novels and movies, such as Harry Potter and the Half-Blood Prince (Warner Brothers 2009).

·······················

Alfred the Great

4. Granucci at 844-45 (discussing the Anglo-Saxon fine schedule and noting that Germanic peoples had fixed punishments called the Gulathing and Frustathing Laws).

Alfred the Great (c. 849–899) was king of the southern Anglo-Saxon kingdom of Wessex (871 to 899) but styled himself "King of the Anglo-Saxons." He is "the Great" for his defense against the Danish Vikings, because he encouraged education, and improved the legal system.

reconciliation of the killer with the victim's family.[3]

The Anglo-Saxons also had the concept of *lex talionis*. King Alfred codified the *lex talionis* in England around 900 AD.[4] Later King Edward the Confessor incorporated proportionality in his laws.[5] Thus the concept that the punishment should fit the crime has a long tradition in English law.

The early punishments for "murder" reflect the proportionality concept. During Anglo-Saxon times the "king's peace," or anything approaching a modern criminal justice system, was centuries away.[6] Thus if you killed someone you answered to his family, clan, or tribe. Either a blood feud would begin or the killer paid reparation, called the

"*wergild*,"[7] to the victim's family, determined by the victim's social rank.[8]

The killer's actual intent was unimportant; all killings from accidents to premeditated murder demanded the *wergild*.[9] The law recognized no mental state—the *mens rea*—to make an act a crime and, indeed, the law recognized no difference between crime and tort.[10]

King Edward the Confessor

5. LEVY at 232; Rumann at 666.

Edward the Confessor (or Eadweard III) (c. 1003–1066), was the son of Æthelred the Unready and the second to last Anglo-Saxon king of England, the last of the House of Wessex. Edward's death in 1066 with no son caused the conflict between three claimants: William, Duke of Normandy; Harold Godwinson; and Edgar Ætheling. The Catholic Church canonized Edward in 1161, and he is the patron saint of kings, difficult marriages, and separated spouses. He was the patron saint of England and remains the royal family's patron saint.

6. Anglo-Saxons generally only had the death penalty for actions that directly hurt the tribe's fighting ability — treason, cowardice, desertion, or sexual nonconformity, which threatened tribal population. LOVELL at 7, 40.

Hywel Dda (King Howell the Good)

7. The word "*wergild*" is composed of "*were*," ("man" in Old English and other Germanic languages—as in "*werewolf*"), and "*geld*" ("payment"). *Geld* is the root of English "gilt" and is the Dutch, Yiddish, and German word for "money." *Wergild* in practice may have existed for long after it officially ended. Green at 694.

Something akin was the Welsh compensation payments to avoid blood feuds in the Laws of Hywel Dda, named after Hywel Dda (Howell the Good, c. 880–950), who was king of most of modern day Wales. BAKER at 30.

On proportionality in homicide cases in ancient Jewish law, see Richard H. Hiers, *The Death Penalty and Due Process in Biblical Law,* 81 U. DET. MERCY L. REV. 751, 806–09 (2004); Irene Merker Rosenberg, Yale L. Rosenberg & Bentzion S. Turin, *Murder by Gruma: Causation in Homicide Cases under Jewish Law,* 80 B.U. L. REV. 1017, 1021, 1052–59 (2000). *See also* EHRLICH at 130 (noting that the Hebrew Bible states that "Thou shalt not commit murder" while the Protestant and Catholic Bibles state that "Thou shalt not kill").

8. Regarding the role of compensation in punishment during the Anglo-Saxon period, see LOVELL at 8 ("*even regicide meant only a higher payment to the royal survivors*").

9. *See* Frederick Pollock, *English Law before the Norman Conquest,* 14 LAW Q. REV. 291, 299, 302 (1898). Private vengeance in Anglo-Saxon times drew no distinction among willful, negligent, or accidental killings; rather, the issue was the number of cattle for payment. *See* Green, *Homicide,* at 417 (noting that the earliest "*dooms,*" i.e., Anglo-Saxon laws or decrees, only record the level of compensation for homicides). For example, a "*thegn*" (or "*thane*"), who was an Anglo-Saxon official, was worth a *wergild* of six times that of a "*ceorle,*" a common freeman.

The word "*ceorle*" is also the basis of the British place and surnames of Carlton and Charlton, meaning "*the farm of the churls.*" The names Carl and Charles are derived from *churl* or *ceorle.* In J. R. R. Tolkien's fictional Middle-earth a "*ceorl*" is a rider of Rohan.

10. On the development of *mens rea,* see A.K.R. KIRALFY, POTTER'S HISTORICAL INTRODUCTION TO ENGLISH LAW 355–60. *See also* FREDERICK G. KEMPIN, HISTORICAL INTRODUCTION TO ANGLO-AMERICAN LAW 182 (1990); George Jarvis Thompson, *History of the English Courts to the Judicature Acts,* 17 CORNELL L.Q. 9, 13–17 (1932). The Anglo-Saxons would have had no O.J. Simpson criminal trial for

murder. The only thing they would have understood was his later civil trial for wrongful death and the resulting damage award against him.

A variation of the *wergild* was the "*murdrum*," which the Normans revived from the older "*Danelaw*" in England.[1] The *murdrum* applied to an Anglo-Saxon who killed a Norman, a likely occurrence since there were a lot of unhappy Anglo-Saxons after the Battle of Hastings in 1066.

The *murdrum* involved a very large fine that went to the king for such a killing. Moreover the Normans assumed that any dead body was Norman, unless the locals could prove he was a Saxon.[2] If not, the village had to pay the murdrum.[3] Our word "murder" comes from *murdrum*.[4]

Surely the *murdrum* was to create political stability for the Norman rulers of England. Like the *wergild*, it had an element of proportionality. The Normans required a set fine for a Norman's killing, not the destruction of the whole village or other reprisal.

Also showing the Anglo-Saxon sense of proportionality was that killing a slave in Anglo-Saxon England did not necessitate the paying of the *wergild* but only the lesser "*manwryth*."[5] Although based on the values of a culture that accepted slavery, it at

---

1. On *murdrum* fines and *wergilds*, see Green, *Homicide* at 419.

The Danes and Normans were cousins, both having originated from Scandinavia. ("Norman" is an adaptation of "Northmen" or "Norsemen.") The *Danelaw* (or the *Danelagh*) applied over the parts of England the Danes had taken from the Anglo-Saxons in the ninth and tenth centuries (the Kingdoms of Northumbria, East Anglia, and the Five Boroughs of Leicester, Nottingham, Derby, Stamford, and Lincoln). The *Danelaw* had its greatest extent under King Canute's empire. Our English word "law" comes from the Danish "*lagh*." BAKER at 3.

Canute is also famous for showing his flattering couriers that even he could not turn back the tide.↓

The *Danelaw* appeared as late as the early twelfth century in the *Laws of King Henry I* ("*Leges Henrici Primi*") and the Laws of King Canute and King Edward the Confessor are our main sources for old English law. BAKER at 3.

King Canute by F. Holl, an engraving after R. E. Pine (1849)

2. Frederick Pollock, *The King's Peace in the Middle Ages*, 13 HARV. L. REV. 177, 178 (1899). *See also* LOVELL at 80 (discussing "*presentment of Englishry*" to avoid the *murdrum*).

Modern forfeiture law also came from this coroner's inquest. Any object that caused a death was a "*deodand*" from "*Deo damdum*," meaning "giving to God" when giving the object to the church expunged the sin of the item. Under the Normans the king, not the church, took it. The *deodand* could be any chattel, like an axe, hoe, dog, horse, mill-will, or tree. By the nineteenth century the *deodand* could be a ship or locomotive, which is why the practice was abolished in 1846.

3. KIRALFY at 366 n.86. Long after the Norman Conquest, the *murdrum* continued to exist. It boosted the king's treasury, which the common people resented, especially when crown officials applied it to any death, not just homicide. Eventually it only applied to felonious killing, and Edward III abolished it in 1340. Green, *Homicide,* at 456 n.157; J.M. Kaye, *The Early History of Murder and Manslaughter,* 83 LAW Q. REV. 365, 366 n.11 (1967).

4. Just the word "murder" creates dramatic effect. *See, e.g.,* Alfred Hitchcock's classic film MURDER! (British International Pictures 1930). Spelling "murder" backwards as "redrum" can be eerie, as in THE SHINING (Warner Brothers 1980), from Stephen King's novel THE SHINING (1977).

"Murder" is also the term for a group of crows. This comes from the folk tale that crows form tribunals to judge each other. If the verdict goes against the offending bird, the murder kills him. In fact, crows will occasionally kill a dying crow that does not belong in their territory and will commonly feed on dead crows. Crows also frequent battlefields, execution sites, and cemeteries to scavenge on human remains. *See* RICHARD SPILSBURY & LOUISE SPILSBURY, A MURDER OF CROWS (2003). Crows commit the nastier killings in another Alfred Hitchcock classic, THE BIRDS (Universal Pictures 1963), and a crow is the evil pet of the witch Maleficent in SLEEPING BEAUTY (Buena Vista 1959).

There is also the movie, A MURDER OF CROWS (1999) that has nothing to do with crows.

Ravens are a type of crow. In England a tombstone is sometimes called a "ravenstone," reflected in the English town names of Ravenstone, Bedfordshire; Ravenstone, Buckinghamshire; and Ravenstone, Leicestershire.

least shows that they did not consider all killings equal. Punishment, then, had to be in proportion to the crime. *Manwryth* is the origin of our word "manslaughter," which incorporates a modern sense of proportionality in our distinction between the crimes of murder and manslaughter.[6]

After the Norman Conquest of England, the Anglo-Saxon system of proportional punishments disappeared, giving the king unfettered discretion on punishment.[7] *Magna Carta's* Chapter 14 sought to correct this imbalance, demonstrating *lex talionis* and the proportionality tradition:

"A free man shall not be amerced [fined] for a trivial offense, except in accordance with the degree of the offence; and for a serious offence he shall be amerced according to its gravity, *saving his livelihood; and a merchant likewise, saving his merchandise; in the same way a villein shall be amerced saving his wainage; if they fall into our mercy. And none of the aforesaid amercements shall be imposed except by the testimony of reputable men of the neighborhood."*[8]

Magna Carta then articulates the fundamental law prohibiting disproportional punishment.[9]

A murder of crows

The Twa Corbies (The Two Ravens) by Arthur Rackham (1919) over a dead body

5. Lovell at 22.

6. All murders are not alike. For a study in the worst kind, premeditated first degree murder, see the Alfred Hitchcock classic Dial M for Murder (Warner Brothers 1954), a thriller about a retired tennis pro (Ray Milland) who wants to have his wife (Grace Kelly) killed. A remake was A Perfect Murder (Warner Brothers 1998), starring Michael Douglas and Gwyneth Paltrow, with some interesting modifications and plot changes.

Grace Kelly in DIAL M for Murder.

7. See *Furman v. Georgia*, 408 U.S. at 242–43 ("Following the Norman conquest of England in 1066, the old system of penalties, which ensured equality between crime and punishment, suddenly disappeared. By the time systematic judicial records were kept, its demise was almost complete. With the exception of certain grave crimes for which the punishment was death or outlawry, the arbitrary fine was replaced by a discretionary amercement. Although amercement's discretionary character allowed the circumstances of each case to be taken into account and the level of cash penalties to be decreased or increased accordingly, the amercement presented an opportunity for excessive or oppressive fines.").

King John signs Magna Carta

8. Levy at 231–32; Granucci at 845–46. Also quoted in *Furman*, 408 U.S. at 243 (noting that "[t]he problem of excessive amercements became so prevalent that three chapters of the Magna Carta were devoted to their regulation. Maitland [the historian] said of Chapter 14 that 'very likely there was no clause in the Magna Carta more grateful to the mass of the people.'"). See also *Solem v. Helm*, 463 U.S. 277 (1983) (noting that an amercement is similar to a modern day fine and was the most common criminal punishment in thirteenth century England) (citing 2 F. Pollock & F. Maitland, The History of English Law 513–15 (2d ed. 1909)). *Solem* traces the origin of the Eighth Amendment's proportionality concept from *Magna Carta*.

This is also the origin of the Eighth Amendment's clause prohibiting "excessive fines."

"nor excessive fines imposed"
—The Eighth Amendment

9. See Schwartz at 787–88 (for *Magna Carta* and proportionality). See also Baker at 512 (noting that judges for misdemeanors could not disproportionately fine an offender).

DOUBLE JEOPARDY AND PROPORTIONALITY

Underscoring the Eighth Amendment's proportionality foundation is the Fifth Amendment's Double Jeopardy Clause:

"[N]or shall any person be subject for the same offense to be twice put in jeopardy of life or limb . . . ."[1]

In preventing a person from having to face a second trial after acquittal (or even conviction), the Double Jeopardy Clause is a key foundation of the rule of law. The Double Jeopardy Clause forbids the government from prosecuting or punishing the same crime more than once,[2] thereby also encompassing the principle of proportionality.

This prohibition against punishing the same offense more than one time is as ancient as the proportionality concept of *"an eye for an eye."*[3] Jewish law prohibited double jeopardy, holding that *"for one offense, only one punishment might be inflicted."*[4] Thus a person condemned to death could not also be flogged.[5]

The story of Cain killing Abel illustrates the principle. After God punished Cain he forbade anyone else from killing Cain upon risk of his sevenfold vengeance.[6]

The Romans believed *nemo debet bis puniri pro uno delicto* ("no one ought to be punished twice for the same offense").[7] This norm passed into canon law, with added biblical justification. Saint Jerome in 391 AD read a verse from *Nahum* 1:9 that *"[a]ffliction shall not rise up the second time"* to

---

1. U.S. Const. amend. V. *See* **Chapter 5: From Testicles to *Dragnet*: How the Fifth Amendment Protects All of Us** for more on the Double Jeopardy Clause.

....

2. *Hudson v. United States,* 522 U.S. 93, 99 (1997); *Missouri v. Hunter,* 459 U.S. 359, 366 (1983); see also *Dep't of Revenue of Mont. v. Kurth Ranch,* 511 U.S. 767, 784 (1994) (holding that a *"drug tax"* assessed after a conviction violates double jeopardy); *North Carolina v. Pearce,* 395 U.S. 711, 718–19 (1969) (holding that *"punishment already exacted must be fully 'credited'"* upon reconviction), *overruled on other grounds by Alabama v. Smith,* 490 U.S. 794 (1989). *But see Witte v. United States,* 515 U.S. 389, 407 (1995) (Scalia, J., concurring in the judgment) (*"I adhere to my view that 'the Double Jeopardy Clause prohibits successive prosecution, not successive punishment.'"* (citation omitted)).

3. David S. Rudstein, *A Brief History of the Fifth Amendment Guarantee against Double Jeopardy* 14 Wm. & Mary Bill Rts. J. 193, 197 (2005). *See also* Justin W. Curtis, *The Meaning of Life (or Limb): An Originalist*

Proposal for Double Jeopardy Reform, 41 U. Rich. L. Rev. 991, 995–96 (2007) (noting the Code of Hammurabi fined and removed a judge that changed a final sentence).

4. *See* Rudstein at 197 (citing George Horowitz, The Spirit of Jewish Law 170 (1973)); Samuel Mendelsohn, The Criminal Jurisprudence of the Ancient Hebrews 35 and n.62 (2d ed. 1968).

....

5. Rudstein at 197 (citing the Babylonian Talmud). *See also id.* for the example of rabbis teaching that when a man forcibly engages in sexual intercourse with his maiden sister he may be flogged for the intercourse with his sister but not also fined for intercourse with a maiden because Deuteronomy 25:2 means that *"you punish him because of one guilt but not because of two guilts."*

    Not punishing *"because of two guilts"* is broader than American law, which allows stacking of multiple punishments for separate crimes even when committed in the same course of conduct and at the same time.

....

6. *"Cain said unto the Lord, 'My punishment is greater than I can bear. Behold, thou hast driven me out this day from the face of the earth; and from thy face shall I be hid; and I shall be a fugitive and a vagabond in the earth; and it shall come to pass, that every one that findeth me shall slay me.' And the Lord said unto him, 'Therefore whosoever slayeth Cain, vengeance shall be taken on him sevenfold.' And the Lord set a mark upon Cain, lest any finding him should kill him."* Genesis 4:13–15 (King James). See Hiers at 755.

Cain Killing Abel, a detail of the Ghent altarpiece (1432)

mean "*that God does not punish twice for the same act*" or "*not even God judges twice for the same act.*"[8] Jerome's reasoning for this basis for canon law ignores that God would not judge twice because, unlike humans, God would not need to.[9]

Thus the Eighth Amendment's proportionality concept finds support in the Fifth Amendment's Double Jeopardy Clause.

The concept of proportionality applies to all punishments. But nowhere is proportionality in punishment more important than the death penalty. If a penalty other than death is disproportionate, even if it involves mutilation, something can be done about it—restitution paid, a good name cleared, fines waived, estates or property restored. But death precludes any restoration.[10]

Thus the history of the Eighth Amendment, as well as the modern debate, focuses on the death penalty.

A HISTORY OF DEATH

The death penalty is nothing "*unusual*" in history.

Governments, be they kings or democracies, readily impose capital punishment on traitors.[11] And the death penalty is biblically old.

Biblical Death: Mosaic law listed thirty-six capital crimes, including

"*adultery, sex perversion, incest, homosexuality, blasphemy, idolatry, false prophecy, profaning the Sabbath, witchcraft, polytheism, sins against parents, kidnapping, treason, and murder.*"[12]

---

7. Rudstein at 200 (citing Jay A. Sigler, Double Jeopardy: The Development of a Legal and Social Policy 2 (1969); Black's Law Dictionary 1736 (8th ed. 2004)). Rudstein notes, however, that because Roman criminal prosecution was generally brought by an accuser/victim and not the state, the law did not prevent other accuser-victims from charging the same defendant for the same crime.

8. *Nahum* 1:9 (King James), *quoted in* Rudstein at 201; *Bartkus v. Illinois*, 359 U.S. 121, 152 n.4 (1959) (Black, J., dissenting).

9. *Noted in* Rudstein at 201.

Saint Jerome by Ghirlandaio (1480)

10. As William Shakespeare wrote in *Measure for Measure:* "Death is a fearful thing . . ." (act 3, sc. 1. l. 116) and "*The weariest and most loathed worldly life / That age, ache, penury, and imprisonment/ Can lay on nature is a paradise / To what we fear of death.*" (act 3, sc. 1. ll. 129–32). Quoted in Daniel J. Kornstein, Kill all The Lawyers: Shakespeare's Legal Appeal 49–50 (1994).

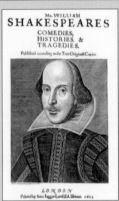

11. **Julius Rosenberg** and **Ethel Greenglass Rosenberg** meet death as traitors. The Rosenbergs were executed on June 19, 1953, after having been found guilty of conspiracy to commit espionage for passing information about the nuclear bomb to the Soviet Union. Their execution has been controversial ever since. Regarding the growth of treason law, see Lovell at 209–10.

12. Ehrlich at 50. *See also* Hiers at 760–62 (discussing capital offenses in Hebrew law, negligent homicide, and killing a burglar).

Although this list seems long to us, executions were actually uncommon.[1] Procedural rules in Jewish law made it very difficult to convict a person. Although the listing had a deterrent value, the rabbis designed the law to protect the sanctity of life.[2]

The trial procedures favored the defendants,

and they had every chance to argue for acquittal. For example, circumstantial evidence was disallowed, and confessions were inadmissible.[3] Jewish law required at least two competent and independent witnesses to prove a fact.[4] Any discrepancy between the witnesses, even on minor matters, disqualified the testimony.

The judges who heard capital cases interrogated the witnesses rigorously on even the most tangential facts. They would then discuss the case overnight, seeking any possible basis for acquittal.[5] In the Sanhedrin, the high court, favorable evidence to the defendant had greater weight than unfavorable evidence, and the voting

1. Irene Merker Rosenberg & Yale L. Rosenberg, *Of God's Mercy and the Four Biblical Methods of Capital Punishment: Stoning, Burning, Beheading, and Strangulation*, 78 Tul. L. Rev. 1169 (2004).

The Supreme Court has recently held that the death penalty in America today only applies when the crime results in death. *Kennedy v. Louisiana*, 128 S. Ct. 2641 (2008) (death penalty for crime of raping a child not allowed).

2. Rosenberg & Rosenberg, *Of God's Mercy*, at 1178 (noting that the proof and evidence rules in the rabbinic codes amounted to a supercharged Bill of Rights). *See also id.* at 1208–09 ("*The difficulty of conviction [in Jewish law] effectively emphasizes the sanctity of beings created in God's image. In America, on the other hand, executions have become almost numbingly routine, particularly in some jurisdictions, making ours, in a sense, a death-oriented society in which life, if not cheap, at least has less value.*"); Hiers at 797–800.

3. *See* Irene Merker Rosenberg & Yale L. Rosenberg, *In the Beginning: The Talmudic Rule against Self-Incrimination*, 63 N.Y.U. L. Rev. 955, 1031–41 (1988) (discussing the nearly absolute Talmudic prohibition against using confessions in criminal cases).

4. Rosenberg & Rosenberg, *Of God's Mercy*, at 1179 (citing *Deuteronomy* 17:6, 19:15). *Numbers* 35:30 states: "*Whoso killeth any person, the murderer shall be put to death by the mouth of witnesses: but one witness shall not testify against any person to cause him to die.*" *See also* Ehrlich at 52.

5. Rosenberg & Rosenberg, *Of God's Mercy*, at 1179, 1190.

6. The Great Sanhedrin served as the Jewish high court and legislature, specified in *Numbers* 11:16, 17 "*Gather unto me seventy men . . . elders of the people . . .*" The Sanhedrin heard the defense evidence first, and testimony favorable to the defendant was irreversible, but unfavorable testimony could be reversed. As for voting in capital cases a majority of one equaled an acquittal, but conviction needed a majority of two. Ehrlich at 146–47.

Christ's Sanhedrin trial by Giotto

7. Rosenberg & Rosenberg, *Of God's Mercy*, at 1190–91, noting that the Jewish law allowed the defendant to return to court as many times as necessary to make all possible exonerating arguments. This is in contrast to contemporary cries that there are far too many appeals in capital cases.

Caiaphas: *We turn to Rome to sentence Nazareth./We have no law to put a man to death./We need him crucified./It's all you have to do./We need him crucified./ It's all you have to do.*

8. Rosenberg & Rosenberg, *Of God's Mercy*, at 1180.

The rock opera and later film Jesus Christ Superstar (Universal Studios 1973) underscore the procedural protections of Hebrew law. As shown, the Hebrews had plenty of laws to "*put a man to death.*" What they lacked was a procedural mechanism to make it practical. Thus the Romans killed Jesus, not the Jews.

9. Rosenberg & Rosenberg, *Of God's Mercy*, at 1192.

10. Rosenberg & Rosenberg, *Of God's Mercy*, at 1191–92 (noting that this law came from *Leviticus* 19:18 to "*love your fellow as yourself*").

11. Rosenberg & Rosenberg, *Of God's Mercy*, at 1186.

Matthew 2:11 notes that frankincense, along with gold and myrrh, were the gifts of the Magi to the Christ child. Frankincense is an aromatic resin from Boswellia trees used in incense and perfumes. The name for this resin possibly comes from "incense of the Franks" because Frankish Crusaders reintroduced the fragrance to Europe. Myrrh is also a resin from trees used in perfumes and medicines.

Adoration of the Magi by Fra Angelico and Filippo Lippi

12. Generally each execution method applied to specific crimes, although there is some overlapping.

Stoning was for (1) sexual offenses like adultery and incest, (2) blasphemy, (3) idol worship and instigation of others to idolatry, (4) Sabbath desecration, (5) cursing one's father or mother, (6) sorcery, and (7) being a stubborn and rebellious son. Rosenberg & Rosenberg, *Of God's Mercy*, at 1183. *Method:* The executioners procedure on the death penalty favored the defendant.[6]

Even after trial, the courts allowed the convicted defendant to return to court with any favorable evidence, even if he was on his way to his execution.[7] On the way to the execution site, at some distance from the court, court officials would shout out the convict's name and crime and call for exculpatory evidence.[8]

The condemned also deserved a humane death, and efforts to minimize suffering and humiliation.[9] In terminology similar to that used in later Christian medieval Europe, the condemned merited "*a favorable death*."[10] The condemned received frankincense and wine "*to dull his senses*," to make the execution less painful.[11] And even though the methods of execution— stoning, burning, beheading, strangulation, etc.—may seem harsh, each was carried out to avoid suffering and degradation.[12]

---

remove all the condemned's clothes except for covering of the genitals. They then pushed the condemned from a cliff twice the height of a man, which if it did not kill him at least stunned him, before throwing stones on him. *Id.* at 1191–92.

The *Gospel of Luke* 4:24–30 recounts that the people wanted to stone Jesus in this way:

"'I tell you the truth,' he continued, 'no prophet is accepted in his hometown. I assure you that there were many widows in Israel in Elijah's time, when the sky was shut for three and a half years and there was a severe famine throughout the land. Yet Elijah was not sent to any of them, but to a widow in Zarephath in the region of Sidon. And there were many in Israel with leprosy in the time of Elisha the prophet, yet not one of them was cleansed—only Naaman the Syrian.' All the people in the synagogue were furious when they heard this. They got up, drove him out of the town, and took him to the brow of the hill on which the town was built, in order to throw him down the cliff. But he walked right through the crowd and went on his way."

Burning was for adultery with a priest's daughter and having sex with a woman and her daughter. Rosenberg & Rosenberg, *Of God's Mercy*, at 1183. *Method:* The executioners put the defendant in manure up to his knees. A coarse scarf was wrapped in a soft scarf and executioners wound them around the defendant's neck in opposite directions, opening his mouth while a "*lighted wick*" or molten lead went into the defendant's mouth, burning his intestines. This is faster and, believe it or not, less painful than being burned at the stake, and the body is left intact. *Id.* at 1194–95.

Beheading was for murderers and inhabitants of a city of idol worshipers. *Method:* The executioners used the edges of a sword specified in *Deuteronomy* 13:16: "[S]mite the inhabitants of that city by the edge of the sword." Rosenberg & Rosenberg, *Of God's Mercy*, at 1183 and 1195–96.

Strangulation was for a child who strikes his parent, a kidnapper, a sage who refuses to follow the Great Sanhedrin's rulings, a false prophet or one who prophesies for a false god, an adulterer, a false witness against a priest's daughter, or one who illicitly cohabits with a priest's daughter. *Id.* at 1183. *Method:* The executioners would place the condemned in manure up to his knees and with a coarse scarf in a soft one wound around his neck they would pull in opposite directions until death. *Id.* at 1199. *See also* Hiers at 791–93 (noting the methods of execution).

Saint Stephen by Carlo Crivelli (1476), showing three stones and the martyrs' palm. In the *Acts of the Apostles* (at 6:11 and 6:13–14) the Sanhedrin tried Saint Stephen for blasphemy against Moses, God, the temple, and the law. A mob stoned him with the encouragement of Saul of Tarsus, the future Saint Paul.

The biblical strangulation method appears similar to the modern "*garrote*" execution device for ligature strangulation

Joan of Arc's burning at the stake was far worse than what ancient Hebrew law allowed. For a Hollywood depiction of Joan, *see* THE MESSENGER: THE STORY OF JOAN OF ARC (1999).

Judith Beheading Holofernes (1598). The Babylonian king Nebuchadnezzar dispatched Holofernes to punish the western nations that had withheld assistance to his reign. Holofernes laid siege to Bethulia (i.e., Meselieh), which almost surrendered. Judith, a beautiful Jewish widow, saved the city by entering Holofernes's camp, seducing him, and beheading him while he was drunk. The Jews defeated his army after she returned with his head. *See* the deuterocanonical *Book of Judith*. This was not, however, a court-ordered execution.

In THE GODFATHER (Paramount Pictures 1972) Michael Corleone has his brother-in-law Carlo garroted in a car because Carlo arranged for Sonny Corleone's death.

Thus although biblical law seems harsh to us,[1] and prosecutors sometimes use it today to argue for harsher punishments, in practice it actually was not so. Certainly the punishments were harsher; but the extensive procedural protections in Jewish law assured that these punishments rarely, if ever, occurred. If they were imposed, the procedures were conducted in a way that minimized pain and indignity.[2]

A CLASSICAL DEATH

The Greeks: Plato, in *The Laws,* supported the death penalty.[3] But in a precursor to the Eighth Amendment, Plato, in the dialogue *Gorgias,* has Socrates identify the goal of all punishment as correction and deterrence, not retribution:

"He who is rightly punished ought either to become better and profit by it, or he ought to be made an example to his fellows, that they may see what

---

1. The closest modern execution method to stoning would be death by firing squad.

Death by Firing Squad or Shooting. Several soldiers or peace officers form the firing squad, which fires simultaneously to prevent identifying who fires the lethal shot. Often a single shot, the *"coup de grâce,"* from an officer or official, follow the initial volley to assure death. Traditionally one unknown squad member has a blank cartridge, allowing each member the chance that he did not fire the fatal shot. Although an experienced marksman can tell the difference between a blank and a live cartridge from the recoil, there is a significant psychological incentive not to pay attention and to remember the recoil as soft (i.e., like the recoil of a blank cartridge). For the procedure and cause of death, see Arif Khan & Robyn M. Leventhal, *Medical Aspects of Capital Punishment Executions,* 47 J. Forensic Sci. 847, 848 (2002).

When courts-martial impose the death penalty they commonly use a firing squad, such as Breaker Morant's execution during the Boer War, rendered into the very good courtroom drama, Breaker Morant (Roadshow Entertainment 1980), or when the U.S. Army executed Private Eddie Slovik in 1945. Some jurisdictions traditionally use the firing squad at first light or sunrise, giving raise to the term "shot at dawn."

Beaker Morant

Norman Mailer's The Executioner's Song (1979) is a Pulitzer Prize–winning novel about the events around Gary Gilmore's execution.

Gary Gilmore was the first person to be executed after the death penalty was reinstated in *Gregg v. Georgia,* 428 U.S. 153 (1976), after *Furman v. Georgia,* 408 U.S. 238 (1972), and he chose to die by firing squad on January 17, 1977, at the Utah State Prison. The five executioners had .30-30 caliber rifles and off-the-shelf Winchester 150 grain (9.7 g) SilverTip ammunition, and fired from 20 feet (6 meters) at his chest.

The Supreme Court upheld the constitutionality of death by shooting in *Wilkerson v. Utah,* 99 U.S. 130 (1878).

The Third of May by Francisco Goya

Eddie Slovik

2. Rosenberg & Rosenberg, *Lone Star,* at 505. This is in contrast, for example, to the English Murder Act of 1751 (25 Geo.2 c.37), which provided that the condemned should receive *"some further terror and peculiar mark of infamy be added to the punishment"* and that *"in no case whatsoever shall the body of any murderer be suffered to be buried."* Rather the convicted murder received either public dissection or *"hanging in chains."* As for procedural protections the act stipulated execution within two days of conviction unless the execution would happen on Friday, in which case the execution should take place on Saturday.

3. Plato, The Laws, bk. VIII, ch. 16: *"If someone is proved guilty of a murder, having killed any of these peoples, the judges' slaves will kill him and throw him naked in a cross-road, out of the city; all the judges will bring a stone in the name of the whole State throwing it on the head of the corpse, then will bring him out of the State's frontier and will leave him there unburied; this is the law."*

4. Plato, *Gorgias,* quoted in Edward M. Peters, *Prison before the Prison: The Ancient and Medieval Worlds, in* The Oxford History of the Prison 5 (Norval Morris & David J. Rothman eds., 1998).

Plato has Socrates note the benefit of pain in correction:

"Those who are improved when they are punished by gods and men, are those whose sins are curable; and they are improved, as in this world so also in another, by pain and suffering; for there is no other way in which they can be delivered from their evil."

As we will see, this foreshadows a key aspect of medieval punishment.

Socrates

he suffers, and fear to suffer the like, and become better."[4]

Plato also presented the problems with the death penalty as applied. In 399 BC the Athenians executed Socrates for impiety; an execution wholly unjust because Socrates, the philosopher, had no need of state correction (as he argued to his detriment to the jury deciding his punishment). His execution was not to deter evil but in fact deterred good.[5] Plato reemphasizes the wrongness of retribution, the true motive behind Socrates's trial and execution.[6]

The Athenians executed Socrates by having him take hemlock.[7] Plato accurately described death by hemlock in *Phaedo*.[8] In addition to hemlock poisoning as a form of execution, the Greeks also executed people by shackling them to wooden planks and left them outside to die from exposure.[9]

---

5. Plato's Socrates went along with the morality lesson by refusing exile to avoid the death penalty and saying in mitigation that Athens should maintain him at state expense for the rest of his life. SADAKAT KADRI, THE TRIAL: A HISTORY, FROM SOCRATES TO O.J. SIMPSON 12 (2005).

6. The Athenian human scapegoats, "*pharmakoi*," were usually the poorest and ugliest inhabitants of the city. They were feasted and venerated at public expense until famine or plague struck. Then they were dethroned and paraded and hounded out of the city with stones. KADRI at 7.

7. *The Death of Socrates* by David (1787). "*The man . . . laid his hands on him and after a while examined his feet and legs, then pinched his foot hard and asked if he felt it. He said 'No'; then after that, his thighs; and passing upwards in this way he showed us that he was growing cold and rigid. And then again he touched him and said that when it reached his heart, he would be gone. The chill had now reached the region about the groin, and uncovering his face, which had been covered, he said—and these were his last words, 'Crito, we owe a cock to Asclepius, pay it and do not neglect it.' 'That,' said Crito, 'shall be done; but see if you have anything else to say.' To this question he made no reply, but after a little while he moved; the attendant uncovered him; his eyes were fixed. And Crito when he saw it, closed his mouth and eyes.*"

Hemlock (*Conium maculatum*). Be careful, it looks like fennel, a common spice,

but fennel smells like licorice when broken, whereas hemlock smells "woody" or "earthy." The red spots on the stem and branches are called "the blood of Socrates."

8. Death by Hemlock. The killing substance in hemlock is coniine, a neurotoxin, which disrupts the peripheral nervous system. It causes death by blocking the neuromuscular junction, creating an ascending muscular paralysis that eventually stops the respiratory muscles by withholding oxygen to the heart and brain. Artificial ventilation can save the person until the toxin wears off.

Death by lethal injection is the closest modern form to the hemlock death penalty. This involves injecting a person with fatal doses of poison. Lethal injection for capital punishment generally replaced other supposedly less humane forms of execution, such as electrocution, hanging, firing squad, gas chamber, or decapitation. *Method:* Although states vary, most jurisdictions have the executioners fasten the condemned to a table and put an intravenous tube in each arm (one is a back up). The executioners attach one tube to the lethal injection machine in another room and start drips into each arm with saline solution. They monitor the condemned with a heart monitor. The executioners then send a "cocktail" down the tube in the following order:
1. sodium thiopental—an ultra–short action barbiturate and anesthetic that renders the condemned unconscious in seconds;
2. pancuronium/tubocurarine—a nondepolarizing muscle relaxant causing complete muscle paralysis, including the diaphragm and the rest of the respiratory muscle, that would eventually cause an asphyxia death; and
3. potassium chloride—a chemical that stops the heart, causing death.

Rosenberg & Rosenberg, *Of God's Mercy*, at 1170; Khan & Leventhal at 847. This cocktail may be truly cruel because the condemned may actually feel great pain from the final agent of death, the potassium chloride, because the second agent, the pancuronium/tubocurarine, renders him completely paralyzed and unable to scream. Death by hemlock may indeed be a much more humane method, as Plato's description of Socrates's death shows.

Hippocrates

The Hippocratic Oath

Part of the problem with lethal injection is that it is a medical means of execution with little or no participation by a medical doctor. *See, e.g.,* W. Noel Keyes, *The Choice of Participation by Physicians in Capital Punishment,* 22 WHITTIER L. REV. 809, 809–10 (2001) (noting American Medical Association policy that doctor participation in any aspect of execution is unethical). This goes back to the Hippocratic Oath, part of which reads "*I will not give a lethal drug to anyone if I am asked, nor will I advise such a plan . . .*" Hippocrates is the father of Western medicine and wrote the oath in Ionic Greek in the late fifth century BC.

9. Adriaan Lanni, "*Verdict Most Just*": *The Modes of Classical Athenian Justice,* 16 YALE J.L. & HUMAN. 277, 287 (2004).

Prometheus, chained to a rock and having an eagle eat his liver each day for having given fire to man, would have been an archetype for exposure execution. Being immortal, though, Prometheus did not die because his liver grew back each night.

Prometheus

Plato, in his general support of the death penalty for deterrence, did not speak for all Greeks. Thucydides did not uphold the value of capital punishment, even as a deterrent. He provides a long dialogue arguing the fallacy of the death penalty's value related to a rebellion in the island of Mitylene:

"We must not, therefore, commit ourselves to a false policy through a belief in the efficacy of the punishment of death, or exclude rebels from the hope of repentance and an early atonement of their error."[1]

Thus the Ancient Greeks reflected a view of capital punishment as complex as our own.[2]

The Romans: The Romans built an empire on death.

The Romans used crucifixion for heinous crimes,

1. THUCYDIDES, THE PELOPONNESIAN WAR 212–22 (Rex Warner trans., 1954).

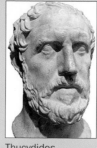

Thucydides

For a modern extension of Thucydides's argument, *see* COMPULSION (20th Century Fox 1959), about two defendants who killed a young boy to commit the "perfect crime." Their attorney, played by Orson Wells, saves them from hanging with an impassioned closing argument against capital punishment. The movie was based on the 1924 trial of Nathan Freudenthal Leopold, Jr., (1904–71) and Richard Albert Loeb (1905–36), the Leopold and Loeb trial, where Clarence Darrow defended the two for murdering fourteen-year-old Bobby Franks. Darrow's closing argument was an influential criticism of capital punishment and the retributive model of justice. Leopold and Loeb received life imprisonment.

Later, the Leopold and Loeb case also inspired the Alfred Hitchcock thriller film ROPE (Warner Brothers 1948), starring Jimmy Stewart.

Clarence Darrow

Leopold and Loeb

Jimmy Stewart in ROPE

2. The Greek cultural heritage is but one reason international law is relevant to any reading of the American Bill of Rights, especially on issues of punishments. First, the Cruel and Unusual Punishment Clause was borrowed verbatim from England's Bill of Rights. Bill of Rights, 1689, 1 W. & M., c. 36, 1 (Eng.). *See* Tepker at 827. Second, the concept of cruel and unusual punishments traces through the history of Western civilization. *See, e.g.,* Granucci at 844–46. Third, the Declaration of Independence, the document announcing America's separation from the Old World, acknowledged a duty to maintain a *"decent Respect to the Opinions of Mankind."* THE DECLARATION OF INDEPENDENCE para. 1 (U.S. 1776). Fourth, the text of the Constitution requires, Congress to create jurisdictions and laws to punish *"Offenses against the Law of Nations."* U.S. CONST. art. I, § 8, cl. 10.

The Supreme Court in its earliest cases dealt with and implemented international law. *See* Tepker at 828. Justice Joseph Story spoke for the Court, holding that kidnapped Africans on the schooner *Amistad* were not pirates or mutineers because they had the right of self-defense under *"eternal principles of justice and international law." The Amistad,* 40 U.S. (15 Pet.) 518, 595 (1841).

See also the movie AMISTAD (Dream-Works 1997); Tepker at 827–28 compares this case to Justice Marshall's decision ten years earlier in the *Antelope* case, which upheld the slave captivity on that ship. *The Antelope,* 23 U.S. (10 Wheat.) 66, 121 (1825) (Marshall, C.J.). *See generally* Youngjae Lee, *International Consensus as Persuasive Authority in the Eighth Amendment,* 156 U. PA. L. REV. 63 (2007) (outlining various aspects of the international consensus on the death penalty).

treason, or to make a political point during conquests and slave revolts.[3] In crucifixion, asphyxiation (i.e., suffocation) is usually the cause of death. The Romans nailed and/or tied the condemned to a large cross, causing him to have to support his whole weight on his outstretched arms. The resulting hyperexpansion of the lungs severely impedes inhaling. Eventually the condemned becomes too exhausted to pull up and is unable to breath.[4] To hasten death Roman executioners often broke the condemned's legs, making it more difficult for the condemned to pull himself up. If death did not come from asphyxiation, eventually shock, exposure, dehydration, or bleeding from the nails would cause it.[5]

3. Rome fought three Servile Wars against slaves, with Spartacus leading the last one, starting in 73 BC. Marcus Crassus crushed it two years later in 71 BC. Stanley Kubrick's SPARTACUS (Universal Pictures 1960) ended with almost all the slaves being crucified.

See KADRI at 14, noting that Roman prisoners of war and those convicted of murder, arson, or sacrilege could be executed in the arena, burned alive, or fed to beasts.

4. The term "excruciating" literally means "out of crucifying."

There is an apocryphal story that Saint Peter died from crucifixion, but he begged to be executed upside down because he was not worthy of the same death as Jesus. See St. Peter, THE CATHOLIC ENCYCLOPEDIA http://www.newadvent.org/cathen/11744a.htm (last visited Feb. 24, 2008).

Crucifixion of Saint Peter by Caravaggio

The gas chamber provides death by asphyxia

5. The gas chamber is the modern version of asphyxia death. Poor Saint Cecilia is again an ancient precedent. Before trying to whack off her head three times, her executioners tried to suffocate her in an overheated sauna.

The modern gas chamber for capital punishment uses gas that asphyxias or poisons the victim: *Method:*
1) potassium cyanide (KCN) pellets are placed below the chair;
2) the chamber is sealed with the condemned inside;
3) concentrated sulfuric acid (H_2SO_4) pours down a tube to the cyanide pellets; and
4) The curtain is opened for witnesses.

A switch or lever causes the cyanide pellets to drop into the sulfuric acid, creating hydrogen cyanide (HCN) gas, which kills.

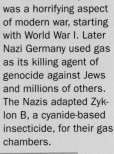

Gas as a weapon was a horrifying aspect of modern war, starting with World War I. Later Nazi Germany used gas as its killing agent of genocide against Jews and millions of others. The Nazis adapted Zyklon B, a cyanide-based insecticide, for their gas chambers.

Empty Zyklon B canisters

Common criminals might be sent to the arena, either to become gladiators or to be executed by one.[1] Indeed, the gladiatorial games themselves probably began as an extension of public executions. Many factors caused the end of gladiatorial games, including the rise of Christianity with its very different morality about death, even the death of a criminal.

Then the Middle Ages arrived, a time of God's mercy.

DEATH IN A TIME OF GOD'S MERCY

Although medieval punishments could be cruel, even gory, they were uncommon. Moreover, retribution was not a justification for punishment, as it is today.[2] Rather the main point was rehabilitation and, to a lesser extent, deterrence. But the rehabilitation was not so much to make the offender a better member of society; it was to redeem him for God.[3]

Through the late twelfth century there was no clean line between "sin" and "crime."[4] English judges were clerics until the late thirteenth century. Penance was the key element of the criminal justice system. Penance acknowledges that under strict justice all is lost. Grace is what you need—God's, the local lord's, or the victim's.[5]

Getting God's Grace: The Ordeal, Sanctuary, Benefit of Clergy, Pardon, and the Jury:

In the medieval system of justice there were many ways to get God's grace or pardon. For a medieval jurist/cleric all wrongdoing, be it sin or crime, was an act of pride against God. Bringing the offender/sinner back to God, often through the intercession of a saint, bishop,

1. The thumb up or down is a Hollywood invention. The Romans did refer to "*pollice verso*" (literally "with a turned thumb"), but no one now knows which way they pointed. A thumb up (called "*pollux infestus*") was an insult to Romans so was probably not the way they would ask to spare a life.

Pollice Verso (With a Turned Thumb) by Gérôme (1872)

2. See, e.g., 18 U.S.C. § 3553.

3. Trisha Olson, *The Medieval Blood Sanction and the Divine Beneficence of Pain: 1100–1450*, 22 J.L. & RELIGION 63 (2007) (arguing "*that while one cannot discount the language of deterrence that crops up in assorted sources, the cultural acceptance of the blood sanction lay less with such utilitarian concerns and more with that set of conciliatory principles that informed dispute resolution more widely*").

Olson does note a few examples of retributive punishments, but they were a rarity in medieval law. See, for example, the rape penalty in early fourteenth century England, allowing a victim to gouge out the eyes and/or sever the offender's testicles herself. *Id.* at 69 (citing The Eyre of Kent: 6 & 7 Edward II, A.D. 1313–1314, at 134 (F.W. Maitland, L.W. Vernon Harcourt & W.C. Bolland eds., Selden Society 1909)).

4. Olson at 81 (citing G.R. EVANS, LAW AND THEOLOGY IN THE MIDDLE AGES 12–13 (Routledge 2002)).

5. Trisha Olson, *Of the Worshipful Warrior: Sanctuary and Punishment in the Middle Ages*, 16 ST. THOMAS L. REV. 473, 423 (2004). See also Olson, *Blood Sanction*, at 73 quoting the Laws of King Henry I ("*Leges Henrici Primi*") that "[w]ith respect to an offender who has either confessed or is of manifest guilt, the proper course is to hand him over to the relatives of the slain man so that he may experience the mercy of those to whom he displayed none." Such a concept of grace or forgiveness is not expressed in today's victims' rights movement.

Augustine by Sandro Botticelli (c. 1480)

or especially the victim, was the ultimate goal.[6]

The Ordeal: Until the mid-thirteenth century, proof was by the ordeal (i.e., *iudicium Dei*). As discussed in Chapter 7, the ordeal was not so much about determining guilt—the court probably already knew that and, if not, God did—but about commutation. The goal of the ordeal ritual was about redeeming the guilty after contrite confession. If the offender did not confess to his judge/confessor/priest and God still acquitted him after the ordeal, the assumption

was that he had confessed in his heart.[7]

Sanctuary and Pilgrimage: The medieval practice of sanctuary had a similar purpose of reconciliation.[8] In Britain the "*dooms*" ("statutes") of King Ine, ruler of the West Saxons from 688 to 725 AD, recognized the practice of sanctuary. If a person facing the death penalty could make it to a church, and if he paid legal compensation, he would be spared.[9] During most of the medieval period, justice was a private matter. Sanctuary sheltered the person from

public justice and avoided the blood feud.[10]

We tend to think of sanctuary as a place to flee. But the intercessor was more important than the place.[11] Again, as with the ordeal, the practice allowed for God's grace through the intercession of the priest, bishop, or saint.[12]

Surely sanctuary would happen "in the church," as a physical place, but more important, sanctuary happened "in the church" as a metaphorical place or community.[13]

6. Olson, *Sanctuary,* at 518. *See also* Olson, *Blood Sanction,* at 72, noting that Saint Augustine writes that "*the more just it is to punish sinners, the more welcome are the favors bestowed by those who intercede for them or spare them.*" Saint Augustine uses the example of Jesus teaching forgiveness for the woman taken in adultery. *Id.* at 79–80.

Christ with the Woman Taken in Adultery by Guercino (1621)

7. For trial by ordeal in the history of the jury trial and our adversarial system, see **Chapter 7: Trial by Jury or . . . by God!** *See* Olson, *Sanctuary,* at 517 (noting that ordeal literature's main theme is not the innocent acquitted but the guilty redeemed because of a contrite confession).

8. *See generally* Olson, *Blood Sanction,* at 64; BAKER at 512–13.

9. Olson, *Sanctuary,* at 476, 491–92. *See also id.* at 479, 499 (noting that sanctuary as a legal concept is in the Theodosian Code and in the Laws of William and Edward the Confessor).

10. *See* Olson, *Sanctuary,* at n.73.

11. Olson, *Sanctuary,* at 477, 482. For Saint Augustine and sanctuary, *see id.* at 480, 502. The great intercessors for the sinner/criminal today are the public defenders like Joyce Davenport (Veronica Hamel) from *Hill Street Blues,* a police drama on NBC television from 1981 to 1987 for 146 episodes. It received high critical acclaim, and its innovations proved highly influential on other television series. The series won eight Emmy Awards in its first season and had ninety-eight Emmy nominations.—

12. On the relationship between ordeal and sanctuary, *see* Olson, *Sanctuary,* at 505, 508. Saint Martin had a special place as an intercessor saint. *See, e.g., id.* at 486, 495. His shrine was also a great stopping point for pilgrims on the road to Santiago de Compostela.

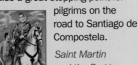

Saint Martin and the Beggar by El Greco (c. 1597–99)

1. The opposite of sanctuary was the law of outlawry. Olson, *Sanctuary,* at 510. To be outside the community meant that the law no longer protected you. It was the civil equivalent to excommunication.

See generally Paul R. Hyams, *The Proof of Villein Status in the Common Law,* 89 ENG. HIST. REV. 721 (1974).

Pilgrimage practice had a similar quality in that the pilgrim did go to a place, and the journey itself had a redemptive value, but it was to gain the intercession of the saint at the shrine. See Olson, *Blood Sanction,* at 63.

Pilgrimage as a journey to redress sin played out in KINGDOM OF HEAVEN (20th Century Fox 2005), directed by Ridley Scott and starring Orlando Bloom, Eva Green, Jeremy Irons, Edward Norton, and Liam Neeson.

One great shrine for pilgrimage was the Cathedral at Santiago de Compostela, Spain

Retribution was not a goal of criminal justice—that was for God—but rehabilitation and deterrence were.[2] Indeed, retribution as a goal would not have been possible because the criminal-sinner would stand before God in no different position from the victim-sinner. Unless, of course, the victim gave the criminal the grace of forgiveness, raising both to heaven.[3]

Benefit of Clergy: Another way of getting grace—or, as we may say, avoiding criminal responsibility—was "*benefit of clergy*." Originally tonsured and clothed clerics could avoid the king's justice and courts by claiming *benefit of clergy* ("*privilegium cleri*") because they were outside the king's jurisdiction.[4] At first the practice was for a charged clerk to claim he was clergy, which a jury would decide after an "inquest of office." Later the clergyman would

---

1. *See* Olson, *Sanctuary,* at 477–78, 532, 535–41 (arguing that the end of sanctuary in the sixteenth century was not because of the rise of temporal power but because the canonists and culture changed regarding sanction and reconciliation). *See id.* at 539–40, 542, discussing Sir Thomas

King Henry VIII

Sir Thomas More

More's new way of looking at sanctuary as a deterrence problem. Through legislation, Henry VIII brought sanctuary practice under the control of the monarchy, *id.* at 547, which is but one of many powers Henry arrogated to himself.

2. *See* Olson, *Blood Sanction,* at 73 (quoting from the *Laws of King Henry I (Leges Henrici Primi)* (c. 1115), one of which provided that acts of disobedience toward one's lord or superior were to be graciously resolved: "*[I]f anyone ma[de] amends to another for his misdeed*" and offered something beyond what was owed "*along with an oath of reconciliation,*" it was commendable of the wronged man to "*give back the whole thing.*" It continued, "*it ought to be sufficient*" that the accused had "*in some measure offered himself to his accuser.*")

3. *See generally* Baker at 513–15. *Benefit of clergy* became established during Henry II's reign as part of his penance for his role in the death of Archbishop Thomas Becket. Baker at 513.

A better and more descriptive translation of *privilegium cleri* would be "clerical privilege" or "privilege of clerics." Later anyone who could read qualified for *benefit of clergy* because usually only clerics could read. Unofficially this legal loophole was even larger because anyone who could memorize Psalm 51 (Psalm 50 in the Vulgate and Septuagint), "*Miserere mei, Deus, secundum misericordiam tuam*" ("*O God, have mercy upon me, according to thine heartfelt mercifulness*") could recive benefit of clergy regardless of whether they really were clergy. Psalm 51 became known as the "*neck verse*" because it could save your neck. *See id.* at 514; George Jarvis Thompson, *History of the English Courts to the Judicature Acts,* 17 Cornell L.Q. 395, 404 (1932); Kiralfy at 361–63; Lovell at 99.

King Henry VII introduced the practice of branding the thumb of a convict who pleaded benefit of clergy with an "M" for murder or "T" for thief. This allowed detection of a second offender. Baker at 515; Thompson at 404 n.405; Green II at 488. His son, King Henry VIII, tried to close

this jurisdictional loophole, and his frustrations in dealing with the church (as well as his sexual frustrations in finding a wife that would give him a male heir) were part of the break with Rome. Green, *Homicide,* at 480 n.241. Benefit of clergy passed into the common law as a basis for granting leniency. *See id.* at 474–76, 483–84 and n.251 (on *benefit of clergy* affecting development of homicide law). Parliament began to place limits on the application of the clergy privilege. *See* Chris Kemmitt, *Function over Form: Reviving the Criminal Jury's Historical Role as a Sentencing Body,* 40 U. Mich. J.L. Reform 93, 98 (2006). The common law already excluded treason, highway robbery, and arson of a house from this privilege, and Parliament later excluded most major crimes. John H. Langbein,

Tonsured monk

Henry VII

accept a trial and claim the benefit if convicted. Given the large numbers of clerics in England, *benefit of clergy* had a huge effect on the criminal justice system.[5]

The punishment in ecclesiastical courts was penance, which even if severe was better than hanging.[6] If the crime was really bad, a clergyman could be defrocked (literally lose his protective clerical clothes), thus assuring his punishment for a repeat offense.[7]

For most of its history *benefit of clergy* was part of the conflict between the church and the king in England. Moreover, its history shows it to have been one of the most abused practices, encouraging impunity for "*crimonious clerks*."[8] But as with the ordeal, sanctuary, and pilgrimage, *benefit of clergy* had the goal of grace, concord, and reconciliation—not retribution.

Shaping the Eighteenth-Century Criminal Trial: A View from the Ryder Sources, 50 U. Chi. L. Rev. 1, 38–40 (1983). In time, *benefit of clergy* would even be applied to women, the literacy requirement removed, and branding of the thumb replaced with the sentence of transportation of seven years indentured servitude in the colonies. Thus instead of hanging, a first time offender convicted of manslaughter would receive the "burnt in the hand" punishment of a branded "M" for "manslayer."

5. On the procedure of "inquest of office," *see* Baker at 513. By the end of the sixteenth century, half of all men convicted of felonies in the king's courts successfully claimed *benefit of clergy. Id.* at 514.

This pleading of *benefit of clergy* became in practice an early form of plea bargaining. Langbein IV at 278 n.43. This was coupled with the jury's role in setting sentences. Id. at 304 (describing early plea bargaining). For a recounting of the prevalence of modern plea practices, *see* George Fisher, *Plea Bargaining's Triumph,* 109 Yale L.J. 857 (2000), and Fisher's expanded presentation in George Fisher, Plea Bargaining's Triumph: A History of Plea Bargaining in America (2003). *See also* Jennifer L. Mnookin, *Uncertain Bargains: The Rise of Plea Bargaining in America (Reviewing George Fisher, Plea Bargaining's Triumph: A History of Plea Bargaining in America),* 57 Stan. L. Rev. 1721 (2005). For modern British plea bargaining practice, *see* Peter W. Tague, *Guilty Pleas and Barristers' Incentives: Lessons from England,* 20 Geo. J. Legal Ethics 287 (2007).

6. For an outline of the ecclesiastical court's punishments, see Thompson at 410–11. Regarding the king's complaints that church courts were too lenient, *see* Lovell at 93.

7. Because women could not be clerics, they could not plead the benefit. However, they could "*pray the benefit of her belly.*" Baker at 517. The court could not order a female felon to be put to death if she was pregnant. Juries would often find this to allow a woman to avoid the automatic death penalty. If the crown contested the pregnancy claim, a jury of "*matrons*" would decide the matter and would generally find for the defendant.

First woman jury in Los Angeles 1911

8. This is what happened to the only two soldiers convicted in the Boston Massacre trials of 1770. It was not just the massacre but this leniency that sparked the American Revolution. It also showed that John Adams, who defended the soldiers, was indeed a clever lawyer. For his defense of the soldiers, however, the patriots widely criticized Adams, who defended the soldiers to uphold the rule of law. Perhaps in reaction to the Boston Massacre case, Congress abolished *benefit of clergy* in 1790, though it survived in some states and may remain technically available even today. Parliament finally abolished *benefit of clergy* in 1827. See Jeffrey K. Sawyer, *Benefit of Clergy in Maryland and Virginia,* 34 Am. J. Legal Hist. 49 (1990).

The Boston Massacre

The King's (i.e., God's) Pardon: Another way of obtaining God's grace was through a pardon from his representative, the king. The Anglo-Saxon kings lacked unfettered pardoning power. The Norman kings, however, enjoyed a much wider pardoning prerogative. The king would give the grace of the pardon and thereby win grace for himself as well.[1]

The distinction between felonies and misdemeanors is important here because the king only had pardon power over felonies. In the common law "misdemeanors" were lesser crimes, although they were still distinct from being what we would call a civil wrong or tort.[2] "Felonies" were a much more serious crime, subjecting the convicted

to loss of life, lands, and personal goods (called "chattels").[3] The felon was at the king's mercy and thus could get the king's pardon or grace.

After time, however, the king's pardoning power became mostly a way to raise royal revenue.[4] The crown would sell pardons and a defendant could

---

1. See Olson, *Blood Sanction,* at 72–73 (noting the literature on good kingship and expressing the value of concord and reconciliation). This would have been part of a longer biblical tradition of mercy starting with the kings of Israel sparing the life of murderers if the execution would leave his parents with no heirs. Hiers at 755.

Or as Shakespeare wrote: *"This is his pardon, purchased by such sin / For which the pardoner himself is in."* WILLIAM SHAKESPEARE, MEASURE FOR MEASURE act 4, sc. 2. And *"If thou do pardon, whosoever pray, / More sins for this forgiveness prosper may."* and *"I pardon him as God shall pardon me."* WILLIAM SHAKESPEARE, KING RICHARD II act 5, sc. 3. *See* KORNSTEIN at 200–01 (discussing Shakespeare in the context of modern presidential pardons).

2. BAKER at 502. The word "misdemeanor" corresponds to the Latin *"malefactum."* Today it is a crime with a punishment of one year or less. *See, e.g.,* 18 U.S.C. § 3559(a)(6). But misdemeanors may have greater significance under the U.S. CONSTITUTION because Congress can impeach and remove from office the president or a judge for *"high crimes and misdemeanors,"* and the definition of a *"high"* misdemeanor is for Congress to decide.

President Bill Clinton's impeachment trial in 1999

3. BAKER at 502. The concept of felony was feudal in that it was an act that destroyed the bond between lord and man, justifying the forfeiture of life, land, and chattels. Generally the felon's lands reverted to his local lord but his goods were forfeited ("escheated") to the king. In cases of treason, however, the crown got chattels *and* land. Green, *Homicide,* at 414, 425 n.48; BAKER at 512. In the gradation of the time, a felony was a crime between treason and trespass. BELLAMY at 8.

4. *See* Green, *Homicide,* at 426–27. The king's pardoning power later had great influence on homicide law. Instead of today's distinctions between various degrees of killing, offenses were either "pardonable" or not, which a jury decided. The king, through his court, would customarily impose the sentence. An excusable defendant—accidental homicide or self-defense—stayed in jail until he obtained the king's pardon, and after the 1340s the defendant's chattels automatically became forfeit, becoming essentially the price the defendant paid to get the pardon. *Id.* at 425.

5. Green, *Homicide,* at 426. American presidents still enjoy the king's pardoning power. The U.S. Constitution states that the president *"shall have Power to grant Reprieves and Pardons for Offenses against the United States, except in Cases of Impeachment."* U.S. CONST. art. II, § 2, cl. 1. Today a request for a pardon goes to the Justice Department's Office of the Pardon Attorney. Though the pardon power was controversial from the start, Alexander Hamilton defended it in THE FEDERALIST PAPERS, at FEDERALIST NO. 74: THE COMMAND OF THE MILITARY AND NAVAL FORCES, AND THE PARDONING POWER OF THE EXECUTIVE. In his final day in office, George Washington granted the first high-profile federal pardon to leaders of the Whiskey Rebellion. Many pardons have been controversial, such as the following:

- Andrew Johnson's sweeping pardons of thousands of former Confederates after the American Civil War;
- Gerald Ford's pardon of President Richard Nixon after Watergate;
- Jimmy Carter's grant of amnesty to draft evaders after the Vietnam War;
- George H. W. Bush's pardon of seventy-five people in connection with the Iran-Contra affair;
- Bill Clinton's pardon of 140 people on his last day in office; and
- George W. Bush's commutation of I. Lewis "Scooter" Libby's prison term.

Alexander Hamilton

Ford signing Nixon's pardon

Scooter Libby

The president's pardon power only applies to federal crimes.

Most state governors also have pardon or reprieve power for state crimes. Today a governor pardoning or commuting a death sentence is a relatively rare event, but historically governors used this power as a matter of course. *See* STUART BANNER, THE DEATH PENALTY: AN AMERICAN HISTORY (2002) (noting that as many as half of those sentenced to death were pardoned, including valuable slaves). For a discussion of modern pardoning power, see Lauren Schorr, *Breaking into the Pardon Power: Congress and the Office of the Pardon Attorney,* 46 AM. CRIM. L. REV. 1535 (2009).

buy a pardon *"of grace"* (*"de gratia"*) before trial to immunize himself from prosecution. After the thirteenth century, the king retained this "prerogative" power to grant a pardon *of grace,* often for a political favor or money.[5]

Related to the king's pardoning power of *grace* were the king's pardons to reward informants who *"turned approver."*[6]

Death was the penalty for felony convictions. By the thirteenth century, a convicted felon could avoid hanging if he provided evidence against his accomplices. The criminals who did this were called *"approvers."* Among many problems with this system is that if the *approver* failed to secure his former associates' conviction, he hanged. This was a powerful incentive for him to commit perjury.[7] Over time the danger of perjured testimony caused the judges to develop the *"corroboration rule"* and other protections excluding testimony of uncorroborated witnesses who gave *"king's evidence."*[8]

6. Baker at 516.

7. An *approver* "approved" or "proved" a matter, that is, he vouched. The custom was only in capital cases and allowed the approver to confess before plea and accuse others to gain pardon. Black's 5th Ed. at 94. Daniel Klerman, *Settlement and the Decline of Private Prosecution in Thirteenth-Century England,* 19 Law & Hist. Rev. 1, 4 (2001). *See also* A.J. Musson, *Turning the King's Evidence: The Prosecution of Crime in Late Medieval England,* 19 Oxford J. Legal Studies 468 (1999); Frederick C. Mamil, *The King's Approvers: A Chapter in the History of English Criminal Law,* 11 Speculum 238 (1936).

Regarding perjurers in ancient Jewish law, see Rosenberg & Rosenberg, *Of God's Mercy,* at 1189, and for the belief that perjurers are cast out forever from the fellowship of God, see Olson, *Sanctuary,* at 528.

8. John H. Langbein, The Origins of the Adversary Criminal Trial 157, 203 (2003). This included the corpus delicti doctrine, which nullifies a conviction based on a statement alone. Matthew Hale warned that *"[h]e would never convict any person of murder or manslaughter unless the fact were proved to be done, or at least the body found dead."* 2 Matthew Hale, Historia Placitorum Coronae: The History of the Pleas of the Crown 290 (P.R. Glazebrook gen. ed., Professional Books 1971) (1736).

Blackstone followed the same reasoning: *"Never convict any person of murder or manslaughter, till at least the body be found dead . . ."* 4 William Blackstone, Commentaries On The Laws Of England 359 (Univ. of Chicago Press, 2002) (1769). Quoted in Bruce P. Smith, *The History of Wrongful Execution,* 56 Hastings L.J. 1185, 1194–95 (2005). Blackstone argued against "presumptive" (circumstantial) evidence and required the prosecutor to prove the crime had occurred: *"[A]ll presumptive evidence of felony should be admitted cautiously: for the law holds, that it is better that ten guilty persons escape, than that one innocent suffer."*

For modern defense of the corpus delicti rule, see David A. Moran, *In Defense of the Corpus Delicti Rule,* 64 Ohio St. L.J. 817 (2003); Note, *Proof of the Corpus Delicti Aliunde the Defendant's Confession,* 103 U. Pa. L. Rev. 638 (1955).

Coke and later Hale also reacted to accounts of executed innocents, such as Coke's account of the Warwickshire case of 1611 where an uncle was executed for the death of his niece only to have her show up later to claim her inheritance. Edward Coke, The Third Part of The Institutes of the Laws of England: Concerning High Treason, and Other Pleas of the Crown, And Criminal Causes 232 (London 1644). Also cited by 2 Hale at 290 and discussed in John Henry Wigmore, A Treatise on the Anglo-American System of Evidence in Trials at Common Law, Including The Statutes and Judicial Decisions of all Jurisdictions of The United States and Canada 417 (3d ed. 1940). See Smith at 1193 (citing the above example and noting the instances in England and America of wrongful executions and the response both in law and culture).

Hale   Blackstone   Coke

The "king's" pardoning power became a key foundation of judicial discretion.[1] During the Middle Ages this had much to do with practicality; a convict was hanged within hours of conviction. Thus for the king's pardoning power to work, the king's representative (i.e., the judge), in conjunction with the jury, had to decide whether the defendant deserved pardon.[2]

By the time of Blackstone (i.e., the mid-1700s), Parliament had become supreme over the king and by implication the "king's judges" became subservient to Parliament's statutes.[3] But for most of their history, English judges had considerable power to do justice on the spot.[4] And they exercised this power in conjunction with the jury.

The *"Pious Perjurers"*— Juries as Sentencers:

If you were a defendant

Aristotle with the *Ethics*

1. On judges gaining the king's discretionary power over pardons, see Green, *Homicide,* at 425. In exercising this discretion the medieval English judge could have looked back to Aristotle, who encouraged equity for the exceptional case. *See* ARISTOTLE, NICOMACHEAN ETHICS k 10.1137534–1138 as; Rhetoric I. 13. 1364233–51. The equitable decision is what the king (or later a legislator) would have done in the particular circumstances if he had been present.

   For a discussion of sentencing discretion in modern federal courts, see John S. Martin, Jr., *Cruel and Usual: Sentencing in the Federal Courts,* 26 PACE L. REV. 489 (2005).

2. *See* Simon Devereaux, *Imposing the Royal Pardon: Execution, Transportation, and Convict Resistance in London, 1789,* 25 LAW & HIST. REV. 101 (2007) (relating to a later period but demonstrating judicial control of a pardoning system allowing for transportation to New South Wales rather than death).

4. *See* LOVELL at 415 (noting that Parliament did not change the king's old prerogative of mercy in criminal cases). *See* Rachel E. Barkow, *The Ascent of the Administrative State and the Demise of Mercy,* 121 HARV. L. REV. 1332 (2008) (arguing that administrative law has weakened these exercises of mercy).

5. *See* **Chapter 7: Trial by Jury or . . . by God!**
   See also Thomas A. Green, Societal Concepts of Criminal Liability for Homicide in Mediaeval England, 47 SPECULUM 669, 671 (1972) (recording the high acquittal rates); J.G. BELLAMY, THE CRIMINAL TRIAL IN LATER MEDIEVAL ENGLAND: FELONY BEFORE THE COURTS FROM EDWARD I TO THE SIXTEENTH CENTURY 37–38 (1998) (noting that Tudor criminal justice reforms showed conviction rates raising in certain cases).

Blackstone

3. *See* 4 BLACKSTONE, COMMENTARIES ON THE LAWS OF ENGLAND 369–72 (1st ed. 1769), quoted in Claus at 144–45; Granucci at 862–63: *"And it is moreover on the glories of our English law, that the nature, though not always the quality of degree, of punishment is ascertained for every offence; and that it is not left in the breast of any judge, nor even of a jury, to alter that judgment, which the has beforehand ordained, for every subject alike, without respect of persons. For, if judgments were to be private opinions of the judge, men would then be slaves to their magistrates; and would live in society, without knowing exactly the conditions and obligations which it lays them under. And besides, as this prevents oppression on the one hand, so on the other it stifles all hopes of impunity or mitigation; with which an offender might flatter himself, if his punishment depended on the humor or discretion of the court. Whereas, where an established penalty is annexed to crimes, the criminal may read their certain consequences in that law, which ought to be the unvaried rule, as it is the inflexible judge of his actions."*

6. THOMAS A. GREEN, VERDICT ACCORDING TO CONSCIENCE: PERSPECTIVES ON THE ENGLISH CRIMINAL TRIAL JURY, 1200–1800, at 28–64 (1985) (noting that medieval law did not provide for manslaughter and juries would often twist facts to support a self-defense verdict); John H. Langbein, *Ryder Sources,* at 52–55 (noting nineteenth century jury nullification to temper overly severe laws).

   Later commentators connected this medieval history of jury power and *Magna Carta* to modern justifications of nullification. *See, e.g.,* Steve J. Shone, *Lysander Spooner, Jury Nullification, and Magna Carta,* 22 QUINNIPIAC L. REV. 651, 658–59, 664–65, 666 (2004).

7. Hanged versus hung. The preferred past tense and past participle in English is "hanged" and refers to a person; an object like a coat is "hung." Samuel Johnson, the author of the first English dictionary stated, *"Depend upon it, sir, when a man knows he is to be hanged in a fortnight, it concentrates his mind wonderfully."*

before a medieval jury you had a better chance of acquittal than today.[5]

Juries eventually became the main way of deciding cases after the Assize of Clarendon in 1166 and the Fourth Lateran Council of 1215. There was no plea bargaining, and the jurors knew the punishments.[6] Thus they effectively were the sentencers with clear and specific choices:

- *"quietus est,"* meaning "he is acquitted";

- *"suspendatus est,"* meaning "he is hanged" (or, literally, "he is suspended");[7]

- *"remittitur ad gratiam domine regis,"* meaning "he is remitted to the king's grace" (this was part of the pardon discussed above, usually for what we would call justifiable homicides and manslaughter).[8]

Hanging has an old European history. In honor of the god Odin, the Norse hanged criminals by the neck from wooden beams and stabbed them repeatedly until dead. The Norse *"galgatre"* became known as the "gallows tree." KADRI at 17.

Samuel Johnson

A gallows

The **hangman's knot** or **hangman's noose** (known as a **collar** during Elizabethan times) is a specially tied knot to break the neck when it is placed just behind the left ear.

Death by Hanging. This was the main method of American and European capital punishment through history and a cheap alternative to prisons. It is the lethal suspension of a person by a ligature. Hanging is also a common suicide method.

There are four ways of hanging: the short drop, suspension hanging, the standard drop, and the long drop.

With the **short drop**, executioners put the condemned on a cart, horse, or other conveyance, with the noose around the neck. They move away, leaving the condemned dangling from the rope. Death is slow and painful as the condemned dies of strangulation.

Suspension hanging is similar to the short drop except a gallows falls out from under the condemned.

The **standard drop** is a calculated fall of the condemned with the noose around his neck designed to immediately break the neck. This causes immediate paralysis and probable unconsciousness. The drop is between four and six feet. The trouble with the method is that it can cause decapitation.

The **long drop** is also called the **measured drop** and is a "scientific" advancement to the standard drop. Instead of everyone falling the same standard distance, the hangman calculates the person's weight to determine the rope's length to ensure the neck is broken without decapitation. Before 1892, the drop was between four and ten feet to deliver a force of 1,260 lbf to fracture the neck from the second to fifth cervical vertebrae. Because of decapitations, the force calculation was reduced to about 1,000 lbf by shortening the rope.

Depending on the method used, a hanging may induce one or more of the following medical conditions: close the carotid arteries, causing cerebral ischemi; close the jugular veins; induce carotid reflex, which reduces heartbeat when the pressure in the carotid arteries is high, causing cardiac arrest; break the neck (cervical fracture), causing traumatic spinal cord injury; or close the airway, causing suffocation.

The table is used as a guide but the hangman decides the drop after seeing the condemned's build and neck strength.

Hanging has had its problems. See, e.g., Carla McClain, *Lethal Injection Bill Getting Little Support,* TUCSON CITIZEN, Apr. 7, 1992, at 2A (noting that Arizona switched from hanging to lethal gas in 1930 when the noose beheaded a heavy woman, Eva Dugan, when the trapdoor opened).

For how hanging works, see L.D.M. Nokes, A. Roberts & D.S. James, *Biomechanics of Judicial Hanging: A Case Report,* 39 MED. SCI. L. 61, 64 (1999) (concluding that the traditional formula for calculating the drop in hanging is unreliable because it is not possible to determine the correct drop on the basis of the victim's mass alone to pull apart the spinal cord or brainstem without pulling off the head). *See also generally* Khan & Leventhal at 848.

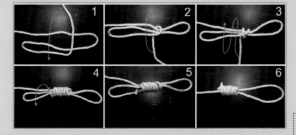

8. Green, *Homicide,* at 423.

The jurors knew that common-law penal policy was simple: misdemeanor convictions meant punishment at the judge's discretion that did not touch life or limb; felony convictions meant the defendant was at the king's mercy and a fixed death sentence.[1] Thus jurors controlled the sentence with their verdict.

For example, acquittal rates for homicide cases in the fourteenth century were 80 to 90 percent.[2] Moreover, from the end of Edward I's reign until the middle of the fifteenth century, the conviction rate for indicted defendants was between 10 and 30 percent.[3] This power of juries, to decide sentences and give mercy as the case demanded, extended well into the modern period and the founding of the United States.[4]

Much of this high acquittal rate can be attributed to the lack of police detectives, crime labs, or medical examiners.[5] But additionally, the medieval English jury was a dependable source of God's grace.

The Medieval Blood Sanction: Assuming you were one of the relatively few persons who did not get some grace through

---

1. BAKER at 512. For misdemeanors this could include punishment or fines or whipping. For felonies the penalty after the thirteenth century was death, though in the Norman and Angevin periods the kings' judges could order mutilations such as castration or blinding instead. Traitors got a cruel death, but for English felons it was generally hanging.

A Medieval Hanging by Pisanello (1436–38)

2. Green, *The Jury,* at 431–32 (noting the lack of distinction in the law for murder versus manslaughter and accounting for the verdicts because the jurors knew the penalty involved).

3. BELLAMY at 37. The conviction rates for the process of "appeal"—i.e., private prosecutions from which our modern tort law derives—the conviction rate was much higher, 50 to 75 percent. This rose to 70 to 90 percent by the mid-fifteenth century.

4. *See generally* Kemmitt (a persuasive historical study on original American juries as sentencers and recommending that courts advise modern juries of sentencing consequences to conform to the Framers' original intent). See also Mark DeWolfe Howe, *Juries as Judges of Criminal Law,* 52 HARV. L. REV. 582, 590–91 (1939) (noting that in Rhode Island, judges held office "*not for the purpose of deciding causes, for the jury decided all questions of law and fact; but merely to preserve order, and see that the parties had a fair chance with the jury*"). See also Apprendi v. New Jersey, 530 U.S. 466, 478–79 (2000) (discussing role of original American juries).

For a more modern discussion of these issues, see Kirk J. Henderson, *Mandatory-Minimum Sentences and the Jury: Time Again to Revisit Their Relationship,* 33 U. DAYTON L. REV. 37 (2007), arguing that juries should find beyond a reasonable doubt any predicate factors that allow for mandatory sentences.

5. But in what we could call *CSI: Medieval,* some jurists believed that the corpse of a victim would rise up in accusation by bleeding or grabbing a suspect brought within its view. Olson, *Blood Sanction,* at 81.

CSI: Crime Scene Investigation is a popular, Emmy Award–winning CBS television series that has aired from 2000. The show follows Las Vegas forensic scientists who discover the causes of mysterious crimes. Numerous spin-offs include *CSI: Miami* and *CSI: NY.*

CSI:
CRIME SCENE INVESTIGATION

6. Olson, *Blood Sanction,* at 65 (noting that benefit of clergy, sanctuary, royal pardon, and high English acquittal rates prevented the blood sanction). See also id. at 74–75.

See Mark Osler, *Christ, Christians and Capital Punishment,* 59 BAYLOR L. REV. 1 (2007), for an account of Jesus's trial and postconviction procedures involved in his execution for a modern comparison.

See also Edward Peters, *Destruction of the Flesh— Salvation of the Spirit: The Paradox of Torture in Medieval Christian Society,* in THE DEVIL, HERESY AND WITCHCRAFT IN THE MIDDLE AGES: ESSAYS IN HONOR OF JEFFREY B. RUSSELL 131, 143, 147 (Alberto Ferreiro ed., 1998) (both ecclesiastical and secular courts primary obligations were to divine justice and this "*required strenuous effort to achieve the restoration and the salvation of even the worst criminals, even of those sent to torture or condemnation to death. . . . [B]y 1300 the principle of destroying the flesh in order to save the spirit had become joined to that of preserving the Christian community and the public good . . .*").

the ordeal, sanctuary, the king's pardon, or a merciful jury, what then? You would face a grueling punishment. But the point was still concord and reconciliation, if not with the community, then with God.[6]

Prison was generally not a punishment in the Middle Ages, mainly because there were no prisons. A king

or local lord might have a dungeon for political undesirables and military captives, but they generally did not waste the space on common criminals. Punishment for them could be scourging, mutilation, or death.

Medieval people had a different notion of the meaning of suffering than we do, perhaps because

they had more of it in their lives.[7]

We generally view suffering as something to avoid.[8] For medieval culture, however, pain had its own benefit.[9] In suffering one could share in the redemptive Passion of Christ.[10] This is because body and soul were believed to be one substance.[11] Thus the pain of the body leads to the cleansing of the soul.[12]

---

7. Sir Thomas More, for instance, wrote: "*Every tribulation which ever comes our way either is sent to be medicinal, if we will take it as such, or may become medicinal, if we will make it such, or is better than medicinal, unless we forsake it.*" DIALOGUE OF COMFORT AGAINST TRIBULATION CWM, v. 12, p. 23. Also, "*We cannot go to heaven in featherbeds.*"

8. An exception, of course, is the almost spiritual experience people seek from exercise to attain the grace of youth and fitness. The descriptions of exercise as being good for "*body and soul*" compare to any purgative a medieval theologian could divine. Add anorexia and bulimia and you have to question how different the psychology is from medieval food asceticism. *See* Olson, *Blood Sanction*, at 91 (discussing Saint Columba of Rieti's food asceticism).

9. ROSELYNE REY, THE HISTORY OF PAIN 49 (1995) (noting that within medieval Christendom, bodily pain possessed an affirmative meaning as a sacrificial offering, allowing one to share in Christ's Passion or as purgation to gain redemption). But one example in imagery is this woodcut by Wolfgang Katzheimer displaying a judicial procession of a shackled man to his execution. A friar with a crucifix attends him and the banner reads, "*If you bear your pain patiently / it shall be useful to you / Therefore give yourself to it willing.*" REPRODUCED IN MITCHELL MERBACK, THE THIEF, THE CROSS, AND THE WHEEL: PAIN AND THE SPECTACLE OF PUNISHMENT IN MEDIEVAL AND RENAISSANCE EUROPE 156 (1999); *discussed in* Olson, *Blood Sanction,* at 88.

10. The two "thieves" who died with Christ, depicted tens of thousands of times. One shared in Christ's redemption and one did not.

Crucifixion by Andrea Mantegna (1457–59)

11. Olson, *Blood Sanction,* at 82–89. For Saints Augustine and Aquinas body and soul were one substance, and thus the pain of the body led to cleansing of the soul. For Aquinas pain was a source of inward joy, meaning that scourging, maiming, and decapitation were for the condemned's spiritual good. Again, if the criminal/sinner could imitate Christ's suffering, redemption could be had. *Id.* at 89.

Saint Augustine by Botticelli (1480)

12. For Augustine and Aquinas evil cannot exist in the absence of good; evil is parasitic and requires good, so as to corrupt it. *See generally* Olson, *Blood Sanction,* at 92. Evil is suffering ("*malum peonae*") and moral wrong ("*malum culpae*"), but it lacks independent essence ("*esse*" in Latin). *Id.* at 94. Evil therefore cannot triumph over good because to eradicate good would mean evil eradicates itself. For this reason Aquinas states that "[i]t is impossible to find anything totally evil." *Id.* Thus, when the human being commits wrong, he acts in "*opposition to [his] fair nature*" and that evil then causes a "disorder" within a man's soul. Pain (even death) equals penance and restores the wrongdoer to "order." *Id.* at 103 ("*by negating the negation that is evil, penal pain affirms [the criminal/sinner's] status as a worthy being*").

Saint Thomas Aquinas

And who would need redemption more than a criminal/sinner?[1] For medieval people, therefore, scourging, maiming, and decapitation were for the condemned's spiritual good, or, as we would say, his rehabilitation. Because of the redemptive nature of punishment the ritual of execution was very important and loaded with spiritual imagery and iconic

1. Writing much later, Milton explained evil's existence as part of a great cosmic battle; God could have created man incapable of evil, but such a mankind would not have been worth the effort. *See generally* Jillisa Brittan & Richard Posner, *Classic Revisited: Penal Theory in Paradise Lost,* 105 MICH. L. REV. 1049, 1053 (2007) (analyzing God's punishments in Milton's *Paradise Lost,* identifying retribution for Satan to deter further angelic rebellion; rehabilitation and deterrence for Adam, Eve, and descendants (us), and strict liability for the serpent).

3. Olson, *Blood Sanction,* at 89.

The ritual of execution is still important today. *See* IVAN SOLOTAROFF, THE LAST FACT YOU'LL EVER SEE: THE PRIVATE LIFE OF THE AMERICAN DEATH PENALTY (2001) (a very interesting chronicle of the psychological toll the death penalty has on executioners as well as descriptions of the death protocols and mechanisms). The film THE GREEN MILE (Warner Brothers 1999), starring Tom Hanks and Michael Clarke Duncan and adapted from Stephen King's 1996 novel, shows the ritual in numerous scenes. *See* Osler at 2 (noting how the condemned's last meal echoes Jesus's Last Supper).

THE GREEN MILE and DEAD MAN WALKING thematically center on the death ritual

Death by Electrocution. The word "electrocution" comes from "electric" and "execution."

The death. The executioners do the following: shave the condemned's head and legs; strap him to a chair; place a natural sponge with saline solution on his head; and attach an electrode to the head and another to his leg, which closes the circuit. Death occurs when the executioners pass electricity through his body in various cycles (differing in voltage and duration); the alternating current fatally damages internal organs, including the brain. Rosenberg & Rosenberg, *Of God's Mercy,* at 1172; Khan & Leventhal at 848. Several states still have electrocution as their primary means of execution or allow the condemned to choose it.

The chair. A dentist, Alfred P. Southwick, conceived of the electric chair, patterning it from his dentist's chair after he saw an intoxicated man die after touching an exposed electric terminal.

Nicknames for various chairs include Sizzlin' Sally, Old Smokey, Old Sparky, Yellow Mama, and Gruesome Gertie. Gruesome Gertie (the Louisiana electric chair) was in the movie MONSTER'S BALL (Lions Gate Films 2001). The electric chair was first used in 1890 after the Supreme Court approved its constitutionality. *In re* Kemmler, 136 U.S. 436 (1890). Andy Warhol made it a statement of political art in *Orange Disaster* (1963).

The chair and the *war of currents*. Harold P. Brown worked for Thomas Edison to make the first electric chair, which became a skirmish in the "war of currents" between Edison, propo-

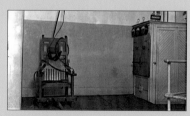

Old Sparky (Texas)

2. Olson, *Blood Sanction,* at 81.

nent and seller of direct current (DC), and George Westinghouse, proponent and seller of alternating current (AC). Edison wanted the electric chair to function on Westinghouse's AC to claim it was more dangerous. (In reality, the difference at the required amperage is marginal.) Edison killed animals with AC for the press to associate it with electrical death. Edison even tried to make up the verb "to Westinghouse" for execution. Westinghouse, who knew what Edison was up to, refused to sell Edison an AC generator. Edison had to pretend he was a university and had Westinghouse's AC generator drop-shipped to New York through South America. On the other side, Westinghouse surreptitiously financed the defense of the first person to be sentenced to death by electric chair so as not to give his AC a bad name. After the first execution went sloppily, Westinghouse commented: "They would have done better using an axe." *See generally* STUART BANNER, THE DEATH PENALTY: AN AMERICAN HISTORY (2002); *see also* Robert J. Cottrol, *Finality with Ambivalence: The American Death Penalty's Uneasy History,* 56 STAN. L. REV. 1641 (2004) (reviewing Banner's THE DEATH PENALTY: AN AMERICAN HISTORY).

The chair and double jeopardy. Despite its seeming technological foundation, the electric chair has produced messy results. In *State of Louisiana ex rel. Francis v. Resweber,* 329 U.S. 459 (1947), the Supreme Court held that a second attempt to electrocute Willie Francis after the first time failed did not violate the Fifth Amendment's Double Jeopardy Clause or the Eighth Amendment's Cruel and Unusual Punishment Clause. They electrocuted Francis again in 1947, this time killing him. *See* GILBERT KING, THE EXECUTION OF WILLIE FRANCIS: RACE, MURDER, AND THE SEARCH FOR JUSTICE IN THE AMERICAN SOUTH (2008); Schwartz at 790; COLIN DAYAN, THE STORY OF CRUEL AND UNUSUAL 27–28 (2007) (giving an account of Willie Francis's story).

symbology.[2] In the execution ritual the bleeding body accessed God, bringing the soul along with it.[3] The key elements were that the criminal/sinner confessed, atoned, and suffered steadfastly.[4]

The scaffold was like an altar, with the sacrifice being the good death.[5]

The scaffold ladder compared to the theological ladder of paradise.[6]

Willie Francis with his fingers crossed for the good luck that the Supreme Court did not give him

4. Olson, *Blood Sanction,* at 112. The movie Dead Man Walking (Gramercy Pictures U.S. 1995) also shows the ritual of death as a prison guard declares *"dead man walking"* during the film. The film adapts Sister Helen Prejean's nonfiction book of the same name, which tells the story of Sister Prejean (Susan Sarandon), who establishes a special relationship with Matthew Poncelet (Sean Penn), a consolidation of two real-life death row prisoners. As with medieval rituals, the film's climax is Poncelet's confession and atonement.

6. Olson, *Blood Sanction,* at 118–19. Compare *The Ladder of Paradise,* showing demons and angels vying for monks, with *Crucifixion of Christ* by Albrecht Altdorfer, showing the thematic ladder associated with Christ, and *The Execution of Hugh Despenser the Younger* from the Froissart manuscript. Though he was not a common criminal, Despenser's execution exemplifies the expected good death. In 1326, Despenser was convicted of treason after Queen Isabella and Roger Mortimer's successful revolt against the English king Edward II. Although Despenser was *"drawn through the whole city of Herford, then hanged, then beheaded,"* he *"humbly and patiently suffered anything and professed publicly to all that he had merited worse, and he often asked pardon of those who stood near and the passerbys."* Id. at 115.

Despenser is displayed with a large penis because he was Edward II's reputed homosexual lover, taking the male role. They also castrated him. Edward II was reportedly killed with a hot iron up his rectum. Peter Hanly played Edward II in the movie Braveheart. In the movie the old king Edward I, throws Edward II's gay lover out the castle window. This was probably not Despenser but an earlier lover, called Peter Giles, who some of Edward II's other courtiers had executed.

5. Olson, *Blood Sanction,* at 103. Saint Catherine of Siena records participating in an execution ritual. *See id.* at 121–24. In 1375, Catherine helped prepare Nicolas Tuldo for a good death. He was sentenced to death in Siena for speaking against the city's magistrates. *"He was so comforted and consoled that he confessed his sins and prepared himself very well,"* hearing mass and taking communion. *"His will was united and submissive to the will of God,"* and he mounted the scaffold as a *"peaceable lamb"* and *"called holy the place of justice [i.e., the gallows!]."* She placed his neck on the block and when the blade struck him he said, *"Gesù!"* and *"Caterina!"* She then caught his head and his eyes *"fixed on divine Goodness."* Christ *"received Nicolas' blood into His own."* The crowd participated in the ritual too, and *"marveled"* at what happened.

Although Saint Catherine writes that Nicolas received communion, medieval authorities and the church often denied the condemned communion because Christ was thought to remain present in the body for three days, and executioners did not want to send Christ to the gallows. *Id.* at 113.

The Execution of Hugh Despenser the Younger, from a manuscript of Froissart

Saint Catherine of Siena by Domenico Beccafumi (c. 1515). Saint Catherine, O.P. (1347–80) was a Dominican lay affiliate, scholastic philosopher, and theologian.

The Ladder of Paradise (twelfth century)

Crucifixion of Christ by Albrecht Altdorfer (1526)

The condemned was expected to forgive his executioner, giving grace in the expectation of receiving grace.[1] Each event was not just public but shared by the public to create reconciliation. In this the criminal/sinner brought the community closer to God.[2]

The ritual, moreover, always allowed for the chance of God's intervention. If the ladder to the scaffold went missing or was too short, jurists took it as a sign that the accused was either innocent or had received God's mercy, *ad iudicium Dei.*[3]

Even the type of execution had spiritual significance.[4] For example, beheading represented the removal of the figurative crown

1. Olson, *Blood Sanction,* at 116–17.

2. Michel Foucault, Discipline And Punish: The Birth of The Prison 46 (1979), discussed in Olson, *Blood Sanction,* at 127.

3. Olson *Blood Sanction,* at 111. Also a woman could interceded for the condemned by asking him to marry her.

4. Generally, beheading was for the upper nobility, hanging for the masses, and burning at the stake for heretics or those who had committed particularly heinous crimes. Olson, *Blood Sanction,* at 117.

5. Olson, *Blood Sanction,* at 117 (citing Samuel Edgerton, Pictures and Punishment: Art And Criminal Prosecution During The Florentine Renaissance 126 (1985)). For example, Giotto's Justice is an enthroned woman with a crown holding the scales of justice. An angel brandishes a sword upon the head of a seated figure who wears a crown while another angel reaches to place a crown upon another seated figure. Personified is "distributive justice" which, according to Saint Aquinas, *"gives to each what his rank deserves . . . good and bad, honour and shame."*

The Seven Virtues—Justice by Giotto (1306)

6. *Jesus Carrying the Cross* by El Greco (1580). Note the crown of thorns.

7. The breaking wheel.

8. "Breaking on the wheel" meant that the condemned would have every major bone in his body broken several times per limb. Depending on the device this could mean he was attached to a wheel and a large hammer or iron bar would break the bones as the executioners would slowly turn the wheel. Then his executioners wove his arms and legs into the spokes of the wheel and mounted it on a pole where they left him to die from exposure and hungry birds. Death could take days. Sometimes the condemned received mercy when his executioner struck him on the chest and stomach, blows known as *coups de grâce* (French: "blows of mercy"), causing death.

from the criminal/sinner's head.[5] The allusion to Christ's crown of thorns naturally followed.[6]

The common criminal's execution was on the "breaking wheel," a torturous capital punishment device causing death by cudgeling (i.e., blunt force trauma with bone-breaking force).[7] The executioner systematically broke all the bones in all the condemned's limbs long before death happened.[8] This manner of execution, which we would today call inhumane, had great spiritual significance.[9]

The wheel was also called "the Catherine wheel" because Saint Catherine of Alexandria was going to be executed on one.[10]

9. The wheel was also an important cultural theme in medieval Europe in the concept of the Rota Fortuna or Wheel of Fortune. God's grace put you at the top one day, but because the earth is a transitory place, the next day you could be at the wheel's bottom, or broken by it.

For instance, *Carmina Burana,* the medieval collection of poems and stories from the eleventh or twelfth to the thirteenth centuries, has two poems about fortune, "O Fortuna" and "Fortunae Plango Vulner," the last line of which translates to *"The wheel of Fortune turns; I sink, debased; another is raised up; lifted too high, a king sits on the top to let him beware of ruin!"*

The Carmina Burana of Carl Orff, http://www.tylatin.org/extras/cb2.html (last visited Oct. 20, 2010). In 1935–36 composer Carl Orff set "O Fortuna" to music in his cantata Carmina Burana. Countless television commercials and films, including Excalibur (Warner Brothers 1981), use Orff's "O Fortuna."

Later Chaucer wrote: *"And thus does Fortune's wheel turn treacherously, / And out of happiness bring men to sorrow."* "The Monk's Tale," in Geoffrey Chaucer, The Canterbury Tales. William Shakespeare, in Hamlet, wrote of the *"slings and arrows of outrageous fortune"* (act 3, sc. 3) and, of fortune personified, to *"break all the spokes and fellies from her wheel"* (act 2, sc. 2). *See also* Henry V act 3, sc. 6; and King Lear, act 2, sc. 2: *"Fortune, good night, smile once more; turn thy wheel!"*

Carmina Burana's original "O Fortuna," showing the Wheel of Fortune

10. Catherine visited Roman Emperor Maxentius to convince him to stop persecuting Christians. Instead the emperor tried to seduce her, and when he failed he ordered her condemned on the breaking wheel. When Catherine touched it, the wheel broke, so the emperor had her beheaded. Saint Catherine was one of the saints that Joan of Arc speaks to in the movie The Messenger: The Story of Joan of Arc (Columbia Pictures 1999). Santa Catalina (Catalina) Island, California, and a lunar crater are named for this Saint Catherine.

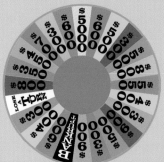

Of course, it would be hard to argue that the modern game show, *Wheel of Fortune*, retains this sense

Wheel of Fortune

Saint Catherine of Alexandria by Caravaggio (c. 1598)

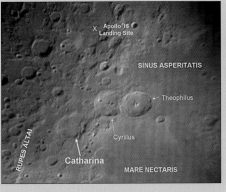

SINUS ASPERITATIS
Apollo 16 Landing Site
Theophilus
Cyrillus
Catharina
RUPES ALTAI
MARE NECTARIS

Detail of *The Last Judgment* by Michelangelo (1534–41), with Saint Catherine holding a broken wheel

Medieval paintings of Christ's Passion sometimes depict the wheel in Christ's crucifixion, despite the fact there is no biblical reference to one.[1]

The disturbing implication of this spiritual focus of redemptive punishment, however, is that it can be all too tolerant of the execution of innocents.[2] If the goal of the death ritual is

the reconciliation of the community, who better than an innocent person suffering in imitation of Christ, the true sacrificial lamb?[3] After all, we are all guilty of something! Thus,

1. For example, *The Procession to Calvary* by Pieter Bruegel (1564) has a Catherine wheel on the far right.

2. Our age can be just as tolerant of innocents executed. For example, Cassell states, "*Perhaps the most successful rhetorical attack on the death penalty has been the claim that innocent persons have been convicted of, and even executed for, capital offenses.*" Paul G. Cassell, *In Defense of the Death Penalty,* in DEBATING THE DEATH PENALTY: SHOULD AMERICA HAVE CAPITAL PUNISHMENT? 183, 205 (Hugo Adam Bedau & Paul G. Cassell eds., 2004). As of February 2008, The Innocence Project has exonerated over 213 death row inmates. The Innocence Project, http://www.innocenceproject.org (last visited Feb. 25, 2008).

INNOCENCE PROJECT

3. The sacrifice of the innocent lamb is metaphor for redemption and is a very old Christian theme evident in the books and movie THE CHRONICLES OF NARNIA. (Buena Vista 2005)

The Mystic Lamb by Van Eyck

4. Thus he would avoid the extension of the earthily blood sanction in hell. This was the premise of Dante's DIVINE COMEDY. Olson, *Blood Sanction,* at 88. The damned are blind to their own vice and thus continue to pursue it. The sin itself causes the suffering, not God. Id. at 100–01, 126 (demonstrating how Dante illustrates the cultural theme of the purpose of punishment). Therefore Dante's hell is not about retribution or "an eye for eye" because the punishments arise from the crime/sin itself, not from the damage. See WHAT DREAMS MAY COME (PolyGram 1998), starring Robin Williams, Cuba Gooding, Jr., and Annabella Sciorra, for a modern rendition of Dante's themes. Dante's punishments are symbolic (e.g., the Neutrals, those who refused to take sides during times of moral crisis, run forever under a symbolic blank banner). In purgatory, the punishments are generally the same as in hell, but the souls are aware of their sin and their penance. Olson, *Blood Sanction,* at 102. Thus, purgatory is about payment of debt and the chance to gain grace. *Id.* at 99.

Expressing the theology of Saint Thomas Aquinas that the soul and body are one essence, Dante notes that so intense is the soul's need of the body that when deprived of it, the soul "imprints" its body in the air. *Id.* at 100. This "imprinting" of the soul idea is a nice plot device allowing Dante to talk to the souls during his guided tour of hell and purgatory. THE MATRIX (Warner Brothers 1999) uses the same plot device, calling it "*residual self-imaging,*" explaining why the characters look the same in both the "real" and the computer-generated Matrix worlds.

Dante and His Poem by Domenico di Michelino (1465)

even if a person did not commit the crime, he was still a sinner like everyone else and would have an easier path to heaven.[4] And the community is reconciled nonetheless. The problem, of course, is that a sacrificial lamb becomes a scapegoat.[5]

Medieval public executions also served to deter crime.[6] But the jurists at the time were very clear that deterrence was not the focus of their justifications.[7] Executions were bloody and public but infrequent in contrast to our age of frequent executions behind sealed prison walls.[8]

5. The priests of ancient Israel would drive a goat into the wilderness as part of the Day of Atonement ceremonies (Yom Kippur) after ceremonially heaping the sins of the community on it. *Leviticus* 16 describes the practice, which foreshadowed the Christian theme of Christ as the Sacrificial Lamb. Today "to scapegoat" is more widely used as a metaphor meaning to blame someone or a group for misfortunes, usually to distract from the real problem.

The Scapegoat by William Holman Hunt (1854)

6. *See The Allegory of Good Government* by Ambrogio Lorenzetti (1328) in Siena's Palazzo Pubblico, showing a winged and draped woman, Securitas, flying over the town holding a gallows with a dead man. *Noted in* Olsen, *Blood Sanction,* at 72.

7. Olson, *Blood Sanction,* at 70–81. For Aquinas the benefit of removing a *"corrupt limb"* from society outweighed the evil of physical punishment to the criminal/sinner. *Id.* at 97. Again, medieval society lacked prisons.

8. "*[E]xecutions which had once been frequent public spectacles became infrequent private affairs. The manner of inflicting death changed, and the horrors of the punishment were, therefore, somewhat diminished in the minds of the general public.*" *Furman v. Georgia,* 408 U.S. 238, 340 (1972) (Marshall, J., concurring).

See also Nicholas Levi, *Veil of Secrecy: Public Executions, Limitations on Reporting Capital Punishment, and the Content-Based Nature of Private Execution Laws,* 55 FED. COMM. L.J. 131, 134–35 (2002).

For a study of modern punishment in general, see Eva S. Nilsen, *Decency, Dignity, and Desert: Restoring Ideals of Humane Punishment to Constitutional Discourse.* 41 U.C. DAVIS L. REV. 111–75 (2007). Modern punishment involves longer and meaner sentences, prison conditions that are more degrading and dangerous, and a lack of meaningful post-release programs. Moreover, the Supreme Court's formalistic reading of the Eighth Amendment has produced *"a legal and moral blindness"* to the constitutional problems of modern punishment.

A modern (semi private) death chamber

KINGS AND DEATH

Much of the history of the English monarchy involved kings wanting to control the death business. From Henry II's attempts to prosecute *"crimonious clerks"*[1] to Henry VIII's use of the death penalty to become the English pope, death became a useful state tool.[2]

The law of homicide developed as kings got into the death business.[3]

---

1. Antonia Fraser, The Lives Of The Kings And Queens Of England 40–41 (1998).

Court of King's Bench (c. 1460), showing a chain gang at the bottom and a jury to the left with judges, lawyers, and clerks (Inner Temple Library)

2. See **Chapter 1: Of Dogma and Desire: Saying What You Believe about the First Amendment** and **Chapter 5: From Testicles to** *Dragnet*: **How the Fifth Amendment Protects** *All* **of Us** regarding Henry VIII and his "inquisition." In the sixteenth century, during Henry VIII's reign there were an estimated 72,000 executions. Levy at 232. This was a staggering number for a nation the size of England and a break from medieval practice. Sir Thomas More, as we have seen in past chapters, stood against Henry's desire to make himself pope of England. More's writings on criminal law and social policy show him at odds with King Henry regarding both. In Utopia, Book 1, More comments on crime and society: "*For if you suffer your people to be ill-educated, and their manners to be corrupted from their infancy, and then punish them for those crimes to which their first education disposed them, what else is to be concluded from this, but that you first make thieves and then punish them.*"

It just so happens that Drew Barrymore's character, Cinderella, quotes this passage in the movie Ever After (20th Century Fox 1998). Obviously, More's thoughts are at odds with King Henry VIII's policies that led to 72,000 executions.

Henry VIII

Utopia

Thomas More

---

3. Executing the Insane. As part of Henry VIII getting into the death business, he had Parliament pass a law that a person convicted of treason should still be executed even if he became insane. 33 Hen. VIII, ch. 20, *cited in Ford v. Wainwright*, 477 U.S. 399, 399 n.1 (1986). This was to get Lady Jane Boleyn (c. 1505–42) for helping Henry's fifth wife, Catherine Howard, commit adultery. During her imprisonment in the Tower of London, she suffered a nervous breakdown and by the beginning of 1542 was pronounced insane. Thus, under the common law, Henry could not chop off her head. The new law allowed Henry to do so. Jane was condemned to death by an act of attainder (a parliamentary declaration of guilt without trial) and executed February 13, 1542, the same day as Catherine Howard.

Common-law writers uniformly condemned the law. Coke wrote that the "*cruel and inhumane Law lived not long, but was repealed, for in that point also it was against the Common Law . . . .*" 3 E. Coke, Institutes 6 (6th ed. 1680), *quoted in Ford*, 477 U.S. at 407–08. Coke also wrote: "*[B]y intendment of Law the execution of the offender is for example, . . . but so it is not when a mad man is executed, but should be a miserable spectacle, both against Law, and of extreme inhumanity and cruelty, and can be no example to others.*" 3 E. Coke, Institutes 6, *quoted in Ford*, 477 U.S. at 407–08 (citing 1 M. Hale, Pleas Of The Crown 35 (1736); 1 W. Hawkins, Pleas Of

Coke

In the sixteenth century, under the Tudors, the concept of *benefit of clergy* passed into common law and produced the outlines of modern homicide law.[4]

Murder, for instance, became a homicide that did not qualify for *benefit of clergy*.[5]

At this point the use of

torture as punishment and as an investigative tool came into question as being "cruel."[6]

THE CROWN 2 (7th ed. 1795)); Hawles, *Remarks on the Trial of Mr. Charles Bateman,* 11 How. St. Tr. 474, 477 (1685).

Blackstone followed a century later: "*[I]diots and lunatics are not chargeable for their own acts, if committed when under these incapacities: no, not even for treason itself. Also, if a man in his sound memory commits a capital offence, and before arraignment for it, he becomes mad, he ought not to be arraigned for it: because he is not able to plead to it with that advice and caution that he ought. And if, after he has pleaded, the prisoner becomes mad, he shall not be tried: for how can he make his defense? If, after he be tried and found guilty, he loses his senses before judgment, judgment shall not be pronounced; and if, after judgment, he becomes of nonsane memory, execution shall be stayed: for peradventure, says the humanity of the English law, had the prisoner been of sound*

Marshall

Blackstone

memory, he might have alleged something in stay of judgment or execution." 4 W. BLACKSTONE, COMMENTARIES 24–25.

Justice Thurgood Marshall, in 1986 writing for the U.S. Supreme Court in *Ford v. Wainwright,* 477 U.S. 399 (1986), finally found the practice of executing the insane unconstitutional.

See generally Robert A. Stark, *There May or May Not Be Blood: Why the Eighth Amendment Prohibition against Executing the Insane Requires a Definitive Standard,* 41 CREIGHTON L. REV. 763 (2008).

---

4. See Green, *Homicide,* at 415, 472–76, on *benefit of clergy* affecting development of homicide law; id. at 480 n. 241 on the power struggle with Henry VIII. Henry VIII, of course, had eliminated the independence of the church courts and terminated the old *benefit of clergy.* This facilitated passage into the common-law courts.

5. Lanham at 90. The courts, not Parliament, first defined manslaughter. Kaye at 369. Over time the older definitions of serious and simple homicide became murder and manslaughter. Green, *Homicide,* at 472–73, 473– 91. These more formal definitions replaced the informal rough justice of the jury system. Thus, though conviction rates increased from the fourteenth century, the condemnation rate remained the same, showing that the law used the manslaughter/murder distinction to replace the old jury justice system. *Id.* at 493; Kaye at 365. The penalty for manslaughter was imprisonment of not more than one year and branding. Green, *Homicide,* at 483, 488.

6. In 1583, Robert Beale condemned "*the racking of grievous offenders, as being cruel, barbarous, contrary to law, and unto the liberty of English subjects.*" LEVY at 232. See **Chapter 5: From Testicles to Dragnet: How the Fifth Amendment Protects All of Us.** Again, as the start of this chapter notes, there is a close relationship between the Fifth Amendment's prohibition on coerced statements and the Eighth Amendment's prohibition on cruel and unusual punishments. See Rumann at 665–66, 668, 679 n.45.

The rack

These objections to torture in criminal procedure, however, cut against long-standing practices.

THE ENGLISH BILL OF RIGHTS

In 1603, the last of the Tudors, Elizabeth I, died, and the Stuarts, starting with James I, took over England.[1]

It was a tumultuous time in English history. James's son, Charles I, lost both the throne and his head.[2] Oliver Cromwell assumed power and kept it until he died in 1658, leading to the restoration of Charles I's son, Charles II.

The Restoration set the stage for Titus Oates and his Popish Plot. As we saw in Chapter 6, Oates hatched an idea that there was a Catholic plot to kill Charles I. As his conspiracy theory spun out and people were tried and executed for treason, his claims became more and more outrageous. The rampant anti-Catholicism of his day gave him a receptive audience.[3]

Oates's escapades finally caught up with him during the reign of James II. Upon Oates's conviction for perjury, Judge George Jeffreys declared him a *"Shame to mankind"* while sentencing him to pillory, public whippings, and prison.[4] Given that Oates was

1. Elisabeth I

James I

2. King Charles I and Oliver Cromwell.

Charles II

The trial of Charles I

3. For the detailed history, *see* JOHN KENYON, THE POPISH PLOT (1972); *also* Claus at 136–37; Parr at 43–45. Regarding English anti-Catholicism, *see* Claus at 135.

Though Oates was a perjuring fraud, he never lost popular support. Following James II, King William and Queen Mary pardoned him in 1688 and Parliament gave him a pension. *Id.* at 141. Oates died in 1705.

4. Claus at 137–39. Jeffreys built his career in the service of Charles II and James II. He presided over the trial of Algernon Sidney, who had been implicated in the Rye House Plot to kill Charles and James. Jeffreys became lord chief justice and privy councilor in 1683 and lord chancellor in 1685. James II made him Baron Jeffreys of Wem.

James II

5. See Claus at 140–42; Parr at 44. *See also* John F. Stinneford, *The Original Meaning of "Unusual": The Eighth Amendment as a Bar to Cruel Innovation,* 102 NW. U. L. REV. 1739 (2008).

clergy, Jeffreys also sentenced Oates to be defrocked. This had implications for the history of the Eighth Amendment because it was "*unusual*"[5] —the twin in our pair, "*cruel and unusual.*"

It was "*unusual*" because whether a common-law court could defrock a clergyman was an open question. After Charles I's deposition, Parliament abolished the Court of High Commission for Ecclesiastical Causes, the body that would have defrocked clergy. Thus it was unclear whether a common-law court now had that power.[6]

For the time, there was nothing "*cruel,*" at least as a legal matter, about each individual part of Oates's sentence. His pillorying, whipping, fine, and prison were standard for the day. But the objections to Oates's sentence were that it was "*cruel and unusual*" and "*cruel and illegal.*"[7] Oates's sentence was "*unusual*" because it was "*illegal,*" since it was unprecedented in the common law or unauthorized by Parliament.[8]

The "Bloody Assizes" of 1685 demonstrated the issues behind unusual punishments.[9] The Bloody Assizes were hundreds of trials beginning in August 1685 after the Monmouth Rebellion.[10]

6. Granucci at 858–59. The House of Commons, where Oates still enjoyed popular support, criticized the House of Lords for allowing a temporal court to render a judgment reserved to the ecclesiastical courts. *See also* Parr at 44.

Oates pilloried

7. *See* Granucci at 859; LEVY at 237 (the "*Oates affair presented the only recorded contemporary uses of the terms 'cruel and unusual' and 'cruel and illegal'*").

8. Granucci at 855–59. *See also* Note, *Original Meaning and Its Limits,* 120 HARV. L. REV. 1279, 1289–92 (2007) (outlining briefly the Oates history as a source of the Eighth Amendment and that the Eighth Amendment prohibits "*the official who assigns the punishment [who] has no legal authority to assign punishments of that kind, or because the law does not provide for punishments of that kind for the relevant offense*").

 See also Jeffrey D. Bukowski, *The Eighth Amendment and Original Intent: Applying the Prohibition against Cruel and Unusual Punishment to Prison Deprivation Cases Is Not Beyond the Bounds of History and Precedent,* 99 DICK. L. REV. 419, 420 (1995) (following Granucci at 860, and thus Justices Thomas and Scalia incorrectly state that the expansion of the Eighth Amendment to prison deprivations is "*beyond all bounds of history and precedent*" in *Helling v. McKinney,* 113 S. Ct. 2475, 2482–83 (1993) (Thomas, J., dissenting), and *Hudson v. McMillian,* 112 S. Ct. 995, 1010 (1992) (Thomas, J., dissenting)).

9. Steve Bachmann, *Starting Again with the Mayflower . . . England's Civil War and America's Bill of Rights,* 20 QUINNIPIAC L. REV. 193, 205–06, 257–59 (2001). *See also* Parr at 47–48; Granucci at 855–59 (arguing that the Bloody Assizes were not the Eighth Amendment's source, but the Titus Oates trial); LEVY at 236 (noting that Henry Pollfexen, chief prosecutor of the Bloody Assizes and backer of the Bill of Rights, did not view the Bloody Assizes as illegal).

James Scott, 1st Duke of Monmouth

10. The **Monmouth Rebellion** of 1685 was to overthrow James II, who was unpopular because he was Catholic. The protestant James Scott, 1st Duke of Monmouth and Charles II's illegitimate son, claimed the throne. James won the Battle of Sedgemoor and executed Monmouth on July 15, 1685. The **Bloody Assizes** followed, resulting in the execution or transportation of Monmouth's followers. *See generally* Bachmann at 257–59.

Judge Jeffreys

Lord Chief Justice George Jeffreys presided.[1]

Of the roughly 1,400 prisoners in the first round of trials in the Bloody Assizes, most received the death sentence. About 292 were hanged, drawn, and quartered, and about 841 were transported to the West Indies as slave labor.[2] Others died in custody of "gaol fever" (i.e., typhus). Later another 500 prisoners were tried, and 144 were hanged, with their remains dis-

played around the country.[3]

In these punishments, the issue was not cruelty, as we define the term, but *unusuality*. The assizes were bloody indeed, but not cruel for the time.[4] It was the fact that the punishments were also unusual that became the issue. This pairing in the law, therefore, of "*cruel*" and "unusual," was important, and the law developed around these concepts as a pair.

"CRUEL AND UNUSUAL" AS A PAIR

King James II's reign was short, from 1685 to 1688. Anti-Catholicism, the Stuart notions of divine right of kings, struggles with Parliament, and rebellions all led to his fleeing the country in the face of the Glorious Revolution of 1688.[5]

The pairing of "*cruel and unusual*" in the law comes from a pair of sovereigns.

1. The infamous executioner Jack Ketch botched the dispatching of the Duke of Monmouth. Ketch was famous for messy executions, either though incompetence or sadism. During his execution of Lord William Russell in 1683, Ketch wrote that he missed with the axe because the condemned did not "*dispose himself as was most suitable*" and that Ketch was interrupted while taking aim. For Monmouth in 1685, Ketch used at least five axe strokes and finally used a knife to sever Monmouth's head. Jack Ketch is now a name for death, Satan, and the gallows. The hangman's knot is sometimes called Jack Ketch's knot. On Ketch, see Gerald D. Robin, *The Executioner: His Place in English Society*, 15 BRIT. J. SOC. 234, 242 (1964). Regarding executioners under Hebrew law, see Hiers at 793–97.

The late D of M beheaded on Tower Hill 15 july 1685

2. LEVY at 234.

3. For his work, King James II made Jeffreys lord chancellor, the highest judicial officer in England. After James was deposed, Jeffreys died a prisoner in the Tower of London of kidney failure in 1689. *See generally* LEVY at 236.

4. Even after the Bill of Rights, executing male rebels with drawing and quartering continued until 1814, when Parliament only eliminated the disemboweling part; beheading and quartering continued until 1870, and the burning of female felons continued until 1790. Granucci at 855–56.

5. On James II losing the throne, *see* Granucci at 852–53.

6. After Mary died in 1694, William of Orange ruled alone until his death in 1702. Their rule was the only time of "joint sovereigns" with equal powers. Usually the spouse of the monarch has no power, being simply a consort.

The College of William & Mary in Williamsburg, Virginia, chartered in 1693, is named for them. Thomas Jefferson, among other notables, is a graduate.

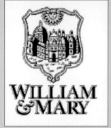

Thomas Jefferson

Parliament in 1689 called William III and Mary II (James's daughter) to replace James II, who was "*deemed to have fled*" the country.[6]

William and Mary brought a new cooperation in governing with Parliament and ended any hope of restoration of Catholism.[7] Part of the deal was that they had to agree to the Bill of Rights, including Article 10:

"*That excessive bail ought not to be required, nor excessive fines imposed; nor cruel and unusual punishments inflicted.*"[8]

WHAT THE ENGLISH MEANT, AND WHO CARES?

What the English meant in 1689 is supposed to have a lot of significance for what the Framers of the Eighth Amendment meant in 1789.[9] And as the start of this chapter notes, the wording is identical, with

the exception of "*ought*" for "*must*," which appears to have no significance. But one hundred years passed between the two, and it was not a static century.

The Enlightenment was the difference. The Eighth Amendment was the product of a different age. In 1689 Parliament passed the Bill of Rights to recognize what existed: common-law liberties of Englishmen from a grasping monarch.[10]

7. These actions led to the nation we now call the United Kingdom under their successor, Mary's sister Anne.

The English colonials brought their anti-Catholicism to America; it flourished to the point of costing Al Smith the presidency in 1928 against Herbert Hoover and was still an issue in John F. Kennedy's close election in 1960. *See* **Chapter 1: Of Dogma and Desire: Saying What You Believe about the First Amendment.**

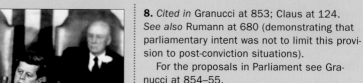

8. *Cited in* Granucci at 853; Claus at 124. *See also* Rumann at 680 (demonstrating that parliamentary intent was not to limit this provision to post-conviction situations).

For the proposals in Parliament see Granucci at 854–55.

For the origins of the English Bill of Rights with the Levelers and the Humble Petition to Parliament of 1648, *see* Bachmann at 256–57.

Again, we call our first ten constitutional amendments "the Bill of Rights" because the English Bill of Rights was an actual legislative bill in Parliament in 1689. *See* **Prequel and Preamble: Did They Forget to Pay the Bill?**

9. *See, e.g.,* Claus at 130 ("*The language of the English Bill of Rights meant for the Founders whatever it meant for the English.*").

10. Claus at 143; Stephen T. Parr, *Symmetric Proportionality: A New Perspective on the Cruel and Unusual Punishment Clause*, 68 TENN. L. REV. 41, 49 (2000–01) (arguing the intent of the English Bill of Rights and the Eighth Amendment was merely to prevent judges from sentencing outside the statutory range). *See also* Parr at 45 (noting the English punished trivial crimes by death for more than one hundred years after the English Bill of Rights).

For example, murder and forgery were the crimes most likely to send a man to the gallows in eighteenth century England. Randall McGowen, *Managing the Gallows: The Bank of England and the Death Penalty, 1797–1821,* 25 LAW & HIST. REV. 241, 243 (2007). Between 1797 and 1821, the Bank of England faced a forgery epidemic, and the bank's solicitors and directors actually decided who got pardoned or executed. *Id.* at 243–44, 280. Robert Peel supported the death penalty for forgery in Parliament in 1830 because the "*punishment of death had checked the crime*" and thus he

Bank of England

"*was in favour of the law as it stood.*" *Id.* at 281 (citing *Parliamentary Debates,* n.s. 1830, xxiii, 1183, xxiv, 1049–50, 1054). Bankers themselves pleaded for reform of the forgery death penalty. LOVELL at 458; Bruce Kercher, *Perish or Prosper: The Law and Convict Transportation in the British Empire, 1700–1850,* 21 LAW & HIST. REV. 527 (2003).

For the English it was not about law reform; they thought nothing of heaping subsequent cruelties on criminals and political dissidents.[1]

For them the only issue from the Oates case, and perhaps the Bloody Assizes, was the unusualness of the punishments.[2]

Americans, however, had a Puritan cultural heritage sensitive to the "*cruel*" punishments suffered in England.[3] Patrick Henry was speaking from (and perhaps to) this heritage when he decried a lack of a bill of rights because

"*congress will lose the restriction of not imposing excessive fines, demanding excessive bail, and inflicting cruel and unusual punishments.*"

John Wilkes

Charles Dickens

Henry Fielding

John Fielding

Culloden by Morier

1. But reform in punishment was coming to England as well. In the 1760 and 1770s our friend John Wilkes, from Chapter 4, as Lord Mayor of London championed punishment and criminal justice reform. See Stephan Landsman, *The Rise of the Contentious Spirit: Adversary Procedure in Eighteenth Century England,* 75 Cornell L. Rev. 497, 581–93 (1990). During this period there was a reduction of capital crimes. This was through reform efforts of Charles Dickens in his novels such as Oliver Twist. The Judicature Acts of 1873–75 implemented this reform. See Thompson at 226 and 452. (Also for the reforms of Jeremy Bentham, see Thompson at 451).

For the reform of policing and criminal justice, see the discussion of Henry and John Fielding in John H. Langbein, *Ryder Sources,* and J.M. Beattie, *Sir John Fielding and Public Justice: The Bow Street Magistrates' Court, 1754–1780,* 25 Law & Hist. Rev. 61 (2007). Arguably, Henry and John started the first police force, the Bow Street Runners, and conducted a magistrate court to treat the criminal justice problems of their day. Henry was the author of The History of Tom Jones, A Foundling (1749), made into a movie in 1963 starring Albert Finny. After Henry's death, his brother John, who was blind, continued the police/magistrate work and reforms.

See also Simon Devereaux, *Imposing the Royal Pardon: Execution, Transportation, and Convict Resistance in London, 1789,* 25 Law & Hist. Rev. 101 (2007) (outlining the need for reforms of an unfair English justice system causing prisoners to refuse transportation and instead opt for the death penalty as a protest). See also James J. Willis, *Transportation versus Imprisonment in Eighteenth and Nineteenth-Century Britain: Penal Power, Liberty, and the State,* 39 Law & Soc'y Rev. 171 (2005); Baker at 516 (on transportation to America and Botany Bay).

2. For "*unusual*" as meaning "*illegal*" at common law, see Claus at 122. Punishments for the second Jacobite Rising of 1745–46, to place James II's grandson, Bonnie Prince Charles, on the throne, were brutal and

As products of the Enlightenment, the Eighth Amendment's Framers were independent thinkers and expansive in their concept of individual rights. Certainly, they wanted to protect individual liberties, like the members of Parliament who wrote the English Bill of Rights. But the Eighth Amendment encompasses an evolving notion of crime, proportionality, and punishment, which Representative Livermore's statements, quoted at the start of this chapter, demonstrate.[4] Indeed, one of the first things the new American states did after independence was to reform criminal law, making it less punitive.[5]

It was, after all, not just a revolt from Great Britain, but the American *Revolution*.

---

unmitigated by the English Bill of Rights. *See* Claus at 144; Granucci at 856; John Prebble, Culloden (1967). The Jacobite Rising gets its name from *"Jacobus,"* Latin for "James."

The Battle of Culloden in 1746 ended the rebellion with great slaughter. The song "Ye'll Take the High Road" comes from the aftermath:
"Oh! ye'll take the high road and I'll take the low road,
And I'll be in Scotland afore ye;
But me and my true love
Will never meet again
On the bonnie, bonnie banks of Loch Lomond."
One man is taking the "high road," the fast road, as in a "highway." But even though the other man takes "the low [slow] road," he will get home first because this "low road" is the one his spirit takes after his execution.

....

3. Levy at 232–33. Although Parr at 42 argues that *"[n]either the English nor the Framers, however, intended to incorporate a guarantee of proportionality,"* he notes that the Eighth Amendment's Framers did *"misinterpret English history and intended to prevent certain modes of punishment." See id.* at 49. On this issue, *see* Granucci at 847, arguing that the Framers, by misinterpreting English history, also intended to prohibit certain modes of punishment.

4. The Italian jurist and philosopher Cesare Beccaria, in On Crimes and Punishments (1763–64), was very influential with the Founding generation. Levi at 135. Beccaria based his thinking regarding punishment on the concept of proportionality. *See generally* Deborah A. Schwartz & Jay Wishingrad, Comment, *The Eighth Amendment, Beccaria, and the Enlightenment: An Historical Justification for the Weems v. United States Excessive Punishment Doctrine,* 24 Buff. L. Rev. 783 (1975) (concluding that the Supreme Court's embracing of the proportionality doctrine in *Weems* was correct when looking at the Eighth Amendment's Enlightenment antecedents). For Beccaria's influence on William Blackstone, *see id.* at 788; on Montesquieu, *see id.* at 810; on Voltaire, *see id.* at 811–13; on Thomas Jefferson, *see id.* at 817–18; and on Benjamin Rush, *see id.* at 823.

In fact, John Adams, in his opening statement defending the soldiers in the Boston Massacre trial, invoked Beccaria:
"May it please your honors, and you, gentlemen of the jury: I am for the prisoners at the bar, and shall apologize for it only in the words of the Marquis Beccaria: If I can be the instrument of preserving one life, his blessing and tears of transport shall be a sufficient consolation to me for the contempt of all mankind." Id. at 814 n.148.

Beccaria

John Adams

---

5. *See* Erwin C. Surrency, *The Transition from Colonialism to Independence,* 46 Am. J. Legal Hist. 55, 56 (2008). Brookhiser at 32 (noting Beccaria's influence and that the Founders lived at a time when people were rethinking crime and punishment).

For example, at the end of the eighteenth century, England had over two hundred capital crimes. Lovell at 458. The traditional power of the jury and pardon system worked to soften this reality. In 1819, 14,000 capital cases came before jurors, who acquitted in 5,000 of them. Of the 9,000 defendants who received a death sentence, all but a few were given the royal prerogative of mercy and were transported to Australia. *See also* Kadri at 95–100 (discussing English punishment during the eighteenth and nineteenth centuries).

Massachusetts, conversely, never had more than fifteen capital crimes. *Id.* at 134.

CHAPTER 9

The Ninth Amendment:

Still a Mystery after All These Years

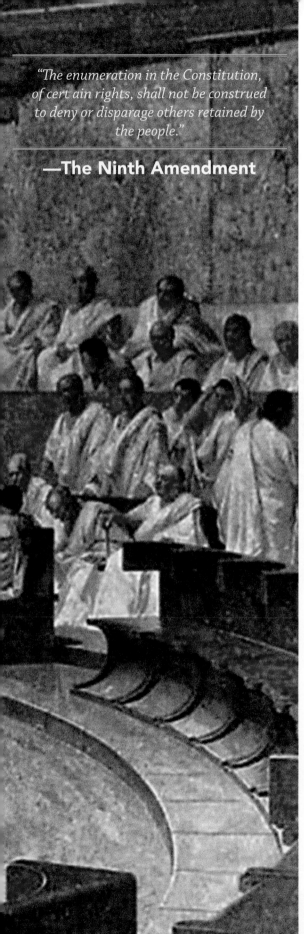

"The enumeration in the Constitution, of certain rights, shall not be construed to deny or disparage others retained by the people."

—The Ninth Amendment

Did you know that neither the original Constitution nor the Bill of Rights gives you the right to vote?[1]

Also forget any right to public education, travel, or marriage. And forget about any right to engage in whatever sex you like, even if you are married and consenting— oh, that means no birth control.[2]

1. See Pamela S. Karlan, *Ballots and Bullets: The Exceptional History of the Right to Vote*, 71 U. CIN. L. REV. 1345, 1345 (2003) ("*At the founding of the Republic, that right [the right to vote] was mentioned in the Constitution only in a backhanded way and was limited essentially to property-owning, taxpaying white males over the age of twenty-one.*").

All the Constitution provides is Article I, Section 2, clause 1: "*the Electors in each State shall have the Qualifications requisite for Electors of the most numerous Branch of the State Legislature.*" Thus state law defined, and as the Florida experience during the 2000 election showed, still defines, the federal right to vote. This underscores the tenuous legal footing of the Supreme Court's 2000 decision in *Bush v. Gore*, 531 U.S. 98 (2000), where the Supreme Court intervened in the federal election to stop the Florida recount and resolved the 2000 presidential election in favor of George W. Bush.

 Al Gore and George W. Bush in 2007 when President Bush congratulated Gore and others for winning the Nobel Prize. Gore also won an Oscar for his movie AN INCONVE-NIENT TRUTH (Paramount Classics 2006).

2. And the list goes on:
* no right to freedom from sterilization,
* no right to refuse medical treatment,
* no right to work,
* no right to political asylum,
* no right to make unrestricted political contributions,
* no right burn a draft card,
* no right to self-preservation,
* no right of access to government files,
* no right to have government officials discharge their duties,
* no right to take drugs,
* no right of civil disobedience,
* no right of conscientious objection, and
* no right to freedom from capital punishment.

Various rights are listed with citations in Eugene M. Van Loan III, *Natural Rights and the Ninth Amendment*, 48 B.U. L. Rev. 1, 46–47 (1968). *See also* SUSAN FORD WILTSHIRE, GREECE, ROME, AND THE BILL OF RIGHTS 172 (1992).

The only individual rights the original Constitution protected were a prohibition against ex post facto laws and bills of attainder in Article I, Section 9, and the right to a jury trial in criminal cases in Article III, Section 2.

True, some of these rights are older than the Constitution, even ancient.[1] Others we eventually added to the Constitution,[2] and the courts or Congress gave us others, but that still leaves out a big chunk of what we take for granted as our "constitutional rights."

Ah, you could say, "don't forget the Ninth Amendment!"[3] It says we get to keep all the rights that the Constitution and the Bill of Rights do not "enumerate" (i.e., list).[4] The trouble is that this does little to tell us what it means.[5]

With refreshing honesty, Justice Robert Jackson

---

1. "Freedom of movement" goes at least as far back as *Magna Carta* in 1215 AD: "*It shall be lawful in future, unless in time of war, for anyone to leave Our Kingdom and to return, safe and secure by land and water, saving his fealty to Us, for any short period, for the common benefit of the realm, except prisoners and outlaws according to the law of the land, and people of a country at war with Us.*" *Magna Carta*, cl. 42, *reprinted in* O. John Rogge, *Unenumerated Rights*, 47 Cal. L. Rev. 787, 806 (1959).

....

2. The Fifteenth Amendment (1870) was the first provision in the Constitution to protect voting: "*The right of citizens of the United States to vote shall be denied or abridged by the United States or by any State on account of race, color, or previous condition of servitude.*" But the popular vote still does not elect the president. *See, e.g.*, Brandon H. Robb, Comment, *Making the Electoral College Work Today: The Agreement Among the States to Elect the President by National Popular Vote*, 54 Loy. L. Rev. 419, 465 (2008).

....

3. Bennett B. Patterson, The Forgotten Ninth Amendment: A Call for Legislative and Judicial Recognition of Rights under Social Conditions of Today (1955). Patterson's little book started an academic cottage industry regarding the Ninth Amendment. His two main points were (1) the Ninth Amendment incorporated preexisting ideas of "natural law" or "natural rights" into the Constitution, and (2) the natural law doctrine restricts both the federal and state governments.

4. The word "enumerate" means the same today as in the eighteenth century—"to number," and an "*enumeration*" was simply "a numbering or count." Kurt T. Lash, *A Textual-Historical Theory of the Ninth Amendment*, 60 Stan. L. Rev. 895, 901 (2008) (citing early English dictionaries). *See generally* Kurt T. Lash, *The Lost Original Meaning of the Ninth Amendment*, 83 Tex. L. Rev. 331 (2004).

....

5. Plenty of academics tell us what they think it means. *See*, for example, Symposium, *The Forgotten Constitutional Amendments*, 56 Drake L. Rev. 829 (2008), with the following three articles laying out the current scholarship: Daniel A. Farber, *Constitutional Cadenzas*, 56 Drake L. Rev. 833 (2008); Kurt T. Lash, *Three Myths of the Ninth Amendment*, 56 Drake L. Rev. 875 (2008); Randy E. Barnett, *The Golden Mean between Kurt & Dan: A Moderate Reading of the Ninth Amendment*, 56 Drake L. Rev. 897 (2008).

As for books on the subject, among others see The Rights Retained by the People: The History and Meaning of the Ninth Amendment (Randy E. Barnett ed., 1989); Thomas B. McAffee, Jay S. Bybee & A. Christopher Bryant, Powers Reserved for the People and the States: A History of the Ninth and Tenth Amendments (2006).

....

6. "*[A] lawyer friend asked me in a friendly way what I thought the Ninth Amendment to the Constitution meant. I vainly tried to recall what it was. . . . What are those other rights retained by the people? To what law shall we look for their source and definition? . . . [T]he Ninth Amendment rights which are not to be disturbed by the Federal Government are still a mystery to me.*" Robert H. Jackson, The Supreme Court and the American System of Government 74–75 (1955). Nearly every scholar treating the Ninth Amendment uses this Jack-

admitted that "the Ninth Amendment rights . . . are still a mystery to me."[6] Later Judge Robert Bork during his failed confirmation hearing for a Supreme Court vacancy called it an "inkblot."[7]

The Ninth Amendment did not feature in a modern Supreme Court case until 1965's *Griswold v. Connecticut*, holding that married couples could buy contraceptives without fear of criminal prosecution.[8]

To make *Griswold* work, the justices had to coin a new constitutional term: *"the penumbra"* of rights in the Constitution.

son quote at some time. *See, e.g.,* LEONARD W. LEVY, ORIGINS OF THE BILL OF RIGHTS 241 (1999); Leslie W. Dunbar, *James Madison and the Ninth Amendment*, 42 VA. L. REV. 627, 629 (1956); Rogge at 787 (demonstrating that lawyers rely on the Fifth and Fourteenth Amendments' Due Process Clauses rather than the Ninth Amendment).

See also Russell L. Caplan, *The History and Meaning of the Ninth Amendment*, 69 VA. L. REV. 223, 267 (1983) (arguing that the Ninth Amendment is limited to the specific *"well-understood"* rights in state law at the time of adoption and that *"[t]he ninth amendment, therefore, has become obscure precisely because of its own success"*).

Justice Robert Jackson was also the main American prosecutor during the 1945–46 Nuremberg trials. Alec Baldwin played him in the television movie *Nuremberg* (Alliance Atlantis Communications 2000).

Robert H. Jackson

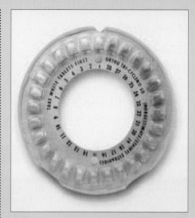

Birth control dispenser

8. *Griswold v. Connecticut*, 381 U.S. 479 (1965).

The Connecticut law stated that any person *"who uses any drug, medicinal article or instrument for the purpose of preventing conception shall be fined not less than fifty dollars or imprisoned not less than sixty days nor more than one year or be both fined and imprisoned."* CONN. GEN. STAT. REV. § 53-32 (1958). The statute also penalized anyone *"who assists, abets, counsels, causes, hires or commands another to commit any offense."* *Id.* § 54-196. For discussions on the lack of a Ninth Amendment Supreme Court case until 1965, see LEVY at 241; WILTSHIRE at 173; Kurt T. Lash, *The Inescapable Federalism of the Ninth Amendment*, 93 IOWA L. REV. 801, 804 (2008); Dunbar at 628 (*"The chronicle of the ninth amendment shows an almost entire neglect"*); Van Loan at 1.

Judge Robert Bork

7. *"I do not think you can use the Ninth Amendment unless you know something of what it means. For example, if you had an amendment that says 'Congress shall make no' and then there is an inkblot and you cannot read the rest of it and that is the only copy you have, I do not think the court can make up what might be under the inkblot if you cannot read it."* Nomination of Robert H. Bork to be Associate Justice of the Supreme Court of the United States: Hearings Before the Senate Comm. on Judiciary 249 (1989), *quoted in* Randy E. Barnett, *A Ninth Amendment for Today's Constitution*, 26 VAL. U. L. REV. 419, 419 (1991) (arguing that the Ninth Amendment encompasses a general right of freedom). Bork also referred to the Privileges and Immunities Clause as an inkblot. *See* Kyle Alexander Casazza, *Inkblots: How the Ninth Amendment and the Privileges or Immunities Clause Protect Unenumerated Constitutional Rights*, 80 S. CAL. L. REV. 1383, 1384 (2007). Bork probably designed his statements to play to the notion that the courts, especially the Warren Supreme Court, had overly expanded individual rights, especially of criminal defendants. These and other statements backfired on him, and the Senate did not confirm his nomination. The entire process gave a new term to the political lexicon of the Supreme Court confirmation process: a nominee can now be "borked," which means to be defamed and vilified in the media to prevent a person's appointment to office (i.e., defeated).

This means that a bunch of rights not explicitly in the Constitution or Bill of Rights are under the umbrella of the whole thing.[1] This notion certainly seems to flow from the Ninth Amendment's wording that the Constitution's relatively few listed rights do not *"deny or disparage others retained by the people."* It sounds like a good idea, and it is![2]

So what's all the fuss about?

MY RIGHT, YOUR RIGHT, AND WHO'S RIGHT?

The problem is deciding on a "right" and whether someone else doesn't want you to have it. Or what if your "right" to something takes away someone else's "right" to something else?

How about the following vexing problems?

- The right to reproductive freedom takes away from

many people's belief in the right to life.[3]

- The *"right to work"* takes away from the right to collectively bargain.[4]

- Letting the public have a right to read about a crime or see a criminal trial can hinder the accused's right to block prejudicial pretrial publicity.[5]

- The right to take drugs butts up against an entire

Justice William O. Douglas

1. *"Penumbra,"* from Latin *"paene"* ("almost") and *"umbra"* ("shadow"). WEBSTER'S NEW INTERNATIONAL DICTIONARY OF THE ENGLISH LANGUAGE 1813 (2d ed. 1942). Regarding *"penumbra"* rights, see John P. Kaminski, *Restoring the Declaration of Independence: Natural Rights and the Ninth Amendment, in* THE BILL OF RIGHTS: A LIVELY HERITAGE 149 (Jon Kukla ed., 1987). Justice William O. Douglas was the great champion of the *"penumbra." See* LEVY at 241–42.

2. *See Bowers v. Hardwick*, 478 U.S. 186, 199 (1986) (Blackmun, J., dissenting) (stating that the Ninth Amendment gives *"the most comprehensive of rights and the right most valued by civilized men . . . the right to be let alone"). See also* Barnett, *Today's Constitution* (arguing that the Ninth Amendment encompasses a general right of freedom). *See also* Kathleen Anne Ward, *Williams v. Attorney General of Alabama: Does a Constitutional Right to Sexual Privacy Exist?* 31 T. JEFFERSON L. REV. 1 (2008).

3. The right to privacy seems pretty basic, even though the Constitution does not explicitly say so. The problem for many, however, is that privacy is the foundation of *Roe v. Wade*, 410 U.S. 113 (1973), the case protecting a woman's right to abortion. Indeed, the Ninth Amendment was the basis of the lower court's decision in *Roe. See* WILTSHIRE at 174. Thus, if you do not believe the Constitution protects, or even should protect, the right to abort, you may want to challenge the foundation of the right to privacy.

For the general concept of the right to privacy, *see* Rogge at 799–804 (citing *Olmstead v. United States*, 277 U.S. 438 (1928)); Samuel D. Warren & Louis D. Brandeis, *The Right to Privacy*, 4 HARV. L. REV. 193 (1890). *See also* Allgeyer v. Louisiana, 165 U.S. 578, 589 (1897) (*"[Liberty] means not only the right of a citizen to be free from the mere physical restraint of his person, as by incarceration, but the term is deemed to embrace the right of the citizen to be free in the enjoyment of all his faculties; to be free to use them in all lawful ways; to live and work where he will; to earn his livelihood by any lawful calling; to pursue any livelihood or avocation; and for that purpose to enter into all contracts which may be proper, necessary, and essential to his carrying out to a successful conclusion the purposes above mentioned."*).

government program of eradicating their use.[6]

The Framers listed some rights for us. With these "enumerated" rights we just argue about their application and extension. Having modern rights takes modern balancing.

RIGHTS, GOVERNMENT, AND STATES

If balancing rights is not hard enough, the question arises about the role of government in this balancing. Although the Ninth Amendment says you get to keep all of your rights, it actually does not specifically give you any one of them. Rather it provides a way to understand the rest of the Constitution.[7]

Our Constitution does two things: It provides us a working government *and* protects us from the very government it provides— an obvious paradox.

But the paradox is an outgrowth of popular sovereignty, the idea that all power comes from the people.[8] Thus the Constitution aspires to limit government from interfering unduly with peoples' lives.

And if all government comes from the people, so the argument goes, the states were closer to the people and the best realization of their popular sovereignty.

---

4. Often the term *"right to work"* is a euphemism for efforts to defeat unions. The concept, however, was not so intended, and the UNIVERSAL DECLARATION OF HUMAN RIGHTS, Article 23.1 states: *"Everyone has the right to work, to free choice of employment, to just and favourable conditions of work and to protection against unemployment."*

5. See *Richmond Newspapers, Inc. v. Virginia*, 448 U.S. 555 (1980) (plurality opinion) (citing the Ninth Amendment as support for the right of public access for criminal trials).

In a case like O.J. Simpson's, of course, the pretrial publicity was the point!

See also Sarah Tupper, Note, *Taking the Ninth: A Victim's Right of Privacy*, 28 WASH. U. J.L. & POL'Y 457 (2008) (arguing the Ninth Amendment allows a crime victim to *"take the Ninth"* and refuse to testify against a family member in a criminal proceeding based on a privacy right).

United Farm Workers César Chávez, Philip Vera Cruz, Dolores Huerta, and Larry Itliong founded the United Farm Workers (UFW) union in 1962 after merging several other unions. The UFW was famous for organizing a boycott of table grapes, which after five years lead to a contract with the major California grape growers.

6. See Kevin S. Toll, Comment, *The Ninth and America's Unconstitutional War on Drugs*, 84 U. DET. MERCY L. REV. 417, 418–19 (2007).

7. *"It is a common error, but an error nonetheless, to talk of 'ninth amendment rights.' The ninth amendment is not a source of rights as such; it is simply a rule about how to read the Constitution."* LAURENCE H. TRIBE, AMERICAN CONSTITUTIONAL LAW 776 n.14 (2d ed. 1988). See also Lash, *Textual Theory*, at 903.

8. See Akhil R. Amar, *Philadelphia Revisited: Amending the Constitution Outside Article V*, 55 U. CHI. L. REV. 1043, 1064 n.77 (1988) (noting that the theory of popular sovereignty *"served as the foundational principle of the Constitution"*). *Id.* at 1071 (*"Thus, our true constitutional rule of recognition is . . . the principle of popular sovereignty that undergirds every Article of the original Constitution and every Amendment in the Bill of Rights."*). See also Lash, *Federalism*, at 811–12, 825–34.

The federal Constitution was the great threat to states' aspirations to be independent sovereign nations, as Patrick Henry unambiguously warned:

"Here is a revolution as radical as that which separated us from Great Britain. Our rights and privileges are endangered, and the sovereignty of the States . . . relinquished."[1]

Henry never bargained for a national government when he supposedly called out *"Give me liberty or give me death!"*[2] Each state was supposed to be an independent government, as in our modern way of talking about "the state" of England or France, as the Declaration of Independence demonstrates:

"We, therefore . . . declare, That these United Colonies are, and of Right ought to be Free and Independent States . . . and that as Free and Independent States, they have full power to levy war, conclude peace . . . and do all other acts and things which Independent States may of right do."[3]

With such passion in play, Alexander Hamilton sought to calm state fears in THE FEDERALIST No. 32:

Patrick Henry

George Mason

The George Mason Memorial at George Mason University

Elbridge Perry

1. Patrick Henry, Speech in Virginia Convention, June 5, 1788, *quoted in* Kaminski at 142. The convention that produced our Constitution was only supposed to amend the Articles of Confederation. What Henry wanted was a constitution that preserved Article II of the ARTICLES OF CONFEDERATION, which provided that *"[e]ach state retains its sovereignty, freedom, and independence, and every power, jurisdiction, and right, which is not by this Confederation expressly delegated to the United States, in Congress assembled."* Caplan at 236. Instead, what Henry and the rest got was a whole new constitution.

George Mason, too, warned that the Constitution would *"commence in a moderate aristocracy,"* then *"vibrate some years between"* monarchy and aristocracy and end up one or the other. *Quoted in* Kaminski at 142. Elbridge Gerry didn't sign the Constitution because it was *"neither consistent with the principles of the Revolution, or of the Constitutions of the several States."* *Quoted in id.* at 141. It did not seem to hurt his career, though, because he still became vice president under President James Madison and died in office in 1814.

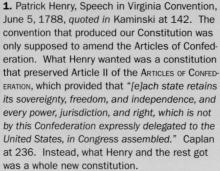

2. Henry throws down the gauntlet..

3. Even John Adams in 1774 referred to Massachusetts as *"our country"* and to the Massachusetts delegation to the Continental Congress as *"our embassy."* Letter from John Adams to Abigail Adams (Sept. 18, 1774), *reprinted in* 1 LETTERS OF MEMBERS OF THE CONTINENTAL CONGRESS 35 (E. Burnett ed., 1921).

James Madison stressed at some length that before the Revolution, the common law *"was the separate law of each colony within its respective limits, and was unknown to them as a law pervading and operating through the whole, as one society."* The common law *"was not the same in any two of the colonies; in some, the modifications were materially and extensively different. There was no common legislature, by which a common will could be expressed in the form of a law."* *Quoted in* Caplan at 244.

"The State governments would clearly retain all the rights of sovereignty which they before had, and which were not by that act exclusively delegated to the United States."[4]

Calming fears about losing rights was the Ninth Amendment's purpose.[5] Although James Madison wanted the Constitution, he also feared the consolidation of federal power.[6] The states were supposed to be repositories of individual rights.[7] And the Founders limited the federal government to protect these rights.[8]

In short, Henry and Madison, though in disagreement about the Constitution, never wanted to lose their identity as Virginians first and Americans second.

History proved Henry's fears right and Hamilton, if not wrong, perhaps disingenuous—the states did lose their identity. No Virginian will tell you today that he is anything other than a citizen of the United States of America.[9]

---

4. THE FEDERALIST No. 32 (Alexander Hamilton), at 194 (Clinton Rossiter ed., 1961). *See* Lash, *Federalism*, at 827 n.90, *citing* GORDON S. WOOD, THE CREATION OF THE AMERICAN REPUBLIC, 1776–1787, 524–32 (1998) (discussing the Federalists' assurances that the Constitution would never consolidate the states into a single national mass). *See id.* at 832 (arguing that before 1791 the *"retained rights of the people"* was synonymous with *"retained rights of the states"*).

5. For a discussion of Madison and the relationship of rights and state power, *see* Joseph L. Call, *Federalism and the Ninth Amendment*, 64 DICK. L. REV. 121, 129 (1959). *Id.* at 126–28 also provides a good outline of the Ninth Amendment's passage in Congress.

6. *See* Call at 122, 125.

....

7. A further example of the centrality of states to the Framers' plan of government is that two years after the Bill of Rights the people added the Eleventh Amendment: *"The Judicial power of the United States shall not be construed to extend to any suit in law or equity, commenced or prosecuted against one of the United States by Citizens of another State, or by Citizens or Subjects of any Foreign State."* U.S. CONST. amend. XI.

8. Lash, *Federalism*, at 831. *See id.* at 807 (arguing that *"the original federalist aspect of the [Ninth] Amendment remains in force and requires judicial protection of local self-government today just as it did in 1791"*). *See also* Lash, *Lost Meaning*, at 401; Raoul Berger, *The Ninth Amendment*, 66 CORNELL L. REV. 1, 10 (1981) (arguing that *"Justice Goldberg [in Griswold] leaps too lightly from the 'existence of rights' retained by the people to a federal power to protect them"*); E. Norman Veasey, *What Would Madison Think? The Irony of the Twists and Turns of Federalism*, 34 DEL. J. CORP. L. 35, 35 (2009) (noting Madison's *"nimble"* view of federalism).

9. Virginia Gets Special Mention. In 1788, the Virginia ratifying convention produced the following proposed amendment to the U.S. Constitution:

> *"That those clauses which declare that Congress shall not exercise certain powers be not interpreted in any manner whatsoever to extend the powers of Congress. But that they may be construed either as making exceptions to the specified powers where this shall be the case, or otherwise as inserted merely for greater caution."*

With Madison's redrafting and congressional committee tinkering, this eventually became the Ninth Amendment.
There is also Owen Wister's THE VIRGINIAN (1902), a Wild West novel having nothing to do with the Constitution but made into a film several times, including THE VIRGINIAN (Paramount Pictures 1929), starring Gary Cooper, and a television series *The Virginian* (NBC, from 1962 to 1971), starring James Drury, Doug McClure, and Lee J. Cobb.

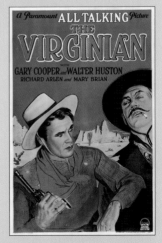

But it was this question of identity about which the Federalists and Anti-Federalists, and later the Federalists and Republican-Democrats, argued.[1]

For us though, the argument has little meaning. Despite the transfer from state to federal power, as well as state to national identity, the basic concept of government remains the same: popular sovereignty.[2] Both the Ninth and Tenth Amendments explicitly refer to "the people," which, regardless of any original intent that this might refer to *"the people"* in the states, it readily transfers to *"the people"* of the United States.[3]

DECLARING OUR RIGHT TO RIGHTS NATURALLY

The Ninth Amendment sounds good[4] and naturally follows the Declaration of Independence. You don't

---

1. Making Academic Careers from Day One. St. George Tucker, a judge and professor at the College of William & Mary, wrote in his influential View of the Constitution that the Ninth Amendment guarded the people's collective right to abolish their government: *"the powers delegated to the federal government, are, in all cases, to receive the most strict construction that the instrument will bear, where the rights of a state or of the people, either collectively, or individually, may be drawn in question."* St. George Tucker, A View of the Constitution of the United States, *in* 1 Blackstone's Commentaries app. 154 (St. George Tucker ed., William Young Birch & Abraham Small 1803). Tucker even refused to accept that the new Constitution had abrogated the Articles of Confederation. Tucker was thus the academic champion of the Jefferson/Madison camp.

Thirty years later along came Joseph Story's Commentaries on the Constitution, attacking Tucker's Ninth Amendment view on states' rights. For Story the proper view was Chief Justice John Marshall's formulation of federal power in *McCulloch v. Maryland*, 17 U.S. 316, 404–05 (1819), and *Martin v. Hunter's Lessee*, 14 U.S. 304, 324 (1816) (*"The constitution of the United States was ordained and established, not by the states in their sovereign capacities, but emphatically, as the preamble of the constitution declares, by 'the people of the United States.'"*); 1 Joseph Story, Commentaries on the Constitution § 417, at 400 (Boston, Hilliard, Gray, & Co. 1833). Thus for Story *"the people"* were the united citizenry, who only happened to live in several states. Story dedicated his commentaries *"to the Honorable John Marshall"* and, given the animosity, both political and personal, between Jefferson and Marshall, Story was the standard bearer of the Federalist academic camp. *See* Lash, *Federalism*, at 833–34, 859–60; Kurt T. Lash, *The Lost Jurisprudence of the Ninth Amendment*, 83 Tex. L. Rev. 597, 632–33 (2005) (for a discussion of Tucker and Story). *See also* Kurt T. Lash, *"Tucker's Rule": St. George Tucker and the Limited Construction of Federal Power*, 47 Wm. & Mary L. Rev. 1343 (2006).

Joseph Story   St. George Tucker

3. Popular sovereignty is an organizing concept of government that in the early modern period (i.e., leaving out a study of the ancient Greeks or Romans) historically happened between absolutism and totalitarianism.

Absolutism. King Louis XIV's statement *"I am the state"* (*"L'état, c'est moi"*) summed up the role of the absolute monarch, with sovereignty literally vested in the sovereign. The monarch had absolute power over all aspects of his or her subjects' lives, though the monarch was expected to follow custom. The system put its trust in well-bred and trained monarchs. The "divine right of kings" justified the absolute monarch—from God to king to people. In England, the Stuart kings tried to import this principle, but lacking the French monarchy's resources and the different English history of recognizing rights, it met with no success.

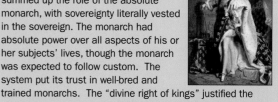

Totalitarianism. Fascism, National Socialism (the ideology of the Nazi Party, or the National Socialist German Workers' Party), and Communism all started with the belief in the absolute state. The Nazis, for example, sought to unite the working class into a proletarian nation while socializing industry and providing a welfare state. Although at odds with Communism, it shared the belief in a proletarian (worker) revolution. Although democratic in concept, the state, through its chosen few in "the party" (Nazi or Communist), maintained *total* control over all aspects of life—civic, economic, educational, etc.

Ironically, both National Socialism and Communism as political ideologies descended from the French and later Russian Revolutions, which were the violent end of French and Russian absolutism.

2. As Chief Justice John Marshall wrote in *McCulloch v. Maryland*, "The government of the Union, then (whatever may be the influence of this fact on the case), is, emphatically and truly, a government of the people. In form, and in substance, it emanates from them. Its powers are granted by them, and are to be exercised directly on them, and for their benefit." 17 U.S. at 404–05. *But see* Lash, *Lost Jurisprudence* (arguing that the Marshall Court ignored the Ninth Amendment and insisted that the *"people"* of the Tenth Amendment were the undifferentiated people of the United States).

John Marshall

just get *"Life, Liberty and the pursuit of Happiness"* because they are *"among"* your *"unalienable"* rights, which implies the list is incomplete.[5] Rather the Declaration, and later the Ninth Amendment, is based on the idea that people have the *"pre-existent rights of nature."*[6]

The Declaration's self-evident truths and the Ninth Amendment's recognition of the *"rights . . . retained by the people"* articulate natural law (*"lex naturalis"*), valid everywhere.[7] This natural law exists regardless of the *"positive law"* (statutes, pronouncements, decrees, etc.) of a given state or country.[8]

These rights spring from nature rather than from a king or government, even a democratic one like ours. This remains as radical an idea today as it was in 1791.

But where did the Framers get this idea of *"natural rights"*?

Justice Goldberg

4. *See* RANDY E. BARNETT, RESTORING THE LOST CONSTITUTION: THE PRESUMPTION OF LIBERTY (2004); Randy E. Barnett, *The Ninth Amendment: It Means What It Says,* 85 TEX. L. REV. 1 (2006). *See also* Van Loan at 17 (noting that Madison's purpose was to protect fundamental natural rights).

As Justice Arthur Goldberg declared: *"[t]he language and history of the Ninth Amendment reveal that the Framers of the Constitution believed that there are additional fundamental rights, protected from governmental infringement, which exist alongside those fundamental rights specifically mentioned in the first eight constitutional amendments." Griswold,* 381 U.S. at 488 (emphasis added).

THE DECLARATION OF INDEPENDENCE

5. WILTSHIRE at 173.
"We hold these truths to be self-evident, that all men are created equal, that they are endowed by their Creator with certain unalienable Rights, that among these are Life, Liberty and the pursuit of Happiness." See generally PAULINE MAIER, AMERICAN SCRIPTURE: MAKING THE DECLARATION OF INDEPENDENCE (1997). *See also* Kaminski at 150 (*"The Founders realized that no statesman could list every liberty in a bill of rights, so they wrote the Ninth Amendment to affirm the natural rights doctrines of the Declaration of Independence."*).

7. Finding the Law? An outgrowth of natural rights is that courts will often write that they *"find"* the law. The thinking is that as society and people develop intellectually, spiritually, and socially, we increase our ability to understand and comprehend the rights that nature endows. Thus judges do not make law but *"find"* it. Obviously, the source is something like God or, as Justice Holmes may have cynically described, *"a brooding omnipresence in the sky." S. Pac. Co. v. Jensen,* 244 U.S. 205, 222 (1917) (Holmes, J., dissenting).

8. *See* Calvin R. Massey, *Federalism and Fundamental Rights: The Ninth Amendment,* 38 HASTINGS L.J. 305, 321 (1987) (noting that the Framers *"understood and observed a distinction between 'natural' rights and . . . 'positive' rights"*).

6. Madison said this upon introducing what would become the Bill of Rights in Congress. *Quoted in* Van Loan at 11 (citing 1 CONGRESSIONAL PROCEEDINGS 454). On Madison discussing *"the preexistent rights of nature"* versus those *"resulting from a social compact,"* see LEVY at 250. *See also* WILTSHIRE at 169 (noting the Ninth Amendment is more closely connected with the doctrine of natural law). *But see* Thomas B. McAffee, *The Bill of Rights, Social Contract Theory, and the Rights "Retained" by the People,* 16 S. ILL. U. L.J. 267 (1992) (arguing that the Framer's had no general understanding of the inherent constitutional status of certain natural rights).

RITES BEFORE RIGHTS—GREEKS AND ROMANS ON RIGHTS AND LAW

The Greeks and Romans gave us a concept of self-government—at least they wrote it down so we can read it.[1] Self-government provides a basis for our later ideas on the individual's liberties and privileges.

The Greeks: Self-government creates an environment where a thinker like Aristotle can work. Aristotle is the origin of natural rights as a concept.[2] By definition, Aristotle did not invent natural rights—he couldn't because they are "natural"—though he originated the articulation.

Although not a major part of Aristotle's work, his idea of a *"law of nature"* broke with prior thinking. Plato, for instance, wrote that

"goodness according to nature and goodness according to the law are two different things, and there is no natural standard of justice at all."[3]

The Sophists also tended to define "law" and "nature" (*"nomos"* and *"physis"*) as opposites.

Aristotle, however, wrote of a justice and law that is *"kata physin"*—"based on" or "in accordance with"—nature.[4] Though various countries have different laws for dealing with everyday justice, there remains an eternal common and natural law. [5]

To learn this natural law you need to study *"what actually happens."* Thus, if a practice is common and *"evident in all communities and peoples,"* it is natural.[6] Because humans tend toward the good, natural law and virtue are related.[7]

Despite Aristotle's notion of natural law, the Greeks did not have a concept of individual civil rights. Your city-state (*"polis"*) defined

---

1. Obviously cavemen governed themselves. What the Greeks and Romans did was to organize the concept of popular government and define it in terminology we can read today. The Greeks had *"politeia"* and the Romans *"constitutio"* as concepts of self-government. WILTSHIRE at 99.

2. *See* John R. Kroger, *The Philosophical Foundations of Roman Law: Aristotle, the Stoics, and Roman Theories of Natural Law*, 2004 WIS. L. REV. 905, 916 (2004) (*"Prior to Aristotle, ancient Greek philosophy possessed no working concept of natural law."*).

3. Kroger at 916, *quoting* PLATO, LAWS 889e, *reprinted in* PLATO: COMPLETE WORKS 1318, 1546–47 (John M. Cooper ed., Trevor J. Saunders trans., 1997).

4. Kroger at 916–17, *quoting* ARISTOTLE, ON RHETORIC: A THEORY OF CIVIC DISCOURSE 1373b, 1375a, at 102, 107–10 (George A. Kennedy trans., 1991).

5. WILTSHIRE at 12, *citing* ARISTOTLE, NICOMACHAEAN ETHICS 1098a7-8, b2-4 (I.7.14).

The School of Athens by Raphael (1510–11) centers on Plato (modeled on Leonardo da Vinci) and Aristotle (modeled on Michelangelo) discoursing

6. Kroger at 919.

7. WILTSHIRE at 13. As we will see, Saint Thomas Aquinas followed this theme to great effect.

8. *See* Keith Werhan, *The Classical Athenian Ancestry of American Freedom of Speech*, 2008 SUP. CT. REV. 293, 298 (noting that in Athens the full right of free speech was *"an attribute of citizenship, not a natural right"*).

9. THE DECLARATION OF INDEPENDENCE para. 2 (U.S. 1776).

10. WILTSHIRE at 17–18, 29.

11. WILTSHIRE at 19. Roman law included Justinian's Code. Edward Gibbon in THE DECLINE AND FALL OF THE ROMAN EMPIRE (1776–88) wrote about Justinian: *"Wise or fortunate is the prince who connects his own reputation with the honour and interest of a perpetual order of men."* Quoted in id. at 21.

your place in the world.[8] If it defined you as a slave, you were a slave without independent status or rights.

But Aristotle's articulation of natural justice was only a short step from the Founding generation's concept of *"unalienable rights."*[9]

The Romans: The idea of the rule of law was more important to the Romans than the Greeks.[10] Roman law spanned centuries, well past the Roman Empire, to include all Byzantine law, the European *ius commune* ("common sense" or "common law"), and the Catholic Church's canon law.[11]

In Rome Cicero espoused the idea of natural law:

"True law is right reason in agreement with Nature; it is of universal application, unchanging and everlasting; . . . It is a sin to try to alter this law, nor is it allowable to attempt to repeal any part of it, and it is impossible to abolish it entirely. We cannot be freed from its obligations by senate or people, and we need not look outside ourselves for an expounder or interpreter of it. And there will not be different laws at Rome and at Athens, or different laws now and in the future, but one eternal and unchangeable law will be valid for all nations and for all times, and there will be one master and one ruler, that

is, God, over us all, for he is the author of this law, its promulgator, and enforcing judge."[12]

Cicero was a Stoic. Stoic philosophy taught that there was a rational and purposeful order to the universe (i.e., divine or eternal law).[13] Building on the relatively brief passages in Aristotle, the Stoics developed the theory of natural law.

Natural law guided a Stoic's life.[14] A rational man tried to live within the order of natural law, which spelled out action and virtue, or as Cicero wrote,

"We are slaves of the law that we may be free."[15]

---

12. *Quoted in* Wiltshire at 23.

Justinian and his Code

Edward Gibbon

Cicero

14. *See generally* Wiltshire at 13–17.

15. Cicero's Latin was "*legume idcirco omnes servi sumus ut liberi esse possimus.*" Wiltshire at 24. See Kroger at 934–35 (regarding Cicero's explanation of divine, universal, and natural law—e.g., "*right reason of supreme Jupiter*"— contrasted with local laws of particular communities).

13. Stoics, the Original Committee Men. Stoics honored family, country, friends, looking after one's health, acting prudently and justly, marrying, conversing, and serving on embassies. Kroger at 925–26. For Stoic origins of natural law through John Locke and the Enlightenment, see Wiltshire at 169.

Cicero Denounces Catiline by Cesare Maccari (1888)

Maccari's painting of Cicero as a consul of Rome in 63 BC, shows when he thwarted Catiline's conspiracy to overthrow the Roman Republic. Cicero started by denouncing Catiline in the Senate with a series of speeches known as the Catilinarian Orations. The Roman Senate eventually executed Catiline without a trial. Today we would call the procedure a "bill of attainder." Article 1, Section 9, of the U.S. Constitution prohibits bills of attainder.

Although Roman law originally had only a limited concept of individual rights, Stoic ideas began to change this. The ideas of individual worth, moral duty, and universal brotherhood were the beginnings of the concept of individual rights.[1] This was because, for Stoics, men had souls.[2]

The Roman Stoic belief in individual equality and inherent natural rights is the Ninth Amendment's foundation; that we retain rights, even if the Constitution does not list them. The exact definition of what our individual rights are, however, remains a difficult problem.[3] Nevertheless, these Roman Stoic ideas formed the basis of recognition of individual rights through the Middle Ages until today. America's classically trained Founding generation asserted:

"We hold these truths to be self-evident, that all men are created equal, that they are endowed by their Creator with certain unalienable Rights, that among these are Life, Liberty and the pursuit of Happiness."[4]

MEDIEVAL RIGHTS

The concept of natural law worked well for Christianity. A universally valid law fit with a universally omnipotent

---

1. Kroger at 924.

2. Stoics, Vegetarianism, and Animal Rights. For the Stoic, animals have souls, too, because they act according to their nature. Kroger at 924, 916–17. Although animals act naturally, they lack speech and comprehension of justice and laws. As Aristotle wrote, only man is *"a political animal."* Animals lack reason, are incapable of participating in civic community, and have no laws. Thus, though both humans and animals exist in nature, only humans understand or follow natural justice and natural laws. *Id.* at n.58. So the Stoics really do not provide an argument for vegetarianism, as any Coliseum scene would confirm.

Gladiators killing animals

The Trial of Bill Burns, the first person prosecuted under the 1822 Martin's Act for cruelty to animals for beating his donkey. The prosecutor, Richard Martin, brought the donkey into court.

3. Romans and Marriage. Romans had a simple view of marriage. A valid marriage only needed a couple to show the intent to be married. There was no specific legal form, or trip to city hall, or registry. Kroger at 941–42. Indeed, the entire modern discussion of getting the government to recognize a marriage, same sex or conventional, would have been a strange topic for a Roman.

Our view of marriage is much more romanticized. *See,* for example, THE PRINCESS BRIDE (20th Century Fox 1987) for a great spoof, especially the pompous clergyman, played by Peter Cook, talking about *"mawwiage, the bwwessed institution."* We see marriage as a legal status the government confers after a couple complies with specified requirements and a formal ceremony.

We also see marriage as a fundamental right, as Chief Justice Earl Warren wrote while striking down Virginia's ban on marriage between blacks and whites: *"Marriage is one of the 'basic civil rights of man,' fundamental to our very existence and survival. . . . To deny this fundamental freedom on so unsupportable a basis as the racial classifications embodied in these statutes, classifications so directly subversive of the principle of equality at the heart of the Fourteenth Amendment, is surely to deprive all the State's citizens of liberty without due process of law."* Loving v. Virginia, 388 U.S. 1, 12 (1967).

Our view of marriage as a fundamental right, but still something that the government confers, makes this issue the subject of modern controversy in the same-sex marriage debate. *See, e.g.,* Bryan K. Fair, *The Ultimate Association: Same-Sex Marriage and the Battle against Jim Crow's Other Cousin,* 63 U. MIAMI L. REV. 269, 299 (2008).

and just God. The early Christian fathers swiped a few terms from Aristotle and the Stoics and had a ready-made theology revealed to them.[5]

Saint Augustine of Hippo, for instance, equated natural law with the Garden of Eden.[6] God's grace and divine law, the law God revealed to man through scripture and tradition, could take you back to the garden.

Saint Thomas Aquinas grabbed Aristotle and added the idea that human reason had a role in the process of revelation:

Mankind is ruled by two laws: Natural Law and Custom. Natural Law is that which is contained in the Scriptures and the Gospel.[7]

Thus to know what is right requires reason that *"seeks the good and avoids evil."*[8] This reason, or conscience,

allows humans to discern between good and evil.[9]

Aquinas's emphasis on human reason is the seed of revolution.[10] Human reason allows men to judge human laws and social norms on whether they conform to natural law or justice.[11] Natural law not only measures the moral worth of various laws but also determines what should be the law in the first place. An unjust law is therefore not binding.[12]

---

4. The Declaration of Independence para. 2 (U.S. 1776).

5. See generally Wiltshire at 34–50.

6. *The Garden of Eden* by Lucas (1536).

7. *Quoted in* Wiltshire at 35.

8. For Aquinas the general principles of natural law *"can nowise be blotted out from men's hearts."* But in their application, *"concupiscence"* or *"passion"* can hinder reason and blot the natural law *"from men's hearts."* Also *"evil persuasions," "vicious customs,"* or *"corrupt habits"* can blot out natural law. Thus some men do not even consider theft or *"unnatural vices"* sinful. Thomas Aquinas, Summa Theologica I–II, Q. 94, A. 2 & 6.

9. Aquinas wrote that disobedience to the state may be a duty, but he does not allow for revolution. Wiltshire at 39.

10. Doing the Right Thing Is Not Enough. Natural moral law is concerned with both exterior and interior acts, also known as action and motive. Simply doing the right thing is not enough; to be truly moral one's motive must be right as well. For example, helping an old lady across the road (good exterior act) to impress someone (bad interior act) is wrong. However, good intentions don't always lead to good actions. The motive must coincide with Aquinas's cardinal or theological virtues, which you acquire through reason applied to nature: (1) prudence, (2) justice, (3) temperance, and (4) fortitude. His theological virtues are faith, hope, and charity.

According to Aquinas, to lack any of these virtues is to lack the ability to make a moral choice. For example, consider a man who possesses the virtues of justice, prudence, and fortitude yet lacks temperance. Due to his lack of self-control and desire for pleasure, despite his good intentions, he will find himself straying from the moral path.

11. Aquinas coined the term *scientia politica*, that is, "political science." Wiltshire at 38.

12. For example, for Aquinas drunkenness is wrong because it injures one's health, and worse, destroys one's ability to reason, which is fundamental to man as a rational animal (i.e., does not support self-preservation). Theft is wrong because it destroys social relations, and man is by nature a social animal.

Aquinas's revolutionary idea, that men have reason and can judge a law's justice for themselves, carries through to our present time.[1] The belief in human reason means that we would expect nothing less than a Ninth Amendment declaring that rights are *"retained by the people."*

And this idea is the foundation of the Declaration of Independence:

"When in the Course of human events, it becomes necessary for one people to dissolve the political bands which have connected them with another, and to assume among the powers of the earth, the separate and equal station to which the Laws of Nature and of Nature's God entitle them, a decent respect to the opinions of mankind requires that they should declare the causes which impel them to the separation."[2]

But the American Revolution was not just the product of Aquinas. Natural law joined with English notions of individual rights to influence the colonists to break with the mother country.

RIGHTS IN ENGLISH HISTORY

England has always been different from the rest of Europe.

English kings could be powerful or not, but they were never absolute monarchs.[3] England had the common law and juries while the rest of Europe had the civil law and inquest.[4]

Magna Carta underscored the difference. In 1215 AD, King John's barons forced him to sign the "Great Charter," affirming the idea that there was justice under the *"law of the land,"* which we today call *"due process."*[5]

And what is *"due process"*? Put simply, it is the "process" (rights) that the individual is "due" (owed) from the king. When *Magna Carta* articulates the *"law of the land"* as our *"due process,"* it shows the preexistence of individual rights under natural law to which the king and his government must conform.[6]

---

1. Other Medieval thinkers agreed. For example, Dante Alighieri relied on Saints Augustine and Aquinas when he wrote that *"[c]itizens are not there for the sake of governors, nor the nation for the sake of the king, but conversely the governors for the sake of the citizens, the king for the sake of the nation."* And freedom was the *"greatest gift conferred by God on man."* DANTE, DE MONARCHIA 1.12, *quoted in* WILTSHIRE at 65. As the author of the DIVINE COMEDY, Dante could also put you in hell, purgatory, or heaven.

2. THE DECLARATION OF INDEPENDENCE para. 1 (U.S. 1776).

3. For example, Edward III's coronation medal in 1327 reads *"The will of the people gives the laws"* (*"Voluntas populi dat jura"*). WILTSHIRE at 60. Of course, the kings had an interest in claiming to represent the will of *"the people"* against powerful barons.

Edward III was the son of Isabella of France and Edward II and thus would have been Sophie Marceau's child in BRAVEHEART (Paramount Pictures 1995). But there is no way William Wallace (Mel Gibson) could have fathered the child because he had been executed long before she ever came to England to marry Edward II. *See* ALISON WEIR, QUEEN ISABELLA (2005).

4. *See, e.g.,* WILTSHIRE at 54 (noting that the recording of English judicial decisions started from Henry II's reign, as well as Glanville and Bracton's early texts on English law, causing English lawyers to rely on their tradition rather than the Roman law of continental Europe).

5. *Magna Carta* Chapter 39 (in some versions Chapter 29) is the basis of the Fifth Amendment's Due Process Clause. WILTSHIRE at 57. Centuries later, Sir Edward Coke called Chapter 39 *"the golden passage."* *Id.* at 56. Under Coke's gloss, Chapter 39 guaranteed common-law procedures, especially grand jury and trial by jury. LEVY at 248. *See* **Chapter 7: Trial by Jury or . . . by God!**

Although it would take until the late eighteenth century for the idea to catch on that the government's purpose is to advance the individual's personal liberty, *Magna Carta* was the starting point.[7] And in the later struggles with the kings, Parliament often referred to the *"Fundamental Laws of England"* embodying not only natural law but also the *"law of the land."*[8]

RIGHTS MARCH ON

As English history progressed, the power of the people through Parliament expanded, as did the common law. But the seventeenth century produced the real foundation of the idea that rights are universal and that government's purpose was to guarantee them.[9]

Parliament started to flex its muscle. In the Petition of Right (1628) and the Grand Remonstrance (1641), Parliament articulated what civil rights should be. A number are now in the Constitution (e.g., due process, trial by jury, and prohibiting of billeting of soldiers in private homes). Other rights such as expedited and inexpensive lawsuits and enhanced employment opportunities for the poor have not made it into the Constitution, though we have some of these rights through legislation and other means.[10]

The seventeenth century was also the time of the Levellers, a movement of the lower and working classes.[11] Levellers used the "petition" as a political tool. Although presented as "petitions" to the king or Parliament, they were really open letters on what a constitution and civil rights should be. The Agreement of the People (1647), the Large Petition (1647), and the Humble Petition (1648) asserted many rights now in the U.S. Constitution, for example, religious tolerance and equal protection of law. Others, like economic safety nets for the poor, minimum standards for the imprisoned, and guaranteed public education, are not in the Constitution but might as well be.

King John signs *Magna Carta* in 1215 AD

---

6. *Magna Carta:* What It Really Said versus What It Is Said to Have Said! Much of *Magna Carta* was just a clarification of feudalism's landlord-tenant relationship. The English king was fundamentally the first of the barons. Wᴉʟᴛsʜɪʀᴇ at 56. *Magna Carta* clarified the preexisting relationships between king, barons, and church. In fact in 1215, after excluding slaves, serfs, and women, *Magna Carta* applied to only about 10 percent of the population. *Id.* at 57.

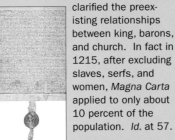

Magna Carta

8. *See generally* Bᴇʀɴᴀʀᴅ Sᴄʜᴡᴀʀᴛᴢ, Tʜᴇ Gʀᴇᴀᴛ Rɪɢʜᴛs ᴏғ Mᴀɴᴋɪɴᴅ: A Hɪsᴛᴏʀʏ ᴏғ ᴛʜᴇ Aᴍᴇʀɪᴄᴀɴ Bɪʟʟ ᴏғ Rɪɢʜᴛs 202 (1977) (due process allows the Supreme Court to be a continuing constitutional convention, allowing for an expanding and evolving notion of what rights are due the individual).

7. *See* Wᴉʟᴛsʜɪʀᴇ at 58 (noting the link from *Magna Carta* to the notion of personal liberty as a goal of government).

9. Steve Bachmann, *Starting Again with the Mayflower. . . England's Civil War and America's Bill of Rights*, 20 Qᴜɪɴɴɪᴘɪᴀᴄ L. Rᴇᴠ. 193, 259–60 (2000) (noting Leveller history and a broader expansion of rights).

10. Bachmann at 260.

11. Other chapters outline the exploits of John Lilburne, but he was only a member of the Leveller movement.

The culmination of much of this petitioning, and indeed the template for our own Bill of Rights, was the English Bill of Rights of 1689, which included the following:

- Parliament, not the king or executive, makes the law and approves taxes;

- freedom to petition the monarch;

- freedom from a standing army in peacetime, and parliamentary control over the army even during war;

- freedom of Protestants

to bear arms for their own defense, but as suitable to their class and as the law allowed;

- freedom to elect Parliament without the monarch interfering;

- freedom of speech in Parliament;

- freedom from cruel and unusual punishment and excessive bail; and

- freedom from fine and forfeiture without trial.[1]

Amidst this seventeenth century stew of history,

petitions, bills, and rights arose someone to articulate their basis: John Locke.

JOHN LOCKE AND THE NATURAL LAW

John Locke grabbed Aristotle and Aquinas and articulated a basis of rights that flowed naturally from being human.[2] You are born *"endowed"* with rights, not granted them by superior authority.

Locke's thinking was directly contrary to King James I's Canons of 1666, which asserted,

---

1. The English Bill of Rights of 1689.

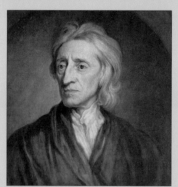

2. For a general, brief discussion of Locke, see LEVY at 252–53; WILTSHIRE at 76–85. Locke quotes Aristotle in his *Essays on the Law of Nature.* WILTSHIRE at 13.

3. The full quote follows:
"*If any man shall affirm that men at the first, without all good education and civility, ran up and down in woods and fields, as wild creatures, resting themselves in caves and dens, and acknowledging no superiority one over another, until they were taught by experience the necessity of government; and that thereupon they chose some among themselves to order and rule the rest, giving them power and authority to do so; and that consequently all civil power, jurisdiction and authority was first derived from the people, and disordered multitude; or either is originally still in them, or else is deduced by their consents naturally from them, and is not God's ordinance originally descending from him and depending upon him; he doth greatly err.*"
Bachmann at 261, *citing* The Canons of 1666 (1666), *in* THE STUART CONSTITUTION 1603–1688: DOCUMENTS AND COMMENTARY 11–12 (J.P. Kenyon ed., 1966).

4. JOHN LOCKE, SECOND TREATISE ON GOVERNMENT, *quoted in* LEVY at 252. As Levy notes, our Constitution uses both senses of the word "property." *Id.* at 253. The Fifth Amendment, for instance, states in the Due Process Clause that no man shall "*be deprived of life, liberty, or property without due process of law,*" and in the Takings Clause that property (i.e., physical goods) will not be taken "*without just compensation.*"

"If any man shall affirm that men at the first . . . acknowledge no superiority . . . until they . . . chose some among themselves to order and rule the rest . . . and that consequently all civil power, jurisdiction and authority was first derived from the people . . . or either is originally still in them, or else is deduced by their consents naturally from them, and is not God's ordinance originally descending from him and depending upon him; he doth greatly err."[3]

Locke, on the other hand, spoke of natural law, although he added at least one word to its vocabulary—"property." Property for Locke did not just mean your car or television. Rather a man owns his rights as well:

"[A] man has property in his opinions and the free communication of them. He has a property of peculiar value in his religious opinions, and in the profession and practices dictated by them. He has property very dear to him in the safety and liberty of his person. He has an equal property in the free use of his faculties and free choice of the objects on which to employ them. In a word, as a man is said to have a right to his property, he may be equally said to have a property in his rights."[4]

Where Locke differs from Aristotle and Aquinas is on government's role.[5] For Locke the state does not define one's humanity but is only a pragmatic arrangement to protect private pursuits and avoid conflicts:[6]

"The great and chief end, therefore, of men's uniting into commonwealths, and putting themselves under government, is the preservation of their property; to which in the state of nature there are many things wanting."[7]

---

5. God Naturally Becomes a Little Less Omnipotent. In the seventeenth century Hugo Grotius formulated a basis of international law and the law of war based on natural law. In particular his writings on "freedom of the seas" and "just war theory" directly appealed to natural law. But he, like the rest of the early Enlightenment thinkers, had a problem explaining the role of an omnipotent God. How could there be a natural law if God was omnipotent, i.e., not subject to it? Grotius's explanation was that *"even the will of an omnipotent being cannot change or abrogate"* natural law, which *"would maintain its objective validity even if we should assume the impossible, that there is no God or that he does not care for human affairs."* (*De iure belli ac pacis*, Prolegomeni XI). Thus even God cannot break natural law or, if there is no God or he just does not care, natural law still applies. For a general discussion of Grotius and arguing that his sources were classical, *see* Benjamin

Grotius

Thomas Hobbs

Straumann, *Is Modern Liberty Ancient? Roman Remedies and Natural Rights in Hugo Grotius's Early Works on Natural Law*, 27 Law & Hist. Rev. 55 (2009).

Other thinkers further separated God from natural law. Rather then emanating from God, natural law for Thomas Hobbes was how a rational human being, seeking to survive and prosper, would act. Jean-Jacques Rousseau and Montesquieu followed Hobbes, expanding this contractual approach to rights. *See* Wiltshire at 73–76.

---

6. Wiltshire at 81. The idea of the "social contract" implies equality of parties, in this case the individual and the state. *Id.* at 71.

7. John Locke, Of the Ends of Political Society and Government ¶ 124, *in* The World's Great Thinkers: Man and the State: The Political Philosophers 129 (Saxe Commins & Robert N. Linscott eds., 1947). Locke's precursor was the ancient Roman Lucretius, who wrote that man invented laws and government as he evolved from nature: *"mankind, tired out with a life of brute force, lay exhausted from its feuds; and therefore the more readily it submitted of its own freewill to laws and stringent codes."* Lucretius, On the Nature of Things 144 (H.A.J. Munro ed., 1900).

Thus, if the ruler went against natural law and failed to protect *"life, liberty, and property,"* people could justifiably overthrow the existing state and create a new one.[1]

LOCKE AND THE FOUNDING GENERATION

Thomas Jefferson and the Founding generation echoed Locke in the Declaration of Independence:[2]

"We hold these truths to be self-evident, that all men are created equal, that they are endowed by their Creator with certain unalienable Rights, that among these are Life, Liberty and the pursuit of Happiness."[3]

James Madison also wrote that the rights *"retained"* in the Ninth Amendment are the *"Lockean rights to self-determination that are retained by the people when they agree to the formation of civil government."*[4]

Madison had gotten himself in a tough spot because he originally opposed the Bill of Rights. People in his home state of Virginia, like Patrick

St. George Tucker

1. St. George Tucker quoted Locke that *"there remains still inherent in the people a supreme power to remove or alter the legislative, when they find the legislative act contrary to the trust reposed in them: for, when such trust is abused, it is thereby forfeited, and devolves to those who gave it."* Following this quotation Tucker notes that *"[t]his principle is expressly recognized in our government, Amendments to the Constitution U.S. Art. 11, 12,"* which became the Nineth and Tenth Amendments. TUCKER at app. 154.

2. Thomas Jefferson wrote and insisted on the following epitaph, listing the writing of the Declaration of Independence as one of his singular achievements: "HERE WAS BURIED THOMAS JEFFERSON / AUTHOR OF THE DECLARATION OF AMERICAN INDEPENDENCE / OF THE STATUTE OF VIRGINIA FOR RELIGIOUS FREEDOM / AND FATHER OF THE UNIVERSITY OF VIRGINIA"

Despite Jefferson's claim of authorship, the ideas he expressed were not original. On Jefferson's fundamental lack of originality, see Alexander Tsesis, *Undermining Inalienable Rights: From Dredd Scott to the Rehnquist Court*, 39 ARIZ. ST. L.J. 1179, 1182–83 (2007) (Jefferson's statement of the *"self-evident"* truth that *"all men are created equal, that they are endowed by their Creator with certain unalienable Rights, that among these are Life, Liberty and the pursuit of Happiness"* distilled philosophical and political thought of his day). *But see* GARRY WILLS, INVENTING AMERICA: JEFFERSON'S Declaration of Independence 172–75 (1978) (arguing that Locke had little, if any, influence on Jefferson's writing the DECLARATION OF INDEPENDENCE). Jefferson, in fact, was the youngest member of a committee of five; the other members of the committee, such as John Adams, had many more important things to do. Whether he was the main mind behind the Declaration of Independence or

Jefferson's gravestone

just a drafter of the committee is still debated.

As for Locke's influence on other revolutionaries, there is James Otis's 1764 pamphlet, *The Rights of the British Colonies Asserted and Proved*, which quoted, paraphrased, or alluded to Locke on almost every page. *See* Caplan at 231–32.

As Otis declared *"[n]o legislative, supreme or subordinate, has a right to make itself arbitrary."* See **Chapter 4: Molasses and the Sticky Origins of the Fourth Amendment** for James Otis's arguments during the Boston writs case.

James Otis, arguing against the writs in the Council Chamber of the Old Town House, Boston, February 1761

3. Although the Declaration of Independence articulates Locke's language, he would not have understood its need. Locke assumed a constitutional system dominated by a parliament. Natural rights were not secure except within a well-governed legal order, and popular legislatures were most likely to strike the necessary balance between liberty and order. The problem for America, however, was that it was the English Parliament that was abusing colonial rights. Indeed, the indictment of *"the King"* in the Declaration was in many ways a fiction given parliamentary supremacy. *See* McAffee at 273–76 (for discussion of parliamentary supremacy issues).

Henry, made this a key issue. This, as well as his friendship and political alliance with Jefferson, propelled Madison to champion the Bill of Rights.[5]

The Ninth Amendment was Madison's answer to himself. Because he had objected to listing rights, he wrote the Ninth Amendment as a "catchall" to refute the argument that listing rights is dangerous to all the ones not listed.[6]

With the Ninth Amendment, Congress did not have to spend all its time listing every possible right. In a sense, it was an insurance policy (or perhaps an investment in the future) on rights not yet articulated.

In fact, Madison was happy that Congress did not have the chance to enumerate specific rights because he feared legislative power. Today we live in a world where the President of the United States is the single most powerful man on earth-the raw military might he has at his disposal would have made a Roman emperor blush.

---

4. Casazza at 1388. For more background on these writings of Locke and their influence on the Ninth Amendment's Framers, see Caplan at 230–38.

5. *See* **Prequel and Preamble: Did They Just Forget to Pay the Bill?**

Madison

Henry

Jefferson

6. Regarding Madison answering his own previous objections, *see* Levy at 247. This is what Madison stated in Congress: "*It has been objected also against a bill of rights, that, by enumerating particular exceptions to the grant of power, it would disparage those rights which were not placed in that enumeration; and it might follow, by implication, that those rights which were not singled out, were intended to be assigned into the hands of the General Government, and were consequently insecure. This is one of the most plausible arguments I have ever heard urged against the admission of a bill of rights unto this system; but, I conceive, that it may be guarded against. I have attempted it, as gentlemen may see by turning to the last clause of the fourth resolution.*" 1 Annals of Cong. 456 (1834), *quoted in* Norman Redlich, *Are There "Certain Rights . . . Retained by the People"?* 37 N.Y.U. L. Rev. 787, 805 (1962). *See also* Levy at 257–58.

Regarding the Ninth Amendment being a catchall to refute the "reserving rights is dangerous" theme, *see id.* at 249; Lash, *Textual Theory*, at 904. *See also* Dunbar (providing a detailed analysis of the legislative history and documents to show Madison's probable thinking on the Ninth Amendment). For a discussion of the Federalist and Anti-Federalist power struggle, *see* Kurt T. Lash, *The Original Meaning of an Omission: The Tenth Amendment, Popular Sovereignty, and "Expressly" Delegated Power*, 83 Notre Dame L. Rev. 1889, 1903–08 (2008).

Justice Story later wrote dismissively of the failure-to-list argument while at the same time recognizing the Ninth Amendment's role in clarifying the issue: "*In regard to another suggestion, that the affirmance of certain rights might disparage others, or might lead to argumentative implications in favor of other powers, it might be sufficient to say that such a course of reasoning could never be sustained upon any solid basis, and it could never furnish any just ground of objection that ingenuity might pervert or usurpation overleap the true sense. That objection will equally lie against all powers, whether large or limited, whether national or state, whether in a bill of rights or in a frame of government. But a conclusive answer is, that such an attempt may be interdicted (as it has been) by a positive declaration in such a bill of rights, that the enumeration of certain rights shall not be construed to deny or disparage others retained by the people.*" 2 Story on the Constitution 626, § 1867. *See also* Knowlton H. Kelsey, *The Ninth Amendment of the Federal Constitution*, 11 Ind. L.J. 309, 319 (1936) (citing Story).

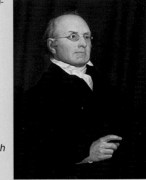

Madison, conversely, lived in a political culture that had just freed itself from the British Parliament; a system of government that even today sets policy through the legislative branch alone.[1] What the colonists fought against was unfettered parliamentary government. Indeed it was Parliament that eventually ended the Revolutionary War, not King George III.

Madison and others feared the unfettered power of a national legislative branch as the greatest threat to liberty and rights.[2] The Ninth Amendment was to be a check on its power.

TAKING THE NINTH AMENDMENT PERSONALLY

If the camp that says the Ninth Amendment pro-vides individual rights is correct, then it protects a whole number of very personal issues, including consensual sexuality.

The Supreme Court seems to be going in this direction in discussing a constitutional right of *"autonomy of self."*[3]

Thus the right to engage in sexual activities, which

---

1. The prime minister of Great Britain comes from the majority party in Parliament and takes over the executive branch (except when there is a coalition government). He selects and can dismiss other members of the cabinet, and allocates posts in the government, including the civil service. He is the actual head of the government, with the head of state, i.e., the monarch, holding a ceremonial position. The prime minister ensures the passage of bills in Parliament, is first lord of the treasury, and minister for the civil service, and can assume other posts. This governmental system worked itself out a generation before the American Revolution under Sir Robert Walpole. Walpole, Massachusetts, is named for him.

Sir Robert Walpole in 1740

2. Casazza at n.41 (discussing Madison's concern about the legislature and quoting him that *"the legislative [branch]. . . is the most powerful, and most likely to be abused, because it is under the least control. Hence, so far as a declaration of rights can tend to prevent the exercise of undue power, it cannot be doubted but such declaration is proper."*). 1 THE DEBATES AND PROCEEDINGS IN THE CONGRESS OF THE UNITED STATES 454 (J. Gales & W. Seaton eds., 1834) (speech of Rep. J. Madison)). Madison expressed similar concerns about the power of democratic majorities to abrogate individual rights.

- -

3. *Lawrence v. Texas,* 539 U.S. 558, 562 (2003) (*"Liberty presumes an autonomy of self that includes freedom of thought, belief, expression, and certain intimate conduct."*). John Locke, Thomas Jefferson, John Stuart Mill, and Justice Louis D. Brandeis's dissent in *Olmstead v. United States,* 277 U.S. 438 (1928), all provide the basis for this *"autonomy of self"* idea. *See* JOHN LOCKE, TWO TREATISES OF GOVERNMENT (Peter Laslett ed., Cambridge Univ. Press 1988) (1690); THOMAS JEFFERSON, THE DECLARATION OF INDEPENDENCE (U.S. 1776); JOHN STUART MILL, ON LIBERTY (Gertrude Himmelfarb ed., Penguin Books 1974) (1859). *See also* Kristin Fasullo, *Beyond Lawrence v. Texas: Crafting a Fundamental Right to Sexual Privacy,* 77 FORDHAM L. REV. 2997 (2009).

4. Madison on Getting High. *"I have received . . .a copy of your Lecture on Tobacco and ardent spirits. It is a powerful dissuasion from the pernicious use of such stimulants. . . . Its foreign translations and its reaching a fifth Edition are encouraging evidences of its usefulness; however much it be feared that the listlessness of non-labourers, and the fatigues of hard labourers, will continue to plead for the relief of intoxicating liquors, or exhilarating plants; one or other of which seem to have been in use in every age and country."* Letter from James Madison to Benjamin Waterhouse (June 22, 1822), *quoted in* Toll at 419 n.2.

James Madison

most Americans take for granted, is now finding judicial support. The argument is that the rights were always there, but the Framers found no need to write them down.[4]

If there is *"autonomy of self,"* how can there be a "war on drugs"?[5] For most of this country's history (until 1914), you could legally buy and ingest any drug you could get your hands on. Thus, in addition to our modern intoxicators of alcohol, tobacco, and caffeine, our great-grandfathers and grandmothers could also imbibe cocaine, cannabis, and opiates.[6] You could buy these substances alone or as ingredients of common over-the-counter medicines.[7]

Only during the early part of the twentieth century did Congress begin regulating, not prohibiting, drugs.[8] In fact, Prohibition in the Eighteenth Amendment (effective in 1920) applied only to alcohol and had nothing to do with the drugs we now spend considerable effort and treasure to eradicate.[9]

5. Toll at 448 (arguing that *"[a]ll laws that criminalize the use of drugs by adults violate the rights of liberty and autonomy of self and, as a result, are unconstitutional under the Ninth Amendment of the United States Constitution, as applied to the federal government, and the Privileges or Immunities Clause of the Fourteenth Amendment, as applied to the states"*). See also Barnett, *Today's Constitution*, at 432 (*"Is it really necessary to criminalize the sale and use of intoxicating substances, or is a 'drug-free' society better achieved in ways that do not infringe upon the liberties of the people—perhaps by the sort of education and social pressure that is currently being used so effectively to combat the use of nicotine in cigarettes and the abuse of alcohol."*).

6. When **Coca-Cola Was "The Real Thing"!** Until 1903 cocaine was the key ingredient in Coca-Cola. Toll at 427, *citing* DAVID F. MUSTO, THE AMERICAN DISEASE: ORIGINS OF NARCOTIC CONTROL 3 (1973). Cocaine comes from the coca leaf. Coca-Cola's other main stimulant, caffeine, comes from kola nuts. The Coca-Cola company replaced the "K" in Kola with a "C" for marketing reasons.

Coca-Cola was not the only company to use cocaine as an ingredient in a product during the nineteenth century. See Toll at 427–29.

A coca plant   The kola nut plant

7. Over-the-counter medicine for babies with colic contained opiates, and common cough suppressants contained heroin. Bayer Pharmaceutical Products introduced heroin in 1898, selling it over the counter before later marketing aspirin. Toll at 427 n.59, *citing* JAMES P. GRAY, WHY OUR DRUG LAWS HAVE FAILED AND WHAT WE CAN DO ABOUT IT 21 (2001).

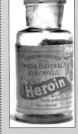 

8. *See* Toll at 427–29 (discussing the process by which many common drugs became illegal). For example, the 1937 Marihuana Tax Act did not outlaw pot per se but instead created registering and reporting requirements. The Marihuana Tax Act of 1937, Pub. L. No. 75-238, 50 Stat. 551 (1937) (repealed 1970).

9. THE EIGHTEENTH AMENDMENT

"Section 1. After one year from the ratification of this article the manufacture, sale, or transportation of intoxicating liquors within, the importation thereof into, or the exportation thereof from the United States and all territory subject to the jurisdiction thereof for beverage purposes is hereby prohibited.

Section 2. The Congress and the several States shall have concurrent power to enforce this article by appropriate legislation.

Section 3. This article shall be inoperative unless it shall have been ratified as an amendment to the Constitution by the legislatures of the several States, as provided in the Constitution, within seven years from the date of the submission hereof to the States by the Congress."

Prohibition was repealed in 1933.

Perhaps the Eighteenth Amendment recognized, before the Twenty-First Amendment repealed it,[1] that alcohol is the most destructive drug in society to lives, families, and productivity.[2]

THE NINTH AMENDMENT: A HAPPY FAILURE

The idea that natural rights would be the entire basis of a new nation was revolutionary.[3] The Ninth Amendment affirms that in a political order that assumes such rights, there is no need to list them.[4]

Thus the Ninth Amendment, as well as the Tenth, allows us to expand our understanding of how we exercise natural rights.[5]

But exercising modern rights creates a paradox: to get them—for example, the right to universal education at the public's expense—we need more

---

1. The Twenty-First Amendment (1933) is the only amendment that state conventions rather than state legislatures ratified and is also the only amendment explicitly repealing an *earlier* amendment:

"*Section 1. The eighteenth article of amendment to the Constitution of the United States is hereby repealed.*

Section 2. The transportation or importation into any State, Territory, or possession of the United States for delivery or use therein of intoxicating liquors, in violation of the laws thereof, is hereby prohibited.

Section 3. This article shall be inoperative unless it shall have been ratified as an amendment to the Constitution by conventions in the several States, as provided in the Constitution, within seven years from the date of the submission hereof to the States by the Congress."

---

2. Toll at 428.

John Locke's Approach to Rehab. "*The care therefore of every man's soul belongs unto himself, and is to be left unto himself. But what if he neglect the care of his soul? I answer, what if he neglect the care of his health, or of his estate; which things are nearlier related to the government of the magistrate than the other? Will the magistrate provide by an express law, that such an one shall not become poor or sick? Laws provide, as much as is possible, that the goods and health of subjects be not injured by the fraud or violence of others; they do not guard them from the negligence or ill husbandry of the possessors themselves. No man can be forced to be rich or healthful, whether he will or no.*" John Locke, *A Letter Concerning Toleration*, in Two Treatises of Government and A Letter Concerning Toleration 227–28 (Ian Shapiro ed., 2003), *quoted in* Toll at 421.

John Locke

3. Kaminski at 141.

---

4. *See* Daniel A. Farber, Retained by the People: The "Silent" Ninth Amendment and the Constitutional Rights Americans Don't Know They Have (2007) (arguing the Ninth Amendment is a better constitutional foundation for a wide variety of rights). There has been a historical trend, however, to list rights. Our American Bill of Rights recognizes twenty-seven rights explicitly. *Magna Carta* stated only six of those rights, or about 20 percent of what our Bill of Rights lists. Colonial documents before the 1689 English Bill of Rights listed twenty-one specific rights or about 75 percent of what our Bill of Rights provides. Using a catchall like the Ninth Amendment started a new trend, with states adding catchalls to their constitutions. Wiltshire at 98–99.

---

5. *See* Levy at 255; Lash, *Textual Theory*, at 908–10 (noting that the Framers allowed for new rights important to future generations).

---

6. For example, on January 8, 2002, Republican President George W. Bush signed into law the No Child Left Behind Act of 2001, Pub. L. No. 107-110 (2001). The law reauthorized many federal programs to improve student performance. It specifically increased accountability standards for states and local school districts.

Thus, for the modern right of a universal education, we want the federal government to encroach on state sovereignty, something the Founders did not desire. *See, e.g.*, *Houston v. Moore*, 18 U.S. (5 Wheat.) 1, 51 (1820) (Story, J., dissenting) ("*What is not taken away by the Constitution of the United States, must be considered as retained by the States or the people.*").

George W. Bush signing the No Child Left Behind Act

government, usually more national government.[6]

The Ninth Amendment was supposed to protect us from exactly what most of us want, such as:

• a Department of Housing and Urban Development to better our lives,

• a Department of Education to help raise up our children,

• an Environmental Protection Agency to clean up and protect our environment,[7] and

• a Food and Drug Administration to assure the safety of our food and medicine.[8]

Few of us want to go back to the "simpler" world of eighteenth century *laize faire*, where government has little or no role in the regulation of American life—besides, we couldn't anyway.[9]

7. Although Upton Sinclair intended his novel THE JUNGLE (1906) to expose the American meatpacking industry's corruption and abuse of workers during the early twentieth century, the public instead fixated on food safety as the novel's most pressing issue. His descriptions of workers falling into rendering tanks and being ground, along with animal parts gripped public attention. It led to the passage of the Meat Inspection Act and the Pure Food and Drug Act of 1906, which established the Food and Drug Administration.

Chicago meat inspectors (1906)

8. Rachel Carlson's SILENT SPRING (1962) was one of the most important books of the twentieth century and helped start the environmental movement by documenting the detrimental effects of pesticides, especially DDT. She also decried the chemical industry's disinformation and public officials' uncritical acceptance of industry claims.

9. The Camel's Nose in the Tent. The Constitution has other "catchalls" and some say that the use of these clauses through the years has eliminated the Framer's original goal of a limited government. The Necessary and Proper Clause (also known as the Elastic, Basket, Coefficient, or Sweeping Clause) states that Congress has the power "[t]o make all Laws which shall be necessary and proper for carrying into Execution the foregoing Powers, and all other Powers vested by this Constitution in the Government of the United States or in any Department or Officer thereof." U.S. CONST. art. 1, § 8, cl. 18.

So the national government has a lot of freedom to use methods to effect legitimate federal subjects. In *McCulloch v. Maryland*, Chief Justice John Marshall held that Maryland could not tax the Second Bank of the United States: "Let the end be legitimate, let it be within the scope of the constitution, and all means which are appropriate, which are plainly adapted to that end, which are not prohibited, but consist with the letter and spirit of the constitution, are constitutional." 17 U.S. at 421. The Necessary and Proper Clause thus trumps the Ninth and Tenth Amendments: "If granted power is found, necessarily the objection of invasion of those rights, reserved by the Ninth and Tenth Amendments, must fail." *United Public Workers of Am. (C.I.O.) v. Mitchell*, 330 U.S. 75, 96 (1947).

First Bank of the United States, in Philadelphia

For example, though controversial when first passed, even the most hard-core capitalist today does not whimper at the federal government's vast role in regulating markets through the Securities and Exchange Commission and the Federal Reserve Board. Modern markets need the regularity and confidence the federal government provides. Madison would roll over in his grave![1]

Certainly sincere thinkers question our modern market system and regulatory state, arguing that *"less government is better."* But very few of us are consistent in this belief.

Sure some of us may want less government regulation of the environment or drug products, but we do want plenty of regulation of other things, say, health care or more military spending. Others may want drugs

legalized with no federal law enforcement of drug laws, but they want bald eagles protected. And almost everyone in America cries *"Don't touch my social security!"*

We want the federal government to fight crime,[2] even though the Framers never intended the national government to have broad jurisdiction to enforce criminal laws.[3] But often the same political voices

---

1. Hamilton, however, from his grave, would applaud.

The first great fight between political parties was over economic regulation in the form of whether the country should have the First Bank of the United States. The Federalists squared up against the Democratic-Republicans. Hamilton, a Federalist, used the Necessary and Proper Clause in 1791 to defend the constitutionality of the First Bank of the United States.

Much of this dispute had to do with regional conflicts. Southern states were concerned that moneyed northerners would use the bank to exploit the South. Hamilton and Madison, the former colleagues in writing THE FEDERALIST PAPERS, were now at odds. Madison opposed

Madison

the bank, and Hamilton argued it was a reasonable means of carrying out powers related to taxation and the borrowing of funds. Hamilton had Madison's earlier FEDERALIST PAPERS read aloud in Congress to embarrass Madison. *See* Lash, *Original Tenth*, at 1927–34. For the account of Madison's speech on the Bank of the United States, see Lash, *Federalism*, at 844–48.

Eventually the South agreed to the bank when the deal included moving the national capital south to a swamp of the Potomac River, to what became Washington D.C. Since the New Deal, the courts have not entertained legal arguments against economic and social governmental action absent a specific constitutional prohibition. Redlich at 794–95. *See also* Lash, *Lost Jurisprudence*, at 597 (noting that *"[u]biquitously paired with the Tenth Amendment, the Ninth suffered the same fate as the Tenth at the time of the New Deal, when both were rendered mere 'truisms' in the face of expansive constructions of federal power"*). *See also* RICHARD BROOKHISER, WHAT WOULD THE FOUNDERS DO?: OUR QUESTIONS, THEIR ANSWERS 92 (2006) (noting the popularity of the Federal Reserve today).

Hamilton

Capitol Building, Washington D.C.

2. *"Don't shoot, G-Men; don't shoot, G-Men!"* So cried gangster Machine Gun Kelly with hands up when the Feds arrested him in 1933. At least that's the version from THE FBI STORY (WARNER BROTHERS 1959), starring Jimmy Stewart. After that every kid in America wanted to be a "G-Man."

Efrem Zimbalist Jr., in *The FBI* (ABC 1965-74)

Machine Gun Kelly

3. The Federal Kidnapping Statute. The General Welfare Clause and the Commerce Clause allow the federal government jurisdiction to prohibit criminal conduct, for example, the Federal Kidnapping Act (18 U.S.C. § 1201(a) (1) (2006)) criminalizes transporting a kidnapped person across state lines. Its enactment followed the abduction and murder of Charles Lindbergh's toddler son. It allows federal authorities to pursue kidnappers who cross a state border with their victim.

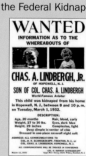

calling for *"less [federal] government in people's lives"* are the same ones calling for more government in people's lives in the form of prosecution for crimes.[4] And the federal government has grown exponentially.

Few in public life dare question the *"military-industrial complex,"* the entire existence of which is contrary to the Founder's belief that standing armies were the greatest danger to democracy. We spend trillions to maintain the best military in the world, all under a Constitution that the Founders intended would never support such an expense and expanse of government power.[5]

If the Ninth Amendment was about limiting government in peoples' lives, it failed. But to be honest, most of us are happy it failed. We want ever-expanding access to the rights and benefits of government.[6]

Because the federal government has increased its power and scope, diminishing the states at every turn, we as a nation can defend ourselves.

And not only more people, but a much higher percentage of *"the people,"* can read this page than ever before.

---

4. **The Mann Act, known as the White Slave Traffic Act** of 1910 (codified as amended at 18 U.S.C. §§ 2421–2424 (2006)) prohibited white slavery and banned the interstate transport of females for *"immoral purposes."* Named after lawmaker James Robert Mann, the statute was enacted to address prostitution, immorality, and human trafficking. Its original ambiguous language allowed selective prosecutions for many years.

The very term *"white slavery,"* for instance, referred to sexual slavery and did not necessarily have to do with the victim's race. The term distinguished it from the hereditary slavery imposed on black people.

Ironically, African-American heavyweight boxing champ Jack Johnson was the first person prosecuted under the act for having sex with a white prostitute named Lucille Cameron. Johnson married Cameron so that she could not testify against him. Another prostitute named Belle Schreiber, however, left a brothel and traveled with Johnson across state lines. Johnson received the maximum penalty of a year and a day in prison.

Johnson's life was the basis of the film THE GREAT WHITE HOPE (20th Century Fox 1970). *See also* GEOFFREY C. WARD, UNFORGIVABLE BLACKNESS: THE RISE AND FALL OF JACK JOHNSON (2004) and the subsequent Ken Burns documentary film *Unforgivable Blackness: The Rise and Fall of Jack Johnson* (PBS television, broadcast Jan. 17, 2005).

In 1910, former undefeated heavyweight champion James J. Jeffries came out of retirement and said *"I am going into this fight for the sole purpose of proving that a white man is better than a Negro."* Johnson beat Jeffries on July 4, 1910. Despite the charged racial atmosphere, Jeffries acknowledged that even in his prime he could not have defeated Johnson.

5. Charles Montesquieu's THE SPIRIT OF THE LAWS (1748) argued that republics could not survive unless they stayed small. Even in the eighteenth century America was huge.

Rome was the only large republic in antiquity that lasted. But this exception proved the rule when Julius Caesar took his legions and marched on Rome, destroying the republic.

Echoing the fears of the Framers, President Dwight D. Eisenhower, in his farewell address as president, warned the American people to fear the *"military-industrial complex,"* a phrase that refers to the relationships between governments, their armies, and industry. Thus the political approval for research, development,

President Eisenhower

production, use, and support for military training, weapons, equipment, and facilities within the national defense and security policy are all part of this military-industrial complex. The Framers' fear of standing armies was the foundation of the Second, Third, and arguably the Fourth Amendments.

Caesar crossing the Rubicon to become Rome's dictator

6. See Kaminski at 150 (*"Quite possibly, in a future marked by astonishing technological development, the ancient wisdom of the Ninth Amendment may protect as yet undefined rights from as yet uninvented dangers."*). In fact, breathing a bit of life into the Ninth Amendment would conform to Chief Justice Marshall's command that *"[i]t cannot be presumed that any clause in the Constitution is intended to be without effect; and therefore such a construction is inadmissible, unless the words require it." Marbury v. Madison,* 5 U.S. (1 Cranch) 137, 174 (1803). *But see* Kelsey at 323 (*"It must be a positive declaration of existing, though unnamed rights, which may be vindicated under the authority of the Amendment whenever and if ever any governmental authority shall aspire to ungranted power in contravention of 'unenumerated rights.'"*).

CHAPTER 10

"Are You Talkin' to Me?":

Just Who Are Those "*People*" in the Tenth Amendment?

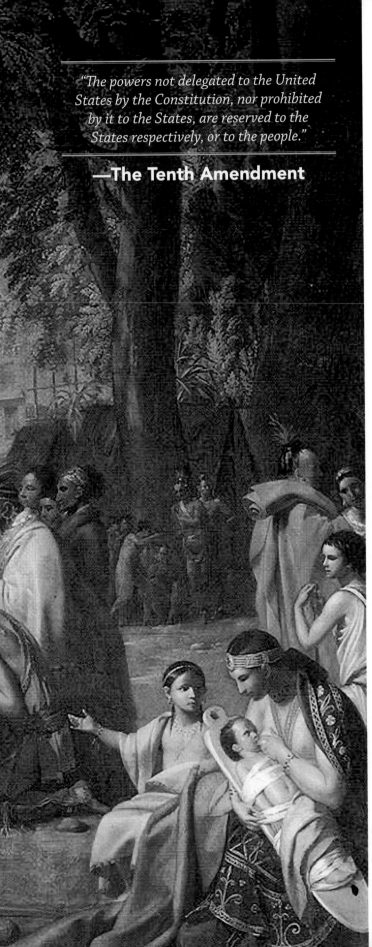

> "*The powers not delegated to the United States by the Constitution, nor prohibited by it to the States, are reserved to the States respectively, or to the people.*"

—The Tenth Amendment

"*We the People*" are the first words of the Constitution,[1] and if you include the Bill of Rights as part of the whole package, the Constitution's last words are the Tenth Amendment's "*the people.*"[2] So "*[w]e the people*" get to keep all our rights. But many of us would not have been "*the people*" in 1789—blacks, Native Americans, women, poor folk, etc.

The states defined "*the people.*" And the Tenth Amendment explicitly says that the states, not the federal government, keep all the power. "*The people*" were tacked on at the end like a nice-sounding afterthought or even an early version of political correctness.

1. *The preamble to the U.S. Constitution states:*
We the People of the United States, in Order to form a more perfect Union, establish justice, insure domestic Tranquility, provide for the common defense, promote the general Welfare, and secure the Blessings of Liberty to ourselves and our Posterity, do ordain and establish this Constitution for the United States of America.

2. "For this very purpose, one of the Constitutional Convention delegates, Mr. Carroll, proposed to add to the end of the proposition, *or to the people.* This was agreed to." 1 ANNALS OF CONG. 761 (Joseph Gales ed., 1834), *quoted in* Kurt T. Lash, *The Original Meaning of an Omission: The Tenth Amendment, Popular Sovereignty, and "Expressly" Delegated Power,* 83 NOTRE DAME L. REV. 1889, 1901 (2008). *See also* Charles F. Hobson, *The Tenth Amendment and the New Federalism of 1789, in* THE BILL OF RIGHTS: A LIVELY HERITAGE 162, 154 (Jon Kukla ed., 1987).

This is why the proponents of "states' rights" love the Tenth Amendment.[1] But as we saw in the last chapter, "states' rights" is not a practical way to run the national government that we love to complain about but really want.

Moreover, "states' rights" has often been synonymous with the power to block any expansion of who gets to be "*the people*"—from the early arguments against federal interference with

1. "States' rights" is the idea that the states have rights and powers over the federal government. The defenders of segregation used "states' rights" as their rallying cry. Alabama Governor **George Corley Wallace, Jr.** famously declared in his inaugural address, "*Segregation now! Segregation tomorrow! Segregation forever!*" He later claimed that he should have said, "*States' rights now! States' rights tomorrow! States' rights forever!*"

Wallace was reacting to the U.S. Supreme Court's decision in *Brown v. Board of Education,* 347 U.S. 483 (1954), which overruled *Plessy v. Ferguson*, 163 U.S. 537 (1896), to end segregated education.

The civil rights movement of the 1950s and 1960s led to the Civil Rights Act of 1964 (42 U.S.C. § 21 (2006)) and the Voting Rights Act of 1965 (42 U.S.C. §§ 1973–1973aa-6). In reaction, several states passed "interposition" resolutions declaring that *Brown* had usurped states' rights.

The first break in the power of the Democratic Party in the "solid South" after World War II occurred in 1948, when Hubert Humphrey of Minnesota told the Southern delegates to "*get out of the shadow of states' rights and walk forthrightly into the bright sunshine of human rights.*" ALFRED W. BLUMROSEN & RUTH G. BLUMROSEN, SLAVE NATION: HOW SLAVERY UNITED THE COLONIES & SPARKED THE AMERICAN REVOLUTION 252 (2005).

Hubert Humphrey at the 1948 Democratic Convention

Reagan assassination attempt

2. George Wallace (1919–98) was Alabama's governor for four terms (1963–67, 1971–79, and 1983–87). He ran for president three times as a Democrat and once as an American Independent but always as a segregationist, a conviction he later abandoned.

In 1972, while running for president, Arthur Bremer shot Wallace, leaving him paralyzed for life. Bremer's AN ASSASSIN'S DIARY (1973) inspired the movie TAXI DRIVER (Columbia Pictures 1976), which then inspired John Hinckley, Jr. to try to assassinate President Ronald Reagan in 1981.

Deputy U.S. Attorney General Nicholas Katzenbach confronts Wallace, standing against desegregation at the University of Alabama in 1963

slavery though the civil rights struggles of the 1950s and 1960s.[2]

Many of the Founders would roll over in their graves to think that *everyone* gets to be "*the people*."[3] But the Declaration of Independence articulated a foundation of individual rights that "*all men are created equal*."[4] The Ninth and Tenth Amendments continued this growing radical idea: rights are *universal*.[5]

3. James Madison in THE FEDERALIST No. 10 noted that in "*pure democracy*" nothing restrained the majority's "*passion or interest*" and that "*democracies have ever been spectacles of turbulence and contention; have ever been incompatible with personal security or the rights of property; and have in general been as short in their lives as they have been violent in their deaths.*" *Quoted in* RICHARD BROOKHISER, WHAT WOULD THE FOUNDERS DO?: OUR QUESTIONS, THEIR ANSWERS 121 (2006). Madison's one-time buddy Alexander Hamilton, in his last letter before getting mortally shot in a duel, wrote "*our real disease . . . is democracy.*" *Id.* at 121.

Morris

The Founder **Gouverneur Morris** at the Constitutional Convention warned that to "*[g]ive the votes to people who have no property, and they will sell them to the rich who will be able to buy them. . . . We should remember that the people never act from reason alone. The rich will take advantage of the passions and make these the instruments of oppressing them.*" *Quoted in id.* at 191.

5. In 1848, the modern women's suffrage movement began with the Seneca Falls Convention, which eventually lead to the Nineteenth Amendment seventy years later, in 1920, which reads:

"*The right of citizens of the United States to vote shall not be denied or abridged by the United States or by any State on account of sex.*

Congress shall have power to enforce this article by appropriate legislation."

The convention was at Seneca Falls, New York, and the Seneca were one of the original "five nations" of the Iroquois Confederacy. *See* below for a brief discussion of the Iroquois Confederacy. Seneca Falls Declaration of Sentiments, http://en.wikipedia.org/wiki/Seneca_Falls_Declaration_of_Sentiments (last visited Apr. 24, 2009).

Wyoming was the first state in the United States to recognize women's right to vote in 1869.

Wyoming state seal, with the motto "Equal Rights," referring to women's suffrage

Abigail Adams

4. Do Girls Get to Play? On March 31, 1776, Abigail Adams advised John "*in the new code of laws . . . , I desire you would remember the ladies, and be more generous and favourable to them than your ancestors . . . . If particular care and attention is not paid to the ladies, we are determined to foment a rebellion, and will not hold ourselves bound by any laws in which we have not voice, or representation.*" *Quoted in* BROOKHISER at 151. This sounds pretty much like "*No taxation without representation!*" *See generally* COKIE ROBERTS, FOUNDING MOTHERS: THE WOMEN WHO RAISED OUR NATION (2004); COKIE ROBERTS, LADIES OF LIBERTY: THE WOMEN WHO SHAPED OUR NATION (2009).

For an award-winning portrayal of Abigail Adams, *see* Laura Linney in the miniseries *John Adams* (HBO March 16 to April 20, 2008).

Perhaps Abigail and the other "Founding Mothers" could note that male grammarians have long written that "he" is gender neutral: "*The use of "he" as pronoun for nouns embracing both genders is a simple, practical convention rooted in the beginnings of the English language.*"

WILLIAM STRUNK, JR. & E.B. WHITE, THE ELEMENTS OF STYLE 60–61 (3rd ed. 1979). So "*all men are created equal*" means women too.

But despite Abigail's entreaties, it would be over one hundred years before women nationally got the right to vote, and over two hundred years before Geraldine Ferraro, in 1984, became the first female vice presidential candidate for a major American political party.

Thus, despite what the states said, everyone gets rights—even blacks, Native Americans, women, and poor folk.[1]

So here it is: when the Tenth Amendment declared in 1789 that the states keep all the power that the Constitution did not specifically give to the federal government, it *was* consistent with *"the people"* keeping their rights. That is because at the time those same states defined a bunch of white guys as *"the [only] people"* who counted.[2]

But when you start to have a broader and universal view of rights and define *"the people"* of the United States as everyone, regardless of what the states say, then there are going to be problems.

THE NINTH AND TENTH AMENDMENTS: TWO SIDES OF THE SAME COIN?

Why do we need the Tenth Amendment?

Not only do we have the whole Constitution saying that the federal government only gets some powers, the Ninth Amendment says *"the people"* keep every right not listed. Comparing the Ninth and Tenth Amendments, it is hard to see how the Tenth brings more to the table. Let's start with the Ninth:

The enumeration in the Constitution, of certain rights, shall not be construed to deny or disparage others retained by the people.

1. Even aliens without documentation are "the people." "Whatever his status under immigration laws, an alien is surely a 'person' in the ordinary sense of the term." *Plyler v. Doe*, 457 U.S. 202, 210 (1982). "Aliens, even aliens whose presence in this country is unlawful, have long been recognized as "persons" guaranteed due process of law by . . . the Fourteenth Amendment." *Plyler* at 210. *See also Zadvydas v. Davis*, 533 U.S. 678, 693 (2001) ("the Due Process Clause applies to all "persons' within the United States, including aliens, whether their presence here is lawful, unlawful, temporary, or permanent").

Such a view of "the people" does not sit well with some in the anti-immigrant crowd.

2. *Patrick Henry's "Give Me Liberty" Speech* by Peter F. Rothermel (1851), without a black, poor person, or Native American to be found! The only women are in the gallery swooning.

3. David M. Sprick, *Ex Abundanti Cautela (Out of the Abundance of Caution): A Historical Analysis of the Tenth Amendment and the Continuing Dilemma Over "Federal" Power*, 27 CAP. U. L. REV. 529, 536 (1999). Although what became the Tenth Amendment was the most frequently proposed of all the amendments, Hobson at 153, Madison regarded it as implied in the whole Constitution. *Id.* at 161. *See generally* Mark R. Killenbeck, *No Harm in Such a Declaration, in* THE TENTH AMENDMENT AND STATE SOVEREIGNTY 1 (Mark R. Killenbeck ed., 2002) (hereafter TENTH AMENDMENT).

John Marshall

4. *McCulloch v. Maryland*, 17 U.S. (4 Wheat.) 316, 363 (1819). This cuts against Marshall's famous dictum years earlier in *Marbury v. Madison* that "[i]t cannot be presumed that any clause in the constitution is intended to be without effect; and therefore such a construction is inadmissible, unless the words require it." 5 U.S. (1 Cranch) 137, 174 (1803).

Followed by the Tenth:

The powers not delegated to the United States by the Constitution, nor prohibited by it to the States, are reserved to the States respectively, or to the people.

James Madison, in fact, thought the Tenth Amendment "*unnecessary*" and "*superfluous*."[3] Could it be that the Framers just put the Tenth Amendment in the Bill of Rights without it having anything more than a symbolic meaning?

The answer is yes, and not only Madison thought so. John Marshall, who was part of the Virginia ratifying convention, wrote in *McCulloch v. Maryland* that

"*[w]e admit, that the 10th amendment to the constitution is merely declaratory; that it was adopted* ex abundanti cautela [*"out of an abundance of caution"*]; *and that with it, nothing more is reserved, than would have been reserved without it.*"[4]

The Supreme Court has generally followed this view.[5]

Despite the history that the Tenth Amendment was a slogan, or as Marshall wrote "*is merely declaratory,*" courts and academics have worked out a formula to explain it: *the Ninth Amendment is about rights while the Tenth Amendment is about powers.*[6]

The idea is that the Ninth Amendment reserves to the people all rights not listed, while the Tenth Amendment reserves the people's power over government.[7]

Justice Joseph Story wrote that the Tenth Amendment is not a rule of law but that "*[t]his amendment is a mere affirmation of what, upon any just reasoning, is a necessary rule of interpreting the constitution.*" Joseph Story, Commentaries on the Constitution of the United States 711–12 (Carolina Academic Press 1987) (1833).

Thus the Tenth Amendment cannot settle a case and instead stands as a mere reminder that federal action must be grounded in enumerated powers or implied as necessary to execute those powers.

Story foresaw the strategy of future "states' rights" advocates, like John C. Calhoun, who would try to use parts of the Constitution, such as the Tenth Amendment, to protect slavery. See Sprick at 536–38. "*Stripped of the ingenious disguises in which they are clothed, they are neither more nor less than attempts to foist into the text the word 'expressly;' to qualify, what is general, and obscure, what is clear, and defined.*" Story at 712–13, quoted in Sprick at 537–38.

6. Kurt Lash, *The Lost Original Meaning of the Ninth Amendment*, 83 Tex. L. Rev. 331 (2004). See Knowlton H. Kelsey, *The Ninth Amendment of the Federal Constitution*, 11 Ind. L.J. 310, 310 (1936) ("*When the two provisions are laid beside each other, it becomes evident that there was some distinction in the minds of the framers of those amendments between declarations of right and limitations on or prohibitions of power.*"); Hobson at 153 (noting that the Tenth Amendment does not guarantee rights of individuals but the distribution of powers between the United States and the people of the states). See also Kurt Lash, *A Textual-Historical Theory of the Ninth Amendment*, 60 Stan. L. Rev. 895, 895 (2008) (arguing that though both the Ninth and Tenth Amendments refer to "*the people,*" contemporary scholars and courts have given them opposite meanings, with the Ninth referring to a single national people and the Tenth referring to the people the several states).

7. Lash, *Textual Theory*, at 920–21 (noting that "*the Ninth Amendment is about rights while the Tenth Amendment is about powers.*"). The "*Tenth limits the federal government to only enumerated powers. The Ninth limits the interpretation of enumerated powers. Both provisions are necessary if federal power is to be effectively constrained.*" Id. at 920. See also Eugene M. Van Loan III, *Natural Rights and the Ninth Amendment*, 48 B.U. L. Rev. 1, 16 (1968) ("*The tenth amendment was viewed essentially as a limit on federal power vis-à-vis the states and the ninth as a limit on federal power vis-à-vis the rights of the people.*"); Norman Redlich, *Are There "Certain Rights . . . Retained by the People"?* 37 N.Y.U. L. Rev. 787, 807–08 (1962) (noting that the Ninth and Tenth Amendments were to limit the power of the federal government because most people at the time of the Founding viewed the states as the protectors of their individual rights). See also Randy E. Barnett, *Reconceiving the Ninth Amendment*, 74 Cornell L. Rev. 1 (1988).

---

5. See United States v. Sprague, 282 U.S. 716 (1931) (the Tenth Amendment "*added nothing to the [Constitution] as originally ratified*"); United States v. Darby, 312 U.S. 100, 124 (1941) ("*The amendment states but a truism that all is retained which has not been surrendered. There is nothing in the history of its adoption to suggest that it was more than declaratory of the relationship between the national and state governments . . . or that its purpose was other than to allay fears that the new national government might seek to exercise powers not granted . . . .*"). See generally William E. Leuchtenburg, *The Tenth Amendment over Two Centuries: More than a Truism*, in Tenth Amendment at 41.

You have to question how these Ninth and Tenth Amendment definitions really matter today. Although Madison stated that the Tenth was *"superfluous,"* history does provide a reason for the distinction between expanding rights as opposed to explicitly limiting government power.[1]

It comes down to who had the power first. At least one interpretation is that *"the step from the Ninth to the Tenth Amendment is one from constitutional monarchy to constitutional democracy."*[2]

A HISTORY OF RIGHTS AND POWERS

No one in 1215 challenged the legitimacy of royal power.[3] For all those assembled at Runnymede it had always been this way and would be for centuries. Although England's barons asserted their rights, *Magna Carta* only *implied* limits on the king.

The sovereign retained all power unless expressly delegated. (Note the word "expressly"; it will come up

again.)[4] This was part of feudalism, where the king was the ultimate landlord renting rights to land in exchange for military service.

It took over four centuries, not until the late 1600s, for a discussion of the king's power to start. The 1600s, in fact, started with King James I lecturing *his* Parliament that

"[t]he state of monarchy is the supremest thing upon earth; for kings are not only God's lieutenants up on earth, and sit upon God's throne,

---

1. Giving the Modern Tenth Amendment Some Scope. Only a few modern cases have used the Tenth Amendment to declare a law unconstitutional when the federal government compels states to enforce federal statutes.

In *New York v. United States*, 505 U.S. 144 (1992), the Supreme Court invalidated a portion of the Low-Level Radioactive Waste Policy Amendments Act of 1985 that obliged states to take title to any waste within their borders not disposed of before January 1, 1996, making each state liable for all damages directly related to the waste. Congress, ruled the Court, cannot directly compel states to enforce federal regulations.

In *Printz v. United States,* 521 U.S. 898 (1997), the Supreme Court held that the Brady Handgun Violence Prevention Act violated the Tenth Amendment because the act required state and local law enforcement officials to conduct background checks on persons attempting to purchase handguns.

2. Steve Bachmann, *Starting Again with the Mayflower . . . England's Civil War and America's Bill of Rights*, 20 QUINNIPIAC L. REV. 193, 260 (2001).

3. *Magna Carta* of 1215.

King John signing Magna Carta

4. *See* Lash, *Original Tenth*, at 1908 (discussing EMMERICH DE VATTEL, THE LAW OF NATIONS (Charles G. Fenwick trans., Carnegie Inst. of Wash. 1916) (1758)). Vattel explained that kings retained all powers not expressly delegated, with delegations of power strictly construed.

Vattel and the title page to THE LAW OF NATIONS (1758)

St. George Tucker in 1803 harnessed Vattel's reasoning to the concept of *"popular sovereignty,"* where *"the people"* not the king, were sovereign. ST. GEORGE TUCKER, VIEW OF THE CONSTITUTION OF THE UNITED STATES, *in* 1 BLACKSTONE'S COMMENTARIES app. 140 (St. George Tucker ed., Phila., William Birch Young & Abraham Small 1803). Thus the people in the states retained all power and jurisdiction not *"expressly delegated"* to the federal government, which was nothing more than the people's agent. The power of the federal government for Tucker was nothing more than a portion of state sovereignty that they delegated to it. Lash, *Original Tenth*, at 1910. For Tucker, following Vattel, Article II of the Articles of Confederation, which was the origin of the Tenth Amendment, was simply *"a declaration of the law of nations."*

St. George Tucker

An early seventeenth century Parliament with James I presiding

but even by God himself they are called gods . . . Kings are justly called god, for that they exercise a manner or resemblance of divine power on earth, for if you will consider the attributes to God, you shall see how they agree in the person of a king . . . ."[5]

How do you start a conversation with a guy like that?

The answer is you don't.[6] James was arguing—and arguing hard—for divine right of kings as the source of government and power. But he was arguing something that King John in 1215 would never have felt compelled to defend. Thus even in James's day a different sense of power and government was emerging, which James felt the need to explicitly condemn.

In the 1640s these populist ideas erupted under James's son, Charles I, who lost his head upon the altar of the divine right of kings.[7]

The populist leaders of seventeenth century England were called Levellers because they wanted to "level" society by making it more equal.[8] In 1647 one Leveller declared that

"all people and all nations whatsoever have a liberty and power to alter and change their constitutions, if they find them to be weak and infirm. Now if the people of England shall find this weakness in their constitution, they may change it if they please."[9]

---

5. Bachmann at 261 (citing The Canons of 1666 (1666), *in* THE STUART CONSTITUTION 1603–1688 DOCUMENTS AND COMMENTARY 11–12 (J.P. Kenyon ed., 1966)). James's lecture went on: *"God hath power to create or destroy, make or unmake at his pleasure: to give life or send death, to judge all and to be judged not accountable to none: to raise low things and to make high things low at his pleasure: and*

James I in 1620

6. As we saw in **Chapter 6: How the Sixth Amendment Guarantees You a Court, a Lawyer, and a Chamber Pot,** it was a famous conversation between King James I and **Sir Edward Coke**, chief justice of the King's Bench, that got Coke in a lot of trouble.

to God are both soul and body due. And the like power have kings: they make and unmake subjects: they have power of raising, and casting down: of life, and of death, judges over all their subjects, and in all causes and yet accountable to none but God only." Id.

7. Charles I losing his head in 1649.

8. The Levellers were a political movement rather than a party. During the English Civil Wars they advanced a disorganized agenda for popular sovereignty and argued for extended suffrage, equality before the law, and religious tolerance. Their manifesto, THE AGREEMENT OF THE PEOPLE, articulated these core beliefs. Levellers were the largest Parliamentary faction during the English Civil Wars. Their strongest support was in some regiments of the New Model Army and in London, where they had national offices in various inns and taverns. Cromwell marginalized the Levellers, and by 1650 they no longer had a serious voice in events.

9. *Quoted in* Bachmann at 262, *citing* G. AYLMER, THE LEVELLERS IN THE ENGLISH REVOLUTION 120 (1975).

On January 4, 1649, the so-called Rump Parliament resolved,

"that the Commons of England, in Parliament assembled, do declare, That the people are, under God, the original of all just power . . . ."[1]

In the seventeenth century, this was as far as populist rights and powers went.[2] The army's Levellers and Independents could not agree on who should vote in their new republic, with the Levellers pushing for a general franchise and the Independents for a franchise of those with property.

Oliver Cromwell eventually took over as England's dictator and quelled populism, famously putting John Lilburne on trial in 1649.[3]

But despite this setback, as well as the restored monarchy of Charles II and James II, the mid- to late seventeenth century witnessed an important change in the progression of the concept of rights and powers. The Framers wrote this into our Tenth Amendment.

The discussion was not about having a king recognize people's traditional rights (the modern equivalent of the Ninth Amendment's statement that rights are *"retained by the people"*). Rather, the people are the source of rights and can thus change their government, as in the Tenth Amendment's statement that all *"powers"*

---

1. *Quoted in* Bachmann at 262, *citing* Cannons Resolutions (Jan. 4, 1649), *in* THE STUART CONSTITUTION at 324.

It was called the Rump Parliament in reference to the hind end of an animal or what remains after the front parts are taken. In 1648, both Levellers and Independents in the army claimed that ultimate political sovereignty resided in the people and that Charles I had to go. When the Presbyterians in Parliament balked, the other members kicked them out, leaving only the remaining, or the rump, to decide King Charles's fate and run the country. It functioned, more or less, until Oliver Cromwell dismissed it in 1653.

Cromwell dismissing the Rump Parliament in 1653

2. *See* Bachmann at 262.

----

3. *See* **Chapter 6: How the Sixth Amendment Guarantees You a Court, a Lawyer, and a Chamber Pot** and **Chapter 7: Trial by Jury or . . . by God!** for more on John Lilburne.

John Lilburne

4. Bachmann at 263, *quoting* MILTON VIORST, THE GREAT DOCUMENTS OF WESTERN CIVILIZATION 124 (1965).

Thomas Rainsborough

5. In 1647, the Leveller leader Colonel Rainsborough remarked: *"I do not find anything in the Law of God, that a lord shall choose twenty burgesses, and a gentleman but two, or a poor man shall choose none . . . ."* Quoted in Bachmann at 264, *citing* The Putney Debates (Oct. 28–29, 1647), *in* THE STUART CONSTITUTION at 314.

The **Putney Debates** were discussions in 1647 between the Levellers in the New Model Army and others regarding the new constitution and who should have the right to vote.

----

6. You can still see this today in the caption of criminal cases in state courts as "People," "Commonwealth," or "State" vs. John Doe," as the film title THE PEOPLE VS. LARRY FLYNT (Columbia Pictures 1996) demonstrates.

----

7. The **Civil Rights Act of 1964** and the **Voting Rights Act of 1965** outlawed discriminatory voting practices, including literacy tests, that caused widespread African American disenfranchisement.

ultimately belong "*to the people.*"

At the very end of the seventeenth century, Parliament got rid of James II and brought in William and Mary as co-monarchs under the express agreement that they agree to a constitutional monarchy and to the DECLARATION OF RIGHTS and the ENGLISH BILL OF RIGHTS OF 1689. Parliament—"*the lords spiritual and temporal, and commons . . . lawfully, fully, and freely representing all the estates of the people of this realm*"—now had the power in England.[4]

But as with the early United States, this definition of "Parliament" did not expand the right to vote to everyone.[5]

One hundred years later, in 1789, the Tenth Amendment affirmed the ideal that "*the people*" had that ultimate sovereignty and power.[6] Maybe the ideal did not fully arrive until Congress passed the Voting Rights Act of 1965.[7] Or we could argue it will not arrive without campaign finance reform.[8] But no one debates that "*the people*" are the source of power and legitimacy.

The Framers wrote the American Constitution to recognize that "*the people*" had that power. Not only did they articulate and define rights, but they created an entire system of government to give them effect.

This is what we call "federalism."

Lyndon B. Johnson signs the Civil Rights Act of 1964, with Martin Luther King, Jr., behind him

Senator Benjamin Tillman positioned himself as a populist with the nickname of Pitchfork Ben. The ugly side of his South Carolina populism was his racism. Upon hearing that Booker T. Washington had dined at the White House with President Theodore Roosevelt, Tillman declared that "*[t]he action of President Roosevelt in entertaining that nigger will necessitate our killing a thousand niggers in the South before they will learn their place again.*" Quoted in JOHN D. WEAVER, THE SENATOR AND THE SHARECROPPER'S SON: EXONERATION OF THE BROWNSVILLE SOLDIERS 90–91 (1997).

8. In 1905, President Theodore Roosevelt argued for campaign finance reform to ban corporate contributions in politics. In 1907, Congress passed the Tillman Act, named for Senator Benjamin Tillman, which barred corporate contributions in political campaigns. Other acts followed. In 1971, Congress consolidated these laws into the Federal Election Campaign Act, with its more stringent disclosure requirements for federal candidates, political parties, and political action committees. This law also provided for financing of presidential general elections and national party conventions. In 1976, the Supreme Court struck down or narrowed several aspects of campaign finance reform by ruling that spending money to influence elections is protected "free speech" and there can be no limit on what a candidate wants to spend of his own money. *Buckley v. Valeo*, 424 U.S. 1 (1976). As mentioned in **Chapter 1: Of Dogma and Desire: Saying What You Believe about the First Amendment**, attempts at reform continue, including the Bipartisan Campaign Reform Act of 2002, known as the McCain-Feingold Act, named after sponsors Senator Russell Feingold (D–Wis.) and John McCain (R–Ariz.).

Theodore Roosevelt

THE TENTH AMENDMENT AND FEDERALISM

The Tenth Amendment came after Article of Confederation II, which stated:

[E]ach state retains its sovereignty, freedom and independence, and every Power, Jurisdiction and right, which is not by this confederation expressly delegated to the United States, in Congress assembled.[1]

That word "expressly" was a big deal because the Framers *expressly* left it out of the Tenth Amendment.[2] This was because

"[t]he men who drew and adopted this amendment had experienced the embarrassments resulting from the insertion of this word [expressly] in the articles of confederation, and probably omitted it, to avoid those embarrassments."[3]

It was an embarrassment because the Articles of Confederation could not provide a true national government.

Following the Revolution, each of the former colonies became an independent, sovereign nation. On March 1, 1781, these

---

1. *Quoted in* Hobson at 154 (emphasis added). *See also* Jack N. Rakove, *American Federalism: Was There an Original Understanding?* in Tenth Amendment at 107.

2. Thomas Tucker of South Carolina and Elbridge Gerry of Massachusetts tried to insert the word "expressly" before the word "delegated," but Madison opposed them *"because it was impossible to confine a Government to the exercise of express powers; there must necessarily be powers by implication, unless the Constitution descended to recount every minutiae."* O. John Rogge, *Unenumerated Rights*, 47 Cal. L. Rev. 787, 792 (1959), *citing* 1 Annals of Congress 790 (Aug. 18, 1789). Madison had argued the same point in The Federalist No. 44:
"Had the convention [followed the] method of adopting the second article of Confederation, it is evident that the new Congress would be continually exposed, as their predecessors have been, to the alternative of construing the term "expressly" with so much rigor as to disarm the government of all real authority whatever, or with so much latitude as to destroy altogether the force of the restriction."
The Federalist No. 44 (James Madison). *See also* Rogge at 793–94.

3. *McCulloch*, 17 U.S. at 406–07. Marshall ruled that the federal government had significant implied, as well as expressly delegated, powers: *"Let the end be legitimate, let it be within the scope of the constitution, and all means which are appropriate, which are plainly adapted to that end, which are not prohibited, but consist with the letter and spirit of the constitution, are constitutional." Id.* at 421. *See* Rogge at 795. *See also* Lash, *Original Tenth*, at 1900–01. But before Marshall's 1801 Supreme Court appointment, the Court ruled through Justice Samuel Chase that *"the several State Legislatures retain all the powers of legislation, delegated to them by the State Constitutions; which are not expressly taken away by the Constitution of the United States." Calder v. Bull*, 3 U.S. (3 Dall.) 386, 387 (1798) (emphasis added), *quoted in* Lash, *Original Tenth*, at 1893 (arguing that Marshall wrongly read the Tenth Amendment).

4. Hobson at 154. *Compare* U.S. Const. pmbl. (*"We the People of the United States . . . do ordain and establish this Constitution for the United States of America."*), with Articles of Confederation art. III (*"The said States hereby severally enter into a firm league of friendship with each other . . ."*).

Justice Brandeis

5. That clause reads: *"The Congress shall have Power . . . [t]o make all Laws which shall be necessary and proper for carrying into Execution the foregoing Powers, and all other Powers vested by this Constitution in the Government of the United States, or in any Department or Officer thereof."* U.S. Const. art. I, § 8, cl. 18.
Justice Louis Brandeis actually coined the label "Necessary and Proper Clause" in *Lambert v. Yellowley*, 272 U.S. 581 (1926) (ruling that a law restricting medicinal use of alcohol was a necessary and proper exercise of power under the Eighteenth Amendment (i.e., Prohibition)).
The Necessary and Proper Clause is also known as the Elastic Clause, the Basket Clause, the Coefficient Clause, and the Sweeping Clause, all of which show the concern about the necessary and proper clause's scope.

6. **Dancing around Federalism.** So with all these limitations on federal power, how does the federal government do it? How does it have the reach and scope in our lives that it does today? The easy answer, as stated in the last chapter, is we want it to!
In addition to the Necessary and Proper Clause, the Constitution allows for the exercise of federal government power through the following mechanisms:
The Commerce Clause. Article I, Section 8, specifically delegates to Congress the power to regulate commerce. As "commerce" has increased so has the federal government's scope. The twentieth century's complex economic challenges of the Great Depression and World War II redirected both Congress and the Supreme Court toward using the Commerce Clause powers to maintain a strong

individual states entered *"a firm league of friendship"* to address matters of national importance under the Articles of Confederation. The government of these articles was only the instrument of the states to effect military and diplomatic goals. It lacked both an executive and judiciary. Unlike the Constitution, the Articles of Confederation existed by agreement of the sovereign states, not directly from *"the people."*[4]

Getting rid of "expressly" allowed for the gradual increase in the power and scope of the federal government. This happened through other parts of the Constitution, such as the Necessary and Proper Clause,[5] as well as other modern mechanisms and ways to read the Constitution.[6]

What the Tenth Amendment did was restate federalism.[7] In American federalism, the central government shares power with the states. Power is also divided among the three branches of the federal government: legislative, executive, and judiciary.[8]

Many of the Founders never thought it would work.

national economy. *See, e.g., Wickard v. Filburn*, 317 U.S. 111 (1942) (during World War II, the Court ruled that federal regulations of wheat production could constitutionally apply to even *"home-grown"* wheat); *Garcia v. San Antonio Metro. Transit Auth.*, 469 U.S. 528 (1985) (upholding the Federal Labor Standards Act's overtime and minimum wage requirements). In *Gonzales v. Raich*, 545 U.S. 1 (2005), the Court upheld federal marijuana laws, turning away a California woman's lawsuit against the Drug Enforcement Administration after it destroyed her medical marijuana crop. The Supreme Court reasoned that growing one's own marijuana *affects* the interstate market of marijuana. The first modern case to limit the Commerce Clause was *United States v. Lopez*, 514 U.S. 549 (1995) (striking down a federal law mandating a *"gun-free zone"* around public schools for lack of a constitutional clause authorizing it). *Lopez*, however, did not mention the Tenth Amendment.

Federal Funding. Although federalism limits the federal government from requiring state governments to act, *see Printz*, Congress can encourage states to do so voluntarily. This allows federal resources to reach local officials closer to local problems. Also it limits the growth of the national bureaucracy. Thus Congress often seeks to exercise its powers by encouraging states to implement national programs with minimum standards. This is known as "cooperative federalism." For example, a state may not accept federal educational funds unless it implements specified education programs. Another example is that states lose federal highway funding if they did not adopt the .08 legal blood alcohol limit and the nationwide twenty-one-year-old drinking age. *See, e.g. South Dakota v. Dole*, 483 U.S. 203 (1987).

7. The word "federal" comes from Latin *"foedus,"* meaning faith, underscoring the bonds between the states despite the fact they retained sovereignty. This is also the origin of the name Fido for a dog, from the Latin for *"I am faithful."*

Jan van Eyck, in his famous *Arnolfini Portrait* (1434), included the pet dog as a symbol of the couple's fidelity

8. Hobson at 155. As Madison explained in THE FEDERALIST No. 39: *"[T]he proposed Constitution, therefore, even when tested by the rules laid down by its antagonists, is, in strictness, neither a national nor a federal Constitution, but a composition of both."* In THE FEDERALIST No. 51 Madison continues: *"In the compound republic of America, the power surrendered by the people is first divided between two distinct governments, and then the portion allotted to each subdivided among distinct and separate departments. Hence a double security arises to the rights of the people. The different governments will control each other, at the same time that each will be controlled by itself."*

Article I, Sections 1 through 7 of the Constitution established federalism by defining the organization of Congress and its function. Section 8 details the positive powers of Congress, and Section 9 enumerates prohibitions. Section 10 lists actions the states cannot take.

A 55 mph speed limit sign erected in response to the National Maximum Speed Law of 1974

Luther Martin, a delegate from Maryland, complained that the new government was unprecedented from

"anything in the history of mankind or in the sentiments of those who have favoured the world with their ideas on government, to warrant or countenance the motley mixture of a system proposed: a system which is an innovation in government of the most extraordinary kind; a system neither wholly federal, nor wholly national— *but a strange hotch-potch of both."*[1]

Governor William Grayson of Virginia declared *"absurd"* what he called the Constitution's *"imperium in imperio"* ("sovereignty within sovereignty").[2]

But others such as James Wilson of Pennsylvania noted that *"the people"* could contract out their sovereignty as they saw fit.[3] For his part, Madison noted the national government's role in protecting the rights of minorities from state majority *"factions."*[4]

And federalism as a division of power was not wholly without precedent in English history. The relationship between the Catholic Church and the English kings reflected a similar concept of division of power and jurisdiction.[5]

But the idea of a federal system of government may have had roots other than

---

1. *Quoted in* Hobson at 155.

2. *Quoted in* Hobson at 157. The term *"imperium in imperio"* referred to the position of the Catholic Church in England before Henry VIII.

3. Hobson at 159.

4. According to Madison, the smallness of state government made it easy for factions (parties) to gain control. Hobson at 159. On the advantages of the national government and *"factions,"* see The Federalist No. 10 where Madison states: *"Extend the sphere, and you take in a greater variety of parties and interests; you make it less probable that a majority of the whole will have a common motive to invade the rights of other citizens."*

   History proved Madison wrong. The national government did not eliminate factions at all; they just got bigger and are now called the Republican and

Democratic Parties. Every four years these factions throw a big party called the Party Convention, involving copious amounts of alcohol and balloons. Almost incidentally to the balloons, they also select (or actually confirm from the primaries) who will run for president.

5. *See* **Chapter 1: Of Dogma and Desire: Saying What You Believe about the First Amendment.**

6. The **Iroquois Confederacy** (or *"Haudenosaunee,"* the "League of Peace and Power," the "Five Nations," the "Six Nations," or the "People of the Longhouse") originally were a confederation of the Mohawk, Oneida, Onondaga, Cayuga, and the Seneca. Later the Tuscarora joined.

   The best known of the tribes is the Mohawks because of James Fenimore Cooper's books and various movies, including the epic The Last of the Mohicans.

   The Mohawks are famous for the haircut of the same name.

Mohawk leader Joseph Bryan (left), with scalp lock in 1806, and the modern stylized punk mohawk (right)

7. *See, e.g.,* **William Penn's 1682 Treaty with the Lenape (Delaware) Indians** by Benjamin West (1771).

Image of a *wampum* belt presented to William Penn at the Great Treaty ceremony in 1682

the old power struggles between church and kings. The Native American Iroquois Confederacy may have influenced it as well.[6]

Although the congressional record does not directly refer to Native American governments as an influence, colonial America by the time of the Revolution had had centuries of contact with Native Americans and their governments.[7] Benjamin Franklin, for one, had

considerable contact with Iroquois government.[8]

COURTS AS UMPIRES OF FEDERALISM AND SEPARATE POWERS

Not only did the new Constitution create our system offederalism, it created its own arbitrators: the federal courts.

The Articles of Confederation allowed for no federal trial courts in America.[9] The Constitution provided for

the first federal judiciary,[10] which did not sit well with many of the Founders, including Patrick Henry:

"I see arising out of [the Constitution], a tribunal, that is to be recurred to in all cases, when the destruction of the State Judiciaries shall happen; and from the extensive jurisdiction of these paramount Courts, the State Courts must soon be annihilated."[11]

The Bell Helicopter **UH-1 Iroquois** (known as the **"Huey"**) was famous during the Vietnam War. It figured prominently in Apocalypse Now (United Artists 1979) and the reworked Apocalypse Now Redux (Miramax Films 2001).

The Iroquois Confederacy flag is a *wampum* belt design

8. In 2004, the U.S. government acknowledged the influence of the Iroquois constitution on the U.S. Constitution. The Iroquois constitution, called the Great Law of Peace, guaranteed freedom of religion and expression. It also had a two-house legislature and a federalist government, dividing jurisdiction and power between the tribes and the confederacy, or as we would say, the states and the national government. The Great Law provided for a commander-in-chief who should present a "state of the union." The Iroquois created their constitution between 1000 and 1400 AD by the record of belts called "*wampum*" (see the Iroquois flag). Franklin, as Pennsylvania's official printer, printed the Iroquois minutes of meetings. See Kathryn McConnell, *Iroquois Constitution Influenced That of U.S., Historians Say,* http://www.america.gov/st/washfile-english/2004/September/20040924120101AKllennoCcM9.930056e-02.html (last visited Apr. 23, 2009). A copy of the Iroquois constitution is available at http://www.indigenouspeople.net/iroqcon.htm. (last visited June 8, 2010).

9. Robert L. Jones, *Finishing a Friendly Argument: The Jury and the Historical Origins of Diversity Jurisdiction,* 82 N.Y.U. L. Rev. 997, 1001 (2007) (noting that only for admiralty cases did a national court exist: the Court of Appeals in Cases of Capture). *See also* John Choon Yoo, *Federalism and Judicial Review, in* Tenth Amendment at 131.

10. "*The judicial Power of the United States, shall be vested in one supreme Court, and in such inferior Courts as the Congress may from time to time ordain and establish. The Judges, both of the supreme and inferior Courts, shall hold their Offices during good Behaviour, and shall, at stated Times, receive for their Services a Compensation, which shall not be diminished during their Continuance in Office.*"U.S. Const. art. III, § 1.

11. *Quoted in* Jones at 1001 n. 12 (Patrick Henry at the Virginia ratifying convention). Before that, at the Constitutional Convention,

delegate Pierce Butler of South Carolina cautioned that the people would not accept "*such innovations*" as lower federal courts and their creation would cause states to "*revolt.*" John Rutledge of South Carolina criticized inferior federal courts as an "*unnecessary encroachmenton the jurisdiction [of the States].*" *Quoted in id.* at 1001 n.11.

Henry was wrong; state courts were not *"annihilated."* The Constitution leaves power to the states, including the state courts. But on drawing the line between state and federal courts, and on what the Constitution means, the federal courts call the shots.

As Alexander Hamilton explained in THE FEDERALIST No. 80, the U.S. Supreme Court in particular had to hear appeals from the states because

"[t]hirteen independent courts of final jurisdiction over the same causes, arising upon the same laws, is a hydra[1] in government from which nothing but contradiction and confusion can proceed."[2]

Henry's countryman (i.e., his fellow Virginian), John Marshall, defined the issue in *McCulloch v. Maryland:*

[T]he question, whether the particular power which may become the subject of contest, has been delegated to the one government, or prohibited to the other, . . . depend[s] on a fair construction of the whole instrument.

And the Supreme Court is the institution that "constructs" the *"whole instrument"* (i.e., the Constitution). It decides where the Constitution allows the federal government to act:

"Let the end be legitimate, let it be within the scope of the constitution, and all means which are appropriate, which are plainly adapted to that end, which are not prohibited, but consist with the letter and spirit of the constitution, are constitutional."[3]

In *McCulloch,* Maryland wanted to tax the Second Bank of the United States.[4] John Marshall's ruling established that a state could not hinder the federal government when it was acting in an area the Constitution allowed it, or when carrying out any action that was *"necessary and proper."[5]*

---

1. In Greek mythology the **Hydra** was an ancient, nine-headed water serpent. Whenever a hapless hero cut off a head, two grew back to replace it, thus doubling the problem with every strike. Heracles finally killed the nasty beast by loping off all its heads and then plunging a burning torch into the severed neck.

   Thus, Hamilton's classical reference argues his point: without an active Supreme Court there can be no national unity.

2. THE FEDERALIST No. 80 (Alexander Hamilton), *quoted in* Raoul Berger, *The Ninth Amendment,* 66 CORNELL L. REV. 2, 4 n.4 (1981). Chief Justice John Marshall's decisions in *McCulloch v. Maryland* (1819) and *Cohens v. Virginia,* 19 U.S. 264 (1821), implemented Hamilton's explanation that the federal judiciary could review and overrule state court decisions that involved federal matters.

3. *McCulloch,* 17 U.S. at 406.

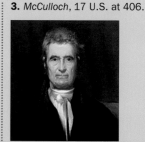
John Marshall

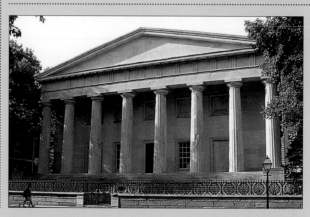

4. The Second Bank of the United States building today.

COURTING RIGHTS

The Framers viewed federalism and the separation of powers as the way to guarantee individual liberty. But the question in their day, as today, was how to directly enforce the Bill of Rights, including the unlisted rights of the Ninth and Tenth Amendments.[6]

Despite modern arguments against "judicial activism"(generally emanating from the losing side of a case on social issues), the Framers intended the courts to be active in both defining and defending individual rights.[7]

According to Madison, courts would be

"independent tribunals of justice [which would] consider themselves in a peculiar manner the guardians of those rights; they will be an impenetrable bulwark against any assumption of power in the Legislative or Executive; they will be naturally led to resist every encroachment upon rights expressly stipulated for in the Constitution by the declaration of rights."[8]

Thus the entire constitutional structure, including the later Bill of Rights, presupposes not only a functioning and independent court system, but judicial review: the power of the courts to review whether acts of Congress and president are legal under the Constitution, i.e., *constitutional.*

This makes sense because the Framers saw their courts as a place to redress the wrongs of the king's government. The Declaration of Independence, in fact, indicted King George's attacks on judicial independence:

"He has made Judges dependent on his Will alone for the tenure of their offices, and the amount and payment of their salaries."

The bank was not popular with Southern rural interests. President Andrew Jackson succeeded in ending it in the 1830s. This 1833 cartoon shows Jackson destroying the bank, with the bank's president as the devil.

5. On the presumption of liberty in the Constitution and natural rights, see Randy E. Barnett, *A Ninth Amendment for Today's Constitution*, 26 VAL. U. L. REV. 419, 426–28 (1991).

6. In a 1788 letter, Madison expressed his lingering misgivings about the effect of a Bill of Rights: "*Repeated violations of these parchment barriers have been committed by overbearing majorities in every state.*" Quoted in Van Loan at 9.

7. Those Nasty Activist Judges. Thurgood Marshall (1908–93) was the first African American to serve on the U.S. Supreme Court after a distinguished career arguing such cases as *Brown v. Board of Education,* which effectively ended legal justifications for racial segregation. He is honored with a postage stamp. In addition, he became for some the poster child of an activist judge. The term "activist judge," however, seems only to apply to those judges who happen to rule in a supposed liberal or progressive way on some issues. Judges who are by any standard extremely activist but who espouse a conservative agenda never get the label "activist judge."

Some conservatives, like Phyllis Schlafly, who tirelessly worked to defeat the Equal Rights Amendment, would excuse a conservative judge's activism as just "correcting" the liberal errors of prior court rulings. See PHYLLIS SCHLAFLY, THE SUPREMACISTS: THE TYRANNY OF JUDGES AND HOW TO STOP IT (2004).

Thurgood Marshall

8. *Quoted in* Hugo L. Black, *The Bill of Rights*, 35 N.Y.U. L. REV. 865, 880 (1960), *citing* 1 ANNALS OF CONGRESS 439 (1789); LEONARD W. LEVY, ORIGINS OF THE BILL OF RIGHTS 259 (1999). Thus, rather than less "judicial activism," Madison called for more. *See also* Lash, *Textual Theory*, at 929 (noting that Madison thought judicial enforcement of the people's retained rights "*indispensable*").

Indeed, judicial review implicates natural law, which Chief Justice Marshall noted in *Fletcher v. Peck*, 10 U.S. (6 Cranch) 87, 135 (1810): "*It may well be doubted whether the nature of society and of government does not prescribe some limits to the legislative power . . .*" See Van Loan at 25.

STOP JUDICIAL ACTIVISM

Thus the Framers wanted an independent court system because Americans had known that since their first days as colonists.[1]

Courts for them were a place where people could seek redress; a place where the accused could have a fair trial; and a place with independent judges to ensure rights and liberties, even in the face of executive or legislative power—be it king and Parliament or president and Congress.

The problem, however, is that, although the Framers implied that judicial review existed, they did not explicitly write it in the Constitution.[2] It took John Marshall in *Marbury v. Madison* (1803) to clinch it.[3]

In *Marbury*, the Supreme Court held the Judiciary Act of 1789 unconstitutional because it expanded the original jurisdiction of the Supreme Court. Marshall, this time in opposition to another fellow Virginian and his distant cousin, Thomas Jefferson, pulled off a judicial sleight-of-hand. By holding that the act could not add to the Court's power, the Supreme Court established the greater power of judicial review.[4]

Jefferson was angered. The Constitution, he now lamented, was

---

1. Upon arriving in America, the colonists set up "courts of common pleas" in Pennsylvania and "courts of oyer and terminer" in Virginia. Frederick G. Kempin, Historical Introduction To Anglo-American Law 45 (1990). See also William E. Nelson, *Government by Judiciary: The Growth of Judicial Power in Colonial Pennsylvania*, 59 Smu L. Rev. 3 (2006); Anthony J. Bellia, *The Origins of Article III "Arising Under" Jurisdiction*, 57 Duke L. J. 263 (2007) (regarding jurisdictional issues related to the exercise of court powers both in English history and the early American republic); Herbert Pope, *The English Common Law in the United States*, 24 Harv. L. Rev. 6 (1911) (discussing the common-law methodology in America). But see Frederick Schauer, *The Failure of the Common Law*, 36 Ariz. St. L.J. 765 (2005) (discussing the difficulty of the common-law methodology in America).

3. 5 U.S. (1 Cranch) 137.

John Lilburne

John Marshall

2. The Origin of Judicial Review. Alexander Hamilton in Federalist No.78 discussed judicial review:

"It is far more rational to suppose, that the courts were designed to be an intermediate body between the people and the legislature, in order, among other things, to keep the latter within the limits assigned to their authority. The interpretation of the laws is the proper and peculiar province of the courts. A constitution is, in fact, and must be regarded by the judges, as a fundamental law. It, therefore, belongs to them to ascertain its meaning, as well as the meaning of any particular act proceeding from the legislative body. If there should happen to be an irreconcilable variance between the two, that which has the superior obligation and validity ought, of course, to be preferred; or, in other words, the Constitution ought to be preferred to the statute, the intention of the people to the intention of their agents."

Hamilton's ideas had a long history in legal thought. Our old friend, John Lilburne, wrote "that which is done by one Parliament, as a Parliament, may be undone by the next Parliament: but an Agreement of the People begun and ended amongst the People can never come justly within the Parliament's cognizance to destroy." For Lilburne, it would be the supreme "law of the land." Quoted in Black at 868, citing Leveller Manifestoes of the Puritan Revolution 423 (Wolfe ed., 1944). This is the basis of the idea that our Constitution is "the supreme law of the land."

Coke also established the principle of judicial review over acts of Parliament in *Dr. Bonham's Case*, stating that "when an Act of Parliament is against Common right and reason, the Common Law will control it and adjudge such Act to be void." Quoted in Kempin at 92. See also Saikrishna B. Prakash & John C. Yoo, *The Origins of Judicial Review*, 70 U. Chi. L. Rev. 887 (2003) (noting the activism of the Rehnquist Court); William Michael Treanor, *Judicial Review before Marbury*, 58 Stan. L. Rev. 455 (2005).

Sir Edward Coke

4. See generally George L. Haskins, *Law versus Politics in the Early Years of the Marshall Court*, 130 U. Pa. L. Rev. 1 (1981).

5. Letter from Thomas Jefferson to Spencer Roane (Sept. 6, 1819), http://press-pubs.uchicago.edu/founders/documents/a1_8_18s16.html (last visited Mar. 16, 2008).

Jefferson's reaction stands in contrast to what he wrote a decade earlier to Madison on March 15, 1789, arguing that a Bill of Rights was good because "the legal check which it puts into the hands of the judiciary." Levy at 279. An independent judiciary, Jefferson then argued, would shield

"a mere thing of wax in the hands of the judiciary, which they may twist and shape into any form they please."[5]

Despite Jefferson's protestation, the power of judicial review makes the system work and is the main mechanism for enforcing individual rights.[6] Although the Constitution and Bill of Rights may guide legislators and presidents when making law, the enforcement of the rights usually happens in court.

Judicial review and the courts' role in protecting individual rights were part of a concept of "separation of powers." Each branch of government has its own sphere of power to check the others, and the states and national government check each other.[7]

This separation of powers distinguishes American government from the British parliamentary system.[8] In the American system of separation of powers, the courts are the best guardians of rights because, as Hamilton noted in THE FEDERALIST No.78, the court

"has no influence over either the sword or the purse . . . [the court is] beyond comparison the weakest of the three departments of power."

How Jefferson looked in 1791, when he believed that the courts should "*check*" the majority

How Jefferson looked in 1800, when he was in the majority and did not like judicial review

against majority impulses by holding acts unconstitutional. After Jefferson rode a wave of popular Republicanism to become the third president in 1801, and thus the majority, he did not like putting power in "*the hands of the judiciary.*" The Supreme Court was the last branch of government under the Federalists, allowing Marshall to write *Marbury v. Madison.*

For a small sampling of all that has been written on Jefferson and the early Federal courts, see, for example, Melvin I. Urofsky, *Thomas Jefferson and John Marshall: What Kind of Court Shall We Have?* 31 J. Sup. Ct. Hist. 109 (2006); Kent R. Newmyer, *Thomas Jefferson and the Rise of the Supreme Court,* 31 J. Sup. Ct. Hist. 126 (2006); Henry J. Abraham, *President Jefferson's Three Appointments to the Supreme Court of the United States: 1804, 1807, and 1807,* 31 J. Sup. Ct. Hist. 141 (2006); John Yoo, *Jefferson and Executive Power,* 88 B.U. L. Rev. 421, 425 (2008) (arguing that Jefferson's success as chief executive was closely "*intertwined with his broad conception of presidential power*").

Regarding Marshall, see Timothy S. Huebner, *Lawyer, Litigant, Leader: John Marshall and His Papers—A Review Essay,* 48 Am. J. Legal Hist. 314 (2006). For an interesting discussion of how Washington and Adams selected the first justices, and how their selections furthered the judiciary's role and the rule of law, see Maeva Marcus, *Federal Judicial Selection: The First Decade,* 39 U. Rich. L. Rev. 797 (2005).

Andrew Jackson

6. Not everyone agreed. For example, President Andrew Jackson would later show no respect for judicial review in at least two cases. After Marshall upheld the rights of Native American tribes against Georgia's anti-Cherokee statutes in *Worcester v. Georgia,* 31 U.S. (6 Pet.) 515 (1832), Jackson refused to follow the decision, declaring, "*John Marshall has made his decision; now let him enforce it.*" Later, when vetoing a law that would have created the Bank of the United States, Jackson asserted, "*[t]he opinion of judges has no more authority over Congress than the opinion of Congress over judges, and on that point the President is independent of both.*" Andrew Jackson, Veto Message (July 10, 1832).

7. According to Madison, "*the permanent success of the Constitution depend[ed] on a definite partition of powers between the general and state governments*" and it was "*of great importance as well as of indispensable obligation, that the constitutional boundary between them should be impartially maintained.*" Quoted in Lash, *Textual Theory,* at 928 (citing, respectively, Madison's Veto Message of Mar. 3, 1817, and a letter to Spencer Roane of May 6, 1821).

8. Madison, during his attack on the Alien and Sedition Acts, explained the difference between judicial review in England and in America:

"*In the British Government the danger of encroachment on the rights of the people is understood to be confined to the executive magistrate. The representatives of the people in the Legislature are not only exempt themselves from distrust, but are considered as sufficient guardians of the rights of their constituents against the danger from the Executive. Hence it is a principle, that the Parliament is unlimited in its power; or, in their own language, is omnipotent. Hence too, all the ramparts for protecting the rights of the people—such as the Magna Carta, their Bill of Rights, [etc.]—are not reared against the Parliament, but against the royal prerogative. . . . In the United States, the case is altogether different. The People, not the Government, possess the absolute sovereignty. The Legislature, no less than the Executive, is under limitations of power.*"

Quoted in William S. Fields & David T. Hardy, *The Third Amendment and the Issue of Maintenance of Standing Armies: A Legal History,* 35 Am. J. Legal Hist. 393, 412 n.85 (1991).

Although the judiciary is the weakest branch, the Framers did give the judges protections like no other government official, namely, tenure and protection from decreases in pay.[1] This was to allow and encourage what the Framers thought crucial: judicial independence.[2]

The Declaration of Independence underscores that King George's encroachments on judicial independence in America were among the reasons for the Revolution:

"He has made Judges dependent on his Will alone for the tenure of their offices, and the amount and payment of their salaries."[3]

The Constitution's Framers specifically desired to protect judges from the political branches, so that federal courts could be a check on them, as well as the states, to protect individual rights without fear of retaliation.[4]

But what were the Framers so jealous to protect?

Henry, Madison, and Jefferson would have answered that federalism and the courts were to ensure "liberty" or the "self-evident truths" of natural law "endowing inalienable rights."

These answers created a problem for many of the Founders, especially

---

1. U.S. Const. art. III, § 1.

Justice Hugo Black

2. As Justice Hugo Black wrote in 1960, "*our Constitution was the first to provide a really independent judiciary. . . . In this country the judiciary was made independent because it has, I believe, the primary responsibility and duty of giving force and effect to constitutional liberties and limitations upon the executive and legislative branches. Judges in England were not always independent and they could not hold Parliamentary acts void.*" Black at 870.

3. The Declaration of Independence.
   The British were working under the premise of Sir Francis Bacon, who stated "*that justices should be 'lions,' but lions under the throne.*" Quoted in Colin Rhys Lovell, English Constitutional and Legal History 329 (1962).

5. Blumrosen & Blumrosen at 178–79.

6. John Adams wrote Thomas Jefferson much later in life that to keep the South in the nation he told Southerners that he would leave slavery up to them: "*I must leave it to you. I will vote for forcing no measure against your judgments [on slavery].*" Quoted in Blumrosen & Blumrosen at 88. See also Alexander Tsesis, *Undermining Inalienable Rights: From Dred Scott to the Rehnquist Court*, 39 Ariz. St. L.J. 1179, 1209 (2007).

Samuel Chase

Aaron Burr

4. The impeachment trial of Justice Samuel Chase also established judicial independence, helping to insulate judges from partisan politics. See William H. Rehnquist, Grand Inquests: The Historic Impeachments of Justice Samuel Chase and President Andrew Johnson 595 (1992); Mark DeWolfe Howe, *Juries as Judges of Criminal Law*, 52 Harv. L. Rev. 582, 588 n.20 (1939). For the *Chase* case and the relationship of judges and juries, see Stephan Landsman, *The Civil Jury in America: Scenes from an Unappreciated History*, 44 Hastings L.J. 579, 603–04 (1993).
   Samuel Chase (1741–1811) remains the only Supreme Court justice ever impeached. This signer of the Declaration of Independence was a Federalist partisan. The Jeffersonian Republicans, controlling Congress, served Chase with six impeachment articles in 1804. Jefferson wanted to control the Federalist-dominated judicial branch. After Chase, the next target would have been Chief Justice Marshall. Vice President Aaron Burr, under indictment for having killed Alexander Hamilton, presided over Chase's trial. Although a Republican, Burr conducted the trial with fairness and impartiality. Fortunately for Chase, and the concept of judicial independence, the Senate acquitted him in early 1805. The Senate Republicans, led by Burr, protected the principle of judicial independence despite the fact that many of them detested Chase and his politics.

7. Benjamin Rush, a member of the Continental Congress and an intimate friend of two presidents, explained in a 1774 letter to the British Abolitionist Granville Sharp, "*[t]he cause of African freedom in America continues to gain ground.*" Letter from Benjamin Rush to Granville Sharp (May 13, 1774), *in The Correspondence of Benjamin Rush and Granville Sharp, 1773–1809*, 1 Journal of American Studies 1, 5 (John A. Woods ed., 1967). He expected slavery in America to end within forty years.

when coupled with the Declaration's statement that *"all men are created equal."* The problem was slavery.

Among the rights they wished to protect was the right to own other people.

SLAVERY: A *"PECULIAR"* RIGHT PERFECTING THE ART OF HYPOCRISY

Slavery was *the* controversy from the first days of the republic. James Madison wrote in his notes during the Constitutional Convention that

"[t]he States were divided into different interests not by . . . size . . . but principally from . . . their having or not having slaves."[5]

The Southern states stayed in the deal only because the antislavery Founders agreed that union was more important than emancipation.[6]

And the emancipationists consoled themselves in the mistaken—perhaps deluded—belief that slavery would end on its own.[7] So they wrote a Constitution that explicitly protected slavery.[8]

But no one seemed to have liked it much, or wanted to overtly say what they were doing. Despite all the protections for slavery, the Constitution actually made no reference to race.[9]

8. The Three-Fifths Clause counted slaves as three-fifths of a person for determining how many representatives a state had in Congress and for tax apportionment (U.S. CONST. art. I, § 2, cl. 3), assuring more Southern representation. Also the Importation Clause (U.S. CONST. art. I, § 9) prohibited Congress from abolishing the international slave trade for twenty years, and the Fugitive Slave Clause (U.S. CONST. art. IV, § 2, cl. 3) required the return of fugitive slaves and prohibited free states from liberating them. *See, e.g., Prigg v. Pennsylvania*, 41 U.S. (16 Pet.) 539, 575 (1842). The Insurrection Clause (U.S. CONST. art. I, § 8, cl. 15) and the Domestic Violence Clause (U.S. CONST. art. IV, § 4) empowered Congress to suppress slave revolts.

The Three-Fifths Clause also assured more Southern representation in the Electoral College, accounting for the fact that four of our first six presidents were not only Southerners but Virginians: Washington, Jefferson, Madison, and Monroe. Indeed, but for the prominence of John Adams and John Quincy Adams of Massachusetts, who each only got one term, the South would have probably had the presidency the whole time.

9. Conversely, the CONSTITUTION OF THE CONFEDERATE STATES OF AMERICA overtly protected "Negro slavery." EMORY M. THOMAS, THE CONFEDERATE NATION, 1861–1865, at 313 (1979). It also provided that "[n]o bill of attainder, ex post facto law, or law denying or impairing the right to property in Negro slaves, shall be passed." See Alexander Tsesis, *The Problem of Confederate Symbols: A Thirteenth Amendment Approach*, 75 TEMP. L. REV. 539, 543 (2002). With the exception of slavery and increased states' rights, it duplicates the U.S. Constitution almost word for word, including the Ninth Amendment at Article VI, Section 5 (1861): *"The enumeration, in the Constitution, of certain rights shall not be construed to deny or disparage others retained by the people of the several States."* Also, Article VI, Section 6, states: *"The powers not delegated to the Confederate States by the Constitution, nor prohibited by it to the States, are reserved to the States, respectively, or to the people thereof."*

The first six presidents: Washington, Adams, Jefferson, Madison, Monroe, and Quincy Adams

The Framers, in fact, conscientiously avoided the terms "slave" or "slavery."

Slavery, more than anything else, underscores the fact that the Framers did not intend everyone to be "*the people*."[1] After

all, argued slaveholders, "*had not slavery existed throughout history?*"[2] Even Aristotle said it was "*natural*."[3]

1. This was contrary to John Locke's statement on slavery that "*[t]he natural liberty of man is to be free from any superior power on earth.*" John Locke, *An Essay Concerning the True Original Extent and End of Civil Government, in* THE WORLD'S GREAT THINKERS, MAN AND THE STATE: THE POLITICAL PHILOSOPHERS 69 (1947).

2. *The Slave Market* by Boulanger (1882). Despite the practice of Roman slavery, Roman Stoic philosophers broke with Aristotle and believed slavery was against natural law. For the Stoics, all men have souls, and their commonalities cannot justify enslavement. *See* John R. Kroger, *The Philosophical Foundations of Roman Law: Aristotle, the Stoics, and Roman Theories of Natural Law*, 2004 WIS. L. REV. 905, 931–32 (2004) (discussing Stoic beliefs on slavery and especially Epictetus's *Discourses*). *See also* Kroger at 938 (discussing the Roman jurist Ulpian and his Stoic views on slavery being unnatural and rejecting Aristotle's natural theory of inequality).

3. Aristotle and slavery: Aristotle did not base slavery on race, which cut against arguments in the American South that blacks were inferior. Generally, slaves in Greece, and later in Rome, became so as the result of war. For Aristotle nature establishes hierarchies: men are superior to animals and women; masters are superior to slaves. The "natural" difference between masters and slaves had to do with different abilities to reason. Some men possess reason while others can only perceive reason. If you possess reason you are by nature a master, and if you lack it

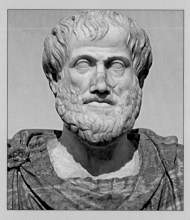

you are by nature a slave. Slavery is therefore "just," as the universality of the practice showed. Of course, if Aristotle followed his own rule to study "what actually happens," he would have seen that any number of "masters" lack any capacity to reason and that any number of slaves are far more intelligent and reasonable than their "masters." As Kroger notes, Aristotle's views on slavery are literally "the classic" example of the naturalist fallacy, where the observer believes as "natural" his own limited historical and social perspective. Because Aristotle could not imagine a world without slavery, it had to be "natural." *See* Kroger at 919–20. *See generally* ARISTOTLE, POLITICS 55–63 (Benjamin Jowett trans., Random House 1943) (providing Aristotle's comprehensive justification of slavery).

In fact, Aristotle's own philosophical tools show the fallacy of his thinking on slavery. The foundation of Aristotle's thought was the "syllogism," as expressed in the simple formula

> *If A = B, and B = C, then (or "ergo" to use the Greek) C = A*

So pervasive is the syllogism in Aristotle's method, textbooks everywhere use the following example to describe it:

> *If all men **are** mortal, and Aristotle **is** a man, then Aristotle is mortal.*
> *A = B, and C = A, ergo C = B*

Roughly applying the syllogism to Aristotle's view on slavery gives us the following:

> *All men **are** naturally different, **and** the natural difference is that masters have reason and slaves do not, **then** slavery is "natural."*

But the value to the syllogism depends on the truth of both the first and second premise, and on the ordering of the equation. Surely men are different, but the second premise that masters have "reason" and slaves do not, does not stand up to observation. Although it may have appeared subjectively true for Aristotle and American slaveholders, it is objectively false.

Perhaps the more honest answer for the slave-holding Framers was *"sure, we want our individual liberties and rights,* including *our right to own other people!"* And even though blacks are still "men" under the Constitution, a sleight of hand maintains them as "property." Thus, *"all men are created equal—except ours!"***[4]**

Instead of a syllogism, it becomes a "tautology," a statement asserted as truth merely by saying the same thing twice.
If A and B; or not A; or not B
Aristotle's view of slavery is really no more sophisticated than the following tautology:
Slavery shows that men are naturally different; or a master is naturally not a slave; or a slave is naturally not a master.
A tautology has limited rhetorical value and no logical value.
The fact that Aristotle had sophisticated tools to see the fallacy of his own views on slavery cuts against excusing him as "just a man of his time." Rather it diminishes him as someone who is otherwise a great thinker.

---

4. How to Count a Man. The Constitution's Three-Fifths Clause said slaves were three-fifths of a person for determining representatives in Congress. U.S. CONST. art. I, §, 2, cl. 3. Thus, even for the slavers, a slave still had to be a man, though only three-fifths of one.

In a segregated, slave-holding society, counting ancestry becomes imperative. A "**mulatto**" is a person with one black and one white parent, or it can refer to anyone with any biracial ancestry. The word comes from Spanish "*mulato*," meaning "small mule," from "*mulo*," ("mule") and the Old Spanish and Latin "*mulus*." A mule is a cross between a donkey and a horse. Mulatto is the general term for the following categories.

A "**quadroon**" usually refers to someone of one-quarter black ancestry, for example, a person with three white grandparents or the reverse: a person of one-quarter caucasian ancestry and three-quarters black ancestry. A quadroon can also have a mulatto parent and one white parent (or black) parent. An "**octoroon**" is a person of fourth generation black ancestry, genealogically meaning one-eighth black. An octoroon usually has one full black great-grandparent and seven great-grandparents who are white. A "**quintroon**" is a person of fifth generation black ancestry, usually meaning someone with an octoroon parent and a white parent. A "**hexadecaroon**" is one-sixteenth black and is not commonly traced. Finally, a **mestee** refers to anyone with less than one-eighth black ancestry.

These words mainly derive from Latin: "quadroon" is borrowed from Spanish "*cuarterón*" (and ultimately from Latin "*quartus*," or "fourth"); "octoroon" from Latin "*octo*," or "eight" (or equivalently Greek "*okto*"); *quintus* is Latin "fifth," but "quintroon" does not follow the same logic and instead refers to the generation rather than racial proportion. The alternative "hexadecaroon", from Greek "*hexadeka*," or "sixteen," expresses this proportion directly.

The caption of this Spanish colonial period painting reads *De negro y española sale mulato.—negro 1. española 2. mulato 3 ("From Black and Spanish comes Mulato")*. The amazing part of this scene is that the black man is a well-dressed husband-father with a white wife-mother, highly unlikely for the period, as the normal combination would have been a black mother coerced by a white slaveholder into sex (i.e., raped).

In addition to being offensively part of racial segregation, all of these designations are faulty because they assume that the ancestors are not themselves of mixed race. In fact the distinctions mattered little in practice because any child of a woman slave took his mother's status. Moreover, under the "one drop rule," any person with any African ancestry was black.

One of the Spanish painter Velazquez's unforgettable portraits is of Juan de Pareja, his mulatto slave whom he taught to paint and later freed. Velazquez painted him with a regal bearing and a lace collar.

The Barbadoes Mulatto Girl, an engraving after a painting by Brunias (1764)

The Mulatto Woman by Eugene Delacroix is fused with sexual overtones

A Mulatto Woman with her White Daughter Visited by Negro Women by Le Masurier (1775)

The easy justification was to believe African slaves were inferior.[1] Over time these arguments became more and more "peculiar."[2]

But the declarers of "*unalienable rights*" who owned other men had a harder time. Most were too intelligent to accept the fallacy of racial inferiority. And they had to maintain some credentials for what

we today call political correctness with their Northern counterparts, as in, "*I really don't believe in slavery, I just have some by accident.*"[3]

Virginians were the most notable among this group of embarrassed apologists.

Young Thomas Jefferson in 1774 tried to have Virginia adopt the statement that

"*the abolition of domestic slavery is the greatest object of desire of these colonies.*"

Virginia did not go for it.

He later wanted to have the Declaration of Independence condemn King George for the slave trade, but Congress did not go for it.[4] Later Jefferson's second and third drafts of the Virginia Constitution provided that

---

1. *See* Tsesis, *Undermining*, at 1199–1200 (discussing early nineteenth century racist views in the Southern states).

In law, this culminated in Chief Justice Roger Taney's *Dred Scott v. Sandford*, 60 U.S. (19 How.) 393 (1856), decision holding that slaves were not full citizens. Before his tenure on the Supreme Court as President Andrew Jackson's Attorney General, Taney had stated that "[t]he African race in the United States even when free are everywhere a degraded class, and exercise no political influence. The privileges they are allowed to enjoy, are accorded to them as a matter of kindness and benevolence rather than of right." Quoted in Tsesis, *Undermining*, at 1202 (noting the proslavery composition of the *Dred Scott* Supreme Court, including that three justices owned slaves). Taney's citizenship perspective distorted history. *Id.* at 1200.

Dred Scott   Chief Justice Roger Taney

2. "Our Peculiar Institution." "Peculiar" in the modern sense means "strange," but the proponents of slavery used the term "*peculiar institution*" as a euphemism for Southern slavery, with "peculiar" having the meaning "personal," "particular," or "one's own." The expression is always possessive, e.g., "*our peculiar institution*" or "*the South's peculiar institution*." It became common in the early 1800s when the actual word "slavery" was "improper" and banned in certain areas. John C. Calhoun used the "*peculiar institution*" to argue slavery was a "*positive good,*" not just a necessary evil. John C. Calhoun, Speech on the Reception of Abolition Petitions (1837).

Later, in 1861, Confederate Vice President Alexander Stephens argued that "*our peculiar institution*" corrected Jefferson's erroneous statement in the Declaration of Independence that "*all men are created equal.*" "Peculiar" derives from the Latin "*pecu*" ("cattle"). Because cattle were a common means of barter, they became a measure of value, and thus the origin of words like "pecuniary"—pertaining to money; "impecunious"—without money; and "peculate"—to embezzle. HENDRICKSON at 554. "Peculiar," in the sense of "pertaining to one's own things or goods" or, literally, "one's own cattle," is the Southern meaning of "*peculiar institution*," as in looking after one's own cattle in the form of slaves. Both the words "cattle" and "chattel" derive from the Latin "*capitale*," for one's capital or financial holdings, *id.* at 139, and underscores the term "chattel slavery," where people are treated as cattle for their peculiar, as in pecuniary, worth.

3. Henry Clay, in an impromptu speech while running for president in 1844, explained that slavery was "*an enormous evil*" but nonetheless an American institution. "*Here is Charles,*" Clay declared pointing to his personal slave. In an interesting precursor to the argument in the later *Dred Scott* case, Clay went on, "*he is in a free state and entirely at liberty to leave me if he desires to do so, and if you who present the petition will prepare a place for my slaves at home where they can be provided for, and enable to make a living, I will gladly release them all; but as it is, it* [i.e., emancipation] *would be an act of cruelty.*" Quoted in MERRILL D. PETERSON, THE GREAT TRIUMVIRATE: WEBSTER, CLAY, AND CALHOUN 351–52 (1987). Of course, Clay did not mention that in 1829 Charles's mother, Charlotte Dupuy, had an attorney file a lawsuit in district court for her freedom, arguing that she should be free because she had lived in the free territory of Washington, D.C., and that her prior owner had promised her freedom. Clay fought the case and eventually won, keeping Charlotte in bondage. See a brief account in JESSE J. HOLLAND, BLACK MEN BUILT THE CAPITOL: DISCOVERING AFRICAN-AMERICAN HISTORY IN AND AROUND WASHINGTON, D.C. 101 (2007). Clay eventually did free Charlotte in 1840 and freed Charles in 1844. Who knows what Charles thought of being Clay's prop?

Calhoun   Stephens   Henry Clay

"[n]o person hereafter coming into this country shall be held in slavery under any pretext whatever."

Again, Virginia did not go for it.

Despite this, Jefferson owned slaves his whole life.[5]

Madison also declared against slavery, stating at the Constitutional Convention that

"[w]e have seen the mere distinction of colour made in the most enlightened period of time, a ground to the most oppressive dominion ever exercised by man over man."[6]

Despite this, Madison also owned slaves his whole life.

Richard Henry Lee, at age twenty-five in his first speech to the Virginia House of Burgesses, advocated ending slave importation. He said importing slaves

"has been, and will be attended with effects, dangerous both to our political and moral interests."

Slaves, Lee extolled, are

"created in the image of God as well as ourselves, and equally entitled to liberty and freedom by the great law of nature."[7]

4. Slavery and the DECLARATION OF INDEPENDENCE. Jefferson may have drafted the Declaration beholden to what was going on in Virginia, and his famous second paragraph about equality was a balancing act. The Virginia legislature, with a filibuster, had rejected John Locke's declaration of rights based on the trilogy of *"life, liberty, and property."* Virginia had also eliminated a statement that men were *"born free"* and had declared that *"natural rights"* only applied to men who the ruling elite had decided *"enter[ed] a state of society."* BLUMROSEN & BLUMROSEN at 129. Jefferson had to declare independence without creating a slavery crisis. He replaced the word *"born"* with *"created,"* eliminated the conditional quality of *"natural rights,"* and changed Locke's classic statement to read *"the pursuit of Happiness."* See id. at 121–43. These changes prevented the Declaration of Independence from being used to support slavery, and rather than denying that slaves had *"natural rights,"* Jefferson created, with Benjamin Franklin's help, an immortally inspiring ambiguity: *"We hold these truths to be self-evident, that all men are created equal, that they are endowed by their Creator with certain unalienable Rights, that among these rights are Life, Liberty and the Pursuit of Happiness . . . ."* Id. at 138–39.

Jefferson also sought to avoid any blame to the Southern states for slavery by condemning the king for waging *"cruel war"* in seeking slaves from Africa and imposing them on the colonies. As to the substance of this claim, from 1713, Britain became the world's main slave merchant. Under a contract with Spain called the *"Asiento",* Britain gained a monopoly over the Spanish colonial slave trade for thirty years, making England "the great slave trader of the world." Congress deleted Jefferson's clause condemning England for slavery. See id. at 139–42.

England did not abolish the slave trade until 1833.

5. For more on Jefferson's complicated relationship with slavery and slaves, see William G. Merkel, *Jefferson's Failed Anti-Slavery Proviso of 1784 and the Nascence of Free Soil Constitutionalism,* 38 SETON HALL L. REV. 555 (2008).

Jefferson made a famous statement about slavery: *"Indeed, I tremble for my country when I reflect that God is just."* Notes on the State of Virginia, quoted in BARTLETT'S FAMILIAR QUOTATIONS 471 (14th ed. 1968). Maybe Jefferson reconciled what he said about slavery with the fact that he owned slaves his whole life by the fact that he may not have believed in God. See **Chapter 1: Of Dogma and Desire: Saying What You Believe about the First Amendment.**

6. *Quoted in* Tsesis, *Undermining,* at 1210.

7. Tsesis, *Undermining,* at 1186–88.

Richard Henry Lee first moved for independence in June 1776, during the Second Continental Congress

Confederate General Robert E. Lee was Richard Henry Lee's great nephew

Yet again, despite his fine sentiments, Lee owned slaves, leaving thirty-seven to his heirs.

Another Virginian, George Mason, argued in opposition to the Constitution that slave importation was "*infamous*" and "*detestable*" and that Great Britain's support for it "*was one of the great causes of our separation*," i.e., the Revolution:

"*Slaves weaken the states; and such a trade is diabolical in itself, and disgraceful to mankind.*"

Of course, restrictions or elimination of slave importation would increase the value of American-born slaves. Mason owned about three hundred slaves and was upset that the Constitution did not secure "*the property of the slaves we have already.*" Connecticut delegate Oliver Ellsworth, among others, charged that Mason's opposition to importation was based on a desire to increase the value of his property.[1]

Patrick Henry, who at least showed honesty, admitted that slavery was wrong but that he could not "conveniently" live without it:

"*Is it not amazing that at a time when the rights of Humanity are defined &*
understood with precision in a Country above all others fond of Liberty: that . . . we find Men, professing a Religion the most humane, mild, meek, gentle & generous, adopting a Principle as repugnant to humanity . . . . Would anyone believe that I am Master of Slaves of my own purchase! I am drawn along by ye general Inconvenience of living without them; I will not, I cannot justify it. . . . I believe a time will come when an oppertunity [sic] will be offered to abolish this lamentable Evil."[2]

With such statements in the air, Samuel Johnson, the great English lexicographer, could thus mockingly quip in 1775,

---

1. *The Old Plantation* (c. 1790).

Virginian Luxuries shows another aspect of southern interest in slaves.

Patrick Henry

Samuel Johnson in 1772

3. Samuel Johnson, *Taxation No Tyranny: An Answer to the Resolutions and Address of the American Congress,* THE SAMUEL JOHNSON SOUND BITE PAGE, http://www.samueljohnson.com/tnt.html (last visited Aug. 5, 2010). Johnson also refuted Aristotle's assertions about the nature of slavery.

"It must be agreed that in most ages many countries have had part of their inhabitants in a state of slavery; yet it may be doubted whether slavery can ever be supposed the natural condition of man. It is impossible not to conceive that men in their original state were equal; and very difficult to imagine how one would be subjected to another but by violent compulsion. An individual may, indeed, forfeit his liberty by a crime; but he cannot by that crime forfeit the liberty of his children. What is true of a criminal seems true likewise of a captive. A man may accept life from a conquering enemy on condition of perpetual servitude; but it is very doubtful whether he can entail that servitude on his descendants; for no man can stipulate without commission for another. The condition which he himself accepts, his son or grandson would have rejected." Quoted at id., Quotes on Slavery, http://www.samueljohnson.com/slavery.html (last visited August 5, 2010).

4. William Murray, **1st Earl of Mansfield.** The Somerset case is cited as *R. v. Knowles, ex parte Somerset,* (1772) Lofft 1, 98 Eng. Rep. 499 (K.B. 1772), *reprinted in* 20 Howell's St. Tr. 1 (1909), or more commonly as *Somerset v. Stewart,* (1772) 98 Eng. Rep. 499 (K.B.). See LOVELL at 455 (noting that in *Somerset* Mansfield applied the Camden dictum about positive law from the *Wilkes* cases. See **Chapter 4: Molasses and the Sticky Origins of the Fourth Amendment**).

"[h]ow is it that we hear the loudest yelps for liberty among the drivers of Negros?"[3]

BRINGING THE SOUTH TO THE CAUSE

In 1772, a court case in England was a key event that helped send the Southern colonies down the road of revolution.

Chief Justice of the King's Bench, Lord Mansfield, ruled that a slave named Somerset became free when he came to England. Lord Mansfield ruled that slavery

"is so odious that nothing can be suffered to support it but positive law."[4]

In other words, slavery is not natural or part of natural law, and the only way it can exist is if there is a law permitting it.[5] Thus, because no law in England made Somerset a slave, his prior slave status in other places did not transfer to England.[6]

Mansfield's ruling did not affect the English slave trade or slavery outside England. America had plenty of specific laws that legalized slavery. Nevertheless, the ruling caused uproar in colonial America.

Virginia, which in the late colonial period exported slaves to the rest of the

South, furtively consulted with the other colonies, leading to the First Continental Congress in Philadelphia in 1774.[7]

Later British conduct heightened Southern fears. Royal governor of Virginia, Lord Dunmore, faced a manpower shortage to defend the colony from the rebels.[8] To bolster British numbers, Dunmore and other British generals proclaimed freedom for any slave that joined the British army, proclaiming in 1775 that

"all indented Servants, Negroes or others . . . [will be] free that are able and willing to bear Arms."[9]

---

5. This is directly against Aristotle's view that slavery was "natural" because it was in all places the custom. *See* **Chapter 9: The Ninth Amendment: Still a Mystery after All These Years.**

Conversely, Blackstone wrote that the *"spirit of liberty is so deeply implicated in our constitution, and rooted even in our very soil, that a slave or a negro, the moment he lands in England, falls under the protection of the laws; and so far becomes a freeman."* 2 WILLIAM BLACKSTONE, COMMENTARIES 1765, *quoted in* SIMON SCHAMA, ROUGH CROSSINGS: BRITAIN, THE SLAVES AND THE AMERICAN REVOLUTION 39 (2005). There was, however, contrary judicial authority in England at the time, and later editions of Blackstone took out the above quote, leaving the question open. *See id.* at 35–36, 38–39.

6. *Somerset* is the precursor of *Dred Scott v. Sanford,* in which Scott advanced essentially the same argument that once a slave has entered a free state he is no longer a slave, but to no avail.

Dred Scott

See generally Symposium, *Dred Scott after 150 Years: A Grievous Wound Remembered,* 17 WIDENER L.J. 1 (2007).

7. For the complete account of *Somerset* and its place in revolutionary history, *see* BLUMROSEN & BLUMROSEN at 9, 33–36; Alfred W. Blumrosen, *The Profound Influence in America of Lord Mansfield's Decision in Somerset v. Stuart,* 13 TEX. WESLEYAN L. REV. 645 (2007); Cheryl I. Harris, *"Too Pure an Air:" Somerset's Legacy from Anti-Slavery to Colorblindness,* 13 TEX. WESLEYAN L. REV. 439 (2007) (arguing that the assertion that England was *"too pure"* for slavery had as much to do with racism as human rights, because black people would destroy the white race); STEVEN M. WISE, THOUGH THE HEAVENS MAY FALL: THE LANDMARK TRIAL THAT LED TO THE END OF HUMAN SLAVERY (2005).

For a general account of the slave trade, *see* SCHAMA; Book Note, *Reimagining Revolution: A Critical Review of Simon Schama's Rough Crossings: Britain, the Slaves, and the American Revolution,* 9 BERKELEY J. AFR.-AM. L. & POL'Y 74 (2007).

8. *See* SCHAMA at 80. Following Lord Dunmore, Sir Henry Clinton, the commander in chief of the British in North America, also offered freedom to slaves who joined the British.

Lord Dunmore (John Murray, 4th Earl of Dunmore)

General Sir Henry Clinton

9. Lord Dunmore's proclamation can be found at http://www.digitalhistory.uh.edu/learning_history/revolution/dunsmore.cfm (last visited May 2, 2009).

Slaves escaped to his ranks, and outraged Virginians threatened to execute them if captured, or send them to the cane fields of the West Indies for a short, miserable life and death.[1]

Lord Dunmore's proclamation counts as the first "emancipation proclamation" in North America

and, as with Lincoln's later Emancipation Proclamation, was born of military necessity.[2] Lest there be any doubt of Dunmore's proclamation's importance in helping lead to the Revolution, look to the Declaration of Independence, where the colonists indicted King George III for having

"*excited domestic Insurrections among us.*"[3]

FIGHTING FOR THE RIGHT TO BE "*THE PEOPLE*"

The great irony of American constitutional and cultural history is that, because the states were the protectors of

---

1. BLUMROSEN & BLUMROSEN at 121–23, 141.

2. Before the Thirteenth Amendment most Constitutionalists, including Abraham Lincoln, thought the national government had no power to outlaw slavery. Thus Lincoln had to justify the Emancipation Proclamation under some constitutional power, and Article II, Section 2, giving the president "war powers" as *Commander in Chief*" served. The **Emancipation Proclamation** was actually two executive orders, The first, of September 22, 1862, declared free all slaves in any Confederate state that did not return to the Union by January 1, 1863. The second, of January 1, 1863, only declared free the slaves in the Confederate states, specifically leaving slavery intact in the border states of Kentucky, Missouri, Maryland, and Delaware. The proclamation also did not apply to Tennessee, New Orleans, and parts of Louisiana that were already under Union control. It also did not apply to the forty-eight counties of Virginia that later became West Virginia. Despite these shortcomings, this second order freed at least 20,000 slaves immediately, and, as the Union armies conquered the Confederacy, the proclamation would free approximately four million slaves by July 1865.

With the war ending, Abolitionists worried that the proclamation's justification as a war measure would end. This led to the Thirteenth Amendment outlawing legal slavery for good on December 18, 1865. *See generally*

Lincoln meeting with his cabinet on July 22, 1862, to read the Emancipation Proclamation

3. Detail from *The Death of Major Pierson* (1782–84) showing a black Loyalist soldier

4. The Tennessee National Guard blocking Beale Street from civil rights marchers on March 29, 1968, in Memphis, Tennessee.

BURRUS M. CARNAHAN, ACT OF JUSTICE: LINCOLN'S EMANCIPATION PROCLAMATION AND THE LAW OF WAR (2008); Robert Fabrikant, Book Note, *Lincoln, Emancipation, and "Military Necessity,"* 52 HOW. L J. 375 (2009) (book review).

individual rights, they remained free to protect slavery. This carried through into modern times, when "states' rights" was the main Southern response to the civil rights movement.[4]

The civil rights movement was not about creating rights but getting them *recognized*.[5] The movement was thus akin to the Declaration of Independence, pronouncing rights that were "*self evident*."

As the Declaration of Independence shows, people have to stand up for their rights and demand them. A slave of American General William Whipple, named Prince, did just that in 1777, when he told his master

"*you are going to fight for your liberty, but I have none to fight for.*"[6]

Whipple freed him, which Prince deserved, because he, like all of us, was born to it.[7]

Homer Plessy

John Marshall Harlan

5. Homer Plessy was a Louisiana shoemaker and octoroon (one-eighth black ancestry) who, under the "one drop rule," could not sit in a railroad car reserved for whites. On June 7, 1892, the thirty-year-old Plessy was arrested and challenged the law. The Supreme Court decided *Plessy v. Ferguson*, upholding the constitutionality of racial segregation even in public accommodations (particularly railroads), under the doctrine of "*separate but equal.*" Justice John Marshall Harlan, a former slaveholder, wrote a forceful dissent where he predicted the court's decision would become as infamous as that in *Dred Scott* and went on to write: "*But in view of the Constitution, in the eye of the law, there is in this country no superior, dominant, ruling class of citizens. There is no caste here. Our Constitution is color-blind, and neither knows nor tolerates classes among citizens. In respect of civil rights, all citizens are equal before the law.*"

Justice Harlan's grandson, John Marshall Harlan II, joined the Supreme Court shortly after *Brown v. Board of Education* was decided and overturned *Plessy*. In subsequent cases, Harlan II carried on his grandfather's legacy from *Plessy*.

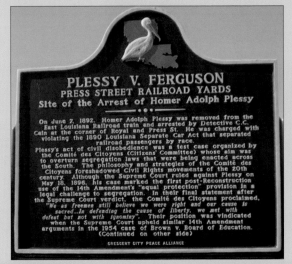

Marker placed at Press and Royal Streets in New Orleans on February 12, 2009, commemorating the planned arrest of Homer Plessy on June 17, 1892, for violating the Louisiana 1890 Separate Car Act.

6. See Tsesis, *Undermining*, at 1190.

John Marshall Harlan II

7. Perhaps Whipple's example influenced George Washington, who freed his slaves in his will and provided for their education and care. See Tsesis, *Undermining*, at 1189.

Given that blacks, Native Americans, women, and gays were there at the start,[1] the recognition of their rights should have been a matter of course.[2] But history showed that "*the people*" still had to fight for recognition, as

Steuben

Steuben was important enough to get his own stamp

A provocative Steuben Monument in Lafayette Square near the White House in Washington, D.C.

1. Baron von Steuben (1730–94) was a Prussian aristocrat (according to him) who taught the Continental Army how to drill, stand, shoot, and fight with the bayonet. He wrote the Revolutionary War Drill Manual and by war's end was George Washington's chief-of-staff. He was most certainly gay. Steuben left Germany in 1776 in scandal after he was accused of improper sexual behavior with boys. On February 23, 1778, Steuben volunteered for duty at Valley Forge. Steuben spoke little English and often yelled to his translator, "Here! Come swear for me!" His training made the American army able to stand toe to toe against British regulars. Without Steuben, we would not have won the Revolution. *See* Paul Douglas Lockhart, The Drillmaster of Valley Forge: The Baron De Steuben and the Making of the American Army (2008).

Steuben never married and had no children. He left his estate to General Benjamin Walker and Captain William North, his aides-de-camp during the war, with whom he had had an "*extraordinarily intense emotional relationship . . . treating them as surrogate sons.*" Arguing that Steuben was gay, see Randy Shilts, Conduct Unbecoming: Lesbians and Gays in the US Military from Vietnam to the Persian Gulf War (1993). Steuben has several places and events named for him as well as the von Steuben Day Parade in Chicago that Ferris Bueller crashed in Ferris Bueller's Day Off (Paramount Pictures 1986).

2. A civil rights march from the Washington Monument to the Lincoln Memorial, on August 28, 1963.

John Locke in his *Essay on Toleration* argued that the government had more than just a passive duty of "not persecuting," but an active obligation to penalize people who were intolerant. Lovell at 400 (noting that Locke's idea that the state might coerce the intolerant into tolerance has reappeared in the twentieth century's fair employment codes to prevent racial discrimination).

Prince Whipple did when he helped row General Washington across the Delaware in 1776.[3]

Thus, the American Revolution and the civil rights movement, among many others, were about

recognition, not only of rights . . .

but who are "*the people*."

3. *Washington Crossing the Delaware* **by Emanuel Leutze (1851).** Prince Whipple is shown rowing to Washington's front right. Lieutenant (later president) James Monroe supposedly is the guy holding the flag. In 1936, David Schulman put this painting to verse:

Washington Crossing the Delaware
A hard, howling, tossing water scene.
Strong tide was washing hero clean.
"How cold!" Weather stings as in anger.
O Silent night shows war ace danger!
The cold waters swashing on in rage.
Redcoats warn slow his hint engage.
When star general's action wish'd "Go!"
He saw his ragged continentals row.
Ah, he stands
sailor crew went going.
And so this general watches rowing.
He hastens
winter again grows cold.
A wet crew gain Hessian stronghold.
George can't lose war with's hand in;
He's astern
so go alight, crew, and win!

Epilogue:
How We Ponied-Up to Pay the Bill

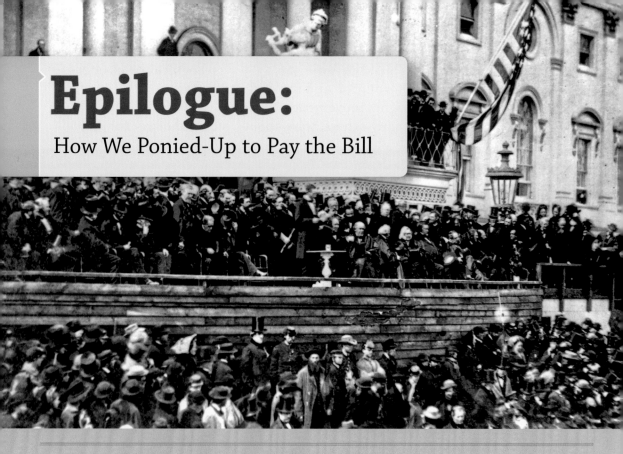

Section 1. Neither slavery nor involuntary servitude, except as a punishment for crime whereof the party shall have been duly convicted, shall exist within the United States, or any place subject to their jurisdiction.

Section 2. Congress shall have power to enforce this article by appropriate legislation.

– THE THIRTEENTH AMENDMENT

Section 1. All persons born or naturalized in the United States . . . are citizens of the United States and of the State wherein they reside. No State shall make or enforce any law which shall abridge the privileges or immunities of citizens of the United States; nor shall any State deprive any person of life, liberty, or property, without due process of law; nor deny to any person within its jurisdiction the equal protection of the laws.

Section 2. Representatives shall be apportioned among the several States according to their respective numbers, counting the whole number of persons in each State, excluding Indians not taxed . . . .

Section 5. The Congress shall have power to enforce, by appropriate legislation, the provisions of this article.

– THE FOURTEENTH AMENDMENT

Section 1. The right of citizens of the United States to vote shall not be denied or abridged by the United States or by any State on account of race, color, or previous condition of servitude.

Section 2. The Congress shall have power to enforce this article by appropriate legislation.

– THE FIFTEENTH AMENDMENT

If the Bill of Rights is supposed to apply to the federal government, why do the states have to follow it?

The Civil War Amendments are the short answer.

After the Civil War, between 1865 and 1870, Congress passed and the states ratified three amendments to the United States Constitution:

- The Thirteenth Amendment (1865) abolished slavery;

- The Fourteenth Amendment (1868)

included the Privileges and Immunities Clause, Due Process, and Equal Protection Clauses;

- The Fifteenth Amendment (1870) granted voting rights regardless of "race, color, or previous condition of servitude."[1]

These Civil War (aka Reconstruction Era) Amendments transformed the United States from "half-slave and half-free" to a nation in which the "blessings of liberty" extend to every man.[2]

Each Amendment ends the same way:

Congress shall have power to enforce this article by appropriate legislation.

None of the original Bill of Rights did this. The First Amendment, for example, specifically states "*Congress shall make no law . . . ,*" meaning that it only applied to Congress, with no application to the states at all.[3]

By their very terms, the Civil War Amendments reshuffled the deck and opened the way for courts to later apply the Constitution to the states. They resulted from the greatest constitutional crisis of the United States: the Civil War.[4]

---

1. *See generally* David P. Currie, *The Reconstruction Congress*, 75 U. Chi. L. Rev. 383 (2008).

2. As Abraham Lincoln declared in his Second Inaugural Address on Saturday, March 4, 1865, slavery drove the Civil War:

One-eighth of the whole population were colored slaves, not distributed generally over the Union, but localized in the southern part of it. These slaves constituted a peculiar and powerful interest. All knew that this interest was somehow the cause of the war.

Second Inaugural Address, *available at* http://avalon.law.yale.edu/19th_century/lincoln2.asp (last visited Feb. 28, 2010). *See also* Garry Wills, *Lincoln's Greatest Speech?* The Atlantic Monthly, September 1999, http://www.theatlantic.com/past/issues/99sep/9909lincoln.htm.

For a moving musical rendition of parts of Lincoln's Second Inaugural and Gettysburg Addresses, *see* Aaron Copland, Lincoln Portrait (1942).

3. The 1st Amendment was James Madison's pet project, and he wanted it to apply to the states. The First Congress voted on the version that specifically did not apply to the states.

4. Originalism is a way of interpreting the Constitution with deference to the Framer's "original intent." Some conservatives espoused originalism in the 1980s as a critique of "liberal" Supreme Court decisions in the 1950s and 60s under Chief Justice Earl Warren. Conservatives argued that the Constitutional text and Framers original intent did not support some Warren Court rulings, such as *Griswold v. Connecticut*, 381 U.S. 479 (1965), striking down a ban on contraceptives as violating privacy rights. But the "original intent" of the Framers in 1791 may not be the end of the discussion. Another source of original intent is the three Reconstruction Amendments ratified after the Civil War. The 13th, 14th, and 15th Amendments radically altered the structure of American federalism, elevating Federal power over the states, and giving individual rights preeminence. "The Framers" in 1868 trumped the Framers of 1791. *See, e.g.,* Risa L. Goluboff, *The Thirteenth Amendment in Historical Perspective*, 11 U. Pa. J. Const. L. 1451 (2009) (arguing the importance of the 13th Amendment's historical context); Michael Scimone, Comment, *More to Lose Than Your Chains: Realizing the Ideals of the Thirteenth Amendment*, 12 N.Y. City L. Rev. 175 (2008) (arguing that the 13th Amendment could provide a unifying theme for workers' rights); Lea S. Vandervelde, *The Labor Vision of the Thirteenth Amendment*, 138 U. Pa. L. Rev. 437 (1989).

Black Union troops marching at Lincoln's second inauguration

The Civil War killed millions.[1] As President Lincoln lamented:

> "*Neither party expected for the war the magnitude or the duration which it has already attained. Neither anticipated that the cause of the conflict might cease with or even before the conflict itself should cease. Each looked for an easier triumph and a result less fundamental and astounding.*"[2]

After the bloodletting, the Civil War Amendments represented a great change.

Before then, Congress and the nation had not amended the Constitution for sixty years.[3]

The Thirteenth Amendment completed the abolition of slavery that President Lincoln's first *Emancipation Proclamation* began in September 1862.[4] States can no longer allow slavery.[5] In abolishing slavery though, the Thirteenth Amendment for the first time put the word "slavery" in the Constitution and even allowed it,

> "*as a punishment for crime whereof the party shall have been duly convicted . . . .*"

Thus, the Thirteenth Amendment actually allowed slavery to continue as punishment for a convicted criminal.[6]

The Fourteenth Amendment has various provisions extending the Constitution to the states the most important is Section 1:

> *nor shall any State deprive any person of life, liberty, or property, without due process of law; nor deny to any*

1. Union dead after the Battle of Gettysburg.

Lincoln delivering his Second Inaugural Address

2. Lincoln's Second Inaugural Address, available at *http://avalon.law.yale. edu/19th_century/lincoln2.asp* (last visited Feb. 28, 2010).

3. The most recent amendment before the Civil War, the Twelfth Amendment in 1804, changed the procedures for election of the President and Vice-President.

4. Paul Finkelman, *Lincoln, Emancipation, and the Limits of Constitutional Change*, 2008 Sup. Ct. Rev. 349, 387 (2008).

President Lincoln signing the Emancipation Proclamation

5. The 13th Amendment.

6. See Scott W. Howe, *Slavery as Punishment: Original Public Meaning, Cruel and Unusual Punishment, and the Neglected Clause in the Thirteenth Amendment*, 51 Ariz. L. Rev. 983 (2009); Kamal Ghali, *No Slavery Except as a Punishment for Crime: The Punishment Clause and Sexual Slavery*, 55 UCLA L. Rev. 607 (2008) (arguing that despite the explicit wording of the 13th Amendment's Punishment Clause, prisoners still have 13th Amendment rights while in prison and that it specifically protects them against sexual slavery).

7. The 14th Amendment with Section 1.

14th Amendment page 2.

8. See Michael P. O'Connor, *Time Out of Mind: Our Collective Amnesia about the History of the Privileges or Immunities Clause*, 93 Kentucky L. J. 659 (2004–05) (regarding the 14th Amendment's privileges and immunities clause's intended broad scope using Freedman Bureau records and other legislation and court records contemporaneous with the 14th Amendment). *See also* Robert G. Natelson, *The Original Meaning of the Privileges and Immunities Clause*, 43 Ga. L. Rev. 1117 (2009); David T. Hardy, *Original Popular Understanding of the Fourteenth Amendment as Reflected in the Print Media 1866–1868*, 30 Whittier L. Rev. 695 (2009); Christopher R. Green, *The Original Sense of the (Equal) Protection Clause: Pre-Enactment History*, 19 Geo. Mason U. Civ. Rts. L.J. 1 (2008); Steven G. Calabresi & Sarah E. Agudo, *Individual Rights under State Constitutions When the Fourteenth Amendment Was Ratified in 1868: What Rights Are Deeply Rooted in American History and Tradition?* 87 Tex. L. Rev. 7 (2008). For arguments against the incorporation doctrine, see Charles Fairman, *Does the Fourteenth Amendment Incorporate the Bill of Rights? The Original Understanding*, 2 Stan. L. Rev. 5 (1949); Stanley Morrison, *Does the Fourteenth Amendment Incorporate the Bill of Rights? The Judicial Interpretation*, 2 Stan. L. Rev. 140 (1949).

person within its jurisdiction the equal protection of the laws.[7]

This is the basis of the idea that the original Bill of Rights is "incorporated" to the states. This is why we, today, talk about the Bill of Rights and how it applies to us directly.[8]

The Fourteenth Amendment also dumped the Supreme Court's terrible 1857 *Dred Scott* decision, which held that blacks could not enjoy the *"privileges and immunities"* of citizenship.[9]

The Fourteenth Amendment fulfilled the Declaration of Independence's promise that "all men are created equal."[10]

The Fifteenth Amendment prohibits using a citizen's race, color, or previous status as a slave to disqualify him from voting.[11] And any office was now open to anyone regardless of race.[12]

Unfortunately, the implementation of the Civil War amendments fell victim to Southern defiance and Northern fatigue. It took the civil rights movement to give the Civil War amendments anything approaching their intended scope.

But the Civil War amendments represented a promise:

"that this nation, under God, shall have a new birth of freedom . . . ."[13]

It was the promise of the original Bill of Rights. The promise remained unfulfilled for generations. And we still have more to do.

But the promise remains.

Dred Scott

9. *Dred Scott v. Sanford*, 60 U.S. (19 How.) 393 (1857).
See generally Louisa M. A. Heiny, *Radical Abolitionist Influence on Federalism and the Fourteenth Amendment*, 49 AM. J. LEGAL HIST. 180 (2007). See also Symposium, *Dred Scott After 150 Years: A Grievous Wound Remembered*, 17 WIDENER L. J. 1 (2007); Paul Finkleman, *Was Dred Scott Correctly Decided? An "Expert Report" for the Defendant*, 12 LEWIS & CLARK L. REV. 1219 (2008) (arguing that under the Constitution at the time, with its proslavery provisions *Dred Scott* was correctly decided).

11. The 15th Amendment.

10. Ohio congressman John Bingham drafted Section 1 to correct what he considered fundamental flaws in the Constitution.
During ratification debates, House Speaker Schuyler Colfax said the 14th Amendment would become *"the gem of the Constitution,"* because *"it is the Declaration of Independence placed immutably and forever"* there.

Schuyler Colfax

John Bingham

Thomas Mundy Peterson

12. Thomas Mundy Peterson was the first African American to vote after the Fifteenth Amendment, casting his ballot in a school board election in Perth Amboy, New Jersey, on March 31, 1870.
The forty-fourth president of the United States of America, Barack Obama, is black. Regardless of your political persuasion, this is a remarkable progression in less than 140 years.

13. Lincoln's Gettysburg Address, Thursday afternoon, November 19, 1863:
Four score and seven years ago our fathers brought forth on this continent a new nation, conceived in Liberty, and dedicated to the proposition that all men are created equal.
Now we are engaged in a great civil war, testing whether that nation, or any nation, so conceived and so dedicated, can long endure. We are met on a great battle-field of that war. We have come to dedicate a portion of that field, as a final resting place for those who here gave their lives that that nation might live. It is altogether fitting and proper that we should do this.
But, in a larger sense, we can not dedicate . . . we can not consecrate . . . we can not hallow this ground. The brave men, living and dead, who struggled here, have consecrated it, far above our poor power to add or detract. The world will little note, nor long remember what we say here, but it can never forget what they did here. It is for us the living, rather, to be dedicated here to the unfinished work which they who fought here have thus far so nobly advanced. It is rather for us to be here dedicated to the great task remaining before us—that from these honored dead we take increased devotion to that cause for which they gave the last full measure of devotion—that we here highly resolve that these dead shall not have died in vain—that this nation, under God, shall have a new birth of freedom—and that government: of the people, by the people, for the people, shall not perish from the earth.

Bibliography

PREQUEL

CASES:
McCulloch v. Maryland, 17 U.S. (4 Wheat.) 316 (1819).

CONSTITUTIONS:
THE BILL OF RIGHTS
UNITED STATES CONSTITUTION

BOOKS:
1 WILLIAM BLACKSTONE, COMMENTARIES ON THE LAWS OF ENGLAND (1765).

2 JOSEPH STORY, COMMENTARIES ON THE CONSTITUTION OF THE UNITED STATES 651 (5th ed. 1891).

3 J. ELLIOT, THE DEBATES IN THE SEVERAL STATE CONVENTIONS ON THE ADOPTION OF THE FEDERAL CONSTITUTION 462 (1891).

4 WILLIAM BLACKSTONE, COMMENTARIES ON THE LAWS OF ENGLAND (1st ed. 1769).

BERNARD SCHWARTZ, THE BILL OF RIGHTS: A DOCUMENTARY HISTORY (1971).

BERNARD SCHWARTZ, THE GREAT RIGHTS OF MANKIND (1977).

CATHERINE DRINKER BOWEN, MIRACLE AT PHILADELPHIA: THE STORY OF THE CONSTITUTIONAL CONVENTION MAY TO SEPTEMBER 1787 (1966).

Leonard W. Levy, *Bill of Rights, in* ESSAYS ON THE MAKING OF THE CONSTITUTION (Leonard W. Levy ed., 1987).

LEONARD W. LEVY, ORIGINS OF THE FIFTH AMENDMENT: THE RIGHT AGAINST SELF-INCRIMINATION (1968).

PATRICK T. CONLEY & JOHN P. KAMINSKI, THE BILL OF RIGHTS AND THE STATES: THE COLONIAL AND REVOLUTIONARY ORIGINS OF AMERICAN LIBERTIES (1992).

RICHARD LABUNSKI, JAMES MADISON AND THE STRUGGLE FOR THE BILL OF RIGHTS (2006).

ROBERT A. DAHL, HOW DEMOCRATIC IS THE AMERICAN CONSTITUTION? (2001).

ROBERT JAMES WALLER, THE BRIDGES OF MADISON COUNTY (1992).

SAINT THOMAS AQUINAS, TREATISE ON LAW 6 (Richard J. Regan 2000).

THE FEDERALIST PAPERS

THE FEDERALIST NO. 84 (Alexander Hamilton) (Clinton Rossiter ed., 1961).

BRIEFS AND ARTICLES:
Carl T. Bogus, *The Hidden History of the Second Amendment*, 31 U.C. DAVIS L. REV. 309 (1998).

Charles A. Rees, *Remarkable Evolution: The Early Constitutional History of Maryland*, 36 U. BALT. L. REV. 217 (2007).

Dan T. Coenen, *A Rhetoric for Ratifications: The Argument of the Federalist and its Impact on Constitutional Interpretation*, 56 DUKE L. J. 469 (2006).

Douglas G. Smith, *An Analysis of Two Federal Structures: The Articles of Confederation and the Constitution*, 34 SAN DIEGO L. REV. 249 (1997).

Douglas O. Linder, *The Two Hundredth Reunion of Delegates to the Constitutional Convention (or, "All Things Considered, We'd Really Rather Be in Philadelphia")*, 1985 ARIZ. ST. L. J. 823 (1985).

Gene R. Nichol, *Toward a People's Constitution*, 91 Cal. L. Rev. 621 (2003).

Gregory E. Maggs, *A Concise Guide to the Federalist Papers as a Source of the Original Meaning of the United States Constitution*, 87 B.U.L. REV. 801 (2007).

Horst Dippel, *Human Rights in America, 1776-1849: Rediscovering the States' Contribution*, 67 ALB. L. REV. 713 (2004).

Hugo L. Black, *The Bill of Rights*, 35 N.Y.U. L. REV. 865 (1960).

Matthew P. Harrington, *The Economic Origins of the Seventh Amendment*, 87 IOWA L. REV. 145 (2001).

Melvyn R. Durchslag, *The Supreme Court and the Federalist Papers: Is There Less Here Than Meets the Eye?*, 14 WM. & MARY BILL RTS. J. 243 (2005).

Randall T. Shepard, *The Bill of Rights for the Whole Nation*, 26 VAL. U. L. REV. 27 (1991).

Randy E. Barnett, *The Ninth Amendment: It Means What It Says*, 85 TEX. L. REV. 1 (2006).

Robert Farley, Comments, *Preventing Unconstitutional Gerrymandering: Escaping the Intent/Effects Quagmire*, 38 SETON HALL L. REV. 397 (2008).

Shlomo Slonim, *The Federalist Papers and the Bill of Rights*, 20 CONST. COMMENT. 151 (2003).

Thurgood Marshall, *Reflections on the Bicentennial of the United States Constitution*, 101 HARV. L. REV. 1 (1987).

William J. Brennan, Jr., *Why We Have a Bill of Rights?*, 26 VAL. U. L. REV. 1 (1991).

MOVIES:

THE BRIDGES OF MADISON COUNTY (Warner Bros. 1995).

MISC.

Documentary History of the Bill of Rights, http://www.constitution.org/dhbr.htm (last visited March 12, 2008).

Madison County, Iowa, http://en.wikipedia.org/wiki/Madison_County%2C_Iowa (last visited March 31, 2006).

CHAPTER ONE
CASES

Abrams v. United States, 250 U.S. 616 (1919).

Barnes v. Glen Theatre, Inc., 501 U.S. 560 (1991).

Brandenburg v. Ohio, 395 U.S. 444 (1969).

Brandenburg v. Ohio, 395 U.S. 444 (1969).

Cohen v. California, 403 U.S. 15 (1971).

County of Allegheny v. ACLU, 492 U.S. 573 (1989).

Dennis v. United States, 341 U.S. 494 (1951).

Edwards v. Aguillard, 482 U.S. 578 (1987).

Epperson v. Arkansas, 393 U.S. 97 (1968).

Everson v. Board of Education, 330 U.S. 1 (1947).

Frederick v. Morse, 439 F.3d 1114 (9th Cir. 2006).

Garland v. Torre, 259 F.2d 545 (2d Cir. 1958).

Gitlow v. New York, 268 U.S. 652 (1925).

Holy Trinity Church v. United States, 143 U.S. 457 (1892).

Hustler Magazine, Inc. v. Falwell, 485 U.S. 46 (1988).

Jacobellis v. Ohio, 378 U.S. 184 (1964).

Korematsu v. United States, 323 U.S. 214 (1944), rh'g denied, 324 U.S. 885 (1945).

Lamont v. Postmaster General, 381 U.S. 301 (1965).

Lee v. Weisman, 505 U.S. 577 (1992).

Lynch v. Donnelly, 465 U.S. 668 (1984).

Masses Publishing Co. v. Patten, 244 F. 535 (S.D.N.Y. 1917), rev'd, 246 F. 24 (2d Cir. 1917).

McCreary County v. ACLU of Kentucky, 545 U.S. 844 (2005).

McIntyre v. Ohio Elections Comm'n, 514 U.S. 334 (1995).

McLean v. Arkansas Board of Education, 529 F. Supp. 1255 (E.D. Ark. 1982).

Morse v. Frederick, 551 U.S. 393 (2007).

National Ass'n of Home Builders v. Defenders of Wildlife, 551 U.S. 644 (2007).

Near v. Minnesota, 283 U.S. 697 (1931).

New York Times Co. v. U.S. (Pentagon Papers), 403 U.S. 713 (1971).

New York Times v. Sullivan, 376 U.S. 254, 273 (1964).

Newdow v. U.S. Congress (Newdow I) 292 F.3d 597 (9th Cir 2002).

Reynolds v. United States, 98 U.S. 145 (1878).

Roth v. United States, 354 U.S. 476 (1957).

Rumsfeld v. Forum for Academic & Institutional Rights, Inc., 547 U.S. 47 (2006).

Schenck v. United States, 249 U.S. 47 (1919).

Scopes v. State, 278 S.W. 57 (Tenn. 1925).

State v. Buchanan, 436 P.2d 729 (Or. 1968).

State v. Knops, 183 N.W.2d 93 (Wis. 1971).

State v. Scopes, 152 Tenn. 424 (Tenn. 1925).

Stromberg v. California, 283 U.S. 359 (1931).

United States v. Schwimmer, 279 U.S. 644 (1929).

Van Orden v. Perry, 545 U.S. 677 (2005).

Vidal v. Girard's Executors, 43 U.S. 127 (1844).

Wallace v. Jaffree, 472 U.S. 38 (1985).

Watts v. Indiana, 338 U.S. 49 (1949).

West Virginia Bd. of Educ. v. Barnette, 319 U.S. 624 (1943).

Whitney v. California, 274 U.S. 357 (1927).

Zorach v. Clauson, 343 U.S. 306 (1951).

CONSTITUTIONS:

UNITED STATES CONSTITUTION

STATUTES:

36 U.S.C. § 301 (2006).

The Catholic Relief Act of 1829, 10 Geo. 4, c. 7 (Eng.).

The Ecclesiastical Appeals Act, 1532, 24 Hen. 8, c. 12.

BOOKS:

1 Historical Collections: Consisting Of State Papers And Other Authentic Documents: Intended As Materials For A History Of The United States Of America (Ebenezer Hazard ed., T. Dobson 1792).

3 Joseph Story, Commentaries On The Constitution Of The United States (1833).

4 William Blackstone, Commentaries.

4 William Blackstone, Commentaries (1769), *reprinted in* L. Levy, Freedom Of The Press From Zenger To Jefferson (1966).

Alan Haynes, Invisible Power: The Elizabethan Secret Services 1570-1603 (1992).

Alf J. Mapp, The Faiths of Our Fathers: What America's Founders Really Believed (2005).

Ann Coulter, Godless: The Church of Liberalism (2006).

Anthony Lewis, Freedom for the Thought That We Hate: A Biography of the First Amendment (2007).

Aristotle, Poetics 1459a (McGill-Queen's University Press 1997).

Arthur Miller, The Crucible (1953).

Brent Tarter, *Virginians and the Bill of Rights*, *in* The Bill of Rights: A Lively Heritage (Jon Kukla ed. 1987).

Brooke Allen, Moral Minority: Our Skeptical Founding Fathers (2006).

Camille Saint-Saëns, Henry VIII (1883).

Catherine Drinker Bowen, Miracle at Philadephia: The Story of the Constitutional Convention May to September 1789 (1966).

Charles Dickens, A Child's History of England, Vol. III (1953) *available at* http://www.archive.org/stream/childshistoryofe03dickrich#page/58/mode/2up (last visited November 7, 2009).

Colin Rhys Lovell, English Constitutional and Legal History (1962).

Cynthia Susan Clegg, Censorship in Jacobean England (2001).

Cynthia Susan Clegg, Press Censorship in Elizabethan England (1997).

Dan Brown, The DaVinci Code (2003).

Danny Danziger & John Gillingham, 1215: The Year of Magna Carta (2003).

David Howarth, 1066: The Year of the Conquest (1977).

David L. Holmes, The Faiths of the founding Fathers (2006).

David Loades, Politics, Censorship and the English Reformation (1991).

David M. O'Brien, *Freedom of Speech and Free Government: The First Amendment, the Supreme Court and the Polity*, *in* Jon Kukla, ed. The Bill of Rights: A Lively Heritage (1987).

David McCullough, John Adams (2001).

Encyclopedia of Catholicism (Richard P. McBrien, gen. ed.) (1995).

E.R. Chamberlin, The Bad Popes (1969).

Floyd Abrams, Speaking Freely: Trails of the First Amendment (2005).

G.R. Elton, The Tudor Constitution: Documents and Commentary (1960).

Garry Wills, Saint Augustine (1999).

Gary Kowalski, Revolutionary Spirits: The Enlightened Faith of America's Founding Fathers (2008).

Geoffrey Chaucer, The Canterbury Tales (14th c.).

Geoffrey Cowan, The People v. Clarence Darrow: The Bribery Trial of America's Greatest Lawyer (1993).

Geoffrey R. Stone, Perilous Times: Free Speech in Wartime, From the Sedition Act of 1798 to the War on Terrorism (2004).

J. W. Ehrlich, The Holy Bible and the Law (1962).

J. William Frost, A Perfect Freedom: Religious Liberty in Pennsylvania (1990).

James Alexander, A Brief Narrative of the Case and Trial of John Peter Zenger, Printer of The New York Weekly Journal (1963).

Janice Connell, Faith of Our Founding Father: The Spiritual Journey of George Washington (2003).

Jeremy D. Bailey, Thomas Jefferson and Executive Power 218 (2007).

John Ayto, Dictionary of Word Origins (1990).

John Foxe, Foxe's Book of Martyrs (1563).

John Gillingham, The Wars of the Roses (1981).

John le Carre, A Murder of Quality (1962).

John le Carre, Call for the Dead (1961).

John le Carre, Smiley's People (1979).

John le Carre, The Honourable Schoolboy (1977).

John le Carre, Tinker, Tailor, Soldier, Spy (1974).

John Milton, Areopagitica: A speech of Mr. John Milton for the liberty of unlicensed printing to the Parliament of England (1644).

John Milton, Paradise Lost (1667–68).

John Stuart Mill, On Liberty (1859).

Jon Meacham, American Gospel: God, the Founding Fathers, and the Making of a Nation (2007).

Joseph J. Ellis, His Excellency: George Washington (2004).

Kurt von S. Kynell, Saxon and Medieval Antecedents of the English Common Law (2000).

Larry D. Eldridge, A Distant Heritage: The Growth of Free Speech in Early America (1994).

Leonard W. Levy, Bill of Rights in Essays on the Making of the Constitution (Leonard W. Levy ed., 1987).

Leonard W. Levy, Emergence Of A Free Press (1985).

Leonard W. Levy, Legacy of Suppression (1960).

Leonard W. Levy, Origins of the Fifth Amendment (1968).

Mark Twain, The Prince and the Pauper (1881).

Michael Farris, From Tyndale to Madison: How the Death of an English Martyr Led to the American Bill of Rights, Ch. 3 (2007).

NATHANIEL HAWTHORNE, THE SCARLET LETTER (1850).

PETER ACKROYD, THE LIFE OF THOMAS MORE (1999).

PETER BROWN, AUGUSTINE OF HIPPO (1967).

Plato, *Apology* 21d *in* PLATO: COMPLETE WORKS (Hackett, 1997) (G. M. A. Grube, trans, rev C. D. C. Reeve, John M. Cooper, ed.).

PLATO, LAWS 225 (R.G. Bury trans., Harvard University Press 1926) (n.d.).

PLATO, THE REPUBLIC, (trans. Benjamin Jowett 2009) *available at* http://classics.mit.edu/Plato/republic.html.

R. BLAIN ANDRUS, LAWYER: A BRIEF 5,000 YEAR HISTORY (2009).

RAY BRADBURY, FAHRENHEIT 451 (1951).

REBECCA L. MCMURRY & JAMES F. MCMURRY, JR. THE SCANDALMONGER AND THE NEWSPAPER WAR OF 1802 (2000).

RICH BEYER, THE GREATEST STORIES NEVER TOLD: 100 TABLES FROM HISTORY TO ASTONISH, BEWILDER & STUPEFY (2003).

RICHARD BROOKHISER, WHAT WOULD THE FOUNDERS DO? (2006).

RICHARD MARIUS, THOMAS MORE: A BIOGRAPHY (1985).

Robert A. Rutland, *Freedom of the Press*, *in* THE BILL OF RIGHTS: A LIVELY HERITAGE (John Kukla ed., 1987).

ROBERT HENDRICKSON, QPB ENCYCLOPEDIA OF WORD AND PHRASE ORIGINS (2004).

RON CHERNOW, ALEXANDER HAMILTON (2004).

S. MUTCHOW TOWERS, CONTROL OF RELIGIOUS PRINTING IN EARLY STUART ENGLAND (2003).

SAMUEL RUTHERFORD, LEX, REX, *available at* The Liberty Library of Constitutional Classics, http://www.constitution.org/sr/lexrex.htm.

STEPHEN E. AMBROSE, D-DAY JUNE 6, 1944: THE CLIMACTIC BATTLE OF WORLD WAR II (1994).

STEPHEN HESS & SANDY NORTHROP, DRAWN & QUARTERED: THE HISTORY OF AMERICAN POLITICAL CARTOONS (1996).

STEVEN WALDMAN, FOUNDING FAITHS: HOW OUR FOUNDING FATHERS FORGED A RADICAL NEW APPROACH TO RELIGIOUS LIBERTY (2009).

SUSAN FORD WILTSHIRE, GREECE, ROME, AND THE BILL OF RIGHTS (1992).

T.S. ELIOT, MURDER IN THE CATHEDRAL (1935).

THE BIBLE

THE FEDERALIST 44 (James Madison).

THE FEDERALIST 51 (James Madison).

THE WORKS OF FLAVIUS JOSPEHUS (trans. William Whiston 1847).

THE WORKS OF PLATO, *Apology* 60 (Irwin Edman ed., Benjamin Jowett trans., Random House 1956).

THOMAS CAHILL, HOW THE IRISH SAVED CIVILIZATION: THE UNTOLD STORY OF IRELAND'S HEROIC ROLE FROM THE FALL OF ROME TO THE RISE OF MEDIEVAL EUROPE (1995).

THOMAS JEFFERSON, THE JEFFERSON BIBLE: THE LIFE AND MORALS OF JESUS OF NAZARETH (2010).

THOMAS MORE, UTOPIA (1516).

THOMAS PAINE, THE AGE OF REASON: PART ONE (1794).

TIM F. LAHAYE, FAITH OF OUR FOUNDING FATHERS (1996).

Umberto Eco, The Name of the Rose (1980).

Walter Scott, Redgauntlet (1824).

Will Durant, The Age of Faith: A History of Medieval Civilization – Christian, Islamic, and Judaic – from Constantine to Dante: A.D. 325-1300 (1950).

William Bradford, History Of Plymouth Plantation (Little, Brown & Co. 1856).

William H. Rehnquist, Grand Inquests: The Historic Impeachments of Justice Samuel Chase and President Andrew Johnson (1992).

William Roper, The Life of Sir Thomas More c. 1556 57 (Gerard B. Wegemer and Stephen W. Smith eds. 2003) *available at* http://www.thomasmorestudies.org/docs/Roper.pdf.

William Shakespeare, The Famous History of the Life of King Henry the Eighth (1613).

William L. Shirer, The Rise and Fall of the Third Reich: A History of Nazi Germany (1950, 1960).

William Tyndale and David Daniell, Tyndale's New Testament (1996).

ARTICLES:

Albert W. Alschuler & Andrew G. Deiss, *A Brief History of the Criminal Jury in the United States*, 61 U. Chi. L. Rev. 867 (1994).

Anuj C. Desai, *The Transformation of Statutes into Constitutional Law: How Early Post Office Policy Shaped Modern First Amendment Doctrine*, 58 Hastings L.J. 671 (2007).

Barbara A. Perry, *Jefferson's Legacy to the Supreme Court: Freedom of Religion*, 31 Sup. Ct. Hist. 181 (2006).

Blake D. Morant, *Lessons from Thomas More's Dilemma of Conscience: Reconciling the Clash Between a Lawyer's Beliefs and Professional Expectations*, 78 St. John's L.Rev. 965 (2004).

Charles P. Sherman, *A Brief History of Imperial Roman Canon Law*, 7 Cal. L. Rev. 93 (1918).

Daniel J. Solove, *The First Amendment as Criminal Procedure*, 82 N.Y.U. L. Rev. 112 (2007).

David A. Anderson, *Levy vs. Levy*, 84 Mich. L. Rev. 777 (1986) (reviewing Leonard W. Levy, Emergence Of A Free Press (1985).

David K. DeWolf, *Ten Tortured Words,* 85 Denv. U. L. Rev. 443, (2007) (reviewing Stephen Mansfield, Ten Tortured Words: How the Founding Fathers Tried to Protect Religion in America and What's Happened Since (2007).

David L. Wardle, *Reason to Ratify: The Influence of John Locke's Religious Beliefs on the Creation and Adoption of the United States Constitution*, 26 Seattle U. L. Rev. 291 (2002).

David M. Rabban, *The Ahistorical Historian: Leonard Levy on Freedom of Expression in Early American History*, 37 Stan. L. Rev. 795 (1985) (book review).

David M. Rabban, *The Emergence of Modern First Amendment Doctrine*, 50 U. Chi. L. Rev. 1205 (1983).

Diana Woodhouse, *United Kingdom: The Constitutional Reform Act 2005 – Defending Judicial Independence the English Way*, 5 Int'l J. Const. L. 153 (2007)

Dinitia Smith, *Writers as Plunderers; Why do they Keep Giving Away Other People's Secrets?* N.Y. Times, October 24, 1998, *available at* http://www.nytimes.com/1998/10/24/books/writers-as-plunderers-why-do-they-keep-giving-away-other-people-s-secrets.html?sec=&spon=&pagewanted=2.

Douglas Laycock, *"Noncoercive" Support for Religion: Another False Claim about the Establishment Clause*, 26 VAL. U. L. REV. 37 (1992).

Douglas Laycock, *Towards a General Theory of the Religion Clauses: The Case of Church Labor Relations and the Right to Church Autonomy*, 81 COLUM. L. REV. 1373 (1981).

Eric Schnapper, *'Libelou'" Petitions for Redress of Grievances: Bad Historiography Makes Worse Law*, 74 IOWA L. REV. 303 (1989).

Erwin Chemerinsky, *History, Tradition, the Supreme Court, and the First Amendment*, 44 HASTINGS L.J. 901 (1993).

Eugene Volokh, *Symbolic Expression and the Original Meaning of the First Amendment*, 97 GEO. L.J. 1057 (2009).

Geoffrey R. Stone, *The World of the Framers: A Christian Nation?* 56 UCLA L. REV. 1 (2008).

Gerald Gunther, *Learned Hand and the Origins of Modern First Amendment Doctrine: Some Fragments of History*, 27 STAN L. REV. 719 (1975).

Gregory C. Downs, *Religious Liberty that Almost Wasn't: On the Origin of the Establishment Clause of the First Amendment*, 30 U. ARK. LITTLE ROCK L. REV. 19 (2007).

Harold J. Berman, *Law and Belief in Three Revolutions*, 18 VAL. U. L. REV. 569 (1984).

Harold J. Berman, *Religious Foundations of Law in the West: An Historical Perspective*, 1 J.L. & RELIGION 3 (1983).

Harold W. Wolfram, *John Lilburne,: Democracy's Pillar of Fire*, 3 SYRACUSE L. REV. 213 (1952).

Herbert W. Titus, *God's Revelation: Foundation for the Common Law*, 4 REGENT U. L. REV. 1 (1994).

Hirad Abtahi, *Reflections on the Ambiguous Universality of Human Rights: Cyrus the Great's Proclamation as a Challenge to the Athenian Democracy's Perceived Monopoly on Human Rights*, 36 DENV. J. INT'L L. & POL'Y 55 (2007).

Hugo L. Black, *The Bill of Rights*, 35 N.Y.U. L. REV. 865 (1960).

Jacob Reynolds, *The Rule of Law and the Origins of the Bill of Attainder Clause*, 18 ST. THOMAS L. REV. 177 (2005).

Jeffrey K. Sawyer, *Benefit of Clergy in Maryland and Virginia*, 34 AM. J. LEGAL HIST. 49 (1990).

John Wertheimer, *Review: Freedom of Speech: Zechariah Chafee and Free-Speech History*, 22 REVS. IN AM. HIST. 365 (1994).

John Witte, Jr., *"A Most Mild and Equitable Establishment of Religion": John Adams and The Massachusetts Experiment*, 41 J. CHURCH & ST. 213 (1999).

John Witte, Jr., *Blest be the Ties that Bind: Covenant and Community in Puritan Thought*, 36 EMORY L.J. 579 (1987).

John Witte, Jr., Book Review, 16 J.L. & RELIGION 565 (2001) (reviewing DANIEL L. DREISBACH, RELIGION AND POLITICS IN THE EARLY REPUBLIC: JASPER ADAMS AND THE CHURCH-STATE DEBATE (1996)).

John Witte, Jr., *How to Govern a City on a Hill: The Early Puritan Contribution to American Constitutionalism*, 39 EMORY L.J. 41 (1990).

John Witte, Jr., *Prophets, Priests, and Kings: John Milton and the Reformation of Rights and Liberties in England*, 57 EMORY L.J. 1527 (2008).

John Witte, Jr., *Tax Exemption of Church Property: Historical Anomaly or Valid Constitutional Practice?*, 64 S. CAL. L. REV. 363 (1991).

Keith Werhan, *The Classical Athenian Ancestry of American Freedom of Speech*, 2008 SUP. CT. REV. 293 (2009).

Lael Daniel Weinberger, *The Monument and the Message: Pragmatism and Principle in Establishment Clause Ten Commandments Litigation*, 14 TEX. WESLEYAN L. REV. 393 (2008).

Leonard W. Levy, *On the Origins of the Free Press Clause*, 32 UCLA L. REV. 177 (1984).

Leonard W. Levy, *The Legacy Reexamined*, 37 STAN. L. REV. 767 (1985).

Mark J. Chadsey, *Thomas Jefferson and the Establishment Clause*, 40 AKRON L. REV. 623 (2007).

Martin E. Marty, *Freedom of Religion and the First Amendment, in* THE BILL OF RIGHTS: A LIVELY HERITAGE 19 (Jon Kukla ed., 1987).

Martin E. Marty, *On A Medial Moraine: Religious Dimensions Of American Constitutionalism* 39 EMORY L.J. 9 (1990).

Matthew C. Berger, Comment, *One Nation Indivisible: How Congress's Addition of "Under God" to the Pledge of Allegiance Offends the Original Intent of the Establishment Clause*, 3 U. ST. THOMAS L.J. 629 (2006).

Patrick M. Garry, *The Myth of Separation: America's Historical Experience with Church and State*, 33 HOFSTRA L. REV. 475 (2004).

Richard Albert, *Religion in the New Republic*, 67 LA. L. REV. 1 (2006).

Robert A. Sedler, *Essay: The Protection of Religious Freedom Under the American Constitution*, 53 WAYNE L. REV. 817 (2007).

Robert Joseph Renaud & Lael Daniel Weinberger, *Spheres Of Sovereignty: Church Autonomy Doctrine and the Theological Heritage of the Separation of Church and State*, 35 N. KY. L. REV. 67 (2008).

Scott J. Street, *Poor Richard's Forgotten Press Clause: How Journalists Can Use Original Intent to Protect their Confidential Sources*, 27 LOY. L.A. ENT. L. REV. 463 (2007).

Stanford E. Lehmberg, *Parliamentary Attainder in the Reign of Henry VIII*, 18 HIST. J. 675 (1975).

Stanley Ingber, *The Marketplace of Ideas: A Legitimizing Myth*, 1984 DUKE L.J. 1 (1984).

Stephen M. Feldman, *Free Speech, World War I, and Republican Democracy: The Internal and External Holmes*, 6 FIRST AMEND. L. REV. 192 (2008).

Steve Bachmann, *Starting Again with the Mayflower . . . England's Civil War and America's Bill of Rights*, 20 QLR 193 (2000).

Susanna Dokupil, *"Thou Shalt Not Bear False Witness": "Sham" Secular Purposes in Ten Commandments Displays*, 28 HARV. J.L. & PUB. POL'Y 609 (2005).

Susanna Frederick Fischer, *Playing Poohsticks with the British Constitution? The Blair Government's Proposal to Abolish the Lord Chancellor*, 24 PENN. ST. INT'L L. REV. 257 (2005).

Thomas B. Colby, *A Constitutional Hierarchy of Religions? Justice Scalia, the Ten Commandments, and the Future of the Establishment Clause*, 100 NW. U.L. REV. 1097 (2006).

Thomas B. McAffee, *The Bill of Rights, Social Contract Theory, and the Rights "Retained" by the People*, 16 S. ILL. U. L.J. 267 (1992).

Thomas Jefferson: Establishing a Federal Republic, http://www.loc.gov/exhibits/jefferson/jefffed.html (last visited November 20, 2009).

Trevor D. Dryer, *"All the News that's Fit to Print": The New York Times, "Yellow" Journalism, and the Criminal Trial 1898-1902,* 8 NEV. L. J. 541 (2008).

Walter B. Hamlin, *The Bill of Rights or the First Ten Amendments to the United States Constitution*, 68 COM. L. J. 233 (1963).

William Trunk, *The Scourge of Contextualism: Ceremonial Deism and the Establishment Clause*, 49 B.C. L. Rev. 571 (2008).

Zechariah Chafee, Jr., *Freedom of Speech in War Time*, 32 Harv. L. Rev. 932 (1919).

Movies:

300 (Warner Bros. 2007).

A Bridge Too Far (United Artists 1977).

A Knight's Tale (Columbia Pictures 2001).

A Man for All Seasons (Columbia Pictures 1966).

A Man for All Seasons (TNT 1988).

Akeelah and the Bee (Lionsgate 2006).

All the President's Men (Warner Bros. 1976).

Anne of the Thousand Days (Universal Pictures 1969).

Becket (Paramount Pictures 1964).

Bee Season (Fox Searchlight Pictures 2005).

Bill & Ted's Excellent Adventure (Orion Pictures 1989).

Bonnie Prince Charlie (London Film Productions 1948).

Braveheart (20th Century Fox 1995).

Bruce Almighty (Universal Studios 2003).

Casino Royal (Metro-Goldwyn-Mayer 2006).

Citizen Kane (RKO Pictures 1941).

Cromwell (Columbia Pictures 1970).

Elizabeth (Gramercy 1998).

Evan Almighty (Universal Studios 2007).

Ever After: A Cinderella Story (20th Century Fox 1998).

Excalibur (Orion Pictures 1981).

Fahrenheit 451 (Universal Pictures 1966).

From Russia with Love (United Artists 1963).

Frost/Nixon (Universal Studios 2008).

Henry VIII (Granada Television 2003).

Hocus Pocus (Walt Disney 1993).

Inherit the Wind (United Artists 1960).

Jesus Christ Superstar (Universal Studios 1973).

King Arthur (Touchstone Pictures 1994).

Kingdom of Heaven (20th Century Fox 2005).

Luther (MGM 2003).

Monty Python's Life of Brian (Warner Bros. 1979).

Network (MGM 1976).

Oh, God (Warner Bros. 1977).

People v. Larry Flynt (Columbia Pictures 1996).

Pleasantville (New Line Cinema 1998).

Queen Margot (Miramax 1994).

Quo Vadis (MGM 1951).

Seven (New Line Cinema 1995).

Shouting Fire: Stories from the Edge of Free Speech (Moxie Firecracker Films 2009).

The 300 Spartans (20th Century Fox 1962).

The Crow (Miramax 1989).

The DaVinci Code (Columbia Pictures 2006).

The Day After Tomorrow (20th Century Fox 2004).

The Devil's Advocate (Warner Bros. 1997).

The Hoax (Miramax Films 2006).

The Last Temptation of Christ (Universal Studios 1988).

The Lion in Winter (Universal Pictures 1968).

The Lovers (Les Amants) (Zenith International Films 1958).

The Magnificent Yankee (Metro-Goldwyn-Mayer 1950).

The Most Dangerous Man in America: Daniel Ellsberg and the Pentagon Papers (First Run Features 2009).

The Mission (Warner Bros. 1986).

The Name of the Rose (20th Century Fox 1986).

The Other Boleyn Girl (Columbia Pictures 2008).

The Paper (Universal Pictures 1994).

The Passion of the Christ (Newmarket Films 2004).

The Prince and the Pauper (1937).

The Prince and the Pauper (Buena Vista Pictures 1990).

The Private Life of Henry VIII (United Artists 1933).

The Prophecy (Dimension Films 1995).

The Scarlet Letter (Hollywood Pictures 1995).

The Sentinel (Universal Pictures 1977).

The Star Chamber (20th Century Fox 1983).

The Ten Commandments (Paramount Pictures 1923).

The Ten Commandments (Paramount Pictures 1956).

The Tudors (Showtime 2007-present).

Misc.:

Abraham Lincoln, Second Inaugural Address (March 4, 1865).

Act of Supremacy, 1534, 26 Hen. 8, c. 1, *available at* http://tudorhistory.org/primary/supremacy.html (last visited 10 February 2006).

Amnesty International, China: No Investigation, No Redress and Still No Freedom of Speech! Human rights activists targeted for discussing the Tiananmen Crackdown, http://www.amnesty.org/en/library/info/ASA17/025/2010/en (last visited August 15, 2010).

Heinrich Heine, Almansor: A Tragedy (1823).

Monty Python, *Oliver Cromwell, on* Monty Python Sings (Virgin Records 1991).

The Catholic Encyclopedia, http://www.newadvent.org/cathen/ (last visited June 12, 2010).

The Prince and the Pauper (Classic Comics Issue 29 1946).

Treaty of Peace and Friendship between the United States of America and the Bey and Subjects of Tripoli of Barbary, art. XI (Nov. 4, 1796) *available at* http:// www.yale.edu/lawweb/avalon/diplomacy/barbary/bar1796t.htm (last visited Oct. 14, 2006).

United States Holocaust Memorial Museum http://www.ushmm.org/research/library/faq/details.php?topic=06#quote_heine (last visited August 21, 2010).

Wikipedia, http://en.wikipedia.org/wiki/Lord_High_Chancellor.

CHAPTER TWO

CASES:

Brown v. Board of Education, 347 U.S. 483 (1954).

District of Columbia v. Heller, 128 S. Ct. 2783 (2008).

Dred Scott v. Sandford, 60 U.S. 393 (1856).

Maryland v. United States, 381 U.S. 41, 46 (1965).

Presser v. Illinois, 116 U.S. 252 (1886).

Silveira v. Lockyer, 312 F. 3d 1052 (9th Cir. 2002).

United States v. Cruikshank, 92 U.S. 542 (1876).

United States v. Emerson, 270 F.3d 203 (5th Cir. 2001).

United States v. Lopez, 514 U.S. 549 (1995).

United States v. Miller, 307 U.S. 174 (1939).

STATUTES:

10 U.S.C. § 311 (2006).

The National Defense Authorization Act for Fiscal Year 1996, 36 U.S.C. § 40701–33.

30 George II, c. 25 (1757) (Eng.).

An Act for the Better Securing the Government by Disarming Papists and Reputed Papists, 1 W. & M., c. 1 (1688) (Eng.).

An Act for Ordering the Forces in the Several Counties of this Kingdom, 13 & 14 Car., c. 3 (1662) (Eng.).

The Statute of Winchester, 13 Edw., cc. 1, 4 (1285) (Eng.).

BOOKS:

1 WILLIAM BLACKSTONE, COMMENTARIES.

ALEXANDER DUMAS, THE THREE MUSKETEERS (1844).

ALEXANDER KEYSSAR, THE RIGHT TO VOTE: THE CONTESTED HISTORY OF DEMOCRACY IN THE UNITED STATES (2000).

ARISTOTLE, POLITICS.

CELIA MILLWARD, HANDBOOK FOR WRITERS (1950).

CHARLES GILDON & JOHN BRIGHTLAND, A GRAMMAR OF THE ENGLISH TONGUE (1711).

COLIN RHYS LOVELL, ENGLISH CONSTITUTIONAL AND LEGAL HISTORY (1962).

DANNY DANZIGER & JOHN GILLINGHAM, 1215: THE YEAR OF MAGNA CARTA (2003).

DAVID HOWARTH, 1066: THE YEAR OF THE CONQUEST (1977).

Dudley Pope, Guns (1965).

E.G. Heath, A History of Target Archery (1973).

Eric H. Monkkonen, Murder in New York City (2001).

Exodus 13:18.

H. Richard Uviller & William G. Merkel, The Militia and the Right to Arms, or, How the Second Amendment Fell Silent (2002).

James Fenimore Cooper, The Leatherstocking Tales (1823–1841).

James William Gibson, Warrior Dreams: Violence and Manhood in Post-Vietnam America (1995).

John E. Warriner, Mary E. Whitten, & Francis Griffith, English Grammar and Composition (1973).

Joseph Story, Commentaries on the U.S. Constitution (5th ed., Melville M. Bigelow 1891) (1833).

Joyce Lee Malcolm, To Keep and Bear Arms: The Origins of an Anglo-American Right (1994).

Juliet Barker, Agincourt: Henry V and the Battle That Made England (2006).

Leonard W. Levy, Origins of the Bill of Rights (1999).

Mark V. Tushnet, Out of Range: Why the Constitution Can't End the Battle Over Guns (2007).

Paul Cartledge, The Spartans: The World of the Warrior-Heroes of Ancient Greece (2002).

Richard Brookhiser, What Would the Founders Do?: Our Questions, Their Answers (2006).

Rick Beyer, The Greatest Stories Never Told (2003).

Robert A. Gross, The Minutemen and Their World (1976).

Robert Baldick, The Duel: A History (1965).

Robert Hardy, Longbow: A Social and Military History (1976).

Robert Hendrickson, QPB Encyclopedia of Word and Phrase Origins (2nd ed. 2004).

Robert Franklin Williams, Negroes with Guns (1961).

Roscoe Pound, The Development of Constitutional Guarantees of Liberty (1957).

Russell F. Weigley, History of the United States Army 202 (1984).

Susan Ford Wiltshire, Greece, Rome, and the Bill of Rights (1992).

The Federalist No. 46 (James Madison).

Thucydides, The Peloponnesian War 313 (Rex Warner trans., 1954).

Thucydides, The Peloponnesian War 265 (T.E. Wick ed., 1982).

Virgil, The Aeneid.

W.F. Paterson, Encyclopaedia of Archery 106 (1984).

Webster's New International Dictionary Of The English Language (2d ed. 1942).

Webster's Word Histories (1989).

William Shakespeare, Henry V. William Strunk, Jr. & E.B. White, The Elements of Style (Macmillan, 3d ed. 1979).

Briefs and Articles:

Adam Winkler, *Scrutinizing the Second Amendment*, 105 Mich. L. Rev. 683 (2007).

Brief for the National Rifle Association and the NRA Civil Rights Defense Fund as Amici Curiae Supporting Respondent, District of Columbia v. Heller, 128 S. Ct. 2783 (2008) (No. 07-290), *available at* http://www.nraila.org/heller/proamicusbriefs/nra_amicus_heller.pdf.

Cameron Desmond, Comment, *From Cities to Schoolyards: The Implications of an Individual Right to Bear Arms on the Constitutionality of Gun-Free Zones*, 39 McGeorge L. Rev. 1043 (2008).

Carl T. Bogus, *The Hidden History of the Second Amendment*, 31 U.C. Davis L. Rev. 309, (1998).

Carl T. Bogus, *The History and Politics of Second Amendment Scholarship: A Primer*, 76 Chi.-Kent L. Rev. 3 (2000).

Carole Emberton, *The Limits of Incorporation: Violence, Gun Rights, and Gun Regulation in the Reconstruction South*, 17 Stan. L. & Pol'y Rev. 615 (2006).

Christopher Keleher, *The Impending Storm: The Supreme Court's Foray Into The Second Amendment Debate*, 69 Mont. L. Rev. 113 (2008).

Clayton E. Cramer & Joseph Edward Olson, *Pistols, Crime, and Public Safety in Early America*, 44 Willamette L. Rev. 699 (2008).

David A. Lieber, *The Cruikshank Redemption: The Enduring Rationale for Excluding the Second Amendment from the Court's Modern Incorporation Doctrine*, 95 J. Crim. L. & Criminology 1079 (2005).

David B. Kopel, Paul Gallant & Joanne D. Eisen, *The Human Right of Self-Defense*, 22 B.Y.U. J. Pub. L. 43 (2007).

David B. Kopel, *The Torah and Self-Defense*, 109 Penn. St. L. Rev. 17 (2004).

David C. Williams, *Civic Constitutionalism, The Second Amendment, and the Right of Revolution*, 79 Ind. L. J. 379 (2004).

David Thomas Konig, *Arms and the Man: What Did the Right to "Keep" Arms Mean in the Early Republic?*, 25 Law & Hist. Rev. 177 (2007).

Dennis A. Henigan, *Arms, Anarchy and the Second Amendment*, 26 Val. U. L. Rev. 107 (1991).

Don B. Kates, Jr., *The Second Amendment and the Ideology of Self-Protection*, 9 Const. Comment. 87 (1992).

Douglas G. Smith, *The Second Amendment and the Supreme Court*, 6 Geo. J. L. & Pub. Pol'y 591 (2008).

Eugene Volokh, *State Constitutional Rights to Keep and Bear Arms*, 11 Tex. Rev. L. & Pol. 191 (2006).

Forum: Rethinking the Second Amendment, 25 Law & Hist. Rev. 139 (2007).

Garry Wills, *To Keep and Bear Arms*, N.Y. Rev. Books, Sept. 21, 1995, at 62.

George A. Mocsary, Note, *Explaining Away The Obvious: The Infeasibility of Characterizing the Second Amendment as a Nonindividual Right*, 76 Fordham L. Rev. 2113 (2008).

Glenn H. Reynolds & Brannon P. Denning, *Heller's Future In The Lower Courts*, 102 Nw. U. L. Rev. 2035 (2008).

John Gibeaut, *A Shot at the Second Amendment*, ABA Journal, November 2007, at 50.

John Levin, *The Right to Bear Arms: The Development of the American Experience*, 48 Chi.-Kent L. Rev. 148 (1971).

John Locke, *An Essay Concerning the True Original, Extent and End of Civil Government* in THE WORLD'S GREAT THINKERS: MAN AND THE STATE: THE POLITICAL PHILOSOPHERS (1947).

John-Peter Lund, *Do Federal Firearms Laws Violate the Second Amendment by Disarming the Militia?*, 10 TEX. REV. L. & POL. 469 (2006).

Jonah Goldberg, *Homer Never Nods: The Importance of The Simpsons,* NAT'L REV., May 1, 2000, at 36, 37.

Jonathan D. Marshall, *Symposium Introduction: District of Columbia v. Heller*, 59 SYRACUSE L. REV. 165 (2008).

Margaret E. Sprunger, *D.C. As a Breeding Ground for the Next Second Amendment Test Case: The Conflict within the U.S. Attorney's Office*, 53 CATH. U. L. REV. 577 (2004).

Mark DeWolfe Howe, *Juries as Judges of Criminal Law*, 52 HARV. L. REV. 582 (1938-1939).

Maxine Burkett, *Much Ado About . . . Something Else: D.C. v. Heller, the Racialized Mythology of the Second Amendment, and Gun Policy Reform*, 12 J. GENDER RACE & JUST. 57 (2008).

Michael Anthony Lawrence, *Second Amendment Incorporation Through the Fourteenth Amendment Privileges or Immunities and Due Process Clauses*, 72 MO. L. REV. 1 (2007).

Mort Luby, Jr., *The History of Bowling*, Bowlers Journal 70 (1983).

Nathan Kozuskanich, *Originalism, History, and the Second Amendment: What Did Bearing Arms Really Mean to the Founders?*, 10 U. PA. J. CONST. L. 413 (2008).

Nelson Lund, *The Second Amendment, Political Liberty, and the Right to Self-Preservation*, 39 ALA. L. REV. 103 (1987).

Pamela S. Karlan, *Ballots and Bullets: The Exceptional History of the Right to Vote*, 71 U. CIN. L. REV. 1345 (2003).

Paul Finkelman, *It Really Was About a Well Regulated Militia*, 59 SYRACUSE L. REV. 267 (2008).

Randall M. Miller, *A Backcountry Loyalist Plan to Retake Georgia and the Carolinas, 1778*, 75 S.C. HIST. MAG. 207 (1974).

Randy E. Barnett, *Book Review Essay: Was the Right to Keep and Bear Arms Conditioned on Service in an Organized Militia?*, 83 TEX. L. REV. 237 (2004).

Richard Brust, *The 25 Greatest Legal Movies: Tales of Lawyers We've Loved and Loathed*, ABA JOURNAL, Aug. 2008, at 38-53.

Robert A. Creamer, *History is not Enough: Using Contemporary Justifications for the Right to Keep and Bear Arms in Interpreting the Second Amendment*, 45 B.C. L. REV. 905 (2004).

Robert H. Churchill, *Gun Regulation, the Police Power, and the Right to Keep Arms in Early America: The Legal Context of the Second Amendment*, 25 LAW & HIST. REV. 139 (2007).

Robert H. Churchill, *Once More Unto the Breach, Dear Friends*, 25 LAW & HIST. REV. 205 (2007).

Sanford Levison, *The Embarrassing Second Amendment*, 99 YALE L. J. 637 (1989).

Saul Cornell & Nathan DeDino, *A Well Regulated Right: The Early American Origins Of Gun Control,* 73 FORDHAM L. REV. 487, 489 (2004).

Saul Cornell, *Early American Gun Regulation and the Second Amendment: A Closer Look at the Evidence*, 25 LAW & HIST. REV. 197 (2007).

Scott D. Gerber, *The Court, The Constitution, and the History of Ideas*, 61 VAND. L. REV. 1067 (2008).

Stephen P. Halbrook, *The Right of the People or the Power of the State: Bearing Arms, Arming Militias, and the Second Amendment*, 26 VAL. U. L. REV. 131 (1991).

Stephen P. Halbrook, *To Keep and Bear Their Private Arms: The Adoption of the Second Amendment, 1787-1791*, 10 N. KY. L. REV. 13 (1982).

Steve Bachmann, *Starting Again With the Mayflower . . . England's Civil War and America's Bill of Rights*, 20 QLR 193 (2000).

Thomas A. Green, *The Jury and the English Law of Homicide, 1200-1600*, 74 MICH. L. REV. 414 (1976).

William G. Merkel, *Mandatory Gun Ownership, the Militia Census of 1806, and Background Assumptions Concerning the Early American Right to Arms: A Cautious Response to Robert Churchill*, 25 LAW & HIST. REV. 187 (2007).

William S. Fields & David T. Hardy, *The Third Amendment and the Issue of the Maintenance of Standing Armies: A Legal History*, 35 AM. J. LEGAL HIST. 393 (1991).

William Sutton Fields, *The Third Amendment: Constitutional Protection from the Involuntary Quartering of Soldiers*, 124 MIL. L. REV. 195 (1989).

MOVIES AND TELEVISION:

2001: A SPACE ODYSSEY (Metro-Goldwyn-Mayer 1968).

A CHRISTMAS STORY (Metro-Goldwyn-Mayer 1983).

A FEW GOOD MEN (Columbia Pictures 1992).

Band of Brothers (HBO 2001).

BONNIE PRINCE CHARLIE (London Film Productions 1948).

BOWFINGER (Universal Pictures 1999).

BRAVEHEART (Paramount Pictures 1995).

Daniel Boone (20th Century Fox September 24, 1964–September 10, 1970).

DAVY CROCKETT, KING OF THE WILD FRONTIER (Buena Vista 1955).

DEATH WISH (Paramount Pictures 1974).

DELIVERANCE (Warner Brothers 1972).

DIRTY HARRY (Warner Bros. 1971).

EXODUS (United Artists 1960).

FIRST BLOOD (Orion Pictures 1982).

FLETCH (Universal Pictures 1985).

FLETCH LIVES (Universal Pictures 1989).

FORT APACHE (RKO 1948).

FRANKENSTEIN (Universal Pictures 1931).

FROST/NIXON (Universal Studios 2008).

FULL METAL JACKET (Warner Bros. 1987).

GLADIATOR (Dreamworks 2000).

GRAN TORINO (Warner Bros. 2008).

HENRY V (Eagle-Lion Distributors Ltd. 1944).

HENRY V (Renaissance Films 1989).

HIGH NOON (United Artists 1952).

INVENTING THE ABBOTTS (20th Century Fox 1997).

MAGNUM FORCE (Warner Bros. 1973).

OUTLAND (Warner Bros. 1981).

PALE RIDER (Warner Bros. 1985).

PLANET OF THE APES (20th Century Fox 1968).

PLATOON (Orion Pictures 1986).

POSSE (Paramount Pictures 1975).

RAIDERS OF THE LOST ARK (Paramount Pictures 1981).

RAMBO (Lionsgate 2008).

RAMBO III (TriStar Pictures 1988).

RAMBO: FIRST BLOOD PART II (TriStar Pictures 1985).

ROBIN HOOD (Buena Vista 1973).

ROBIN HOOD: MEN IN TIGHTS (20th Century Fox 1993).

ROBIN HOOD: PRINCE OF THIEVES (Warner Bros. 1991).

SANDS OF IWO JIMA (Republic Pictures 1949).

SERGEANT YORK (Warner Bros. 1941).

SERPICO (Paramount Pictures 1973).

SHANE (Paramount Pictures 1953).

SNIPER (TriStar Pictures 1993).

SNIPER 2 (TriStar Pictures 2002).

SNIPER 3 (Destination Films 2004).

Star Trek: Arena (NBC television broadcast January 19, 1967).

SUDDEN IMPACT (Warner Bros. 1983).

THE ADVENTURES OF ROBIN HOOD (Warner Bros. 1938).

THE BIRTH OF A NATION (Epoch Film Co. 1915).

THE DEAD POOL (Warner Bros. 1988).

THE ENFORCER (Warner Bros. 1976).

THE FOUR MUSKETEERS (20th Century Fox 1974).

THE LAST OF THE MOHICANS (20th Century Fox 1992).

THE MESSENGER: THE STORY OF JOAN OF ARC (Columbia Pictures 1999).

THE PATRIOT (Columbia Pictures 2000).

The Rifleman (ABC television broadcast 1958–1963).

THE SEARCHERS (Warner Bros. 1956).

The Simpsons: The Cartridge Family (Fox television broadcast Nov. 2, 1997).

THE TEN COMMANDMENTS (Paramount Pictures 1956).

THE THREE MUSKETEERS (20th Century Fox 1973).

TOOTH FAIRY (20th Century Fox 2010).

TROY (Warner Bros. 2004).

Wanted: Dead or Alive (Four Star Productions 1958–1961).

WAY OF THE DRAGON (Golden Harvest 1972).

WINCHESTER '73 (Universal Pictures 1950).

Xena: Warrior Princess (Pacific Renaissance Pictures Ltd. 1995–2001).

Misc.

Civilian Marksmanship Program, http://www.odcmp.com.

How Stuff Works, science.howstuffworks.com/flintlock2.htm.

NRA-ILA: Who We Are, And What We Do, http://www.nraila.org/About/ (last visited August 4, 2008).

President Abraham Lincoln, The Emancipation Proclamation (Jan. 1, 1863), *available at* http://avalon.law.yale.edu/19th_century/emancipa.asp.

Ralph Waldo Emerson, *Concord Hymn*.

U.S. Dep't of Defense, Department of Defense Budget for Fiscal Year 2007: Program Acquisition Costs by Weapon System, (2006), at http://www.defenselink.mil/comptroller/defbudget/fy2007/fy2007_weabook.pdf (last visited July 28, 2008).

About.Com, *Dick Cheney Shooting Jokes*, at http://politicalhumor.about.com/od/cheneyshooting/
a/cheneyshooting.htm (last visited September 11, 2010).

CHAPTER THREE

CASES:

Engblom v. Carey, 677 F.2d 957 (2d Cir. 1982).

Griswold v. Connecticut, 381 U.S. 479 (1965).

Jones v. United States Secretary of Defense. 346 F. Supp. 97 (D. Minn. 1972).

Securities Investor Protection Corp. v. Executive Securities Corp., 433 F. Supp. 470 (S.D.N.Y. 1977).

United States v. Miller, 307 U.S. 174 (1939).

United States v. Valenzuala, 95 F. Supp. 363 (S.D. Cal. 1951).

CONSTITUTIONS:

C.S. CONST. art. I, §. 9, cl. 14.

CAL. CONST. art. I, § 5.

CONN. CONST. art. I, § 17.

MAGNA CARTA, cl. 51.

THE DECLARATION OF INDEPENDENCE (U.S. 1776).

UNITED STATES CONSTITUTION

STATUTES:

13 Edw. 3, rot. 35 (1340).

42 U.S.C. § 1994 (2006).

Anti-Quartering Act of 1679, 31 Car. 2, ch. 1.

Petition of Right, 1628, 3 Car. 1, cap. 1, § VI (Eng.).

Quartering Act of 1774, 14 Geo. 3, ch. 54.

BOOKS:

V THE FOUNDERS' CONSTITUTION (Philip B. Kurland & Ralph Lerner eds., 1987).

ADRIAN GOLDSWORTHY, ROMAN WARFARE (2000).

BARBARA W. TUCHMAN, THE MARCH OF FOLLY: FROM TROY TO VIETNAM *Chapter 4: The British Lose America* (1984).

Colin Rhys Lovell, English Constitutional and Legal History (1962).

Danny Danziger & John Gillingham, 1215: The Year of Magna Carta (2003).

Eric Schultz & Michael J. Touglas, King Philip's War: The History and Legacy of America's Forgotten Conflict (2000).

James Madison, Political Observations (1795).

J.R.R. Tolkien, The Hobbit (1937).

Kurt von S. Kynell, Saxon and Medieval Antecedents of the English Common Law (2000).

Lois G. Schwoerer, The Declaration of Rights, 1689 (1981).

Marilyn Yalom, Birth of the Chess Queen (2004).

Mark V. Tushnet, Out of Range: Why the Constitution Can't End the Battle Over Guns (2007).

Maurizio Viroli, Niccolo's Smile, A Biography of Machiavelli (2000).

Niccolo Machiavelli, The Prince and the Discourses (Mod. Library ed., 1950) (1513).

Richard Holmes, Redcoat: The British Soldier in the Age of Horse and Musket (2001).

Ronald Chernow, Alexander Hamilton (2004).

Sources of Our Liberties (R. Perry ed., 1952).

Susan Ford Wiltshire, Greece, Rome, and the Bill of Rights (1992).

The Federalist No. 46 (James Madison).

The Roots of the Bill of Rights (B. Schwartz ed., 1980).

Webster's New International Dictionary Of The English Language (2d ed.1942).

William Shakespeare, King Lear.

Articles:

Ann Marie C. Petrey, *The Third Amendment's Protection Against Unwanted Military Intrusion: Engblom v. Carey*, 49 Brooklyn L. Rev. 857 (1983).

Dennis A. Henigan, *Arms, Anarchy and the Second Amendment*, 26 Val. U. L. Rev. 107 (1991).

Frank B. Lewis, *Whatever Happened to the 3rd Amendment?*, N.Y.L.J., Feb. 26, 1979, at 1.

Jeffrey L. Scheib, *Barracks for the Borough: A Constitutional Question in Colonial Lancaster*, 87 J. Lancaster County Hist. Soc'y 53 (1983).

Morton J. Horwitz, *Is the Third Amendment Obsolete?*, 26 Val. U. L. Rev. 209 (1992).

Robert A. Gross, *Public and Private in the Third Amendment*, 26 Val. U. L. Rev. 215 (1992).

Seymour W. Warfel, *Quartering of Troops: The Unlitigated Third Amendment*, 21 Tenn. L. Rev. 723 (1951).

Tom W. Bell, *The Third Amendment: Forgotten but Not Gone*, 2 William & Mary Bill of Rights J. 117 (1993).

William S. Fields, *The Third Amendment: Constitutional Protection from the Involuntary Quartering of Soldiers*, 124 Mil. L. Rev. 195 (1989).

William S. Fields & David T. Hardy, *The Third Amendment and the Issue of the Maintenance of Standing Armies: A Legal History*, 35 Am. J. Legal Hist. 393 (1991).

MOVIES AND TELEVISION:

300 (Warner Bros. 2007).

CROMWELL (Columbia Pictures 1970).

PLATOON (Orion Pictures 1986).

MEET THE SPARTANS (20th Century Fox 2008).

NATIONAL LAMPOON'S ANIMAL HOUSE (Universal Pictures 1978).

Police Squad! (1982).

THE 13TH WARRIOR (Touchstone Pictures 1999).

THE 300 SPARTANS (20th Century Fox 1962).

THE NAKED GUN: FROM THE FILES OF POLICE SQUAD! (Paramount Pictures 1988).

THE NAKED GUN 2½: THE SMELL OF FEAR (Paramount Pictures 1991).

THE NAKED GUN 33⅓: THE FINAL INSULT (Paramount Pictures 1994).

MISC.:

IV Convention – The Laws and Customs of War on Land of the Hague Conventions of 1907, Article 23.

Department of Housing and Urban Development, http://www.nhl.gov/about/budget/fy07/fy07budget.pdf (last visited Jul. 28, 2008).

Office of the Under Secretary of Defense, Dept. of Defense, Program Acquisition Costs By Weapon System, Fiscal Year 2007(2006), available at http://www.defenselink.mil/comptroller/defbudget/fy2007/fy2007_weakbook.pdf (last visited Jul. 4, 2008).Petition of Right, 1628, 3 Car. 1, cap. 1, § VI (Eng.), *reproduced at* http://www.constitution.org/eng/petright.htm (last visited Jul. 12 2008).

The Nuremberg Trials, October 1946.World Military Spending, http://www.globalissues.org/article/75/world-military-spending#USMilitarySpending (Sept. 13, 2009).

CHAPTER FOUR

CASES:

Arizona v. Gant, 129 S.Ct. 1710 (2009).

Johnson v. United States, 333 U.S. 10, 14-15 (1948).

Mapp v. Ohio, 367 U.S. 643 (1961).

Semayne's Case, 77 Eng. Rep. 194, 195 (K.B.) (1604).

State v. Bolt, 689 P.2d 519 (Ariz. 1984).

Richards v. Wisconsin, 117 S. Ct. 1416 (1997).

United States v. Dale Juan Osife, 398 F.3d 1143 (9th Cir. 2005).

United States v. Leon, 468 U.S. 897 (1984).

United States v. Thornton, 124 S. Ct. 2132 (2004).

Weeks v. United States, 232 U.S. 383 (1914).

CONSTITUTIONS:

Arizona Constitution, Art. II § 8.

STATUTES:

18 U.S.C. § 3105 (2006).

BOOKS:

ADAM NICOLSON, SEIZE THE FIRE: HEROISM, DUTY AND THE BATTLE OF TRAFALGAR (2005).

AKHIL REED AMAR, THE CONSTITUTION AND CRIMINAL PROCEDURE: FIRST PRINCIPLES (1997).

ALDEN BRADFORD, BIOGRAPHICAL NOTICES OF DISTINGUISHED MEN IN NEW ENGLAND: STATESMEN, PATRIOTS, PHYSICIANS, LAWYERS, CLERGYMEN, AND MECHANICS (1842).

ANDREW E. TASLITZ, RECONSTRUCTING THE FOURTH AMENDMENT: A HISTORY OF SEARCH AND SEIZURE 1789-1868 (2006).

ANTONIA FRASER, THE LIVES OF THE KINGS AND QUEENS OF ENGLAND (1975).

ARTHUR H. CASH, JOHN WILKES: THE SCANDALOUS FATHER OF CIVIL LIBERTY (2006).

CHARLES RAPPLEYE, SONS OF PROVIDENCE: THE BROWN BROTHERS, THE SLAVE TRADE, AND THE AMERICAN REVOLUTION (2006).

CLIFFORD LINDSEY ALDERMAN, RUM, SLAVES AND MOLASSES: THE STORY OF NEW ENGLAND'S TRIANGULAR TRADE (1972).

COLIN RHYS LOVELL, ENGLISH CONSTITUTIONAL AND LEGAL HISTORY (1962).

DANNY DANZIGER & JOHN GILLINGHAM, 1215: THE YEAR OF MAGNA CARTA (2003).

DAVID MCCULLOUGH, JOHN ADAMS (2001).

DEAN KING, ET. AL., A SEA OF WORDS: A LEXICON AND COMPANION TO THE COMPLETE SEAFARING TALES OF PATRICK O'BRIAN (3rd ed. 2000).

Deuteronomy 24:10–11.

EVAN THOMAS, JOHN PAUL JONES: SAILOR, HERO, FATHER OF THE AMERICAN NAVY (2003).

Exodus 22:2-3.

FRED ANDERSON, THE WAR THAT MADE AMERICA: A SHORT HISTORY OF THE FRENCH AND INDIAN WAR (2005).

HUNTER S. THOMPSON, THE RUM DIARY (1999).

IAN LENDLER, ALCOHOLICA ESOTERICA: A COLLECTION OF USEFUL AND USELESS INFORMATION AS IT RELATES TO THE HISTORY AND CONSUMPTION OF ALL MANNER OF BOOZE (2003).

IAN WILLIAMS, RUM: A SOCIAL AND SOCIABLE HISTORY OF THE REAL SPIRIT OF 1776 (2005).

JAMES L. SWANSON, MANHUNT: THE 12-DAY CHASE FOR LINCOLN'S KILLER (2007).

JOHN J. MCCUSKER & RUSSELL R. MENARD, THE ECONOMY OF BRITISH AMERICA1607–1789 (1985).

JOHN J. MCCUSKER, RUM AND THE AMERICAN REVOLUTION: THE RUM TRADE AND THE BALANCE OF PAYMENTS OF THE THIRTEEN CONTINENTAL COLONIES, VOLUME 1 (1989).

LEONARD W. LEVY, ORIGINS OF THE BILL OF RIGHTS (1999).

LEONARD W. LEVY, ORIGINS OF THE FIFTH AMENDMENT: THE RIGHT AGAINST SELF-INCRIMINATION (1968).

NATHANIEL PHILBRICK, SEA OF GLORY: AMERICA'S VOYAGE OF DISCOVERY, THE U.S. EXPLORING EXPEDITION 1838–1842 (2003).

NELSON B. LASSON, THE HISTORY AND DEVELOPMENT OF THE FOURTH AMENDMENT TO THE UNITED STATES CONSTITUTION (1937).

RAYMOND POSTGATE, THAT DEVIL WILKES (rev. ed., Dobson Books Ltd 1956).

RICHARD BROOKHISER, WHAT WOULD THE FOUNDERS DO?: OUR QUESTIONS, THEIR ANSWERS (2006).

ROGER KNIGHT, THE PURSUIT OF VICTORY: THE LIFE AND ACHIEVEMENT OF HORATIO NELSON (2005).

ROY ADKINS, NELSON'S TRAFALGAR: THE BATTLE THAT CHANGED THE WORLD (2004).

SAMUEL DASH, THE INTRUDERS: UNREASONABLE SEARCHES AND SEIZURES FROM KING JOHN TO JOHN ASHCROFT (2004).

SAMUEL ELIOT MORISON, JOHN PAUL JONES: A SAILOR'S BIOGRAPHY (1959).

SUSAN FORD WILTSHIRE, GREECE, ROME, AND THE BILL OF RIGHTS (1992).

THE NEW ENCYCLOPEDIA BRITANNICA, John Wilkes, 661–62 (15th ed. 2002).

WEBSTER'S NEW INTERNATIONAL DICTIONARY OF THE ENGLISH LANGUAGE 1579 (2d ed. 1942).

WILLIAM J. CUDDIHY, THE FOURTH AMENDMENT: ORIGINS AND ORIGINAL MEANING (2009).

William Cuddihy, From General to Specific Warrants: The Origins of the Fourth Amendment, in THE BILL OF RIGHTS: A LIVELY HERITAGE (JON KUKLA ed., 1987).

WILLIAM STRUNK JR. AND WHITE, THE ELEMENTS OF STYLE (2007).

WILLIAM G. SUMNER, A HISTORY OF AMERICAN CURRENCY (1874).

ARTICLES:

Akhil Reed Amar, Fourth Amendment First Principles, 107 HARV. L. REV. 757 (1994).

Benjamin D. Barros, Home As a Legal Concept, 46 SANTA CLARA L. REV. 255 (2006).

Carol S. Steiker, Second Thoughts About First Principles, 107 HARV. L.REV. 820 (1994).

David B. Kopel, The Torah and Self-Defense, 109 PENN. ST. L. REV. 17 (2004).

David E. Steinberg, An Original Misunderstanding: Akhil Amar and Fourth Amendment History, 42 SAN DIEGO L. REV. 227 (2005).

David E. Steinberg, The Original Understanding of Unreasonable Searches and Seizures, 56 FLA. L. REV. 1051 (2004).

David E. Steinberg, Restoring the Fourth Amendment: The Original Understanding Revisited, 33 Hastings Const. L.Q. 47 (2005).

David E. Steinberg, Sense-Enhanced Searches and the Irrelevance of the Fourth Amendment, 16 WM & MARY BILL RTS. J. 465 (2007).

David E. Steinberg, The Uses and Misuses of Fourth Amendment History, 10 U. PA. J. CONST. L. 581 (2008).

Donald A. Dripps, Reconstruction and the Police: Two Ships Passing in the Night?, 24 CONST. COMMENT. 533 (2007).

Fabio Arcila, Jr., In the Trenches: Searches and the Misunderstood Common-Law History of Suspicion and Probable Cause, 10 U. PA. J. CONST. L. 1 (2007).

Frederick Pollock, English Law before the Norman Conquest, 14 L. Q. REV. 301 (1898).

George C. Thomas III, Time Travel, Hovercrafts, and the Framers: James Madison Sees the Future and Rewrites the Fourth Amendment, 80 NOTRE DAME L. REV. 1451 (2005).

Jeffrey Sturgeon, A Constitutional Right to Reasonable Treatment: Excessive Force and the Plight of Warrantless Arrestees, 77 TEMP. L. REV. 125 (2004).

John Williams, False Arrest, Malicious Prosecution, and Abuse of Process in §1983 Litigation, 20 TOURO L. REV. 705 (2004).

Karen M. Blum, Qualified Immunity in the Fourth Amendment: A Practical Application of § 1983 as it Applies to Fourth Amendment Excessive Force Cases, 21 TOURO L. REV. 571 (2005).

Karen M. Blum, Support Your Local Sheriff: Suing Sheriffs Under § 1983, 34 STETSON L. REV. 623 (2005).

Morgan Cloud, Quakers, Slaves and the Founders: Profiling to Save the Union, 73 MISS. L. J. 369 (2003).

Stephanos Bibas, Originalism and Formalism in Criminal Procedure: The Triumph of Justice Scalia, the Unlikely Friend of Criminal Defendants?, 94 GEO. L.J. 183 (2005).

Thomas K. Clancy, The Fourth Amendment's Concept of Reasonableness, 2004 UTAH L.REV. 977 (2004).

Thomas Y. Davies, Recovering the Original Fourth Amendment, 98 MICH. L. REV. 547 (1999).

Timothy P. O'Neill, Rethinking Miranda: Custodial Interrogation as a Fourth Amendment Search and Seizure, 37 U.C. DAVIS L. REV. 1109 (2004).

Tracey Maclin, The Central Meaning of the Fourth Amendment, 35 WM. & MARY L. REV. 197 (1993).

Tracey Maclin, The Complexity of the Fourth Amendment: A Historical Review, 77 B.U.L.REV. 925 (1997).

William Cuddihy & B. Carmon Hardy, A Man's House was not His Castle: Origins of the Fourth Amendment to the United States Constitution, 37 WM. & MARY Q. 371 (1980).

William J. Stuntz, The Substantive Origins of Criminal Procedure, 105 YALE L.J. 393 (1995).

MOVIES:

1776 (Columbia Pictures 1972).

AMISTAD (Dreamworks 1997).

THE MADNESS OF KING GEORGE, (The Samuel Goldwyn Company 1994).

PIRATES OF THE CARIBBEAN: DEAD MAN'S CHEST (Buena Vista Pictures 2006).

ROBIN HOOD (Universal Pictures 2010).

THE LAST OF THE MOHICANS (Morgan Creek Productions 1992).

MISC.

Charles Paxton – Biography, http://www.famousamericans.net/charlespaxton/.

Code of Justinian, Encyclopedia Britannica, available at http://www.britannica.com/EBchecked /topic/308835/Code-of-Justinian.

Entick v. Carrington, 19 Howell's State Trials 1029 (1765), available at http://www.constitution.

org/trials/entick/ entick_v_carrington.htm.

How Much is That?, http://eh.net/hmit/.

Mohican Press, Fort William Henry. . . The Siege & Massacre, http://www.mohicanpress.com/ mo08009.html.

Paxton Historical Commission, http://www.orgsites.com/ma/paxton/.

Pusser's, http://www.pussers.com.

Pusser's Rum History, http://www.pussers.com/rum/history.

The Dunk Warrant, available at http://www.montaguemillennium.com/ familyresearch/ dunk.htm.

CHAPTER FIVE

CASES:

Adamson v. California, 332 U.S. 46 (1946).

Boyd v. United States, 116 U.S. 616 (1886).

Chavez v. Martinez, 123 S. Ct. 1994 (2003).

Couch v. United States, 409 U.S. 322 (1973).

Dickerson v. United States, 530 U.S. 427 (2000).

Entik v. Carrington, 19 How. St. Tr. 1029-1073 (1765).

Fisher v. United States, 425 U.S. 391 (1976).

Gideon v. Wainwright, 372 U.S. 335 (1963).

Malloy v. Hogan, 378 U.S. 1 (1964).

Mapp v. Ohio, 367 U.S. 655 (1960).

Marbury v. Madison, 5 U.S. 137 (1803).

McCulloch v. Maryland, 7 U.S. 316 (1918).

Miranda v. Arizona, 384 U.S. 436 (1966).

Mitchell v. United States, 526 U.S. 314 (1999).

Murphy v. Waterfront Commission, 378 U.S. 53 (1964).

Pennsylvania v. Muniz, 496 U.S. 582 (1990).

Rock v. Arkansas, 483 U.S. 44 (1987).

Santobello v. New York, 404 U.S. 257 (1971).

Twining v. New Jersey, 211 U.S. 78 (1908).

Ullmann v. United States, 350 U.S. 422 (1956).

United States v. Hubbell, 530 U.S. 27 (2000).

United States v. McCrary, 643 F.2d 323 (5th Cir. 1981).

Watts v. Indiana, 338 U.S. 49 (1949).

Withrow v. Williams, 507 U.S. 680 (1993).

STATUTES:

Codex Iuris Canonici, 1983 CODE c. 1538.

CODE OF CANON LAW, *Codex Iuris Canonici,* 1983 CODE.

Magna Carta 29.

U.S. Const. Art. I, § 9.

Books:

2 Corinthians, 1:23.

4 William Blackstone, Commentaries on the Laws of England (Univ. of Chicago Press, 2002) (1769).

Akhil Reed Amar, The Constitution and Criminal Procedure: First Principals (1997).

Alan Haynes, Invisible Power: The Elizabethan Secret Services 1570-1603 (1992).

Alberto Ferreiro, ed., The Devil, Heresy and Witchcraft in the Middle Ages: Essays in Honor of Jeffrey B. Russell 131 (1998).

Anthony Lewis, Gideon's Trumpet (Reissue ed. 1989).

Antonia Fraser, The Lives of the Kings and Queens of England (1975).

Black's Law Dictionary (5th ed. 1979).

Burnham Holmes, The American Heritage History of the Bill of Rights: The Fifth Amendment (1991).

Catechism of the Catholic Church (1994).

Catherine Drinker Bowen, The Lion and the Throne (1956).

Charles M. Gray, Prohibitions and the Privilege Against Self-Incrimination in Tudor Rule and Revolution (Delloyd J. Guth and John W. McKenna, eds, 1982).

Colin Rhys Lovell, English Constitutional and Legal History (1962).

Danny Danziger & John Gillingham, 1215: The Year of Magna Carta (2003).

David McCullough, John Adams (2001).

Deuteronomy 5:11.

Deuteronomy 17:6.

Deuteronomy 19:15.

Deuteronomy 24:16.

E.R. Chamberlin, The Bad Popes (1969).

Edward Peters, Inquisition (1988).

Edward W. Cleary, et al, McCormick on Evidence (3rd ed. 1984).

Essays on the Making of the Constitution (Leonard W. Levy ed., 1987).

Eve LaPlante, American Jezebel: The Uncommon Life of Anne Hutchinson, the Woman Who Defied the Puritans (2004).

Exodus 20:7.

Gary L. Stuart, Miranda: The Story of America's Right to Remain Silent (2004).

Genesis 21:23-24.

George Fisher, Plea Bargaining's Triumph (2004).

Isaiah 62:8.

Jay A. Sigler, Double Jeopardy: The Development of a Legal and Social Policy Ch, 1 (1969).

John 8:10-11.

John Gillingham, The Wars of the Roses (1981).

John H. Langbein, Torture and the Law of Proof (1976).

John Lilburne, The Just Offense of John Lilburne in the Leveler Tracks (William Haller and Godfrey Davies eds., 1944).

John H. Wigmore, Evidence in Trials At Common Law (McNaughton ed. 1961).

John Winthrop, History of New England (J. Savage, ed., Boston, Phelps & Farnham 1826).

Judges 7:16-22.

Leonard W. Levy, Origins of the Bill of Rights (1999).

Leonard W. Levy, Origins of the Fifth Amendment: The Right Against Self-Incrimination (1968).

Leonard W. Levy, Bill of Rights in Essays on the Making of the Constitution (Leonard W. Levy ed., 1987).

Leviticus 19:12.

Maguire, Attack of the Common Lawyers on the Oath Ex Officio As Administered in the Ecclesiastical Courts in England in Essays in History and Political Theory in Honor of Charles Howard McIlwain (1936).

Marion L. Starkey, The Devil in Massachusetts (1949).

Marqis Beccaria of Milan, An Essay on Crimes and Punishments with a Commentary by M. de Voltaire (New Ed., 1872).

Matthew 5:33-37.

Nahum 1:9 (King James).

Nelson B. Lasson, The History and Development of the Fourth Amendment to the United States Constitution (1937).

Numbers 35:30.

Patricia M. Dugan, The Penal Process and the Protection of Rights in Canon Law (2005).

Peter Ackroyd, The Life of Thomas More (1999).

Peter Charles Hoffer, The Salem Witchcraft Trials: A Legal History (1997).

Rich Beyer, The Greatest Stories Never Told: 100 Tales from History to Astonish, Bewilder & Stupefy (2003).

Richard Marius, Thomas More: A Biography (1985).

Robert Hendrickson, Encyclopedia of Word and Phrase Origins (1997).

Sadakat Kadri, The Trail: A History, from Socrates to O.J. Simpson xvii (2005).

Samuel Dash, The Intruders: Unreasonable Searches and Seizures from King John to John Ashcroft (2004).

Steven J. Rubenzer, Thomas R. Faschingbauer, Personality, Character, and Leadership in the White House: Psychologists Assess the Presidents, 101 (2004).

The Barnhart Dictionary of Etymology (Robert K. Barnhart et al. ed. 1988).

The New Encyclopedia Britannica (15th ed. 2002).

The Privilege Against Self-Incrimination: Its Origins and Development (R.H. Helmholz ed. 1997).

Walter B. Schaefer, The Suspect in Society (1967).

Webster's New International Dictionary of the English Language (2d ed. 1934).

William H. Woestman, O.M.I., Ecclesiastical Sanctions and the Penal Process: A Commentary on the Code of Canon Law (2003).

ARTICLES:

Aaron M. Clemens, *The Pending Reinvigoration of Boyd: Personal Papers are Protected by the Privilege Against Self-Incrimination*, 25 N. Ill. U. L. Rev. 75 (2004).

Abe Fortas, *The Fifth Amendment: Nemo Tenture Prodere Seipsum*, 25 Cleve. D. Ass'n. J. 95 (1954).

Alexandra Natapoff, *Speechless: The Silencing of Criminal Defendants*, 80 N.Y.U. L. Rev. 1449 (2005).

Alan Hirsch, *Threats, Promises, and False Confessions: Lessons of Slavery*, 49 How. L. J. 31 (2005).

Albert R. Alschuler, *A Particular Privilege in a Historical Prospective: The Right to Remain Silent*, 94 Mich. L. Rev. 2626 (1996).

Albert R. Alschuler, *Plea Bargaining and Its History*, 70 Col. L. Rev. 1 (1979).

Alison L. LaCroix, *To Gain the Whole World and Lose His Own Soul: Nineteenth Century American Dueling as Public Law and Private Code*, 33 Hofstra L. Rev. 501 (2004).

Blake D. Morant, *Lessons from Thomas More's Dilemma of Conscience: Reconciling the Clash Between a Lawyer's Beliefs and Professional Expectations*, 78 St. John's L. Rev. 965 (2004).

Charles H. Randall, Jr., *Sir Edward Coke and the Privilege Against Self-Incrimination*, 8 S.C.L.Q. 417 (1955-56).

Charles T. McCormick, *Law And the Future: Evidence*, 51 N.W. U.L. Rev. 218 (1956).

Chris Blair, *Miranda and the Right to Silence in England*, 11 Tulsa J. Comp. & Int'l L. 1 (2003).

Daniel J. Hulsebosch, *The Ancient Constitution and the Expanding Empire: Sir Edward Coke's British Jurisprudence*, 21 Law & Hist. Rev. 439 (2003).

David S. Romantz, *"You Have the Right to Remain Silent": A Case for the Use of Silence as Substantive Proof of the Criminal Defendant's Guilt*, 38 Ind. L. Rev. 1 (2005).

David S. Rudstein, *A Brief History of the Fifth Amendment Guarantee Against Double Jeopardy*, 14 Wm. & Mary Bill Rts. J. 193 (2005).

David S. Rudstein, *Retrying the Acquitted in England, part I: The Exceptions to the Rule Against Double Jeopardy for "New and Compelling Evidence"*, 8 San Diego Int'l L. J. 387 (2007).

E.M. Morgan, *The Privilege Against Self-Incrimination*, 34 Min. L. Rev. 1 (1949).

Eben Moglen, *Taking the Fifth, Reconsidering the Constitutional Origins of the Privilege Against Self-Incrimination*, 92 Mitch. L. Rev. 1086 (1994).

Edward Coke, *The Third Part of the Institute of the Law of England: Concerning High Treason and Other Pleas of the Crown in Criminal Causes*, 29 (London M. Flesher, 1644).

Frank Riebli, *The Spectre of Star Chamber: the Rule of an Ancient English Tribunal and the Supreme Court's Self-incrimination Jurisprudence*, 21 Hastings Const. L. Q. 807 (2002).

Harold W. Wolfram, *John Lilburne: Democracy's Pillar of Fire*, 3 Syracuse L. Rev. 213 (1952).

Horowitz, *the Privilege Against Self-incrimination–How Did It Originate?*, 31 Temple L. Q. 121 (1958).

Irene M. Rosenberg and Yale L. Rosenberg, *In the Beginning: The Talmudic Rule Against Self-Incrimination*, 63 N.Y.U. L. Rev. 955 (1988).

James Franklin, *Evidence Gained From Torture: Wishful Thinking, Checkability, And Extreme Circumstances*, 17 Cardozo J. Int'l & Comp. L. 281 (2009).

James Morice, *A briefe treatise of Oathes exacted by Ordinaries and Ecclesiasticall Judges* (1598).

James Oldham, *Truth-Telling in the Eighteenth-Century English Courtroom*, 12 LAW & HIST. REV. 95 (1994).

Jeffrey M. Gaba, *John Locke and the Meaning of the Takings Clause*, 72 MO. L. REV. 525 (2007).

Jeffrey K. Sawyer, *Benefit of Clergy in Maryland and Virigina*, 34 AM. J. LEGAL HIST. 49 (1990).

Joel N. Bodansky, *The Abolition of the Party Witness Disqualification: An Historical Survey*, 70 KY. L. J. 91 (1982).

John H. Langbein, *The Criminal Trial Before the Lawyers,* 45 U. CHI. L. REV. 263 (1978).

John H. Langbein, *The Historical Origins of the Privilege Against Self-Incrimination at Common Law*, 92 MICH. L. REV. 1047 (1994).

John H. Wigmore, *Nemo Teneur Seipsum Prodere*, 5 HARV. L. REV. 71 (1891-92).

John H. Wigmore, *The Privilege Against Self-Crimination*; Its History, 15 HARV. L. REV. 10 (1901-02).

Justin W. Curtis, *The Meaning of Life (Or Limb): An Originalist Proposal for Double Jeopardy Reform*, 41 U. RICH. L. REV. 991 (2007).

Katharine B. Hazlett, *The Nineteenth Century Origins of the Fifth Amendment Privilege Against Self-Incrimination*, 42 AM. J. LEGAL HIST. 235 (1998).

Kyden Creekpaum, *What's Wrong with a Little More Double Jeopardy? A 21st Century Recalibration of an Ancient Individual Right*, 44 AM. CRIM. L. REV. 1179 (2007).

Leonard W. Levy, *Origins of the Fifth Amendment and Its Critics*, 19 CARDOZO L. REV. 821 (1997).

Michael J. Hunter, *The Man on the Stairs Who Wasn't There: What Does a Defendant's Pre-Arrest Silence have to do with Miranda, the Fifth Amendment or Due Process?*, 28 HAMLINE L. REV. 277 (2005).

Michael R.T. MacNair, *The Early Development of the Privilege Against Self-Incrimination*, 10 OXFORD J. LEGAL STUD. 66 (1990).

Mitchell Franklin, *The Encyclopediste Origin and Meaning of the Fifth Amendment*, 15 LAW. GUILD REV. 41(1956).

Paul Raffield, *Contract, Classicism, And The Common-Weal: Coke's Reports and the Foundations of the Modern English Constitution*, 17 Law & Literature 69 (2005).

Peter Westen, *The Compulsory Process Clause*, 73 MICH. L. REV. 71 (1974).

R. Carter Pittman, *The Colonial and Constitutional History of the Privilege Against Self-Incrimination in America*, 21 VA. L. REV. 763 (1934-35).

R. H. Helmholz, *Origins of the Privilege Against Self-Incrimination: The Role of the European Ius Commune*, 65 N.Y.U. L. REV. 962 (1990).

Ronald J. Allen, Bard Ferrall, & John Rathaswamy, *The Double Jeopardy Clause, Constitutional Interpretation and the Limits of Formal Logic*, 26 VAL. U. L. REV. 281 (1992).

Steve Bachmann, *Starting Again With the Mayflower. . . England's Civil War and America's Bill of Rights*, 20 Q.L. REV. 193 (2001).

Susanna Frederick Fischer, *Playing Poohsticks with the British Constitution: The Blair Government's Proposal to Abolish the Lord Chancellor*, 24 PENN. ST. INT'L L. REV. 257 (2005).

Thomas Y. Davies, *Farther and Farther from the Original Fifth Amendment: The Recharacterization of the Right Against Self-Incrimination as a "Trial Right" in Chavez v. Martinez*, 70 TENN. L. REV. 987 (2003).

Wesley MacNeil Oliver, *Magistrates' Examinations, Police Interrogations, and Miranda-Like Warnings in the Nineteenth Century*, 81 Tul. L. Rev. 777 (2007).

William J. Stuntz, *The Substantive Origins of Criminal Procedure*, 105 Yale L. J. 393 (1995).

MOVIES AND TELEVISION:

Brother Sun, Sister Moon (Paramount 1972).

Cromwell (Columbia Pictures, 1970).

Dirty Harry (Warner Brothers 1971).

Double Jeopardy (Paramount 1999).

Dragnet (TBS 1987).

Frost/Nixon (Universal Studios 2008).

History of the World, Part I (20th Century Fox 1981).

JFK (Warner Brothers 1991).

Squanto: A Warrior's Tale (1994).

The Crucible (20th Century Fox 1996).

The Name of the Rose (20th Century Fox 1986).

The Star Chamber (20th Century Fox 1983).

The Ten Commandments (Paramount Studios 1956).

Witness (Paramount Pictures 1985).

Witness for the Prosecution (United Artists 1957).

MISC.:

Bill Clinton and the Meaning of "Is" by Timothy Noah, Slate, Posted Sunday, Sept. 13, 1998, at 9:14 PM ET http://www.slate.com/id/1000162/ (last visited July 30, 2010).

Dirty Harry, http://en.wikipedia.org/wiki/Dirty_Harry (Last visited May 29, 2010).

Dragnet (series), http://en.wikipedia.org/wiki/Dragnet_%28drama%29 (last visited May 29, 2010).

Fleet Prison, http://en.wikipedia.org/wiki/Fleet_prison (last visited June 2, 2010).

Jeopardy!, http://en.wikipedia.org/wiki/Jeopardy! (last visited May 29, 2010).

Law & Order, http://en.wikipedia.org/wiki/Law_%26_Order (Last visited May 29, 2010).

Madison County, Iowa, http://en.wikipedia.org/wiki/Madison_County%2C_Iowa (last visited March 31, 2006).

Nathaniel Bacon (died 1622), http://en.wikipedia.org/wiki/Nathaniel_Bacon (last visited January 6, 2006).

New Advent, The Catholic Encyclopedia, St. Edmund Campion, http://www.newadvent.org/cathen/05293c.htm (last visited August 8, 2005).

Thomas More, *Apology of Syr Thomas More Knight*, 219a-227b (1533).

Witness (1985 film), http://en.wikipedia.org/wiki/Witness_%281985_film%29 (last visited May 29, 2010).

Witness for the Prosecution, http://en.wikipedia.org/wiki/Witness_For_the_Prosecution (last visited May 29, 2010).

CHAPTER SIX
CASES:

Berghuis v. Thompkins, 560 U.S. ___ (2010).

Coffin v. U.S., 156 U.S. 432 (1895).

Coy v. Iowa, 487 U. S. 1012 (1988).

Crawford v. Washington, 541 U.S. 36 (2004).

Gideon v. Wainwright, 372 U.S. 335 (1963).

Hamdi v. Rumsfeld, 542 U.S. 507 (2004).

In re Winship, 397 U.S. 358 (1970).

Johnson v. Zerbst, 304 U.S. 458 (1938).

Marbury v. Madison, 5 U.S. (1 Cranch) 137 (1803).

Miranda v. Arizona, 384 U.S. 436 (1966).

Rock v. Arkansas, 483 U.S. 44 (1987).

CONSTITUTIONS:

MASSACHUSETTS CONSTITUTION, Part The First, art. XXX (1780).

The DECLARATION OF INDEPENDENCE.

UNITED STATES CONSTITUTION.

STATUTES:

Federal Rules of Civil Procedure.

Habeas Corpus Act of 1679 *available at* http://press-pubs.uchicago.edu/founders/documents/a1_9_2s2.html (last visited February 26, 2008).

The County Courts Amendment Act, ending the Hundred Courts.

BOOKS:

4 BLACKSTONE COMMENTARIES ON THE LAWS OF ENGLAND (1st ed. 1769).

8 WIGMORE, EVIDENCE (3d ed. 1940).

A.E. DICK HOWARD, MAGNA CARTA: TEXT AND COMMENTARY (1964).

A.K.R. KIRALFY, POTTER'S HISTORICAL INTRODUCTION TO ENGLISH LAW (4th ed. 1958).

ALEXANDRE DUMAS, THE THREE MUSKETEERS (1844).

ALISON WEIR, QUEEN ISABELLA (2005).

ANTHONY LEWIS, GIDEON'S TRUMPET (Reissue ed. 1989).

ANTONIA FRASER, THE LIVES OF THE KINGS AND QUEENS OF ENGLAND (1975).

ARISTOTLE, ETHICS (Penguin Classics ed. 1955).

ARTHUR SCHLESINGER, PRELUDE TO INDEPENDENCE: THE NEWSPAPER WAR ON BRITAIN, 1764–1776 (1958).

BARBARA J. SHAPIRO, "BEYOND REASONABLE DOUBT" AND "PROBABLE CAUSE" (1991).

BLACK'S LAW DICTIONARY (5th ed. 1979).

CATHERINE DRINKER BOWEN, THE LION AND THE THRONE: THE LIFE AND TIMES OF SIR EDWARD COKE (1956).

CHARLES MONTESQUIEU, THE SPIRIT OF THE LAWS (1748).

CHRISTOPHER HIBBERT, THE VIRGIN QUEEN: ELIZABETH I, GENIUS OF THE GOLDEN AGE (1992).

COLIN RHYS LOVELL, ENGLISH CONSTITUTIONAL AND LEGAL HISTORY (1962).

DANIEL J. KORNSTEIN, KILL ALL THE LAWYERS?: SHAKESPEARE'S LEGAL APPEAL (1994).

DANNY DANZIGER & JOHN GILLINGHAM, 1215: THE YEAR OF MAGNA CARTA (2003).

Deuteronomy 19:18, 19.

Ecclesiastics 20:25.

Exodus 20:16.

FREDERICK G. KEMPIN JR. HISTORICAL INTRODUCTION TO ANGLO-AMERICAN LAW (3d ed. 1990).

G. R. ELTON, THE TUDOR CONSTITUTION (2d ed. 1982).

GEORGE GARNETT, LAW AND JURISDICTION IN THE MIDDLE AGES (1988).

HENRY WADSWORTH LONGFELLOW, THE COURTSHIP OF MILES STANDISH (1858).

J.G. BELLAMY, THE CRIMINAL TRIAL IN LATER MEDIEVAL ENGLAND: FELONY BEFORE THE COURTS FROM EDWARD I TO THE SIXTEEN CENTURY (1998).

J.H. BAKER, AN INTRODUCTION TO ENGLISH LEGAL HISTORY (2002).

J.M. BEATTIE, CRIME AND THE COURTS IN ENGLAND: 1660 – 1800 (1986).

J.R.R. TOLKIEN, LORD OF THE RINGS (1954).

J. W. EHRLICH, THE HOLY BIBLE AND THE LAW (1962).

John 8: 3-7.

JOHN AYTO, DICTIONARY OF WORD ORIGINS (1990).

JOHN H. WIGMORE, EVIDENCE IN TRIALS AT COMMON LAW § 2250 (McNaughton ed. 1961).

JOHN JAY OSBORN, JR, THE PAPER CHASE (1970).

Judges 7:16-22.

KURT VON S. KYNELL, SAXON AND MEDIEVAL ANTECEDENTS OF THE ENGLISH COMMON LAW (2000).

LEONARD W. LEVY, ORIGINS OF THE FIFTH AMENDMENT: THE RIGHT AGAIN SELF-INCRIMINATION (1968).

LORD MACAULAY, THE HISTORY OF ENGLAND (1979).

Luke 11:46 (King James).

MANUAL FOR COURTS-MARTIAL, UNITED STATES (2008).

NELSON B. LASSON, THE HISTORY AND DEVELOPMENT OF THE FOURTH AMENDMENT TO THE UNITED STATES CONSTITUTION (1937).

PATRICIA M. DUGAN, THE PENAL PROCESS AND THE PROTECTION OF RIGHTS IN CANON LAW (2005).

Proverbs 11:9.

R. BLAIN ANDRUS, LAWYER: A BRIEF 5,000 YEAR HISTORY (2009).

R.C. VAN CAENEGEM, THE BIRTH OF THE ENGLISH COMMON LAW (2d ed. 1988).

RICH BEYER, THE GREATEST STORIES NEVER TOLD: 100 TALES FROM HISTORY TO ASTONISH, BEWILDER & STUPEFY (2003).

RICHARD BROOKHISER, WHAT WOULD THE FOUNDERS DO: OUR QUESTIONS THEIR ANSWERS (2006).

ROBERT R. PEARCE, A HISTORY OF THE INNS OF COURT AND CHANCERY (1848).

ROSCOE POUND, THE DEVELOPMENT OF CONSTITUTIONAL GUARANTEES OF LIBERTY (1957).

ROSCOE POUND, THE LAWYER FROM ANTIQUITY TO MODERN TIMES (1953).

S.E. THORNE, *The Early History of the Inns of Court with Special Reference to Gray's Inn*, ESSAYS IN ENGLISH LEGAL HISTORY (1985).

SADAKAT KADRI, THE TRIAL: A HISTORY, FROM SOCRATES TO O.J. SIMPSON (2005).

SAMUEL DASH, THE INTRUDERS: UNREASONABLE SEARCHES AND SEIZURES FROM KING JOHN TO JOHN ASHCROFT (2004).

Susanna 1:164.

SUSAN FORD WILTSHIRE, GREECE, ROME, AND THE BILL OF RIGHTS (1992).

T.S. ELIOT, MURDER IN THE CATHEDRAL (1935).

THE COLUMBIA ENCYCLOPEDIA (4th ed. 1975).

THE COLUMBIA ENCYCLOPEDIA (4th ed. 1963).

THE NEW ENCYCLOPEDIA BRITANNICA (15th ed. 2002).

THE OXFORD CLASSICAL DICTIONARY (1970).

THE WORKS OF PLATO, *Apology* (Irwin Edman ed., Benjamin Jowett trans., Random House 1956).

WEBSTER'S NEW INTERNATIONAL DICTIONARY OF THE ENGLISH LANGUAGE (2d ed. 1942).

WEBSTER'S WORD HISTORIES (1989).

WINSTON CHURCHILL, A HISTORY OF THE ENGLISH-SPEAKING PEOPLES, VOL. 1 (1958).

ARTICLES:

Alexander Volokh, n Guilty Men, 146 U. PENN. L. R.173 (1997).

A.W.B. Simpson, *The Early Constitution of the Inns of Court* 28 CAMBRIDGE L. J. 241 (1970).

Allen D. Boyer, *The Trial of Sir Walter Ralegh: The Law of Treason, The Trial of Treason and the Origins of the Confrontation Clause*, 74 MISS. L. J. 869 (2005).

Anthony Morano, *A Reexamination of the Development of the Reasonable Doubt Rule*, 55 B.U.L. Rev. 507 (1975) .

Bruce P. Smith, *The Emergence of Public Prosecution in London, 1790-1850*, 18 YALE J. L. & HUMAN. 29 (2006).

C.A. Morrison, *Some Features of the Roman and the English Law of Evidence*, 33 TUL. L. REV. 577 (1958).

Charles Donahue, Jr., *Ius Commune, Canon Law, and Common Law in England*, 66 TUL. L. REV. 1745 (1992).

Charles M. Gray, *Prohibitions and the Privilege Against Self-Incrimination*, in TUDOR RULE AND REVOLUTION: ESSAYS FOR G.R. ELTON FROM HIS AMERICAN FRIENDS (Delloyd J. Guth & John W. McKenna eds., 1982).

Daniel Klerman, *Was the Jury Ever Self-Informing*, 77 S. CAL. L. REV. 123 (2003-2004).

Daniel R. Coquillette, The *Legal Education of a Patriot: Josiah Quincy Jr.'s Law Commonplace (1763)*, 39 ARIZ. ST. L. J. 317 (2007).

Daniel Shaviro, *The Confrontation Clause Today in Light of Its Common Law Background*, 26 VAL. U. L. REV. 337 (1991).

David R. Stras, *Why Supreme Court Justices Should Ride Circuit Again*, 91 MINN. L. REV. 1710 (2007).

Deborah A. Schwartz & Jay Wishingard, *The Eighth Amendment, Beccaria, and the Enlightenment: An Historical Justification for Weems v. United States Excessive Punishment Doctrine*, 24 BUFF. L. REV. 781 (1975).

Diana Woodhouse, *United Kingdom: The Constitutional Reform Act 2005 – Defending Judicial Independence the English Way*, 5 INT'L J. CONST. L. 153 (2007).

Diane Parkin-Speer, *John Lilburne: a Revolutionary Interprets Statutes and Common Law Due Process*, 1 LAW & HIST. REV. 276 (1983).

Frank R. Herrmann, S.J. & Brownlow M. Speer, *Facing the Accuser: Ancient and Medieval Precursors of the Confrontation Clause*, 34 VA. J. INT'L. L. 481 (1994).

Fred O. Smith, Jr., *Crawford's Aftershock: Aligning the Regulation Of Nontestimonial Hearsay With The History And Purposes Of The Confrontation Clause*, 60 STAN. L. REV. 1497 (2008).

George C. Thomas III, *History's Lesson for the Right to Counsel*, 2004 U. ILL. L. REV. 543 (2004).

George Fisher, *The Jury's Rise as Lie Detector*, 107 YALE L.J. 575 (1997).

George Jarvis Thompson, *The Development of the Anglo-American Judicial System*, 17 CORNELL L. Q. 9 (1932).

George Jarvis Thompson, *The Development of the Anglo-American Judicial System*, 17 CORNELL L. Q. 395, 399 (1931-32).

George Jarvis Thompson, *The Development of the Anglo-American Judicial System*, 203, 209, *et seq.* (1932).

Harold J. Berman, *Religious Foundations of Law in the West: An Historical Perspective*, 1 J.L. & RELIGION 3 (1983).

Harold W. Wolfram, *John Lilburne: Democracy's Pillar of Fire*, 3 SYRACUSE L. REV. 213 (1952).

J.H. Baker, *Cousellors and Barristers: An Historical Study*, 27 CAMBRIDGE L.J. 205 (1969).

J.M. Beattie, *Scales of Justice: Defense Counsel and the English Criminal Trial in the Eighteenth and Nineteenth Centuries*, 9 Law & Hist. 221 (1991).

Jacob Reynolds, *The Rule of Law and the Origins of the Bill of Attainder Clause*, 18 ST. THOMAS L. REV. 177 (2006).

James A. Brundage, *The Medieval Advocate's Profession*, 6 LAW & HIST. REV. 439 (1988).

James Oldham, *Truth-Telling in the Eighteenth-Century English Courtroom*, 12 LAW & HIST. REV. 95 (1994).

James Robertson, *Quo Vadis, Habeas Corpus?*, 55 BUFF. L. REV. 1063 (2008).

Jeffrey K. Sawyer, *Benefit of Clergy in Maryland and Virginia*, 34 AM. J. LEGAL HIST. 49 (1990).

Joel N. Bodansky, *The Abolition of the Party-Witness Disqualification: An Historical Survey*, 70 KY. L. J. 91 (1981-82).

John Langbein, *The Criminal Trial Before the Lawyers*, 45 U. CHI. L. REV. 263 (1978).

John H. Langbein, *Shaping the Eighteenth-Century Criminal Trial: A View from the Ryder Sources*, 50 U.CHI. L. REV. 1 (1983).

John H. Langbein, *The Historical Origins of the Privilege Against Self-incrimination at Common Law*, 92 MICH. L. REV. 1047 (1994).

John H. Langbein, *The Origins of Public Prosecution at Common Law*, 17 AM. J. LEGAL HIST. 313 (1973).

John H. Langbein, *The Prosecutorial Origins of Defense Counsel in the Eighteenth Century: The Appearance of Solicitors*, 58 CAMB. L. J. 314 (1999).

John H. Wigmore, *Required Numbers of Witnesses; A Brief History of the Numerical System in England*, 15 HARV. L. REV. 83 (1901-02).

Justin C. Barnes, *Lessons from England's "Great Guardian of Liberty": A Comparative Study of English and American Civil Juries*, 3 U. ST. THOMAS 345 (2005).

Kenneth Graham, *Confrontation Stories: Raleigh on the Mayflower*, 3 OHIO ST. J. CRIM. L. 209 (2005).

Laura Ikins Stern, *Inquisition Procedure and Crime in Early Fifteenth-Century Florence*, 8 LAW & HIST. REV. 297 (1990).

Louis J. Sirico, Jr., *The Federalist and the Lessons of Rome*, 75 MISS. L. J. 431 (2006).

Martin R. Gardner, *The Mens Rea Enigma: Observations on the Role of Motive in the Criminal Law Past and Present*, 1993 UTAH L. REV. 635 (1993).

Michael MacNair, *Sir Jeffrey Gilbert and His Treatises*, 15 LEGAL HIST. 252 (1994).

P.R. Glazebrook, *The Making of English Criminal Law: The Reign of Mary Tudor*, 1977 CRIM. L.R. 582 (1977).

Paul Brand, *Courtroom and Schoolroom: the Education of Lawyers in England prior to 1400*, 60 BULL. INST. OF HIST. RESEARCH 147 (1987).

Paul M. Rashkind, *Gideon v. Wainwright: A 40th Birthday Celebration and the Threat of a Midlife Crisis*, THE FLORIDA BAR JOURNAL, March 2003, Volume 77: No. 3.

Peter Westen, *The Compulsory Process Clause*, 73 MICH. L. REV. 71 (1974).

Rafael Alberto Madan, *The Sign and Seal of Justice*, 7 AVE MARIA L. REV. 123 (2008).

Randolph N. Jonakait, *The Rise of the American Adversary System: America Before England*, 14 WIDENER L. REV. 323 (2009).

Richard Burst, *The 25 Greatest Legal Movies: Tales of Lawyers We've Loved and Loathed*, ABA JOURNAL August 2008.

Richard M. Fraher, *Conviction According to Conscience: The Medieval Jurists' Debate Concerning Judicial Discretion and the Law of Proof*, 7 LAW & HIST. R. 23 (1989).

Richard M. Fraher, *The Theoretical Justification for the New Criminal Law of the High Middle Ages: "Rei Publicae Interest, Ne Crimina Remaneant Impunita,"* 1984 U. ILL. L. REV. 577 (1984).

Robert Kry, *Confrontation Under the Marian Statutes: A Response to Professor Davies*, 72 BROOK. L. REV. 493 (2007).

Robert Popper, *History and Development of the Accused's Right to Testify*, 1962 WASH. U.L.Q. 454 (1962).

Robert Stein, *Rule Of Law: What Does It Mean?*, 18 MINN. J. INT'L L. 293 (2009).

Roger D. Groot, *The Jury in Private Criminal Prosecutions Before 1215*, 27 AM. J. LEGAL HIST. 113 (1983).

Scott D. Gerber, *The Court, the Constitution, and the History of Ideas,* 61 VAND. L. REV. 1067 (2008).

Seymour W. Warfel, *Quartering of Troops: The Unlitigated Third Amendment*, 21 TENN. L. REV. 723 (1951).

Sir Fredrick Pollock, *English Law Before the Norman Conquest*, 14 L. Q. REV. 291 (1898).

Stephan Landsman, *From Gilbert to Bentham: The Reconceptualization of Evidence Theory*, 36 WAYNE L. REV. 1149 (1990).

Stephan Landsman, *The Rise of the Contentious Spirit: Adversary Procedure in Eighteenth Century England,* 75 CORNELL L. REV. 497 (1990).

Steven G. Calabresi, *The Historical Origins of the Rule of Law in the American Constitutional Order*, 28 HARV. J. L. & PUB. POL'Y 273 (2005).

Susanna Frederick Fischer, *Playing Poohsticks with the British Constitution: The Blair Government's Proposal to Abolish the Lord Chancellor*, 24 PENN. ST. INT'L L. REV. 257 (2005).

Theodore Waldman, *Origins of the Legal Doctrine of Reasonable Doubt*, 20 J. Hist. of Ideas 299 (1959).

Thomas Davis, *What Did the Framers Know, and When Did They Know It? Fictional Originalism in Crawford v. Washington*, 71 Brook. L. Rev. 105 (2005).

Thomas A. Green, *The Jury and the English Law of Homicide, 1200-1600*, 74 Mich L. Rev. 414 (1976).

W. Peter Westen, *The Compulsory Process Clause*, 73 Mich. L. Rev. 71 (1974).

Walter Ullmann, *Medieval Principles of Evidence*, 62 The Law Quarterly Rev. 77 (1946).

Walter Ullmann, *Some Medieval Principles of Criminal Procedure*, in Jurisprudence in the Middle Ages (1980).

William F. Duker, *English Origins of the Writ of Habeas Corpus: A Peculiar Path to Fame*, 53 N.Y.U. L. Rev. 983 (1978).

William E. Nelson, *Authority and the Rule of Law in Early Virginia*, 29 Ohio N.U.L. Rev. 305 (2003).

William E. Nelson, *Government by Judiciary: The Growth of Judicial Power in Colonial Pennsylvania*, 59 SMU L. Rev. 3 (2006).

William E. Nelson, *The Utopian Legal Order of the Massachusetts Bay Colony, 1630-1686*, 47 Am. J. Legal Hist. 183 (2005).

MOVIES AND TV:

A Few Good Men (Columbia Pictures 1992).

A Funny Thing Happened on the Way to the Forum (United Artists 1966).

Anatomy of a Murder (Columbia Pictures 1959).

Becket (Paramount 1964).

Braveheart (Paramount Pictures 1995).

COPS (Fox 1989-present).

Dog the Bounty Hunger (A&E 2004–present).

Elizabeth (Gramercy 1998).

Elizabeth: The Golden Age (2008).

Frost/Nixon (Universal Studios 2008).

Gunsmoke (CBS 1952–61).

History of the World, Part I (20th Century Fox 1981).

Judd, for the Defense (ABC 1967–1969).

Judgment at Nuremberg (United Artists 1961).

Kingdom of Heaven (20th Century Fox 2005).

L.A. Law (NBC 1986–94).

Laugh-In (NBC 1968–73).

Law and Order (NBC 1990-present).

Matlock (NBC 1986–92).

Minority Report (DreamWorks and 20th Century Fox 2002).

My Cousin Vinny (20th Century Fox 1992).

Nancy Grace (HLN February 21, 2005 – present).

National Lampoon's Animal House (Universal Pictures 1978).

Owen Marshall: Counselor at Law(ABC 1971–1974).

Petrocelli's (NBC 1974–1976).

Perry Mason (CBS 1957–66).

PRESUMED INNOCENT (Warner Bros. 1990).

RESTORATION (Miramax 1995).

ROBIN HOOD (Buena Vista Pictures 1973).

Rumpole of the Bailey (BBC 1975–92).

SEVEN BRIDES FOR SEVEN BROTHERS (Metro-Goldwyn-Mayer 1954).

STAR WARS (20th Century Fox 1977).

THE ADVENTURES OF ROBIN HOOD (Warner Brothers 1938).

THE ADVOCATE (Europe = THE HOUR OF THE PIG) (1993).

The Bold Ones: The Lawyers (NBC 1968–1972).

THE COURTSHIP OF EDDIE'S FATHER (Metro-Goldwyn-Mayer 1963).

THE GODFATHER (Paramount Pictures 1972).

THE LIFE AND TIMES OF JUDGE ROY BEAN (Cinerama Releasing 1972).

THE LION IN WINTER (Universal Pictures 1968).

THE LORD OF THE RINGS (New Line Cinema 2001–2003).

THE PAPER CHASE (20th Century Fox 1973).

The Practice (20 Century Fox TV 1997–2004).

THE SAINT (Paramount Pictures 1997).

THE THREE MUSKETEERS (20th Century Fox 1973).

THE FOUR MUSKETEERS (20th Century Fox 1974).

THE VIRGIN QUEEN (20th Century Fox 1955).

THE WESTERNER (Samuel Goldwyn 1940).

TO KILL A MOCKINGBIRD (Universal Pictures 1962).

TOMBSTONE (Hollywood Pictures 1993).

V FOR VENDETTA (Warner Bros. 2006).

Wanted: Dead or Alive (CBS 1958–61).

WITNESS (Paramount Pictures 1985).

WITNESS FOR THE PROSECUTION (United Artists 1957).

YOUNG MR. LINCOLN (20th Century Fox 1939).

MISC.:

Boston Massacre Trial *available at* http://www.bostonmassacre.net/trial/index.htm (last visited 13 June 2007).

CRIMINAL TRIALS 389–520 (DAVID JARDINE ed., 1850) *available at* http://www.wfu.edu/~chesner/Evidence/Linked%20Files/Additional%20Assigned%20Readings/TRIAL%20OF%20SIR%20WALTER%20RALEIGH.htm (last visited 3 June 2007).

Doom (id Software 1993).

George Hodak, ABA Journal, March 2009.

Inner Temple Library at http://www.innertemplelibrary.org.uk/welcome.htm (last visited 15 May 2007).

MANUAL FOR COURTS-MARTIAL, UNITED STATES (2008).

Old Bailey *available at* http://www.oldbaileyonline.org.

Quintilian, http://www.thelatinlibrary.com/quintilian.html (last visited 7 July 2007).

Quintilian, http://www.public.iastate.edu/~honeyl/quintilian/index.html (last visited 7 July 2007).

THE CATHOLIC ENCYCLOPEDIA at http://www.newadvent.org/cathen/08256b.htm (last visited 7 July 2007).

THE CATHOLIC ENCYCLOPEDIA http://www.newadvent.org/cathen/11173c.htm (last visited 11 July 2007).

The State of Florida, Department of Corrections, http://www.dc.state.fl.us/oth/timeline/1963-1965.html (last visited 8 July 2007).

The Liberty Library of Constitutional Classics http://www.constitution.org/sr/lexrex.htm (last visited 5 December 2005).

Thomas Smith, *De Repvblica Anglorvm available at* http://www.constitution.org/eng/repang.htm (last visited 31 May 2007).

CHAPTER SEVEN
CASES:

Allen v. United States, 164 U.S. 492 (1896).

Apodaca v. Oregon, 406 U.S. 404 (1972).

Ashford v. Thornton, 1 B. & Ald. 405 (1818).

Batson v. Kentucky, 476 U.S. 79 (1986).

Bushell's Case, Vaughan's Reports 135 (1670).

Coffin v. U.S., 156 U.S. 432 (1895).

Duncan v. Louisiana, 391 U.S. 145 (1968).

Georgia v. Brailsford, 3 U.S. (3 Dall.) 4 (1794).

Griffin v. State, 100 Tex. Crim. 641, 274 S.W. 611 (1925).

Horning v. District of Columbia, 249 U.S. 596 (1920).

Ring v. Arizona, 536 U.S. 584 (2002).

Sparf and Hansen v. United States, 156 U.S. 51 (1895).

United States v. Navarro, 408 F.3d 1184 (9th Cir. 2005).

United States v. Powell, 469 U.S. 57 (1984).

United States v. Singer, 380 U.S. 24 (1965).

United States v. Thomas, 116 F. 3d 606 (2d Cir. 1997).

United States v. Washington, 705 F.2d 489 (D.C. Cir. 1983).

United States v. Wills, 88 F.3d 704 (9th Cir. 1996).

Ward v. Commonwealth, 132 Ky. 636, 116 S.W. 786 (1909).

Williams v. Florida, 399 U.S. 78 (1970).

CONSTITUTIONS:

UNITED STATES CONSTITUTION.

THE DECLARATION OF INDEPENDENCE (U.S. 1776).

Statutes:

Fed. R. Crim. Pro. 23.

Fed. R. Evid. 608.

Fed. R. Evid. 801 (a)(c).

Books:

1 Samuel 17.

A.K.R. Kiralfy, Potter's Historical Introduction to English Law, 4th ed. (1958).

Alexis de Tocqueville, Democracy in America (Arthur Goldhammer trans., The Library of America 2004) (1835).

Alison Weir, Queen Isabella (2005).

Anti-Federalist No. 83.

Barbara J. Shapiro, "Beyond Reasonable Doubt" and "Probable Cause" (1991).

Baron Jeffrey Gilbert, THE LAW OF EVIDENCE (1754).

Black's Law Dictionary (5th ed. 1979).

Blackstone, Commentaries on the Laws of England (University of Chicago Press 1979 (1765-69).

Bryce Lyon, A Constitutional and Legal History of Medieval England (1960).

Colin R. Lovell, English Constitutional and Legal History (1962).

Daniel J. Kornstein, Shakespear's Legal Appeal (1994).

Danny Danziger & John Gillingham, 1215: The Year of Magna Carta (2003).

Dante, The Divine Comedy

Exodus 20:13.

Frederick G. Kempin, Jr., Historical Introduction to Anglo-American Law (3d ed. 1990).

H.W. Fowler, A Dictionary of Modern English Usage (2nd ed. 1965).

G.K. Chesterton, Tremendous Trifles (1968).

Genesis 18, 20-32.

George J. Edwards, The Grand Jury: An Essay (1906).

Howard W. Goldstein, Grand Jury Practice (2005).

J.G. Bellamy, The Criminal Trial in Later Medieval England (1998).

J. H. Baker, An Introduction to English Legal History (4th ed. 2002).

John Ayto, Dictionary of Word Origins (1990).

John Phillip Reid, The Ancient Constitution and the Origins of Anglo-American Liberty (2005).

Kurt von S. Kynell, Saxon and Medieval Antecedents of the English Common Law (2000).

Laws of William, c. 6.

Leonard W. Levy, Origins of the Fifth Amendment: The Right Against Self-Incrimination (1969).

Lewis Carroll, Alice's Adventures in Wonderland (1865).

Nelson B. Lasson, The History and Development of the Fourth Amendment of the United States Constitution (1937).

O.F. ROBINSON, THE CRIMINAL LAW OF ANCIENT ROME (1995).

Peter Earle, *Richard II* in THE LIVES OF THE KINGS AND QUEENS OF ENGLAND (Antonia Fraser ed. 1975).

Proverbs 11:29.

R.C. VAN CAENEGEM, THE BIRTH OF THE ENGLISH COMMON LAW (1988).

ROBERT BALDICK, THE DUEL: A HISTORY (1965).

Roger D. Groot, *The Early Thirteenth Century Criminal Jury*, in TWELVE GOOD MEN AND TRUE: THE CRIMINAL TRIAL JURY IN ENGLAND, 1200-1800 (J.S. Cockburn & Thomas A Green eds., 1988).

ROSCOE POUND, THE LAWYER FROM ANTIQUITY TO MODERN TIMES (1951).

SADAKAT KADRI, THE TRIAL: A HISTORY, FROM SOCRATES TO O.J. SIMPSON (2005).

SEAMUS HEANEY, BEOWULF: A NEW VERSE TRANSLATION 39 (2000).

SIR WALTER SCOTT, IVANHOE (1819).

SUSAN FORD WILTSHIRE, GREECE, ROME, AND THE BILL OF RIGHTS (1992).

THE FEDERALIST No. 83 (Alexander Hamilton).

THE *Placita Corone* (circa 1274–75).

THE WORKS OF ARISTOTLE TRANSLATED INTO ENGLISH (W.D. Ross trans., Clarendon Press 1925).

THE WORKS OF PLATO, *Apology* (Irwin Edman ed., Benjamin Jowett trans., Random House 1956).

THOMAS ANDREW GREEN, VERDICT ACCORDING TO CONSCIENCE: PERSPECTIVES ON THE ENGLISH CRIMINAL TRIAL JURY, 1200–1800 (1985).

THOMAS JEFFERSON, NOTES ON THE STATE OF VIRGINIA (J.W. Randolph ed., 1853).

WALTER ULLMANN, JURISPRUDENCE IN THE MIDDLE AGES (1980).

WEBSTER'S NEW INT'L DICTIONARY (2d ed. 1942).

WILLIAM H. REHNQUIST, GRAND INQUESTS: THE HISTORIC IMPEACHMENTS OF JUSTICE SAMUEL CHASE AND PRESIDENT ANDREW JOHNSON (1992).

ARTICLES:

Adriaan Lanni, *"Verdict Most Just": The Modes of Classical Athenian Justice*, 16 YALE J.L. & HUMAN. 277 (2004).

Albert W. Alschuler & Andrew G. Deiss, *A Brief History of the Criminal Jury in the United States*, 61 U. CHI. L. REV. 867 (1994).

Alison L. LaCroix, *To Gain the Whole World and Lose His Own Soul: Nineteenth Centruy American Dueling as Public Law and Private Code*, 33 HOFSTRA L. REV. 501 (2004).

Amalia D. Kessler, *Our Inquisitorial Tradition: Equity Procedure, Due Process, And The Search For An Alternative To The Adversarial*, 90 CORNELL L. REV. 1181 (2005).

Andrea McKenzie, *"This Death Some Strong and Stout Hearted Man Doth Choose": The Practice of Peine Forte Et Dure in Seventeen- and Eighteenth-Centrury England*, 23 LAW & HIST. REV. 279 (2005).

Andrew J. Parmenter, *Nullifying the Jury: "The Judicial Oligarchy" Declares War on Jury Nullification*, 46 WASHBURN L. J. 379 (2007).

Anthony Morano, *A Reexamination of the Development of the Reasonable Doubt Rule*, 55 B.U.L. REV. 507 (1975).

Anthony Musson, *Twelve Good Men and True? The Character of Early Fourteenth-Century Juries,* 15 LAW & HIST. REV. 115 (1997).

B. Michael Dann, *"Must Find the Defendant Guilty": Jury Instructions Violate the Sixth Amendment,* 91 JUDICATURE 12 (2007).

C.A. Morrison, *Some Features of the Roman and the English Law of Evidence,* 33 TUL. L. REV. 577 (1958-59).

Charles Gross, *The Early History and Influnce of the Office of Coroner,* 7 POLITICAL SCIENCE QUARTERLY 656 (1892).

Charles H. Haskins, *The Early Norman Jury,* 8 AM. HIST. REV. 613 (1903).

Chris Kemmitt, *Function Over Form: Reviving The Criminal Jury's Historical Role As A Sentencing Body,* 40 U. MICH. J.L. REFORM 93 (2006).

Daniel D. Blinka, *Jefferson and Juries: The Problem of Law, Reason, and Politics in the New Republic,* 47 AM. J. LEGAL HIST. 35 (2005).

David Crook, *Triers and the Origin of the Grand Jury,* 12 J. LEG. HIST. 103 (1991).

Daniel Klerman, *Settlement and the Decline of Private Prosecution in Thirteen-Century England,* 19 LAW & HIST. REV. 1 (2001).

Daniel Klerman, *Was the Jury Ever Self-Informing?,* 77 S. CAL. L. REV. 123 (2003).

Diane Parkin-Speer, *John Lilburne: a Revolutionary Interprets Statutes and Common Law Due Process,* 1 LAW & HIST. REV. 276 (1983).

Donald M. Middlebrooks, *Reviving Thomas Jefferson's Jury: Sparf and Hansen v. United States Reconsidered,* 46 AM. J. LEGAL HIST. 353 (2004).

Edith Guild Henderson, *The Background of the Seventh Amendment,* 80 HARV. L. REV. 289 (1967).

Ellen E. Sward, *A History of the Civil Trial in the United States,* 51 U. KAN. L. REV. 347 (2003).

Ellen E. Sward, *The Seventh Amendment and the Alchemy of Fact and Law,* 33 SETON HALL L. REV. 573 (2003).

Eric G. Barber, *Judicial Discretion, Sentencing Guidelines, and Lessons from Medieval England,* 1066-1215, 27 W. NEW ENG. L. REV. 1 (2008).

Ethan J. Leib, *Supermajoritarianism and the American Criminal Jury,* 33 HASTINGS CONST. L.Q. 141 (2006).

Frank R. Herrmann, S.J., *The Establishment of a Rule Against Hearsay in Romano-Canonical Procedure,* 36 VA. J. INT'L L. 1 (1995).

George C. Thomas, III, *History's lesson for the right to counsel,* 2004 U. Ill. L. Rev. 543 (2004).

George Jarvis Thompson, *The Development of the Anglo-American Judicial System: History of the English Court to the Judicature Acts,* 17 CORNELL L.Q. 9, (1931-32).

Harold W. Wolfram, *John Lilburne: Democracy's Pillar of Fire,* 3 SYRACUSE L. REV. 213 (1952).

Helene E. Schwartz, *Demythologizing the Historic Role of the Grand Jury,* 10 AM. CRIM. L. REV. 701 (1972).

Honorable William G. Young, *Vanishing Trials, Vanishing Juries, Vanishing Constitution,* 40 SUFFOLK U. L. REV. 67 (2006).

Ian Ayres, *Pregnant with Embarrassments: An Incomplete Theory of the Seventh Amendment,* 26 VAL. U. L. REV. 385 (1992).

Irwin Langbein, *The Jury of Presentment and the Coroner,* 33 COLUM. L. REV. 1329 (1933).

Jacob Reynolds, *The Rule Of Law And The Origins Of The Bill Of Attainder Clause,* 18 ST. THOMAS L. REV. 177 (2005).

James B. Thayer, *The Jury and Its Development*, 5 HARV. L. REV. 249 (1891-92).

James B. Thayer, *The Older Modes of Trial*, 5 HARV. L.REV. 45 (1891-92).

James C. Oldham, *The Origins of the Special Jury*, 50 UNIV. CHICAGO L. REV. 137 (1983).

James C. Oldham, *Truth-Telling in the Eighteenth-Century English Courtroom*, 12 LAW & HIST. REV. 95 (1994).

James Forman, Jr. *Juries and Race in the Nineteenth Century*, 113 YALE L.J. 895 (2004).

Jeffrey Omar Usman, *Ancient and Modern Character Evidence: How Character Evidence Was Used in Ancient Athenian Trials, Its Uses in the United States, and What This Means for How These Democratic Societies Understood the Role of Jurors*, 33 OKLA. CITY U.L. REV. 1 (2008).

John F. Decker, *Legislating New Federalism: The Call for Grand Jury Reform in the States*, 58 OKLA. L. REV. 341 (2005).

John W. Baldwin, *The Intellectual Preparation for the Canon of 1215 Against Ordeals*, 36 SPECULUM 613 (1961).

John H. Langbein, *Historical Foundations of the Law of Evidence: A View from the Ryder Sources*, 96 COLUM. L. REV. 1168 (1996).

John H. Langbein, *Shaping the Eighteenth-Century Criminal Trial: A View from the Ryder Sources*, 50 U. CHI. L. REV. 1 (1983).

John H. Langbein, *The Criminal Trial Before the Lawyers*, 45 U. CHI. L. REV. 263 (1977-78).

John H. Wigmore, *The History of the Hearsay Rule* 17 HARV. L. REV. 437 (1903-04).

Julian S. Waterman, *Thomas Jefferson and Blackstone's Commentaries*, 27 ILL. L. REV. 629 (1932-33).

Justin C. Barnes, *Lessons Learned from England's "Great Guardian of Liberty": A Comparative Study of English and American Civil Juries*, 3 U. ST. THOMAS L.J. 345 (2005).

Kenneth Graham, *Confrontation Stories: Raleigh on the Mayflower*, 3 Ohio St. J. Crim. L. 209 (2005).

Kevin K. Washburn, *Restoring The Grand Jury*, 76 FORDHAM L. REV. 2333 (2008).

Margaret C. Klingelsmith, *New Readings of Old Law*, 66 U. PA. L. REV. 107 (1917-18).

Margaret H. Kerr, Richard D. Forsyth, and Michael J. Plyley, *Cold Water and Hot Iron: Trial by Ordeal in England*, 22 J. INTERDISCIPLINARY HIST. 573 (1992).

Mark DeWolfe Howe, *Juries as Judges of Criminal Law*, 52 HARV. L. REV. 582 (1938-39).

Matthew P. Harrington, *The Economic Origins of the Seventh Amendment*, 87 IOWA L. REV. 145 (2001).

Michael D. Gordon, *The Perjury Statute of 1563: A Case History of Confusion*, 124 PROCEEDINGS OF THE AM. PHILOSOPHICAL SOCIETY 438 (1980).

Mike MacNair, *Vicinage and the Antecedents of the Jury*, 17 LAW & HIST. REV. 537 (1999).

Morgan, *A Brief History of Special Verdicts and Special Interrogatories* 32 YALE L. J. 575 (1923).

Morris S. Arnold, *Law and Fact in Medieval Jury Trial: Out of Sight, Out of Mind*, 18 AM. J. LEGAL HIST. 267 (1974).

Naomi D. Hurnard, *The Jury of Presentment and the Assize of Clarendon*, 56 ENGLISH HIST. REV. 374 (1941).

Niki Kuckes, *The Democratic Prosecutor: Explaining the Constitutional Function of the Federal Grand Jury*, 94 GEO. L. J. 1265 (2006).

Patrick Wormald, *Neighbors, Courts, and Kings: Reflections on Michael Macnair's Vicini*, 17 LAW & HIST. REV. 597 (1999).

Paul D. Carrington, *The Civil Jury and American Democracy*, 13 Duke J. Comp. & Int'l L. 79 (2003).

Paul F. Kirgis, *The Right to a Jury Decision on Questions of Fact Under the Seventh Amendment*, 64 Ohio St. L. J. 1125 (2003).

Paul R. Hyams, *The Charter as a Source for the Early Common Law*, 12 J. Legal Hist. 173 (1991).

Peter Brown, *Society and the Supernatural: A Medieval Change*, 104 Daedalus 133 (1975).

Peter Westen, *The Compulsory Process Clause*, 73 Mich. L. Rev. 71 (1974).

Phillip B. Scott, *Jury Nullification: An Historical Perspective on a Modern Debate*, 91 W. Va. L. Rev. 389 (1988).

R.H. Helmholz, *Crime, Compurgation and the Courts of the Medieval Church*, 1 Law & Hist. Rev. 1 (1983).

R.H. Helmholz, *The Early History of the Grand Jury and the Canon Law*, 50 U. Chi. L. Rev. 613 (1983).

Ralph V. Turner, *The Origins of the Medieval Jury: Frankish, English, of Scandinavian?*, 7 J. of British Studies 1 (1968).

Rebecca V. Colman, *Reason and Unreason in Early Medieval Law*, 4 J. of Interdisciplinary Hist. 571 (1974).

Roger A. Fairfax, Jr., *The Jurisdictional Heritage of the Grand Jury Clause*, 91 Minn. L. Rev. 398 (2006).

Roger D. Groot, *The Jury in Private Criminal Prosecutions before 1215*, 27 Am. J. Legal Hist. 116 (1983).

Roger D. Groot, *The Jury of Presentment Before 1215*, 26 Am. J. Legal Hist. 1 (1992).

Simon Stern, *Between Local Knowledge and National Politics: Debating Rationales for Jury Nullification after Bushell's Case*, 111 Yale L. J. 1815 (2002).

Sir Frederick Pollock, *The King's Peace in the Middle Ages*, 13 Harv. L. Rev. 177 (1900).

Stanton D. Krauss, *An Inquiry into the Right of Criminal Juries to Determine the Law in Colonial America*, 89 J. Crim. L. & Criminology 111 (1998).

Stephan Landsman, *The Civil Jury in America: Scenes from an Unappreciated History*, 44 Hastings L. J. 579 (1993).

Steve Bachmann, *Starting Again with the Mayflower … England's Civil War and America's Bill of Rights*, 20 QLR 194 (2001).

Steve J. Shone, *Lysander Spooner, Jury Nullification, and Magna Carta*, 22 Q. L. R. 651, 658 (2004).

Suja A. Thomas, *The Seventh Amendment, Modern Procudure, and the English Common Law*, 82 Wash. U. L. Q. 687 (2004).

Theodore Waldman, *Origins of the Legal Doctrine of Reasonable Doubt*, 20 J. of Hist. of Ideas 299 (1959).

Trisha Olson, *Of Enchantment: The Passing of the Ordeals and the Rise of the Jury Trial*, 50 Syracuse L. Rev. 109 (2000).

W.A. Morris, *The Sheriff and the Justices of William Rufus and Henry I,* 7 Cal. L. Rev. 235 (1910).

Walter Ullmann, *Some Medieval Principles of Criminal Procedure*, 59 (LIX) Juridical Rev. 1 (1947).

MOVIES AND TELEVISION:

... AND JUSTICE FOR ALL (Columbia Pictures 1979).

12 ANGRY MEN (United Artists 1957).

A KNIGHT'S TALE (Colombia Pictures 2001).

BILL & TED'S EXCELLENT ADVENTURE (Orion Pictures 1989).

CAMELOT (Warner Brothers 1967).

CHEAPER BY THE DOZEN (20th Century Fox 2003) and (20th Century Fox 1950).

COP (1988).

COP OUT (Warner Bros. 2010).

Cops (March 11, 1989 March 21, 2009).

EL CID (Allied Artists 1961).

EXCALIBUR (Warner Brothers 1981).

HIGH NOON (United Artists 1952).

INHERIT THE WIND (United Artists 1960).

IVANHOE (MGM 1952).

Law & Order: Trial by Jury (March 3, 2005 - May 6, 2006).

MONTY PYTHON AND THE HOLY GRAIL (1975).

PHILADELPHIA (TriStar Pictures 1993).

STAR WARS (20th Century Fox 1977).

THE 13TH WARRIOR (Touchstone Pictures 1999).

THE CRUCIBLE (20th Century Fox 1996).

THE DIRTY DOZEN (MGM 1967).

THE DUELISTS (Paramount Pictures 1977).

THE JUROR (Sony 1996).

TOMBSTONE (Hollywood Pictures 1993).

TRIAL BY JURY (1875).

TRIAL BY JURY (Morgan Creek 1994).

THE VERDICT (Warner Bro. 1946).

THE VERDICT (20th Century Fox 1982).

MISC.:

http://www.constitution.org/liberlib.htm (last visited 1 June 2007).

CHAPTER EIGHT
CASES:

Alabama v. Smith, 490 U.S. 794 (1989).

Apprendi v. New Jersey, 530 U.S. 466 (2000).

Atkins v. Virginia, 536 U. S. 304 (2002).

Bartkus v. Illinois, 359 U.S. 121 (1959).

Baze v. Rees, No. 07-5439 (2007).

Dep't of Revenue of Mont. v. Kurth Ranch, 511 U.S. 767 (1994).

Dred Scott v. Sandford, 60 U.S. 393, 19 How. 393 (1856).

Ewing v. California, 538 U.S. 11 (2003).

Ford v. Wainwright, 477 U.S. 399 (1986).

Furman v. Georgia, 408 U.S. 238 (1972).

Gregg v. Georgia, 428 U.S 153 (1979).

Harmelin v. Michigan, 501 U.S. 957 (1991).

Helling v. McKinney, 113 S. Ct. 2475 (1993).

Hudson v. McMillian, 112 S.Ct. 995 (1992).

Hudson v. United States, 522 U.S. 93 (1997).

Ingraham v. Wright, 430 U.S. 651 (1977).

In re Kemmler, 136 U.S. 436 (1890).

Kennedy v. Louisiana, 128 S. Ct. 2641 (2008).

McGautha v. California, 402 U.S. 183 (1971).

Mickle v. Henrichs, 262 Fed. 687 (D. Nev. 1918).

Missouri v. Hunter, 459 U.S. 359 (1983).

North Carolina v. Pearce, 395 U.S. 711 (1969).

Roper v. Simmons, 125 S. Ct. 1183 (2005).

Rummel v. Estelle, 100 S. Ct. 1133 (1980).

Solem v. Helm, 463 U.S. 277 (1983).

South Carolina v. United States, 199 U.S. 437 (1905).

State v. Cannon, 1900 A.2d 514 (1963).

State of Louisiana Ex Rel. Francis v. Resweber, 329 U.S. 459 (1947).

The Amistad, 40 U.S. (15 Pet.) 518 (1841).

The Antelope, 23 U.S. (10 Wheat.) 66 (1825).

Trop v. Dulles, 356 U.S. 86 (1958).

Weems v. United States, 217 U.S. 349 (1910).

Wilkerson v. Utah, 99 U.S. 130 (1878).

Witte v. United States, 515 U.S. 389 (1995).

CONSTITUTIONS:

Bill of Rights, 1689, 1 W. & M., c. 36, 1 (Eng.).

English Bill of Rights (1689).

Magna Carta Chapter 39.

THE DECLARATION OF INDEPENDENCE para. 1 (U.S. 1776).

UNITED STATES CONSTITUTION, AMENDMENT V.

UNITED STATES CONSTITUTION, Art. I, § 8, cl. 10.

STATUTES:

18 U.S.C. § 3142(f) (2006).

18 USC § 3559 (2006).

Bail Reform Act of 1984, 18 U.S.C. §§ 3141-3150.

Federal Rule of Criminal Procedure 11 (a)(4).

Statute of Westminster (1275) (Eng.).

Books:

1 W. Hawkins, Pleas of the Crown (7th ed. 1795).

2 Matthew Hale, Historia Placitorum Coronae: The History of the Pleas of the Crown (P.R. Glazebrook gen. ed., Professional Books, 1971) (1736).

4 William Blackstone, Commentaries on the Laws of England (Univ. of Chicago Press, 2002) (1769).

A.K.R. Kiralfy, Potter's Historical Introduction to English Law (1948).

Alberto Ferreiro, ed., The Devil, Heresy and Witchcraft in the Middle Ages: Essays in Honor of Jeffrey B. Russell (1998).

Antonia Fraser, The Lives of the Kings and Queens of England (1998).

Aristotle, Ethics (Penguin Classics ed. 1955).

Black's Law Dictionary (8th ed. 2004).

Cesare Beccaria, On Crimes and Punishments (1763-64).

Colin Dayan, The Story of Cruel and Unusual (2007).

Colin Rhys Lovell, English Constitutional and Legal History (1962).

Daniel J. Kornstein, Kill All the Lawyers: Shakespeare's Legal Appeal (1994).

Deuteronomy 25:2.

Deuteronomy 25:3.

Dr. Benjamin Rush, An Enquiry into the Effects of Public Punishments Upon Criminals and Upon Society (1787).

Dr. Benjamin Rush, Considerations of the Injustice and Impolicy of Punishing Murder by Death (1792).

Ecclesiastics 8:5.

Edward Coke, The Third Part of the Institutes of the Laws of England: Concerning High Treason, and Other Pleas of the Crown, and Criminall Causes (London, 1644).

Frederick G. Kempin, Historical Introduction to Anglo-American Law (1990).

Genesis 4:13-15 (King James).

George Fisher, Plea Bargaining's Triumph: A History of Plea Bargaining in America (2003).

George G. Killinger & Paul F. Cromwell, Jr., eds., Penology: The Evolution of Corrections in America (1973).

Gilbert King, The Execution of Willie Francis: Race, Murder, and the Search for Justice in the American South (2008).

Henry Fielding, The History of Tom Jones, A Foundling (1749).

Ivan Solotaroff, The Last Fact You'll Ever See: The Private Life of the American Death Penalty (2001).

J.G. Bellamy, The Criminal Trial in Later Medieval England: Felony Before the Courts from Edward I to the Sixteenth Century (1998).

J.H. Baker, An Introduction to English Legal History (4th ed. 2002).

J.W. Ehrlich, The Holy Bible and the Law (1962).

John Kenyon, The Popish Plot (1972).

John H. Langbein, The Origins of the Adversary Criminal Trial (2003).

John Henry Wigmore, A Treatise on the Anglo-American System of Evidence in Trials at Common Law including the Statutes and Judicial Decisions of all Jurisdictions of the United States and Canada (3d ed. 1940).

John Prebble, Culloden (1967).

Kurt von S. Kynell, Saxon and Medieval Antecedents of the English Common Law (2000).

Leonard W. Levy, Origins of the Bill of Rights (1999).

Louis P. Masur, Rites of Execution: Capital Punishment and the Transformation of American Culture, 1776-1865 (1989).

Michel Foucault, Discipline and Punish: The Birth of the Prison (1979).

Mitchell Merback, The Thief, the Cross, and the Wheel: Pain and the Spectacle of Punishment in Medieval and Renaissance Europe (1999).

Nahum 1:9 (King James).

Nathaniel Hawthorne, The Scarlet Letter: A Romance (1850).

Norman Mailer, The Executioner's Song (1979).

Norval Morris and David J. Rothman, eds. The Oxford History of the Prison (1998).

Numbers 11:16.

Numbers 35:30.

Paul G. Cassell, *In Defense of the Death Penalty*, in Debating the Death Penalty: Should America Have Capital Punishment? (Hugo Adam Bedau & Paul G. Cassell eds., 2004).

Plato, The Laws, Book VIII, Chapter 16.

Richard Brookhiser, What Would the Founders Do? (Our Questions Their Answers) (2006).

Richard Spilsbury and Louise Spilsbury, A Murder of Crows (2003).

Roselyne Rey, The History of Pain (1995).

Sadakat Kadri, The Trial: A History, from Socrates to O.J. Simpson (2005).

Samuel Mendelsohn, The Criminal Jurisprudence of the Ancient Hebrews (2d ed. 1968).

Stephen King, The Shining (1977).

Stuart Banner, The Death Penalty: An American History (2002).

The Debate on the Constitution (Bernard Bailyn ed., 1993).

The Gospel of Matthew 2:11.

The Jerusalem Bible (Jones ed. 1966).

The Merchant of Venice, (5.3.81-82) (5.3.111-16).

Thomas Andrew Green, Verdict According to Conscience: Perspectives on the English Criminal Trial Jury, 1200-1800 (1985).

Thucydides, The Peloponnesian War (1954 Rex Warner trans.).

Articles:

A.J. Musson, *Turing the King's Evidence: the Prosecution of Crime in Late Medieval England*, 19 Oxford Journal of Legal Studies 468 (1999).

Adriaan Lanni, *"Verdict Most Just": The Modes Of Classical Athenian Justice*, 16 Yale J.L. & Human. 277 (2004).

Aimee Logan, Note. *Who Says So? Defining Cruel And Unusual Punishment By Science, Sentiment, And Consensus*. 35 HASTINGS CONST. L.Q. 195 (2008).

Alex Kozinski, Sanhedrin II, New Republic, Sept. 13, 1993, at 16

Andrea McKenzie, *"This Death Some Strong And Stout Hearted Man Doth Choose": The Practice Of Peine Forte Et Dure In Seventeenth- And Eighteenth-Century England"*, 23 LAW & HIST. REV. 279 (2005).

Ann M. Overbeck, Editorial Note, *Detention for the Dangerous: The Bail Reform Act of 1984*, 55 U. CIN. L. REV. 153 (1986).

Anthony F. Granucci, *"Nor Cruel and Unusual Punishments Inflicted:" the Original Meaning*, 57 CAL. L. REV. 839 (1969).

Antonin Scalia, *Originalism: The Lesser Evil*, 57 U. CIN. L. REV. 849 (1989).

Arif Khan and Robyn M. Leventhal, *Medical Aspects of Capital Punishment Executions*, 47 J. FORENSIC SCI. 847 (2002).

Bruce Kercher, *Perish or Prosper: The Law and Convict Transportation in the British Empire, 1700-1850*, 21 LAW & HIST. REV. 527 (2003).

Bruce P. Smith, *The History of Wrongful Execution*, 56 HASTINGS L. J. 1185 (2005).

Caleb Foote, *The Coming Constitutional Crisis in Bail: I*, 113 U. PA. L. REV. 959 (1965).

Celia Rumann, *Tortured History: Finding Our Way Back to the Lost Origins of the Eighth Amendment*, 31 PEPP. L. REV. 661 (2004).

Chad Flanders, *Shame and the Meanings of Punishment*, 54 CLEV. ST. L. REV. 609 (2006).

Charles Walter Schwartz, *Eighth Amendment Proportionality Analysis and the Compelling Case of William Rummel*, 71 J. CRIM. L. & CRIMINOLOGY 378 (1980).

Chris Kemmitt, *Function Over Form: Reviving the Criminal Jury's Historical Role as a Sentencing Body*, 40 U. MICH. J. L. REFORM 93 (2006).

Daniel Klerman, *Settlement and the Decline of Private Prosecution in Thirteenth-Century England*, 19 LAW & HIST. REV. 1 (2001).

David S. Rudstein, *A Brief History Of The Fifth Amendment Guarantee Against Double Jeopardy*, 14 WM & MARY BILL OF RTS. J. 193 (2005).

Deborah A. Schwartz & Jay Wishingrad, *The Eighth Amendment, Beccaria, and the Enlightenment: A Historical Justification for the Weems v. United States Excessive Punishment Doctrine*, 24 BUFF. L. REV. 783 (1975).

Erwin C. Surrency, *The Transition from Colonialism to Independence*, 46 AM. J. LEGAL HIST. 55 (2008).

Eva S. Nilsen, *Decency, Dignity, And Desert: Restoring Ideals Of Humane Punishment To Constitutional Discourse*. 41 U.C. DAVIS L. REV. 111 (2007).

Frederick C. Mamil, *The King's Approvers: A Chapter in the History of English Criminal Law*, 11 SPECULUM 238 (1936).

Frederick Pollack, *The King's Peace in the Middle Ages*, 13 HARV. L. REV. 177 (1899).

Frederick Pollock, *English Law Before the Norman Conquest*, 14 L. Q. REV. 291 (1898).

George Fisher, *Plea Bargaining's Triumph*, 109 YALE L. J. 857 (2000).

Gerald D. Robin, *The Executioner: His Place in English Society*, 15 BRITISH J. OF SOCIOLOGY 234 (1964).

George Jarvis Thompson, *History of the English Courts to the Judicature Acts*, 17 CORNELL L. Q. 9 (1932).

Gregg Mayer, *The Poet and Death: Literary Reflections on Capital Punishment Through the Sonnets of William Wordsworth*, 21 ST. JOHN'S J. LEGAL COMMENT 727 (2007).

Harold J. Berman, *Religious Foundations of Law in the West: An Historical Perspective*, 1 J.L. & RELIGION 3 (1983).

Harry F. Tepker, *Tradition & The Abolition of Capital Punishment for Juvenile Crime*, 59 OKLA. L. REV. 809 (2006).

Hawles, *Remarks on the Trial of Mr. Charles Bateman*, 11 How. St. Tr. 474 (1685).

Irene Merker Rosenberg & Yale L. Rosenberg, *In the Beginning: The Talmudic Rule Against Self-Incrimination,* 63 N.Y.U.L. REV. 955 (1988).

Irene Merker Rosenberg & Yale L. Rosenberg, *Lone Star Liberal Musings on "Eye for Eye" and the Death Penalty*, 1998 UTAH L. REV. 505 (1998).

Irene Merker Rosenberg & Yale L. Rosenberg & Bentzion S. Turin, *Murder by Gruma: Causation in Homicide Cases Under Jewish Law*, 80 B.U. L. REV. 1017 (2000).

Irene Merker Rosenberg & Yale L. Rosenberg, *Of God's Mercy and the Four Biblical Methods of Capital Punishment: Stoning, Burning, Beheading, and Strangulation*, 78 TUL. L. REV. 1169 (2004).

J.M. Beattie, *Sir John Fielding and Public Justice: The Bow Street Magistrates' Court, 1754-1780*, 25 LAW & HIST. REV. 61 (2007).

J.M. Kaye, *The Early History of Murder and Manslaughter,* 83 LAW QUARTERLY REV. 365 (1967).

Jack B. Weinstein, *Does Religion Have A Role In Criminal Sentencing*? 23 TOURO L. REV. 539 (2007).

James J. Beha II, *Redemption to Reform: The Intellectual Origins of the Prison Reform Movement*, 63 N.Y.U. ANN. SURV. AM. L. 773 (2008).

James J. Willis, *Transportation versus Imprisonment in Eighteenth and Nineteenth-Century Britain: Penal Power, Liberty, and the State*, 39 LAW & SOC'Y REV. 171 (2005).

Jeffrey D. Bukowski, *The Eighth Amendment and Original Intent: Applying the Prohibition Against Cruel and Unusual Punishment to Prison Deprivation Cases is Not Beyond the Bounds of History and Precedent,* 99 DICK. L. REV. 419 (1995).

Jeffrey K. Sawyer, *Benefit of Clergy in Maryland and Virginia*, 34 AM. J. LEGAL HIST. 49 (1990).

Jennifer Bellott, *To Humiliate or Not To Humiliate: Does the Sentencing Reform Act Permit Shaming as a Condition of Supervised Release?*, 38 U. MEM. L. REV. 923 (2008).

Jennifer L. Mnookin, *Uncertain Bargains: The Rise of Plea Bargaining in America. (Reviewing George Fisher, Plea Bargaining's Triumph: A History of Plea Bargaining in America.)* 57 STAN. L. REV. 1721 (2005).

Jillisa Brittan and Richard Posner, *Classic Revisited: Penal Theory in Paradise Lost*, 105 MICH. L. REV. 1049 (2007).

John Braithwaite, *A Future Where Punishment Is Marginalized: Realistic or Utopian?*, 46 UCLA L. REV. 1727 (1999).

John H. Langbein, *Shaping the Eighteenth-Century Criminal Trial: A View from the Ryder Sources*, 50 U. CHI. L. REV. 1 (1983).

John F. Stinneford, *The Original Meaning of "Unusual": The Eighth Amendment as a Bar to Cruel Innovation,* 102 NW. U. L. REV. 1739 (2008).

John S. Martin, Jr., *Cruel and Usual: Sentencing in the Federal Courts*, 26 PACE L. REV. 489 (2005).

Justin W. Curtis, The Meaning of Life (or Limb): An Originalist Proposal for Double Jeopardy Reform, 41 U. RICH. L. REV. 991 (2007).

Kirk J. Henderson, *Mandatory-Minimum Sentences and the Jury: Time Again to Revisit Their Relationship*, 33 U. DAYTON L. REV. 37 (2007).

L.D.M. Nokes, A. Roberts & D.S. James, *Biomechanics of Judicial Hanging: A Case Report*, 39 MED. SCI. L. 61 (1999).

Lauren Schorr, *Breaking Into The Pardon Power: Congress And The Office Of The Pardon Attorney*, 46 AM. CRIM. L. REV. 1535 (2009).

Laurence Claus, *The Antidiscrimination Eighth Amendment*, 28 HARV. L. J. & PUB. POL'Y 119 (2005).

Margaret Jane Radin, *The Jurispurdence of Death: Evolving Standards of Cruel and Unusual Punishments Clause*, 126 U. PA. L. REV. 989 (1978).

Mark DeWolfe Howe, *Juries as Judges of Criminal Law*, 52 HARV. L. REV. 582 (1939).

Mark Osler, *Christ, Christians and Capital Punishment*, 59 BAYLOR L. REV. 1 (2007).

Nicholas Levi, *Veil of Secrecy: Public Executions, Limitations on Reporting Capital Punishment, and the Content-Based Nature of Private Execution Laws*, 55 FED. COMM. L. J. 131 (2002).

Note, *Original Meaning and It's Limits*, 120 HARV. L. REV. 1279 (2007).

Note, *Proof of the Corpus Delicti Aliunde the Defendant's Confession*, 103 U. PA. L .REV. 638 (1955).

Note, *The Eighth Amendment, Proportionality, And The Changing Meaning Of "Punishments"*, 122 HARV. L. REV. 96 (2009).

Paul R. Hyams, *The Proof of Villein Status in the Common Law*, 89 ENGLISH HIST. REV. 721 (1974).

Peter W. Tague, *Guilty Pleas and Barristers' Incentives: Lessons from England*, 20 GEO. J. LEGAL ETHICS 287 (2007).

Rachel E. Barkow *The Ascent Of The Administrative State And The Demise Of Mercy*, 121 HARV. L. REV. 1332 (2008).

Randall McGowen, *Managing the Gallows: The Bank of England and the Death Penalty, 1797-1821*, 25 LAW & HIST. REV. 241 (2007).

Richard H. Hiers, *The Death Penalty and Due Process in Biblical Law*, 81 U. DET. MERCY L. REV. 751 (2004).

Robert J. Cottrol, *Finality with Ambivalence: The American Death Penalty's Uneasy History*, 56 STAN. L. REV. 1641 (2004).

Robert A. Stark, *There May or May Not Be Blood: Why the Eighth Amendment Prohibition Against Executing the Insane Requires a Definitive Standard*, 41 CREIGHTON L. REV. 763 (2008).

Samuel B. Lutz, *The Eighth Amendment Reconsidered: A Framework For Analyzing The Excessiveness Prohibition*, 80 N.Y.U. L. REV. 1862 (2005).

Simon Devereaux, *Imposing the Royal Pardon: Execution, Transportation, and Convict Resistance in London, 1789*, 25 LAW & HIST. REV. 101 (2007).

Stephan Landsman, *The Rise of the Contentious Spirit: Adversary Procedure in Eighteenth Century England*, 75 CORNELL L. REV. 497 (1990).

Stephen T. Parr, *Symmetric Proportionality: A New Perspective on the Cruel and Unusual Punishment Clause*, 68 TENN. L. REV. 41 (2000-01).

Steve Bachmann, *Starting Again with the Mayflower . . . England's Civil War and America's Bill of Rights*, 20 QLR 193 (2001).

Steve J. Shone, *Lysander Spooner, Jury Nullification, and Magna Carta*, 22 Q. L. R. 651 (2004).

Thomas A. Green, *Societal Concepts of Criminal Liability for Homicide in Mediaeval England*, 47 SPECULUM 669 (1972).

Thomas A. Green, *The Jury and the English Law of Homicide, 1200-1600*, 74 MICH. L. REV. 414 (1976).

Trisha Olson, *Of the Worshipful Warrior: Sanctuary And Punishment In The Middle Ages*, 16 ST. THOMAS L. REV. 473 (2004).

Trisha Olson, *The Medieval Blood Sanction And The Divine Beneficence Of Pain: 1100-1450*, 22 J.L. & RELIGION 63 (2007).

W. Noel Keyes, *The Choice of Participation by Physicians in Capital Punishment*, 22 WHITTIER L. REV. 809 (2001).

Youngjae Lee, *International Consensus As Persuasive Authority In The Eighth Amendment*. 156 U. PA. L. REV. 63 (2007).

MOVIES, TV, AND MUSIC:

A MURDER OF CROWS (1999).

AMISTAD (DreamWorks 1997).

A PERFECT MURDER (Warner Bro. 1998).

BRAVEHEART (20th Century Fox 1995).

BREAKER MORANT (Roadshow Entertainment 1980).

COMPULSION (20th Century Fox 1959).

DIAL M FOR MURDER (Warner Bros. 1954).

EVER AFTER (20th Century Fox 1998).

EXCALIBUR (Warner Bros. 1981).

HARRY POTTER AND THE HALF-BLOOD PRINCE (Warner Bros. 2009).

JESUS CHRIST SUPERSTAR (Universal Studios 1973).

Johnny Cash, AT FOLSOM PRISON (Columbia 1968).

Johnny Cash, AT SAN QUENTIN (Columbia 1969).

GLORY (Tri-Star 1989).

JAILHOUSE ROCK (Metro-Goldwyn-Mayer 1957).

KINGDOM OF HEAVEN (20th Century Fox 2005).

MONSTER'S BALL (Lions Gate Films 2001).

MURDER! (British International Pictures 1930).

PAPILLON (Allied Artists Pictures 1973).

RESTORATION (Miramax 1995).

ROPE (Warner Bros. 1948).

SHAWSHANK REDEMPTION (Columbia Pictures 1994).

SLEEPING BEAUTY (Buena Vista 1959).

SPARTACUS (Universal Pictures 1960).

THE BIRDS (Universal Pictures 1963).

THE CHRONICLES OF NARNIA (Buena Vista 2005).

THE GODFATHER (Paramount Pictures 1972).

THE GREEN MILE (Warner Bros. 1999).

THE MATRIX (Warner Bros. 1999).

THE MESSENGER: THE STORY OF JOAN OF ARC (1999).

THE SCARLET LETTER (Hollywood Pictures 1995).

THE SHINING (Warner Bros. 1980).

WHAT DREAMS MAY COME (PolyGram 1998).

MISC.:

BrainyQuote, Mohandas Gandhi Quotes, http://www.brainyquote.com/quotes/quotes/m/mohandasga107039.html (last visited Jaunuary 20, 2008).

Carla McClain, *Lethal Injection Bill Getting Little Support*, TUCSON CITIZEN, Apr. 7, 1992, at 2A.

Inner Temple Library, http://www.innertemplelibrary.org.uk/welcome.htm (last visited 15 May 2007).

LyricsFreak, Don't Be Cruel Lyrics, http://www.lyricsfreak.com/e/elvis+presley/dont+be+cruel_20048329.html (last visited January 13, 2008).

Songfacts, Don't Be Cruel by Elvis Presley, http://www.songfacts.com/detail.php?id=1140 (last visited January 13, 2008).

The Carmina Burana of Carl Orff, http://www.tylatin.org/extras/cb2.html (last visited October 20, 2010).

THE CATHOLIC ENCYCLOPEDIA, http://www.newadvent.org/cathen/12565a.htm (last visited February 28, 2008).

The Innocence Project, http://www.innocenceproject.org/ (last visited 25 February 2008).

CHAPTER NINE

CASES:

Allgeyer v. Louisiana, 165 U.S. 578 (1897).

Bush v. Gore, 531 U.S. 98 (2000).

Bowers v. Hardwick, 478 U. S. 186 (1986).

Griswold v. Connecticut, 381 U.S. 479 (1965).

Houston v. Moore, 18 U.S. (5 Wheat.). 1 (1820).

Lawrence v. Texas, 539 U.S. 558 (2003).

Loving v. Virginia, 388 U.S. 1 (1967).

Marbury v. Madison, 5 U.S. (1 Cranch). 137 (1803).

Martin v. Hunter's Lessee, 14 U.S. 304 (1816).

McCulloch v. Maryland, 17 U.S. 316 (1819).

Olmstead v. United States, 277 U. S. 438 (1928).

Richmond Newspapers, Inc. v. Virginia, 448 U.S. 555 (1980).

Roe v. Wade, 410 U.S. 113 (1973).

Southern Pacific Co. v. Jensen, 244 U.S. 205 (1917).

United Public Workers of America (C.I.O.). v. Mitchell, 330 U.S. 75 (1947).

STATUTES:

Conn. Gen. Stat. Rev. § 53–32 (1958).

Conn. Gen. Stat. Rev. § 54–196 (1958).

The Marihuana Tax Act of 1937, Pub. L. No. 75-238, 50 Stat. 551 (1937). (repealed 1970).

No Child Left Behind Act of 2001, Public Law 107-110 (2001).

18 U.S.C. § 1201(a).(1). (2006).

18 U.S.C. § 2421–2424 (2006).

BOOKS:

1 JOSEPH STORY, COMMENTARIES ON THE CONSTITUTION (Boston, Hilliard, Gray, & Co. 1833).

3 J. ELLIOT, THE DEBATES IN THE SEVERAL STATE CONVENTIONS ON THE ADOPTION OF THE FEDERAL CONSTITUTION (1891).

Alexander Hamilton, *The Federalist No. 32 in* THE FEDERALIST PAPERS (Clinton Rossiter ed., 1961).

ALISON WEIR, QUEEN ISABELLA (2005).

BENNETT B. PATTERSON, THE FORGOTTEN NINTH AMENDMENT: A CALL FOR LEGISLATIVE AND JUDICIAL RECOGNITION OF RIGHTS UNDER SOCIAL CONDITIONS OF TODAY (1955).

BERNARD SCHWARTZ, THE GREAT RIGHTS OF MANKIND: A HISTORY OF THE AMERICAN BILL OF RIGHTS (1977).

CHARLES MONTESQUIEU, THE SPIRIT OF THE LAWS (1748).

DANIEL A. FARBER, RETAINED BY THE PEOPLE: THE "SILENT" NINTH AMENDMENT AND THE CONSTITUTIONAL RIGHTS AMERICANS DON'T KNOW THEY HAVE (2007).

GARRY WILLS, INVENTING AMERICA: JEFFERSON'S DECLARATION OF INDEPENDENCE (1978).

GEOFFREY C. WARD, UNFORGIVABLE BLACKNESS: THE RISE AND FALL OF JACK JOHNSON (2004).

GORDON S. WOOD, THE CREATION OF THE AMERICAN REPUBLIC, 1776–1787 (1998).

John Locke, *A Letter Concerning Toleration, in* TWO TREATISES OF GOVERNMENT AND A LETTER CONCERNING TOLERATION 227-28 (Ian Shapiro ed., 2003).

JOHN LOCKE, OF THE ENDS OF POLITICAL SOCIETY AND GOVERNMENT, PARAGRAPH 124 *in* THE WORLD'S GREAT THINKERS: MAN AND THE STATE: THE POLITICAL PHILOSOPHERS (Saxe Commins & Robert N. Linscott eds., 1947).

John P. Kaminski, *Restoring the Declaration of Independence: Natural Rights and the Ninth Amendment, in* THE BILL OF RIGHTS: A LIVELY HERITAGE 150 (Jon Kukla ed., 1987).

JOHN STUART MILL, ON LIBERTY (Gertrude Himmelfarb ed., Penguin Books 1974). (1859).

LAURENCE H. TRIBE, AMERICAN CONSTITUTIONAL LAW (2d ed. 1988).

LEONARD W. LEVY, ORIGINS OF THE BILL OF RIGHTS (1999).

LUCRETIUS, ON THE NATURE OF THINGS (H. A. J. Munro ed., 1900).

PAULINE MAIER, AMERICAN SCRIPTURE: MAKING THE DECLARATION OF INDEPENDENCE (1997).

RACHEL CARLSON, SILENT SPRING (1962).

RANDY E. BARNETT, RESTORING THE LOST CONSTITUTION: THE PRESUMPTION OF LIBERTY (2004).

RICHARD BROOKHISER, WHAT WOULD THE FOUNDERS DO: OUR QUESTIONS THEIR ANSWERS (2006).

Robert H. Jackson, The Supreme Court and the American System of Government (1955).

St. George Tucker, A View of the Constitution of the United States, in 1 Blackstone's Commentaries (St. George Tucker ed., Phila., William Young Birch & Abraham Small 1803).

Susan Ford Wiltshire, Greece, Rome, and the Bill of Rights (1992).

The Rights Retained by the People: The History and Meaning of the Ninth Amendment (Randy E. Barnett ed., 1989).

Thomas B. McAffee, Jay S. Bybee, and A. Christopher Bryant, Powers Reserved for the People and the States: A History of the Ninth and Tenth Amendments (2006).

Owen Wister, The Virginian (1902).

Upton Sinclair, The Jungle (1906).

Articles:

Akhil R. Amar, *Philadelphia Revisited: Amending the Constitution Outside Article V*, 55 U. Chi. L. Rev. 1043 (1988).

Alexander Tsesis, *Underminding Inalienable Rights: From Dredd Scott to the Rehnquist Court*, 39 Ariz. St. L. J. 1179 (2007).

Benjamin Straumann, *Is Modern Liberty Ancient? Roman Remedies and Natural Rights in Hugo Grotius's Early Works on Natural Law*, 27 Law & Hist. Rev. 55 (2009).

Brandon H. Robb, Comment, *Making the Electoral College Work Today: The Agreement Among the States to Elect the President by National Popular Vote*, 54 Loy. L. Rev. 419 (2008).

Bryan K. Fair, *The Ultimate Association: Same-Sex Marriage and the Battle Against Jim Crow's Other Cousin*, 63 U. Miami L. Rev. 269 (2008).

Calvin R. Massey, *Federalism and Fundamental Rights: The Ninth Amendment*, 38 Hastings L.J. 305 (1987).

Daniel A. Farber, *Constitutional Cadenzas*, 56 Drake L. Rev. 833 (2008).

E. Norman Veasey, *What Would Madison Think? The Irony of the Twists and Turns of Federalism*, 34 Del. J. Corp. L. 35 (2009).

Eugene M. Van Loan, III, *Natural Rights and the Ninth Amendment*, 48 B. U. L. Rev. 1 (1968).

John R. Kroger, *The Philosophical Foundations of Roman Law: Aristotle, the Stoics, and Roman Theories of Natural Law*, 2004 Wis. L. Rev. 905 (2004).

Joseph L. Call, *Federalism and the Ninth Amendment*, 64 Dick. L. Rev. 121 (1959).

Kathleen Anne Ward, *Williams v. Attorney General of Alabama: Does a Constitutional Right to Sexual Privacy Exist?*, 31 T. Jefferson L. Rev. 1 (2008).

Keith Werhan, *The Classical Athenian Ancestry of American Freedom of Speech*, 2008 Sup. Ct. Rev. 293 (2008).

Kevin S. Toll, Comment, *The Ninth and America's Unconstitutional War on Drugs*, 84 U. Det. Mercy L. Rev. 417 (2007).

Knowlton H. Kelsey, *The Ninth Amendment of the Federal Constitution*, 11 Ind. L. J. 309 (1936).

Kristin Fasullo, *Beyond* Lawrence V.Texas: *Crafting a Fundamental Right to Sexual Privacy*, 77 Fordham L. Rev. 2997 (2009).

Kurt T. Lash, *The Inescapable Federalism of the Ninth Amendment*, 93 Iowa L. Rev. 801 (2008).

Kurt T. Lash, *The Lost Jurisprudence of the Ninth Amendment*, 83 Tex. L. Rev. 597 (2005).

Kurt T. Lash, *The Lost Original Meaning of the Ninth Amendment*, 83 Tex. L. Rev. 331 (2004).

Kurt T. Lash, *The Original Meaning of an Omission: The Tenth Amendment, Popular Sovereignty, and "Expressly" Delegated Power*, 83 Notre Dame L. Rev. 1889 (2008).

Kurt T. Lash, *A Textual-Historical Theory of the Ninth Amendment*, 60 Stan. L. Rev. 895 (2008).

Kurt T. Lash, *Three Myths of the Ninth Amendment*, 56 Drake L. Rev. 875 (2008).

Kurt T. Lash, *"Tucker's Rule": St. George Tucker and the Limited Construction of Federal Power*, 47 Wm & Mary L. Rev. 1343 (2006).

Kyle Alexander Casazza, *Inkblots: How the Ninth Amendment and the Privileges or Immunities Clause Protect Unenumerated Constitutional Rights*, 80 S. Cal. L. Rev. 1383 (2007).

Leslie W. Dunbar, *James Madison and the Ninth Amendment*, 42 Va. L. Rev. 627 (1956).

Norman Redlich, *Are There "Certain Rights ... Retained by the People"?*, 37 N.Y.U. L. Rev. 787 (1962).

O. John Rogge, *Unenumerated Rights*, 47 Cal. L. Rev. 787 (1959).

Pamela S. Karlan, *Ballots and Bullets: The Exceptional History of the Right to Vote*, 71 U. Cin. L. Rev. 1345 (2003).

Randy E. Barnett, *The Golden Mean Between Kurt & Dan: A Moderate Reading of the Ninth Amendment* 56 Drake L. Rev. 897 (2008).

Randy E. Barnett, *A Ninth Amendment for Today's Constitution,* 26 Val. U. L. Rev. 419 (1991).

Randy E. Barnett, *The Ninth Amendment: It Means What It Says*, 85 Tex. L. Rev. 1 (2006).

Raoul Berger, *The Ninth Amendment* 66 Cornell L. Rev. 1 (1981).

Russell L. Caplan, *The History and Meaning of the Ninth Amendment*, 69 Va. L. Rev. 223 (1983).

Samuel D. Warren & Louis D. Brandeis, *The Right to Privacy*, 4 Harv. L. Rev. 193 (1890).

Sarah Tupper, Note, *Taking The Ninth: A Victim's Right Of Privacy*, 28 Wash. U. J.L. & Pol'y 457 (2008).

Steve Bachmann, *Starting Again with the Mayflower. . . England's Civil War and America's Bill of Rights*, 20 QLR 193 (2000).

Symposium, *The Forgotten Constitutional Amendments*, 56 Drake L. Rev. 829 (2008).

Thomas B. McAffee, *The Bill of Rights, Social Contract Theory, and the Rights "Retained" by the People*, 16 S. Ill. U. L. J. 267 (1992).

Zelma W. Price, *The Ninth Amendment*, 48 Women Law. J. 19 (1962).

Movies/Television:

An Inconvenient Truth (Paramount Classics 2006).

Braveheart (Paramount Pictures 1995).

Nuremberg (Alliance Atlantis Communications 2000).

The FBI Story (Warner Brothers 1959).

The Great White Hope (20th Century Fox 1970).

The Princess Bride (20th Century Fox 1987).

Unforgivable Blackness: The Rise and Fall of Jack Johnson (PBS television broadcast Jan. 17, 2005).

The Virginian (Paramount Pictures 1929).

The Virginian (NBC 1962–1971).

MISCELLANEOUS:

1 The Debates and Proceedings in the Congress of the United States (J. Gales & W. Seaton eds., 1834).

JOHN LOCKE, TWO TREATISES OF GOVERNMENT (Peter Laslett ed., Cambridge Univ. Press 1988). (1690).

John Adams to Abigail Adams Letter (Sept. 18, 1774)., *reprinted in* 1 Letters of Members of the Continental Congress (E. Burnett ed., 1921).

HOWARD SACKLER, THE GREAT WHITE HOPE (1967).

Summa Theologica I–II, Q. 94, A. 2 & 6.

THE DECLARATION OF INDEPENDENCE

UNITED STATES CONSTITUTION

UNIVERSAL DECLARATION OF HUMAN RIGHTS

CHAPTER TEN

CASES:

Brown v. Board of Education, 347 U.S. 483 (1954).

Buckley v. Valeo, 424 U.S. 1 (1976).

Calder v. Bull, 3 U.S. (3 Dall.) 386 (1798).

Cohens v. Virginia, 19 U.S. 264 (1821).

Dred Scott v. Sandford, 60 U.S. (19 How.) 393 (1856).

Fletcher v. Peck, 10 U.S. (6 Cranch) 87 (1810).

Garcia v. San Antonio Metropolitan Transit Authority, 469 U.S. 528 (1985).

Gonzales v. Raich, 545 U.S. 1 (2005).

Hustler Magazine, Inc. v. Falwell, 485 U.S. 46 (1988).

Lambert v. Yellowley, 272 U.S. 581 (1926).

Marbury v. Madison, 5 U.S. (1 Cranch) 137 (1803).

McCulloch v. Maryland, 17 U.S. (4 Wheat.) 316 (1819).

New York v. United States, 505 U.S. 144 (1992).

Plessy v. Ferguson, 163 U.S. 537 (1896).

Plyler v. Doe, 457 U. S. 202 (1982).

Prigg v. Pennsylvania, 41 U.S. (16 Pet.) 539 (1842).

Printz v. United States, 521 U.S. 898 (1997).

R. v. Knowles, ex parte Somerset, (1772) Lofft 1, 98 Eng. Rep. 499 (K.B. 1772) reprinted in 20 Howell's State Trials 1 (1909).

Somerset v. Stewart, (1772) 98 Eng. Rep. 499 (K.B.).

South Dakota v. Dole, 483 U.S. 203 (1987).

United States v. Darby, 312 U.S. 100 (1941).

United States v. Lopez, 514 U.S. 549 (1995).

United States v. Sprague, 282 U.S. 716 (1931).

Wickard v. Filburn, 317 U.S. 111 (1942).

Worcester v. Georgia, 31 U.S. (6 Pet.) 515 (1832).

Zadvydas v. Davis, 533 U.S. 678 (2001).

CONSTITUTIONS:

ARTICLES OF CONFEDERATION

THE DECLARATION OF INDEPENDENCE

UNITED STATES CONSTITUTION

STATUTES:

42 U.S.C. § 21 (2006).

BOOKS:

ALFRED W. BLUMROSEN & RUTH G. BLUMROSEN, SLAVE NATION: HOW SLAVERY UNITED THE COLONIES & SPARKED THE AMERICAN REVOLUTION (2005).

ARISTOTLE, POLITICS (Benjamin Jowett trans., Random House 1943).

ARTHUR H. BREMER, AN ASSASSIN'S DIARY (1973).

BURRUS M. CARNAHAN, ACT OF JUSTICE: LINCOLN'S EMANCIPATION PROCLAMATION AND THE LAW OF WAR (2008).

Charles F. Hobson, *The Tenth Amendment and the New Federalism of 1789*, *in* THE BILL OF RIGHTS: A LIVELY HERITAGE 162 (Jon Kukla ed., 1987).

COKIE ROBERTS, FOUNDING MOTHERS: THE WOMEN WHO RAISED OUR NATION (2004).

COKIE ROBERTS, LADIES OF LIBERTY: THE WOMEN WHO SHAPED OUR NATION (2009).

COLIN RHYS LOVELL, ENGLISH CONSTITUTIONAL AND LEGAL HISTORY (1962).

EMORY M. THOMAS, THE CONFEDERATE NATION, 1861–1865 (1979).

FREDERICK G. KEMPIN, HISTORICAL INTRODUCTION TO ANGLO-AMERICAN LAW (1990).

Jack N. Rakove, *American Federalism: Was There an Original Understanding? in* THE TENTH AMENDMENT AND STATE SOVEREIGNTY (Mark R. Killenbeck ed., 2002).

JESSE J. HOLLAND, BLACK MEN BUILT THE CAPITOL: DISCOVERING AFRICAN-AMERICAN HISTORY IN AND AROUND WASHINGTON, D.C. (2007).

JOHN AYTO, DICTIONARY OF WORD ORIGINS (1990).

JOHN D. WEAVER, THE SENATOR AND THE SHARECROPPER'S SON: EXONERATION OF THE BROWNSVILLE SOLDIERS 90-91 (1997).

John Choon Yoo, *Federalism and Judicial Review*, *in* THE TENTH AMENDMENT AND STATE SOVEREIGNTY (Mark R. Killenbeck ed., 2002).

John Locke, *An Essay Concerning the True Original, Extent and End of Civil Government*, *in* THE WORLD'S GREAT THINKERS, MAN AND THE STATE: THE POLITICAL PHILOSOPHERS (1947).

JOSEPH STORY, COMMENTARIES ON THE CONSTITUTION OF THE UNITED STATES (Carolina Academic Press 1987) (1833).

LEONARD W. LEVY, ORIGINS OF THE BILL OF RIGHTS (1999).

Mark R. Killenbeck, *No Harm in Such a Declaration*, *in* THE TENTH AMENDMENT AND STATE SOVEREIGNTY (Mark R. Killenbeck ed., 2002).

PAUL DOUGLAS LOCKHART, THE DRILLMASTER OF VALLEY FORGE: THE BARON DE STEUBEN AND THE MAKING OF THE AMERICAN ARMY (2008).

PHYLLIS SCHLAFLY, THE SUPREMACISTS: THE TYRANNY OF JUDGES AND HOW TO STOP IT (2004).

Randy Shilts, Conduct Unbecoming: Lesbians and Gays in the US Military from Vietnam to the Persian Gulf War (1993).

Richard Brookhiser, What Would the Founders Do? Our Questions, Their Answers (2006).

Robert Hendrickson, QPB Encyclopedia of Word and Phrase Origins (2d ed. 2004).

Simon Schama, Rough Crossings: Britain, the Slaves and the American Revolution (2005).

St. George Tucker, View of the Constitution of the United States, in 1 Blackstone's Commentaries (St. George Tucker ed., Phila., William Birch Young & Abraham Small 1803).

Steven M. Wise, Though The Heavens May Fall: The Landmark Trial that Led to the End of Human Slavery (2005).

The Federalist No. 10 (James Madison).

The Federalist No. 39 (James Madison).

The Federalist No. 44 (James Madison).

The Federalist No. 51 (James Madison).

The Federalist No. 78 (Alexander Hamilton).

The Federalist No. 80 (Alexander Hamilton).

William E. Leuchtenburg, *The Tenth Amendment over Two Centuries: More than a Truism*, in The Tenth Amendment and State Sovereignty (Mark R. Killenbeck ed., 2002).

William H. Rehnquist, Grand Inquests: The Historic Impeachments of Justice Samuel Chase and President Andrew Johnson (1992).

William Strunk, Jr. and E.B. White, The Elements of Style (3rd ed. 1979).

ARTICLES:

Alexander Tsesis, *The Problem of Confederate Symbols: A Thirteenth Amendment Approach*, 75 Temp. L. Rev. 539 (2002).

Alexander Tsesis, *Undermining Inalienable Rights: From Dred Scott To The Rehnquist Court*, 39 Ariz. St. L.J. 1179 (2007).

Alfred W. Blumrosen, *The Profound Influence in America of Lord Mansfield's Decision in Somerset V. Stuart*, 13 Tex. Wesleyan L. Rev. 645 (2007).

Anthony J. Bellia, *The Origins of Article III "Arising Under" Jurisdiction*, 57 Duke L.J. 263 (2007).

Book Note, *Reimagining Revolution: A Critical Review of Simon Schama's Rough Crossings: Britain, the Slaves, and the American Revolution*, 9 Berkeley J. Afr.-Am. L. & Pol'y 74 (2007).

Cheryl I. Harris, *"Too Pure an Air:" Somerset's Legacy from Anti-Slavery to Colorblindness*, 13 Tex. Wesleyan L. Rev. 439 (2007).

David M. Sprick, *Ex Abundanti Cautela (Out of the Abundance of Caution): A Historical Analysis of the Tenth Amendment and the Continuing Dilemma Over "Federal" Power*, 27 Cap. U. L. Rev. 529 (1999).

Eugene M. Van Loan, III, *Natural Rights and the Ninth Amendment*, 48 B. U. L. Rev. 1 (1968).

Frederick Schauer, *The Failure of the Common Law*, 36 Ariz. St. L. J. 765 (2005).

George L. Haskins, *Law Versus Politics in the Early Years of the Marshall Court*, 130 Penn. L. Rev. 1 (1981).

Henry J. Abraham, *President Jefferson's Three Appointments to the Supreme Court of the United States: 1804, 1807, and 1807*, 31 J. Sup. Ct. Hist. 141 (2006).

Herbert Pope, *The English Common Law in the United States*, 24 HARV. L. REV. 6 (1911).

Hugo L. Black, *The Bill of Rights*, 35 N.Y.U. L. REV. 865 (1960).

John R. Kroger, *The Philosophical Foundations of Roman Law: Aristotle, the Stoics, and Roman Theories of Natural Law*, 2004 WIS. L. REV. 905 (2004).

John Yoo, *Jefferson and Executive Power*, 88 B.U. L. REV. 421 (2008).

Kent R. Newmyer, *Thomas Jefferson and the Rise of the Supreme Court*, 31 J. SUP. CT. HIST. 126 (2006).

Knowlton H. Kelsey, *The Ninth Amendment of the Federal Constitution*, 11 IND. L. J. 310 (1936).

Kurt T. Lash, *A Textual-Historical Theory Of The Ninth Amendment*, 60 STAN. L. REV. 895 (2008).

Kurt Lash, *The Lost Original Meaning of the Ninth Amendment*, 83 TEX. L. REV. 331 (2004).

Kurt T. Lash, *The Original Meaning of an Omission: The Tenth Amendment, Popular Sovereignty, and "Expressly" Delegated Power,* 83 NOTRE DAME L. REV. 1889 (2008).

Maeva Marcus, *Federal Judicial Selection: The First Decade*, 39 U. RICH. L. REV. 797 (2005).

Mark DeWolfe Howe, *Juries as Judges of Criminal Law*, 52 HARV. L. REV. 582 (1939).

Melvin I. Urofsky, *Thomas Jefferson and John Marshall: What Kind of Court Shall We Have*, 31 J. SUP. CT. HIST. 109 (2006).

Norman Redlich, *Are There "Certain Rights ... Retained by the People"?*, 37 N.Y.U. L. REV. 787 (1962).

O. John Rogge, *Unenumerated Rights*, 47 CAL. L. REV. 787 (1959).

Randy E. Barnett, *A Ninth Amendment for Today's Constitution*, 26 VAL. U. L. REV. 419 (1991).

Randy E. Barnett, *Reconceiving the Ninth Amendment,* 74 CORNELL L. REV. 1 (1988).

Raoul Berger, *The Ninth Amendment*, 66 CORNELL L. REV. 2 (1981).

Robert Fabrikant, *Lincoln, Emancipation, and "Military Necessity"*, 52 HOW. L. J. 375 (2009).

Robert L. Jones, *Finishing A Friendly Argument: The Jury and the Historical Origins of Diversity Jurisdiction*, 82 N.Y.U. L. REV. 997 (2007).

Saikrishna B. Prakash & John C. Yoo, *The Origins of Judicial Review*, 70 U. CHI. L. REV. 887 (2003).

Stephan Landsman, *The Civil Jury in America: Scenes from an Unappreciated History*, 44 HASTINGS L. J. 579 (1993).

Steve Bachmann, *Starting Again with the Mayflower ... England's Civil War and America's Bill of Rights*, 20 QLR 193 (2001).

Symposium, Dred Scott After 150 Years: A Grievous Wound Remembered, 17 WIDENER L. J. 1 (2007).

Timothy S. Huebner, *Lawyer, Litigant, Leader: John Marshall and His Papers-A Review Essay*, 48 AM. J. LEGAL HIST. 314 (2006).

William E. Nelson, *Government by Judiciary: The Growth of Judicial Power in Colonial Pennsylvania,* 59 SMU L. REV. 3 (2006).

William G. Merkel, *Jefferson's Failed Anti-Slavery Proviso of 1784 and the Nascence of Free Soil Constitutionalism*, 38 SETON HALL L. REV. 555 (2008).

William Michael Treanor, *Judicial Review Before Marbury*, 58 STAN. L. REV. 455 (2005).

William S. Fields & David T. Hardy, *The Third Amendment and the Issue of Maintenance of Standing Armies: A Legal History*, 35 AM. J. LEGAL HIST. 393 (1991).

Movies and Television:

Apocalypse Now (United Artists 1979).

Apocalypse Now Redux (Miramax Films 2001).

Forrest Gump (Paramount Pictures 1994).

John Adams (HBO March 16 through April 20, 2008).

Taxi Driver (Columbia Pictures 1976).

The Last of the Mohicans (20th Century Fox 1992).

The Maltese Falcon (Warner Bros. 1941).

The People vs. Larry Flynt (Columbia Pictures 1996).

Misc.:

Andrew Jackson, *Veto Message* (July 10, 1832).

Iroquois Constitution *available at* http://www.indigenouspeople.net/iroqcon.htm (last visited June 8, 2010).

John C. Calhoun, Speech on the Reception of Abolition Petitions (1837).

Letter from Benjamin Rush to Granville Sharp (May 13, 1774), *in* The Correspondence of Benjamin Rush and Granville Sharp, 1773–1809, 1 J. Am. Stud. 1, 5 (John A. Woods ed., 1967).

Letter from Thomas Jefferson to Spencer Roane (Sept. 6, 1819), *available at* http://press-pubs. uchicago.edu/founders/documents/a1_8_18s16.html (last visited March 16, 2008).

Lord Dunmore's Proclamation *available at* http://www.digitalhistory.uh.edu/learning_history/revolution/dunsmore.cfm (last visited May 2, 2009).

Kathryn McConnell, *Iroquois Constitution Influenced That of U.S., Historians Say*, http://www.america.gov/st/washfile-english/2004/September/20040924120101AKllennoCcM9.930056e-02.html (last visited April 23, 2009).

Samuel Johnson Sound Bite Page: Quotes on Slavery, http://www.samueljohnson.com/tnt.html (last visited August 5, 2010).

Seneca Falls Declaration of Sentiments *available at* http://en.wikipedia.org/wiki/Seneca_Falls_Declaration_of_Sentiments (last visited April 24, 2009).

EPILOGUE

Cases:

Dred Scott v. Sandford, 60 U.S. (19 How.) 393 (1857).

Griswold v. Connecticut, 381 U.S. 479 (1965).

Constitutions:

United states Constitution

Articles:

Charles Fairman, *Does the Fourteenth Amendment Incorporate the Bill of Rights?: The Original Understanding*, 2 Stan. L. Rev. 5 (1949).

Christopher R. Green, *The Original Sense of the (Equal) Protection Clause: Pre-Enactment History*, 19 Geo. Mason U. Civ. Rts. L.J. 1 (2008).

David P. Currie, *The Reconstruction Congress*, 75 U. CHI. L. REV. 383 (2008).

David T. Hardy, *Original Popular Understanding of the Fourteenth Amendment as Reflected in the Print Media 1866–1868*, 30 WHITTIER L. REV. 695 (2009).

Kamal Ghali, *No Slavery Except as a Punishment for Crime: The Punishment Clause and Sexual Slavery*, 55 UCLA L. REV. 607 (2008).

Lea S. Vandervelde, *The Labor Vision of the Thirteenth Amendment*, 138 U. PA. L. REV. 437 (1989).

Louisa M. A. Heiny, *Radical Abolitionist Influence on Federalism and the Fourteenth Amendment*, 49 AM. J. LEGAL HIST. 180 (2007).

Michael P. O'Connor, *Time Out of Mind: Our Collective Amnesia about the History of the Privileges or Immunities Clause*, 93 KENTUCKY L. J. 659 (2004–2005).

Michael Scimone, Comment, *More to Lose than your Chains: Realizing the Ideals of the Thirteenth Amendment*, 12 N.Y. City L. Rev. 175 (2008).

Paul Finkelman, *Lincoln, Emancipation, and the Limits of Constitutional Change*, 2008 SUP. CT. REV. 349 (2008).

Paul Finkleman, *Was Dred Scott Correctly Decided? An "Expert Report" for the Defendant*, 12 LEWIS & CLARK L. REV. 1219 (2008).

Risa L. Goluboff, *The Thirteenth Amendment in Historical Perspective,* 11 U. PA. J. CONST. L. 1451 (2009).

Robert G. Natelson, *The Original Meaning of the Privileges and Immunities Clause*, 43 GA. L. REV. 1117 (2009).

Scott W. Howe, *Slavery as Punishment: Original Public Meaning, Cruel and Unusual Punishment, and the Neglected Clause in the Thirteenth Amendment*, 51 ARIZ. L. REV. 983 (2009).

Stanley Morrison, *Does the Fourteenth Amendment Incorporate the Bill of Rights?: The Judicial Interpretation,* 2 STAN. L. REV. 140 (1949).

Steven G. Calabresi & Sarah E. Agudo, *Individual Rights Under State Constitutions when the Fourteenth Amendment was Ratified in 1868: What Rights are Deeply Rooted in American History and Tradition?,* 87 TEX. L. REV. 7 (2008).

Symposium, *Dred Scott After 150 Years: A Grievous Wound Remembered*, 17 WIDENER L. J. 1 (2007).

MOVIES:

GLORY (Tri-Star 1989).

MISC.:

AARON COPLAND, LINCOLN PORTRAIT (1942).

Abraham Lincoln, Second Inaugural Address (Mar. 4, 1865), *available at http://avalon.law.yale.edu/19th_century/lincoln2.asp* (last visited February 28, 2010).

Garry Wills, *Lincoln's Greatest Speech?*, THE ATLANTIC MONTHLY, September 1999, http://www.theatlantic.com/past/issues/99sep/9909lincoln.htm.

Index

ABOUT THE AUTHOR

Photo used with permission & John Hall photography, www.johnhallphotography.com/

Robert J. McWhirter is a nationally and internationally know speaker and author on trial advocacy, immigration law, and the history of the bill of rights. He is a Certified Specialist in Criminal Law with the State Bar of Arizona and first chair qualified to defend capital cases by the Arizona Supreme Court. Mr. McWhirter has lived and worked in El Salvador administering a USAID contract to reform the justice system. He is currently in private practice specializing in Criminal Defense law in Arizona.

Robert J. McWhirter received his Juris Doctorate from Arizona State University College of Law in 1988. Upon graduation, Mr. McWhirter clerked for Vice Chief Justice Stanley G. Feldman of the Supreme Court of Arizona.

Mr. McWhirter was an Assistant Federal Public Defender from 1989 until 2007 representing Native Americans and other clients in a broad range of Federal cases including homicide, sexual abuse, and bank robbery. In addition, Mr. McWhirter specialized in criminal immigration law publishing articles in the GEORGETOWN IMMIGRATION LAW REVIEW and the CRIMINAL PRACTICE LAW REPORT and two books, THE CRIMINAL LAWYER'S GUIDE TO IMMIGRATION LAW: QUESTIONS AND ANSWERS, 2nd Ed. (ABA Books 2006) and THE CITIZENSHIP FLOWCHART (ABA Books 2007). In 2010, the United States Supreme Court, through Justice Alito's concurring opinion, extensively quoted from Mr. McWhirter's THE CRIMINAL LAWYER'S GUIDE TO IMMIGRATION LAW, in the ground-breaking case of *Padilla v. Kentucky*.

Mr. McWhirter also served from 2007-2010 as a Senior Attorney with the Maricopa Legal Defender's Office defending death penalty and other serious felonies.

Mr. McWhirter has been an adjunct professor in Trial Advocacy at the Phoenix School of Law as well as a visiting professor of law at the Catholic University of Chile and the University of Chile. Mr. McWhirter has taught trial advocacy and criminal procedure in Venezuela, Mexico, Ecuador, Nicaragua, Colombia, and Chile. He also served as an advisor to the Venezuelan Constitutional Assembly drafting the 1999 Venezuelan Constitution as a grant recipient from the United States State Department.

Mr. McWhirter has served on the American Bar Association Criminal Justice Section Council and on the Standards Committee writing the ABA CRIMINAL JUSTICE STANDARDS.
Mr. McWhirter is a past president of Arizona Attorneys for Criminal Justice. He has served on the corporate board of directors of Catholic Charities of Arizona. He is a past president of the St. Thomas More Society of Phoenix Arizona and a recipient of its St. Thomas More Award.

But Mr. McWhirter's best achievement is that he is the father of three great boys.